Justice, Liberty,
New Challenges for EU

Bernd Martenczuk and Servaas van Thiel (Eds.)

Justice, Liberty, Security:
New Challenges for EU
External Relations

VUBPRESS

Brussels University Press

Institute for European Studies - publication series, nr. 11

The Institute for European Studies is a Jean Monnet Pole of Excellence.
It promulgates European Studies in general, and studies of Globalisation, European and Comparative Law, Environment and Regional (European) Integration specifically. The IES is an education and research centre, carrying out research on various European issues, and responsible for the Programme on International Legal Cooperation (PILC), an advanced Masters programme leading to an internationally renowned LL.M.

Institute for European Studies (IES)
Vrije Universiteit Brussel
Pleinlaan 2
B-1050 Brussels
ies@vub.ac.be
http://www.ies.be

Cover design: Koloriet, Sterrebeek
Book design: Style, Hulshout
Print: Flin Graphic Group, Oostkamp

© 2008 VUBPRESS Brussels University Press
VUBPRESS is an imprint of ASP nv (Academic and Scientific Publishers nv)
Ravensteingalerij 28
B-1000 Brussels
Tel. ++ 32 2 289 26 50
Fax ++ 32 2 289 26 59
E-mail info@vubpress.be
www.vubpress.be

ISBN 978 90 5487 472 0
NUR 754
Legal Deposit D/2008/11.161/016

Table of Contents

List of contributors

Philippe Boillat, Director General, Council of Europe

Jonathan Faull, Director-General, Directorate General for Justice, Freedom and Security, European Commission; Professor of Law, Vrije Universiteit Brussel

Fabrice Filliez, Head of Political Coordination, European Integration Office, Swiss Ministry of Foreign Affairs

Madeline Garlick, Head of the EU Policy Unit at the Office of the United Nations High Commissioner for Refugees (UNHCR) in Brussels

Dick Heimans, Administrator, Directorate General for Justice, Freedom and Security, European Commission

Paul de Hert, Professor of Law, Vrije Universiteit Brussel; Associated Professor, Tilburg University

Jan-Peter Hix, Legal Advisor in the Legal Service, Council of the European Union

Pieter Jan Kuijper, Professor of Law, University of Amsterdam

Judith Kumin, Regional Representative for the Benelux countries and the EU Institutions, Office of the United Nations High Commissioner for Refugees (UNHCR) in Brussels

Stéphane Leyenberger, Administrator, Council of Europe

Hans van Loon, Secretary General, Hague Conference on Private International Law

Bernd Martenczuk, Member of the Legal Service, European Commission; Professor of Law, Vrije Universiteit Brussel

Steven Peers, Professor of law, University of Essex

Martin Schieffer, Head of Sector, DG Justice and Home Affairs, European Commission

Andrea Schulz, Head of the German Central Authority for matters of international child protection and child abduction; formerly First Secretary at the Permanent Bureau of the Hague Conference on Private International Law

Bart de Schutter, Professor of Law, Vrije Universiteit Brussel; Belgian Representative in the Schengen and Europol Common Control Authority; Belgian Data Protection Commissioner

Luigi Soreca, Head of Unit, External Relations and Enlargement, Directorate General for Justice, Freedom and Security, European Commission

Guy Stessens, Administrator, Council of the European Union

Servaas van Thiel, Head of Unit, Council of the European Union; Director PILC Program (LL.M) and Professor of Law, Vrije Universiteit Brussel; Judge in the Regional Court of Appeal Den Bosch (NL)

Introduction

The External Dimension of EU Justice and Home Affairs: Evolution, Challenges and Outlook

Bernd Martenczuk and Servaas van Thiel[1]

I.   Introduction

The present volume is dedicated to the external relations of the European Union in the field of Justice and Home Affairs.[2] It contains contributions from both practitioners and academics covering all areas of EU Justice and Home Affairs, including migration policy, asylum and border controls, civil law, and criminal law, including the fight against terrorism and international crime. Most of the contributions were presented as part of a lecture series organised by the LL.M Program on International Legal Cooperation (PILC) and the Institute of European Studies (IES) of the Vrije Universiteit Brussels in the fall of 2007.

The external dimension of EU Justice and Home Affairs is a relatively novel topic. Traditionally, "justice and home affairs" has been considered as a matter primarily of domestic policy and national sovereignty, and it is only recently that the need for international cooperation and regulation in this field has acquired its current urgency. Moreover, it is only with the Treaty of Amsterdam that the EU began building a European area of freedom, security and justice, and has started to give this area an external dimension.

This simultaneous building of a European Area of Justice, Liberty, and Security and the increasing need for international cooperation have given rise to numerous challenges for the external relations of the EU. Indeed,

---

1.   The article expresses the personal view of the authors only.
2.   In the parlance of the EU institutions, the field is also frequently referred to as "Justice, Liberty, Security". Indeed, with the taking of office of the Barroso Commission in 2004, the name of the European Commission's Directorate General "Justice and Home Affairs" was changed to "Justice, Liberty, Security". This terminology reflects not only that of the Treaties, but also underlines that this policy area is not, as might be suggested by the term "home affairs", purely a domestic one. In this introduction, as throughout the book, the terms "Justice and Home Affairs" and "Justice, Liberty, Security" are used interchangeably.

EU external relations is at its most complex when it comes to justice, liberty and security. At the same time, however, justice and home affairs matters also have a direct bearing on human rights and civil liberties, which increases the sensitivity of international cooperation in this area.

The present introduction will provide a general overview of the issues covered in this book. First, it will briefly retrace the gradual evolution of the external dimension of EU justice and home affairs. Second, based on the contributions contained in this book, it will set out the main institutional and substantive challenges facing EU external relations in this area. Finally, the editors will draw some conclusions, and make some attempt at looking ahead. In this context, the possible effects of the entry into force of the Treaty of Lisbon on EU external relations in justice and home affairs will also briefly be considered.

II.   The External Dimension of EU Justice and Home Affairs

The international dimension of EU justice and home affairs began with the entry into force of the Treaty of Amsterdam in May 1999. It is true that the Treaty of Maastricht had already established a third pillar of the European Union dedicated to cooperation in the field of justice and home affairs. However, the third pillar as set up by the Maastricht Treaty was purely intergovernmental in nature, and did not confer on the European Union the necessary tools for acting on the international scene.

This situation changed fundamentally with the Treaty of Amsterdam, which introduced the goal of the creation of a Europe-wide area of freedom, security and justice.[3] First, the Treaty of Amsterdam transferred a substantial part of the former third pillar, namely the competences relating to migration, asylum, border controls and private international law to a new Title IV of Part III of the EC Treaty. This meant that the European Community as an established actor in international relations could now become active in these areas. Second, the Amsterdam Treaty also inserted provisions into the EU Treaty which allow the EU to conclude international agreements in the remaining field of the third pillar, i.e. police and judicial cooperation in criminal matters. It thereby confirmed that the third pillar also has an international dimension.

---

3.   Cf. Articles 29 EU and 61 EC. Cf. generally also Jörg Monar, *The EU as an International Actor in the Domain of Justice and Home Affairs*, [2004] European Foreign Affairs Journal 395.

In fact, in each of the major policy areas of EU justice and home affairs, as defined in the Treaties, there is a pressing need for international cooperation. Moreover, as a result of globalisation and increased international mobility also between the EU and third countries, this international dimension has grown considerably in recent years.

Immigration, asylum and border controls by definition concern nationals of third countries and cross-border movements of natural persons. Moreover, in recent years, international migration flows have become a global phenomenon. Accordingly, there is an inherent need for international cooperation to ensure the appropriate management of migration flows. At the same time, there is also a need for international standards to protect the rights of migrants, asylum seekers and refugees.

In the area of civil law, the EC's competences are currently limited essentially to issues of private international law, i.e. the regulation of conflicts of law and conflicts of jurisdiction.[4] However, such conflicts of law do not only arise between Member States, but also between the EU and third countries, and their importance has grown with increasing international trade and cross-border mobility. In addition, private international law is traditionally regulated by multilateral international conventions elaborated by organisations such as the Hague Conference on Private International Law. Therefore, the EC's activity in the area of private international law is inseparably intertwined with international issues.

Finally, as regards the third pillar, police and judicial cooperation in criminal matters has equally acquired an international dimension. This is most obvious as regards the fight against international terrorism. Since the attacks of September 11, 2001, the fight against international terrorism has been a major topic for international cooperation, not least between the EU and the US, and has become a major driving force in the internationalisation of EU Justice and Home Affairs. At the same time, however, international cooperation in the fight against international crime and terrorism also raises complex questions regarding the protection of the rights of individuals and the rule of law, such as may be the case, for instance, but not only, where the transfer of personal data is concerned.

Since the entry into force of the Treaty of Amsterdam, the EU institutions have actively sought to develop the external dimension of EU Justice and Home Affairs. Already the European Council of Tampere of 15 and 16 October 1999 demanded that in the area of Justice and Home Affairs, "the Union should also develop a capacity to act and be regarded as a

---

4.   Cf. Article 65 EC.

significant partner on the international scene".[5] The European Council of Feira of 19 and 20 June 2000 approved a set of priorities for the EU's external relations in Justice and Home Affairs, and requested that these be incorporated into the overall strategy of the EU's external relations.[6]

The Brussels European Council of 4 and 5 November 2004 approved the Hague Programme, which sets out the priorities of EU Justice and Home Affairs for the five-year period until 2009.[7] The Hague Programme places a great emphasis on the international dimension of justice, liberty and security; accordingly, international activities are mentioned for nearly all of the policy objectives and priorities set out in the programme. Moreover, in the Hague Programme, the European Council also called for the elaboration of a strategy on the external aspects of EU justice and home affairs.[8] Accordingly, in 2005, the Council, on the basis of a communication from the Commission[9] adopted an EU Strategy for the External Dimension of Justice and Home Affairs.[10]

III. Main Challenges for EU External Relation in the Field of Justice and Home Affairs

As the contributions contained in the present volume show, remarkable progress has been achieved in the development of the external dimension of EU Justice and Home Affairs. However, the contributions at the same time also show the considerable challenges and difficulties that the EU has to face in developing its external activity in this field. These challenges relate essentially to two main factors. First, the EU remains a highly fragmented and complex international actor, and this fragmentation and complexity weighs particularly heavily in the area of justice and home affairs. Second, international cooperation in the area of justice and home affairs also requires a delicate process of reconciling the often competing values of justice, liberty and security, in particular where human rights, fundamental freedoms, and the rule of law are concerned.

5. Presidency Conclusions, para. 8 (available under http://www.consilium.europa.eu/ ueDocs/cms_Data/docs/pressData/en/ec/00200-r1.en9.htm).
6. Presidency conclusions, para. 51 (available under: http://www.consilium.europa.eu/ ueDocs/cms_Data/docs/pressData/en/ec/00200-r1.en0.htm).
7. OJ C 53, 3.3.2005, p. 1.
8. Id., point 4.
9. A Strategy on the External Dimension of the Area of Freedom, Security and Justice, COM (2005) 491 final.
10. Council Doc 14366/3/05 REV 3 (30 November 2005).

A.   The EU as a Fragmented International Actor

The first factor contributing to the complexity of EU external relations in this area is the pillar structure of the European Union. The European Union, as set up by the Treaties of Maastricht and Amsterdam, is not a uniform actor. Rather, it is in fact composed of two separate, and sometimes competing, international entities, with the European Community holding competences over the matters governed in the EC Treaty, including, but not only, those in Title IV, whereas the European Union is competent for the matters governed by the second and third pillar. Moreover, the actions of these entities are governed by entirely different, and often incompatible, rules and procedures concerning international representation, internal decision-making, and the negotiation and conclusion of international agreements.

However, international cooperation in the field of justice and home affairs frequently has a cross-pillar nature, i.e. requires the competences of more than one pillar to be exercised. For instance, border controls do not only take place for immigration law purposes, but also have a criminal law component. The resulting difficulties for the association of third countries with the cross-pillar Schengen acquis are described in the contribution by **Filliez**. Moreover, effective action in fighting crime or terrorism frequently also touches upon competences of the European Community, be it in the field of customs cooperation, transport policy, data protection, or visa policy. Such cross-pillar issues are raised in many of the contributions, but are most prominently featured in the contributions by **Faull and Soreca** and **de Schutter and de Hert**. Additional complications arise from the recourse to second-pillar sanctions in the fight against international terrorism, as described in the contribution by **van Thiel**.

Another factor of complexity of the EU's external relations in the area of Justice and Home Affairs results from its uneasy coexistence with its Member States. The Member States, with their long tradition and bureaucratic expertise in the field, have only recently transferred competences to the Union, and the delimitation of competences between the Union and its Member States therefore remains an uneasy and delicate exercise. This is most obvious in the area of the first pillar, where the Community is slowly but steadily in the process of acquiring exclusive competences, with the consequence that its Member States may no longer act internationally. The resulting slow shift in external competences is described by **Martenczuk** for EC visa policy, and by **Kuijper** for private international law. Moreover, where competences are shared between the EC and its Member States, very complex legal constellations can arise for the exercise of the EC's external competences, as illustrated by **Hix** with respect to mixed agreements in the field of private international law, and by **van Loon and Schulz** for the example of an international organisation. Finally, in the area of the third pillar, it is less the delimitation of competences between the EU and its Member States which is problematic, but rather the strong limitations which are still placed on the exercise of the EU's external competences, as illustrated by the EU-US Agreements on Extradition and Mutual Legal Assistance discussed in the contribution by **Stessens**.

The third source of fragmentation is the strong degree of variable geometry of the EU's Justice and Home Affairs. As explained in the contribution by **Martenczuk**, the various opt-ins and opt-outs benefiting Denmark, Ireland and the United Kingdom, have led to an additional- this time territorial- fragmentation of the EU as an international actor, and have created numerous difficulties in the treaty-making procedures of the EU. At the same time, the EU has also had to accommodate its special links with Norway, Iceland and, in the future, Switzerland and Liechtenstein; the resulting complex arrangements are described in the contribution by **Filliez**.

Finally, the multiplicity of actors and organisations in the field of Justice and Home Affairs has also a certain impact on EU external relations. As the "newcomer" in this area, the EU has had to define its relationship with international organisations which have been active in the field for much longer than the EU. **Van Loon and Schulz** discuss the example of the relationship between the EU and the Hague Conference on Private International Law, which was put rather quickly on a formal footing with the accession of the EU to the Hague Conference in 2007; **Boillat and Leyenberger** discuss the relationship between the Council of Europe and the EU, which remains far more fluid. Finally, the contribution by **Heimans** on the external relations of Europol shows that, even within the EU, individual actors or agencies can have a role to play in external relations, which need to be integrated into the overall external relations strategy of the Union.

B.   Reconciling Liberty, Security, Justice in an International Context

The second challenge of EU Justice and Home Affairs is of a more substantive nature. Justice and Home Affairs is a human-rights sensitive area. Measures to combat illegal immigration or to regulate legal immigration affect the rights of migrants; in fighting crime and terrorism, the innocent need to be protected, and due process must be guaranteed for the accused; and even private international law and complex fundamental rights questions may arise when regulating matters concerning family law, divorce and child care.

This challenge becomes even greater in the context of international cooperation. Between the EU and third states, divergences may sometimes arise concerning key human rights issues in the area of justice and home affairs. Still, international cooperation in all these areas has become indispensable, which means that a balance may sometimes have to be struck between the EU's values and principles and those of other cooperating partners.

The resulting tension is discussed in a number of contributions contained in this book. **Schieffer** describes the need for effective international cooperation to ensure the readmission and repatriation of illegal migrants, whereas **Garlick and Cumin** describe the dangers to refugee protection and the right to asylum resulting from migration control policies. **Peers** describes the complex relationship between the guarantees for third-country workers included in association agreements and the sometimes divergent rules of EC migration law.

As regards more specifically the fight against terrorism and international crime, the relationship between the US and the EU has been particularly complex in this respect. It is examined from a general angle by **Faull and Soreca**, whereas **Stessens** focuses more specifically on the issues which arose in the negotiation of the EU-US Agreements on extradition and mutual legal assistance. **De Hert and de Schutter** examine the difficulties of information-sharing for law enforcement purposes in the absence of common privacy standards, which is compounded by the internal fragmentation of the EU, where comprehensive data protection rules currently apply only in the first pillar, but not in the second or third. **Van Thiel**, finally, examines the complex issues arising from the need to reconcile UN anti-terrorism sanctions and EU standards of human rights protection and judicial review.

IV.   Conclusions and Outlook

Overall, the development of the international dimension of EU justice and home affairs can be regarded as a success. In less than a decade since the entry into force of the Treaty of Amsterdam, the EU has become an established actor in international justice and home affairs. When it comes to fighting crime and international terrorism, managing migration flows or regulating private international law issues, third countries and international organisations turn to the EU as their natural interlocutor. The EC, and increasingly also the EU, has negotiated countless international agreements, and is active in international organisations and in other fora. In this context, the EC has also generally stood firm on the protection of fundamental rights and the rule of law, on which all policies in the area of Justice and Home Affairs must be based.

Success, however, has been achieved not because, but rather despite the current framework governing the external relations of the EU in the field of justice and home affairs. The legal difficulties surrounding cross-pillar coordination, mixed competences, and variable geometry have resulted in a high degree of complexity of EU Justice and Home Affairs, which in turn at times impede the achievement the EC's substantive objectives and the protection of its values.

It is therefore appropriate to also briefly address the likely impact of the entry into force of the Treaty of Lisbon,[11] as signed on 13 December 2007, on EU external relations in the field of Justice and Home Affairs.[12] Of course, it is still too early for a full evaluation of the Treaty of Lisbon. However, a few major changes with a direct bearing on the subject-matter of this volume can already be noted.

First of all, the Treaty of Lisbon will create a single legal personality for the European Union, which will absorb the current European Community and the European Union, as limited to the second and third pillar. Moreover, the current third pillar will be fully integrated into the framework of the European Union and become subject to the same decision-making procedures as other Union policies. The second pillar will remain as a separate policy area with separate procedures, but even here there will be a single treaty-making procedure. There will also be a uniform representation of the Union through the High Representative for the Common Foreign Security Policy, and the European Commission for all other areas, including also the current third pillar.[13]

---

11. OJ C 306, 17.12.2007, p. 1.
12. More broadly on the impact of the European Constitution on EU external relations, cf. Bernd Martenczuk, The Constitution for Europe and the External Relations of the European Union, in: Servaas van Thiel/Karel de Gucht/Richard Lewis (ed.), Understanding the new European Constitutional Treaty, VUB Press p. 253 (2005).
13. Cf. Article 9D (1) EU (future Article 17 EU) as amended by the Treaty of Lisbon.

Accordingly, the Treaty of Lisbon will finally allow the EU to act externally as a unified legal actor for all matters falling under its competence. Therefore, the cross-pillar difficulties which currently beset much of EU justice and home affairs will become a thing of the past. The EU will finally be able to negotiate international agreements contributing to the fight against crime or terrorism without having to artificially distinguish between matters falling under the competences of the EC, and others which fall under the second or third pillar. Moreover, it will be able to speak with one voice for all aspects of Justice and Home Affairs. This alone will be a major improvement for EU external relations generally, and for Justice and Home Affairs in particular.

The Treaty of Lisbon also strengthens the EU's commitment to fundamental rights and the rule of law underpinning Justice and Home Affairs. First of all, the EU Charter of Fundamental Rights, which was proclaimed on 12 December 2007,[14] will become legally binding for all EU policy areas, including justice and home affairs.[15] Second, the competences of the Court of Justice will fully extend to the former third pillar, from which the Court has so far been partially excluded. Third, the Court of Justice will equally become competent to review restrictive measures taken against individuals in the context of the common foreign and security policy.[16] Moreover, it is also provided that specific rules will be adopted to ensure the protection of personal data in the context of the common foreign and security policy.[17]

Of course, the Treaty of Lisbon does not solve all the difficulties that have been outlined above. For instance, the current awkward division of competences between the Union and its Member States is likely to continue for some time. In fact, the incorporation of the third pillar is likely to give rise to new disputes concerning the extent and the exclusive character of the Union's external relations powers. Similarly, the Treaty of Lisbon does not reduce the variable geometry of EU justice and home affairs, but rather increases it by extending the current Danish, Irish and British op-outs to the provisions of the current third pillar, which were so far applied uniformly to all Member States.

Overall, however, the Treaty of Lisbon will bring a major improvement to the EU's capacity to act at the international level in the area of justice and

---

14. OJ C 3003, 14.12.2007, p. 1.
15. Cf. Article 6 (1) EU as amended by the Treaty of Lisbon.
16. Cf. Article 240a EC (future Article 275 of the Treaty on the Functioning of the European Union) as amended by the Treaty of Lisbon.
17. Cf. Article 25 b EU (future Article 40 EU) as amended by the Treaty of Lisbon.

home affairs. It is therefore to be hoped that this Treaty can enter into force as soon as possible. Even then, building the external policy of the European area of Justice, Liberty and Security will remain a challenging task, which is likely to occupy the Union for years to come.

Part I

Immigration, Asylum, and Border Controls

1. Visa Policy and EU External Relations

Bernd Martenczuk[1]

I.   Introduction

Visa policy is both sensitive and complex. It is first and foremost an instrument of border control, through which States regulate the entry of persons into their territory. In this perspective, visa policy is an instrument to fight against illegal immigration and to safeguard internal security. However, visa policy is also a tool for promoting tourism, commerce, and people-to-people exchanges. Moreover, visa policy affects third countries and their nationals, and therefore is also a matter of foreign policy.

At the same time, controlling external borders is an important prerogative of State sovereignty. In the European Community, this traditional conception has long since been modified as regards the crossing of external borders by goods. Under the EC Treaty, trade in goods falls under the exclusive competence of the Community, which therefore is solely responsible for setting the rules under which goods may cross the external borders of the Community. Harmonising the external border regime for goods was also a necessary corollary of the abolition of all restrictions on internal trade within the customs union established by the EC Treaty.

A similar process of supra-nationalisation of external borders has been set in motion by the Amsterdam Treaty with respect to the movement of persons. The Amsterdam Treaty introduced the goal of the establishment of an area of freedom, security and justice, which included the abolition of all internal border controls. At the same time, the Amsterdam Treaty also foresaw the adoption by the Community of flanking measures with respect to external border controls. These measures were adopted partially through the integration of the existing Schengen acquis into the framework of the European Community, and have led to a considerable harmonisation of visa policy in the Community.

However, unlike in the area of trade policy, the harmonisation of the rules on the crossing of external borders by persons has remained partial and

1.   The author is grateful to Carmel O'Reilly for useful comments and suggestions. The article expresses the personal view of the author only.

incomplete. This is particularly true in the area of visa policy, where Community harmonisation only covers short-term visas up to three months, and not long-term visas or residence permits, which are considered to be more sensitive from the point of view of immigration policy. This more hesitant approach to harmonisation with regard to the cross-border movement of persons is due to the politically sensitive nature of migration policy. The result, however, is the current awkward situation in which the crossing of the external border of the Union by persons is governed by a mix of national and Community rules.

The present contribution will examine the consequences of this incomplete harmonisation for the external competences of the Community and – by implication – of its Member States. It will focus particularly on the issue of visa policy, since the granting or refusal of visas[2] is the most visible act affecting the movement of persons across borders. At the same time, visa policy is also increasingly becoming an issue in the negotiation of international agreements. The question whether it is the Community or its Member States which may conclude such agreements is therefore also an important question in practice.

The present contribution will first trace the historical development of EC visa policy from the Treaty of Maastricht to the Treaty of Amsterdam (II). It will then set out the current state of harmonisation of visa policy in Community law (III). The contribution will go on to examine the principles governing the EC's external competence in the field of visa policy, and in particular the question whether this competence may be regarded as exclusive (IV). On this basis, the contribution will examine some examples of international agreements concluded by the EC or its Member States in the field of visa policy (V). The contribution will also examine the relationship between EC visa policy and some other EU external relations policies, in particular the common commercial policy and the Common Foreign and Security Policy (CFSP) (VI).

II.   The Evolution of EC Visa Policy

The EC's competences in the field of visa policy have developed gradually, and the current state of EC visa rules still bears the traces of this historical development. For this reason, this section will provide a brief overview of the historical development of EC visa rules.

---

2.   For the purposes of the present contribution, a visa is understood as an authorisation required with a view to entry of a person into the territory of the issuing state.

A.   The Treaty of Maastricht

The first provision of EC law to deal explicitly with visa policy was Article 100c of the EC Treaty, which was inserted by the Treaty of Maastricht. Until the Treaty of Amsterdam, this provision was the only element of visa policy subject to the "Community method". Article 100c, which was contained in the chapter of the Treaty dealing with the harmonisation of laws in the common market, covered two matters: a) the list of third countries whose nationals must be in possession of a visa; and b) a uniform format for visas.

The Community legislated on both matters. The first Community measure on visas was Regulation 1683/95 laying down a uniform format for visas[3]. The second recital to that regulation emphasised its "internal market" objectives and, in terms of a Community visa policy, stated that the uniform format was an important step towards the harmonisation of visa policy.

As regards the list of third countries whose nationals must be in possession of a visa, the Commission had equally promptly submitted a proposal.[4] However, the adoption of this proposal proved rather more difficult and time-consuming. In the explanatory memorandum to its proposal, the Commission had stated that "ideally it would have wished to place every third country either on a negative list or on a positive list but acknowledged that this was impossible because of the very large number of third countries for which the practices of MS diverged and the sensitive nature of the decision to be taken with respect to many of those countries."[5] It was the Commission's clear view that Article 100c was designed to achieve a complete harmonisation in terms of the listing of third countries and that two exhaustive lists should have been its outcome – one list of all third countries whose nationals had to be in possession of a visa (the so-called "black list") and the other a list of all countries whose nationals are free from the visa requirement (the "white list"). However, political reality being what it was, the Commission's proposal only included a black list and for the rest allowed Member States to decide whether or not to impose visa requirements on the nationals of countries not listed, though this

---

3.   Council Regulation (EC) No 1683/95 of 29 May 1995, OJ L 164, 14.7.1995, p. 1.
4.   Com (93) 684 of 10 December 1993. This proposal covered not only a proposal on the visa list, but also a proposal based on Article K.3 of the Treaty on European Union establishing the Convention on the crossing of the external borders of the Member States.
5.   Com (93) 684.

could only be applied for a limited period until June 1996. The limited period proposed by the Commission did not survive Council deliberations. Regulation 2317/95[6], as finally adopted on 25 September 1995, allowed Member States to determine, for an indefinite period, the visa requirements for nationals of third countries not on the common list. However, this modification was deemed by the Court of Justice in Case C-392/95 to have been "substantial", and therefore necessitating the re-consultation of Parliament. The fact that the Council had not re-consulted the Parliament entailed the annulment of Regulation No 2317/95.[7]

The regulation which was adopted following the annulment – Regulation 549/1999[8] – took the same form as the 1995 version in as much as only a black list was drawn up and the Member States were left free to determine the visa requirements for nationals of third countries not on the common list. However, despite the fact that the regulation did not, as the Commission might have wished, achieve a complete harmonization in terms of the countries subjected to the visa requirement and those that were not did not signify that the matter was completely in the hands of national policy. Rather, by the time of the adoption Regulation 549/1999, visa policy had become the subject of the intense cooperation in the context of the Schengen agreement.

B.   The Schengen Cooperation

In June 1985, five Member States[9] had signed an agreement in the Luxembourg village of Schengen "on the gradual abolition of checks at their common borders". The delicate balance of the agreement was encapsulated in Article 17[10] thereof – an area of free movement to be made possible by the adoption of compensatory or flanking measures to safeguard internal security and prevent illegal immigration. Crystallizing

6.   OJ L 234, 3.10.1995, p. 1.
7.   Case C-392/95, Parliament/Council, [1997] ECR I-3213, para. 24.
8.   Council Regulation (EC) No 574/1999 of 12 March 1999 determining the third countries whose nationals must be in possession of visas when crossing the external borders of the Member States, OJ L 72, 18.3.1999, p. 2.
9.   The Benelux States, Germany and France.
10.   Article 17 reads: *With regard to the movement of persons, the Parties shall endeavour to abolish checks at common borders and transfer them to their external borders. To that end they shall endeavour first to harmonise, where necessary, the laws, regulations and administrative provisions concerning the prohibitions and restrictions on which the checks are based and to take complementary measures to safeguard internal security and prevent illegal immigration by nationals of States that are not members of the European Communities.*

the objectives of the Schengen agreement, and particularly the compensatory measures, was left to the Schengen Implementing Convention ("the Schengen Convention"), signed, on 19 June 1990, also in Schengen, and which became operational on 26 March 1995[11].

The harmonization of visas policies had always been envisaged by the Schengen Agreement[12] and so, the Schengen Convention devoted a chapter to the matter, setting out the broad outlines of a visa policy. In terms of broad outlines, the visa policy as conceived by the Convention was based on three essential elements – common arrangements relating to third states whose nationals were subject to a visa requirement, the notion of a uniform visa valid for the entire territory of the Contracting Parties and uniform criteria for issuing the uniform visa. It was left to the Schengen Executive Committee[13] to fill in the details of those essential elements particularly as regards common rules for the examination of visas, their form, content and validity and the fees to be charged for their issue. By 1999 and the entry into force of the Treaty of Amsterdam, the "filling in of the details" represented a rather impressive body of work. Essentially, almost all aspects of visa policy had been harmonized.

Work on visa policy had, indeed, begun even before the entry into force of the Convention. By December 1993, the nine countries at that date participating in Schengen had completed the work on a uniform visa. This work was acknowledged by the Commission in its Explanatory Memorandum[14] to the proposal on a uniform visa; it was, indeed, stated that the "Schengen" model fulfilled the technical specifications set out in the proposal. Thus, and although this is obviously not specified in the regulation itself, the uniform format as set up by Regulation 1683/95 did in actual practice replace the Schengen version[15].

With respect to the requirement for a visa, Schengen had at the time of the adoption of Regulation 574/ 1999, developed three lists, the so-called black, white and grey lists. The black list of countries whose nationals required visas included 130 countries; the white list of countries whose nationals did not require visas included 30 countries. The other countries (18 of them) were included in a grey list allowing the Parties to decide

---

11. By which time, the original five had been joined by Italy, Spain, Portugal and Greece. By 1999, 13 of the 15 Member States were "Schengen" States.
12. See Article 20 thereof.
13. See Articles 12(3) and 17.
14. Com (1994) 287.
15. Confirmed in SEC(1999)1213.

whether or not to impose the visa requirement[16]. In the Explanatory Memorandum to the visa regulation, the Commission stated somewhat cryptically that "the Commission has naturally had regard to all these texts when drafting this proposal and has drawn on them where appropriate".

However, the Schengen harmonization of visa policy went far beyond what was contemplated by Article 100c of the Treaty. In particular, and most importantly, it harmonized the procedures and conditions which would govern the issuing of visas and in doing so, it dealt with such matters as how to complete the application form, the accompanying documentation, the examination procedure, the fees and the matter of consular organization and cooperation. The results of this activity were consolidated in the Common Consular Instructions (the CCI)[17] which was essentially a guidebook for the benefit of consular agents for the daily treatment of applications for visas.

C.   The Amsterdam Treaty

At the time of the entry into force of Treaty of Amsterdam, visa policy, thus, derived from two sources – Community acts and the Schengen Convention. By virtue of the Protocol integrating the Schengen *acquis* into the framework of the European Union (hereinafter referred to as the "Schengen protocol"), the Schengen Convention and all rules adopted thereunder were incorporated into the Union framework and thereby essentially became instruments of secondary Community law, or of Union law for those matters that remained with the "third pillar".[18] On 20 May 1999, the Council, acting on the basis of the Schengen protocol, adopted Decision 1999/436/EC[19] which determined, in conformity with the provisions of the Treaty establishing the European Community and the

---

16. By the time of the integration of the Schengen *acquis* there remained only one country on the grey list.
17. The operative version in 1999 had been adopted by a Decision of the Executive Committee of 28 April – Sch/Com-Ex (99) 13 and was later published in the Official Journal No L 239 of 22.9.2000, p. 317. Until that publication, the CCI were secret and unpublished outside the Schengen circle. The current version is to be found in OJ C 326, 22.12.2005, p. 1.
18. On the special arrangements applicable to Denmark, Ireland and the UK in this context, cf. the contribution by Martenczuk in this book.
19. OJ L 176, 10.07.1999, p. 17.

Treaty on European Union, the legal bases for each of the provisions or decisions which constitute the Schengen *acquis*.[20]

This integration of the Schengen acquis into the framework of the European Community also had significant implications for the external relations of the Member States in the field of visa policy. The Schengen cooperation had been intergovernmental in character, and had therefore left the foreign relations powers of the Schengen Member States relatively unaffected.[21] In contrast, with the communitarization of the Schengen acquis, the principles of the case law of the Court of Justice on the exclusive competence of the Community would become applicable, with the potential consequence that the Member States might lose some of their competences in this area. Conscious of this fact, the Member States therefore concluded with the Treaty of Amsterdam a "Protocol on external relations of the Member States with regard to the crossing of external borders". This Protocol, which was annexed to the EC Treaty, provides that "[t]he provisions on the measures on the crossing of external borders included in Article 62 (2) (a) of Title IV of the Treaty shall be without prejudice to the competence of Member States to negotiate or conclude agreements with third countries as long as the they respect Community law and other relevant international agreements".[22] The significance of this Protocol for the external relations of the EC in the field of visa policy will be examined in more detail in Section IV below.

III. The Current State of Harmonisation of EC Visa Policy

This section will provide an overview of the current state of harmonisation of EC visa policy. In this context, it must be noted that EC visa law remains

---

20. Cf. Pieter Jan Kuijper, Some Legal Problems Associated with the Communitarization of Policy on Visas, Ayslum, and Immigration under the Amsterdam Treaty and Incorporation of the Schengen acquis, 37 [2000] CMLR 345.
21. However, Article 136 of the Schengen Implementing Convention had already provided that agreements on border checks should be negotiated in consultation with other Schengen Member States, and that agreements simplifying or abolishing border checks should be concluded with the agreement of the other Schengen Member States.
22. The Intergovernmental Conference equally adopted Declaration No. 16, which is attached to the Treaty of Amsterdam, and states that "the Conference agrees that foreign policy considerations of the Union and the Member States shall be taken into account in the application of Article 62 (2) (b) of the Treaty establishing the European Community". Since Article 62 (2) (b) EC is the legal basis for EC visa policy, this declaration underlines the foreign policy significance of visa policy.

rather fragmented. This fragmentation has two main causes. The first cause is the historical evolution of EC visa policy, as a result of which important questions are still regulated in texts which have their origin in the Schengen cooperation, notably the Schengen Convention and the CCI. However, this fragmentation of the legal bases of EC visa law is likely be temporary, since the Commission has proposed the adoption of a Community Code on Visas, which will replace and consolidate most of the legal acts governing short-term visas, including the Schengen Convention and the CCI.[23]

The second and more permanent source of fragmentation of EC visa law is the distinction between short-term visas on the one hand, and long-term visas and residence permits, on the other.[24] Already the Schengen cooperation had focused on short-term visas for stays not exceeding three months, whereas long-term stays were left to be regulated by the Member States. This basic distinction was upheld by the Treaty of Amsterdam, which introduced distinct legal bases for short-term and long-term visas with more demanding procedural requirements for the latter. As a consequence, the state of harmonisation of visa policy is far more advanced in the field of short-term visas than when it comes to long-term stays. The following discussion will therefore mainly focus on short-term visas; long-term stays will be dealt within only briefly at the end of this section (D).

A.   The EC Treaty and Visa Policy

The Treaty of Amsterdam moved visa policy from the third pillar of the Union to the first pillar. The legal basis for EC visa policy is now exclusively to be found in Title IV of Part III of the EC Treaty.

Article 62 EC is the legal basis for measures in the field of border controls and short-term visas. According to this provision, the Council shall, within

---

23.   COM (2006) 403 final. The Community Code on Visas would not, however, replace Regulation 539/2001 listing the countries whose nationals must be in possession of visas when crossing the external borders and those who are exempt from that requirement, and Regulation 1683 on the uniform format for visas.

24.   It should be noted that it is doubtful whether, and to which extent, visas should still be required from third-country nationals who are long-term residents. However, in the present contribution, the terms long-term visa and residence permit will be used interchangeably.

a period of five years after the entry into force of the Treaty of Amsterdam, adopt the following measures:

1. measures with a view to ensuring, in compliance with Article 14, the absence of any controls on persons, be they citizens of the Union or nationals of third countries, when crossing internal borders;
2. measures on the crossing of the external borders of the Member States which shall establish:
   (a) standards and procedures to be followed by Member States in carrying out checks on persons at such borders;
   (b) rules on visas for intended stays of no more than three months, including:
      (i) the list of third countries whose nationals must be in possession of visas when crossing the external borders and those whose nationals are exempt from that requirement;
      (ii) the procedures and conditions for issuing visas by Member States;
      (iii) a uniform format for visas;
      (iv) rules on a uniform visa.
3. measures setting out the conditions under which nationals of third countries shall have the freedom to travel within the territory of the Member States during a period of no more than three months.

Within Article 62, it is paragraph (2) (b) which is the legal basis for measures concerning short-term visas, which are defined as visas for intended stays of no more than three months. The measures listed under Article 62 (2) (b) cover essentially all relevant aspects of short-term visa policy as developed under the EC Treaty and the Schengen Convention by the time of the Treaty of Amsterdam.[25] As regards the procedure for the adoption of Community acts, however, there still remain some differences between the various matters listed in Article 62 (2) (b) EC. According to Article 67 (3) EC, measures falling under Article 62 (2) (b) (i) and (iii), i.e. the visa list and the uniform format for visas, are adopted by the Council acting by qualified majority and after consultation of the European Parliament. These are the measures which had already fallen within Community competence since the Maastricht Treaty. In contrast, the measures falling under Article 62 (2) (b) (ii) and (iv), which were originally subject of the Schengen cooperation, are, since the end of the transitional period of five years from the Treaty of Amsterdam, adopted

---

25. It should be noted, however, that according to the wording of Article 62 (2) (b) ("including"), the enumeration of measures in this provision is not exhaustive.

according to the co-decision procedure.[26] The main difference between the various measures listed in Article 62 (2) (b) is therefore the involvement of the European Parliament, which is only consulted on measures referred to in letters (i) and (iii) of that provision.

The remaining provisions of Article 62 do not directly concern visa policy, but rather measures concerning the abolition of internal borders, the controls at external borders, and the freedom of travel for third-country nationals within the territory of the Member States. Nonetheless, these provisions are closely linked to visa policy, and should therefore be briefly mentioned as important context. Importantly, Article 62 (1), with its explicit reference to nationals of third countries, clarifies that the abolition of internal borders shall not benefit only EU nationals, but equally the nationals of third countries. Article 62 (2) (a), which concerns the standards and procedures for checks at external borders, is equally relevant, since it is at the external border that the obligation to be in possession of a visa is normally enforced.[27] Finally, Article 63 (3) EC allows regulating the right of third-country nationals to move freely through the territory of the Member States for a period of no more than three months, including both third-country nationals who have entered with a visa, and third country nationals who are exempted from the requirement of a visa.

As regards long-term stays, the relevant legal basis is Article 63 (3) (a) EC, which allows the adoption of measures on immigration policy in the area of "conditions of entry and residence, and standards on procedures for the issue by Member States of long-term visas and residence permits, including those for the purpose of family reunion". Under Article 18 of the Schengen Convention, long-term visas were national visas which in principle remained subject to national rules. This hesitant approach to harmonisation with respect to long-term stays is still present in the EC Treaty. Measures under Article 63 (3) (a) are still decided by the Council with unanimity, and after mere consultation of the European Parliament. When the Council, at the end of the transitional period, decided to render the co-decision procedure applicable to most remaining matters under Articles 62 and 63, it consciously excluded Article 63 (3) (a) EC from these

26. Cf. Article 67 (4) EC. During the transitional period, such measures were adopted by the Council acting unanimously on a proposal from the Commission or on the initiative of a Member State and after consulting the European Parliament, Article 67 (1) EC.
27. Cf. Article 5 (1) (b) of the Schengen Borders Code (Council Regulation 562/2006, OJ L 105, 13.4.2006, p. 1), which makes the entry by third-country citizens subject to the possession of a valid visa, if required by Regulation 539/2001.

improvements.[28] This clearly reflects the political sensitivity of long-term migration, including economic migration, which makes Member States reluctant to relinquish control of this policy area.[29]

Another important difference between long-term and short-term visa policy results from the last paragraph of Article 63, which provides that measures in the field of long-term migration are not subject to the five-year transitional period. Reflecting this difference, the progress of harmonisation in the area of long-term visas and migration policy has been far slower than it has been in the area of short-term visas.

B.   Visa Requirements and Visa Exemptions

The first question of visa policy is the definition of which individuals must be in possession of a visa for crossing the external borders of the Union. This question is regulated by Council Regulation 539/2001,[30] which replaced the earlier regulation 549/1999 still adopted on the basis of the Maastricht Treaty. Regulation 539/2001, which was adopted on the basis of Article 62 (2) (b) (i) EC, contains the common lists both of the countries whose nationals must be in possession of a visa in order to cross the external borders, and the countries whose nationals are exempted from that requirement.[31]

The fifth recital of the Regulation explains that the determination of the countries subject to the visa requirement and those exempt from it is to be made on a case-by-case basis, taking into account factors such as illegal immigration, public policy and security, the EC's external relations with third countries, and regional coherence and reciprocity. The condition of reciprocity has taken on particular importance for the application of Regulation 539/2001. Under the regulation as originally in force, the introduction of a visa requirement by an exempted third country for the nationals of any Member States would automatically have led to the re-

---

28.   Cf. Article 1 (2) of Council Decision 2004/927/EC, OJ L 396, 31.12.2004, p. 45.
29.   Similar concerns underlie a provision to be introduced by the Treaty of Lisbon, according to which the competences of the Union in the field of long-term migration would not affect the right of Member States to determine the volumes of admission of third-country nationals coming from third countries in order to seek work, whether employed or self-employed (Article 79 [5] TFEU).
30.   OJ L 81, 21.3.2001, p. 1.
31.   On this Regulation, cf. Annalisa Meloni, The Development of a Common Visa Policy under the Treaty of Amsterdam, 42 [2005] CMLRev. 1357, 1365 et seq.

introduction of a visa requirement for the nationals of the third country within a period of 30 days. This provision was likely to cause considerable difficulties following the enlargement of the EU by 10 new Member States in May 2004. Since a number of third countries still required visas for most of the new Member States, a strict application of the reciprocity mechanism would have meant the reintroduction of visa requirements for a number of important third countries, including the US, Canada, and Australia. This reintroduction might then in turn have triggered the reintroduction of visa requirements for all EU citizens.

In order to avoid this consequence, Regulation 539/2001 was amended[32] to render the reciprocity mechanism more flexible and allow more time for negotiations. Under the new mechanism, as set out in Article 1 (4) of Regulation 539/2001, where a visa-exempted third country introduces a visa requirement for nationals of a Member State, the Member State concerned shall notify this to the Council and the Commission. The Commission shall then make the necessary contacts with the third countries in order to seek the reestablishment of reciprocity, and shall report on the outcome of its efforts to the Council. If reciprocity has not been re-established, the Commission may also propose the temporary or definitive reintroduction of the visa requirement for the third country concerned. However, contrary to the old system, there is no automaticity towards the reestablishment of the visa requirement, since the Commission is not obliged to propose the reintroduction of the visa requirement at any given point. On the basis of these provisions, the Commission has conducted negotiations with a number of third countries, which have led to the reestablishment of visa reciprocity in certain cases. In contrast, in the case of the United States, no progress has been made, since the United States still maintains visa requirements for 12 of the 27 EU Member States. This has led the Commission recently to consider the re-imposition of visa requirements on US nationals holding diplomatic or official passports.[33]

Pursuant to Article 1 (2) of Regulation 539/2001, certain further categories of persons are exempted from the visa requirement. This includes in particular the holders of a local border traffic card issued by Member States pursuant to the provisions of Regulation 1931/2006 on local border traffic.[34] However, the local border traffic card must be limited to the

---

32. Cf. Regulation 851/2005, OJ L 141, 4.6.2005, p. 3.
33. On EU-US cooperation in the field of visas, cf. the contribution by Soreca/Faull, in this book. Cf. equally the report from the Commission on visa reciprocity, COM (2006) 568 final.
34. OJ L 29, 3.2.2007, p. 3.

border area of the Member State, and thus does not give full freedom to travel in the territory of all Member States. Article 13 of Regulation 1931/ 2006 authorises Member States to conclude or maintain international agreements with third countries concerning local border traffic. However, before concluding any such agreement, the Member States concerned must consult with the Commission as to the compatibility of the agreement with the Regulation. Article 13 of the Regulation also foresees that agreements with third countries must ensure comparable rights to those granted to the border residents of the third country to any of the border residents of the Member States, including Community nationals and third-country nationals legally resident in the border area. Under 4 (1) of Regulation 539/ 2001, Member States may also exempt from the visa requirement certain other categories of persons, including holders of diplomatic or official passports, and civilian air and sea crews.

According to Article 20 (1) of the Schengen Convention, the legal basis of which is Article 62 (3) EC, nationals who are exempted from the visa requirement may move freely within the territories of the Member States for a period of maximum three months during the sixth month following the date of their first entry. The purpose of the stay is not regulated. However, according to Article 4 (3) of Regulation 539/2001, Member States may provide for exceptions from the visa exemptions for persons carrying out a paid activity during their stay.

C.   Schengen Visas: Conditions, Procedures, Legal Effect

The conditions and procedures for issuing short-term visas are regulated in general terms in Articles 12 et seq. of the Schengen Convention. However, considerably more detail is provided in the Common Consular Instructions (CCI). The CCI were originally a guidebook elaborated by the Schengen Committee, but have been integrated into the EC framework and allocated Articles 62 and 63 EC as their legal basis.[35]

The CCI have subsequently been amended by the Council on numerous occasions.[36] The procedure of the amendment of the CCI is contained in Council Regulation 789/2001, by which the Council reserved certain

---

35.   Council Decision 1999/436, OJ L 176, 10.7.1999, p. 27.
36.   The current version is published in OJ C 326, 22.12.2005, p. 1.

powers to amend the CCI.[37] Despite their intergovernmental origins and their atypical denomination, the CCI are therefore an act of the EC institutions which is binding for the Member States.

The CCI contain detailed rules governing the issuance of short-term visas, including the type of visa, the Member State responsible for the issuance, the forms to be used for visa applications, documentation to be provided by the applicant, conditions regarding the return and means of subsistence, the possibility of personal interviews, criteria for the examination of applications, etc.[38] Equally harmonised is the fee payable for a Schengen visa, which came into effect from 1 January 2007 and was increased from € 35 to € 60.[39]

The EC has also adopted special rules to facilitate the issuance of short-term visas in specific cases or for specific categories of persons. Such cases include the issuance of visas at the border, and in particular to seamen in transit;[40] the issuance of visas to members of the Olympic family taking part in the Olympic or Paralympic Games;[41] and the admission of researchers from third countries.[42] A further specific regime is the Facilitated Transit Document and Facilitated Rail Transit Document established by Council Regulation (EC) 693/2003.[43] These documents, which replace the visa and are issued according to facilitated procedures, are intended to facilitate transit by land for third-country nationals who must necessarily pass through the territory of EC Member States in order to travel between two parts of their country which are not geographically contiguous. This scheme was put into place to address the difficulties of transit between the Russian region of Kaliningrad and the rest of Russia following the 2004 enlargement of the EC, which led to Kaliningrad being separated from the rest of Russia by EU Member States.

---

37. This regulation was challenged by the Commission as an infringement of the provisions of the Treaty on the implementing powers of the Commission. However, the action was dismissed by the Court of Justice; cf. Case C-257/01, Commission/ Council, [2005] ECR I-345.
38. Cf. in more detail Steven Peers, EU Justice and Home Affairs Law, p. 162 et seq. (2006)
39. Council Decision 2006/440/EC, OJ L 175, 29.6.2006, p. 77.
40. Council Regulation (EC) 415/2003, OJ L 64, 7.3.2003, p. 1.
41. Council Regulation (EC) 1295/2003, OJ L 183, 22.7.2003, p. 1 (concerning the Games in Athens); Regulation of the European Parliament and the Council (EC) 2046/2005, OJ L 334, 20.12.2005, p. 1 (concerning the Winter Games in Turin).
42. Recommendation of the European Parliament and the Council 2005/761/EC, OJ L 289, 3.11.2005, p. 23. This recommendation, which oddly enough was adopted under the co-decision procedure, is not legally binding.
43. OJ L 99, 17.4.2003, p. 8.

In accordance with Article 11 (1) of the Schengen Convention, the period of stay authorised under the common visa, which is also called "Schengen visa", shall not exceed a total period of three months in any half-year period from the date of first entry. According to Article 19 of the Schengen Convention, third-country nationals who hold a Schengen visa may move freely through the territory of all Schengen states.[44] Interestingly, there are no limitations on the purpose of the stay. Finally, it should also be noted that the format of short-term visas is harmonised by Regulation 1683/1995.[45]

D.   Long-term stays

Compared to short-term visas, which are subject to an exhaustive harmonisation, the Community legislation on long-term stays is far more limited.[46] Since the entry intro force of the Amsterdam Treaty, the Community has succeeded in adopting only a very small number of measures governing the issuance of long-term visas or residence permits, namely regarding the admission of third country nationals for the purposes of research,[47] and for the purposes of studies, pupil exchanges, unremunerated training or voluntary service.[48] An important measure adopted on the basis of Article 63 (3) (a) EC was also Directive 2003/86/EC regarding the right to family reunification.[49] In contrast, the EC has not adopted any significant measures affecting economic migration. In particular, a Commission proposal for a directive on the conditions of entry and residence of third-country nationals for the purpose of paid employment and self-employed economic activities[50] did not find support in the Council, and was subsequently withdrawn.[51] To the extent that no measures of the Community have been adopted, long-term visas remain national visas, and are issued in accordance with the law of each Member State.

---

44.   On the variable geometry of the Schengen area, cf. the Contribution by Martenczuk in this book.
45.   OJ L 164, 14.7.1995, p. 1. It is interesting to note that this regulation, which was adopted already before the entry into force of the Amsterdam Treaty, is one of the few measures in the field of visa policy also applicable to the UK and Ireland.
46.   On the state of harmonisation in this area, cf. in more detail the contribution by Peers in this book.
47.   Council Directive 2005/71/EC, OJ L 289, 3.1.2005, p. 15.
48.   Council Directive 2004/114/EC OJ L 375, 23.12.2004, p. 12.
49.   OJ L 251, 3.10.2003, p. 12.
50.   COM (2001) 386 final.
51.   OJ C 64, 17.3.2006, p. 3. Cf. also Peers, above note 38, p. 222 et seq.

IV. Visa Policy and EC External Competence

According to the settled case law of the ECJ, it is clear that the EC has external competences not only when such competences are explicitly attributed to it in the Treaty, but also when the negotiation or conclusion of an international agreement is necessary to attain the objectives of the Treaty.[52] There is no reason why such an implied external competence may not also arise in the field of visa policy, when it is found that the conclusion of an international agreement is necessary to further the objectives of the Treaty. Therefore, Articles 62 (2) or 63 (3) EC imply an external competence of the EC.

However, far more difficult to answer is the question whether, and to which extent, the external competences of the EC in the field of visa policy are exclusive in nature, or shared with the Member States. This section will try to provide an answer to this question by examining the three basic cases in which the ECJ has recognised that EC external competences may become exclusive: first, it will examine whether exclusive competence can be regarded as the consequence of the very nature of visa policy; second, it will examine whether exclusive EC competence can be regarded as necessary for the attainment of the objectives of the Treaty; and third, it will examine whether EC exclusive competence in this field follows from the internal harmonisation of EC visa policy.

A. Exclusive Competence "by Nature"?

For a small number of policy areas, the ECJ has recognised that EC competence is exclusive by definition, without having recourse to any additional criteria such as necessity or internal harmonisation. The most prominent such policy area is the common commercial policy.[53]

---

52. Opinion 1/76, Laying-up Fund for Inland Waterway Vessels, [1977] ECR 741, para. 3; Opinion 1/03, Lugano Convention, [2006] ECR I-1145, para. 114; generally on EC external competence, cf. David O'Keeffe, Exclusive, Concurrent and Shared Competence, in Allan Dashwood/Christophe Hillion (ed.), The General Law of E.C. External Relations, p. 179 (2000).

53. Another area for which the ECJ recognised the exclusivity of EC powers is the conservation of marine living resources (cf. Joined cases C-3, 4 and 6/76, [1976] ECR 1279]. An explicit list of the areas of exclusive competence will be provided in Article 3 (1) of the Treaty on the functioning of the European Union, which lists the customs union, the establishing of competition rules necessary for the functioning of the internal market, monetary policy, the conservation of marine biological resources, and the common commercial policy.

The exclusive nature of the Community's powers in the field of trade is not explicitly stated in the Treaty. Rather, it was developed by the Court of Justice taking into account the objectives and the nature of the policy area as established by the Treaty. In its Opinion on the OECD's Local Cost Standard, the ECJ referred to the need to avoid differences in conditions of competition for the undertakings of Member States in export markets.[54] In *Donckerwolcke*, the ECJ focussed more sharply on the internal working of the EC customs union. The ECJ began by noting that according to Article 24 EC, goods originating in third countries which have cleared customs may circulate freely throughout the customs union just like EC goods.[55] The Court continued by noting that this assimilation of third-country goods to EC goods could only take full effect if goods are subject to the same conditions of importation regardless of the state in which they were put in free circulation.[56] Moreover, the Court also noted the existence of a transitional period, by the end of which all necessary measures should have been adopted, and concluded that after the end of the transitional period, Member States could no longer take measures in the field without authorisation from the EC.[57] Finally, in its Opinion on the International Agreement on Natural Rubber, the ECJ emphasised the need to avoid "disturbances in intra-Community trade by reason of the disparities which would then exist in certain sectors of economic relations with non-Member countries".[58]

There are some striking similarities between the characteristics of the CCP referred to in this case law, and the characteristics of EC visa policy in the Schengen area.[59] As in the customs union, third country nationals are to some extent – although not completely – assimilated to EC nationals in the sense that they are dispensed from internal border controls, and have the right – within certain limits – to travel throughout the Schengen area. This means that the visa practice of each Member State can have an immediate impact on all other Member States. This is most obvious for the risk of illegal immigration: a third-country national who decides to overstay his or her visa may very well do so not in the Member State which has issued the visa, but in any other Member State. Similarly, if a Member State issues a

---

54. Opinion 1/75, OECD Local Cost Standard, [1975] ECR 1355, pt. 2.
55. Case C-41/76, Donckerwolcke, [1976] ECR 1921, para. 17.
56. Donckerwolcke, para. 25.
57. Donckerwolcke, para. 26, 32.
58. Opinion 1/78, International Agreement on Natural Rubber, [1979] ECR 2871, para. 45.
59. On this comparison, cf. also Steven Peers, EU Borders and Globalisation, in Kees Groenendijk/Elspeth Guild/Paul Minderhoud (ed.), In Search of Europe's Borders, p. 45 (2003).

visa to a person which presents a security risk, this risk is borne not just by the issuing Member State, but by all Member States part of the Schengen area. Finally, recognising this need for uniformity, there is also a transitional period of five years from the entry into force of the Treaty of Amsterdam within which the measures foreseen in Article 62 must be adopted.

However, the parallels end here. Contrary to trade in goods, not all cross-border movements of persons have been made subject to Community disciplines. This is most obvious for all persons entering the EC for the purpose of long-term stays. Even though in an area without internal borders, long-term migration can equally have an impact on all Member States, and not just on the Member State which authorises the entry, the Member States have not drawn the same consequence for short-term visas, namely that the issuance of long-term visas and residence permits should be made subject to uniform principles. This is also made clear by the explicit exclusion of the matters governed by Article 63 (3) from the five-year transitional period.

Also relevant is Declaration No. 18 to the Treaty of Amsterdam, according to which "Member States may negotiate and conclude agreements with third countries in the domains covered by Article 63 (3) (a) of the Treaty establishing the European Community as long as such agreements respect Community law". A similar provision is also found in the Protocol on external relations of the Member States with regard to the crossing of external borders, which provides that the "provisions on the measures on the crossing of external borders included in Article 62 (2) (a) of Title IV [...] shall be without prejudice to the competence of Member States to negotiate or conclude agreements with third countries as long as they respect Community law and other relevant international agreements".

It is true that neither of these two texts actually refers to short-term visas, which fall under Article 62 (2) (b). However, overall, it is clear that at the time of the conclusion of the Amsterdam Treaty, Member States did not have the will to accept that the conferral of competences to the EC in the field of visa policy and external border controls would automatically deprive them of all external competences in the area. For this reason, and given the only partial approach to the harmonisation of visa policy under the Amsterdam Treaty, it appears difficult to argue that visa policy has become an exclusive competence of the EC by its very nature, as desirable as this might appear in an area without any internal borders.

B.   Exclusive Competence "by Necessity"?

In Opinion 1/76, the Court of Justice held that the EC had an external competence when the conclusion of an international agreement was necessary for the attainment of the objectives of the EC Treaty.[60] The concrete agreement at issue in Opinion 1/76 was aimed at reducing over-capacity in shipping on the Rhine through the creation of a laying-up fund. The ECJ considered that the conclusion of an international agreement, as opposed to autonomous measures, was necessary for the attainment of the EC's objectives in the field of transport because Swiss vessels were also navigating on the Rhine, and therefore had to be brought into the mechanism.[61]

In the later case law of the Court, Opinion 1/76 has frequently been referred to as authority for the proposition that EC external competence will be exclusive when the Community's internal competence can be exercised only at the same time as its external competence.[62] In other words, the external competence will be exclusive, to use the formulation adopted in the Treaty of Lisbon,[63] when the conclusion of an international agreement is necessary to enable the Community to exercise its internal competence. Thus, there must not only been an internal competence, but the internal and external competence must be linked in such a way that the former cannot be exercised without the latter.

It is clear, therefore, that the test established by Opinion 1/76 is an important one. This is illustrated by the fact that the Court of Justice has never since Opinion 1/76 found Community competence to be exclusive on account of the necessity to attain a Community objective. For instance, in the Open Skies judgments, the Court found that the conclusion of an international air transport agreement was not necessary to achieve the

---

60.   Opinion 1/76, Laying-up Fund for Inland Waterway Vessels, [1977] ECR 741, para. 3.
61.   Opinion 1/76, para. 2.
62.   Opinion 1/94, Accession to the WTO, [1994] ECR I-5267, para. 85; Case C-467/98, Commission/Denmark (Open Skies), [2002] ECR I-9519, para. 57; Opinion 1/2003, Lugano Convention, [2006] ECR I-1145, para. 115. Even though in Opinion 1/76, the Court had not explicitly referred to exclusive competence, this interpretation appears to be based on para. 7 of Opinion 1/76, in which the Court had found that the participation of certain Member States in the Agreement was justified exclusively for the purpose of making amendments to certain pre-existing conventions to which the Member States were parties.
63.   Cf. Article 3 (2) of the Treaty on the Functioning of the Union.

objectives of the Community in the field of air transport. In particular, the Court found that the conclusion of a Community agreement was not necessary to avoid distortions in the common market resulting from bilateral air transport agreements, arguing that the Community institutions could prescribe a uniform approach to be followed through autonomous measures.[64]

On this basis, it is not clear that visa policy would meet the test of Opinion 1/76. It is clear that the conclusion of international agreements may be desirable for attaining the objectives of visa policy. For instance, international agreements may be a useful way of securing reciprocity as regards matters of visa facilitation or visa exemptions. However, as the reciprocity mechanism of Regulation 539/2001 illustrates, international agreements are not the only mechanism for ensuring reciprocity.[65] Moreover, as far as ensuring a uniform approach to the entry of third country-nationals into the EC is concerned, it is clear that autonomous measures can ensure the same result. Accordingly, it is unlikely that international agreements in the field of visa policy would be regarded as indispensable for the attainment of the objectives of the Treaty.

C.   Exclusive Competence by Virtue of Internal Harmonisation?

The third and arguably most important ground for exclusive external competence is the one set out by the Court in its ERTA judgment, in which the Court held that, to the extent that the Community has adopted common rules, the Member States may no longer accept international obligations which might affect those rules or alter their scope.[66] Given the

---

64.   Case C-467/98, Commission/Denmark (Open Skies), [2002] ECR I-9519, para. 59.
65.   A different situation may arise, however, when the granting of visa facilitation or visa exemptions is made conditional to commitments by the third country to accept repatriation of any of its nationals who remain illegally in the Community. This was in fact the situation underlying the ADS Agreement with China, which will be discussed below. Since legal commitments of the third country can be obtained only through the conclusion of an international agreement, it may indeed be argued that the agreement to this extent is indispensable for the attainment of the EC's objectives (on EC external competence for the conclusion of readmission agreements, cf. Schieffer in this book and Pieter-Jan Kuijper, The Evolution of the Third Pillar from Maastricht to the European Constitution: Institutional Aspects, 41 [2004] CMLRev. 609, 617-618).
66.   Case C-22/70, ERTA, [1971] ECR 263, para. 22.

relatively developed character of Community rules in this area, it is clear that the ERTA case law is a potential ground for exclusive EC competence in the field of EC visa policy.[67] However, the application of the ERTA doctrine to visa policy raises a number of complex questions, which shall be examined hereunder.

A first question as to how the ERTA doctrine relates to the Protocol on the external relations of the Member States with regard to the crossing of external borders and to Declaration No 18 to the Amsterdam Treaty. In this respect, it must be noted that these two texts only apply to Articles 62 (2) (a) and 63 (3) (a), and therefore are not applicable to international agreements concerning short-term visas based on Article 62 (2) (b). Moreover, both texts allow Member States only to negotiate international agreements to the extent that they "respect Community law". It appears that this must also include the respect of the ERTA case law, which the Court of Justice has derived directly from the duty of Member States under Article 10 not to jeopardise the objectives of the Community.[68] This means, therefore, that if the Community has legislated on the basis of Article 63 (3) (a) on a matter of long-term migration, the Member States may no longer conclude any international agreements which would affect the common rules. The same also applies for all agreements affecting the Community legislation on the control of external borders, and in particular the Schengen Borders Code.[69]

In a number of cases, the Court of Justice has considered that where a policy area is covered "to a large extent" by Community rules, any agreement falling within this policy area will fall under exclusive competence, without it being necessary for the subject-matter of the agreement and the internal rules to coincide in every respect.[70] An interesting question is therefore whether the harmonisation of EC visa policy has already reached a stage of completeness at which it may be said that visa policy is harmonised "to a large extent", even if isolated matters are not specifically addressed in EC legislation. The response to this

---

67. It must be noted that measures which were originally elaborated under the Schengen Cooperation, but later given a legal basis under the EC Treaty, must equally be regarded as EC measures for the purposes of the ERTA case law. This applies notably for the Schengen Convention and the CCI.
68. Cf. Peers, above note 38, p. 177.
69. It should be recalled that in this respect, the external competences of the Member States are already limited by Article 136 (1) and (2) of the Schengen Convention; cf. above footnote 21.
70. Cf. Opinion 2/91, ILO Convention No. 170, [1993] ECR I-1064, para. 25-26; Opinion 1/2003, Lugano Convention, [2006] ECR I-1145, para. 126.

question would presumably have to be negative for visa policy as a whole, given the rather rudimentary state of Community legislation on long-term stays. However, the questions poses itself more seriously for short-term visas, where the Community has regulated essentially all relevant questions including the definition of the nationals who need to be in possession of a visa, the procedure and conditions for obtaining a visa, and the format and legal effect of the visa. Even where a specific condition or procedural requirement for the obtention of a short-term visa is not specifically addressed in Community legislation, it is doubtful that Member States may negotiate and conclude international agreements on such a matter, since any such agreement would most likely also have an effect on other aspects of EC short-term visa rules.

A related question arises with respect to the numerous provisions of the Schengen acquis, which provide a certain discretion to Member States in the application of visa rules. It is clear that the fact that Member States implement the common rules as such does not affect the exclusivity of the EC's external competence, which depends merely on the extent of the EC's legislation. In this context, therefore, the fact that the common visa rules allow the administrative authorities to exercise a certain level of discretion does not mean that the question is not harmonised by EC rules. Otherwise, Member States could bind themselves through international agreements to exercise the discretion conferred upon them in a particular way. Such an approach would not be conducive to the uniform application of EC visa rules, and must therefore be regarded as incompatible with the ERTA case law.

V.   International Agreements and Visa Policy

On this basis, the article will now consider some examples of international agreements in the field of visa policy which have arisen in the recent practice of the European Community. Some of these examples will provide further illustrations for the difficult division of competences between the EC and its Member States in this field.

A.   The ADS Agreement with China

The first agreement negotiated and concluded by the EC in the field of visa policy was the ADS (Authorised Destination Status) Agreement with

China.[71] The full title of the agreement is "Memorandum of Understanding on visa and related issues concerning tourist groups from the People's Republic of China". However, despite its denomination as a Memorandum of Understanding, the ADS Agreement is in fact a full-fledged international agreement. This is made clear in Article 8 (6) of the Agreement, which explains that the agreement shall be legally binding on both parties.

The ADS Agreement is essentially an agreement facilitating the entry of Chinese tourist groups into the Community. For this purpose, Article 4 of the Agreement establishes a simplified procedure for the granting of tourist visas, under which designated Chinese travel agencies obtain, under certain conditions, the right to lodge visa applications on behalf of Chinese group travellers. The main facilitation compared to the normal rules is that the applicant is not called upon to appear in person to explain the reasons for the application.[72] The visa to be issued will be a Schengen visa limited to a period of validity of 30 days, and marked "ADS". Article 5 deals with issues relating to the illegal overstay of tourists who have entered with an ADS visa; it also contains a readmission clause obliging the Chinese authorities to readmit any Chinese national who has overstayed illegally. Article 6 of the Agreement establishes an ADS Committee composed of representatives of both sides, who will monitor the implementation of the agreement and decide on implementing arrangements. Some further issues regarding the selection of travel agencies, tour leaders and tour guides are dealt with in a non-binding declaration attached to the Agreement.[73]

The Agreement was concluded by the Council on the basis of Articles 62 (2) b) (ii) and (iv) and Article 63 (3) (b). In accordance with Article 300 (6) EC, the Agreement is binding on the institutions and the Member States, and thus constitutes an integral part of EC law. Its provisions concerning the granting of Schengen visas therefore prevail over the provisions of the CCI, and must be directly applied by the consular authorities of the Member States. In order to ensure uniform application of the agreement by the Member State's consular authorities, the Commission

---

71. OJ L 83, 20.3.2004, p. 12. The term "Approved Destination Status" refers to the requirements of Chinese law, according to which Chinese tourists are generally granted exit permission only for travel through "approved destinations", with which China has previously concluded an agreement regulating the modalities of such travel. On the complex variable geometry of this agreement, cf. the contribution by Martenczuk in this book.
72. Cf. Point III.4 of the CCI.
73. This solution was chosen since it was not certain that these matters fell under EC competence under Title IV.

issued a recommendation setting out further details.[74] This recommendation foresees *inter alia* that the withdrawal of accreditation of a Chinese travel agency by one Member State shall have immediate effect for all other Member States. Both the Agreement and the recommendation are unique in setting out a complex scheme for the granting of Schengen visas, which requires a high degree of consular cooperation between the Member States in the third country concerned.

It is also worth noting that the conclusion of the ADS agreement by the Community was preceded by important disagreements as to the nature of Community competence.[75] Before China had started negotiating with the Community, it had already concluded a bilateral ADS MoU with Germany. This bilateral MoU was similar to the later EC agreement in most respects, in particular as regards the issuance of Schengen visas by the German authorities. However, unlike the later EC agreement, it did not contain a readmission clause for Chinese over-stayers. When apprised of the German agreement, the Commission took the position that this agreement violated the exclusive competence of the Community over visas matters since it dealt with issues regulated in the CCI. This applied in particular to the requirement of a personal interview in the CCI, which was waived in the MoU. The fact that the CCI left Member States to decide not to require a personal interview in concrete cases did not mean that Member Sates have an external competence to waive such a requirement through the conclusion of an international agreement.

Moreover, it was clear that the bilateral agreement could lead to serious distortions within the Schengen area and the common market. As a result of the agreement, all Chinese group travellers would enter the Schengen area through Germany and typically use German airlines and travel operators. However, since the visas were Schengen visas, the tour groups would then travel throughout the Schengen area. And so, whereas the economic benefits of the agreement would be reaped largely by German operators, the risks in terms of illegal immigration and security would be borne by all Member States. It was therefore clear that the bilateral agreement was incompatible with the uniform application of the Schengen acquis, as well as with the necessary solidarity required in an area without internal borders.

---

74. OJ L 296, 21.9.2004, p. 23.
75. Cf. Kuijper, above note 65, p. 619.

Since the EC finally succeeded in negotiating a Schengen-wide agreement which superseded the German agreement,[76] the question of the compatibility of the bilateral agreement did not have to be decided by the ECJ. However, the case of the German ADS MoU illustrates the risks and costs of bilateralism in the area of visa policy in general, and short-term visas in particular. A strict application of the ERTA case law is therefore necessary in order to protect the uniform application of the harmonised rules in the field of short-term visas.

B.   Seafarers' Identity Document Convention

A somewhat similar question also arose in connection with the ILO's Convention No 185 on the Seafarers' Identity Document. This Convention, which was adopted in 2003, establishes a Seafarer's Identity Document. According to Article 6 of the Convention, the Contracting Parties shall allow seafarers who hold the document to go on shore for the purposes of shore leave and transit and transfer to other vessels. In other words, the holder of the Seafarer's Identity Document is exempted from any visa requirement which might otherwise apply.

The EC was not involved with the negotiation of the Convention, and, like all ILO Conventions, the Seafarers' Identity Document Convention does not contain a clause allowing the Community to become a party. However, the question arose whether the Convention did not partially fall under exclusive EC competence, given that the requirement to be in possession of a visa for crossing the external EU borders is harmonised through Regulation 539/2001. As the same time, however, Article 4 of that Regulation allows Member States to exempt from the visa requirement the civilian crew of ships navigating in international waters. Accordingly, the question was whether this authorisation contained in Regulation 539/2001 also implied the power of Member States to conclude international agreements.

In the final result, the Community institutions opted for a cautious approach and concluded that the Member States needed to be authorized to conclude the ILO Convention No. 185. This authorisation was granted to all Member States through a Council decision based on Articles 62 (2) (b) (i) in conjunction with Article 300 EC.[77] The ILO's Seafarers' Identity

---

76.   Article 7 of the EC-China ADS Agreement provides that any similar MoU or Agreement shall no longer be applied.

77.   Council Decision 2005/367/EC, OJ L 136, 30.5.2005, p. 1. On similar authorisations in the field of private international law, cf. the contribution by Hix in this book.

Document Convention therefore constitutes another example for a strict application of the ERTA case law in the field of short-term visas.

C.   Visa Facilitation Agreements

More recently, the Community has begun negotiating and concluding full-fledged visa facilitation agreements with a number of third countries. From the point of view of the Community, such agreements are a *quid pro quo* for the conclusion of readmission agreements by third countries. At the same time, to the extent that Community nationals are also subjected to a visa requirement by the third country, visa facilitation agreements also aim at ensuring reciprocal visa facilitation for EC nationals.

The first visa facilitation agreement to have been concluded by the EC is the agreement with Russia, which entered into force on 1 June 2007. This agreement contains reciprocal commitments in the field of visa facilitation on issues such as documentary evidence regarding the purpose of the journey, the issuance of multiple entry-visas, fees for processing visas, length of application procedures, and the like. The agreement also contains an exemption from visas requirements for the holders of diplomatic passports.[78] The entry into force of the visa facilitation agreement was linked to the entry into force of the readmission agreement, thus reflecting the close link between the two agreements.[79]

In the meantime, the EC has concluded further visa facilitation agreements with Albania,[80] Bosnia and Herzegovina,[81] Macedonia,[82] Montenegro,[83] Moldova,[84] Serbia,[85] and Ukraine.[86] To the extent that Community nationals are exempted from visa requirements by these countries, the objective of the agreement is primarily to facilitate the issuance of visas to the nationals of the third country. However, the agreements also contain a clause which renders the visa facilitation applicable to Community

---

78.   Article 11 of the Agreement. Because of this clause, the conclusion of the agreement had to be based, in addition to Article 62 (2) (b) (ii), also on letter (i) of that provision.
79.   Article 15 (2) of the Agreement.
80.   OJ L 334, 19.12.2007, p. 84.
81.   OJ L 334, 19.12.2007, p. 96.
82.   OJ L 334, 19.12.2007, p. 120.
83.   OJ L 334, 19.12.2007, p. 108.
84.   OJ L 334, 19.12.2007, p. 168
85.   OJ L 334, 19.12.2007, p. 136.
86.   OJ L 332, 18.12.2007, p. 66.

nationals in the event of the reintroduction of visa requirements by the third country.[87]

D.   Visa Exemption Agreements

Another specific type of agreement in the field of visa policy is visa exemption agreements. The idea of a visa exemption agreement has arisen in particular in connection with Brazil. Brazil still continues to require visas for the nationals of a number of Member States. When approached by the Commission pursuant to the reciprocity mechanism of Regulation 539/2001, Brazil indicated its willingness to lift these visa requirement, but subject to two conditions.[88] First, for reasons linked to its internal constitutional requirements, Brazil insisted on the conclusion of an international agreement on this matter. Second, Brazil also wished to maintain in force bilateral visa exemption requirements concluded with a number of Member States prior to the entry into force of the Amsterdam Treaty. These agreements have the advantage of allowing a stay of up to six month, compared to only three months under the rules of Regulation 539/2001. Moreover, according to Article 20 (2) of the Schengen Convention, these agreements are not affected by the Schengen Rules, and can therefore continue to be applied.[89] For this reason, Brazil proposed to negotiate with the Community an international agreement covering only those EU Member States with which it does not have a bilateral agreement.

In response, the Commission has indicated its openness to the negotiation of a bilateral exemption agreement, subject to the necessary negotiating authorisation from the Council. However, the Commission rejected the idea of an agreement applying only to some of the EU Member States. This position appears to be the only tenable position, since the Brazilian proposal would have been incompatible with the principle that, subject to exceptions in primary law, Community law, including international agreements, must apply uniformly throughout the Community. Moreover, there is no doubt that the Community has exclusive competence over the matter, and in particular could agree with Brazil that the bilateral agreements with Member States shall no longer be applied. Article 20 (2) of the Schengen Convention, which is merely a provision of secondary law,

---

87. Cf. for instance Article 1 (2) of the Visa Facilitation Agreement between the EC and Ukraine.
88. Cf. on this and the following, the Commission reports under Article 1 (5) of Regulation 539/2001, COM (2006)568 final, p. 5, and COM(2006) 3 final, p. 7.
89. Cf. Peers, above note 38, p. 177-178.

would not therefore constitute a legal obstacle to the conclusion of an agreement. The only remaining question is therefore under which conditions Brazil is willing to accept an agreement; and particularly, in this context, the question might arise whether the Community can agree, in certain specific cases, to a period of stay longer than three months.[90]

VI. Visa Policy and Other EU External Policies

This section will examine the relationship between visa policy and certain other external relations policies, namely trade policy[91] and the common foreign and security policy (CFSP).

A. Visa Policy and Trade in Services

Classical trade policy concerns trade in goods and as such does not directly concern visa policy. However, visa policy and trade policy may come into contact when it comes to trade in services. As the Court of Justice explained in Opinion 1/94, all modes of service provision other than mode 1 (cross-border provision of services) are characterised by the movement of persons, be it the consumer or the provider of the service. This close link with the movement of persons was the reason why the Court considered in Opinion 1/94 that all modes of service provision other than cross-border provision of services could not be assimilated to trade in goods, and therefore did not fall under the common commercial policy.[92]

This legal situation has changed since the entry into force of the Treaty of Amsterdam. Article 133 (5) EC confers upon the Community the competence to conclude international agreements in the area of trade in services.[93] Wherever the service providers or service consumers of the

---

90. Cf. COM(2006) 568 final, p. 5.
91. It is interesting to note that visa issues can also arise in the context of investment protection agreements; cf. on the practice in this field UNCTAD, Bilateral Investment Treaties 1995- 2006: Trends in Investment Rulemaking, pp. 69 et seq. Investment protection agreements are still generally concluded as bilateral agreements of the Member States. However, to the extent that such agreements contain clauses on visa which may affect Community rules, such agreements may fall under exclusive EC competence.
92. Opinion 1/94, Accession to the WTO, [1994] ECR I-5267, para. 44-47.
93. For a detailed analysis of this provision, cf. Christoph W. Herrmann, *Common Commercial Policy after Nice: Sisyphus would have done a better job*, 39 [2002] CMLR 7.

parties crossing a frontier are subject to visa requirements, the question arises how such agreements relate to visa policy. On the one hand, it is clear that trade agreements should not normally prevent the application of general visa rules, for instance the right to refuse a visa to an individual who presents a security risk or a risk of illegal immigration. On the other hand, neither should visa rules be used in such a way as to frustrate the free flow of services in accordance with the commitments of the agreement.[94]

As long as the provisions contained in an agreement on trade in services involving cross-border movement of persons remain at this level of generality, they can arguably be based on Article 133 (5) alone. In contrast, if more specific rules on visa facilitation or visa exemptions are required, it may be necessary to also have recourse to the relevant provisions of Title IV. To the extent that the visas concerned are short-term visas, the Community would be exclusively competent to deal with the issues. In contrast, to the extent that the visas are long-term visas, and the Community has not yet legislated on the specific issue on the basis of Article 63 (3) (a), the matter is likely to fall within the shared competence of the EC and its Member States.

B.   Visa Policy and CFSP

An important question in practice is the relationship between visa policy and the common foreign and security policy. In recent years, visa policy has increasingly become a foreign policy tool commonly used in the context of the CFSP. Most importantly, the EU has in a number of cases imposed visa bans on the leaders of third countries or organisations which the EU intends to sanction.[95] Such visa bans are adopted purely through second-pillar measures and implemented by the Member States individually.[96] In contrast to trade sanctions or measures affecting capital

94.   A similar rule is contained in para. 4 of the Annex on Movement of Natural Persons Supplying Services under the WTO Agreement on Trade in Services (GATS). Cf. more generally also Roman Grynberg/Veniana Qalo, Migration and the World Trade Organisation, 41 (4) [2007] Journal of World Trade Law 751.

95.   Cf. Council Common Position 2001/542/CFSP on a visa ban against extremists in FYROM, OJ L 194, 18.7.2001, p. 55; Common Position 2004/293/CFSP on measures in support of the effective implementation of the mandate of the International Criminal Tribunal for the former Yugoslavia, OJ L 94, 31.3.2004, p. 65; Common Position 2004/661/CFSP concerning restrictive measures against certain officials of Belarus, OJ L 301, 28.9.2004, p. 67; Common Position 2006/318/CFSP on restrictive measures against Burma/Myanmar, OJ L 116, 29.4.2006, p. 77.

96.   Each Member State may also issue an alert through the Schengen Information System in accordance with Article 97 of the Schengen Convention.

movements and payments, for which there are specific legal bases for implementing EC measures, the EC is not involved with the adoption or implementation of visa bans.

However, in some cases, it may also be the granting of a visa which becomes a foreign policy instrument. In 2002, the EU adopted a common position concerning the temporary reception of 12 Palestinians who had to be evacuated from the Bethlehem Church of Nativity.[97] The common position stated that the Palestinians concerned shall obtain national permits to enter the territory of the Member States and stay for a period of up to twelve months.[98]

This practice of regulating visa matters in CFSP actions is highly doubtful from a legal point of view.[99] It follows from Article 47 EU that no action taken in the context of the 2nd pillar may affect the 1st pillar. The Court of Justice has clarified that Article 47 is violated whenever a measure adopted on the basis of the EU Treaty could also have been adopted on the basis of the EC Treaty.[100] However, precisely this seems to be the case for both visa bans and reception measures. Regardless of whether the intended stay is short-term or long-term, the Community clearly has competence, on the basis of Articles 62 (2) (b) and 63 (3) (a) EC, to establish the conditions under which visa shall be granted or refused.

The fact that such measures may be politically motivated does not exclude that they fall within the scope of the EC Treaty. In fact, in its settled case law, the Court has held that a trade ban does not cease to be a commercial policy measure merely because it is also motivated by foreign policy considerations.[101] It is not clear why a different approach should apply to immigration policy. This view is also confirmed by Declaration No 16 to the Treaty of Amsterdam, which provides that "foreign policy considerations of the Union and the Member States shall be taken into account in the application of Article 62 (2) (b) of the Treaty". Obviously, this implies that the fact that foreign policy considerations apply does not preclude the application of Article 62 (2) (b) EC.

It should also be noted that the fact that visa bans are decided under CFSP without any EC involvement has considerable implications for judicial review. Against an EU common position, there is no judicial review

---

97. Common Position 2002/400/CFSP, 28.5.2002, p. 33.
98. Article 3 of Common Position 2002/400/CFSP.
99. Cf. equally Peers, above note 38, p. 111.
100. Case C-176/03, Commission/Council, [2005] ECR I-7879, para. 40; Case C-170/96, Commission/Council, [1998] ECR I-2763, para. 17.
101. Case C-70/94, Werner, [1995] ECR I-3139; Case C-83/94, Leifer, [1995] ECR I-3231.

available at Community level.[102] Therefore, any individual affected by a visa ban would have to seek to obtain judicial review from a national court. National courts would however decide without any guidance at EU level,[103] which is not conducive to a uniform application of EU law. This legal situation contrasts with the situation applicable to measures affecting capital movements, in particular the freezing of funds, where at least the implementing regulation adopted by the EC is subject to judicial review by the Community courts.[104]

Overall, the relationship between the CFSP and visa policy remains delicate and fraught with legal difficulties. It appears that the current practice does not comply with Article 47 EU, which demands that the competences of the EC in the field of visa policy should be respected. De lege ferenda, a possible solution could lie in the creation of a legal basis for visa bans similar to Articles 301 and 60 (1) EC. However, in the absence of such provisions, it would appear that it is exclusively the EC, and not the EU, which has competence to adopt visa bans and similar measures.

VII. Conclusion

The European Community is increasingly asserting itself as an international actor in the field of immigration policy, and in particular in the field of visa policy. This development is the logical consequence of the increased harmonisation in this field of EU law. It also reflects the increased sensitivity of visa policy in international relations, as illustrated by the ongoing negotiations between the EC and the US on questions of visa reciprocity.

However, the division of competences between the Community and its Member States in this area still remains uneasy. Visa policy is not yet an area which could be regarded as falling in its entirety under the exclusive

---

102. However, this would change with the entry into force of the Treaty of Lisbon. According to Article 275 of the future Treaty on the Functioning of the Union (Article 240a in the numbering of the Treaty of Lisbon), the Court of Justice shall have jurisdiction to review the legality of restrictive measures against natural and legal persons adopted in the context of CFSP.
103. However, in analogy to the Court's case law cited above under footnote 100, it appears possible that a national court could refer to the ECJ, in accordance with Article 233 EC, the question whether a common position imposing a visa ban is in accordance with Article 47 EU.
104. Cf. T-228/02, Modjahedines, [2006] ECR II-4665. On the judicial review of EU sanctions, cf. van Thiel in this book.

competence of the EC. Rather, the EC has exclusive competence only to the extent that it has achieved internal harmonisation. Whereas the state of internal harmonisation for short-term visas must be regarded by now as almost complete, with the consequence that Member States can no longer negotiate international agreements in this area, this is not so for the rules governing long-term stays. Accordingly, with respect to long-term visas and residence permits, the Community and its Member States still share competences. Accordingly, the rules governing the entry into the EC by persons may be Community rules or national rules, depending on the intended length of the stay.

A legally problematic area is the relationship between the first and the second pillar in the field of visa policy. Measures affecting visa policy, notably visa bans, are currently adopted under the second pillar and implemented by Member States without any involvement of the EC. This practice ignores the existence of EC competence in the field, and is therefore legally doubtful. It appears that in the future, visa bans and similar measures should be implemented through regulations on the basis of the EC Treaty, similar to the current practice for trade bans and measures affecting capital movements.

It is likely that the current mix between Community and national competence will only be of a transitional nature. For trade in goods, it has been recognised since decades that rules governing the external customs regime of the Community must be uniform, and must be applied in a uniform manner. The same will also have to apply to the external borders of the area of justice, liberty and security, in which not only EU nationals, but also third-country nationals are able to move freely and unimpeded by internal borders. Since a chain can only be as strong as it weakest link, the goal of EU immigration policy must therefore be the full harmonisation of all rules governing entry into the Community by third-country nationals. At the end of this process, EU visa policy should become an area of exclusive competence similar to what the common commercial policy is today.

2. EU Migration Law and Association Agreements

Steven Peers

I. Introduction

In recent years, the EC institutions have adopted a great deal of detailed immigration and asylum legislation. However, for many third-country nationals, this legislation is not the only source of Community law regulating their immigration status. Rather, the legislation interacts with the association agreements the Community has negotiated with favoured third countries. This chapter examines in detail the interaction between the substantive rules in these two sources of law.

II. Legal framework

A. Applicable legislation and treaties

The EC immigration legislation, which is particularly closely connected to EC association agreements, comprises Directives 2003/86 on family reunion and 2003/109 on the rights of long-term residents, along with Regulation 859/2003 on social security rights of third-country nationals.[1] Directives 2004/114 on the entry and residence of students and other categories of persons and 2005/71 on researchers are also relevant,[2] as is Directive 2004/83 on the qualification of persons for refugee or subsidiary protection status.[3] However, the latter Directive is only discussed indirectly in this chapter, which focuses on immigration law.

There is no EC legislation on migration for employment to consider, since the Commission's proposal on this issue dating from 2001 has been

---

1. Respectively OJ L 251, 3.10.2003, p. 12, applicable 3 Oct. 2005, OJ L 16, 23.1.2004, p. 44, applicable 23 Jan. 2006, and OJ L 124, 20.5.2003, p. 1, applicable 1 June 2003.
2. Respectively OJ L 375, 23.12.2004, p. 12, applicable 12 Jan. 2007, and OJ L 289, 3.11.2005, p. 15, applicable 12 Oct. 2007.
3. OJ 2004 L 304, 30.9.2004, p. 12, applicable 10 Oct. 2006.

withdrawn,[4] and the five further Directives which the Commission intends to propose from 2007-2009 have not yet been tabled.[5]

As for association agreements, the principal treaty concerned is the EC-Turkey Association Agreement, which provides for the eventual extension of the free movement of workers, services and establishment between the EC and Turkey. However, in the view of the EU's Court of Justice, the relevant provisions of the agreement cannot confer direct effect, as they simply set out political objectives.[6] On the other hand, a 'standstill' clause in the 1970 Protocol banning any new restrictions on establishment or the provision of services is directly effective,[7] as are a number of provisions of Decision 1/80 of the EC-Turkey Association Council, which sets out interim steps to govern the position of Turkish workers and their family members in the EU. In fact, the Court of Justice has delivered no fewer than twenty-eight judgments on Decision 1/80.[8]

4. COM (2001) 386, 11 July 2001; withdrawn in 2006 (OJ 2006 C 64/3).
5. See the Commission's 'policy plan' on legal migration (COM (2005) 669, 21 Dec. 2005), which announces an intention to propose two Directives in Sep. 2007 (on the admission of highly-skilled workers and for a general framework on the status of all persons admitted for employment), one Directive in 2008 (on seasonal workers), and two Directives in 2009 (on intra-corporate transferees and remunerated trainees).
6. Case 12/86 *Demirel* [1987] ECR 3719 (workers), Case C-37/98 *Savas* [2000] ECR I-2927 (self-employed persons), and Joined Cases C-317/01 and C-369/01 *Abatay and others* [2003] ECR I-12301 (services).
7. *Savas* and *Abatay* (ibid); see the pending Cases C-16/05 *Tum and Dari* (Opinion of 12 Sep. 2006), C-296/05 *Gunes*, C-228/06 *Soysal* and C-92/07 *Commission v Netherlands*.
8. Cases: C-192/89 *Sevince* [1990] ECR I-3461; C-237/91 *Kus* [1992] ECR I-6781; C-355/93 *Eroglu* [1994] ECR I-5113; C-434/93 *Bozkurt* [1995] ECR I-1475; C-171/95 *Tetik* [1997] ECR I-329; C-351/95 *Kadiman* [1997] ECR I-2133; C-386/95 *Eker* [1997] ECR I-2697; C-285/95 *Kol* [1997] ECR I-3095; C-36/96 *Günaydin* [1997] ECR I-5143; C-98/96 *Ertanir* [1997] ECR I-5179; C-210/97 *Akman* [1998] ECR I-7519; C-1/97 *Birden* [1998] ECR I-7747; C-340/97 *Nazli* [2000] ECR I-957; C-329/97 *Ergat* [2000] ECR I-1487; C-65/98 *Eyup* [2000] ECR I-4747; C-188/00 *Kurz* [2002] ECR I-10691; C-171/01 *Birklite* [2003] ECR I-1487; *Abatay and others*, n. 6 above; C-275/02 *Ayaz* [2004] ECR I-8765; C-467/02 *Cetinkaya* [2004] ECR I-10895; C-136/03 *Dorr and Unal* [2005] ECR I-4759; C-373/03 *Aydinli* [2005] ECR I-6181; C-374/03 *Gurol* [2005] ECR I-6199; C-383/03 *Dogan* [2005] ECR I-6237; C-230/03 *Sedef* [2006] ECR I-157; C-502/04 *Torun* [2006] ECR I-1563; C-4/05 *Guzeli* [2006] ECR I-10279; and judgment of 18 July 2007 in C-325/05 *Derin*, not yet reported. See further Cases C-242/06 *Sahin*, C-294/06 *Payir and others* (Opinion of 18 July 2007), C-349/06 *Polat* and C-92/07 *Commission v Netherlands* (n. 7 above), all pending. See also Case C-465/01 *Commission v Austria* [2004] ECR I-8291.

The EC-Turkey Association Council has also adopted Decision 3/80, which governs the issue of social security for Turkish workers and their family members.[9] The Court of Justice has delivered four judgments on this Decision.[10]

The next main source of litigation has been the EC's agreements with Maghreb States (Morocco, Algeria and Tunisia), which confer the right to equal treatment on social security for workers and their families,[11] along with the right to equality in working conditions for workers.[12]

A third main source of case law has been the EC's agreements with Central and East European countries (Europe Agreements),[13] which provided for the right to establishment,[14] to equal treatment in working conditions,[15] and to access to employment for family members.[16] While these agreements are no longer in force following the enlargement of the EU in 2004 and 2007 to include the relevant countries, similar provisions appear in the Stabilisation and Association Agreements with Croatia, the former Yugoslav Republic of Macedonia and Albania,[17] and are likely to appear in agreements with Montenegro, Serbia, and Bosnia-Herzegovina once such

9.   OJ C 110, 25.4.1983, p. 60.
10. Case C-277/94 *Taflan-Met* [1996] ECR I-4085, Case C-262/96 *Surul* [1999] ECR I-2685, Joined Cases C-102/98 *Kocak* and C-211/98 *Ors* [2000] ECR I-1287 and Case C-373/02 *Ozturk* [2004] ECR I-3605.
11. Cases: C-18/90 *Kziber* [1991] ECR I-119; C-58/93 *Yousfi* [1994] ECR I-1353; C-103/94 *Krid* [1995] ECR I-719; C-126/95 *Hallouzi-Choho* [1996] ECR I-4807; C-113/97 *Babahenini* [1998] ECR I-183; C-314/96 *Djabali* [1998] ECR I-1149; C-179/98 *Mesbah* [1999] ECR I-7955; C-33/99 *Fahmi and Cerdeiro-Pinedo Amadao* [2001] ECR I-2415; C-23/02 *Alami* [2003] ECR I-1399; C-336/05 *Echouikh* [2006] ECR I-5223; and C-276/06 *El-Youssfi*, order of 17 April 2007, not yet reported.
12. Cases C-416/96 *El-Yassini* [1999] ECR I-1209 and C-97/05 *Gattoussi* [2006] ECR I-11917. See also *Commission v Austria* (n. 8 above).
13. Agreements with Poland, OJ L 348, 31.12.1993, p. 1; Hungary, OJ L 347, 31.12.1993, p. 1; Romania, OJ L 357, 31.12.1994, p. 1; Bulgaria, OJ L 358, 31.12.1994, p. 1; the Slovak Republik, OJ L 359, 31.12.1994, p. 1; the Czech Republic, OJ L 360, 31.12.1994, p. 1; Latvia, OJ L 26, 2.2.1998, p. 1; Lithuania, OJ L 51, 20.2.1998, p 1; Estonia, OJ L 68, 9.3.1998, p. 1; and Slovenia, OJ L 51, 26.2.1999, p. 1.
14. Cases C-63/99 *Gloszczuk* [2001] ECR I-6369, C-257/99 *Barkoci and Malik* [2001] ECR I-6557, C-235/99 *Kondova* [2001] ECR I-6427, C-268/99 *Jany* [2001] ECR I-8615, and C-327/02 *Panayotova* [2004] ECR I-11055.
15. Cases C-162/00 *Pokrzeptowicz-Meyer* [2002] ECR I-1049 and C-438/00 *Calpak* [2003] ECR I-4135. See also *Commission v Austria* (n. 8 above).
16. This issue was never litigated before the Court of Justice.
17. OJ L 84, 20.3.2004, p. 1 (Former Yugoslav Republic of Macedonia); OJ L 26, 28.1.2005, p. 1 (Croatia); and Council doc. 8164/06, 22 May 2006 (Albania; not yet in force).

agreements are concluded.[18] The only difference between the Europe Agreements and the SAAs (in the SAAs agreed to date) is that there is a five-year waiting period before the provisions on the establishment of natural persons become applicable.

Also, there are Partnership and Cooperation Agreements (PCAs) in force with Russia and all other ex-Soviet states except Belarus, Tadjikistan and Turkmenistan.[19] These agreements provide for the right to equal treatment in working conditions, and the Court of Justice has ruled that at least in the agreement with Russia, this right has direct effect and has the same meaning as the Europe Agreement treaties.[20]

Finally, the EC has concluded the Cotonou agreement with African, Caribbean and Pacific countries, which contains a right to equal treatment in working conditions in the main text of the Convention.[21] The Court of Justice has not yet ruled on the interpretation or legal effect of this provision.

This paper does not examine the EEA (European Economic Area) treaty between the EC and its Member States and Norway, Iceland and Liechtenstein,[22] or the EC-Switzerland agreement on the free movement of persons,[23] because these two treaties simply extend EC free movement law to the States concerned. These States are also currently associated with the Schengen *acquis*, or will be associated with it in future.[24] Also, this paper

---

18. An agreement with Montenegro was initialled early in 2007, but the text has not yet been published. Negotiations with Bosnia-Herzegovina were finished shortly afterward, but the text of the agreement reached has not yet been initialled or made public. Negotiations with Serbia are ongoing.

19. See OJ L 327, 28.11.1997, p. 1 (Russia); OJ L 49, 19.2.1998, p. 1 (Ukraine); OJ L 181, 24.6.1998, p. 1 (Moldova); OJ L 196, 28.7.1999, p. 1 (Kazahkstan); OJ L 196, 28.7.1999, p. 44 (Kyrgyz Republic); OJ L 205, 4.8.1999, p. 1 (Georgia); OJ L 229, 31.8.1999, p. 1 (Uzbekistan); OJ L 239, 9.9.1999, p. 1 (Armenia); and OJ L 246, 17.9.1999, p. 1 (Azerbaijan). Agreements with Turkmenistan (COM (97) 693, 6 Feb. 1998) and Tajikistan (COM (2004) 520, 26 July 2004) have been signed, but not yet ratified, while an agreement with Belarus (COM (95) 44, 22 Feb. 1995) was signed but ratification was frozen due to EU concerns about human rights.

20. Case C-265/03 *Simutenkov* [2005] ECR I-2579, regarding limits on the fielding of foreign football players during professional matches.

21. Art 13 of Cotonou Convention (OJ L 317, 13.12.2000, p. 1), in force 1 Apr. 2003.

22. OJ L 1, 3.1.1994, p. 1. See Case C-92/02 *Kristiansen* [2003] ECR I-14597, para 24.

23. OJ L 114, 30.4.2002, p. 6. See the Opinion of 6 June 2006 in Case C-339/05 *Zentralbetriebsrat der Landeskrankenhäuser Tirols and Land Tirol* (case withdrawn).

24. OJ L 176, 10.7.1999, p. 36 (Norway and Iceland; COM (2004) 593, 14 Sep. 2004 (agreement with Switzerland, not yet in force); COM (2006) 752, 1 Dec. 2006 (agreement with Liechtenstein, not yet in force).

does not examine the interplay between EC migration law and the application of the General Agreement on Trade in Services (GATS) to the movement of persons.[25]

B.   Jurisdiction of the Court of Justice

The Court of Justice has ruled that association agreements and similar treaties, such as Partnership and Cooperation Agreements, form an integral part of EC law;[26] that it can interpret their provisions, even those relating to immigration;[27] that provisions in these agreements can have 'direct effect' allowing individuals to rely on them in their national courts, where those provisions are clear, precise, and unconditional;[28] and that where the agreements have similar or identical wording to EC free movement rules, the agreements will not *necessarily* be similarly interpreted,[29] although they frequently are.[30]

On the other hand, the Court's jurisdiction over immigration and asylum issues is currently restricted to references from the final courts of Member States,[31] which has almost certainly led (and will continue to lead) to a substantial restriction in the number of cases reaching the Court of Justice.[32] The Commission has suggested that the 'normal' rules concerning the Court's jurisdiction should apply to this area,[33] and this proposal was still under discussion in the Council as of summer 2007. It seems unlikely that any changes to the Court's jurisdiction will be applicable, if agreed at all, before late 2007, and it is possible that no change will be agreed, or that the rules will be only partly reformed (for instance, to permit appeal courts, but not courts of first instance, to send questions to the Court of Justice).

---

25. See S. Peers, *EU Justice and Home Affairs Law*, 2nd edition (OUP, 2006), 212-213. Also, this paper does not examine the rules in the bilateral agreement with Chile as regards free movement of services (ibid, 209).
26. Case 181/73 *Hagemann* [1974] ECR 449.
27. Case 12/86 *Demirel* (n. 6 above).
28. *Demirel,* ibid; see also Case 104/81 *Kupferberg* [1982] ECR 3641.
29. Case 270/80 *Polydor* [1982] ECR 329.
30. See in particular the case law starting with *Bozkurt* (n. 8 above) and *Kziber* (n. 11 above).
31. See Art. 68 EC.
32. See Peers, 'The ECJ's Jurisdiction over EC Immigration and Asylum Law: Time for a Change?' in Toner, Guild and Baldaccini, eds., *EU Immigration and Asylum Law and Policy* (Hart, 2007), forthcoming.
33. COM (2006) 346, 28 June 2006.

While the planned Reform Treaty,[34] like the aborted Constitutional Treaty,[35] would apply the normal rules on the Court's jurisdiction in this area, the ratification and entry into force of this Treaty can hardly (in light of the fate of the Constitutional Treaty) be taken for granted.[36]

This issue has important implications for the substantive issues discussed in this paper, which focuses on the circumstances in which the EC's association agreements are closely intertwined with its immigration law. In such cases, there is the question of which jurisdiction applies: the wider jurisdiction over association agreements, or the more limited jurisdiction over immigration law? It is even technically possible that the Court's jurisdiction over criminal law and policing, which is subject to another distinct set of rules,[37] will be applicable simultaneously when the dispute concerns the application of the current Schengen Information System (SIS).[38] I have suggested elsewhere that in cases of 'mixed jurisdiction', the Court should apply a 'most favourable jurisdiction' rule, where the issues in question span different jurisdictional rules and are inextricably intertwined.[39]

The Court of Justice has not yet ruled on such an issue, but the pending *Soysal* case,[40] which involves questions relating to association agreements and immigration law, provides it with an opportunity to do so.[41]

---

34. For the text of the first draft of this Treaty, the mandate for which was agreed in June 2007, see CIG 1/07, 23 July 2007, online at: http://www.consilium.europa.eu/uedocs/cmsUpload/cg00001.en07.pdf
35. OJ C 310, 16.12.2004, p. 1.
36. The plan, at time of writing, was to finalise discussions on the Treaty by October 2007 and to sign it by December 2007. According to the conclusions of the June 2007 European Council, the Treaty should be ratified in time to enter into force by June 2009 at the latest.
37. See Art. 35 EU.
38. The third pillar jurisdiction rules apply, even as regards SIS immigration data, because the Council could not agree how to allocate the SIS provisions to the EC and EU Treaties back in May 1999 (see OJ L 176, 10.7.1999, p. 17). However, the SIS II legislation on immigration data will be subject to the Court's immigration and asylum law jurisdiction (Reg. 1987/2006, OJ L 381, 28.12.2006, p. 4).
39. S. Peers, 'Who Judges the Watchmen', 18 YEL (2000) 337 at 397-399.
40. Case C-228/06, n. 7 above.
41. The point is relevant since the case has been referred from lower courts. In its order in the *El-Youssfi* case (n. 11 above), which also raised questions on free movement law, the Court did not address the mixed jurisdiction issue, but simply answered the questions (sent by a lower court) on immigration law, free movement law and an association agreement. See also the opinion in *Panayatova* (n. 14 above), para. 71.

C. Relationship between EC legislation and association agreements

The Court of Justice has made clear that international agreements ratified by the Community take precedence over EC legislation.[42] So in the event of any conflict between the legislation and the treaties, the treaties will take precedence. This is reflected expressly in the text of the relevant immigration legislation, which is 'without prejudice to more favourable provisions of' any treaties between the Community, or the EC and its Member States, with third countries.[43] Moreover, this interpretation has been accepted by Advocates-General of the Court.[44] On the other hand, the most relevant EC asylum legislation (Directive 2004/83) makes no reference to the possible precedence of such prior treaties.

It might be argued that in principle, there is no relationship between EC immigration legislation on the one hand, and EC association agreements on the other. On this view, these are two separate sources of law that must be relied upon separately, with any conflict (if one exists) regulated by giving priority to the association agreements. If this is correct, then there will be few, if any, 'mixed jurisdiction' cases, except perhaps to establish whether there is a conflict in a particular case between EC migration legislation and an association agreement.

However, this interpretation should be rejected. There is nothing in the text of any association agreement or any EC immigration legislation to suggest that these are two separate sources of law. On the contrary, an examination of the substantive rules in EC immigration legislation and association agreements will show that there will be many circumstances in which the two sets of rules will be closely interconnected. It would be artificial to treat these two sources of rules as entirely separate. Moreover, in one pending case, the Advocate-General's Opinion explicitly assumes that in principle the international agreements and the internal legislation can become intertwined, as do the Member States submitting observations

---

42. Case C-61/94 *Commission v Germany* [1996] ECR I-3989.
43. Recital 16, Reg. 859/2003; Art. 3(4)(a), Directive 2003/86; Art. 3(3)(a), Directive 2003/109; Art. 4(1)(a), Directive 2004/114; and Art. 4(1)(b), Directive 2005/71.
44. See the opinion in *Payir* (n. 8 above), and earlier *Barkoci and Malik* (para. 70: n. 14 above). This can be compared with the highly doubtful reliance on a Council Resolution on immigration to interpret the Europe Agreements in the opinion in *Kondova* (para. 107: n. 14 above).

and the Commission.[45] But it must be conceded that, for those Member States which are not covered by some or all EC immigration law, the association agreements must still be considered in isolation from the relevant legislation.[46]

III. Substantive issues

A. Family reunion

Rules governing family reunion can most usefully be analysed by examining separately the issues of the definition of the sponsors of family members, the definition of family members, the conditions for entry, and the status of family members after their entry.[47] While the relevant association agreements do not give any right to the initial entry of family members,[48] they are nonetheless relevant to defining the initial issue of the sponsors of family members.

45. See the opinion in *Payir* (n. 8 above), paras. 55 to 61. However, on the facts of the case, the Advocate-General argues for an independent interpretation of the international measure in question. The Opinion in Case C-16/05 *Tum and Dari* (n. 7 above) does not directly address the question as to whether the standstill clause in the Protocol to the EC-Turkey Association Agreement would, if applicable, prevail over the Dublin Convention on responsibility for asylum applications, which would otherwise be applied to the Turkish businessmen who seek to rely on the standstill clause in that case. The Opinion in *Derin* (n. 8 above) argues that Decision 1/80 should be interpreted so as to confer more rights than those applicable by virtue of EC immigration law (paras. 135-137), and the earlier opinion in *Cetinkaya* (ibid) argues very similarly that Decision 1/80 should be interpreted in light of the long-term residents' Directive (paras. 43 and 44), but the judgments in these cases do not touch on these issues.
46. The UK, Ireland and Denmark are not covered by Directives 2003/86, 2003/109 and 2004/114; the UK and Denmark are not covered by Directive 2005/71; and Denmark is not covered by Directive 2004/83 or Reg. 859/2003.
47. See S. Peers, 'Family Reunion and Community Law', in Walker, ed., *Towards an Area of Freedom, Security and Justice*, (OUP, 2004), 143.
48. The point was most recently emphasised, as regards the EC-Turkey agreement, in the *Derin* judgment (n. 8 above), although in light of the family reunion Directive, it is no longer accurate, with respect, to state that the admission of family members is governed wholly by national law (para. 64 of the judgment; compare to para. 146 of the Opinion), leaving aside the Member States which have opted out of that Directive.

1. Definition of sponsors

The EC's family reunion Directive states that it applies to sponsors who are 'holding a residence permit issued by a Member State for a period of validity of one year or more who has reasonable prospects of obtaining the right of permanent residence'.[49] However, it does not apply to sponsors who are asylum-seekers, or who have requested or received temporary or subsidiary protection.[50] The connection with EC migration law here is that EC-Turkey Association Council Decision 1/80 strengthens the immigration status of Turkish workers; the standstill on new restrictions on the right of establishment in the Protocol to the Ankara Agreement may strengthen the rights of Turkish nationals; the right to equal treatment in 'working conditions' in at least the EC-Turkey agreement and the EC-Maghreb agreements can in some cases strengthen the immigration status of a sponsor as well; and the right to establishment (when it becomes applicable) will strengthen the immigration status of self-employed persons from the Western Balkans. The practical relevance of these points will be considered in turn.

According to Article 6(1) of Decision 1/80, '…a Turkish worker duly registered as belonging to the labour force of a Member State' is entitled to a renewed work permit after one year's 'legal employment' in order 'to work for the same employer, if a job is available'. That worker is then entitled to respond to another job offer 'in the same occupation' after three years' legal employment, subject to priority for EC workers. Finally, the Turkish worker has free access to any paid employment after four years' legal employment. Article 6(2) provides that annual holidays, maternity absences, work accidents, and short sicknesses count as 'legal employment', and that involuntary unemployment duly certified and long absences due to sickness 'shall not affect rights acquired as the result of the preceding period of employment'. The Court of Justice has ruled that: it has jurisdiction to interpret Decision 1/80;[51] Article 6 of the Decision is directly effective;[52] and the right to employment brings with it a right to residence.[53]

Substantively, the case law has made clear that the definition of a 'Turkish worker' follows the same broad definition applicable in EC free movement

---

49. Art. 3(1).
50. Art. 3(2).
51. *Sevince*, n. 8 above.
52. *Sevince* and *Kus*, ibid.
53. *Sevince*, ibid.

law.[54] The concept of registration in labour force simply means that Turkish workers must comply with rules on entry to the Member States' territory and initial access to employment,[55] plus maintain a territorial link with a Member State;[56] it does not permit Member States to establish distinct labour markets on which Turkish workers cannot participate.[57] Next, the requirement of 'legal employment' means that the Turkish worker must have a 'stable and secure situation on labour force', or in other words authorised residence.[58] However, it is clear that Turkish workers can obtain rights under Article 6 of Decision 1/80 even if their entry and employment was authorised on grounds other than entry for employment, such as to marry a host state national,[59] or where the worker was initially permitted to enter for a limited period only,[60] although it has been argued by an Advocate-General that an exception must be made where a person was admitted for entry as a student.[61]

As for the time periods set out in Article 6, the Court has established that Turkish workers cannot claim rights under the first indent of that Article if they changed employers during the first year,[62] and similarly cannot claim rights after three or four years if they changed employers before that point.[63] However, after four years, their access to employment must be fully equal to that of EU citizens.[64] Turkish workers lose status under Article 6 once they have completely retired or become permanently disabled,[65] but they do not lose status immediately upon voluntary unemployment, but have a 'reasonable period' to find work.[66] Moreover, they do not lose status under Article 6 just because they have been in prison for any reason.[67] The list of circumstances set out in Article 6(2) where the clock either 'keeps ticking' for the acquisition of a Turkish worker's rights

---

54. See particularly *Ertanir, Gunaydin, Birden, Kurz* and (to an extent) the opinion in *Payir* (ibid).
55. See *Birden* (ibid).
56. *Bozkurt* (ibid.).
57. *Birden* (ibid).
58. Turkish workers cannot gain the status of legal employment just because national law allows them to work while contesting a deportation order, or if it is proven that the workers entered on the basis of fraud: *Sevince, Kus* and *Kol* (ibid).
59. *Kus*, ibid.
60. *Ertanir* (ibid).
61. See the opinion in *Payir* (ibid).
62. *Eker* (ibid).
63. *Eroglu* and *Sedef* (ibid).
64. *Tetik* (ibid).
65. *Bozkurt* (ibid).
66. *Tetik* (ibid).
67. *Nazli* and *Dogan* (ibid).

under Article 6 or where the clock is 'stopped' is non-exhaustive; rights can also be acquired or frozen where comparable legitimate reasons for interruption of employment exist.[68] However, Article 6(2) only applies once the worker has acquired at least one year of prior employment.[69]

According to Article 14 of Decision 1/80, the rights in the Decision are 'subject to limitations justified on grounds of public policy, public security or public health'. The Court of Justice has ruled that Article 14(1) of the Decision must be interpreted consistently with Article 39(3) EC, meaning that Turkish workers and their family members cannot be expelled as part of a policy of treating foreigners harshly as a deterrent for the committing of crimes or of imposing automatic expulsions; they can only be expelled where their personal conduct is a serious present threat to one of the fundamental interests of society.[70] Also, the procedural protections of EC free movement law also apply to Decision 1/80.[71]

It follows from this case law that a Turkish worker as defined by the case law interpreting Decision 1/80 has a 'reasonable prospect of obtaining the right of permanent residence' after four years of legal employment, given the corollary right to residence that results from four years of legal employment and the very limited prospects of losing that right (definitive retirement, permanent total disability, very serious criminal activity). In fact, a Turkish worker with four years of legal employment could be regarded as having already attained permanent residence status, not merely the prospect of attaining it. It should be emphasised that the Directive does not refer to national law as regards the definition of 'permanent residence status', so that where applicable EC legislation or agreements can be relevant to determining whether there is a 'reasonable prospect' of obtaining this status.[72]

A Turkish worker surely also has such a 'reasonable prospect' after three years' legal employment, given the right at that point to look for any job within the same occupation (and a corresponding obligation to renew the work permit and guarantee residence rights), the short period remaining until compliance with the four years of legal employment requirement, and the protection guaranteed by Article 6(2) of the Decision in the event of any interruption of employment. Indeed, even after one year of legal

---

68. *Sedef* (ibid).
69. *Guzeli* (ibid.).
70. *Nazli*, ibid.
71. See *Cetinkaya* and particularly *Dorr and Unal* (n. 8 above).
72. See further Peers and Rogers, eds., 'EU Immigration and Asylum Law: Text and Commentary' (Martinus Nijhoff, 2006), at 593-595.

employment it is arguable that there is a 'reasonable prospect' of obtaining permanent residence for Turkish workers, in light of the right to renewal of the work permit to remain with the same employer (not just for the same *job* with that employer) and the protection conferred by Article 6(2). The reasonableness of the 'prospect' of obtaining permanent residence in such cases may depend on factors such as the size and economic stability of the employer and the time remaining until the worker has reached the three-year threshold.

Moving on to self-employed Turkish nationals in the EU, the standstill on new restrictions on the right of establishment should mean that the relevant rules in force relating to the residence of self-employed Turks when the Protocol to the Ankara Agreement became applicable continue to apply. This will in some cases contribute to securing the immigration status of self-employed Turks, depending on the content of the national rules which are thereby preserved in force.

Next, to what extent does the right to 'equal treatment in working conditions' in various agreements strengthen the immigration status of the sponsor? In the *El-Yassini* judgment,[73] regarding an EC-Maghreb agreement, the Court of Justice ruled that the right to equal treatment in working conditions does not generally require the extension of a residence permit in order to continue working when the grounds for the initial admission of the person concerned are no longer valid. However, the situation is different when a Member State grants a period of employment which is shorter than the period of authorised residence; in that case, a host Member State breaches the Maghreb association agreements if it 'had granted the person concerned a residence permit for a period shorter than the duration of his work permit and if, before the work permit expired, it then refused to extend the residence permit without justifying its refusal on grounds relating to the protection of a legitimate national interest, such as public policy, public security or public health'.[74] This judgment was later clarified in the *Gattoussi* judgment, in which the Court ruled that 'concept of public policy presupposes the existence of a genuine and sufficiently serious threat to one of the fundamental interests of society', referring to its case law on both free movement rights and the EC-Turkey agreement.[75]

Does this case law apply to other agreements which grant a right to equal treatment in working conditions? The Court has only been asked this question as regards Turkish workers, who are beneficiaries by such a right

73. N. 12 above.
74. Para. 63 of the judgment, ibid.
75. Para. 41 of the *Gattoussi* judgment, n. 12 above.

conferred by Article 10 of Decision 1/80 of the EC-Turkey Association Council. In its *Guzeli* judgment, the Court does not give a very clear answer to the question, focussing instead on the issue of whether a person in the circumstances of Mr. Guzeli could rely on Article 6 of Decision 1/80. After summarising Mr. Guzeli's argument on the possible application of Article 10, the Court simply stated that '[i]t is for the national court to establish whether such a situation arose in the main proceedings, taking account in particular of Mr. Güzeli's conviction for breach of the conditions set out in his residence permit'.[76] This appears to mean that the Court has accepted that Article 10 of Decision 1/80 can confer a right to stay in the same circumstances as the EC-Maghreb agreements, provided that on the facts, Mr. Guzeli could indeed be considered as being in 'legal employment'.

As for other agreements, the Court has already established that its other interpretations of the right to equal treatment in working conditions apply equally to the Europe Agreements and to the Partnership and Cooperation agreement with Russia.[77] It should follow that the Court's rulings regarding the circumstances in which this right will lead to extended residence also apply to the EC-Russia agreement and to the Stabilisation and Association Agreements (as successors of the Europe Agreements). Also, it should follow that the Court's interpretation of the right (and also the direct effect of the right) is applicable to the Cotonou Agreement, which has a similar aim to the EC-Morocco agreement,[78] considering also that the Court has drawn analogies between the EC-Turkey agreements, EC-Maghreb agreements, the Europe Agreements and EC-ACP agreements.[79]

---

76. Para. 53 of the judgment.
77. See *Commission* v *Austria* and *Simutenkov* (notes 8 and 20 above). See also the equal approach to the EC-Turkey, EC-Maghreb, and Europe Agreements in para. 60 of *Birklite* (n. 8 above).
78. Compare para. 29 of the judgment in *El-Yassini* ('it must be recalled that…the object of [the EC-Morocco] agreement is to promote overall cooperation between the Contracting Parties with a view to contributing to *the economic and social development* of the Kingdom of Morocco and helping to strengthen relations between them') with para. 32 of the judgment in Case C-469/93 *Chiquita Italia* [1995] ECR I-4533 ('[The EC-ACP agreements'] general aim is to promote the *economic and social development* of the non-member countries participating in them').
79. See para. 72 of the judgment in *Surul* (n. 10 above) and para. 53 of the judgment in *Savas* (n. 6 above), in which the Court draws an analogy between the EC-Turkey, EC-Maghreb and EC-ACP agreements. The analogy was extended to the Europe Agreements in the judgments in: *Gloszczuk*, para. 36; *Barkoci and Malik*, para. 37; and *Kondova*, para. 37 (all n. 14 above), referred to again in para. 28 of *Pokrzeptowicz-Meyer* (ibid). See also para. 65 of the *Birklite* judgment (n. 8 above).

Also, as the Court reasoned in *Simutkenov*, the reasoning of the EC-Russia agreement as regards the right to equal treatment in working conditions is 'very similar' to the wording of the Europe Agreements. So although the EC-Russia agreement 'is not intended to establish an association with a view to the gradual integration of that non-member country into the European Communities but is designed rather to bring about "the gradual integration between Russia and a wider area of cooperation in Europe"....it does not in any way follow from the context or purpose of that Partnership Agreement that it intended to give to the prohibition of 'discrimination based on nationality, as regards working conditions ... as compared to [the Member State's] own nationals' any meaning other than that which follows from the ordinary sense of those words'.[80] Similarly, there is no reason to assume that the context or purpose of the EC-ACP agreements should lead to a different interpretation of the right to equal treatment in working conditions than applies to the EC-Turkey or EC-Maghreb agreements, especially given (as just noted) the similarity between the context and purpose of the EC-ACP agreements and the EC-Maghreb agreements.

Finally, to what extent will the right to establishment of self-employed persons, once that right is applied in the context of the Stabilisation Agreements, strengthen the immigration status of such persons with a view to securing for them a reasonable prospect of permanent residence? According to the Court of Justice, the right to establishment under the Europe Agreements was directly effective and carried with it a corollary right of entry and residence, and it precluded the imposition of 'economic needs' tests upon nationals of Central and Eastern Europe who wished to enter the EU to create a company or work as self-employed persons. The concept of 'establishment' had the same broad meaning as it does under EC free movement law as regards the types of activities covered (even potentially prostitution), but since the Europe Agreements permitted EU Member States to maintain immigration law restrictions, checks could be imposed in advance of taking up self-employment to ensure that the planned activity did not constitute disguised employment, and Member States could oblige persons without existing residence rights to submit an application from outside the territory.[81] While the right of establishment under the Europe Agreements could be restricted on grounds of public policy, public security or public health, the Court ruled that these restrictions had the same substantive meaning as the restrictions permitted

---

80. Paras 34-36 of the judgment (n. 20 above).
81. See the cases cited at n. 14 above.

by EC free movement law.[82] There is no reason to doubt that an identical interpretation will apply to the provisions of the Stabilisation Agreements, once implemented, given the similarity in the wording, purpose and context of those agreements as compared to the Europe Agreements, unless the Stabilisation and Association Councils, when they adopt measures to implement the right of establishment, take the opportunity to provide for limitations.

It follows that after the implementation of the relevant provisions of the Stabilisation Agreements, persons who are exercising the right of establishment pursuant to those Agreements in a Member State will have a strong argument that they have a reasonable prospect of obtaining permanent residence, given the wide scope of their right to continue self-employed activities on an equal basis with nationals of the host State and the very limited circumstances in which Member States can restrict those rights.

2. Definition of family

The definition of family members has limited relevance for the EC's association agreements, since these agreements do not confer a right to family reunion as such (leaving aside the EEA and Switzerland, as noted above). However, since the association agreements do regulate in part the *status* of family members after entry, it is useful to compare the association agreements with the family reunion Directive. According to Article 4 of the family reunion Directive, the spouse and minor unmarried children must be admitted, subject to certain qualifications regarding adopted children and children whose custody is shared. However, Member States have an option to retain their existing law, which sets a special 'integration requirement' for children as young as 12, if they arrive separately from the rest of their family. Admission of dependent parents or other relatives in the ascending line, adult disabled children of the sponsor or unmarried partners of the sponsor, along with relevant children, is also optional. Member States can also set age limits for spouses to enter, and can require, on the basis of their existing law, that applications by children must be submitted before the children turn 15. If the application is submitted at a later time, then the Member State concerned 'shall authorise the entry and residence of such children on grounds other than family reunification'. The Court of Justice has upheld the validity of the possible restrictions on the

---

82. *Jany* judgment, paras 58-62 (ibid). Arguably, following the case law on the EC-Turkey agreement (*Dorr and Unal*, n. 8 above), it must also follow that the same procedural protection applies.

admission of children over 12 or over 15, but in doing so it set certain limits on the application of those restrictions by Member States.[83]

In contrast, 'family members' who have rights conferred by Article 7 of Decision 1/80 of the EC-Turkey Association Council are defined by reference to EC free movement law,[84] which is also applicable to any children under 21 or who are dependent on the EU worker, as well as parents of the worker and his or her spouse. Unlike free movement law, the family members of Turkish workers gain fully independent rights three years after living with the worker,[85] or (with regard to the children of Turkish workers) after graduation from a course of vocational training.[86] Of course, it should be emphasised again that this does not mean a wider right of *admission* for the family members of Turkish workers as compared to the family reunion Directive, but rather that a wider category of persons are the beneficiaries of Article 7 of Decision 1/80 as compared to the Directive regarding the status of family members after entry.

It should also be emphasised that Decision 1/80 also has a wider scope with regards family members born on the territory,[87] whereas presumably the family reunion Directive does not, unless the Court of Justice takes a similarly broad interpretation of its scope.[88] It is assumed that both the Decision and the Directive apply to persons who were admitted on grounds other than family reunion, and who were then authorised to stay on family reunion grounds,[89] and that both the Directive and the Decision apply to persons who were already resident before they took effect.[90]

As for the family of Maghreb workers, the Court of Justice has held that the right to equal treatment in social security for a worker's family members

---

83. Case C-540/03 *EP v Council* [2006] ECR I-5769.
84. See particularly *Ayaz*, n. 8 above, and confirmation by the *Derin* judgment, ibid.
85. See *Ergat, Eyup, Ayaz, Cetinkaya, Aydinli* and *Derin*; during the first three years, see *Kadiman* (ibid.)
86. See *Eroglu, Akman, Torun* and *Derin* (ibid.).
87. See *Cetinkaya*, ibid.
88. In the *Cetinkaya* judgment, the Court ruled that merely because Article 7 of Decision 1/80 limited its scope to persons who were 'authorised to join' the worker, this did not mean that persons who were born on the territory were excluded from its scope, but only that persons who were *not* authorised to join the worker were excluded from its scope.
89. This is explicit in Article 5(3) of the Directive; as regards the Decision, it is implicit in the *Cetinkaya* judgment.
90. This has been implicitly accepted by the Court in many cases concerning family members who entered or were born on the territory of Member States before 1980. On the temporal scope of the Directive, see S. Peers, *EU JHA Law* (n. 25 above), 215-16.

extends not just to blood relatives, but also to ascending relatives of the worker or his or her spouse who reside with the worker.[91]

Finally, Court has not yet ruled on the definition of 'family members' pursuant to the Europe Agreements, or now the Stabilisation Agreements, although declarations to those agreements state that 'family members' must be defined by the national law of the relevant Member States.

3.   Conditions of entry

The family reunion Directive states that Member States may reject an application on grounds of public policy, public security or public health; may impose requirements relating to accommodation, sickness insurance and stable and regular resources; may require the satisfaction of integration measures; and may impose a waiting period of two or, under certain conditions, three years.[92] The EC's association agreements impact upon the sickness insurance requirement, because of the requirement of equal treatment in social security matters for Turkish and Maghreb workers and their family members.[93] Also, the right to equal treatment in working conditions under various agreements will have a *de facto* impact upon the satisfaction of these conditions, because the right will assist in ensuring that workers have stable and regular resources (which they will in turn be able to use to purchase sickness insurance and to secure suitable accommodation). Turkish workers' rights of expanded access to employment will also have the same impact.

4.   Status of family members

Article 14 of the family reunion Directive requires Member States to give sponsor and family members alike access to education, employment or self-employment, and vocational training.

Starting with the family members of Turkish workers, it should first of all be emphasised that those family members can apparently obtain the status of Turkish workers themselves, pursuant to Article 6 of Decision 1/80.[94] Although the Court of Justice has recently ruled that Article 7 of Decision 1/80 (which governs family members) takes priority over

---

91. *Mesbah*, n. 11 above.
92. Arts. 6-8. On the waiting period, see again *EP v Council*, n. 83 above.
93. See ns. 10 and 11 above. Also, refugees and stateless persons can rely on EC free movement law to the same end (see Joined Cases C-95/99 to 98/99 *Khalil and others* and C-180/99 *Addou* [2001] ECR I-7413), although most refugees will not have to satisfy the requirements of Art. 7 of the Directive (see Arts. 9 and 12(1)).
94. See the judgments in *Eroglu* and *Kadiman* (n. 8 above).

Article 6,[95] this presumably means only that the position of Turkish workers' family members must first be examined to see if they fall within the scope of Article 7, and failing that to see whether they fall within the scope of Article 6. It should not mean that family members of Turkish workers are unable to gain benefits from Article 6 even if they satisfy the conditions of that Article before they satisfy the conditions of Article 7.

Family members who fall within the scope of Article 7 of Decision 1/80 *and* the family reunion Directive will have earlier access to employment pursuant to the Directive (one year's wait at most, instead of three),[96] but unlike the Decision, the Directive provides only for the same level of access as that enjoyed by the sponsor. For the family of Turkish workers, this presumably will entail access as extensive as that which the sponsor enjoys pursuant to *Article 6* of Decision 1/80 (or to a greater degree of access, if national law allows for this), and indeed it will entail access to the sponsor's *current* level of access pursuant to Article 6 (i.e., the family member will not have to start from scratch accruing rights pursuant to Article 6). If Article 14 only conferred the right to the sponsor's *initial* level of access to employment, it could well mean that family members would initially only be permitted to take up a particular job with a particular employer, a job which could be unavailable because someone else – perhaps still the sponsor – is holding it, or because it no longer exists. This cannot have been the intention of the legislator, as it would render access to employment nugatory.[97]

But it must be admitted that if the sponsor has been working between one and three years in the host Member State for his or her current employer, he or she only has access to work under Article 6 of Decision 1/80 (unless national law is more generous) for that employer,[98] and so the sponsor will only enjoy such access as well – which could be meaningless if that employer does not have jobs available for which the family member is suitably qualified. Even if the Turkish worker/sponsor has between three

---

95. *Aydinli* (ibid).
96. Art. 14(1)(b) of the Directive.
97. This point is equally valid as regards the access to employment of family members of other third-country nationals under the Directive.
98. It should be emphasized however that if national law was more generous as regards access to employment, when Decision 1/80 first became applicable, for Turkish workers who have not yet qualified for full access to employment under Decision 1/80, then the standstill in that Decision would preclude any tightening of the rules of access. If Turkish workers who are sponsoring their family members thereby benefit from the standstill, this would have a knock-on effect on family members' access to employment under the Directive.

and four years' work experience for the purpose of Decision 1/80, then the family member will only gain access to the same occupation as the worker – which may be useless if the family member is not qualified for that occupation or if there are no jobs available within it. Again, to avoid rendering access to the labour market nugatory, and to facilitate achieving the objectives of the Directive,[99] it should be concluded that the family member's access to the labour market on the same terms as the sponsor is dynamic: in other words, when the sponsor is 'upgraded' to obtain greater access to employment under Decision 1/80, then the family member enjoys a simultaneous upgrade under the Directive. In fact, this interpretation would apply by analogy to *any* upgraded access to employment obtained by *any* sponsor (Turkish worker or not) according to national law, but that issue is outside the scope of EC external relations law.

It is therefore possible, depending on the circumstances of the individual family member, that access to the labour market pursuant to the Directive on the same terms as the Turkish worker sponsor is of limited use – assuming that the earlier argument about the 'reasonable prospect' of permanent residence for Turkish workers who have not yet qualified for full access to employment under Decision 1/80 is correct. Where the sponsor already has full labour market access under Decision 1/80, though, the combination of the Directive and Decision 1/80 will give family members of Turkish workers full access to the employment market after a maximum wait of one year.

Also, it could be argued that if, in accordance with the Directive, family members have access to employment before they could possibly have access under Article 7 of Decision 1/80, then they will begin accruing rights as a Turkish worker (if in fact they are Turkish nationals) under Article 6 of Decision 1/80 because, in these circumstances, Article 7 could not be regarded as *lex specialis* to Article 6 (since access to the labour market stemmed from another source). If this is correct, though, will Article 7 nevertheless become a *lex specialis* as regards Article 6 once the time period for the application of Article 7 is satisfied? It is not easy to apply the principle that one legal rule is *lex specialis* in relation to another legal rule once a third legal rule comes into play. The point is relevant because the access to employment for family members granted by the family reunion Directive will likely lead to more cases where family members satisfy Article 6 before Article 7.

---

99. See paras. 3, 4 and 15 of the preamble to the Directive.

Also, it should be noted that even if a Member State refuses access to employment to the extended family members of a Turkish worker, pursuant to Article 14(3) of the Directive (i.e. restricting access to employment for parents, in-laws or adult dependent children), such persons will still be able to obtain access to employment pursuant to Decision 1/80.

The Directive is wider than the Decision to the extent that it also gives family members of Turkish workers access to self-employment on the same terms as the sponsor. Of course, if such family members are Turkish and they take up self-employment, then they will be able to rely upon the standstill regarding self-employment rules in the Protocol to the Ankara Agreement. Moreover, the family members' *level of access* to self-employment (if the sponsor is a worker) or employment (if the sponsor is self-employed) may be facilitated respectively by the standstills in the Protocol and the Decision respectively, since the standstills presumably apply to 'switching rules' (i.e. the ability of a person admitted for employment to switch to self-employment, or vice versa).[100] This would mean that even if the sponsor is a worker, for instance, a family member who wished to take up *self-employment* could rely on the switching rules which were applicable under national law when the Protocol to the Ankara Agreement came into force – for those are the rules which govern the sponsor's (and therefore the family members') access to self-employment.

The Directive also gives the family members access to education on the same terms as the sponsor. This may be of limited utility if the sponsor has limited access to education, and in any event it is not entirely clear whether access to education entails access to the relevant benefits which facilitate access. Arguably it does, as this would facilitate the objectives of the Directive (fair treatment, integration and social and economic cohesion, according to the preamble to the Directive). But again, this is of limited utility if the sponsor has limited access to education benefits.

Family members of Turkish workers are therefore clearly better off relying upon Article 9 of Decision 1/80, if they meet the relevant conditions. It provides as follows:

Turkish children residing legally in a Member State of the Community with their parents who are or have been legally employed in that Member State, shall be admitted to courses of general education, apprenticeship and vocational training under the same educational entry qualifications as the

---

100. This point is explicitly acknowledged by the Opinion in *Tum and Dari* (n. 7 above), para. 67.

children of nationals of that Member State. They may in that Member State be eligible to benefit from the advantages provided for under the national legislation in this area.'

According to the Court's judgment in *Gurol*,[101] both sentences of Article 9 are directly effective, the first sentence does not require the student to be resident with his or her parents during the period of education, and the second sentence creates a mandatory right to equal treatment in education grants, including even grants for study in Turkey. The level of access to education of the sponsor is therefore irrelevant. Moreover it is clear from the wording of Article 9 that it applies whether or not the Turkish children have been admitted to join their parents, or were born on the territory,[102] and regardless of the retirement of the parents.[103] There is no age limit for equal treatment for access to education under Article 9,[104] although there is none under the Directive either.[105]

However, there might still be some children of Turkish nationals who would need to rely upon the Directive, for example if the parents are self-employed, or have departed or died (since the children would no longer be legally residing with them).[106] Other family members besides children could also obtain access to education under the Directive.

As for other benefits, the family reunion Directive confers no right to equal treatment as regards social assistance or social security. However, Turkish workers and their family members can rely upon Decision 3/80 of the EC-Turkey Association Council to secure equal treatment as regards asocial security. It should not, of course, be forgotten that independently of the Directive and association agreements, third-country nationals enjoy equal treatment as regards social security and aspects of social assistance as a

---

101. N. 8 above.
102. Even Article 7 of the Decision applies to children of Turkish workers born on the territory, despite its apparent restriction to family members 'authorised to join' the worker: see *Cetinkaya*, ibid.
103. See by analogy *Akman*, ibid.
104. See by analogy the lack of age limits applicable to children of Turkish workers under Article 7, most recently confirmed in *Derin*, ibid.
105. While Article 14 permits Member States to limit access to self-employment and employment for some categories of family members (paragraph 3), there is no provision for limiting access to education for any family member, and surely, in light of the objectives of the Directive, paragraph 3 must be considered to be an exhaustive list of possible restrictions on family members' rights.
106. On the other hand, the Court of Justice might nevertheless be inclined to interpret Article 9 of the Decision generously on these points (see the *Gurol* judgment).

consequence of the jurisprudence of the European Court of Human Rights.[107]

Next, access to autonomous residence status for spouses, unmarried partners and minor children who have reached the age of majority is guaranteed by the Directive after five years' residence.[108] Member States may limit this status to spouses and partners who have suffered from the breakdown of the family relationship, and other detailed rules are provided for. This can be compared with the right of family members of Turkish workers under Article 7 of Decision 1/80 to stay after three years' residence with the sponsor, regardless of whether they have actually taken up employment. It is hard to imagine why Turkish workers' family members who would qualify for this status under Article 7 would wish to qualify instead under the Directive, although an *additional* qualification under the Directive might be useful since the Directive confers a right of formal documentation of the autonomous status in the form of a residence permit, and holding this permit might moreover under national law grant further access to benefits and employment, et al.

In any event, any Turkish workers' family members completing five years of legal residence would be better advised to seek long-term residence status under the relevant EC Directive – considered further below – as would any family member of a third-country national, if they meet the relevant conditions.[109] If they do not, then autonomous residence status under the family reunion Directive might be a useful supplement to their status under Decision 1/80 (for Turkish workers' family members) or better than nothing (for everyone else within the scope of the Directive).

Finally, Turkish workers' family members who fall within the scope of Decision 1/80 and who possibly face expulsion are probably better off in all cases relying upon Decision 1/80, which limits expulsion to the grounds of public policy, public security and public health as defined under EC free

---

107. *Gaygusuz v. Austria* (Reports of Judgments and Decisions 1996-IV) and *Poirrez v France* (Reports of Judgments and Decisions 2003-IX). See also the non-discrimination right secured by Article 26 of the International Covenant on Civil and Political Rights, as interpreted by the Human Rights Committee (S. Joseph, J. Schulz and M. Castan, *The International Covenant on Economic, Social and Political Rights: Cases, Materials and Commentary* (2nd edition, OUP 2004), 679-751.
108. Art. 15 of the Directive.
109. On the relationship between the two Directives, see n. 72 above.

movement law (including the relevant procedural protection),[110] and lengthy departure from the territory. Arguably, by analogy with Article 6 of Decision 1/80, Article 7 cannot benefit those who are convicted of a fraudulent pretence of a family relationship.[111]

On the other hand, the Directive permits non-renewal or withdrawal of a residence permit where the conditions of entry (i.e., accommodation, sickness insurance, stable resources and possibly integration requirements) are no longer satisfied, where the family member is now in a relationship with another person, or where there is no longer a 'real' marital relationship with the sponsor, the marriage was contracted for the purpose of gaining entry, or where the family member does not yet have an autonomous permit.[112] Member States may also withdraw or refuse to renew a residence permit on grounds of public policy, public security or public health.[113] However, any decisions to withdraw or refuse to renew a permit, or to order removal, are subject to a requirement to take account of the nature and solidity of family relationships, the duration of residence in the Member State and the extent of ties with the country of origin,[114] along with (as regards public policy and public security), the extent of the danger presented or the severity and type of offence committed by the person concerned. The Court of Justice has confirmed that the general balancing factors have been derived from the case-law of the European Court of Human Rights,[115] and the balancing factors specific to public policy and public security appear to have been derived from that case law also.

The grounds of non-renewal or withdrawal of a permit, and removal, therefore appear broader under the Directive than under Decision 1/80, unless the requirements which must be considered before deciding on the removal, etc. of family members under the Directive are interpreted to be identical to the requirements applicable to Decision 1/80 (i.e., the free movement law criteria). Equally the Directive appears to set lower procedural requirements than Decision 1/80, stating merely that there must be a right to 'mount a legal challenge', with the relevant procedure to

---

110. See particularly *Aydinli* and *Derin* (n. 8 above), and on procedural rights, *Dorr and Unal* (ibid). A pending case asks whether the expanded substantive and procedural protection against expulsion of EU citizens in Directive 2004/38 also applies to Decision 1/80: see *Polat*, ibid.
111. See by analogy *Kol*, ibid; but even here the comparable grounds under the family reunion Directive are broader: see Art. 16(2)(a) of the Directive.
112. Art. 16 of the Directive.
113. Art. 6(2) of the Directive.
114. Art. 17 of the Directive.
115. Case C-540/03 *EP v Council* (n. 83 above), para. 64.

be established by national law.[116] Although the Court of Justice has held that the right to mount a legal challenge confers access to courts,[117] and the Directive must arguably be interpreted consistently with the case law of the European Court of Human Rights setting out detailed procedural rights where the right to family life could be infringed by an expulsion,[118] the standards under Decision 1/80 (again, corresponding to EC free movement law) are probably higher and certainly more precise.[119]

As for the other agreements, the status of family members is enhanced by the right of access of family members to the workforce under the Stabilisation and Association Agreements, and by their equal access to social security under the Maghreb agreements. In the absence of case law, it is arguable that family members' access to employment under the SAAs is more generous than under the Directive (since the agreements do not refer to any power for Member States to delay family members' access to the workforce or to limit the access of family members to the same level of access as the sponsor. Finally, under a number of association agreements, family members, once authorised to work in accordance with the Directive, will enjoy the benefit of equal treatment in working conditions pursuant to the agreements, which could also (if their residence permit lasts for longer than the work permit) confer some degree of protection against expulsion, which might possibly confer greater substantive and procedural protection than under the Directive.

B.   Long-term residents

Moving on to the Community's long-term residence (LTR) Directive, the right to long-term residence status which that Directive confers can broadly be compared with the secure status which a Turkish worker or family member can ultimately attain under Decision 1/80. However, full

---

116. Art. 18 of the Directive.
117. Case C-540/03 (n. 83 above), para. 106.
118. *Al-Nashif v Bulgaria* (judgment of 20 June 2002), paras. 117 to 129 and 133 to 138 and *Lupsa v Romania* (judgment of 8 June 2006), paras. 32-44.
119. With the exception of the open point as to whether the standards in more recent EC legislation are now applicable to Decision 1/80 – see the pending *Polat* case (n. 8 above) – although this issue will likely be resolved with a judgment in this case by late 2007 or early 2008.

status under Decision 1/80 only confers a right of access to employment and a corollary right of secure residence.

In contrast, the right of LTR status under the Directive also confers the right to equal treatment with nationals as regards in particular: self-employment; working conditions, education and vocational training (including study grants as defined in national law); recognition of diplomas, et al; and social security, social assistance and social protection as defined by national law.[120] However, Member States may retain a territorial condition on access to some benefits and existing restrictions on access to employment, and may also limit equal treatment as regards social assistance and social protection to 'core benefits'.[121]

However, Turkish workers also have a right under Decision 1/80 to equal treatment in working conditions, regardless of whether they have attained full access to the workforce under that Decision.[122] Also, Turkish workers and their family members derive a right to equal treatment in social security separately from Decision 3/80; again, this right applies regardless of the extent of status which Turkish workers and their families do, or do not, enjoy under Decision 1/80.[123] So it is hard to see what the Directive will add as regards these issues – on the contrary, Turkish workers and their family members might have to remind national authorities that for them, such rights are *not* dependent on gaining long-term residence status under the Directive.

As for the right to education, it can be enjoyed, subject to certain conditions, by Turkish workers' children in accordance with Article 9 of Decision 1/80.[124] The Directive will therefore only be useful for those children who do not meet the conditions for the application of Article 9 of

---

120. Art. 11(1) of the Directive.
121. Art. 11(2), (3) and (4) of the Directive.
122. See Art. 10 of the Decision, as interpreted in the *Birklite* and *Guzeli* judgments (n. 8 above).
123. See the judgments of the Court of Justice (n. 10 above).
124. See the text at notes 101-105 above.

Decision 1/80 -- assuming that the equal treatment rights under the Directive can apply to the children of long-term residents at all.[125]

LTR status also confers the right, subject to detailed conditions, to move between Member States. In contrast, Decision 1/80 does not regulate the initial admission of a Turkish national into the territory of a Member State.[126]

The Directive and Decision 1/80 will intertwine indirectly, in the sense that securing status under Decision 1/80 will bolster the access by Turkish workers to 'stable and secure resources', and the application of Decision 3/80 will ensure that Turkish workers have sickness insurance.[127] Similarly, the secure status, and enhanced access to employment, conferred upon family members by Article 7 of Decision 1/80 – and in particular the immediate secure status and full employment access conferred upon Turkish workers' children who graduate from vocational training, as long as one of their parents is or has been employed in the territory of the relevant Member State – will assist those family members to meet the conditions to obtain LTR status. However, gaining status under Decision 1/80 will not, in itself, entail satisfaction of any integration conditions which may be set by Member States as a condition of gaining long-term residents status,[128] since Member States are not allow to impose integration conditions for gaining status under Decision 1/80.

---

125. Article 11 of the Directive does not state expressly that the equal treatment rights apply to family members of the long-term resident, although arguably that is a necessary implication – otherwise the long-term resident (if he or she lives, like many people, as part of a family unit), will not, after all, enjoy fully equal treatment in practice due to the ancillary effect of the discrimination suffered by his or her family members. It would also be inconsistent for the position of family members to be considered when applying the conditions for acquiring long-term resident's status (see Article 5(1) of the Directive), but not as regards equal treatment. Finally, accepting that family members implicitly enjoy equal treatment as regards access to benefits would be consistent with he Court's interpretation of EC free movement law, where the family members of EU migrant workers enjoy rights under Titles I and II of Reg. 1612/68 even though the Regulation only expressly confers rights on the workers under those Titles (see Cases 131/85 *Gul* [1986] ECR 1573 and C-3/90 *Bernini* [1992] ECR I-1071).
126. See, most recently, the judgment in *Derin* (n. 8 above), para. 66. With respect, in light of the LTR Directive, the Court should no longer refer without qualification to sole national competence to admit Turkish nationals for the first time (compare to para. 143 of the Opinion), leaving aside the position of the Member States which have opted out of that Directive.
127. Art. 5(1) of the Directive.
128. Art. 5(2) of the Directive.

While many Turkish workers and family members are likely to obtain rights under Decision 1/80 and then under the Directive,[129] it should be emphasised that it is possible (particularly in the case of workers) that the conditions of the Directive could be satisfied first, for example if a worker has changed jobs every two years or so. In that case it would still be possible to obtain status under Decision 1/80 *after* obtaining status under the Directive. Obtaining status under Decision 1/80 could still be a useful addition to long-term residence status if, for example, a Member State still retains its existing restrictions on access to employment under the Directive (such restrictions would not be allowed under Decision 1/80),[130] or if it turns out that Decision 1/80 offers greater protection from expulsion than the Directive does.

In some cases, it is possible that a Turkish worker will obtain full status under Decision 1/80 quite simply after four years' employment, but then might have difficulty obtaining long-term residence (LTR) status a year later.[131] This could result from the exclusions from the scope of the Directive of students, persons who enjoy, or who have applied for, international protection status, diplomats, or persons who 'reside on temporary grounds such as au pair or seasonal worker, or as workers posted by a service provider for the purposes of cross-border provision of services, or as cross-border providers of services or in cases where their residence permit has been formally limited'. It is clear from the case law on Decision 1/80 that if a Turkish worker meets the condition of working one year with the same employer, any limitation in their residence permit that prevents them continuing to work with that employer must be set aside.[132] It is also arguable that students and au pairs can obtain rights as Turkish workers.[133] Equally it could be argued that diplomats and employed service providers can meet the definition of 'Turkish worker',[134] and that persons who enjoy or seek international protection can be considered as workers if they have been authorised to work (pursuant to national law, the Geneva

---

129. The Opinion in *Derin* clearly assumes that Turkish workers may, in addition to status under Decision 1/80, obtain rights under the Directive (para. 143).
130. This leaves open the question as to whether the restrictions on access to employment or self-employment connected with 'official authority' permitted by the Directive could also apply in the context of Decision 1/80.
131. Or, mutatis mutandis, that a Turkish worker's family member might obtain status under the Directive only after obtaining it under the Decision.
132. See, for instance, *Ertanir, Gunaydin* and *Kurz*, n. 8 above.
133. See the opinion in the pending case of *Payir*, ibid., which accepts this argument as regards au pairs but rejects it as regards students.
134. However, see the distinction between workers and service providers set out in *Abatay*, ibid.

Convention, and more recently Community law),[135] since Decision 1/80 is not limited in application only to people who were authorised to enter as workers.[136] The exclusion of refugees and beneficiaries of subsidiary protection, would, however, be removed if a Commission proposal to this effect is adopted.[137]

It is also possible that a Turkish worker or worker's family member with status under Decision 1/80 might fail, or at least fail after five years' legal residence, to obtain LTR status, because the worker or family member has not satisfied integration conditions or has become unemployed (or in the case of family members, never was employed).[138] This might also happen even where a Turkish worker has a continuing job, if the 'resources' requirement for LTR is interpreted strictly by some Member States in order to disqualify Turkish workers with low income and/or who work part-time, who nonetheless qualify for status under Decision 1/80.[139]

Another point of comparison between Decision 1/80 and the Directive is the rules on the calculation of time periods to acquire status. The Decision contains detailed rules on the effect of interruption of work, which the Court has interpreted on several occasions.[140] In contrast, the Directive excludes time spent on the territory as a diplomat or on a temporary basis from the calculation, and discounts by half the time spent as a student on the territory;[141] arguably such time would count towards status under the Decision, if the person concerned indeed counts as a worker and was actually working at the time. The Directive also contains detailed rules on

135. See Art. 12 of Directive 2001/55 (OJ L 212, 7.8.2001, p. 12); Art. 11 of Directive 2003/9 (OJ L 31, 6.2.2003, p. 18); and Art. 26 of Directive 2004/83 (n. 3 above). It is arguable, however, that persons merely seeking protection status are covered by the case law which excludes persons with a merely provisional and fundamentally disputed residence status from benefiting from Decision 1/80 (see particularly *Sevince* and *Kus*, ibid).

136. See particularly *Kus*, ibid, but see the opinion in *Payir*, ibid, which argues that persons admitted as students constitute an exception to that rule.

137. COM (2007) 298, 6 June 2007.

138. Family members need not be employed to obtain status under Article 7 of Decision 1/80: see implicitly *Ergat*, paras. 45 to 48, *Cetinkaya*, para. 36 and *Torun*, para. 25, and explicitly *Aydinli*, para. 29 and *Derin*, para. 56 (n. 8 above). But the Directive appears to require that the applicant for LTR status must have access to funds on his/her own account: Art. 5(1).

139. This assumes that this would be a valid interpretation of the LTR Directive, which is highly contestable. On the irrelevance of income levels and part-time status for qualifying as a Turkish worker under Decision 1/80, see the opinion and judgment in *Birden* and the opinion in *Payir* (n. 8 above).

140. See particularly the judgments in *Tetik*, *Guzeli* and *Sedef* (ibid).

141. Art. 4(2) of the Directive.

cases where a departure from the territory either interrupts the calculation period or must be taken into account; in contrast, the Court of Justice ruled more broadly that while short departures from the territory must be taken into account towards acquiring rights under Article 6 of Decision 1/80, longer departures 'stop the clock'.[142] Departure from the territory also has an impact upon the acquisition of rights under Article 7 of that Decision.[143]

A parallel issue is the loss of rights under the Directive and the Decision. The Directive provides that LTR status can be lost because of detection of fraudulent acquisition of status, adoption of an expulsion measure on the grounds set out in the Directive, or absence from the *Community* for over 12 months,[144] although this period could be extended for 'specific or exceptional reasons'.[145] It is also possible to terminate LTR status for less serious breaches of public policy, which do not justify expulsion,[146] or after obtaining LTR status in another Member State, or in any event after six years have passed since leaving the first Member State, although this period can be extended.[147]

In contrast, full rights under Articles 6 or 7 of Decision 1/80 can only be lost on grounds of public policy, public security or public health, or (in the case of Article 7) because of departure from the territory for a considerable period without legitimate excuse, or (in the case of Article 6) because of failure to find new employment within a reasonable period or permanent departure from the labour force.[148] It is not clear from the case law whether temporary departure from the territory could entail the loss of full rights under Article 6. It might also be assumed that status can be lost should a person be convicted of having acquired it fraudulently.[149]

The wording of the Directive and the case law on the Decision is not entirely clear, but it is possible that the ground for expulsion (or at least for loss of LTR status) on grounds of public policy, public security and public health is subject to lower procedural and/or substantive standards under the Directive. Also, it is possible that a lower threshold applies under the Directive in relation to fraud as compared to the Decision (where there is probably an obligation, by analogy with *Kol*, to convict a person for fraud

---

142. *Sedef* (n. 8 above).
143. See in particular the judgments in *Kadiman* and *Ergat*, confirmed in *Derin* (ibid).
144. Art. 9(1).
145. Art. 9(2).
146. Art. 9(3); see Art. 9(7).
147. Art. 9(4).
148. As regards Article 6, see *Bozkurt, Tetik, Nazli, Kurz* and most recently *Dogan*, n. 8 above; As regards Article 7, see n. 143 above.
149. See *Kol* (n. 8 above).

before stripping him or her of status). With regard to departure from the territory, it is not clear whether this ground applies at all to Turkish workers under Article 6 of the Decision, and if so whether the rules are more generous, less generous, or equally generous to those applicable under the Directive. While this ground does apply to the family members of Turkish workers, the Decision is probably less generous than the rules in the Directive regarding movement within the Community, and probably more generous than the rules in the Directive regarding departures outside the Community. But both the Directive and (the case law on) the Decision lack much precision on this issue. Moreover, it is not even clear from the Directive whether an LTR departing to reside in the UK, Ireland or Denmark should be regarded as leaving the Community or not.

A Turkish worker and/or family member would be wise to acquire full status under the Decision and under the LTR Directive before contemplating a move to another Member State. Moreover, the considerable uncertainty regarding this issue means that if a dispute on this issue reaches the national courts, the substantive issues are sufficiently intertwined (because it is arguable that the Decision should not set standards lower than the Directive, or should be interpreted in light of the Directive)[150] that even lower national courts should be able to send questions on this issue to the Court of Justice.

There should surely be no doubt, however, that whatever happens to their Decision 1/80 status in the first Member State, Turkish workers and their family members who move to a second Member State pursuant to the LTR Directive begin to acquire Decision 1/80 status in the second Member State, and will (if the conditions are satisfied) eventually acquire full Decision 1/80 status there. There is nothing in the Directive or Decision 1/80 to rule this out, and this interpretation would be consistent with the objective of the association agreement of facilitating Turkish membership of the Community, as well as with Decision 3/80, which expressly contemplates the situation of Turkish workers moving between Member States.

As for self-employed Turkish nationals, the effect of the standstill relating to establishment might be that a secure residence status can be obtained under national law sooner than LTR status can be obtained under the Directive, because the waiting period and/or the other conditions for obtaining this status are more generous.[151]

---

150. See the opinions referred to in note 45 above.
151. On the effect of more favourable national rules, see Art. 13 of the Directive.

As for the other agreements, the right to equal treatment in working conditions in various agreements has an equivalent under the LTR Directive, but it is not clear whether this right in the LTR Directive also (like the association agreements) confers a right to protection against expulsion if the residence permit lasts longer than the work permit. If so, the question is whether this special protection against expulsion provides for higher procedural and substantive protection than the general protection against expulsion of LTRs provided for in the Directive, and whether the special protection under the LTR Directive sets identical, higher or lower standards to those under the agreements. If not, the question is simply whether the agreements set an identical, higher or lower standard as regards protection against expulsion on this point than the general protection against expulsion under the LTR Directive. In any event, it should be recalled that there is no need to obtain LTR status before benefiting from this protection under the agreements.

C.   Students

The association agreements examined in this Chapter do not generally address the status of students. However, an important question is the status of students who work, given that the relevant EC Directive requires Member States to permit students to undertake employment, although the 'situation of the labour market in the host Member State may be taken into account' (whatever that means), Member States must set a maximum time period for student work (but there must be minimum access of at least 10 hours/week, or the equivalent pro rata), and access to employment may be restricted during the first year of studies.[152]

This provision raises the question of whether students who work are to be considered 'workers' for the purpose of EC-Turkey Association Council Decision 1/80,[153] who are therefore entitled to a renewal of their work permit to work for the same employer after one year of employment, and ultimately entitled to even wider workforce access. Their family members would also, as a consequence, enjoy rights under Articles 7 and 9 of Decision 1/80, although there would be no direct link with the Directive as regards family members, since the Directive is silent on the issue of the admission and status of students' family members.

---

152. Art. 17, Directive 2004/114 (n. 2 above).
153. On the social security position of students under Decision 3/80, see *Surul*, n. 10 above.

The pending case of *Payir* addresses this issue.[154] In her opinion in this case, the Advocate-General argues that the Directive cannot influence the interpretation of the Decision, since the former provides that it is without prejudice to rights conferred by the agreements between the Community and/or the Member States with third countries.[155] In any case, she points out that the application of that Directive is not relevant in *Payir*, since that case was referred from the British courts, and the UK has opted out of the Directive. Instead, she argues for an interpretation of Decision 1/80 independent of the Directive. If her argument is adopted by the Court, it would sever any link between the Directive and the Decision, since, in her view, persons admitted as students (whether under the Directive or on the basis of national law) should not be able to obtain 'worker' status under Article 6 of Decision 1/80.

However, this still leaves open the prospect that persons admitted as students will obtain status under Article 7(2) of Decision 1/80,[156] as long as they graduate from their course of vocational training and one of their parents is or has been employed in the territory of the relevant Member State.[157] But access to employment (and the corollary access to residence status) under this route – which would, moreover, eventually lead to long-term residence status under the LTR Directive, as mentioned above – is not dependent upon having access to employment, or taking up employment, during the period when the person concerned was a student. At least the Directive makes the prospect of obtaining access to the workforce of a Member State via this route more attractive to Turkish students who can satisfy the conditions set out in Article 7(2) of the Decision, since the access to employment guaranteed by the Directive can defray their costs in the meantime.

It also leaves open the prospect that students covered by Article 9 of Decision 1/80 will also have access to employment in accordance with the Directive, to supplement the right of access to education under the Decision. It will be recalled that Turkish workers' children can enjoy rights under Article 9 of the Decision even if they have not been admitted as students.[158]

---

154. Note 8 above.
155. Art. 4(1) of the Directive.
156. The two situations are expressly distinguished in para. 81 of the *Payir* opinion.
157. See particularly *Eroglu, Akman, Torun* and *Derin* (n. 8 above).
158. See the text starting at note 101 above.

D. Researchers

Directive 2005/71 provides for a fast-track system for the entry and residence of researchers, who must be admitted onto the territory and given residence permits if the conditions in the Directive are satisfied.[159] The residence permits must be for at least one year, if the project lasts longer than that, and must be renewed if the conditions are still satisfied.[160] There is nothing in the Directive to regulate the acquisition of any further status for the persons concerned once the research project ends, but it is obvious that any Turkish workers employed as part of such a project will acquire rights pursuant to Article 6 of Decision 1/80 and will therefore ultimately be able to pursue other employment pursuant to that Decision. Of course, this is still without prejudice to Turkish workers' ability to obtain long-term residence status as well under the LTR Directive. In fact, the interaction of this Directive with Decision 1/80 shows the continued importance of the rights which the Decision confers upon Turkish workers. Their right to take up other work within the same occupation after three years, and any work after four years, will mean that they have the right to stay and probably acquire LTR status even if the research project ends between three and five years after their entry, whereas other third-country nationals would not have such a right under Community law as it stands.

As for family members of researchers, the Directive requires that they have the same period of validity of residence permits as that of the researcher, on the condition that the Member State decides to give them a residence permit and that their travel documents are valid for the relevant period. Member States are exempt from this obligation in 'duly justified' cases (whatever this means). Also, the issue of a residence permit to family members cannot be made dependent on a minimum period of residence of the researcher.[161] The precise relationship between this provision and the family reunion Directive is not clear. However, for Turkish workers' family members, any longer period of holding a residence permit may be useful in enabling them to stay long enough to qualify for independent status under Article 7 of Decision 1/80.

There are provisions on equal treatment in working conditions and social security, but they add nothing for the persons covered by the relevant treaties.

159. Arts. 7 and 8 of the Directive.
160. Art. 8.
161. Art. 9.

Finally, the Directive contains a right to carry out research in another Member State if the research project requires it. It is arguable that any departure from the host Member State on these grounds does not entail the loss of status under Decision 1/80 (if it has already been attained) or interrupt the acquisition of such status. An alternative interpretation would threaten both the objectives of the Directive (as set out in the preamble) of attracting more research workers to the European Union, and the objectives of the association agreement. A Turkish worker could, moreover, begin obtaining Decision 1/80 status in the second Member State. Similarly, if family members are allowed to accompany the worker during such periods in another Member State (an issue not addressed in the Directive) this should not entail the loss of, or interrupt the acquisition of, their status under Decision 1/80 either. If, alternatively, family members stay behind in the original host State either because they are not allowed to accompany the Turkish worker or because they decide not to for reasons of their own (such as not interrupting the children's schooling, the cost of the move or the family member wishing to keep or obtain a job in the first host Member State's workforce), then this should be considered an objective reason for a break in the family relationship, which does not threaten the acquisition of rights under Decision 1/80.[162]

E.   Social security

Regulation 859/2003 only governs the social security position of third-country nationals who have moved between Member States.[163] As such, it only connects with other EC immigration legislation (the LTR directive and the researchers' directive) and EC free movement law (as regards third-country nationals who have been posted from one Member State to another by their employer).[164] On the other hand, the EC's association agreements govern the position in a *single* Member State, ensuring equal treatment there for Turkish and Maghreb workers and their family members.[165]

There is therefore no overlap in practice between the Regulation and the association agreements,[166] although the association agreements do overlap

---

162. See *Kadiman*, n. 8 above.
163. The Reg. only extends to the currently applicable social security rules for EU citizens to third-country nationals; a proposed further Reg. would extend the *future* social security rules for EU citizens to third-country nationals (COM (2007) 439, 23 July 2007).
164. See the case law beginning with case C-43/93 *Van der Elst* [1994] ECR I-3803.
165. See the case law at notes 10 and 11 above.
166. See in particular the order in *El-Youssfi* (n. 11 above).

with the requirements to grant equal treatment in social security in a single Member State as set out in the LTR Directive and the researchers' Directive and (more ambiguously) the refugee qualification Directive.[167] While Decision 3/80 does contain inoperative rules on the position of Turkish workers who have moved between Member States,[168] it is doubtful whether the Community now needs to adopt measures implementing Decision 3/80 on this point, given the adoption of Regulation 859/2003.

IV. Conclusion

It can be seen that the immigration status of any person falling within the scope of both the EC's association agreements and its immigration law is liable to be affected by both sources of law, and that there are many direct or indirect links between the two sources, even though there are no explicit links. This is particularly true of Turkish nationals. Even in cases where it appears that only one of the two sources is relevant, because the Member State in question has opted out from EC immigration legislation, the third-country national concerned is not covered by an association agreement, or the facts in the particular case point to the application of only one of the sources of law, it is possible that both sources are relevant, because arguably these two sources of law must be interpreted in light of each other. The interaction between these two sources is likely to lead to significant case law of the Court of Justice and should not be overlooked by anyone with an interest in advising third-country nationals about their immigration status.

---

167. Art. 11(1)(d), LTR Directive and Art. 12(c), Directive 2005/71; Art. 14(6) of the LTR Directive defers to Regulation 859/2003 as regards the position of an LTR who moves to a second Member State. According to Art. 26(5) of the qualification Directive, the 'law in force' in each Member State regarding social security related to employment or self-employment shall apply; cf. Art. 12 of Directive 2001/55 (temporary protection).
168. See *Taflan-Met* (n. 10 above). On the distinction between the operative equal treatment rule in Decision 3/80 governing Turkish workers and their families within a single Member State, and the inoperative rules governing their movement between Member States, see *Ozkurt* (ibid).

3. Readmission and Repatriation of Illegal Residents

Martin Schieffer[1]

I. Introduction

For quite some time now, the issue of illegal immigration figures high on the agenda of the European Union as it has become a major concern for Europe's Governments and citizens. The migratory pressure on the EU´s external borders has been constantly mounting over the past years and, in particular, daily arrivals of boats of illegal immigrants on the shores of southern Member States during successive summers have kept this issue in the public eye. Due to the demographic forecasts and the economic and political situation in many developing countries, especially on the African continent, and given Europe's own demographic decline and growing labour needs, this migration pressure is very likely to even further increase during the next decades. Developing an effective migration management has therefore become an absolute priority for the European Union.

Building upon the Tampere milestones of October 1999 and the Hague Programme of November 2004, European leaders decided in December 2006 that the policy needed to attain this objective should be a comprehensive one, comprising various policy areas of the EU and requiring a much stronger cooperation with countries of origin and transit. To gain this cooperation, the future strategy will be multi-facetted and, in particular, foresees the opening of new channels for legal migration to reduce migratory pressures and fill demands in the EU for temporary and seasonal work while also allowing for more circular migration. This approach, however, can only work if, at the same time, the EU significantly reinforces its efforts to combat illegal immigration. The future priorities in this regard, identified by the Commission in a communication in July 2006[2], comprise a broad range of actions inside and outside the EU. In particular, measures aimed at facilitating the return and readmission of illegally staying third-country nationals have repeatedly been identified as

---

1.   All views expressed in this article are purely personal and do not necessarily reflect the views of the European Commission.
2.   COM (2006) 402 final.

a key element and an integral component of any effective migration management by the EU.

Today, it is generally acknowledged that an effective policy on return and readmission is an indispensable cornerstone of the EU's broader efforts to develop a comprehensive migration policy and to ensure public support for further measures on legal migration and refugee protection. Already in its communication for the June 2003 Thessaloniki European Council, the European Commission described the policy objectives in the area of return in very clear terms and warned that *"the credibility and integrity of the legal immigration and asylum policies are at stake unless there is a Community return policy on illegal residents. Moreover, all efforts to fight illegal immigration are questionable, if those who manage to overcome these measures succeed finally to maintain their illegal residence. The signal effect of a failed return policy on illegal residents cannot be underestimated."*[3]

The development of a common policy on return and readmission is far from being complete and much still remains to be done – inside the Union and in cooperation with third-countries. The present paper seeks to focus on the external dimension of these undertakings and, following a brief outline of the policy context, provide an overview on the state of the Community's readmission negotiations with third-countries, raise a number of legal and institutional issues, analyse some lessons learned and try to sketch out the way forward. Internal policy developments, such as the proposed directive harmonising Member States' return procedures[4] or the future functioning, as of 2008, of the new European Return Fund[5], will be referred to where necessary.

II.   Policy context: from Maastricht to Amsterdam and beyond

For the European Union, dealing with issues related to the return and readmission of illegal immigrants is a relatively new phenomenon. Under the terms of the Maastricht Treaty, Member States were solely competent for dealing with these and, if discussed at EU level, topics were addressed on a strictly intergovernmental basis only.[6] This situation changed on 1 May 1999 with the entry into force of the Amsterdam Treaty, which "communitarized" all issues related to visa, border controls, asylum and

3.   COM (2003) 323 final of 3 June 2003, p. 8.
4.   COM (2005) 391 final of 1 September 2005.
5.   OJ L 144, 6.6.2007, p. 45.
6.   See Article K.1 (3) lit. c) of the Maastricht Treaty ("third pillar").

immigration and conferred explicit powers to the European Community in Title IV of Part 3 of the EC Treaty (EC). Art. 63 (3) (b) EC now enables the Council to adopt measures within the area of *"illegal immigration and illegal residence, including repatriation of illegal residents"*. The Community's powers under this Article include the external competence to conclude readmission agreements with relevant third-countries in order to accelerate and facilitate the return of such persons.

One of the reasons for this transfer of powers was certainly that, in the years following the fall of the iron curtain, Member States had all realised that, individually and on their own, they were no longer able to react appropriately to the increasing difficulties of their authorities to return illegally staying third-country nationals and that, therefore, a common European approach had to be found. In practice, the main obstacle to return is unclear identity and the lack of proper travel documents. Potential returnees are mostly responsible for this lack of documentation since it is generally known that countries of origin often delay or deny the issuing of return travel documents because of missing information about nationality or identity. In order to avoid removal, many illegal residents therefore hide or destroy their travel documents and not infrequently claim a completely false identity and/or nationality. As a consequence, lengthy and expensive procedures often need to be carried out; these include presentation at several embassies of neighbouring third countries or a language or dialect analysis.[7]

In the light of the above return problems and with a view to preparing the entry into force of the Amsterdam Treaty, in December 1998, the JHA Council adopted an action plan[8] on how best to implement the new provisions of Title IV. This action plan identified the establishment of a coherent policy on readmission and return as one of the EU's priorities in the field of immigration.

In May 1999, when debating the effects of the entry into force of the Treaty of Amsterdam on the future EU policy in the field of repatriating illegal residents, the JHA Council became more specific and concluded that readmission agreements would constitute a valuable instrument for an active return policy. In suitable cases, the Commission would, therefore, be authorised to conduct negotiations with relevant third countries on such agreements. The Tampere European Council broadly backed these conclusions in October 1999, when EU Heads of State or Government

---

7.   For more details, see COM (2002) 564 final of 14 October 2002, p. 13.
8.   OJ C 19, 23.1.1999, p. 1.

explicitly confirmed that the Amsterdam Treaty conferred powers on the Community in the field of readmission. In addition, the Tampere European Council invited the Council to start concluding readmission agreements with relevant third-countries or groups of third-countries.

The Laeken European Council of 14/15 December 2001 took stock of the state of implementation of the Tampere agenda and, among others, emphasised the need for new priorities and enhanced efforts to conclude Community readmission agreements with further third-countries. To this end, at its meeting in April 2002, the JHA Council identified 6 concrete selection criteria: (1) the migration pressure exerted by a third country; (2) its geographical position in relation to the EU; (3) the fact that the country must not be a candidate country with which the EU is already negotiating about accession; (4) considerations of geographical balance and regional coherence; (5) the existence of an EU association or co-operation agreement containing a readmission clause, and (6) the added value of a Community agreement in comparison to individual Member State agreements.[9]

The importance of concluding further readmission agreements with relevant third-countries and, more generally, the valuable role such agreements play in the fight against illegal immigration was also strongly confirmed in the February 2002 EU Action Plan to combat illegal immigration[10], as well as by the Seville European Council of 21/22 June 2002. In paragraph 30 of its conclusions, the Seville summit explicitly called for the speeding up of the conclusion of readmission agreements currently being negotiated and the approval of new negotiating mandates for further third countries. Moreover, in the same paragraph of these conclusions, the Seville European Council also asked for the development of an EU Return Action Program, which the JHA Council adopted in November 2002[11]. In paragraph 64 of this Action Program, considerable emphasis was put on the conclusion of readmission agreements which, as a matter of principle, should cover own nationals as well as third-country nationals and stateless persons. Depending on the Commission's assessment of the state of play of negotiations on readmission agreements, the Council reserved the right to take appropriate action with regard to relevant third countries. In addition, it also underlined the importance for

---

9. Council Doc. 7990/02 COR 1. In this context, see also the Council conclusions of 18 November 2002 on intensified cooperation with third-countries on the management of migration flows (Council Doc. 13894/02).
10. OJ C 142, 14.6.2002, p. 23 (31).
11. Council doc. 14673/02.

the European Union to consider the use of all appropriate instruments available in the context of the Union's external relations, in order to further negotiations with third countries without jeopardising the fundamental legal position, that at least the readmission of own nationals is a non-negotiable obligation incumbent on any state.

The European Commission has repeatedly stated it shared this approach and was in agreement with this policy line, e.g. in its Communication on a Common Policy on Illegal Immigration[12], in its Green Paper[13] and Communication[14] on a Community Return Policy on Illegal Residents and in its Communication on the development of a common policy on illegal immigration, smuggling and trafficking of human beings, external borders and the return of illegal residents.[15]

In July 2004, as requested by the Brussels European Council of 15/16 October 2003, the Commission presented a restricted report[16] in which it outlined some strategic orientations and future priorities for a successful development of a common readmission policy. In response to this communication, in November 2004, the Council adopted conclusions[17] on the matter, essentially confirming the Commission's suggested (future) course of action. Moreover, as requested in the Hague programme adopted in November 2004 by EU Heads of State and Government[18], the Commission appointed a Special Representative (and a Deputy) for a common readmission policy in an effort to achieve a more timely conclusion of Community readmission negotiations.[19] Finally, the Hague Programme[20] also asked for the development, in the context of the EC readmission policy, of a common approach on visa facilitation in order to facilitate, on a case-by-case basis and in full reciprocity, the issuance of short-stay visa to third-country nationals as part of a real partnership on migration-related issues. On 21 December 2005, COREPER approved such

12. COM (2001) 672 final of 15 November 2001.
13. COM (2002) 175 final of 10 April 2002.
14. COM (2002) 564 final of 14 October 2002.
15. COM (2003) 323 final of 3 June 2003.
16. SEC (2004) 946 final of 19 July 2004.
17. Council doc. 13758/04.
18. See section 1.6.4 (return and readmission policy) (OJ C 53, 3.3.2005, p. 6).
19. C (2005) 4124 of 17 October 2005. The Commission appointed as Special Representative the Deputy Director-General in DG RELEX, Mr Karel Kovanda, and as his deputy the Director responsible for Immigration, Asylum and Borders in DG JLS, Mr Jean-Louis De Brouwer. They act in agreement with DG ELARG and DG DEV services in the readmission negotiations with all third countries that come under the responsibility of these two Directorates General.
20. See section 1.7.3 (visa policy) (OJ 2005 C 53, 3.3.2005, p. 7).

a common approach[21] and several EC visa facilitation agreements have already been negotiated (e.g. Russia, Ukraine, Western Balkan countries, Moldova), a fact which contributed significantly to securing parallel readmission agreements with the third-countries concerned.[22]

As in the Hague programme, the need for an effective EU policy on removal and repatriation was also highlighted in the Commission's Communication of 30 November 2005[23] on priority actions for responding to the challenges of migration. With this paper the Commission reacted to critical events and recurring waves of illegal immigration in Ceuta and Melilla, Lampedusa, Malta and some Greek Islands and developed a series of immediate, practical measures to be taken forward in cooperation with source and transit countries from the southern Mediterranean area and Africa ("Global approach to Migration"). In its conclusions of December 2005, the European Council endorsed most of the suggested measures for the EU´s southern flank and called, in particular, for a swift conclusion of readmission agreements with Algeria and Morocco.

In December 2006, building upon a follow-up communication[24] from the Commission, the European Council[25] decided to further enlarge the geographical scope of the Global Approach to the EU's Eastern Flank, and to also include other policy areas, with a view to developing a "Comprehensive EU Migration Policy".[26] As an integral part of this new policy, the European Council identified, among other factors, improving cooperation with relevant third countries on return and readmission, including effective identification and documentation, while putting special emphasis on the reintegration of returned migrants. Furthermore, the European Council requested that negotiations on EC readmission agreements should be stepped up. To this end, the Council was invited to explore further ways and means by which Member States could support the Commission in its efforts to conclude such agreements at EU level and to ensure their effective implementation. This task has been taken up in the

---

21. Council doc. 15593/05.
22. For details on the substance and implementation of these agreements, see Council doc. 9501/07.
23. COM (2005) 621 final of 30 November 2005.
24. COM (2006) 735 final of 30 November 2006.
25. Council doc. 16879/1/06 REV1.
26. The goal of developing a comprehensive EU Migration Policy is not something new although it is the first time that the main elements of such a policy have been set out in European Council conclusions. The Commission formulated the main components of such a policy several years ago already. For more details, see in particular COM (2002) 703 final of 3 December 2002, p. 17.

joint work programme of the German, Portuguese and Slovenian Presidencies (January 2007 to June 2008), which foresees an evaluation of the progress made to date in negotiating and implementing EC readmission agreements with a view to identifying means for concluding such agreements in a more targeted and timely manner.[27] Following intensive discussions, the JHA Council of 12 June 2007 adopted Council conclusions[28] in which it calls on the Commission and Member States to take a number of actions to improve the efficiency of the Community's readmission policy.

III. Objectives and substance of Community readmission agreements

Even though it is clear that Community readmission agreements alone are not able to solve the problem of illegal immigration, such agreements are generally recognised to be an indispensable tool for an effective management of migration flows. Their necessity and practical usefulness does not only result from the fact that they facilitate the swift return of illegally staying third-country nationals. They also help to undermine the activities of internationally operating smuggling networks, which are behind a significant part of the illegal immigration into the EU. Although, at EU level, readmission agreements are a new "post-Amsterdam" phenomenon, they can partly build upon standard readmission clauses[29], which have already featured since the mid-nineties in EC association and co-operation agreements, e.g. with Algeria, the Andean Community,

27.   For details, see Council doc. 17025/06.
28.   Council doc. 9850/07.
29.   The present EU standard clauses were adopted by the Council on 3 December 1999 (Council doc. 13409/99), revising the 1996 standard clauses (Council doc. 4272/96) in order to adapt them to the new legal situation arising from the entry into force of the Amsterdam Treaty. These clauses do not constitute readmission agreements in themselves but establish a framework for negotiating such agreements in the future ("enabling clauses"). The conclusions of the 2002 European Council in Seville requested that any future cooperation, association or equivalent agreement which the European Community concludes with any country should include a clause on joint management of migration flows and on compulsory readmission in the event of illegal immigration. The elements to be contained in such a clause have been laid down by the General Affairs Council in its conclusions of 18 November 2002 (Council doc. 14183/02 PRESS 350). For more details, see in particular COM (2002) 175 of 10 April 2002, p. 24; COM (2002) 703 of 3 December 2002, p. 23; Council doc. 8512/05; MEMO/05/351 of 5 October 2005.

Armenia, Azerbijan, Chile, Croatia, Egypt, Georgia, Lebanon, FYROM and Uzbekistan.[30]

In substantive terms, Community readmission agreements are usually defined as bilateral agreements which set out, for the Community and its partner third country, reciprocal obligations as well as detailed administrative and operational procedures to facilitate the return or the transit of persons who do not, or no longer fulfil the conditions for entry or stay in their respective territories.[31] In this context it is worth recalling that, as far as own nationals are concerned, there is already a well-established rule under international customary law, which obliges each State to readmit its own nationals who are illegally staying in the territory of another State, without any further formalities and irrespective of the will of the person concerned.[32] This general rule, however, often requires further procedural arrangements for its proper implementation in practice, which is usually done through the conclusion of readmission agreements. These agreements may also include additional obligations and procedural modalities for the readmission of third-country nationals and stateless persons. To the extent that they also include these categories of persons, readmission agreements are not only "declaratory" in nature, confirming an existing obligation under international law, but they create new obligations between the Parties which did not exist before.

It is important to stress that EC readmission agreements do not define the conditions for the legality or illegality of a person's presence in the EU. They are purely technical agreements, which only come into play once the competent Member State authority – or a Member State court, as the case might be – has finally established that a third-country national does not under any circumstances, including humanitarian ones, have a right to stay. Although, according to Article 300 EC, the Commission is

---

30. OJ L 265, 10.10.2005 (Algeria); COM (2003) 695 final of 14 November 2003 (Andean Community); OJ L 239, 9.9.1999 (Armenia); OJ L 246, 17.9.1999 (Azerbijan); OJ L 352, 30.12.2002 (Chile); OJ L 26, 28.1.2005 (Croatia), OJ L 304, 30.9.2004 (Egypt); OJ L 205, 4.8.1999 (Georgia); OJ L 143, 30.5.2006 (Lebanon); OJ L 84, 20.3.2004 (FYROM); OJ L 229, 31.8.1999 (Uzbekistan).

31. COM (2002) 564 final of 14 October 2002, p.26; SEC (2004) 946 final of 19 July 2004 (annex).

32. See, for instance, Ian Brownlie, Principles of Public International Law, p. 382, 397 (Oxford 1991); Guy S. Goodwin-Gill, International Law and the Movements between States, p. 137 (Oxford 1978); Kai Hailbronner, Rückübernahme eigener und fremder Staatsangehöriger, p. 36 (Heidelberg 1996). This generally recognised rule flows from the country of residence's sovereign right to determine which foreigners are to stay on its territory and of the home country's responsibility for all persons holding its citizenship.

responsible for negotiating Community readmission agreements, it is not responsible for their day-to-day implementation. The actual physical return of a given person rests entirely with the competent authorities of Member States. They have to comply with all relevant obligations under international law, including the principle of *non-refoulement,* and they can be held liable for their expulsion decisions before their national courts. In the not so distant future, however, a stronger "involvement" of the Commission in the preparatory stages of Member States' return operations may result from the fact that, in September 2005, it tabled a proposal for a directive harmonising Member States' expulsion procedures and return standards[33], which should be adopted by the end of 2007.

Looking at the key features of the Community readmission agreements so far concluded, they all set out clear and unambiguous (reciprocal) obligations for both the third country and the EU Member States as to when and how to take back persons who are illegally staying in the other side's territory. This includes not only own nationals but also, subject to certain conditions, non-nationals and stateless persons.[34] In the agreements with countries which have a common border with the EU (e.g. Russia, Ukraine, Moldova), a special accelerated procedure applies to persons apprehended in these border regions, who will be able to be returned within a few days. The agreements all contain technical provisions governing the readmission procedure and transit operations, including readmission applications, means of evidence, time limits, means of transit, rules on costs and the necessary safeguards with regard to data protection and the protection of other international rights and obligations. A joint committee is to be set up under each of the agreements, which will monitor their development and implementation.

It is important to note that Community readmission agreements fully respect human rights and fundamental freedoms, and as such are consistent with the EU's human rights policies. Provisions are being included in all agreements so that, if the competent authorities of the Member States wish to make use of them, their (national) individual expulsion decisions will have to comply, in particular, with the 1951 Geneva Convention and the 1967 Protocol on the Status of Refugees as well as with the 1950 Human Rights Convention. No one may be removed,

33. COM (2005) 391 final of 1 September 2005.
34. Since they are not sovereign and independent States, but autonomous regions of the People's Republic of China, which enjoy, under their Basic Laws, a high degree of autonomy over their internal affairs including border and immigration controls, the agreements with Hong Kong and Macao refer to *"residents"* and *"persons of another jurisdiction"*.

expelled or extradited to a State where there is a serious risk that he or she would be subjected to the death penalty, torture or other inhuman or degrading treatment or punishment.

IV. State of Community readmission negotiations

Based on the Community's powers under Article 63 (3) (b) EC, the Council has so far authorised the Commission to negotiate Community readmission agreements with Morocco, Sri Lanka, Russia, Pakistan (in September 2000), Hong Kong, Macao (in May 2001), Ukraine (in June 2002), Albania, Algeria, China, Turkey (in November 2002), Montenegro, FYROM[35], Serbia, Bosnia and Herzegovina (in November 2006)[36] and Moldova (in December 2006)[37]. No further negotiating mandates are currently being prepared or planned.

Of these 16 third countries, negotiations could be successfully completed with Hong Kong (in November 2001), Macao (in October 2002), Sri Lanka (in May 2002), Albania (in November 2003), Russia (in September 2005), Ukraine (in October 2006), Bosnia and Herzegovina, Montenegro, FYROM and Moldova (in April 2007) and Serbia (in May 2007). The agreement with Hong Kong was formally signed in November 2002 and concluded in December 2003; it entered into force on 1 March 2004 as the first ever Community readmission agreement.[38] The next agreement to follow was the one with Macao, which entered into force on 1 June 2004.[39] The agreement with Sri Lanka was signed in Colombo in June 2004 and its formal conclusion by the Council took place in March 2005; it entered into force on 1 May 2005.[40] The agreement with Albania was signed in the margins of the JHA Council of 14 April 2005; it was concluded in November 2005 and entered into force on 1 May 2006.[41] The readmission agreement with Russia was signed at the occasion of the EU–Russia Summit in Sochi on 25 May 2006; it was formally concluded by the JHA

35. IP/06/570 of 4 May 2006.
36. IP/06/1035 of 20 July 2006; MEMO/06/429 of 15 November 2006.
37. IP/06/1833 of 19 December 2006.
38. OJ L 17, 24.1.2004, p. 23. On 20 September 2004, with Hong Kong, the first ever readmission committee meeting between the EC and a third country took place (se IP/04/1113). At this occasion the two sides adopted rules of procedure (C(2004)2102 of 11 June 2004), which served as a model for the rules of procedure of readmission committees under all other EC readmission agreements.
39. OJ L 143, 30.4.2004, p. 99; OJ L 258, 5.8.2004, p. 17.
40. OJ L 124, 17.5.2005, p. 41.
41. OJ L 124, 17.5.2005, p. 21; OJ L 304, 23.11.2005, p. 12.

Council of 19 April 2007 and entered into force on 1 June 2007.[42] For the agreement with Ukraine[43], the process of ratification has only just been launched and the agreement was formally signed on 18 June 2007; its entry into force is not expected before the end of 2007. As in the case of Russia, it will also be supplemented by a parallel visa facilitation agreement. The agreements with Montenegro, FYROM, Bosnia and Herzegovina, Serbia and Moldova could be initialled in April and May 2007, and their final texts will soon be submitted for ratification, together with parallel visa facilitation agreements between the EC and these countries.[44]

Negotiations with Pakistan, Morocco and Turkey are ongoing and will not be supplemented by parallel visa facilitation agreements with the Community. Negotiations with Pakistan are already far advanced and may be completed before end 2007. Even after more than 11 rounds of negotiations since 2003, talks with Morocco remain difficult and the same is true for the negotiations with Turkey where a break-through is not yet in sight. Regarding Turkey, negotiations were authorised before it obtained the status of candidate country, and the crucial question now is whether the EU should insist on a prior completion of readmission negotiations before agreeing to open the JHA chapter in the framework of accession negotiations with this country.

Informal consultations on readmission have also taken place with China and Algeria, but formal negotiations have not yet been launched.

V.   Legal and institutional issues

The European Court of Justice (ECJ) has not yet had an opportunity to rule on the scope of Article 63 (3) (b) EC, although there are a few outstanding issues with regard to the legal interpretation of this provision, which would need to be further clarified. These questions, which will only be briefly touched upon in this paper, concern in particular the interpretation of the words *"repatriation of illegal residents"*, the procedures for the negotiation and conclusion of Community readmission agreements, the nature of the Community's treaty-making power under Article 63 (3) (b) EC, the

---

42.   OJ L 129, 17.5.2007, p. 38; COM (2006) 191 final of 27 April 2006; IP/05/1263 of 12 October 2005; Council doc. 9170/06 (Press 132) of 22 May 2006; IP/06/678 of 24 May 2006; Council doc. 9850/06 (Press 157) of 25 May 2006; Speech/07/80 of 14 February 2007; IP/07/533 of 19 April 2007.
43.   COM (2007) 197 final of 18.4.2007; IP/07/849 of 18 June 2007.
44.   IP/07/497 of 12 April 2007; IP/07/680 of 16 May 2007.

implications on Member States' bilateral readmission agreements or arrangements, and the special position of the United Kingdom, Ireland and Denmark with regard to measures adopted in the area of return.

A.   Interpretation of Article 63 (3) (b) EC

Concerning the question of how to interpret the word *"repatriation of illegal residents"* in Article 63 (3) (b) EC, it is today beyond doubt that this term is intended to have a broad meaning and, therefore, also includes the *"readmission"* of such persons by the States of their origin or nationality. This interpretation has not only been confirmed by the Tampere European Council[45], which explicitly stated that *"the Amsterdam Treaty conferred powers on the Community in the field of readmission"*; it also corresponds to the practical use that has so far been made of this provision[46], in conjunction with Article 300 EC. For the same reason, the term *"repatriation"* should be construed broadly to also include returns to, and readmission by possible transit countries; it should not be given a narrow interpretation by restricting it to returns to the home country only. In other language versions, e.g. in the German version ("Rückführung"), this ambiguity does not exist thanks to the use of a broader, more neutral term.

The words *"illegal resident"* should not be interpreted narrowly either. This term is not limited to persons having illegally entered since there is a systematic link to the preceding paragraphs: once asylum seekers have been refused asylum, displaced persons have not been granted or have ceased to benefit from a protected status or a third-country national's residence permit or visa has expired, they are in principle "illegal residents" within the meaning of Article 63 (3) (b) EC.

In this context it is worth noting that Article 63 (3) (b) EC does not employ the words *"return"* or *"readmission"*. In order to avoid linguistic confusions and to streamline terminology in the area of return and readmission, the Commission elaborated in 2002 a set of common definitions[47], which – although of a non-binding nature – have been used since then in all policy documents and might thus also contribute to a consistent teleological interpretation of Article 63 (3) (b) EC. According to these definitions, which are also in conformity with definitions to be found in existing EC readmission agreements, "return" is the generic term described as "[t]he process of going back to one's country of origin, transit or another third

45. See paragraph 27 of the summit conclusions.
46. See above part IV.
47. COM (2992) 564 final of 14.10.2002, p. 26 (annex).

country, including preparation and implementation; the return may be voluntary or enforced." In contrast, the term "readmission" is defined to describe the very same process from the perspective or angle of the receiving State, namely as an "Act by a state accepting the re-entry of an individual (own national, third-country national or stateless person), who has been found illegally entering to, being present in or residing in another state".[48] Finally, "illegal resident" is to mean "Any person who does not, or no longer, fulfill the conditions for presence in, or residence on the territory of the Member State of the European Union."

B.   Conduct of Negotiations and Ratification Process

According to Article 300 EC, negotiations on the conclusion of international agreements between the Community and third countries are conducted by the Commission, in consultation with a special committee appointed by the Council in order to assist it in its task. Regarding Community readmission negotiations, on 19 December 2002, the JHA Council decided[49] not to establish a new committee, but to formalise the status quo and to appoint the Working Party on Migration and Expulsion (MEG) as the responsible body for assistance and consultations to the Commission in relation to all ongoing and future negotiations. The Commission alone conducts negotiations, i.e. representatives of Member States, the Presidency or the Council Secretariat have no right to be present and, so far, have never been present in negotiations. However, in September 2006, the MEG examined possible ways for the intensification of co-operation between the Member States and the Commission in the process of negotiating Community Readmission Agreements, which resulted in the informal understanding that, at the Commission's initiative, Member States could make available the necessary technical expertise and in particular expert staff, throughout the negotiations, on a case-by-case basis.[50]

---

48.   The only EC readmission agreement which contains a definition of „readmission" is the one with Russia.
49.   Council doc. 15649/02.
50.   Council doc. 13186/06. Similarly, in a letter sent to the Commission in March 2006, also the Interior Ministers of the G6 EU Member States (Germany, France, UK, Spain, Italy, Poland) offered technical support by their experts in the negotiations. This offer has been declined by the Commission, which had repeatedly pointed out that what was needed most in negotiations would be more political flanking support by Member States, not more technical expertise.

Once negotiations could be completed and a final text be initialled, the Commission formally submits this text to the Council, together with a summary of the outcome of negotiations and two proposals for Council Decisions concerning the signature and the conclusion of the readmission agreement (two-step "ratification" procedure).[51] Until the end of 2004, pursuant to Article 300 (2) in conjunction with Article 67 EC, the Council decided by unanimity on both the signing and the conclusion of the agreement. This legal situation changed in December 2004 when the Council made use of the bridging clause in Article 67 (2) EC and unanimously decided that, with effect of 1 January 2005, inter alia measures falling under Articles 63 (3) (b) EC should be adopted in accordance with the procedure laid down in Article 251 EC.[52] Although this transition to co-decision procedure meant that the Council can now adopt decisions relating to the negotiation, signature or conclusion of EC readmission agreements with qualified majority, the role of European Parliament did not change. According to Article 300 (3) EC, Parliament continues only to be consulted on the decision concerning the conclusion of EC readmission agreements.

C.   Nature of the Community's treaty-making power

According to the case law of the Court of Justice, the EC has a competence to conclude international agreements when this is necessary to attain an objective of the Treaty.[53] On this basis, it is common knowledge that the Community may conclude readmission agreements with third-countries, as explicitly confirmed by Article III-167 (3) of the draft Treaty establishing a Constitution for Europe.

In contrast, it is still unclear whether this treaty-making power is of an *"exclusive"* or of a *"concurrent"* nature. The answer to this question is contingent upon the interpretation and application, to the field of readmission, of the long-standing case law of the European Court of Justice (ECJ) on the Community's treaty-making power in the first pillar,

---

51.   See e.g. SEC (2002) 412 final of 18 April 2002 (Hong Kong); SEC (2003) 255 final of 21 March 2003 (Sri Lanka); COM (2003) 151 final of 31 March 2003 (Macao); COM (2004) 92 final of 12 February 2004 (Albania); COM (2006) 191 final of 27 April 2006 (Russia).
52.   OJ L 396, 31.12.2004, p. 45.
53.   Opinion 1/76, Laying-Up Found, [1977] ECR 741, para. 3.

especially the AETR ruling (case 22/70)[54] and opinions 1/76[55] and 1/94[56]. Pursuant to this case law, the key question is whether the conclusion of readmission agreements is "necessary" or "indispensable" for the repatriation of illegal residents, i.e. for attaining one of the Community objectives. There are indications that, by now, the Commission seems to take the view that this is the case and, consequently, regards the Community's treaty-making power under Article 63 (3) (b) EC as being *"exclusive"* in nature. Member States, on the other hand, constantly deny such a strong link and, therefore, see this power being of a *"concurrent"* nature only.[57]

This divergence of views is not just a theoretical dispute, but has significant practical consequences: If one were to conclude that the Community enjoyed exclusive treaty-making powers, Member States would have to abstain entirely from any new readmission negotiations, even if the Commission were not engaged in Community readmission negotiations with the third country in question. In addition, transitional rules would have to be established at Community level in order to provide for a gradual replacement of Member States' existing agreements by Community agreements. If, in contrast, one were to assume concurrent powers, Member States would retain their treaty-making power and would be free to exercise it in respect of any third country, as long as the Commission had not yet presented to the Council a recommendation for the opening of negotiations on the conclusion of a Community readmission agreement with that very country. Only once such a recommendation had been presented, would Article 10 EC require Member States to abstain from carrying on bilateral negotiations or finalising a bilateral readmission agreement with the third country concerned. In this context, it is however important to note that – irrespective of the nature of the Community's treaty-making power – Member States could not *collectively* conclude a readmission agreement with a third country since this would equally be in contradiction with their good faith obligations under Article 10 EC. Similarly, in accordance with Article 300 (7) EC, it is also clear that a Community readmission agreement would always supersede any existing Member State readmission agreement or arrangement with the same third country.

54. Commission/Council, [1971] ECR, 263.
55. Laying-up Fund, [1977] ECR 741.
56. Accession to the WTO, [1994] ECR I-5267.
57. See, in particular, the conclusions of the JHA Council of 27/28 May 1999 on the effects of the entry into force of the Treaty of Amsterdam on the future EU policy in the field of repatriating illegal residents.

The decision on whether or not readmission agreements are indispensable or necessary for the repatriation of illegal immigrants, ultimately lies with the Council, which enjoys – in view of the facts and under the supervision of the ECJ – a certain margin of discretion in judging this prerequisite. The ECJ has not yet had an opportunity to directly rule on the matter. However, the Court's judgement in cases C-466/98 et al.[58] in the field of civil aviation seem to further point in the direction of exclusive competence. On the other hand, negotiating practice since the entry into force of the Treaty of Amsterdam rather seems to support the assumption of "concurrent" powers, as Member States continue to conclude bilateral readmission agreements with third-countries, without the Commission having formally intervened so far.

D. Special position of UK, Ireland and Denmark

According to Article 300 (7) EC, international agreements concluded by the Community are automatically binding upon Member States. Regarding Community readmission agreements, however, this is only true for 24 of the 27 Member States, with the *United Kingdom, Ireland and Denmark* being in a special situation.

1. UK and Ireland

Since they are based upon Article 63 (3) (b) EC, i.e. a provision of Title IV, Community readmission agreements are neither binding upon nor applicable to the *United Kingdom and Ireland,* unless these two Member States "opt-in" in the manner provided for by Articles 3 or 4 of the Protocol on their special position, annexed to the EU Treaty and to the EC Treaty in Amsterdam. Up till now, the UK – but not Ireland – has always made use of this right and notified the Council of its intention to participate in all Community readmission agreements. In this context it is worth noting that, in particular, the UK did not only "opt-in" to the Council decisions concerning the signing and conclusion of the agreements. In addition, it has regularly decided to notify the Council of its intention to participate also in the earlier stages of the negotiating process, i.e. in the adoption of the Council decisions authorising the Commission to open negotiations ("mandates"). This means that, e.g. in the case of the Community readmission agreements with Hong Kong and Macao, there were 2 "opt-

---

58. ECJ reports 2002, p. I-9427; OJ C 323, 21.12.2002, p. 1.

ins" from the UK, one for each stage of the negotiating process (mandate[59] – signature and conclusion[60]).

This "opt-in practice" with respect to EC readmission agreements has raised serious legal concerns which relate to the question of how and at what stage the UK and Ireland exercise their opt-in possibility under Article 3 (1) of the Protocol. Since the negotiation of EC readmission agreements involves three different Council acts – adoption of the negotiating mandate, adoption of the decision authorising the signature and adoption of the decision authorising the conclusion on behalf of the Community – this issue has been put into focus in particular by Ireland's failure, in 2004 and 2005, to participate in the adoption of the Council Decisions regarding the conclusion of the readmission agreements with Macao, Sri Lanka and Albania. The respective Council Decisions state explicitly that Ireland does not participate in their adoption and that this Member State will not be bound by the said readmission agreements, although Ireland is not excluded from the scope of application of these agreements. The result is that the legal situation under Community law now conflicts with the situation under international law.

This untenable situation could arise since it appears that Ireland considers that negotiating authorisations are purely internal acts to which it does not have to opt-in and that the only moment of opt-in is when the Commission has submitted the official proposals for signature and conclusion of a readmission agreement. The UK, on the other hand, follows the practice of already notifying its intention to participate in the adoption of the decision regarding the negotiating mandate. However, the UK's notifications have also indicated that they are *"without prejudice to the right of the UK to decide whether or not to participate in the adoption of future Council Decisions to conclude the resulting agreements"*. With regard to the three readmission agreements in question, it appears that, in practice, the negotiating directives given by the Council foresaw that they should apply to the UK and Ireland. This put the Commission in the unfortunate position of having to negotiate readmission agreements with Macao, Sri Lanka and Albania which would include the UK and Ireland in their territorial scope, although these two Member States had not yet unequivocally exercised their right to opt-in. The solution to this legally problematic situation can only be that either Ireland exercises an opt-in pursuant to Article 4 of the Protocol to all three readmission agreements or the Commission will have

---

59. Notification of 18 May 2001 (Hong Kong and Macao).
60. Notification of 21 May 2002 (Council doc. 9225/02 – Hong Kong); notification of 27 May 2003 (Council doc. 10148/03 – Macao).

to take the initiative to have these agreements amended to exclude Ireland from their scope of application. As regards all future negotiating directives and agreements, they should only foresee the application to Ireland and the UK, if these two Member States have explicitly opted into the Council decision authorising the negotiations in a clear and unreserved way. In the most recent Council Decisions authorising the launch of readmission negotiations with the Western Balkan countries[61] and Moldova[62], the UK seems to have adjusted its opt-in practice in as much as it no longer includes any reservations.

2.   Denmark

For the same reason as for the UK and Ireland, Community readmission agreements are also not binding upon *Denmark* by virtue of the Protocol on Denmark's special position, annexed to the EU Treaty and the EC Treaty. However, the situation of Denmark is different in as much as this Member State is always "out" and – unlike the UK and Ireland – does not have the possibility to "opt-in". Article 5 of the Protocol is of no help in this context since, in March 2000, Member States unanimously agreed at the level of COREPER[63] that Community readmission agreements would not be a measure building upon or supplementing the Schengen acquis.

VI.   Difficulties encountered in Community readmission negotiations

It is beyond doubt that, once successfully concluded, Community readmission agreements do provide a clear added-value compared to Member States' individual agreements. This is not only due to the abolition of internal borders within the Schengen area, which requires a common approach on readmission rather than bilateral agreements. It is also due to their more comprehensive scope of application, which systematically includes third-country nationals and transit rules. However, not all Community readmission negotiations could be concluded in a timely manner and, for some of them, the Commission has encountered severe problems and delays.

---

61.   Council doc. 15465/06.
62.   Council doc. 17055/06.
63.   SI (2000) 249 of 17 March 2000.

In its report of July 2004[64], the Commission identified a series of external and internal factors of a political and technical nature which complicate its negotiating position and explain (to a large extent) the delay in the conclusion of some of the agreements. There are essentially three categories of difficulties encountered: (1) the third countries themselves and the negative economic and political consequences readmission agreements can have for them, (2) the technical substance and format of Community readmission agreements, especially the standard inclusion of provisions on the readmission of third-country nationals, and (3) the need for full and unreserved diplomatic and political support from all Member States.

The difficulties *related to the third countries themselves* result from the fact that readmission agreements can have severe economic and political consequences, which may negatively influence their domestic public opinion. Even the reintegration of own nationals can generate additional constraints for the domestic labour market or social programmes as the move entails taking back persons who are often low-skilled. Another negative consequence can be a reduction in remittance flows. Neither is it in the interest of third countries to take back non-nationals who have transited through their territory *en route* to the EU, or who have remained on their territory for a period of time. As transit countries, they can be confronted with considerable burdens, of both a technical and financial nature, since they will have to deal with the repatriation of the non-nationals readmitted from the EU. Such concerns have been amplified by the fact that third-countries concluding a readmission agreement with the Community would be confronted with potential returns from, by now, a block of twenty-seven countries.

There are also several *technical aspects related to the substance and format of Community readmission agreements* which have been a complicating factor in negotiations. The negotiating directives given to the Commission are not only detailed and elaborate in technical terms but also ambitious in policy terms for full use of the Community's "negotiating weight". This sometimes limits the room for manoeuvre for the Commission in negotiations at a technical level since the stakes are set high by the standard inclusion of provisions on the readmission of third-country nationals, and on transit. As has been stated before, especially the readmission of third-country nationals who have transited through the territory of the partner third country, or have remained there for a certain time, is often a difficult issue on which to reach agreement.

64.   SEC (2004) 946 final.

Thirdly, Community readmission negotiations also require the *full and unreserved diplomatic and political support from all Member States*. Without this support, the Commission's credibility and negotiating position is severely weakened and advantages possibly gained by individual Member States from this situation are detrimental to the Community in its entirety. Such negative undermining of the Commission's negotiating efforts could be noted, for instance, in the case of negotiations with Sri Lanka and Pakistan where some Member States held parallel bilateral negotiations and meetings with these countries without informing the Commission.

VII. Conclusions: "Lessons learned" and the way forward

As their conclusion is primarily in the EU's interest, the main lesson learned from negotiations so far conducted is that Community readmission agreements always require compensatory offers ("incentives"), in particular if the agreement is also supposed to cover third-country nationals and stateless persons. Unlike in the case of own nationals, there is no obligation under (customary) international law regarding the readmission of third-country nationals, which could be invoked by the Commission in support of its negotiating position. Consequently, as all of the existing agreements and negotiating directives foresee the inclusion of third-country nationals, the Community needs to use all means and to activate all policy areas at its disposal to set sufficient incentives and to provide a better negotiating position. The areas where a greater generosity from the EU is expected include visa facilitation arrangements, enhanced legal migration opportunities, financial and technical support[65], trade concessions or an intensification of the overall relations with the EU.

A recurring request on the part of the third countries concerned is the *facilitation of visa* issuance and the lifting of visa requirements for all or at least some of their nationals. Since the granting of visa-free status is limited to very exceptional cases (e.g. Hong Kong, Macao), visa facilitation is the only realistic option. In December 2005, as requested in the Hague Programme[66], the Permanent Representatives of Member States reached agreement in COREPER on a common approach on visa facilitation, aimed at facilitating – on a case by case basis and in full reciprocity – the

---

65. See, in particular, the AENEAS Regulation of 10 March 2004 (OJ L 80, 18.3.2004, p. 1) and its successor instrument, the new thematic programme Asylum and Migration in the framework of the new Development framework Programme (COM (2006) 26 final of 25 January 2006).
66. See section 1.7.3 (visa policy) (OJ C 53, 3.3.2005, p. 7).

Community's readmission negotiations. The underlying idea is that the granting of visa facilitations should enable the Community to obtain progress on readmission as both negotiations will proceed in parallel. When granting "visa facilitation" to a third country it is important to note that there are several "facilitation options" to choose from, which can be considered appropriate depending on each individual case. These options include multiple entry visas for bona-fide applicants, increasing the number of consular services facilitating the issuance of visas, the lifting or expediting of consultation procedures or a reduction in visa fees. The EU's new approach on visa facilitation undoubtedly gave a strong impetus to a number of pending Community readmission negotiations which, had previously dragged on for years and were somewhat stalled. Successful examples of this new approach are the recent agreements on visa facilitation and readmission with Russia and Ukraine, and similar agreements with the Western Balkan countries are expected to follow soon. In broader policy terms, a successful example of the linkage between readmission and visa facilitation has also been the 2004 ADS agreement with China[67], where the Chinese side for the first time agreed to incorporate a binding readmission clause as a "quid pro quo" in what is, essentially, a visa facilitation agreement for group visits of Chinese tourists to the European Union.

Another incentive that has proven to be able to play an important role in facilitating the conclusion of a readmission agreement is the quality and intensity of the EU's overall relations with a third country. The Community's bargaining position vis-à-vis a third country is usually strongest at the time when negotiations on the conclusion of an association, cooperation or similar agreement are being launched or are ongoing. To wait until the agreement has been finalised would effectively mean that most of the "leverage" the agreement represents is lost. For this reason, building upon the 1996 and 1999 readmission standard clauses, the Seville European Council of 21/22 June 2002 decided to include clauses concerning the joint management of migration flows in all future association, cooperation or equivalent agreements concluded between the EC or EU and third countries. Besides addressing cooperation on a wide variety of migration issues, these clauses establish the principle of readmission and include the commitment to enter into negotiations on a readmission agreement if so requested by one of the parties to the agreement. However, depending on the extent to which they leave the actual operational arrangements and procedural modalities to

67.   OJ L 83, 20.3.2004, p. 12.

implementing agreements to be concluded at a later stage, such readmission "enabling clauses" do not make full use of the high bargaining potential of EU association or cooperation agreements, and thus risk to become a missed opportunity concerning readmission. This needs to be taken into consideration in future association or cooperation negotiations with third-countries with which the Community would like to conclude a readmission agreement. For instance in the soon to be launched negotiations with China on a new Partnership and Cooperation agreement (PCA), the EU will have to decide whether to follow an approach whereby the readmission element in its standard migration clause will have to be beefed up (to become a kind of a "mini" readmission agreement within the PCA) or whether the envisaged Community readmission agreement should be negotiated in parallel while remaining politically linked to the PCA, and possibly even becoming a protocol or an annex to it.

Finally, a new tool to speed up and advance the conclusion of Community readmission agreements could be seen in the concepts of "circular migration schemes" and "mobility partnerships" with third-countries. This concept has been taken up by the December 2006 European Council which invited the Commission to present a report by mid-2007 on how to facilitate the legal movements between the EU and third-countries, especially those which, in exchange, cooperate with the EU on illegal immigration and readmission. In its report of 16 May 2007[68], the Commission focussed on developing further the concept of circular migration and mobility partnerships between the EU and third countries. Mobility partnerships in particular could significantly improve the management of migration flows by forming the framework for a series of political and legal arrangements between a given third country and the EU (Community and Member States) in the area of migration, including legal and labour migration, visa facilitation and readmission. Once agreed at EU level and implemented in practice, they could provide a fresh impetus for the Community readmission policy.

---

68. COM (2007) 248 final.

4. Seeking Asylum in the EU: Disentangling Refugee Protection from Migration Control

Madeline Garlick and Judith Kumin[1]

I.   Introduction

At the opening of the 2007 session of UNHCR's Executive Committee, High Commissioner António Guterres noted that '[t]he present century is a time of human displacement. With each economic opportunity and departing vessel, every calamity and conflict, the 21st century is being marked by people on the move.'[2] It should therefore come as no surprise that within the European Union, the management of migration has become a more dominant political topic than asylum.

The Office of the United Nations High Commissioner for Refugees ('UNHCR')[3] is not a migration management agency. Yet its mandate for refugee protection means that it cannot avoid responding to the fact that today's population movements encompass asylum-seekers and refugees, as well as other people who are on the move for a variety of reasons. Economic and family migration occur alongside migration driven by conflict, persecution and environmental factors. Not only are the flows mixed in character, but the motivations of the individuals may also be mixed.

Within these mixed flows, persons seeking international protection have to be identified and given access to a fair consideration of their claims. Those who have international protection needs must also be able to find asylum and a long term solution to their plight. These are important areas for cooperation among international organizations, governments and civil society, and explain UNHCR's growing engagement with the subject of migration.

---

1.   The article expresses the personal view of the authors only, and does not necessarily reflect the views of UNHCR.
2.   Opening statement by Mr. António Guterres, United Nations High Commissioner for Refugees, at the Fifty-eighth session of Executive Committee of the High Commissioner's Programme, 1 October 2007, available at: http://www.unhcr.org/admin/ADMIN/4700eff54.html
3.   See the United Nations Convention relating to the Status of Refugees (1951); ('1951 Convention').

At the EU level, the attention being paid to migration by the European institutions and the Member States presents both risks and opportunities for refugee protection. On the one hand, it provides new opportunities to bring international protection issues to the fore. The inclusion of migration in discussions with third countries offers a chance to highlight State responsibility for refugee protection, as well as prospects for international solidarity with countries facing particular challenges, including through refugee resettlement programmes. The broad interest in human trafficking provides an opportunity to raise awareness not only of the vulnerability of refugees to trafficking, but also that the fact of being trafficked may give rise to a refugee claim. Discussions about migration and development create opportunities to discuss not only the need for developmental support to make the return and reintegration of refugees sustainable, but also the contribution refugees can make to the development of their host countries.

On the other hand, the high level of attention being devoted to migration control makes it increasingly difficult to maintain a focus on core values of international protection. Refugee advocates, including UNHCR, find it necessary to engage in a widening and ever-more-complex network of themes, in order to ensure that refugee protection challenges do not become inextricably entangled in migration control matters. There is a risk that the accomplishments of the first phase of work toward the ambitious goal of a Common European Asylum System may be sidelined by migration control imperatives.

The first phase of work toward a Common European Asylum System coincided with the period between the European Councils at Tampere in 1999 and The Hague in 2004. At Tampere, the EU Member States agreed to 'work towards establishing a Common European Asylum System, based on the full and inclusive application of the Geneva Refugee Convention.'[4] This conclusion followed the entry into force of the Amsterdam Treaty,[5] which aimed to set common minimum standards for all EU States in key areas of asylum law.

UNHCR was intimately associated with this first, legislative phase. Article 63 of the Amsterdam Treaty specifies that measures on asylum must be in accordance with the 1951 Convention. UNHCR's responsibility for

4.   Presidency Conclusions, Tampere European Council, 15-6 Oct. 1999, Council Document SN 200/99 ('Tampere Conclusions'), paras 13-14.
5.   Treaty of Amsterdam amending the Treaty on European Union, the Treaties establishing the European Communities and related acts, OJ C 340, 3.10.1997, p. 1('Amsterdam Treaty').

supervising the application of that Convention is set out in its Article 35, and is reinforced in the EU context by Declaration Number 17 to the Amsterdam Treaty which states: 'Consultations shall be established with the United Nations High Commissioner for Refugees ... on matters relating to asylum policy'.[6]

Over the five years from 1999-2004, legally binding EC measures were adopted on the grant of temporary protection in situations of mass influx,[7] reception conditions for asylum-seekers,[8] criteria for 'qualification' for refugee status or other forms of protection[9] and procedures for dealing with protection claims.[10] The Treaty also mandated the establishment of criteria and mechanisms for determining which State is responsible for considering an asylum application[11] as well as measures promoting a 'balance of effort' between Member States in 'receiving and bearing the consequences' of the arrival of refugees and displaced persons.[12] Adoption of these instruments marked the end of the first stage of work toward establishing a Common European Asylum System.

---

6. *Ibid.*
7. Council Directive 2001/55/EC of 20 July 2001 on Minimum Standards for Giving Temporary Protection in the Event of a Mass Influx of Displaced Persons and on Measures Promoting a Balance of Efforts Between Member States in Receiving Such Persons and Bearing the Consequences Thereof, OJ L 212, 7.8.2001, p. 12.
8. Council Directive 2003/9/EC of 27 January 2003 laying down minimum standards for the reception of asylum seekers, OJ L 31, 6.2.2003, p. 18.
9. Council Directive 2004/83/EC of 29 April 2004 on minimum standards for the qualification and status of third country nationals or stateless persons as refugees or as persons who otherwise need international protection and the content of the protection granted, OJ L 204, 30.09.2004, p. 12 ('Qualification Directive').
10. Council Directive 2005/85/EC of 1 December 2005 on minimum standards on procedures in Member States for granting and withdrawing refugee status, OJ L 326, 13.12.2005, p. 13 ('Asylum Procedures Directive').
11. Council Regulation (EC) No 343/2003 establishing the criteria and mechanisms for determining the Member State responsible for examining an asylum application lodged in one of the Member States by a third-country national, OJ L 50, 23.02.2003, p. 1 ('Dublin II').
12. Council Decision 2000/596/EC of the 28 September 2000 establishing the European Refugee Fund, OJ L 252, 6.10.2000, p. 12, and Council Decision 2004/904/EC of the 2 December 2004 establishing the European refugee Fund for the period of 2005 – 2010, OJ L 381, 28.12.2004, p. 52. See also Communication from the Commission to the Council and the European Parliament establishing a framework programme on Solidarity and the Management of Migration Flows for the period 2007-2013. Proposal for a Decision of the European Parliament and the Council establishing the European Refugee Fund for the period 2008-2013 as part of the General programme 'Solidarity and Management of Migration Flows", COM (2005) 123, 6.04.2005.

In November 2004, the European Council adopted the Hague Programme on 'Strengthening Freedom, Security and Justice in the European Union,'[13] which *inter alia* sets out the main lines of the second stage of work toward the Common European Asylum System. Again the Council committed itself to 'provide protection in accordance with the Geneva Convention on Refugees and other international treaties...'[14] However, there was a clear shift in the overall emphasis. Along with a section devoted to the development of a Common European Asylum System, Part I of the Hague Programme, entitled 'Strengthening Freedom', addressed extensively the external dimension of asylum and migration, including partnership with third countries of origin and transit; return and readmission policy; border checks and the fight against illegal immigration; as well as biometrics and information systems and visa policy[15].

In its September 2004 recommendations to the European Union in advance of the adoption of the Hague Programme, UNHCR warned of the need to ensure that 'measures on border management and procedures, and other measures to combat irregular migration, human smuggling and trafficking, *are designed and implemented in a protection-sensitive manner*, which does not deprive the right to asylum of practical meaning.'[16]. The extent to which these measures are indeed 'protection-sensitive' continues to preoccupy UNHCR and other refugee advocacy organizations. This article explores the shifting framework within which asylum issues are being addressed in the European Union, and the challenge of safeguarding refugee protection in the context of the EU's growing focus on migration management and control.

II.   EU Relations with third countries on asylum and migration: new developments and debates

The EU's attention to migration in the context of its relations with third countries has primarily focused on the control of irregular migration. Nonetheless, it offers potential opportunities for strengthening refugee

---

13. Hague Programme: Strengthening Freedom, Security and Justice in the European Union, OJ C 53, 3.3.2005, p. 1.
14. *Ibid.*
15. *Ibid.*
16. UNHCR, 'The European Union, Asylum and the International Refugee Protection Regime: UNHCR's recommendations for the new multiannual programme in the area of freedom, security and justice', September 2004, available at http://www.unhcr.org/protect/PROTECTION/43661f532.pdf [emphasis added].

protection in regions of origin and transit of refugees. Already in 1999 it was decided that the fight against irregular migration would be integrated into all association and cooperation agreements, including with countries in the European Neighborhood as well as the African, Caribbean and Pacific (ACP) countries[17]. The 2002 Seville European Council called for 'top priority' to be given to measures to combat illegal immigration, and urged inclusion of a mandatory readmission clause in all EU agreements with third countries.[18] Later that year the Commission issued a Communication entitled 'Integrating migration issues in the European Union's relations with third countries', which set out a three-pronged strategy for the Community's action, including addressing root causes of migratory movements; integration of migration issues into the EU's political dialogue with third countries, including not only illegal immigration but channels for legal immigration; and specific initiatives to assist third countries to increase their capacity in the area of migration management.[19]

The European Neighborhood Policy (ENP), as developed in 2004, took the Seville Conclusions forward. The ENP aims at establishing a 'privileged relationship' between the EU and its neighbors to the East and South (with the exception of Libya, for the present), based on a mutual commitment to common values.[20] An Action Plan is to be developed for each ENP country, in which issues of asylum and refugee protection can feature.[21] Yet the ENP gives considerably more emphasis to migration control than to refugee protection, insofar as visa policy, readmission agreements, the control of land and sea borders, the exchange of information on irregular migration and training of officials in border management are priorities which extend to all countries. Still, the negotiation of the Action Plans offers the EU an opportunity to address with its partners questions concerning capacity and political will to protect refugees.

Wile the Commission continued to develop and implement financial instruments and programmes relating to migration within the framework established at Seville, events of September 2005 in Spain's North African enclaves of Ceuta and Melilla brought new urgency to the need for

---

17. European Parliament, DG External Policies, 'Analysis of the External Dimension of the European Union's Asylum and Immigration Policies,' DT\619330EN.doc, August 2006, p.7.
18. Presidency Conclusions, Seville European Council, 21-22 June 2002, Doc/02/13.
19. COM (2002) 703 final.
20. Communication from the Commission: European Neighborhood Policy Strategy Paper, COM(2004)373 fin, 12.05.2004.
21. *Ibid.*, page 12.

partnership with countries of origin and transit on migration issues, in particular in North and sub-Saharan Africa. The spectre of large numbers of sub-Saharan Africans using Morocco as a 'waiting room' to enter the EU loomed large on the political scene. Against this background, when the Heads of State and Government met in October 2005, they agreed to step up action toward a comprehensive EU migration policy.[22]

On 30 November 2005, the European Commission issued a Communication entitled 'The Global Approach to Migration'[23] which was followed soon thereafter by European Council Conclusions[24] on the same subject. The 'Global Approach' focused on three aims: (1) combating illegal migration and trafficking, (2) ensuring respect for human rights and fundamental freedoms of migrants and refugees and (3) harnessing the benefits of legal migration. During 2006, two important Commission Communications were issued on controlling irregular migration,[25] underlining that of the three goals encompassed in the 'Global Approach', the emphasis has indisputably been on this issue.

UNHCR's concerns about the EU's attention to migration control and border management policies centre on their failure to address asylum and protection issues, notwithstanding their potential impact on people in need of international protection. It is true that in recent years, a number of EU proposals specifically focused on asylum and refugees have also emerged in the external dimension of JHA policy, which have acknowledged positively the basic right of people to seek and enjoy asylum. Yet these proposals have also aroused concerns that the underlying intention is to shift responsibility for international protection from EU Member States to countries less equipped to bear this responsibility.

Efforts to find new ways to ensure refugee protection through inter-regional responsibility-sharing can strengthen the institution of asylum. However, where they fail to acknowledge the EU's own key role in taking on a fair share of refugees, they also carry the risk of 'burden-shifting'. This risk has been highlighted in particular in discussions about readmission

---

22. Hampton Court Informal European Council, 27-28.10.2005.
23. COM (2006) 735 of 30.11.2005.
24. European Council Conclusions, CONCL3, 15914 of 15-16.12.2005, at: http://europa.eu/rapid/pressReleasesAction.do?reference=DOC/05/4&format=HTML&aged=0%3Cuage=EN&guiLanguage=en.
25. Communication from the Commission on policy priorities in the fight against illegal immigration of third country nationals, COM (2006) 402 final of 19.07.2006 and Communication from the Commission on Reinforcing the Management of the European Union's Southern Maritime Borders, COM (2006) 733 final of 30.11.2006.

agreements as well as in connection with two new concepts which have provoked intensive discussion in the EU and beyond: first, the notion of 'extraterritorial processing'; and second, EU 'Regional Protection Programmes', or 'RPPs', including their refugee resettlement component.

A.   Readmission Agreements

The EU has focused on readmission as a key element in the fight against illegal immigration. For many years, Member States had worked to conclude readmission agreements on a bilateral basis with third countries, including many non-EU countries of origin and transit of refugees. In its conclusions at Tampere in 1999, the European Council placed readmission strategies squarely on the EU agenda, proposing the integration of readmission clauses into cooperation agreements with non-EU countries, as well as the conclusion of express agreements on readmission with such countries.[26]

In a short time, readmission had risen to the level of a key external relations priority. Successive Councils expressed the EU's commitment to address migration issues, including readmission, through political dialogue, with the aim of creating 'strict obligations on the readmission of illegal immigrants' for third countries, and thereby 'establishing a prevention policy'[27] on irregular movement.

In Seville, the European Council proposed that compulsory readmission clauses should be inserted in '**any** future cooperation, association or equivalent agreement which the European Union or the European Community concludes with any country'.[28] In addition, the Council also resolved to give the Commission a wide-ranging mandate to negotiate stand-alone agreements on behalf of the European Community with eleven countries: Albania, Algeria, China, the Hong Kong Special Administrative Region, Macao, Moldova, Morocco, Pakistan, Russia, Turkey and Ukraine. The list was expanded in 2006 to include Bosnia and Herzegovina, Montenegro and Serbia. As of the time of writing, ten agreements had been

---

26.   European Council Conclusions, Tampere, December 1999, paras 26-7.
27.   General Affairs Council Conclusions on cooperation with third countries of origin and transit to jointly combat illegal immigration, 9717/2, 17.6.02, p. 12.
28.   European Council Conclusions, Seville, June 2002, para. 33 [emphasis added].

negotiated or concluded.[29] While the agreement with Pakistan was expected 'soon', negotiations with the four remaining priority countries – Algeria, China, Morocco and Turkey – appeared blocked.

Concerns persist about the compatibility of this readmission policy with international protection concerns. A real risk exists that asylum-seekers whose claims have not been examined substantively in the EU will be removed to third countries under the terms of readmission agreements, but without adequate guarantees of access to asylum procedures or effective protection thereafter. Defenders of the EU's readmission policy point out that all of the specific agreements concluded and placed in the public domain to date contain a general provision repeating the parties' obligations under the 1951 Convention. Beyond this, however, the contracting parties have not been prepared to include more explicit protection safeguards, as advocated by UNHCR and human rights organizations. These organizations have asked what steps are being taken to ensure compliance with the 1951 Convention. No monitoring arrangements for readmitted asylum-seekers are in place or under contemplation and there is thus no data on whether people are returned, directly or indirectly, to persecution, through the application of EC readmission agreements or clauses.

In its negotiating efforts to date, the EC has concentrated on concluding readmission agreements covering not only EU nationals and citizens of the contracting country in question, but also others who have transited through the territory of the contracting parties. The inclusion of third country nationals has in fact been promoted as the main element of 'added value' of the EC agreements, beyond the benefits that many Member States already enjoy under their bilateral readmission agreements with the countries in question. It would appear, however, that the EC's focus on imposing obligations to admit third country nationals is a major sticking-point in discussions with the remaining countries on the Commission's mandate list, namely Algeria, China, Morocco and Turkey – all pivotal States for the EU on returns.[30] For this reason, it is expected that the EC might start to shift its focus from securing readmission agreements with countries of transit of irregular migrants covering third nationals as well as own-nationals, to concluding own-national readmission agreements with a

---

29. Agreements negotiated or concluded by October 2007 covered Albania, Bosnia and Herzegovina, the Hong Kong Special Administrative Region, Macao, Moldova, Montenegro, Russia, Serbia, Sri Lanka and Ukraine (cf. in more detail the contribution by Schieffer in this book).
30. Roig A. and Huddleston T., 'EC Readmission Agreements: A Re-evaluation of the Political Impasse', European Journal of Migration and Law 9 (2007) 363-387.

larger number of States, including countries of origin.[31] The result would be more effort invested in securing return of people directly to more countries of origin.

For those States with which the EC has already concluded agreements covering third country nationals, however, serious concerns also arise from a protection and human rights viewpoint. The problem is exemplified by practices involving apparently systematic and unregulated detention upon readmission. By way of illustration, Albania, Ukraine and Russia are all heavily engaged in constructing immigration detention facilities, in many cases with significant levels of EU funding. Reports suggest that third country nationals readmitted to these States are detained as illegal entrants (although they have been admitted under the terms of a legal agreement with the EC), while the readmitting country seeks, in turn, to secure their onward movement to their countries of origin or other countries of transit.

It is not clear that people in such situations are subject to any defined maximum detention periods, nor what the detention conditions might be, whether minors are detained, or how rules on judicial review of detention are applied, if at all. Given that these countries have concluded few readmission agreements to date outside their own immediate region, it could be expected that at least some of those in detention will not be sent onwards soon. This appears to raise the possibility of indefinite detention, in facilities constructed with EU support, for people returned under EC agreements.

B.   Extraterritorial processing

One of the most controversial debates around asylum and third countries in the post-Amsterdam phase has centered around the question of 'extraterritorial processing' – that is, whether and how the EU should seek to establish facilities outside its borders for processing asylum claims from people seeking protection in the EU, where such claims would otherwise be the responsibility of Member States.

The discussion was ignited when the UK government in early 2003 put forward a proposal on 'transit processing centres' and 'regional protection

---

31. It has been proposed that the aim should be to 'operationalise' Article 13 of the Cotonou Agreement, which would provide for readmission to sub-Saharan African countries (among many others in the Africa, Caribbean and Pacific (ACP) regions). However, some observers consider that the high level of resistance and sensitivity on readmission in African States is also likely to confound this new strategy.

zones.'[32] These concepts foresaw the establishment of centres in countries outside the EU, to which asylum-seekers from certain so-called 'safe' countries of origin would be transferred after filing claims in the UK or other Member States. 'Screening' of their claims would occur in the designated non-EU State, with the possibility for those granted refugee status to be resettled within the EU, and others found not to need protection being returned to their countries of origin, under reinforced readmission arrangements. Possible host States for such centres which were initially suggested were Albania, Croatia, Tanzania and Ukraine. UNHCR expressed its strong reservations about the idea,[33] and NGOs and other observers sharply criticized the proposals.[34] Some Member States were also said to oppose the notion. Objections centered mainly on the idea that States would attempt to evade their refugee protection obligations by transferring asylum seekers to countries where the availability of protection could not be guaranteed.

In early 2003, the European Council asked the European Commission to examine the UK ideas further, and to seek other innovative approaches to international protection.[35] In response, the EC prepared a Communication entitled 'Towards more accessible, equitable and managed asylum systems',[36] which laid out an important set of parameters for the discussion which followed. The Commission placed particular emphasis on the need for Member States fully to respect international legal obligations, to ensure 'full and inclusive application' of the 1951 Convention, and to find new

---

32. A first version of the UK Home Office paper emerged as 'A new vision for refugees', Feb. 2003, referred to in 'Safe havens plan to slash asylum numbers', The Guardian, 5 Feb. 2003. A later version, entitled 'New international approaches to asylum processing and protection' and presented to the European Council in March 2003, was analysed in the Communication from the European Commission to the Council and the European Parliament, 'Towards more accessible, equitable and managed asylum systems' COM(2003)315 final, 3 Jun. 2003.

33. Op-Ed by Ruud Lubbers, High Commissioner for Refugees, 20 Jun. 2003; 'EU's 'safe country' asylum plans attacked', The Guardian, 30 Mar. 2004.

34. Amnesty International, 'UK/EU/UNHCR: Unlawful and Unworkable: Amnesty International's views on proposals for extraterritorial processing of asylum claims', 18 Jun. 2003.

35. Conclusion 63, Presidency Conclusions, Brussels European Council, 20-1 March 2003, Council doc. 8410/03.

36. Communication from the European Commission to the Council and the European Parliament, 'Towards more accessible, equitable and managed asylum systems' COM(2003)315 final, 3.06.2003.

ways to achieve 'genuine burden-sharing within the EU and with third countries, rather than shifting the burden to them'.[37]

At Thessaloniki in June 2003, the Council adopted a new set of carefully-formulated conclusions, calling on the European Commission again to 'explore all parameters in order to ensure more orderly and managed entry in the EU of persons in need of international protection and to examine ways and means to enhance the protection capacity of regions of origin.' The Council asked for a comprehensive report to be presented by June 2004 proposing 'measures to be taken, including legal implications'.[38]

Before the Commission could respond, the German Minister of Interior, Otto Schily, launched a verbal proposal which sparked further controversy. Schily raised the idea of establishing EU-operated 'asylum camps' (later referred to as 'reception facilities') in North Africa, for people rescued or intercepted by EU vessels on the high seas.[39] The initiative raised many of the unanswered questions which had also dogged the UK ideas (what legal basis would support such an initiative? What durable solutions would be available for those found to be refugees? How to avoid a 'pull factor'? Who is responsible for removing those without protection needs?) However, in legal terms it was not so easily dismissed, as it relied on the argument that the EU might not be solely responsible for asylum-seekers who were encountered in international waters, and who had never reached Member State territorial seas. While the idea was never carried further, it showed that the extraterritorial processing notion was not off the political agenda.

C.   Regional Protection Programmes and Resettlement

At the July 2004 meeting of Justice and Home Affairs Ministers where German Minister Schily launched his controversial idea, the Commission tabled a Communication which took a more subtle approach. The Communication focused on 'more managed entry in the EU of persons in

---

37. *Ibid.*, section V, points 1 and 5.
38. Presidency Conclusions, Thessaloniki European Council, 19.06.2003, conclusion 26.
39. The proposal came in July 2004, shortly after a maritime incident in which a German-flagged vessel owned by an NGO, the 'Cap Anamur' rescued a group of asylum seekers in distress at sea, and sought to disembark them in Italy or Malta. Neither State accepted responsibility for them, and for several days the dispute continued, with some observers proposing that Germany should be responsible, as flag state of the host ship. Minister Schily was known to be fiercely opposed to the idea that Germany should take the asylum seekers.

need of international protection',[40] among other things; and contrary to some fears,[41] it did not propose any moves towards external processing of asylum claims received from people already in the EU, or from people *en route* to Member States.

Instead, the Commission proposed the concept of 'Regional Protection Programmes', or 'RPPs'. The RPPs comprised two key elements: firstly, EC-funded activities to 'strengthen the protection capacity' of countries in regions of origin and transit. Secondly, resettlement, through a proposal that Member States should examine the concept of resettlement, with a view to creating a common EU resettlement scheme to provide durable solutions for refugees in overburdened host States in regions of origin. While the Communication hinted that this kind of investment could in theory reduce the numbers of people compelled to move on irregularly from host countries to Europe in search of protection, it acknowledged that such a correlation could not be guaranteed.

Importantly, the Communication reiterated that any and all new measures adopted with the aim of facilitating more orderly entry to the EU of people in need of international protection must be supplementary to, rather than in place of, grants of asylum to people arriving spontaneously in the Union. In other words, any proposed initiatives involving third countries would not reduce the obligations of Member States to protect people seeking asylum through their domestic systems. It was an acknowledgement by the Commission that the creation of more opportunities for international protection for refugees, through resettlement and regional capacity-building, did not affect the responsibility of European Union Member States to grant protection to those in their territory who need it, and by implication, to afford access for asylum seekers to their national asylum systems and territories for that purpose.

40. European Commission, Communication to the Council and the European Parliament, 'On the Managed Entry in the EU of Persons in Need of International Protection and Enhancement of the Protection Capacity of the Regions of Origin: Improving Access to Durable Solutions' COM(2004) 410 final, 4 Jun. 2004. The Communication discussed the outcomes of two independent studies prepared for the Commission in late 2003 on (1) the possibilities for expanded resettlement to the EU, and (2) 'protected entry schemes' as potential mechanisms for improving systems for granting protection in the EU.
41. European Council for Refugees and Exiles ('ECRE'), 'Comments of ECRE on the Communication from the Commission to the Council and the European Parliament: Towards a more accessible, equitable and managed international protection regime, COM (2003) 315 final'; 18.06.2004.

In its conclusions of November 2004, the Council endorsed the Commission's proposals for launch of Regional Protection Programmes based on 'principle of solidarity and fair sharing of responsibility, which should be situation-specific and protection oriented'. In 2005, the Commission issued detailed plans for the launch of the first pilot RPPs, to be undertaken in two priority regions: Tanzania, in the Great Lakes region of Africa; and in three countries in Eastern Europe, namely Belarus, Moldova and Ukraine.

UNHCR, which had observed the discussions around extraterritorial processing with concern, took the view that the RPP concept offered positive opportunities for strengthening refugee protection, if implemented in the spirit and within the limitations that the Commission had expressed. As long as they were undertaken as complementary measures to the provision of protection in Europe, and based on genuine cooperation with the countries and regions of origin, the RPPs had the potential to benefit refugees in those regions. UNHCR encouraged the EU in its professed desire to engage with third countries, including through investment of financial resources.

A year after the first pilot projects were launched, some of the limits on the concept were apparent. First among these was the limited funds available. UNHCR was charged with implementing one capacity-building project in each of the two target regions: one in Tanzania[42] and one in Belarus[43], the latter complemented by two projects in Ukraine led by the Danish Refugee Council and Caritas Austria. With the small allocations available in comparison to the scale of needs, UNHCR had warned of the risks of excessive expectations.[44] The investment represented by these new JLS funds was small, compared to the EC humanitarian, development and other forms of aid channeled to the target countries – for instance, in exchange for readmission agreements. The RPPs could not be expected to solve any major problems overnight.

Still, for Eastern Europe (Belarus, Moldova and Ukraine) in particular, it would appear that the Member States maintain great interest in 'asylum capacity building', which among other things could be seen as designed to help those States offer protection *in situ* for people who might otherwise move on to the EU. Member States are less willing to engage in resettlement, although it could be an important gesture of responsibility-

---

42. Budget: EUR 1.5 million for 2007-8.
43. Budget: EUR 575,000 for 2007-8.
44. UNHCR, Observations on the Communication on Regional Protection Programmes, COM(2005)388, 1.09.2005.

sharing with the Eastern States as they adjust to their new role as countries of asylum, and despite the humanitarian needs and apparent lack of local integration prospects. An imbalance in the emphasis within RPPs is apparent, as in the many other external dimension policies which seek to address asylum and migration through cooperation with third countries. The problems could be attributed in part to a heavy emphasis on what is in the EU's interests, and less on what the countries and regions of origin might need or be capable of offering in the migration and protection area.

This has been particularly evident in Member States' reluctance to offer new commitments on resettlement. Despite the affirmation in the Council Conclusions of October 2004 that 'the targeted use of resettlement will demonstrate the Community's commitment towards international efforts to find comprehensive and effective solutions to protracted refugee situations,'[45] Member States have so far proved unwilling to offer substantial numbers of new resettlement places, whether through new or increased resettlement quotas. Although there have been positive signs from some countries which have not traditionally resettled refugees, resettlement to the EU remains very modest, whether from the RPPs' so-called 'priority regions' or elsewhere.

At present, of the 27 EU Member States, only seven have established annual resettlement programmes,[46] which resettled just over 3,700 people in 2007. However, as some of these places are reserved for family reunification with refugees already recognized in the European countries, the real capacity of these programmes to offer durable solutions is even more limited. Political will is needed to reach a substantial and sustained EU commitment to resettlement. Moreover, it is important to make clear that resettlement must be a complement to – and not a substitute for – the provision of protection where needed to persons who apply for asylum in the EU or at its borders.

III. Border management and migration control: Protection for whom?

While EU migration policy offers opportunities for enhanced engagement with third countries, including in such positive areas as strengthening of

---

45. Council of the European Union, Doc. C/04/295 of 2 November 2004.
46. Denmark, Finland, Ireland, Netherlands, Portugal, Sweden and United Kingdom. France has announced that it will commence resettlement in 2008 with around 100 persons.

their capacity to protect refugees, migration and development and legal migration, the undisputed focus of EU political attention and resource allocation has been in the areas of border control and halting irregular migration. This carries inherent risks for the protection of refugees, as access to EU territory becomes more difficult, including for persons seeking asylum.

A.   External borders

As progress has continued towards abolition of internal border checks within the European Union, the EU has moved increasingly to reinforce controls at its external frontiers. This process began in 1990, when Schengen Convention established a 'single external frontier' and common rules on border checks for all of its signatory States, and took a significant step forward with the entry into force of the Amsterdam Treaty in 1999.

In its Title IV, Amsterdam brought 'asylum, immigration, visas and other policies related to free movement of persons' from the sphere of jurisdiction of Member States' national governments, into the 'first pillar' of Community competence. It also incorporated the full set of measures relating to Schengen into the Union's legal and institutional framework. Under the key principles governing the Schengen system, the freedom of movement that comes with the abolition of checks at internal borders is balanced with a range of 'compensatory measures' to secure the area's external borders. In addition to common procedures and formats for external border checks, and the database of detailed information on movements of people and goods known as the 'Schengen Information System' (SIS), these 'compensatory measures' include increased coordination between national police, customs and judiciaries; a common visa regime; and further steps to combat organized crime, terrorism and other threats. Progress in developing the Schengen acquis and EU policies on external border management has been swift and enjoys widespread political support. There are significant grounds for concern, however, that these developments have not been accompanied by adequate safeguards for people in need of international protection.

In the Hague Programme, the European Council included a key section entitled 'Border Checks and the Fight Against Illegal Migration'[47] under the broad heading of 'Management of Migration Flows'. In its first paragraph, the Council stressed 'the importance of swift abolition of internal border

---

47. *Op cit.*, note 12, section 1.7.1.

controls, and the strengthening of controls at and surveillance of the external borders of the Union'[48] as key priorities. It drew a clear link between the aim of combating illegal migration and effective border management. By contrast, no connection was made anywhere in the section on 'Management of Migration Flows' with another major stated objective of the Hague Programme as a whole: 'to provide protection in accordance with the Geneva Convention on Refugees and other international treaties to persons in need'.[49]

UNHCR, in its 'Ten Point Plan of Action' on Refugee Protection and International Migration,[50] has argued repeatedly that the challenges around migration management must be addressed with regard for the rights of people who may be refugees or otherwise in need of protection. It is largely uncontested that while 'refugees and asylum-seekers account for a relatively small portion of the global movement of people, they increasingly move from one country.. to another alongside other people whose reasons for moving are different and not protection-related.'[51] To ensure respect for States' obligations towards people who need protection within these 'mixed flows', safeguards are required to guarantee access to territory and asylum procedures. This requires attention to protection concerns as part of the development of border and migration management systems.

There is little evidence of a 'comprehensive'[52] approach to borders and migration, which also addresses the critical dimension of asylum, in the EU's policy- and law-making framework to date. The security imperatives overshadow the need for safeguards to ensure respect for fundamental principles of refugee law.

---

48. *Ibid.*
49. *Ibid.*, Introduction, para 7.
50. UNHCR: 'Refugee Protection and Mixed Migration: A Ten Point Plan of Action', Revision 1, Jan. 2007.
51. *Ibid.*, Introduction.
52. See UNHCR's call for a coherent and comprehensive approach to borders, migration and asylum: Ten Point Plan, *ibid*, para 3; and UNHCR, 'Response to the EC's Green Paper on the Future Common European Asylum System', Sept. 2007, at: http://www.unhcr.org/protect/PROTECTION/46e53de52.pdf.

B. Integrated Border Management

The EU's concept of 'Integrated Border Management' (or 'IBM'), first elaborated by the Commission[53] and endorsed by the Council[54] in 2002, refers to a range of measures and functions which has grown in scope and political importance over time. In 2006, the Finnish Presidency placed significant priority on border issues, and the JHA Council adopted Conclusions aimed at defining the framework of 'IBM'. Elements forming part of the IBM concept included: border control (checks and surveillance, including risk analysis and criminal intelligence); detecting and investigating 'cross-border crime' with law enforcement authorities; measures in third countries of origin or transit of people seeking to enter the EU, including neighbouring countries; measures on border control at external frontiers surrounding the area of free movement; inter-agency cooperation on border management; and 'coordination and coherence' at the national and transnational level.[55]

Measures and safeguards to ensure respect for the fundamental rights of people seeking to cross the Union's external borders, including the right to seek asylum, were not referred to as part of this 'integrated' border system. The use of the term 'integrated' thus does not refer to the integration of all relevant and binding international or EU *acquis* principles which should guide border management, but rather to the 'integration' of all involved States under a single, uniform set of border rules and procedures. One observer has suggested alternatively that it refers to 'all border-related threats that the EU is supposed to be facing'.[56] The catalogue of IBM measures, as defined and elaborated by the JHA Council, implies a logic that focuses heavily on security and risks, rather than transparency and individual rights.

---

53. European Commission Communication: 'Towards Integrated Management of the External Borders of the Member States of the European Union', COM(2002)233, 7.5.2002.
54. Council of the European Union, 'Plan for the Management of the External Borders of the Member States of the European Union', Document 10019/02, 14.6.2002.
55. Council of the European Union, Conclusions of the Justice and Home Affairs Council meeting, Brussels, 4 -5 December 2006, Press Release 15801/06.
56. See Carrera, S: 'The EU Border Management Strategy – Frontex and the Challenges of Irregular Immigration in the Canary Islands', CEPS Working Document no. 261/ March 2007, p. 3.

Two key measures forming part of the IBM framework will be examined in more detail to assess their compatibility with and accommodation of refugee protection concerns, namely: the Schengen Borders Code; and the EU's External Borders Management Agency, or 'Frontex'.

C. Schengen Borders Code

The Schengen Borders Code[57], adopted in 2006, brought together and replaced provisions from a range of instruments governing EU external borders. The instruments it succeeded include the Schengen Convention, the 'Common Manual' on borders, Council Decisions on external border control, airports, border crossing signs, and others.[58] As such, it codified and developed further the pre-existing *acquis* on internal and external frontiers, thus binding all Member States under a 'common corpus' of border legislation.[59]

The Schengen Borders Code incorporates a general provision on international protection, providing that the Regulation as a whole applies to 'any person crossing the internal or external borders of Member States, without prejudice to the rights of persons enjoying the Community right of free movement; [and] *the rights of refugees and persons requesting international protection, in particular as regards non-refoulement'*.[60]

The Preamble – which is not legally binding, but is accepted as an important guide to interpretation of the main legal instrument – also states that the Code 'respects fundamental rights and observes the principles recognized in particular by the Charter of Fundamental Rights of the European Union'[61], which includes the right to asylum and the principle of *non-refoulement*. Moreover, the Preamble underlines that the Code 'should be applied in accordance with the Member States' obligations as regards international protection and *non-refoulement'*.

These general provisions are also echoed in specific articles dealing with admission and refusal of entry to the EU. Article 5, on the conditions for entry to a Member State, states that an exception to general entry requirements may apply to third country nationals who do not fulfil the

---

57. Council Regulation 562/2006 establishing a Community Code on the rules governing the movement of persons across borders (also known as the 'Community Border Code' or 'Schengen Borders Code'), OJ L 105, 13.4.2006, p. 1.
58. See: Peers, S: 'EU Justice and Home Affairs Law', 2006, p. 145.
59. *Op cit* note 56, Preamble para. 4.
60. *Ibid.*, Article 3(b) (emphasis added).
61. *Ibid.*, Preamble para. 20.

relevant conditions, but who 'may be authorized by a Member State to enter its territory on humanitarian grounds, on grounds of national interest or because of international obligations.'[62]

Article 13 provides that persons who do not fulfil the criteria for entry to the Union shall be refused entry to the territories of the Member States – but that this 'shall be without prejudice to the application of special provisions concerning the right of asylum and to international protection...'[63]

As the first measure in the borders field to be adopted under the new co-decision procedure applying since 2004[64], the Schengen Borders Code also demonstrated the importance of the Parliament's role in ensuring safeguards for individual rights in Community laws. The Parliament insisted that Article 13 contain a specific provision stating that 'persons refused entry shall have the right of appeal'[65], and in that connection, requiring a 'substantiated decision stating the precise reasons for refusal' of entry at an EU external border.[66] The final text also states that refused persons must be given 'a written indication of contact points able to provide information on representatives competent to act on behalf of the third country national'. This appeal right represents a vital element of procedural fairness, which should correspond to the right to an effective remedy established by the European Convention on Human Rights. The obligation for border authorities to provide written reasons for refusal, and a list of contact persons through whom refused would-be entrants could seek advice and representation, are also important practical elements, which could in principle help such people to take legal action.

Notwithstanding these positive provisions, concerns arise about whether they are sufficient to ensure that refugees and other people in need of protection will not be turned back at borders or returned, potentially to situations where they may face persecution. The right to appeal against refusal of entry, for instance, is not suspensive[67], meaning that the refusal decision stands and the person must await the outcome of an appeal in a

---

62. *Ibid.,* Article 5(4)(c).
63. *Ibid.,* Article 13(1).
64. Articles 67 and 251 EC. The new decision making process involved qualified majority voting, rather than unanimity, among Member States within the Council; and co-decision with the European Parliament, replacing the previous consultation mechanism, under which the Council was obliged to seek the Parliament's view, but was not bound to follow it.
65. *Op cit.,* note 56, Article 13(3).
66. *Ibid.,* Article 13(2).
67. *Ibid.,* Article 13(3).

country of transit or his or her country of origin, where dangers may be imminent.

The exemption from general admission requirements for persons whose entry 'may be authorised' to a Member State 'because of international obligations'[68] is phrased as a permissive (entry 'may' be authorised) rather than mandatory ('shall') provision. Furthermore, it is not specified how Article 5(4)(c) should be applied by Member States in practice. Personnel conducting entry checks may not always be trained or authorized to identify a person who is seeking asylum, and there is no specific provision in the Schengen Borders Code obliging border personnel to refer any such applicants to competent asylum authorities. Despite the existence of a right to appeal against refusal of entry, asylum-seekers stranded at a border are unlikely to be aware of their rights or in a position to exercise them. The interaction between the Code and the Asylum Procedures Directive is not clarified. Thus there is a risk that the 'international obligations' in this context may remain a dead letter.

The Code also requires Member States to impose penalties which 'shall be effective, proportionate and dissuasive' on people who cross borders in an irregular fashion.[69] Although this provision is also said to be subject to 'international protection obligations', it fails to mention Article 31(1) of the 1951 Convention, which explicitly prohibits States under certain conditions from penalizing refugees for entering their territory without authorization. There is a risk that the 'dissuasive' penalties required by the Code will effectively prevent refugees from accessing the territory of States where they could claim the protection to which they are entitled.

The Code contains a list of categories of people for whom 'special' – generally reduced and accelerated – border checks shall apply.[70] Despite the references in the Code to the international obligations which should qualify the general border rules, asylum-seekers and people in need of international protection are not included. This omission fails to utilize a further opportunity to give practical effect to the general requirement to respect international obligations. As a result, asylum-seekers remain subject to the same checks and restrictions as other third country

---

68. *Ibid.*, Article 5(4)(c).
69. *Ibid.*, Article 4(3).
70. *Ibid.*, Article 19 – includes Heads of State and their delegations; aircraft crew; seamen, diplomats, cross-border workers and minors (Note: minors are in fact to be subject to special scrutiny under the 'special' rules, but these provisions are directed at preventing the risk of child abduction, and are not connected to possible refugee protection needs).

nationals. At most of the Union's busy external border entry points, the concrete result is that border personnel may not be aware, or equipped to ensure, that the necessary exceptions are made to ensure practical implementation of international protection obligations.

D.   Frontex

A further key step towards creation of an integrated EU border management system is the establishment of the European Agency for the Management of Operational Cooperation at the External Borders, or 'Frontex'. After passage of its founding Regulation in 2004[71], Frontex became operational in mid-2005, with a wide-ranging mandate requiring it, among other things, to:
- assist Member States in training activities;
- coordinate operational cooperation between Member States in managing their external borders, including in the context of joint [border control] operations;
- support cooperation in 'emergencies';
- carry out risk analysis;
- follow up on 'research relevant for border control and surveillance'; and
- support Member States in organizing return operations.[72]

Frontex's establishment demonstrates the will of Member States to work more closely together in order to reinforce external borders. The accession of ten new members in 2004 significantly extended the Union's external frontiers, and placed at the external borders States with varying capacities in border management. The Frontex Regulation thus emphasized the 'need for promoting solidarity between Member States in the field of external borders'[73] and obliged the Agency to 'provide [...] the Member States with the necessary technical support and expertise in the management of the external borders.'[74] It also reiterated the security focus of Community border policy, which should 'aim at an integrated management, ensuring a uniform and high level of control and surveillance, which is a necessary corollary to the free movement of persons within the European Union [...]'[75] Equipped with a far-reaching legal mandate and a high level of

---

71. Council Regulation (EC) No. 2007/2004 of 26 October 2004 establishing a European Agency for the Management of Operational Cooperation at the External Borders of the Member States of the European Union, OJ L 349, 25.11.2004, p. 1.
72. *Ibid.*, Article 2.
73. *Ibid.*, Preamble para. 5.
74. *Ibid.*, Article 3.
75. *Ibid.*, Preamble para 1.

political support, Frontex's activities have the potential significantly to increase the effectiveness of border management across the EU.

However, a number of limitations are placed on its autonomy and scope for action, as articulated in the Agency's Regulation, which emphasizes clearly 'the responsibility for the control and surveillance of external borders lies with the Member States.'[76] Frontex's work focuses on 'the coordination of Member States' actions... thereby contributing to an efficient, high and uniform level of control on persons and surveillance of the external borders of the Member States'.[77] Joint operations and projects under its coordination can only be initiated at the request of a Member State or by the Agency with the agreement of the Member State(s) concerned.[78] Equipment and personnel for carrying out joint operations must be provided by Member States which voluntarily place it at Frontex's disposal for the purpose of assisting the State requesting the operation, but who retain their prior ownership, control and command.[79] This close supervision of the Agency's work is reinforced by the structure of Frontex's Management Board, consisting of representatives from the 27 Member States' border authorities and the European Commission. These arrangements ensure that the activities of Frontex are directed by Member States' political priorities and concerns, such as securing of the frontiers against identified external 'risks'[80] which are seen to require a coordinated response.

Frontex's founding Regulation affirms in its Preamble that it 'respects the fundamental rights and observes the principles recognised by [the ECHR and other international treaties] and reflected in the Charter of Fundamental Rights of the European Union'[81], thereby including the right to asylum and the principle of *non-refoulement*. While Frontex representatives in public statements have emphasized strongly the Agency's commitment to respecting international law, they have also underlined that the mandate of Frontex does not extend to refugee protection, or other functions outside the narrow remit of border control and law enforcement, such as rescue at sea.[82]

---

76. *Ibid.*, Article 1.
77. *Ibid.*
78. *Ibid.*, Article 3.
79. *Ibid.*, Articles 3 and 7.
80. Risk analysis is a key part of Frontex's responsibilities, under Article 2 of its Regulation, with an intelligence-based and non-public risk assessment carried out before each joint operation is defined and launched.
81. *Op cit.,* note 70, Preamble, para. 22.
82. Frontex press release of 11.07.2007, 'Frontex – Facts and Myths' by Ilkka Laitinen.

The limits on Frontex's mandate could be seen to create positive opportunities for refugee protection. Its Regulation provides for cooperation between Frontex and international organizations 'in matters covered by this Regulation in the framework of working arrangements concluded with those bodies, in accordance with the relevant provisions of the Treaty and the provisions on the competence of those bodies'.[83] The organizations with which Frontex has begun discussions on cooperation include Europol, UNHCR and IOM. The fact that Europol alone is explicitly mentioned in the Frontex Regulation as an organization with which Frontex should cooperate suggests that Member States see the law enforcement dimension of Frontex's activities as paramount.

Nevertheless, by conferring this power to enter into cooperative working arrangements with other organs, the Council has given Frontex the scope to ensure that tasks touching on issues outside the strict terms of its competence and expertise can be addressed with input from those with the relevant mandates and experience. Frontex should be in a position to consult and seek guidance from those bodies, in cases where border management activities or incidents raise issues in their fields of responsibility, such as refugee protection. However, the question of whether the envisaged cooperation arrangements can provide the requisite degree of flexibility – and whether Member States will accept a major role for the recommendations of other bodies – remains to be seen. Another concern is what might occur in situations where border control and law enforcement imperatives come into conflict with other principles, such as refugee protection or other fundamental rights. This will be a test of the Member States' will to respect their international and *acquis* obligations.

For the purpose of assessing whether Frontex's processes place due emphasis on the need to balance border controls with safeguards for basic rights, a relevant issue is how its success is measured. Under Frontex's Rules of Procedure[84], an evaluation is undertaken upon completion of each joint operation. However, these evaluations are not public, and it is thus not possible to determine whether they devote any attention to whether Member States' international protection obligations were met in the context of a given operation.

The Agency's public statements following different joint operations provide some insight into how its achievements are assessed. Press Releases have been issued on maritime border operations in 2007,

---

83. *Op cit* note 70, Article 13.
84. Decision of the Management Board of 24 March 2006: 'Rules of procedure for taking decisions related to the operational tasks of Frontex'.

including 'Poseidon' in the Central Mediterranean and 'Nautilus I and II' in the Eastern Mediterranean, as well as 'Hera II' around the Canary Islands. In each case, detailed statistics were provided on how many vessels were intercepted, how many migrants arrived in EU Member States, and how many were prevented or diverted back to their ports of departure. For instance, Frontex emphasized that Hera II had successfully diverted several thousand 'migrants' back to the West African coast, 'thus preventing them to risk their lives on the dangerous journey'[85] (*sic*).

No mention was made of whether any among the people diverted back might have been seeking international protection, or whether measures to ascertain their status were or could have been taken. Following Nautilus I in late 2006, the Frontex Executive Director announced that the exercise had succeeded in ensuring that no 'irregular migrant' had landed on the shores of Malta, in accordance with the exercise's aims.[86] The statement did not, however, elaborate on the fate of those who were prevented from landing in Malta.

It would appear at least from public statements that there has been a tendency for Frontex to characterize its achievements based on the number irregular migrants prevented from landing in Europe. However, if joint operations are to be seen as successful in ensuring fulfillment of Member States' duties to provide international protection, a more nuanced analysis and explanation will be required.

UNHCR has proposed that Member States could enhance Frontex's capacity to ensure that international law is respected in border control operations through some specific amendments to its Regulation.[87] For instance, an explicit reference to international protection obligations, particularly the principle of *non-refoulement*, would recall Member States' voluntarily assumed responsibilities and emphasise their importance in the planning and execution of joint operations, including those involving third countries. In addition, Member States could insert into Article 1 of the Frontex Regulation a requirement for the Agency to work to develop protection-sensitive entry management systems, which could complement

85. See 'Frontex's Accomplished Operations: Canary Islands – HERA', 16.09.2007, at: http://www.frontex.europa.eu/examples_of_accomplished_operati/art5.html

86. See press article Malta Media of 11.11.2006, at: http://www.maltamedia.com/news/2005/eu/article_12300.shtml

87. 'UNHCR: Response to the European Commission's Green Paper on the future Common European Asylum System.', *op cit* note 52, page 48.

the objective of achieving 'an efficient, high and uniform level of control on persons and surveillance of the external borders of the Member States.'[88]

E.   Interception and rescue at sea

Among the Frontex-coordinated joint border operations undertaken since the Agency's inception, a significant number have involved maritime border patrols or related border checks at or near the coastal frontiers of the Union. Some observers argue that the intensive focus on sea border controls is disproportionate, given the larger numbers of people believed to arrive irregularly in the EU via land entry points, and the even greater total who enter regularly and who overstay their visas within EU territory. It is apparent, however, that the maritime context has served to throw into sharp relief many difficult and unresolved questions about States' responsibilities, including their extraterritorial obligations under the principle of *non-refoulement* – and the highly sensitive questions of where intercepted or rescued people should be disembarked and who should be responsible for them.

For many years, the summer period has seen significant numbers of people in small boats seeking to reach the southern coastal borders of EU Member States. While precise figures are unknown, it is acknowledged that many of people drown each year in the Mediterranean and Atlantic waters, as they seek to make the hazardous journey, usually facilitated by people smugglers and often in overcrowded and unseaworthy vessels.

The significant numbers of people arriving in the EU – chiefly in Cyprus, Greece, Italy, Malta and Spain – have drawn intensive media and political attention, and sparked fears that 'floods' of irregular migrants are waiting in North and Sub-Saharan Africa, among other places, for the chance to come to the EU. These fears appear to be largely unfounded, but they have contributed to an atmosphere in which EU political leaders have felt impelled to adopt tough positions, and resist arguments that their States are responsible for receiving the arrivals.

A number of maritime 'incidents' during 2007 illustrated the dilemma. In February 2007, the Guinean-flagged vessel 'Marine I' departed from Guinea-Conakry and broke down in Senegalese waters whilst headed towards the Canary Islands. Spanish Maritime Rescue Services came to the boat's aid, and negotiated an agreement with the Mauritanian authorities to disembark the people on board at the nearest port, in Nouadhibou,

---

88.   *Op cit.,* note 70, Article 1(2).

Mauritania. After UNHCR met and interviewed the people on a preliminary basis, a number were transferred to Spain for substantive asylum determinations, while some others were deported to their countries of origin. A further group of people were detained in unsatisfactory conditions in a fish processing plant in Nouadhibou, a stay that ultimately continued for some of them for several months, with no country willing to accept them on a long-term basis. Ad hoc solutions were eventually achieved for each remaining individual, including the last one in July 2007.

In May 2007, a group of 27 people from sub-Saharan African countries, whose boat had foundered in the sea between Malta and Libya, were encountered by a Maltese fishing boat, the 'Budafel'. Due to the captain's professed concerns about losing his commercial catch, the people were not permitted to board the fishing boat, but held on instead to a tuna pen structure being towed by the boat, which was en route to Spain. The boat continued its journey with the people clinging to the pen for three days, while discussions involving Malta and Libya continued over how to respond. Ultimately, the people were rescued by an Italian coast guard vessel and landed on the Italian island of Lampedusa, where they were admitted to a reception centre and interviewed by UNHCR.

In each of these, and other relevant cases, disagreements have centred around which State is responsible to disembark and subsequently deal with the intercepted or rescued people. The disputes have been exacerbated by the lack of clarity or agreement among States about the extent of the responsibilities imposed by international law. UNHCR's Executive Committee in 2003 adopted a Conclusion on Protection Safeguards in Interception Measures.[89] Among other things, this Conclusion defined the purposes of interception activities, which could include preventing embarkation or onward travel of people without permission; to protect lives and security; and prevent smuggling or transport contrary to maritime laws. The Conclusion emphasizes that primary responsibility for any protection needs of intercepted persons lies with the State in whose territorial waters the interception occurs. It moreover reiterates States' obligations to respect human rights and refrain from *refoulement*, and urges them to ensure that the special needs of vulnerable people are met; that refugees are not criminally punished for smuggling; and relevant state officials receive appropriate training to deal with intercepted persons who may seek protection.

89.   No. 97(LIV)2003.

While the EXCOM Conclusion is an important source of basic principles in this area, it does not answer all of the difficult questions. These include the extent of obligations when interception occurs outside States' territorial waters, i.e. on the high seas. UNHCR in 2007 has issued an advisory opinion on extraterritorial application of *non-refoulement,* which takes the discussion a step further, clarifying that responsibility for *non-refoulement* binds a State wherever it exercises jurisdiction over a person. This is interpreted as all situations where a person is subject to the State's effective authority and control.[90]

At EU level, meanwhile, the European Commission has sought to assist Member States to clarify the position. Against the background of some of the problematic maritime incidents involving Member States undertaking interception and rescue, the Commission in May 2007 issued a 'Study on international law instruments relevant to illegal immigration by sea'.[91] The Study aimed to analyse the relevant international legal framework governing maritime rescue, border control and surveillance, and to propose solutions, potentially including legislative reform. While the Commission confirmed that the *non-refoulement* principle (along with other elements of international law and the asylum *acquis*) was binding on all Member States in their own territories and maritime zones, it left open the question of how far this obligation applies outside Member States' borders or territorial waters.

The Commission's report noted that all vessels, including Member State border patrol boats as well as private vessels under Member States' flags, were bound to render assistance to persons and ships in distress. Under amendments to the relevant Search and Rescue ('SAR') and Safety of Life at Sea ('SOLAS') Conventions, the State in whose search and rescue zone the rescue occurs is responsible to ensure cooperation and coordination of disembarkation of rescued people in a safe place.[92] However, the international instruments do not define what constitutes a 'safe' place for disembarkation of people who may be in need of international protection. Moreover, a key Member State – Malta – has not accepted those

---

90. 'UNHCR: Advisory Opinion on the Extraterritorial Application of *Non-Refoulement* Obligations under the 1951 Convention relating to the Status of Refugees and its 1967 Protocol', January 2007, para. 35, at: http://www.unhcr.org/cgi-bin/texis/vtx/refworld/rwmain?page=search&docid=45f17a1a4&skip=&query=opinion%20on%20extraterritorial%20application
91. SEC(2007)691, 15.5.2007.
92. 1974 International Convention for the Safety of Life at Sea (SOLAS), Chapter V, Regulation 33.

amendments, and does not consider itself bound by the requirement to 'facilitate and coordinate' disembarkation of vessels rescued in its large search and rescue zone.

The Study usefully highlighted and articulated other outstanding issues for Member States, such as how to determine the most appropriate port for disembarkation following rescue at sea or interception, including during States' participation in border operations outside their territorial waters. It noted that disembarkation would generally imply responsibility for examining the protection needs of any asylum-seekers among those intercepted or rescued. It did not, however, provide comprehensive answers to the many associated questions raised.

In the absence of agreed or standard procedures for border operations, the Commission suggested the elaboration of 'practical instructions' to guide Member States participating in joint Frontex operations. Member States and Frontex welcomed the suggestion, and an *ad hoc* drafting group was set up among Member States, the EC, UNHCR, IOM and Frontex. However, the decision to delegate responsibility for preparation of joint 'technical' guidelines did not address the broader outstanding questions of principle in relation to maritime law. At the time of writing, the drafting exercise has not progressed far. Discussions around the basic principles applicable to rescue and interception continue, before the more complex questions are even broached. The lack of progress could be attributed to sensitivities around the question of where to disembark, and in particular of which State should bear responsibility for the longer-term needs of the persons concerned, including potentially for asylum determinations and the grant of protected status.

Even more problematic issues arise in relation to Member States' dealings with non-EU States in the interception and rescue context. Member States and Frontex have spoken repeatedly about the importance of securing more cooperation from non-EU States, including in North Africa, to improve the effectiveness of their border operations.[93] It is argued that this aim also has a humanitarian rationale. If North African countries agree to maritime patrols by EU States in their territorial waters, small and unseaworthy boats can be prevented from departing – thereby saving the lives of people who could otherwise perish at sea attempting to reach Europe.

---

93. See for example 'Frontex's External Relations', at: http://www.frontex.europa.eu/external_relations/

This attractive statement fails to address the complex range of unanswered questions around asylum-seekers and refugees who could be trying to leave North or other parts of Africa for Europe. If an asylum-seeker has transited through North Africa after leaving the country of origin in which she or he faced persecution, return to a North African state may not be safe, or consistent with refugee law obligations, if there is no guarantee that the asylum-seeker would have access to a fair asylum process, and to a secure status upon recognition. In case the transit country subsequently expels him or her to the country of origin, there is a risk that the EU Member State may have contributed to chain refoulement.

If the asylum-seeker is a national of the country from which she or he is departing, 'diverting' the boat back to shore may expose him or her to the risk of further persecution. As such, it could violate the prohibition on *refoulement* and the right to seek asylum from persecution.

There are no simple answers to the sensitive questions raised by interception and rescue at sea. UNHCR has sought to give States some guidance in its Ten Point Plan. In addition to protection-sensitive entry measures, the Office recommends positive elements to ensure appropriate standards of reception, and procedures which can effectively identify people to be channeled into the asylum procedure, or other alternatives, as appropriate. UNHCR has confirmed it would be prepared to help States and Community mechanisms through 'profiling' of people who could be disembarked in EU Member States, and contributing otherwise as appropriate within its mandate and available resources. Other partners, including IOM, NGOs and different levels of government can also play a constructive role, including through working with asylum and border authorities, based on their respective mandates and areas of expertise.[94]

F.   Return standards

Return or removal of people who do not have permission to remain, including those found not to be in need of international protection, is seen by the EU as a cornerstone of its migration management strategy. While EU interest in and commitment to cooperate on return had been evident for

---

94.   *See* notes 49 and 51.

some time,[95] the 2004 Hague Programme foreshadowed the first move to prepare binding Community legislation and devote large-scale Community resources to return.[96] As such, it appeared to signal the intention to ensure that more Member States would actually carry out a substantial number of returns, thus enforcing Member State laws against irregular stay, and aiming to deter other would-be irregular movers. For at least some Member States, this would represent an important shift from long-standing (if not well-publicised) practices which had not been effective in removing rejected asylum-seekers or others without rights to stay from their territories.

The European Council in The Hague called for 'the establishment of an effective removal and repatriation policy based on common standards for persons to be returned in a humane manner and with full respect for their human rights and dignity.'[97] The objective of ensuring the return of people who do not require protection is widely accepted, particularly when cast in language reiterating individual rights and humane treatment. This was emphasized by UNHCR's Executive Committee in 2003, which concluded that 'the efficient and expeditious return of persons found not to be in need of international protection is key to the international protection system as a whole', and that 'the credibility of individual asylum systems is seriously affected by the lack of prompt return' of such persons.[98]

When the European Commission first proposed a Directive on common standards on return, UNHCR welcomed the proposal for an instrument as a 'key component of a comprehensive migration management policy which takes into account the responsibilities of States of origin, transit and

---

95. For the legal basis for Community action on return, see Amsterdam Treaty, article 63(3) (b), op cit note 4, establishing the power to adopt 'measures on immigration policy [...] in the area of illegal immigration and illegal residence, including repatriation of illegal residents'. See also European Commission Communication on a Common Policy on Illegal Immigration, COM(2001) 672 final, 15.11.2001; Green Paper on a Community Return Policy, 10.04.02; Commission Communication on a Community Return Policy on Illegal Residents, COM(2002) 564 final, 14.10.02; European Council, Return Action Programme, 28.11.02. In the last document, the Council called for improved operational co-operation among Member States, intensified co-operation with third countries and the establishment of common standards with the aim of facilitating operational return.
96. OJ C 53/6, 3.3.2005, section 1.6.4.
97. OJ C 53/6, 3.3.2005, section 1.6.4.
98. EXCOM Conclusion No. 96(LIV)2003 on the return of persons found not to be in need of international protection.

destination as well as the rights of the affected individuals.'[99] In addition to Member States' interest in ensuring more efficiency in returns, many in the asylum advocacy community also saw an opportunity to lay down valuable safeguards and restraints on the manner in which returns could be conducted. Tragic cases had been documented in which serious injuries or death had occurred after excessive force was used in the course of involuntary returns, and strong criticism had been levelled at some Member States about the conditions and terms of pre-removal detention, the handling of children and families, and other unregulated areas. With the expectation of a large financial programme to support returns after 2007,[100] it was felt that Community standards were needed to regulate, harmonise and make transparent the return activities on which significant amounts of EU taxpayers' funds would be spent.[101]

While accepting the general idea of common standards, UNHCR in its initial response laid down a number of cautions and recommendations[102] about the text as proposed, bearing in mind also the political context in which migration control objectives were (and remain) dominant. Welcoming requirements that the proposed Directive's provisions be applied in line with international law, including refugee protection and human rights standards, UNHCR argued that those standards, and specific procedures to ensure their implementation, should be set out in more detail. In particular, UNHCR called for the draft Directive explicitly to state that no return decision may be issued and no removal carried out which would violate the *non-refoulement* principle in Article 33 of the 1951 Convention or related human rights instruments. Despite the fact that this would have recalled binding and undisputed principles of the *acquis*, the recommendation was not taken up.

UNHCR also noted that particular safeguards were needed in relation to the proposed removal or return to third countries of asylum-seekers whose applications had not been determined on substance in a Member State. In those cases, it was submitted that removal should be implemented only if access to an asylum procedure in the third country would be assured, and

---

99. UNHCR, 'Observations on the EC's Proposal for a Directive on Common Standards and procedures in Member States for returning illegally staying third-country nationals, COM(2005)291', Dec. 2005, at: http://www.unhcr.org/cgi-bin/texis/vtx/protect/opendoc.pdf?tbl=PROTECTION&id=43a6c2352
100. See the proposal for the Return Fund as under discussion at that time, 'Solidarity and Management of Migration Flows', COM(2005)123 of 6.4.05.
101. The final amount of the Return Fund as ultimately agreed in 2007 will be EUR 676 million for the period 2008-2013.
102. *Op cit.,* note 98.

to effective protection where required. In this connection, the need for effective monitoring mechanisms was also stressed by UNHCR and others, to ensure that such safeguards and arrangements would be respected, as well to help efforts to achieve sustainable return. These recommendations were also not taken up.

The concerns of UNHCR and others about the risks of removal to persecution are real. The Asylum Procedures Directive[103] permits wide-ranging safe third country rules at national level, accelerated procedures which could be applied to people on formal grounds without regard to the strength of their claims and non-suspensive appeals against negative decisions. These provisions all mean that people could be removed to countries in which they could be exposed to the risk of persecution or serious harm, or from which they could be further expelled to countries where they would be at risk. Nevertheless, the proposed Returns Directive has retained its wide scope, permitting removal of asylum- seekers prior to a substantive claim determination. This wide scope has been retained throughout two years of Council negotiations, and was not challenged in a Report adopted by the relevant European Parliament Committee in late 2007.[104]

In addition, the proposal incorporated a provision to establish a mandatory, EU-wide re-entry ban of five years on all people who would be forcibly removed under the Directive. The option was also left open to States to impose such a ban on people ordered to leave, who had not yet complied with the return decision.[105] While the text provided that the ban should 'not prejudice the right to seek asylum in the European Union', it is hard to see how this qualification would be applicable in practice. There is always a possibility that circumstances may change in the removed person's country of origin, or in his or her profile or activities, which could create a need for international protection. But without clear provisions setting out an accessible procedure through which the ban could be challenged and lifted, it is likely that the re-entry ban would constitute an insurmountable obstacle for people potentially in need of protection to secure access to EU territory.

---

103. *Op cit.*, note 9.
104. Report on the proposal for a directive of the European Parliament and of the Council on common standards and procedures in Member States for returning illegally staying third-country nationals (COM(2005)0391), Committee on Civil Liberties, Justice and Home Affairs, 20.09.2007.
105. COM(2005)291, Article 9.

At the time of writing, the European Parliament, after intensive debate which exposed significant divisions along political lines, is about to vote in plenary on a report proposing extensive amendments to the draft, some of which raise protection-related concerns, including those expressed above. Meanwhile, differences persisted also in the Council – although on different grounds. A number of Member States were reportedly opposed to provisions in the draft which were seen to be too strongly focused on the rights of returnees. Nevertheless, both the Council and Parliament were hopeful of reaching conclusions – which would then provide a basis for them to begin negotiating with each other on the text. As one of the first instruments for adoption under the co-decision procedure for asylum and immigration, it is an important test of the ability of the Council and Parliament to reach agreement in this sensitive area. But with vast gaps between their positions, a risk exists that no common standards will be agreed.

The outcome of such a stalemate would be a text with none of the sought-after safeguards for individual rights, and scope for Member States to undertake returns without reference to any common standards. In a Union where removal is permitted of asylum-seekers whose claims have not been examined in substance, and the quality of asylum decision-making is acknowledged as needing improvement,[106] this can only raise concerns about the risk of violations of international refugee law.

IV. Conclusion

It could be argued that the inevitable result of EU migration control policy will be that non-EU countries will have to bear a greater share of the responsibility – and the cost, in financial and other terms – of hosting and providing for people in need of protection. As a result of reinforced controls at the EU's external frontiers, non-EU States along its outer perimeter will necessarily be left with more people who could have claims to refugee protection. This applies both to land and sea borders, and to situations where people may be intercepted or rescued in international waters or conceivably in the waters of third States – where they could be turned back to those States' shores. With several bilateral agreements in place between southern EU Member States and some West and North

---

106. Green paper on the future Common European Asylum System (COM(2007)301), 6.6.2007, at:http://eur-lex.europa.eu/LexUriServ/LexUriServ.do?uri=CELEX:52007 DC0301:EN:NOT

African countries, the potential for this practice to affect large numbers of people is great. Some of those turned back will inevitably be in need of international protection, and the risk arises that they will be returned to persecution, directly or indirectly, as a result.

Readmission agreements can also serve to externalize responsibility for international protection, if they are applied to people who are rejected before their asylum claims have been examined in substance in the EU, including under wide-ranging 'safe third country' rules. While the EU's readmission agreements contain standard wording on the need for parties to respect the 1951 Convention, it is not evident that these provisions are applied in practice, monitored or enforced. The EU's readmission efforts generally are backed by a large injection of financial support for the partner country, in particular for the building of detention centres to hold third country nationals who are sent back. Without any agreement on common standards to govern the conduct of return, risks arise that basic rights will not be respected, including those of refugees.

Relationships and agreements with third countries, including for the provision of financial assistance, are increasingly focused on migration management priorities. The EU has invested considerable political effort in encouraging (or compelling) non-EU countries more effectively to control their borders, including through enlargement negotiations, the European Neighbourhood Policy, region-specific processes and instruments and others. It would appear, however, that there is a danger that the message on asylum which non-EU states should receive from the Union is being lost. Capacity-building activities on migration management, supported readily by the EU in many countries, frequently focus on control-related systems, tools and infrastructure.

EU capacity-building in the area of asylum can significantly improve the likelihood of protection being offered to those in need, if it is well-targeted, sufficiently resourced, and planned and implemented in a collaborative spirit with the States concerned. However, it should not be undertaken with the aim of containing refugees in countries and regions outside the EU, and should also be coupled with an EU commitment to share the responsibility of those countries by implementing significant refugee resettlement programmes. Efforts to transfer responsibility for providing protection to refugees are not only potentially contrary to international law, but have the potential to undermine the international protection system as a whole. This is not in the long-term interests of the European Union, nor its relations with third countries.

5. Schengen/Dublin: The Association Agreements with Iceland, Norway, and Switzerland

Fabrice Filliez[1]

I.   Introduction

France, Germany, Belgium, Luxembourg and the Netherlands decided in 1985 to create an area without internal borders. The first agreement between the five original group members was signed on 14 June 1985[2] and a further implementing convention was signed on 19 June 1990 (Schengen Convention).[3] When it came into effect in 1995, it abolished the internal borders of the signatory States and created a single external border where immigration checks for the Schengen area were carried out.

Step by step, the Schengen area has been extended to include most EU Member States. Italy signed the agreement on 27 November 1990, Spain and Portugal joined on 25 June 1991, Greece followed on 6 November 1992, then Austria on 28 April 1995. Denmark, Finland and Sweden finally joined on 19 December 1996. In February 1995, just after the accession of Sweden and Finland to the European Union (EU)[4], the Heads of State of the Nordic countries decided to initiate cooperation with the Schengen States with the aim to maintain the Nordic Passport Union,[5] which was the

1.   The opinions expressed are those of the author and not necessarily of the Institution for which he works.
2.   Agreement of 14 June 1985 between the Governments of the States of the Benelux Economic Union, the Federal Republic of Germany and the French Republic on the gradual abolition of checks at their common borders, OJ L 239, 22.9.2000, p. 13.
3.   Convention of 19 June 1990 implementing the Schengen Agreement of 14 June 1985 between the Governments of the States of the Benelux Economic Union, the Federal Republic of Germany and the French Republic on the gradual abolition of checks at their common border, OJ L 239, 22.9.2000, p. 19.
4.   See joint declaration on Nordic Cooperation in the Accession treaties of the Republic of Austria, the Kingdom of Sweden, the Republic of Finland and the Kingdom of Norway to the European Union, OJ C 24, 29.8.1994: "*The Contracting Parties record that Sweden, Finland and Norway, as members of the European Union, intend to continue, in full compliance with Community law and the other provisions of the Treaty on European Union, Nordic Cooperation amongst themselves as well as with other countries and territories*".
5.   Aziza Arifkhanova, *The Origins of the Schengen Agreement*, p. 44 (2006).

existing regime between the five Nordic States pursuant to the Convention on the Abolition of Passport Controls at Intra-Nordic borders of 12 July 1957. The 1996 Schengen accession treaties of Sweden, Finland and Denmark explicitly refer to the need to preserve the Nordic Passport Union, once the Nordic States which are also members of the EU take part in the regime on the abolition of checks on persons at internal borders set out in the Schengen agreements.[6] That political statement was an important element which made it possible to open the Schengen cooperation to the non EU-members Norway and Iceland.

This contribution gives an overview of co-operation between Schengen and third countries, focusing specifically on the associated States. It is divided into four main sections. The first section describes the early days of Schengen and the first Cooperation Agreement concluded in 1996 between Schengen and Iceland and Norway. It also gives a short presentation on the integration of the Schengen acquis into the institutional framework of the EU, highlighting the specific consequences for Denmark, the United Kingdom, Ireland, Norway and Iceland. It then describes the main features of the 1999 Association Agreement with Iceland and Norway. The second section is devoted to Switzerland. The historical background of the negotiations and the general political process are outlined. Some legal questions that arose with the adoption of the EU negotiating mandate are taken up. In addition, the main features of the Association Agreement with Switzerland are described, including the possible future participation of Liechtenstein. In a third section, the functioning of Schengen and the specific issue of the Schengen-relevance of acts adopted by the EU institutions are discussed. This issue is important because it decides whether the associated States do or do not participate in the decision-shaping. Some elements of the recent practice of the EU Council with regard to this difficult issue are underlined. Finally, the last section gives an overview of the ratification procedures in Switzerland and in the EU, including the role of the European Parliament.

---

6. Stephen Kabera Karanja, *Norwegian Border Control in a Europe without International Frontiers*, Complex 6/01, p. 15 (2001).

II. Cooperation between Schengen and Iceland and Norway

A. The 1996 Cooperation Agreement with Iceland and Norway

The question of accepting non Member States in Schengen had to be addressed as a consequence of the accession of Finland and Sweden to the European Union. Full membership in Schengen was restricted to EU Member States in accordance with Article 140 of the Schengen Convention. In order to enable Denmark and the new Member States Sweden and Finland to become parties to the Schengen Convention without prejudice to the Nordic Passport Union, the Schengen Executive Committee adopted two decisions. One granted observer status to Denmark, Finland and Sweden.[7] The other invited Iceland and Norway to attend as observers, and from 1 May 1996, they attended all Schengen meetings with a view to concluding a Cooperation Agreement.[8] Denmark, Finland and Sweden finally signed the Schengen Convention in December 1996[9], when the other two Nordic Passport Union members and non-EU countries, Norway and Iceland, were given associate membership.[10]

The Cooperation Agreement granted specific participation rights to Norway and Iceland.[11] While not being EU members, these two countries accepted the Convention as well as the full Schengen acquis thus agreeing to all Schengen obligations. The only difference with Schengen Member States was that Iceland and Norway were formally not allowed to vote. They were, however, fully involved in the decision-shaping process and, for all practical purposes, they were also involved in decision-taking. Accordingly, they had to accept all subsequent decisions emanating from

7. Decision of the Schengen Executive Committee, SCH/Com-ex (96) 3.
8. Decision of the Schengen Executive Committee, SCH/Com-ex (96) 4.
9. Agreement on the Accession of the Kingdom of Denmark to the Convention implementing the Schengen Agreement of 14 June 1985 on the gradual abolition of checks at the common borders signed at Schengen on 19 June 1990, OJ L 239, 22.9.2000, p. 96; Agreement on the Accession of the Republic of Finland to the Convention implementing the Schengen Agreement of 14 June 1985 on the gradual abolition of checks at the common borders signed at Schengen on 19 June 1990, OJ L 239, 22.9.2000, p. 106; Agreement on the Accession of the Republic of Sweden to the Convention implementing the Schengen Agreement of 14 June 1985 on the gradual abolition of checks at the common borders signed at Schengen on 19 June 1990, OJ L 239, 22.9.2000, p. 115.
10. Illka Laitinen, Latest Developments of Schengen: Implementation in the Nordic Countries, in: Claudia Faria (ed.), *Managing Migration Flows and Preventing Illegal Immigration: Schengen –Justice and Home Affairs Colloquium,* 2002.
11. No publication source available for the 1996 Cooperation Agreement.

the Schengen process, or otherwise they would have been expelled from Schengen co-operation.[12] In substance, Iceland and Norway were involved in all measures proposed on the basis of the Schengen agreement, and since every measure was – by definition – Schengen related, Iceland and Norway participated in all working parties and in all of the debates. However, this does not include the actual decision-taking in Schengen which can be seen as a downside of the Schengen association for the associated countries. However, this position was in line with the political objectives of Iceland and Norway to fully participate in all Schengen developments. The solution found can be considered as balanced from the point of view of the associated States. It must be underlined that no other association agreement has granted similarly far-reaching decision-shaping rights to third States, not even the European Economic Area.[13]

B. Integration of the Schengen acquis into the legal framework of the EU/EC

1. The Schengen Protocol of the Amsterdam Treaty

At Maastricht, EEC cooperation became EC and EU cooperation, and with the third pillar (Title VI EU), the EU entered into the field of justice and home affairs. In the years between the entry into force of the Maastricht Treaty and the signing of the Amsterdam Treaty, third pillar cooperation in the EU not only led to the adoption of many instruments, but also to the creation of a specific structure in the Commission and the Council dealing with the new forms of cooperation. When the Maastricht Treaty extended EU competence to the fields of Justice and Home Affairs (new Title K), the integration of the Schengen acquis into the EU became unavoidable. The legal bases created in the Schengen agreement were indeed so broad that they covered large parts of Title VI TEU and Title IV EC, and it would have been inconceivable to let Schengen co-exist with the EU/EC Treaty, thus allowing a number of EU Member States to do together what they should do in the broader context under the EU/EC Treaties. Unsurprisingly, therefore, a Protocol attached to the Treaty of Amsterdam incorporates Schengen into

---

12. Niels Bracke, *Presentation of the Development of Schengen Co-operation with Iceland and Norway*, Seminar in Reykjavik, 19 September 2003, not published.
13. See Jean-Claude Piris, *Justice and Home Affairs and the EEA Agreement – Integration?* Seminar in Reykjavic, 8 September 2006, not published yet.

the European Union framework (Schengen Protocol).[14] The Schengen area is in fact the first concrete example of enhanced cooperation between thirteen EU Member States. In accordance with Article 1 of the Schengen Protocol, this cooperation between the Schengen States shall be conducted within the institutional and legal framework of the European Union and with respect for the relevant provisions of the EU and of the EC.[15]

In order to make this integration possible, the EU Council took a number of decisions.[16] Firstly, the Council took the place of the Executive Committee created under the Schengen Agreement, and on 1 May 1999 it established a procedure for incorporating the Schengen Secretariat into the General Secretariat of the Council.[17] Subsequently, new working groups were set up in the Council to manage the work. Secondly, the Council also had to select those acts from among the provisions and measures taken by the signatory states, which formed a genuine Schengen *acquis*, i.e. a body of law which could serve as a basis for further cooperation. A list of the elements which made up the acquis, setting out the corresponding legal basis for each of them in the Treaties (EC or EU), was adopted on 20 May 1999.[18]

---

14. Treaty of Amsterdam, Protocol integrating the Schengen acquis into the framework of the European Union (Schengen Protocol), OJ C 340, 10.11.1997, p. 93; Charles Elsen, Incorporation juridique et institutionnelle de Schengen dans l'UE, in: Monica de Boer (ed), *Schengen still going strong*, p. 11-20 (2000).

15. Monica Den Boer, The Incorporation of Schengen into the EU: a Bridge Too Far?, in: Jörg Monar and Wolfgang Wessels (eds), *The European Union after the Treaty of Amsterdam*, (2001). Also Jaap De Zwaan, Schengen and its Incorporation into the New Treaty: The Negotiating Process, in: Monica den Boer (ed.), *Schengen's Final Days? The Incorporation of Schengen into the New EU, External Borders and Information Systems*, (1998).

16. Some of the texts quoted are reproduced in: Henri Labayle et Anne Weyembergh, *Code de droit pénal de l'Union européenne*, 1134 p. (2005)

17. Council Decision (EC) No 307/1999 of 1 May 1999 laying down the detailed arrangements for the integration of the Schengen Secretariat into the General Secretariat of the Council, OJ L 119, 7.5.1999, p. 49.

18. Council Decision (EC) No 435/1999 of 20 May 1999 concerning the definition of the Schengen acquis for the purpose of determining, in conformity with the relevant provisions of the Treaty establishing the European Community and the Treaty on European Union, the legal basis for each of the provisions or decisions which constitute the acquis, OJ L 176, 10.7.1999, p. 1; Council Decision (EC) No 436/1999 of 20 May 1999 determining, in conformity with the relevant provisions of the Treaty establishing the European Community and the Treaty on European Union, the legal basis for each of the provisions or decisions which constitute the Schengen acquis, OJ L 176, 10.7.1999, p. 17, corrigendum: OJ L 9, 13.1.2000; The Schengen acquis as referred to in Article 1 (2) of Council Decision 1999/435/EC of 20 May 1999 is published in OJ L 239, 22.9.2000, p. 1-473.

2.   *The new Schengen Association Agreement with Norway and Iceland*

By incorporating Schengen into the EU framework, the future of cooperation between Schengen and Iceland and Norway became unclear and required a special solution. To allow the two non-EU states to continue participating in Schengen, a new agreement had to be concluded, and for that reason, Article 6 of the Schengen Protocol requires the Council to conclude two agreements with Norway and Iceland so as to allow their continued participation in Schengen.[19] Under the Association Agreement that was signed between Iceland, Norway and the EU on 18 May 1999[20], these two countries continue to participate in the drafting of new legal instruments building on the Schengen acquis. Even though these acts are adopted by the EU Member States alone, they apply to Iceland and Norway as well.

Together with this new agreement, the Council adopted a Decision laying down the areas in which the Mixed Committee would operate in the future and providing a procedure to solve the question whether an act or a measure builds upon the Schengen acquis and is therefore relevant for the Mixed Committee or not (Schengen-relevant act).[21] The question of Schengen-relevance is of importance and will be discussed below.

3.   *The position of the United Kingdom and Ireland*

In the Amsterdam Treaty the United Kingdom and Ireland negotiated an opt-out provision enabling them to join Schengen fully or in part, in accordance with Article 4 of the Schengen Protocol, and under the condition that the other Schengen States would agree unanimously.[22]

19. Michael Emerson, Marius Vahl, Stephen Woolcock, Navigating by the Stars – Norway, the European Economic Area and the European Union, p. 72-81 (2000).
20. Council Decision (EC) No 439/1999 of 17 May 1999 on the conclusion of the Agreement with the Republic of Iceland and the Kingdom of Norway concerning the latter's association with the implementation, application and development of the Schengen acquis, OJ L 176, 10.7.1999, p. 17.
21. Council Decision (EC) 1999/437 of 17 May 1999 on certain arrangements for the application of the Agreement concluded by the Council of the European Union and the Republic of Iceland and the Kingdom of Norway concerning the association of those two States with the implementation, application and development of the Schengen acquis, OJ 176, 10.7.1999, p. 31. See section IV.
22. Schengen Protocol, *op. cit.* note 14; also Treaty of Amsterdam, Protocol on the application of certain aspects of Article 14 of the Treaty establishing the European Community to the United Kingdom and to Ireland, OJ C 340, 10.11.1997, p. 97.

The United Kingdom[23] and Ireland[24] do indeed participate in certain provisions of the Schengen acquis, in accordance with the decisions taken on the basis of the Schengen Protocol, and these countries were granted a wide participation, in particular in police and judicial cooperation. Parts of the Schengen acquis were put into effect by the United Kingdom on 1 January 2005.[25] The Council Decision concerning Ireland's request to take part in some of the provisions of the Schengen acquis has not yet been fully implemented. Both countries however keep their special position in respect of matters covered by Title IV of the EC Treaty, as recognised in two special Protocols.[26] Accordingly, both States remain excluded from all provisions concerning external borders of the 1990 Schengen Convention and subsequent developments of the Schengen acquis.[27]

On the basis of the second indent of Article 6 of the Schengen Protocol, the Council also signed an Agreement with Norway and Iceland governing the relations between these two countries, on the one hand, and the United Kingdom and Ireland (to the extent that Ireland and the United Kingdom, or both, participate in the Schengen acquis), on the other.[28] The agreement enables Iceland and Norway and the United Kingdom and Ireland to co-operate through the Mixed Committee on areas which apply to these States in accordance with the rules laid down in the Association Agreement.

23. Council Decision (EC) No 365/2000 of 29 May 2000 concerning the request of the United Kingdom of Great Britain and Northern Ireland to take part in some of the provisions of the Schengen acquis, OJ L 131, 1.6.2000, p. 43.
24. Council Decision (EC) No 192/2002 of 28 February 2002 concerning Ireland's request to take part in some of the provisions of the Schengen acquis, OJ L 64, 7.3.2002, p. 20.
25. Council Decision (EC) No 2004/926 of 22 December 2004 on the putting into effect of parts of the Schengen acquis by the United Kingdom of Great Britain and Northern Ireland, OJ L 395, 31.12.2004, p. 70.
26. Protocol on the position of United Kingdom and Ireland and in the Protocol on the application of certain aspects of Article 14 of the EC Treaty to the United Kingdom and Ireland, OJ C 340, 10.11.1997, p. 99 and p. 97.
27. In more detail on the arrangements concerning the UK and Ireland the contribution by Martenczuk in this book.
28. Council Decision (EC) No 29/2000 of 28 June 1999 on the conclusion of the Agreement with the Republic of Iceland and the Kingdom of Norway on the establishment of rights and obligations between Ireland and the United Kingdom of Great Britain and Northern Ireland, on the one hand, and the Republic of Iceland and the Kingdom of Norway, on the other, in areas of the Schengen acquis which apply to these States, OJ L 15, 20.1.2000, p. 1.

4. The Position of Denmark

Denmark has an opt-out under the Amsterdam Treaty for all measures adopted by the Council pursuant to Title IV TCE and cannot participate in the adoption of developments of the Schengen Acquis by the Council, but may decide, according to Article 5 of the Protocol on the position of Denmark, to transpose them into its national law and to apply them as obligations under international law.[29] Under Article 3 of the Schengen Protocol, Denmark maintains the same rights and obligations with respect to the Schengen signatory states. It fully participates in the third pillar measures.

5. The Dublin Association Agreement with Iceland and Norway

The European Community also entered into an agreement with Norway and Iceland concerning the criteria and mechanisms for establishing the State responsible for examining a request for asylum (Dublin acquis), which is intricately linked to the Schengen acquis.[30] In accordance with Article 12 of that agreement, Denmark may request to participate and it did request such a participation by letter dated 16 February 2001, which again required clarification of the conditions for such participation (by the Contracting Parties acting with the consent of Denmark), in a protocol to the agreement. Before the protocol could be negotiated, it was necessary, in the first place, for Denmark and the European Community to conclude an agreement to settle, in particular, the coordination between the Community and Denmark regarding international agreements.[31] That agreement was concluded by the European Community (and is thus binding for the Member States by virtue of Article 300 (7) EC) and entered

---

29. Treaty of Amsterdam, Protocol on the position of Denmark, OJ C 340, 10.11.1997, p. 101.
30. Council Decision (EC) No 258/2001 of 15 March 2001 concerning the conclusion of an Agreement between the European Community and the Republic of Iceland and the Kingdom of Norway concerning the criteria and mechanisms for establishing the State responsible for examining a request for asylum lodged in a Member State or Iceland or Norway, OJ L 93, 3.4.2001, p. 38.
31. Council Decision (EC) No 188/2006 of 21 February 2006 on the conclusion of the Agreement between the European Community and the Kingdom of Denmark extending to Denmark the provisions of Council Regulation (EC) No 343/2003 establishing the criteria and mechanisms for determining the Member State responsible for examining an asylum application lodged in one of the Member States by a third-country national and Council Regulation (EC) No 2725/2000 concerning the establishment of Eurodac for the comparison of fingerprints for the effective application of the Dublin Convention, OJ L 66, 8.3.2006, p. 37.

into force on 1 April 2006.[32] Subsequent to that agreement, a protocol was concluded between the European Community and Iceland and Norway to set the conditions under which Denmark participates in the Association Agreement between the European Community, Iceland and Norway and in particular to establish rights and obligations between Iceland and Norway and Denmark.[33]

By opting into the adoption and application of the Dublin II regulation and the Eurodac regulation[34], the United Kingdom and Ireland were allowed to participate in the conclusion procedure of the Association Agreement which became binding for them.

C. Main features of the 1999 Schengen Association Agreement with Iceland and Norway

The main features of the new Association Agreement, based on the first indent of Article 6 of the Schengen Protocol, can be summarized as follows:[35]

Procedurally, Iceland and Norway have the same position as they had during the Schengen days. However, instead of being observers, in Council bodies, they became member, of the so-called Mixed Committee. This reflects the fact that outside observers are not allowed to participate in Council meetings, with the exception of candidate countries for EU accession during the interim period between the signature of the act of accession and its entry into force. The Mixed Committee is a body working from a legal point of view "outside the institutional structure of the Union".[36] The Mixed Committee allows Iceland and Norway to be fully involved in the decision-shaping process of Schengen-relevant EU/EC measures, but decision taking will take place in Council bodies. They can also make draft proposals; these proposals must, however, be taken over and formally introduced by the Commission or one of the Member States in accordance with the provisions of the EC or the EU Treaty. The Mixed

32. Information concerning the entry into force, OJ L 96, 5.4.2006, p. 9.
33. Council Decision (EC) No 167/2006 of 21 February 2006 on the conclusion of a Protocol to the Agreement between the European Community and the Republic of Iceland and the Kingdom of Norway concerning the criteria and mechanisms for establishing the State responsible for examining a request for asylum lodged in a Member State or in Iceland or Norway, OJ L 57, 28.2.2006, p. 15.
34. Council Doc 13427/01, 13428/01 and 9568/02, http://register.consilium.europa.eu
35. Peter Cullen, The Schengen Agreement with Iceland and Norway: Its Main Features, 4 [2001] ERA – Forum, p. 71-75.
36. Preamble of the Association Agreement, Recital 8.

Committee will normally meet at Working Party and Article 36 Committee level, but it can also meet at the level of COREPER or Council. In practice the Mixed Committee works quite well.[37]

Acts adopted by the EU institutions following this procedure have to be accepted and implemented by Norway and Iceland. In case of non-acceptance, their co-operation with the EU would normally be terminated automatically.[38] In case of acceptance obligations are created under international law between the EU and Iceland and Norway. The Agreement contains a procedure to guarantee a homogeneous interpretation of the Schengen acquis by all partners. In case of conflict about the interpretation or application of the acquis or the application of the Agreement itself, a conflict resolution procedure is foreseen, which in last resort could result in the termination of the Agreement.

The Agreement not only provides for the formal decision-shaping procedure in the Mixed Committee as set out before, but also states that the Mixed Committee shall be informed about relevant topics which, although not regarded as Schengen development, are still of importance for Iceland and Norway. This second procedure does not, however, provide for anything more than that Norway and Iceland are informed about these topics, without providing for any involvement of Norway and Iceland in the decision-shaping process related to these issues.[39]

III. Switzerland and Schengen

A. The bilateral agreements of 1999

The legal bases of the relationship between Switzerland and the EU are the Free Trade Agreement of 1972, around twenty important bilateral agreements and over one hundred minor agreements of varying scope and significance.[40] Following the rejection of the European Economic Area (EEA) in 1992, the membership application lodged by Switzerland earlier that year was not withdrawn, but frozen. In order to minimise the negative

---

37. Niels Bracke, Norway and Iceland: an Adventure in the Field of Justice and Home Affairs, in Gilles de Kerchove and Anne Weyembergh (eds), *Sécurité et justice: enjeu de la politique extérieure de l'Union européenne*, p. 225 (2003).
38. Cf. Article 8 (4) of the Agreement between the Schengen Association Agreement with Norway and Iceland.
39. Art. 5 of the Association Agreement.
40. An overview can be found on the website of the European Integration Office, http://www.europa.admin.ch/themen/

consequences of the refusal of the EEA, Switzerland started in 1994 a lengthy process of negotiation of seven bilateral agreements with the EU.[41] The agreements were signed in 1999 and entered into force in June 2002.[42]

Over the years Switzerland gradually became an "island" surrounded by EU Member States, and even though it never became an EU member, it nonetheless kept very close relations with the EU.[43] Through its specific geographic and economic position, Switzerland is increasingly dependent on and directly affected by the decisions taken in Brussels – including for example EU decisions on the important issues of internal security, migration, asylum. This contradiction between non-membership on the one hand and close involvement and interdependence on the other[44], presents a series of challenges for Switzerland, especially in the field of Justice and Home Affairs.[45]

B.   The Swiss interest in an association to the Schengen/Dublin cooperation

From the beginning, Switzerland closely followed Schengen developments and it indicated its interest at an early stage.[46] In October 1990, an "Expert Commission on Border Controls" was established to study the impact of Schengen on Switzerland. In its intermediate report of 1991, the commission was of the opinion that without accession, Switzerland would degenerate into an "island of insecurity" and become the "country of last asylum" for asylum seekers whose applications were refused in EC/EU countries. Informal meetings also took place with the so-called Schengen Presidency. The final report published on 31 January 1993 came to the

---

41. Concerning free movement of persons, air and land transport, agriculture, research, public procurement and the mutual recognition of conformity assessments.

42. For a general overview Christine Kaddous, The Relations between the EU and Switzerland, in: Alan Dashwood et Marc Maresceau (eds), *Recent Trends in External Relations of the EU*, 45 p. to be published (2007).

43. Marius Vahl, Nina Grolimund, *Integration without Membership – Switzerland's Bilateral Agreements with the European Union*, p. 36 (2006)

44. Fabrice Filliez and Hanspeter Mock, La Suisse et l'Union européenne: état des lieux d'une relation *sui generis*, 14 [2006] Journal des tribunaux – Droit européen 130, p. 161-167.

45. For a general overview, Daniel Möckli, Schengen und Dublin: Die Bedeutung der europäischen Zusammenarbeit in den Bereichen Justiz und Inneres für die Schweiz, in: Kurt Spillmann and Andreas Wenger (eds), *Bulletin 2001 zum schweizerischen Sicherheitspolitik*, (2001).

46. For a historical overview, see Philippe Kaeser, Le dilemne de Schengen, La Suisse face au projet de politique migratoire européenne, 107 p. (1997).

conclusion that it was not in the interest of Switzerland to remain outside of Schengen and that the best solution would be to find a kind of association with Schengen.[47] The report suggested to enter into exploratory talks on Schengen and possibly also on Dublin.[48]

In June 1995, the Swiss Federal Council commissioned an expert group to analyse the consequences of the entry into force of the Schengen Convention. The expert group delivered its report on 15 September 1997 and recommended exploring the possibilities of a partial association to Schengen.[49] In the second half of 1997, Austria took over the presidency of the Schengen Executive Committee and it declared that an intensification of police cooperation with Switzerland would be one of the focal points of its working programme. In 1998, the German Schengen Presidency made a proposal to the Schengen Executive Committee to progressively integrate Switzerland into the Schengen area, but on 16 September 1998, the Executive Committee opposed any form of cooperation with Switzerland. They argued that Schengen would soon be integrated in the institutional framework of the European Union and that any form of partial cooperation with Switzerland would be out of the question.

Concerning asylum, the EFTA States were invited in 1992 to conclude a parallel agreement to the Dublin Convention.[50] Negotiations could not start because it was necessary to first wait for the entry into force of the Convention[51] and then some Member States suggested waiting until the conclusion of the bilateral negotiations with Switzerland, in particular the agreement on free movement of persons.

47. Message du Conseil fédéral relatif à l'approbation des accords bilatéraux II entre la Suisse et l'UE du 1er octobre 2004, FF 2004 5593, p. 5689.
48. Convention determining the State responsible for examining applications for asylum lodged in one of the Member States of the European Communities – Dublin Convention, OJ C 254, 19.8.1997, p. 1.
49. See the answer of the Swiss Federal Council of 25 February 1998 to the Swiss Parliament on the consequences of the exclusion of Switzerland of the Schengen agreements, Interpellation 97.3676, www.parlament.ch.
50. The Convention, signed in Dublin on 15 June 1990, entered into force on 1 September 1997 for the twelve original signatories, on 1 October 1997 for Austria and Sweden and on 1 January 1998 for Finland, OJ L 242, 4.9.1997, p. 63, OJ L 176, 20.6.1998, p. 39.
51. See Press Release 6712/93 (Presse 90) of the Council, Meeting of the Ministers responsible for Immigration, Copenhagen, 1-2 June 1993: "They therefore asked the Presidency to continue talks with a view to the conclusion in due course of parallel Convention with other interested European States; negotiations proper could not take place until the Dublin Convention had been ratified by the twelve Member States".

C.   Paving the way towards a new set of bilateral agreements

1.   The so-called "left-overs"

After conclusion of the first set of bilateral agreements[52], the EU and Switzerland explored how to proceed from there. The parties had already made joint declarations indicating an interest to negotiate agreements in a number of other sectors, the so-called "left-overs".[53] In an additional declaration, Switzerland reaffirmed its wish to reinforce cooperation with the EU and its Member States in the area of migration and asylum policy, and it proposed negotiations for the conclusion of a convention parallel to the Dublin Convention.[54]

2.   New areas of interest for the EU and Switzerland

In addition to the "left-overs", the EU expressed an interest to come to an agreement with Switzerland in two other areas, which were considered to be a priority[55]: the fight against fraud and other illegal activities affecting the EU's financial interests[56] and the adoption of equivalent measures by Switzerland (and other third countries) in the area of taxation of savings income in accordance with the conclusions of the European Council of Santa Maria da Feira of 19-20 June 2000.

Switzerland, for its part, expressed an interest to include as part of the items to be discussed the cooperation in justice, police, asylum and migration matters[57], and explicitly mentioned Schengen/Dublin.

---

52. Cédric Dupont and Pascal Sciarini, Back to the future, the first round of bilateral negotiations with the EU, in: Clive H. Church (ed), *Switzerland and the European Union*, p. 202-214 (2007).
53. Processed agricultural products, Swiss participation in Community programmes regarding training, youth and media, Swiss participation in the European Environment Agency, Liberalisation of service provisions on the basis of the acquis communautaire, co-operation in the area of statistics.
54. Swiss Declaration attached to the Final Act to Agreement between the European Community and its Member States, of the one part, and the Swiss Confederation, of the other, on the free movement of persons, OJ L 114, 30.4.2002, p. 71.
55. Council Doc 9524/01, 18.6.2001, http://register.consilium.europa.eu.
56. A mandate authorising the Commission to negotiate with Switzerland a cooperation agreement to combat fraud was adopted by the Council on 14 December 2000.
57. Letters of Federal Counsellor Joseph Deiss of 31 January 2001 to Commissioners Patten and Vitorino, and of 23 February 2001 to Commissioner Patten; Letter of Mr. von Däniken, State Secretary in the Swiss Federal Department of Foreign Affairs to Mr. Lars Danielson, State Secretary for International and EU Affairs in the Swedish Cabinet Office, dated 5 June 2001, all letters are reproduced in Council Doc 9524/01.

As illustrated above, Schengen is of utmost importance to the internal security of Switzerland. An association of Switzerland to Schengen and Dublin was therefore considered as crucial to strengthen domestic security and fight against illegal immigration.[58] Excluded from increasingly intensive EU co-operation in matters of internal security and asylum, Switzerland expressed its wish to intensify its co-operation in the fields of justice and home affairs.[59] With the entry into force of the agreement on free movement of persons, on 1 June 2002, a pre-requisite set by the EU for an association to Schengen/Dublin was fulfilled.[60]

3. A long political process to launch negotiations

The Council Presidency declared the EU's willingness to conduct exploratory talks with Switzerland. A letter of 1 March 2001 from the President of the European Council, Prime Minister Persson, to the President of the Swiss Confederation, restated the interest of the Union to start formal negotiations on increased co-operation in the fight against fraud and on savings tax. For its part, the EU would be prepared to start exploratory talks with Switzerland on the Union's Schengen acquis and the Dublin Convention in order to clarify the conditions under which co-operation could be enhanced. Switzerland made it clear that it was ready to find solutions in both areas of interest to the EU, but made the start of the negotiations dependent on a firm EU commitment that some other issues of prime importance to Switzerland would also be negotiated.[61]

Subsequently, exploratory talks were conducted between the Commission and Switzerland on the areas of possible new negotiations. In the discussions of the EFTA Working Party, a special focus was dedicated to a Swiss participation in the Schengen/Dublin acquis. The Legal Service of the Council was asked to make a written evaluation of the legal instruments required for a Swiss participation in this area.

On 31 May 2001, a coordination meeting was held in Bern between the Commission and the Swiss authorities to review the results of the various

---

58. Fabrice Filliez, Le rapprochement de la Suisse à l'Espace pénal européen à l'exemple des négociations en cours avec l'Union européenne, in: *Sécurité et justice: enjeu de la politique extérieure de l'Union européenne*, p. 231 (2003).
59. Sandra Lavenex, Switzerland: Between Intergovernmental Co-operation and Schengen Association, in: Marina Caparini and Otwin Marenin (eds), *Borders and Security Governance: Managing Borders in a Globalised World*, (2006).
60. Alexandre Afonso and Martino Maggetti, *Bilaterals II: reaching the limits of the Swiss third way?*, in: Clive H. Church (ed), *Switzerland and the European Union*, p. 215-233 (2007).
61. Council Doc 9283/01, 30.5.2001.

exploratory talks and to consider next steps. With regard to procedure, the Commission had suggested that negotiations be started immediately in those four areas where both sides had mandates (fraud, processed agricultural products, statistics, environment). The Swiss side did not, in principle, oppose such an approach with a view to an "early harvest", but stressed the need for a commitment by the EU (a further "positive signal" in addition to the letter of the President of the European Council, Prime Minister Persson of 1 March 2001) to negotiate all issues under consideration, especially a Swiss participation in the Schengen/Dublin acquis. The EFTA Working Party took note of the Swiss desire to receive "a clear political signal from the EU confirming the Union's determination to embark on negotiations in all areas".

The Presidency then considered that a sufficient degree of convergence existed to invite COREPER to request that the technical, institutional and legal questions related to the Swiss request of participation in the Schengen/Dublin acquis be examined without further delay in order to prepare for the discussion of a negotiating mandate. The Commission was asked to propose, at the appropriate time and within its competence, draft mandates to the Council in the respective areas.[62]

Upon recommendation from the Commission, the EU Council adopted its mandate on 17 June 2002. Moreover, the General Affairs Council of 30 September 2002 adopted the following declaration:

> The European Union attaches great importance to achieving a successful outcome, well before the end of the year, to the on-going negotiations with Switzerland on the taxation of savings. (...) The Swiss authorities insisted that the tax negotiations could not start until the EU had adopted the mandates for negotiations in other areas in which Switzerland has shown a particular interest. To accommodate this approach, the EU adopted on 17 June 2002 the relevant mandates. The EU is fully prepared to press ahead in all negotiations with a view to achieving positive results as soon as possible. However, it is in this perspective crucial that the Swiss authorities should adopt the necessary steps so that the negotiations on the taxation of savings make progress quickly. The Council shares the disappointment of ECOFIN Ministers on the lack of progress so far in the negotiations on taxation of savings. Should a successful outcome not be achieved, the Council considers it would be difficult to reach agreement in Council to conclude negotiations with Switzerland in other areas [...].[63]

---

62. Press Release of the 2362nd Council meeting, General Affairs, Luxembourg 25 June 2001, Council Doc 10228/01 (Presse 250)
63. Council Doc 12516/02, minutes of the 2450th meeting of the Council of the European Union (General Affairs and External Relations), held in Brussels on 30 September 2002.

D.   The legal discussion on the negotiating mandate

The question whether an agreement associating Switzerland to Schengen was legally possible was extensively debated and doubts were expressed from the outset.[64] A first question concerned the capacity of Switzerland to fully accept and implement the Schengen Acquis, due to its constitutional complexities (referendum, federalism). A second concern was expressed over the growing institutional complexity of Schengen for the EU[65], whereby extension to third States could be detrimental to legal security and to the homogeneity of the Area of Security, Freedom and Justice. Some felt that it had never been the intention to extend Schengen to third States and that including Switzerland could be a dangerous precedent.[66] As sole exception, Norway and Iceland were admitted on the basis of the Schengen Protocol, which provided a clear legal base for the conclusion of an Association Agreement with Norway and Iceland. Moreover, Norway and Iceland were in a situation that was considered not to be comparable that of Switzerland, given the historic links in the form of the Nordic Passport Union, the pre-existing 1996 Association Agreement, and the participation of Norway and Iceland in the European Economic Area. Moreover, Article 6 of the Schengen Protocol had provided a specific legal basis for the association of Norway and Iceland, which did not exist in the case of Switzerland.

The Council Working Party on EFTA examined the main institutional and legal questions related to Switzerland's possible association with the Schengen acquis and the Dublin Convention after the model of Iceland and Norway's association. Following this examination the Working Party identified the following elements[67]:

Community powers for concluding an agreement with Switzerland would not cover the provisions of the Schengen acquis which came under Title VI EU (notably those relating to police and judicial cooperation). As a result,

---

64.   The following elements are given under the sole responsibility of the author.

65.   On Schengen "variable geometry" and the technical complications, Pieter Jan Kuijper, The Evolution of the Third Pillar from Maastricht to the European Constitution: Institutional Aspects, 41 [2004] *Common Market Law Review,* p. 609-626, 620.

66.   In a 1997 Resolution on the functioning and future of Schengen, the European Parliament expressed the opinion that the inclusion of Norway and Iceland may not set a precedent for the enlargement of Schengen to include other countries which are not members of the European Union, PE 219.570, A4-0014/97.

67.   Partial transcription of the pertinent elements of the outcome of proceedings of the Working Party EFTA, Council Doc 14637/01, public, 28.11.2001.

the conclusion of an agreement with Switzerland in this area would require the application of the procedures laid down by the EU on negotiating and concluding international agreements (Article 24 in conjunction with Article 38 the EU).

An agreement associating Switzerland with the Schengen acquis could be concluded on the basis of the EC (for the parts of the Schengen acquis under Community jurisdiction). As for the relevant legal bases, the options were, firstly, Article 310, and, secondly, the EC articles which allow the Community to implement the Schengen acquis, primarily the relevant provisions of Title IV, and in particular Article 62(1) (in both cases in conjunction with Article 300). In the case of the second option, it should be nonetheless established, in accordance with the case law of the Court of Justice,[68] whether the conclusion of an agreement between the Community and Switzerland would be "necessary" in order to attain the objectives of the Treaty. Whatever the case, on the basis of the ERTA case law of the Court of Justice, the Community would have sole competence for the conclusion of such an agreement since it would inevitably affect the Schengen acquis.[69] Some emphasised that the question of the "necessity" of a possible agreement with Switzerland called for political, rather than legal, considerations, particularly in view of the geographical situation of Switzerland and its links with the Community and its Member States.

Doubts were also expressed on the scope of the Community's external powers, in particular the scope of Article 62(1) of the Treaty and whether this provision, relating to measures at the internal borders (of the Community), allowed the conclusion of an agreement with a third State which had, as its main objective, the abolition of checks on persons at common borders (external borders vis-à-vis that State). Some held the view, however, that it followed from the ERTA case law of the CJEC, and more specifically the Opinion 1/76 on the exercise of the Community's implicit external powers, that Article 62 would allow an agreement on the abolition of controls of persons at borders to be concluded with a third country. In order to dispel these legal doubts, the possibility was raised of submitting a request to the Court of Justice for an opinion on the compatibility of the proposed agreement with the Treaty, pursuant to Article 300 (6) EC. However, this was eventually not pursued further.

In relation to the Dublin Convention, it was noted that the Regulation dealing with the subject matter of the Convention had not yet been

---

68. Opinion 1/76, Laying-up fund for inland waterway vessels, [1977] ECR 741, para. 3.
69. Case 22/70, Commission/Council, [1971] ECR 263, para. 22.

adopted. It was suggested that the Commission could nevertheless already be authorised to start the necessary negotiations on behalf of the Community. However, the agreement could only be concluded after the adoption of the Regulation. The possibility of adopting such a mandate in the absence of the previous exercise of an internal Community competence was discussed.

While a negotiating mandate was being proposed doubts were expressed on the legal form of the agreement. In a written statement made in the framework of the Convention for the Future of Europe, the legal dispute was summarized as follows:

> In one "mandate" the Council authorized the opening of negotiations with Switzerland, about the latter's participation in the Schengen acquis. These negotiations are to be conducted in part by the Commission in consultation with a special Council group for the Community side of the Schengen acquis and in part by the Presidency in consultation with the Commission for the third pillar aspects of the Schengen acquis, but the result must be *one* agreement, presumably to be concluded under articles 24 and 38 EU and articles 62 and 63 EC. The Commission was so worried about this awkward precedent that it made a rather detailed declaration why it did not agree to such cross pillar mixity. The Council in turn was so worried about this declaration that it reaffirmed that such cross-pillar mixity was nothing new and wholly lawful.[70]

The declaration of the Commission was not made public, but when approving the negotiating mandates, the Council agreed to enter in its minutes the following joint statement in reply to the unilateral statement by the Commission in its draft negotiating mandate for an EU/EC Agreement concerning the participation of Switzerland in the Schengen acquis:

> The Council has authorised the Commission and the Presidency to negotiate a single Agreement with Switzerland on behalf of both the European Community and the European Union, on the model of the Agreement concluded with Iceland and Norway in 1999. With regard to the institutional issues raised by the Commission in its statement, the Council considers that the joint conclusion of an agreement by

---

70. Pieter Jan Kuijper, International Personality of the Union, Speaking notes for a meeting of the Working Group III "Legal Personality" of the European Convention, WG III – WD3, 3 July 2002. Also in the same document the speaking points of Jean-Claude Piris on the Legal personality of the Union (in French). In general, Ramses A. Wessel, The European Union as a Party to International Agreements: Shared Competences, Mixed Responsibilities, in: Alan Dashwood et Marc Maresceau (eds), *Recent Trends in External Relations of the EU*, 45 p. (2007), to be published.

the Community and the Union is legally comparable to the situation where international agreements are negotiated and concluded jointly by the three Communities and the Member States. Joint conclusion of such agreements, which relies on different procedures under the different Treaties, is established practice of the Council and the Commission, and its legality has been repeatedly confirmed by the Court of Justice. All the issues raised by the Commission have already been settled in that context. Lastly, the Council considers that, in this specific case, the negotiation and conclusion with Switzerland of two separate Agreements on its participation in the Schengen *acquis* would raise legal and institutional difficulties which could jeopardise the proposed Agreement's aims, given that the Schengen *acquis* forms an inseparable whole.[71]

On this basis, a single agreement between the European Union, the European Community and the Swiss Confederation concerning the latter's association with the implementation, application and development of the Schengen acquis was negotiated.

In the explanatory memorandum of its proposal for the signature and conclusion of the agreement, the Commission recalled its declaration made at the time of the adoption of the directives for negotiation and restated its regrets that these directives foresaw a single agreement, including elements from the first as well as from the third pillar. These elements from different pillars are of a fundamentally different nature (the elements from the first pillar are of a Community law nature, including supremacy and possible direct effect, whereas the elements from the third pillar are not), they are subject to different procedures with respect to approval and conclusion (e.g. the third pillar elements are not subject to an opinion of Parliament) and are subject to the ECJ's jurisdiction to different degrees. In order to take account of these differences, the Commission proposed to adopt the Agreement on the Schengen acquis, by two separate acts, one based on the Community Treaty and the other on the Union Treaty.

---

71. Council Doc 10096/02, minutes of the 2437th meeting of the Council (GENERAL AFFAIRS), held in Luxembourg on 17 June 2002.

Following the approach proposed by the Commission, the Council adopted two separate decisions on the signature of the Schengen agreement.[72] The first decision concerned the conclusion of the agreement on behalf of the European Union, based on Art. 24 and 38 EU Treaty; the other decision concerned the conclusion of the agreement on behalf of the European Community, based on Articles 62, 63 (3), 66 and 95 in conjunction with the second sentence of the first subparagraph of Article 300 (2) thereof.[73] Interestingly, however, the decisions do not indicate which part of the agreement falls under the competence of the EU, and which under the competence of the EC. This cross-pillar agreement constitutes a *novum* in the external relations of the EU. It remains to be seen whether such a format could constitute a precedent and be applied in other fields of cross-pillar competences.[74]

Simultaneously with the Schengen Association Agreement, the EC and Switzerland also negotiated an agreement concerning the association of Switzerland with the Dublin/Eurodac acquis.[75] Given that Dublin and Eurodac exclusively falls within EC competence, this agreement did not give rise to the same complex cross-pillar issues as the Schengen association. However, given the close link between Schengen and asylum

72. Council Decision (EC) No 2004/849 of 25 October 2004 on the signing, on behalf of the European Union, and on the provisional application of certain provisions of the Agreement between the European Union, the European Community and the Swiss Confederation concerning the Swiss Confederation's association with the implementation, application and development of the Schengen acquis, OJ L 368, 15.12.2004, p. 26.
Council Decision (EC) No 2004/860 of 25 October 2004 on the signing, on behalf of the European Community, and on the provisional application of certain provisions of the Agreement between the European Union, the European Community and the Swiss Confederation, concerning the Swiss Confederation's association with the implementation, application and development of the Schengen acquis, OJ L 370, 17.12.2004, p. 78.
73. On the treaty-making power of the EU, Stephan Marquard, The Conclusion of International Agreements und Article 24 of the Treaty on European Union, in: Vincent Kronenberger (ed.), *The European Union and the International Legal Order: Discord or Harmony?*, p. 333 (2001); Stephan Marquard, La capacité de l'Union européenne de conclure des accords internationaux dans le domaine de la coopération policière et judiciaire en matière pénale, in: *Sécurité et justice: enjeu de la politique extérieure de l'Union européenne*, p. 179 (2003); Pieter Jan Kuijper, *op. cit.* note 64, p. 622.
74. Jörg Monar, The EU as an International Actor in the Domain of Justice and Home Affairs, 9 [2004] European Foreign Affairs Review, p. 395-415, p. 411.
75. The proposal for the signature and conclusion of both agreements was submitted by the Commission in one single package containing six proposed decisions (cf. COM [2004]593 final).

issues, the Schengen Agreements establishes a close link between the implementation and the termination of the two Agreements.[76]

E. Content of the Swiss EU/EC Schengen Association Agreement

1. *Negotiating objectives of the Commission*

According to the negotiating directives of the Commission, the agreements had to follow the model of the agreement with Norway and Island adapted to the specific constitutional requirements of Switzerland. In addition, the negotiating directives insisted that Switzerland must accept the Schengen acquis and its further development without exception and derogation.

Since the Agreement with Switzerland is indeed based on the model of the agreement with Norway and Iceland, all that has been said above regarding this latter agreement is *mutatis mutandis* applicable to the Swiss Agreement. The following explanations will therefore mainly focus on the specific solutions negotiated and granted to Switzerland.

2. *Specific derogation in respect of the acceptance of future acquis*

The purpose of the agreement is to associate Switzerland with the work of the EU in the area of the Schengen acquis.[77] The adoption of new acts or measures will, however, remain the monopoly of the European institutions. In this way, Switzerland will contribute *de facto* to the development of legislation on the Schengen acquis, without participating in the decision making *de iure*.[78] The sole exception to the principle of full acceptance of the current and future Schengen acquis is the derogation granted to Switzerland in respect of the acceptance of future acquis related to requests for search and seizure in respect of offences in the field of direct taxation, which, if committed in Switzerland, would not be punishable under Swiss law with a custodial penalty. In that case, the mechanism for the acceptance of the future acquis does not apply until such time when the contracting parties, based on consultations, decide otherwise in the Mixed

76. Cf. Articles 15 (4) and 17 (2) of the Schengen Association Agreement and Articles 14 (2) and 16 (2) of the Dublin Association Agreement. For more detail on the latter agreement, cf. below section F.
77. Anne Cornu, Les aspects institutionnels des Accords d'association de la Suisse à Schengen et Dublin, in: Christine Kaddous et Monique Jametti Greiner (éd.), *Accords bilatéraux Suisse-UE et autres accords récents*, p. 207-244 (2006).
78. European Parliament, Report of the Committee on Civil Liberties, Justice and Home Affairs, Explanatory statement, A6-02012005, 7.6.2005.

Committee.[79] This derogation was deemed necessary in order to conclude an agreement with Switzerland in the field of savings taxation. COREPER approved this derogation on 17 May 2004 as part of an overall compromise with Switzerland in a wide range of sectors, which was agreed upon in the high level EU/Switzerland summit on 19 May 2004.[80]

3.   *Judicial cooperation in the field of indirect taxation: problems of interpretation*

As far as indirect taxation is concerned, no derogation was granted from both the current and the future acquis. Switzerland accepted to grant full judicial cooperation in cases of indirect tax evasion.[81] But there was a substantial legal dispute on the interpretation to be given to Article 51 Schengen Convention concerning the admissibility of letters rogatory for search or seizure. Article 51 a) states that the requested state may make the admissibility of letters rogatory dependent on the condition that the act giving rise to the letter rogatory is [either] punishable by a deprivation of liberty of six months in both parties, or that the act is punishable under the law of one Party by six months and under the law of the other Party as an infringement of the rules of law with respect to the conditions for the admissibility of letters rogatory for search and seizure. In the Swiss view, Article 51 (a) is divided into two half-sentences providing for two

79. Article 7 (5) of the Association Agreement reads as follows:
"(a) If provisions of a new act or measure have the effect of no longer allowing Member States to subject compliance with requests for mutual assistance in criminal matters or the recognition of orders from other Member States to search premises and/or seize items of evidence to the conditions set out in Article 51 of the Convention Implementing the Schengen Agreement, Switzerland may notify the Council and the Commission within the period of thirty days referred to in paragraph 2, point (a) that it will not accept or implement those provisions in its internal legal order where they apply to search and seizure requests or orders made for the purposes of investigating or prosecuting offences in the field of direct taxation which, if committed in Switzerland,would not be punishable under Swiss law with a custodial penalty. In that case this Agreement shall not be considered terminated, contrary to the provisions of paragraph 4.
(b) The Mixed Committee shall convene within two months following a request by one of its members and, taking into account international developments, shall discuss the situation resulting from notification pursuant to point (a). Once the Mixed Committee has unanimously reached an agreement on the full acceptance and implementation by Switzerland of the relevant provisions of the new act or measure, paragraphs 2, point (b), 3 and 4 shall apply. The information referred to in the first sentence of paragraph 2, point (b) shall be provided within thirty days of the agreement reached in the Mixed Committee."
80. Council Doc 9544/04, Conclusions for the EU-Switzerland Summit, 19 Mai 2004.
81. Council Doc 9544/04.

alternative options to limit the execution of letters rogatory. Providing for several possibilities in the same sentence as in Article 51 (a) would only make sense if they are understood as alternatives. The Swiss authorities are therefore of the opinion that Article 51 (a) lays down two alternative conditions on which the *requested* Party may make the admissibility of letters rogatory dependent.[82]

The Commission and the Swiss authorities exchanged legal opinions without finding a common understanding. For the Commission, since indirect tax evasion is prosecuted in Switzerland by administrative authorities where the decision may give rise to proceedings before a court having jurisdiction in particular in criminal matters, Article 51 a) second alternative of the Schengen Convention is applicable.[83] In practice, there should be no application problem though, since the Agreement on the Fight against Fraud provides for full judicial cooperation in the field of indirect taxation, including search and seizures in matters of indirect tax evasion and smuggling.[84]

4.   The practical functioning of the Mixed Committees

The Agreement with Iceland and Norway, as well as the Agreement with Switzerland have established legally separate Mixed Committees.[85] This is the consequence of having two separate agreements, one with Iceland and Norway, the other with Switzerland. Initially, two conceptual solutions were discussed. According to one option, the agreement could be concluded as a multilateral agreement, where Switzerland, under specific conditions relating to its position, accedes to the existing agreement with Norway and Iceland. According to another option, Switzerland could first conclude an association agreement with the Community, and then

---

82. Swiss position expressed in a non-paper during the negotiations. Monique Jametti Greiner and Hanspeter Pfenninger, Der Schutz des schweizerischen Bankgeheimnisses im Abkommen zur Assoziierung der Schweiz an Schengen, 14 [2005] Allgemeine Juristische Praxis (AJP), p. 159.
83. Non-paper of the services of the Commission on the Schengen acquis concerning letters rogatory for search and seizure, MD 59/03 (EFTA group).
84. Fabrice Filliez, Les sources du droit de l'UE en matière de protection des intérêts financiers et leur signification pour l'Accord sur la lutte contre la fraude, in: Christine Kaddous et Monique Jametti Greiner (ed.), *Accords bilatéraux Suisse-UE et autres accords récents*, p. 621-654 (2006).
85. On the works of the Mixed Committee, Susanne Gutzwiller, Komitologie und Gemischte Ausschüsse im Rahmen der Assoziierung der Schweiz an Schengen/ Dublin, in: Christine Kaddous et Monique Jametti Greiner (éd.), *Accords bilatéraux Suisse-UE et autres accords récents*, p. 245-266 (2006).

conclude a parallel agreement with Norway and Iceland.[86] The second option was eventually followed by the parties. However, in order to facilitate the functioning of the two "formal" mixed committees, all parties agreed, in a joint declaration attached to the Final Act, that the meetings of these two Mixed Committees shall be held jointly.

In order to facilitate the functioning of the Mixed Committees, all associated countries expressed their wish to cede, if necessary, the exercise of their presidencies and rotate these among them in alphabetical order of name. As a consequence, a new article was inserted into the Rules of procedure of the Mixed Committee Iceland/Norway stipulating that Norway and Iceland may cede the Chair of the Mixed Committee meeting at the level of senior officials and Ministers to another delegation prepared to perform that function.[87] A corresponding article was also included in the Rules of Procedure of the Mixed Committee under the Agreement with Switzerland.[88]

5.   *Swiss constitutional clause for implementation*

Article 7 (2) (b) of the Agreement stipulates that Switzerland is granted a two-year period for acceptance and implementation of future acquis into its internal legal order in case a referendum is requested. If possible, Switzerland has to apply the development of the acquis on a provisional basis. If Switzerland cannot apply the content of the development on a provisional basis, the EU and EC may take proportional and necessary measures against Switzerland in order to ensure the efficient functioning of Schengen. The two year period was deemed necessary to accommodate the Swiss constitutional constraints, for cases where the approval of the parliament is necessary, including the possibility of having a referendum.

86.   Pieter Jan Kuijper, *op. cit.* note 65, p. 622.
87.   Decision N° 1/2004 of the EU/Iceland and Norway Mixed Committee amending Decision N° 1/1999 of 29 June 1999 adopting its Rules of Procedure, OJ C 308, 14.12.2004, p. 1. New sentence in Article 1: "The delegations representing the Governments of Iceland and Norway may cede the chair of the Mixed Committee meeting at the level of senior officials and Ministers to another delegation prepared to perform that function".
88.   Decision N° 1/2004 of the EU/Switzerland Mixed Committee established by the Agreement concluded between the European Union, the European Community and the Swiss Confederation concerning the latter's association in the implementation, application and development of the Schengen acquis of 26 October 2004 adopting its Rules of Procedure, OJ C 308, 14.12.2004, p. 2. Article 1 in fine: "The delegation representing the Government of Switzerland may cede the chair of the Mixed Committee meeting at the level of senior officials and Ministers to another delegation prepared to perform that function".

6.   *Agreements to be concluded with Iceland and Norway and Denmark,*
      and accession of Liechtenstein

Switzerland also needed to conclude an agreement with Iceland and
Norway in order to create rights and obligations between all associated
partners applying the Schengen acquis. This agreement was signed on 17
December 2004 and was ratified by Norway on 27 October 2006, by
Iceland on 17 November 2006 and by Switzerland on 31 January 2008. In
accordance with its special position, Denmark also needed to conclude a
separate Agreement with Switzerland in order to create rights and
obligations with Switzerland in relation to the Schengen acquis adopted
pursuant to Title IV. Such agreement was signed on 28 April 2005 and
ratification is still pending.

Article 16 of the Swiss Association Agreement allows Liechtenstein to
accede to the agreement. This provision avoids the conclusion of a separate
Agreement with Liechtenstein and thus the creation of a third Mixed
Committee once Liechtenstein is associated with the Schengen acquis.[89]

F.   The main elements of the Dublin Association Agreement

In this second agreement Switzerland will be linked to the Dublin acquis
as well as the Eurodac legislation.[90] Switzerland will have to accept,
implement and apply the current and future Dublin/Eurodac acquis with
no exception, as well as the relevant provisions of the data protection
directive. This Agreement mostly adopted the structure of the Agreement
on the Schengen acquis. Article 4 (3) corresponds in substance to Article 7
(2) (b) of the Schengen Association Agreement and grants Switzerland a
two-year period for acceptance and implementation of future acquis into
its internal legal order. As far as the maintenance and termination of the
Agreement is concerned, the Mixed Committee has basically the same
functions as those set up by the Agreement on the Schengen acquis.[91]

According to Denmark's special position with regard to acts adopted
pursuant to Title IV of the Treaty establishing the European Community,

---

89. This is a relatively rare example of an international agreement conferring rights on a
     third state (cf. Article 36 of the Vienna Convention on the Law of Treaties).
90. The proposal for the signature and conclusion of this agreement was submitted by
     the Commission in the single package containing all proposed decisions on Schengen
     and Dublin(cf. COM [2004]593 final). It was signed on 26 October 2004 together
     with all agreements forming the so-called "Bilateral Agreements II", in particular the
     Schengen Association Agreement.
91. European Parliament, *op. cit.* note 78.

Denmark needed to be associated via a protocol in order to create rights and obligations between Denmark and Switzerland in relation to the provisions of Dublin/Eurodac. Such a protocol was negotiated between the European Commission, Switzerland and Liechtenstein. In addition, Norway and Iceland needed to conclude an agreement with Switzerland in order to create rights and obligations between all associated partners applying the Dublin/Eurodac acquis.

G.   The Liechtenstein protocols

By letter dated 12 October 2001, Liechtenstein had already expressed its interest in joining Switzerland as a contracting party to a possible Schengen and Dublin association agreement, since an open border policy for the movement of persons had existed between Liechtenstein and Switzerland for decades.[92] In response to the interest expressed by the Principality of Liechtenstein in being associated with the Schengen acquis and the Dublin Convention at the same time as Switzerland, for which the Council adopted the negotiating mandate on 17 June 2002, the Council approved the following conclusions:

> The Council takes note of the request by the Government of Liechtenstein to be associated with the implementation of the Schengen acquis and the implementation of the legislation on asylum, at the same time as Switzerland. Taking into account the mandates for negotiations with Switzerland on the Schengen acquis and on asylum, the Council asks the Commission to present rapidly a recommendation to negotiate with Liechtenstein an agreement for the association of Liechtenstein with the implementation of the Schengen acquis and for the implementation of the legislation establishing Eurodac and the forthcoming legislation establishing the State responsible for examining requests for asylum.[93]

However, Liechtenstein was not associated with the negotiations with Switzerland on account of the absence of an agreement on savings taxation between the European Community and Liechtenstein. After the conclusion of such an agreement, Liechtenstein confirmed in June 2005 that it wished to be associated with the Schengen and Dublin/Eurodac acquis. Following the authorization given by the Council to the Commission on 27 February 2006, negotiations were held with Liechtenstein and Switzerland. On 21 June 2006 a draft protocol on Liechtenstein's accession to the Schengen

---

92. Council Doc 10024/02, Annex 1.
93. Press Release of the 2439nd Council meeting, Environment, 25 June 2002, Council Doc 10013/02 (Presse 180)

agreement with Switzerland was initialled[94], as well as a draft protocol on its accession to the Dublin/Eurodac Agreement with Switzerland[95] and a draft protocol on Denmark's participation in the agreement on Dublin/Eurodac with Switzerland and Liechtenstein.[96]

Given the fact that the Schengen agreement with Switzerland, to which Liechtenstein acceded, covers both first and third pillar items, the Commission proposed to follow the approach chosen for the signature and adoption of the Schengen agreement with Switzerland. The Commission thus proposed to adopt the Protocol by two separate acts, one based on the EC Treaty (Articles 62, 63 [3], 66 and 95 EC) and one based on the EU Treaty (Articles 24 and 38 EU).

The final content of the agreement can be summarized as follows: Liechtenstein accedes to the Schengen agreement with Switzerland and will have the same rights and obligations as Switzerland. Liechtenstein will have to accept the entire Schengen acquis and the development thereof, with the sole exception granted also to Switzerland (Article 7 paragraph 5 of the Schengen agreement with Switzerland).[97] Liechtenstein will become a member of the Mixed Committee. The putting into effect of the Schengen protocol is linked to the putting into effect of the Dublin/Eurodac protocol, as well as to the putting into effect of the respective agreements between Liechtenstein and Denmark and between Liechtenstein and Norway and Iceland on Schengen. Specific provisions are laid down for Liechtenstein concerning the time period needed for the implementation of a

94. COM (2006) 752, Proposal for a Council Decision on the signature, on behalf of the European Union, and on the provisional application of certain provisions of the Protocol between the European Union, the European Community, the Swiss Confederation and the Principality of Liechtenstein on the accession of the Principality of Liechtenstein to the Agreement between the European Union, the European Community and the Swiss Confederation on the Swiss Confederation's association with the implementation, application and development of the Schengen acquis, 1.12.2006.

95. COM (2006) 754, Proposal for Council Decision on the signature of a Protocol between the European Community, the Swiss Confederation and the Principality of Liechtenstein on the accession of the Principality of Liechtenstein to the Agreement between the European Community and the Swiss Confederation concerning the criteria and mechanisms for establishing the State responsible for examining a request for asylum lodged in a Member State or in Switzerland, 4.12.2006.

96. COM (2006) 753, Proposal on the signature of a Protocol between the European Community, Switzerland and Liechtenstein to the Agreement between the European Community and the Swiss Confederation concerning the criteria and mechanisms for establishing the State responsible for examining a request for asylum lodged in a Member State or in Switzerland

97. See *supra* note 79.

development of the Schengen acquis, in case constitutional requirements need to be fulfilled by Liechtenstein (18 months).

Liechtenstein will also accede to the Dublin/Eurodac Association Agreement with Switzerland and will have to accept the entire Dublin/ Eurodac acquis and the development thereof. An 18-month time period was granted to Liechtenstein for the implementation of a development of the Dublin/Eurodac acquis in case of constitutional requirements. It was also appropriate to establish the participation of Denmark in relation to both Switzerland and Liechtenstein. A protocol makes the Dublin and Eurodac regulations and their implementing rules applicable to the relations between Denmark on the one hand and the Confederation of Switzerland and the Principality of Liechtenstein on the other. The putting into effect of the Dublin/Eurodac protocol is linked to the putting into effect of the Schengen Protocol, as well as to the putting into effect of the protocol between the European Community, Switzerland and Liechtenstein on the participation of Denmark and of the Agreement between Liechtenstein and Norway and Iceland on Dublin/Eurodac. These instruments have been signed on 28 February 2008. The Commission and some Member States were reluctant to proceed with the signature as long as Liechtenstein did not commit itself to negotiate an agreement to combat fraud and other illegal activities.[98]

IV.   The definition of acts building upon the Schengen acquis (Schengen-relevance)

A.   Background

In the following section, the notion of "Schengen-relevance" refers to the acts and measures amending or building upon the Schengen acquis which, according to Article 2 (3) of the Agreement, must be implemented by Switzerland and the other associated States. It does not refer to Art. 5 of the Schengen Association agreement, which describes the conditions under

---

98.   The Council approved on 7 November 2006 a negotiating mandate for the Commission to open negotiations for an Agreement between the European Community and its Member States, of the one part, and the Principality of Liechtenstein, of the other part, to combat fraud and other illegal activity to the detriment of their financial interests, see Council Doc 14502/06.

which the Mixed Committee must be informed of "any acts or measures which may be relevant to this Agreement".[99]

It must be acknowledged that it is not always easy to decide what falls under Schengen development and what is a normal form of EC/EU co-operation. Schengen co-operation, as illustrated above, has become institutionally quite complex. By deciding that a measure is Schengen-relevant, the Council triggers the procedure of the Mixed Committee and the participation of the associated States Norway, Iceland and Switzerland. As a consequence, the Schengen associates are legally obliged to implement it, even if they disagree with it. The Association Agreements do not provide a clear solution for the crucial question of what is covered by the agreements. They simply refer to the development of the acquis that is given a legal basis. For the purpose of helping to determine in advance in which areas legislative proposals would constitute acts building upon the Schengen acquis, the Council has adopted its Decision 1999/437[100] in which it has listed a number of relevant areas. The description of these areas inevitably leaves room for divergent interpretation. This is the case in areas of Title VI EU, such as police and judicial cooperation, or issues of Title IV, such as asylum, where the Schengen acquis constitutes a limited set of rules tat do not cover the whole range of possible EU cooperation.[101] Given that the Schengen acquis has been undergoing developments since 1999, the question of the Schengen-relevance of an act or measure is of considerable importance.[102] It can directly affect the interest of the associated States. Depending on the interests at stake, one can imagine that the EU considers an act as Schengen-relevant and would wish to see the associates apply it, whereas the Schengen associates do not wish to do so. Up to now, the tendency has rather shown a restrictive approach of the EU institutions, as illustrated below.

In 1999, the Finnish Presidency suggested some principles in a note sent to the Chairpersons of the Committees and Working Parties of the Council in the field of Justice and Home Affairs.[103] The note recalls that it is up to

---

99. The information procedure under Article 5 concerns matters that will not entail any future rights and obligations for the associated States.
100. Decision (EC) No 437/1999, *op. cit.* note 21.
101. Council Doc 12164/99, How to decide whether a particular subject matter is "Schengen related" and has to be dealt with through "Mixed Committee" procedures, 22.10.1999.
102. For a good discussion of the question of Schengen-relevance, cf. Nicole Wichman, The Participation of the Schengen Associates, Inside or Outside, 11 [2006] European Foreign Affairs Review, p. 87-107, p. 103.
103. Council Doc 12164/99, *op. cit.* note 101, p. 2.

the Union, and the Union alone, to determine which proposed acts or measures purport to amend or modify the provisions of the Schengen acquis. But the Union has to apply the Agreement in good faith and Iceland and Norway may always raise questions in the Mixed Committee as to the way in which the Union interprets and applies the Agreement. The note also refers to the Council Decision of 17 May 1999 which lists a number of relevant areas[104] and recognises that the description of these areas inevitably leaves room for divergent interpretation. It mentions in particular the areas of "police co-operation" and "judicial co-operation in criminal matters" as well as some Title IV issues, where the Schengen acquis constitutes a limited set of rules, which do not cover the whole range of possible co-operation. In case the Member States fail to agree on whether a certain proposal or initiative is Schengen-relevant, the Presidency shall convene a meeting of the Committee of Permanent Representatives of the Member States to enable a discussion to be held on whether an initiative or proposal falls within an area covered by Article 1 of that Council Decision.

B.   Problems encountered

1.   *The Schengen-relevance test*

Many Working Parties of the Council have encountered problems in determining whether certain proposals or initiatives are Schengen-relevant. The Presidency proposed an approach that would constitute the basis on which consensus can be reached at Working Party level and, if need be, at Coreper level. The main test for determining whether a particular proposal or initiative should be considered Schengen-relevant could be the following:

> Does this proposal or initiative concern a matter which is essential to the free move-ment of persons within an area where checks on persons at internal borders have been eliminated and a common system of control at the external borders has been set up and by which Iceland and Norway therefore should be bound?[105]

For the Presidency, the mere fact that it would be desirable or practical if Iceland and Norway were also bound would not be sufficient to apply the association procedures. It should be essential in terms of the realization of

---

104. Decision (EC) No 307/1999, *op. cit.* note 17. This decision only gives rules in order to decide whether an act is relevant for the Mixed Committee and consequently the Agreements apply. It does not however answer the more general question whether an act is Schengen-relevant and thus the rules of the Schengen Protocol apply or not.
105. Council Doc 12164/99, *op. cit.* note 101, p. 4.

the objectives of Schengen co-operation: abolition of checks on persons at internal borders and the taking of inevitable and essential flanking measures in the interest of immigration control, public order and internal security. In other words, the Presidency was of the opinion that the association with Iceland and Norway serves the narrow objective of establishing an area of free movement of persons (for third country nationals for periods up to three months), as distinct from the much wider substantive objective of the Union in the field of Justice and Home Affairs, i.e. the creation of an area of freedom, security and justice. This test looks simple, but opinions as to what is essential and what is not may continue to vary.

When the Commission drafts a proposal, it usually indicates whether the proposal is Schengen relevant and builds upon the Schengen acquis. The Council then decides whether it agrees with the Commission's suggestion. If it does not agree, discussions take place in the framework of the EU and not as part of the agenda of the Mixed Committee with the associated States.

2.   The European Arrest Warrant

The first important discussion on the Schengen-relevance of an EU act took place in the context of the negotiations on a European Arrest Warrant in 2001. In its proposal, the Commission was of the opinion that the Framework Decision was a development of the Schengen acquis.[106] By letter dated 28 September 2001, the Chairman of the Mixed Committee, the Icelandic Ambassador Gunnarsson, indicated that Iceland and Norway were of the opinion that the Arrest Warrant was to be considered as a development of the Schengen acquis to which the Mixed Committee procedure should apply.[107] The letter was discussed in Coreper, which rejected the Schengen-relevance of the European arrest warrant, but noted the keen interest expressed by both Iceland and Norway in the mechanism of the European arrest warrant.[108]

On the basis of the guidelines of the Presidency quoted above, a measure can only be considered Schengen-relevant if it is strictly necessary for the

---

106. COM(2001) 522, Proposal for a Council Framework Decision on the European arrest warrant and the surrender procedures between the Member States, 19.9.2001, draft article 44.
107. Council Doc 12434/01 ADD 1, 2.5.2002.
108. Philippe de Koster, Bref état des lieux sur les accords de coopération conclus sur la base de l'article 38 du traité UE, in: *Sécurité et justice: enjeu de la politique extérieure de l'Union européenne*, p. 195 (2003).

abolition of internal borders and as flanking measure to realization of the free movement of persons. The measure needs to be inevitable and essential for the purpose of immigration control, public order and internal security. On the contrary, the simple fact that it would be desirable or practical, for instance to associate the two non-Member States in the framework of the decision-shaping procedure is not sufficient to include them in the adoption of a measure. It was agreed that only the development of those provisions on extradition which have a direct relation to the existing provisions of the Schengen Convention were to be considered Schengen-relevant. New mechanisms based on the principle of mutual recognition did not belong to the Schengen cooperation, as opposed to some elements of the EU Conventions of 1995 and 1996 relating to extradition.[109] The mere fact that some provisions of the Schengen Acquis are repealed between Member States does not automatically make a proposal Schengen-relevant.

The Belgian Presidency informed Iceland of the above position, and suggested that, once the Council had adopted the Framework Decision on the European arrest warrant, the European Union could envisage concluding separate agreements with Iceland and Norway on the basis of Articles 24 and 38 of the Treaty on European Union, in order to make the mechanism of the European arrest warrant applicable to Iceland and Norway.[110] Norway and Iceland were disappointed in their hope that Schengen cooperation would pave the way for a wider participation in the Area of Justice, Liberty and Security.

In a public statement, the Icelandic Minister of Justice underlined the deep concerns of the associated States about the decision of the Council:

> The EU States have under the third pillar co-operation decided on several measures to fight this serious menace but it came as a surprise to us when we realised that topics which we consider Schengen-relevant are to be dealt with outside our joint Schengen political fora. One of these measures is to introduce the European Arrest

109. The provisions of the 1995 Convention on simplified extradition procedure between the Member States of the European Union (OJ C 78, 30.3.1995, p. 2) and of the 1996 Convention relating to extradition between the Member States of the European Union (OJ C 313, 23.10.1996, p. 12) referred to in Council Decision 2003/169/JHA of 27 February 2003 determining which provisions of the 1995 Convention on simplified extradition procedure between the Member States of the European Union and of the 1996 Convention relating to extradition between the Member States of the European Union constitute developments of the Schengen acquis in accordance with the Agreement concerning the Republic of Iceland's and the Kingdom of Norway's association with the implementation, application and development of the Schengen acquis, OJ L 67, 12.3.2003, p. 25.
110. Council Doc 11080/02, 19.7.2002.

Warrant. (...) If such matters are not to be considered Schengen-relevant, the result will be to divide the Schengen States into two categories which we strongly object to.[111]

3. The European Evidence Warrant

A similar controversy has arisen in the debates surrounding the European Evidence Warrant.[112] The Commission considered its proposal as a development of the Schengen acquis. According to the explanatory memorandum, the proposal builds upon Article 51 of the Schengen Convention by improving co-operation with respect to search and seizure. It also contains provisions which build upon Articles 3, 6 and 23 of the EU 2000 Convention[113], all of which the Council has decided represent developments of the Schengen acquis.

It was basically confirmed that mutual recognition is not part of the Schengen acquis and that instruments incorporating this new principle are by definition not Schengen-relevant. The new instruments based on mutual recognition cannot be considered as forms of cooperation, as applied between the Member States at the time of entry into force of the Treaty of Amsterdam, in the meaning of Decision (EC) 307/1999.[114] Furthermore, the proposal could not be divided between Schengen and non-Schengen related provisions.

The same reasoning has been applied to the principle of information availability in the field of police cooperation developed in the Hague Programme[115], where new initiatives of the Commission have not been considered Schengen relevant.[116]

---

111. Sólveig Pétursdóttir, Minister of Justice, speech given at the EU & EEA Conference – developing towards a European Legal Order, 12.10.2001, http://eng.domsmalaraduneyti.is/minister/speeches-and-articles/
112. COM(2003) 688, Proposal for a Council Framework Decision on the European Evidence Warrant for obtaining objects, documents and data for use in proceedings in criminal matters, 14.11.2003.
113. Council Act of 29 May 2000 establishing in accordance with Article 34 of the Treaty on European Union the Convention on Mutual Assistance in Criminal Matters between the Member States of the European Union, OJ C 197, 12.7.2000, p. 1.
114. Decision (EC) No 437/1999, *op. cit.* note 21.
115. The Hague Programme: strengthening freedom, security and justice in the European Union, OJ C 53, 3.3.2005, p. 1-14. The principle is explained under point 2.2.1, p. 7.
116. Proposal for a Council framework decision on the exchange of information under the principle of availability, COM (2005) 490 final.

C.   Ways to go beyond the limits of Schengen in judicial affairs

The Council's position seems to reflect the belief that instruments incorporating mutual recognition, such as the European Arrest Warrant or the Evidence Warrant, are conceived within the logic of creating a European Area of Criminal Justice and not with the more traditional forms of cooperation in mind.[117] Another conclusion would, from the point of view of the Union, open the cooperation to the associated States for the entire working programme of the Union concerning mutual recognition of judicial decisions in the field of criminal law. A the same time, the EU has taken into account the interests of Iceland and Norway to develop cooperation beyond Schengen in judicial affairs and it proposed negotiations to complement the Schengen acquis on mutual judicial assistance in criminal matters and to extend mechanisms similar to the arrest warrant with regard to extradition.

The Council authorised the Presidency on 10 July 2001 to negotiate agreements with Norway and Iceland on judicial cooperation on the basis of Articles 24 and 38 EU.[118] The objective of the agreement is to extend the application of certain provisions on judicial cooperation, which do not constitute a development of the provisions of the Schengen acquis, to Iceland and Norway. The mechanisms of the European Arrest Warrant and a large number of provisions of the 2000 MLA and the Protocol 2001 thereto are concerned. The agreement with Iceland and Norway on Mutual Assistance in Criminal Matters was signed on 19 December 2003.[119] Ratification is still pending.[120] And on 27 June 2006 the Council adopted the Decision on the signature of the Agreement with Iceland and Norway

---

117. Wichman, op. cit. note 102, p. 105.
118. Gilles De Kerchove, Introduction, in: Gilles de Kerchove et Anne Weyembergh (ed.), *Sécurité et justice: enjeu de la politique extérieure de l'Union européenne*, p. 24-25 (2003).
119. Council Decision (EC) No 2004/79 of 17 December 2003 on the signing of the Agreement between the European Union and the Republic of Iceland and the Kingdom of Norway on the application of certain provisions of the Convention of 29 May 2000 on Mutual Assistance in Criminal Matters between the Member States of the European Union and the 2001 Protocol thereto, OJ L 26, 29.1.2004, p. 1.
120. The following delegations made statements under Article 24(5) EU: Belgium, Cyprus, Czech Republic, Deutschland, Denmark, Spain, Finland, Hungary, Ireland, Italy, Latvia, Luxemburg, Lithuania, the Netherlands, Portugal, Poland, Sweden, Slovenia, Slovakia, United Kingdom, and most recently Bulgaria, see Council Doc 7097/1/07, State of play of constitutional declarations, 19.3.2007, and Doc 7988/07, 2.4.2007.

on the surrender procedure.[121] The objective is to apply the mechanisms of the European arrest warrant to Iceland and Norway. Ratification is still pending.[122]

V.   Ratification of the agreements with Switzerland

A.   Swiss ratification and declarations

According to the Swiss Constitution, international agreements which contain important dispositions establishing legal norms or whose implementation requires the adoption of a federal law are submitted to the vote of the People at the request of 50'000 citizens within 100 days.[123] Proposals submitted to the vote of the People shall be accepted if the majority of those voting approves them.[124]

Such a request was supported by 86,732 Swiss citizens and a referendum was organized on 5 June 2005 after a very intense internal debate during the referendum campaign before the vote.[125] The population of Switzerland approved the Schengen/Dublin association agreements by 54.6% with a participation of 56%.

Switzerland ratified the Schengen/Dublin Association Agreements at the end of March 2006, and therefore these agreements will enter into force once the EU has ratified them. The entry into force will prepare the ground for the evaluation procedure in view of the effective application of the agreements in principle in autumn 2008. Switzerland also informed the

---

121. Council Decision (EC) No 2006/697 of 27 June 2006 on the signing of the Agreement between the European Union and the Republic of Iceland and the Kingdom of Norway on the surrender procedure between the Member States of the European Union and Iceland and Norway, OJ L 292, 21.10.2006, p. 1.
122. The following delegations made statements under Article 24(5) EU: Belgium, Cyprus, Deutschland, Denmark, Estonia, Spain, Finland, Hungary, Ireland, Italy, Latvia, Lithuania, Malta, the Netherlands, Poland, Portugal, Sweden, Slovenia, and most recently Bulgaria, see Council Doc 7097/1/07, State of play of constitutional declarations, 19.3.2007, and Doc 7988/07, 2.4.2007.
123. Art. 141 (1) d) (3) of the Swiss Federal Constitution, as amended in 2003 by popular vote. RS. 101, http://www.admin.ch/ch/f/rs/rs.html. See also Federal Law on Political Rights, RS. 161.1.
124. Art. 142 of the Swiss Federal Constitution.
125. The explanatory memorandum of the Federal Council summarizes the arguments of the opponents, available under http://www.admin.ch/ch/f/pore/va/20050605/explic/index.html.

General Secretariat of the Council of a series of declarations and communications on the Schengen Association Agreement.[126]

B. Ratification by the EU: the role of the European Parliament and the constitutional reservations according to Articles 24/38 TUE

1. Schengen Association Agreement

As mentioned before, the Schengen Association Agreement is a single "cross-pillar" agreement to be concluded by way of two separate decisions: one in relation to the conclusion of the Agreement on behalf of the Community (first pillar part), and the other in relation to the conclusion on behalf of the Union (third pillar part). From a procedural point of view, this means that the practice of qualified majority rule, possible for the conclusion of Community agreements under Article 300 (2) EC, is absorbed by the requirement of unanimity applied to agreements under the Articles 24 and 38 EU. Moreover, the conclusion of the Agreement by the European Union is subject to the procedural requirements of Article 24 and 38 EU before the decision on the conclusion of the Agreement can be taken. A number of Member States have made use of the possibility to make constitutional reservations.[127]

As regards the European Parliament, the cross-pillar character of the agreement creates a peculiar situation in which it will be required to give an opinion (or its assent) on the first-pillar part of the Agreement, but would not be entitled to deliver such an opinion insofar as the Agreement falls under the third pillar. Another open question will be the legal effects of such "cross-pillar" agreement in relation with the competence of the ECJ, which differ considerably between the first and the third pillar.[128] Given the fact that there is no clear indication as to which parts of the agreement fall under the first and which under the third pillar, there appears to be no obvious solution to this problem.

---

126. Declarations and communications sent to the CATS on 23 January 2007, Council Doc 5520/07.
127. According to the available information, Sweden, Germany, Denmark, Italy, the Netherlands, Czech Republic, Greece and Belgium have announced such reservations. All reservations have been lifted in January 2008 allowing the Council to ratify on 1 February 2008. The Council decisions concerning the conclusion of the agreement are published in OJ L 53, 27.2.2008, pp. 1, 50.
128. Christine Kaddous, *op. cit.* note 42, II. B. 2.

2.   Dublin Association Agreement

The ratification of the Dublin Association Agreement in principle follows the normal first-pillar procedures of Article 300 EC. However, the Council will have to wait for the lifting of the parliamentary reservations concerning the conclusion of the Schengen Association Agreement on behalf of the EU before it can proceed with ratification, since the entry into force of the Dublin Association Agreement is linked to the entry into force of the Schengen Association Agreement.

3.   Role of the European Parliament

As regards the consultation of the European Parliament on the Agreements concerning the Schengen acquis and the Dublin/Eurodac Regulations, the EFTA Working Party had not finalised its discussions at the time of signature of the agreements. The Working Party's examination in November 2004 ended in unanimous agreement in favour of a simple opinion of the European Parliament for both Association Agreements[129], according to the first subparagraph of Article 300 (3) EC. The European Parliament was consulted accordingly.

By letter of 27 January 2005, the Committee on Civil Liberties, Justice and Home Affairs requested an opinion from the Legal Affairs Committee on the legal basis proposed. On 31 March 2005, the Legal Affairs Committee expressed the view that the Mixed Committees created by the Agreements, due their competencies, could be considered a specific institutional framework in the sense of the second subparagraph of Article 300 (3) EC, which implies the assent procedure. The Committee adopted its report on 20 June 2005 approving the proposed Council decisions subject to two amendments concerning the legal basis.[130] In a first discussion in the plenary, the EP asked the Commission to clarify its position on the proposed amendments. The Commission maintained its position. The EP then decided to postpone the vote and to refer back to the committee for reconsideration.[131] On 13 October 2005, it then approved the proposals as amended on 7 July 2005[132] and reserved the right to defend its prerogatives as conferred by the Treaty.

129. Council Doc 14298/04, Working Party on EFTA, Consultation of the European Parliament, 18.11.2004.
130. European Parliament, *op. cit.* note 78.
131. EC-Switzerland Agreement (asylum requests) / EU and EC-Switzerland Agreement (Schengen), OJ C 157 E, 6.7.2006, p. 405.
132. Texts adopted P6_TA(2005)0293 and P6_TA(2005)0292, OJ C 233 E, 28.9.2006, p. 90-91.

The question whether the mixed committees in Schengen/Dublin are a specific institutional framework within the meaning of Article 300 (3) EC is difficult to answer. No precedent is to be found in the jurisprudence of the ECJ. This article provides that by way of derogation from the previous subparagraph, agreements referred to in Article 310 EC, other *agreements establishing a specific institutional framework by organising cooperation procedures*, agreements having important budgetary implications for the Community and agreements entailing amendment of an act adopted under the procedure referred to in Article 251 EC shall be concluded after the assent of the European Parliament has been obtained. ECJ has been asked once to examine the notion of "agreements having important budgetary implications for the Community"[133]. The ECJ supported the view of the Council that the fisheries agreement with Mauritania did not have important budgetary implications for the Community and dismissed the action. Although the judgement does not directly deal with the question at hand, one can find in the conclusions of the Advocate General a sentence saying that agreements establishing a specific institutional framework are quite close to association agreements according to Article 310 EC.[134] Such a reference is also to be found in the literature.[135] It is difficult to assess the position of the European Parliament without having the legal arguments supporting the assent procedure. But this legal question is worth reflecting upon.

One could argue that almost all international agreements have established mixed or joint committees responsible for the management and proper implementation of the agreement and which are empowered to make recommendations and take decisions in the cases provided for by the agreement. Considering a joint or mixed committee as a "specific institutional framework" would extend the assent procedure to almost all international agreements concluded by the EC. Such a conclusion would have as a consequence to generalise the assent procedure for the conclusion of international agreements. That does not seem to correspond to the *ratio* of Article 300 (3), making the exception the general rule.

---

133. Case C-89/97, European Parliament/Council, [1999] ECR I-4741.
134. Conclusions of Advocate General Mischo, European Parliament/Council, [1999] ECR I-4741, para. 54.
135. "... les accords qui, sans être des accords d'association au sens juridique du terme, n'en sont pas moins des accords de coopération étroite, requérant des structures institutionnelles...". Jean-Victor Louis, La procédure de conclusion des accords internationaux, in: Jean-Victor Louis et Marianne Dony (ed.), *Relations extérieures* (Commentaire J. Mégret), p. 101.

On the contrary, one could argue, and that could explain the approach followed by the European Parliament, that the Schengen/Dublin agreements with Switzerland are indeed very close to an association. Their title indicate clearly that these agreements establish an "association" between the EU, EC and Switzerland. Looking closely to the institutional framework could also lead to the observation that the so-called mixed committees differ considerably from classical joint or mixed committees. The system was designed to enable the associate countries to fully participate in the decision-shaping of EC Law. This is a unique example of associating third countries in the decision-making procedure of the EC. That could be considered as specific. Since many of the activities of the mixed committee concern domains falling internally into the co-decision procedure (external borders, illegal migration, visas), one could also argue that the prerogatives of the European Parliament would be affected in a comparable manner to the classical association agreements concluded in accordance with Article 310 EC.

Depending on the final position of the Council, it cannot be excluded that the EP might be tempted to start a procedure before the Court of Justice for the violation of its institutional prerogatives against the Council decisions on the conclusion of the Association Agreements (first pillar Schengen and Dublin). If successful, the Council decision would be annulled, but the effects of the agreement would be maintained until the Council adopts a new decision.[136] In addition, it must be noted that the Commission proposed to follow the approach chosen with Switzerland for the signature and the conclusion of the Liechtenstein protocols. The Committee on Civil Liberties, Justice and Home Affairs has not yet drafted a report, but given the similarities between the agreements, the approach is likely to be similar.

VI. Conclusion

With the entry into force of these agreements on 1 March 2008, Switzerland will become a close partner to the EU in crucial parts of the Area of Freedom, Security and Justice. But like the other associated EFTA partners, this close relation will not allow a complete and full participation in the ambitious objective of the European Union to create a European Area of Freedom, Security and Justice. This is not yet the end of the story.

---

136. For an example, ECJ, Case 211/01, *Commission/Council*, [2001] ECR I-8913, para. 54.

Part II

Private Law

1. The Opinion on the Lugano Convention and the Implied External Relations Powers of the European Community

Pieter Jan Kuijper

I. Introduction

The Opinion on the Lugano Convention constitutes a major effort on the part of the European Court of Justice to create greater clarity with respect to its line of case law on the implied external relations powers of the European Community. This line of case law started more than 35 years ago with the well-known ERTA- or AETR-case[1] and has developed through different stages, marked by the Opinions 1/76[2], 2/91[3] and 1/94[4]and the so-called "Open Skies" cases.[5]

As is well-known, this line of cases relies on the notion that there should be some kind of parallelism between the internal powers of the Community and its external powers. As long as the internal powers remain "potential" and have not been exercised, the corresponding external powers will also retain a purely potential character and there is no obligation on the Council and the Commission, whether on a contractual basis (through international agreements) or on an autonomous basis (through unilateral action in the international arena) to exercise such competence. Once the Council (and the Parliament) have used their internal legislative powers, however, the recourse to external measures can only be taken at Community level, otherwise individual external action by the Member States will affect the proper functioning of the internal Community legislation.

This so-called ERTA jurisprudence has suffered from two problems that are interrelated. As will be recalled below, the fundamental idea behind these cases is basically sound, given the nature of the Community. However,

---

1.   Case 22/70, Commission v. Council (ERTA), [1971] ECR, 263.
2.   Opinion 1/76 (Laying-up Fund for the Rhine), [1977] ECR, 741.
3.   Opinion 2/91 (ILO Convention No. 170), [1993] ECR, I-1061.
4.   Opinion 1/74 (WTO Agreement), [1994] ECR, I- 5267.
5.   Cases C-466 -469, 471-472, and 475-476 (Open Skies), [2002] ECR, I-9427 ff.

over the years cases have come up which have nuanced and complicated the basic conception to such a point that its application by the Commission in its proposals and by the Council in its approval of international agreements has become very difficult. It is not easy to predict beforehand whether or not an agreement needs to be concluded by the Community acting alone, as a Community agreement, or acting together with the Member States in the form of a mixed agreement.

This lack of predictability in the application of the AETR doctrine has contributed to the negative effect that the doctrine tends to have on the internal legislative activity of the Community. Since if there is a link between internal legislation and external competence in the domain of that legislation the link can also be made backwards by the Member States in the Council: if we do not want to lose our external powers in this field, we had better not adopt internal legislation. "What will be the AETR effect of this legislation?" was an oft-heard question at the Legal Service of the Council in the seventies and eighties.[6]

It is a question which is currently no longer put so openly in the Council, but one that does probably play a role in the background with respect to internal legislation in the field of civil law, especially since that is a field that was only fully integrated into Community law when the Treaty of Amsterdam came into force (1999). At that time the Commission took the decision to propose an immediate conversion of the Brussels Convention, concluded under Article 293, fourth indent, of the EC Treaty, into a Regulation under Article 65 of that treaty, thereby actually bringing about the "feared" ERTA effect.

Therefore, the central question in the following essay will not only relate to the direction in which the AETR doctrine will be moving under the influence of the Lugano Opinion, but it will also relate to whether there will now be greater clarity and predictability about its application in general and in the field of private international law in particular. To this end, this contribution will begin with sketching the state of the AETR line of cases just before the Lugano Opinion was handed down and after that it will attempt (1) to set out the direction where the Lugano Opinion will take this line of cases in general and (2) to assess the immediate influence of the Opinion on the division of power in external relations in general, and in the field of private international law in particular.

---

6. In reality, this question should be read as: "is my Member State going to lose external power?" or, more egoistically: "I am afraid that I might not be able to make these nice trips for my Member State to New York/Geneva/Lugano any longer".

II. The development of the ERTA doctrine up to the Lugano case

A. Implied powers: the fundamentals

The ERTA case itself clearly sets out where the notion of implied power in the field of external relations of the Community comes from, namely from the (international) legal personality of the Community laid down in what was then Article 210 (now Article 281) EC. This provision and its place in the Treaty, at the head of the "General and Final Provisions", implied, according to the Court, that in its external relations the Community had the capacity "to establish contractual links with third countries", i.e. to conclude international agreements with them, over the whole field of the objectives of the treaty, since there is a direct link between the first part, on objectives, and the final part of the treaty. This was, even at the time, a rather unsurprising approach, given that the International Court of Justice, already more than two decades earlier, had made a similar implied powers link between the international personality of international organizations and their capacity to act on the international scene (in that case to make international claims).[7] This was, therefore, largely a straightforward application of well-known international law principles on the part of the Court.

However, at the same time, the Court needed to take account of the special character of the Community as an organization that produces legislation that is applicable in the law of its Member States, either directly or through transformation (in the case of directives)[8] and whose treaties are not only binding on the organization, but also on its Member States[9]. In short the Court needed to take account of the federation-like characteristics of the Community, in particular the fact that, though the Community had been equipped with wide-ranging internal powers, it had not necessarily exercised all of them (yet). This is where the difference lies between having a potential power to negotiate and conclude international agreements across the breadth of the Community's internal powers and having the exclusive right to do so. Here the Court uses a principle that is applied primarily internally in federal states, namely pre-emption, also on the external side of the Community. At the time, the Court had neither the

---

7. Reparations for Injuries suffered in the Service of the United Nations, ICJ Reports 1949, pp. 9-23.
8. See Art. 249 EC Treaty.
9. See Art. 300(7) EC Treaty.

time nor did it have the opportunity to make this difference clear and to spell out its consequences, since it was confronted with only one major question: who had the power in this case: the Community or the Member States? Hence, the Court went seamlessly from one issue (implied powers in general) to the next (the exclusive nature of implied powers) and formulated its famous position on exclusivity for the first time, straight after its assertion of (potential) competence co-equal to the scope of the Treaty, as follows:

> In particular each time the Community [...] adopts provisions laying down common rules, [...], the Member States no longer have the right, acting individually, or even collectively to undertake obligations with third countries which affect those rules.

> As and when such common rules come into being, the Community alone is in a position to assume and carry out contractual obligations towards third countries which affect those rules.[10]

In short, "the system of internal Community measures may not ... be separated from that of external relations."[11] The fundamental reason why the Member States cannot act at the international level outside the Community framework, once there are common internal rules in the same domain is very simple and repeated once more later in the judgment: the Member States might assume obligations which might affect those rules or alter their scope. This rationale remains fully valid today and regularly recurs in one form or another in later judgments based on the ERTA principle. Pre-emption, as it is called in the US and many federal states does not only operate on the internal level, but also for the Community's external powers, whereas in most federal states, the external powers have been granted by the constitution "en bloc" to the federation.

In the Community system, as interpreted by the Court, this creeping pre-emption in the field of external relations following hard on the heels of recourse to the corresponding internal powers (in the ERTA case: the harmonization of driving and rest times for lorry-drivers inside the Community) is also based on the duty of co-operation of the Member-States (Article 10 EC Treaty).[12] Helping to create tension or contradiction between their individual international agreements and the Community (internal) legislation clearly cannot be squared with what in the German doctrine is called "Gemeinschaftstreue" (allegiance to the Community).

---

10. Case 22/70, points 17 – 18.
11. Ibid, point 19.
12. Ibid, point 21 and Opinion 2/91, point 10.

It is interesting to note that the Court based its reasoning on the above principles, relating only in passing that this principled approach is "expressly recognized" by an article in the regulation on the harmonization of some social legislation in road transport, which stated that "[t]he Community shall enter into any negotiations with third countries which may prove necessary for the purpose of implementing this regulation."[13] In later case law, we will see such articles being interpreted as, in the Court's view, laying down express exclusive competence.[14]

B.   Potential implied powers: can recourse to them be obligatory? Opinion 1/76 and its progeny

The relationship between implied external relations powers with a potential character and the same powers as exclusive competencies was clarified in the Opinion 1/76 concerning the laying-up fund for the Rhine.[15] This Opinion made it implicitly clear that potential external relations powers could always be used by the Community, if the Council made the political judgment that this was useful. The Opinion went a step further in deciding that such potential powers could become exclusive, if for the realization of one of the objectives of the Community it was necessary to have recourse to the potential power, which thereby became exclusive.

In this way, this case seemed to create a link between the exclusive character of the external relations power in question and the obligation of the Member States in Council (or of the Council itself) to have recourse to that power. This is not a link which is inevitable. Speaking in general terms, it is possible that the Council decides not to use a power which is or has become exclusive. However, in such a situation the Member States are also doomed to inaction, since they would infringe Community law by acting alone, or even collectively. Hence, though there may be no absolute obligation to use an exclusive external competence, in practice, if the Member States acting in Council want to achieve certain goals, such as the reduction of shipping capacity on the Rhine, they cannot but have recourse to the exclusive external power.

The other major issue that was raised by this Opinion was the question of the meaning of the word "necessary" in the phrase "necessary for the realization of one of the objectives of the Community". Was it what the

---

13.   Art. 3 of Reg. 543/69, see ERTA, fn. 1 above, para. 30.
14.   See Opinion 1/94, points 94-95.
15.   See fn. 2 above.

Council deemed necessary or was it necessary to establish some kind of objective necessity that the Council had to accept existed? In Opinion 1/76 the Court argued that, if the Community's objective was to absorb overcapacity in Rhine shipping by the creation of the laying-up fund, it was necessary to conclude an agreement with the Swiss. The Court saw this as a kind of inevitable economic link: if the Swiss created new capacity, the objective of Community transport policy on the Rhine would be frustrated. Hence, it was necessary to agree with the Swiss on their sharing the objective and joining in the policy of capacity reduction. This was indeed a bit more than a political "necessity" established at the Council's say-so; it was an economically compelling necessity. But this was clearly an aspect of the case that was in need of further development. And develop the Court it did, as we will see below in the discussion of Opinion 2/91 and 1/94.

C.   Opinion 2/91: the Court takes with one hand and gives back with the other

In Opinion 2/91, the Court was confronted with the question whether the EC could conclude (alone) Convention N° 170 of the ILO concerning safety in the use of chemicals at work. The Court briefly recalls its approach distinguishing between potential and exclusive Community competences in external relations and begins the analysis of the case with the normal ERTA approach.[16]

The Court divides its analysis of Convention N° 170 in the light of existing internal Community rules into two: insofar as the legislation is based on the social policy provisions of the treaty and insofar as it is based on Articles 95 (then 100a) and 100. In respect of the directives based on the social policy provisions (now Article 136 ff EC), it is pointed out that these provisions provide for minimum rules of Community law (Art. 137 (2)(b) EC). The same is true for the directive on the protection of workers from the risks related to exposure to chemical, physical and biological agents at work based on Article 100. This implies that the Member States still have a certain upward freedom of manoeuvre not only at the Community, but also at the international level. Insofar as Community rules on the safety of chemicals at work might fall below the standards of Convention N° 170,

---

16.   Although it leaves to one side the "seeming" restriction of the ERTA doctrine to the "common policies" of the EC alone, which in any case was untenable. If *any* Community rule is capable of being affected by an international agreement, it is the latter that should become exclusive Community competence, regardless of whether the rule in question is part of a common policy.

the Member States could independently compensate that shortfall and be in conformity with both Community and international obligations. The ILO Constitution also indicates that its Conventions are minimum norms (Article 19(a) ILO Constitution), which in turn means that, should the Community lay down more stringent rules than the ILO Convention N° 170, the Member States would still be in conformity with the ILO Convention,[17] insofar as they satisfy at least its level of protection (they would however breach Community minimum rules).

Insofar as other relevant internal Community law based on the internal market and general harmonisation provisions of the EC Treaty, in particular directives on classification, packaging and labelling of dangerous substances is concerned, the Court notes that they are not minimum standards and confer more extensive protection than Convention N° 170, in particular with respect to labelling. On the other hand, the scope of the Convention is wider than that of these Community rules: the definition of chemicals is broader and it also covers their transport. On balance, however, the Court arrives at the conclusion that the relevant part of the Convention, though Community law is not in contradiction with it, is concerned with an area which is already covered to a large extent by Community rules progressively adopted over a long period of time with a view to achieving progressive harmonization aimed at removing barriers to trade in the Community as well as providing protection for human health and the environment. The Court concluded, therefore, that the relevant Community rules were affected by the commitments of Part III of Convention N° 170 and that Member States could not subscribe to that Part outside the Community framework.[18] Obviously, therefore, the whole of Convention N° 170 was of mixed competence, according to the logic of the Court.

What is interesting here is the contradiction in the Court's approach: the cold logic and meticulous approach, without any analysis whether the Community rules in actual fact fall below the norms of the ILO Convention, in on the one hand the analysis of the effect of the minimum norms approach in the EC Treaty as well as in the ILO Convention, and the willingness to look at the factual conformity of EC law with ILO law and at the bigger picture and not just the individual common rules in a certain area of Community law on the other. The minimum norms approach also shows that there is no complete neutrality, as between Community and Member States, in the choice of whether or not there is exclusive

17. Points 16-18 and 21 of Opinion 2/91.
18. Points 24-26 of Opinion 2/91.

competence, for the simple reason that the Member States are Members of the ILO and the Community is not. The perspective of the Court is entirely determined by the fact that the Member States are already there and must be able to conform to the ILO Convention while escaping international responsibility vis-à-vis the ILO –and while also remaining in line with their (minimum) Community obligations – precisely because of the upward flexibility this entails.

Insofar as the minimum norms approach is based on minimum norms on the EC side, the Member States will be able to conform to ILO law, even if the EC does not (and in the Court's view it seems entirely irrelevant whether EC law conforms or not). In other words the "question préalable" whether or not the Community has (exclusive) competence is determined entirely by the result of whether the Member States will be able to escape international responsibility (which they can on their own, and even without infringing Community law). In other words, the Community has legislative power in the field covered by the international convention, has even comprehensively exercised it, but because the Member States could theoretically escape international responsibility by going further than Community minimum norms, the Community could never conclude an international agreement in an area of Community law where minimum norms were used. Therefore, the international personality of the Community counts for very little in all those areas where Community law-making is based on minimum norms (social affairs and many other areas of harmonisation).[19] In spite of extensive Community legislation in these domains, the Community is doomed to remain a nonentity on the international scene, as long as the Member States in Council do not decide to exercise the potential external power of the Community in those areas, which will be the case only in exceptional situations at this stage of the development of the Community.

On the other hand, insofar as the minimum norms approach is based on the fact that the international organization or convention in question allows such minimum norms,[20] it is legally unacceptable to allow Community exclusive competence to be determined by the "constitutional law" of another organization. It may indeed be true, as the Court seems to

---

19. It shows that the "functional character" of the Community's international legal personality in such situations is totally out of proportion (in a negative sense) with the internal competence actually exercised. This is perhaps less true for areas where there are primarily minimum norms, but where the Treaty recognizes up front that the external power in the area is "shared", such as environmental policy.
20. We do not discuss here the situation where both the EC and the organization allow minimum norms in the same domain, as in the ILO case.

intimate in Opinion 2/91, that in such a situation "delinquent" Member States that fall below the international minimum standards, may be "saved" by Community law above that standard. This implies that the "delinquent" Member States are in breach not only of the international rule in question, but also of Community law. The Community can maintain that it is indeed in conformity with the international norm, but the Commission would need to sue the Member State under Article 226 for breach of Community law (and the international norm)[21] in order to fully guarantee the conformity of the Community, and thus of the Member States who are Members of the organization, with the international minimum norms in question. This is in stark contradiction with the reasoning of the Court in the case, where the minimum norms approach is to be found on the side of the Community.

In short, there are many anomalies in this Opinion and the Member States perspective is clearly prevalent, but that should not perhaps cause surprise in an EC and a world where States are still regarded as basically sovereign, even if many sovereign powers have actually been transferred to the European Community.

D.   Further development of potential and exclusive powers: Opinions 2/92 and 1/94

Opinions 2/92 and 1/94, which were actually given in reverse order did not relate primarily to the question of exclusive implied powers under the ERTA approach, but were rather about the scope of the notion of trade policy. But indirectly, because some second line arguments of the Commission built on Opinion 1/76 and on the ERTA case, the Court was compelled to clarify, or rather to give a more objective legal underpinning to its original approach in these two cases, and thus to restrict their effect.

As to the question of the obligatory direct recourse to potential external competence in line with Opinion 1/76, the Court stressed that, indeed, the

---

21.   For a case of this kind, see the infringement case against Germany for breach of the Community dairy regulations and the International Dairy Agreement concluded in the framework of the GATT (now defunct), Case C-61/94, Commission/Germany, [1996] ECR I-3989. Another case which illustrates the important link between Community powers and Member State powers in mixed agreements, to the point of recognizing that the Community has an interest to prevent a Member State from causing international responsibility for breach of a mixed agreement, even in the area of Member State competence, Case C-239/03, Commission v. France (Etang de Berre), [2004] ECR I- 9325.

necessity of reaching a treaty objective was not something to be left to the broad political judgment of the Community legislator. Some objective link between recourse to the potential external power and the objective to be reached under the Treaty had to be present. The reduction in Swiss capacities was a necessity in order to reach a balance between demand and offer in Community Rhine shipping. Agreements on fisheries with third States were indispensable for preserving the living resources of the sea for Community fishermen. In short, if objectives under the treaties[22] cannot be reached by autonomous Community measures alone, direct recourse to potential external powers without pre-existing internal legislation, is possible and even necessary.[23]

With respect to ERTA itself, the Court followed a similar path to objectification. The fact that, if no international agreement was concluded, there would be competitive distortions within the internal market for services or goods (in the latter case because of differences in legislation on intellectual property), was no valid substitute for, or equivalent of, the possible affectation of internal legislation within the meaning of the ERTA judgment. Moreover, a considerable quantity of internal legislation contained clauses relating to treatment of third-country service providers or third-country firms establishing themselves in the Community. And here, the Court returned to what it had seen in the ERTA case itself as a mere confirmation or symptom of the fact that the internal rules were capable of being affected by the international agreement about to be concluded, namely clauses granting the power to negotiate on external aspects of legislation internal to the Commission.[24] Such clauses and the above-mentioned clauses on the treatment of third country natural and moral persons were considered sufficient by the Court to impart exclusive external competence on the Community.

Finally, the Court, as a kind of afterthought, said that such exclusive external competence, even without specific grant of negotiating authority, also exists if the Community has achieved a complete harmonisation in a certain domain.[25] How this statement had to be understood in connection with the criterion used in Opinion 2/91 to the effect that exclusive external competence would arise already in respect of an area already covered to a large extent by Community rules remained unclear.

---

22. The Court speaks of "objectives of the treaties". However, its own example of the restriction of shipping capacities on the Rhine is not a direct Treaty objective.
23. See Opinion 1/94, § 82-86; Opinion 2/92, para. 4.
24. Opinion 1/94, point 95.
25. Opinion 1/94, point 96.

So, even after the greater precision and objectification of both Opinion 1/76 and the ERTA doctrine, there still remained much room for interpretation.

E.   The Open Skies cases: ERTA risks losing any operational effectiveness and predictability by becoming too detailed and detached from reality

In the so-called Open Skies cases, which were infringement cases brought by the Commission against several Member States for having concluded the agreements with the same title with the USA, the Court had another chance to clarify the doctrines of Opinion 1/76 and ERTA.

With respect to Opinion 1/76, the Court manages to even further restrict the doctrine of the necessity to exercise a potential external competence in order to achieve an objective under the EC Treaty by pretending that it had ruled in Opinion 1/94 that such direct recourse to an external competence was only possible in connection with the simultaneous exercise of both powers, which was supposed to establish the necessity of the recourse to the exclusive external power. However, the Court said nothing about simultaneity in Opinion 1/94[26]; it only spoke about the internal and external competence being inextricably linked in order to establish the necessity of the direct recourse to a potential external competence.

Moreover, the Court reacted negatively to a new argument advanced by the Commission during the procedure, which introduced an element of ERTA reasoning in order to establish the necessity of exercising directly an external competence in the field of aviation, namely that the measures adopted by the Council in relation to the internal aviation market contain a number of provisions relating to nationals from non-member countries. The Commission thus tried to establish in a legal and objective manner that such inextricable link between internal and external competence in the field of air transport existed. However, the Court rejected this novel approach by a qualitative argument, namely the relatively limited character of those provisions, which was not sufficient to establish the inextricable link, in the Court's view.

The Court rejected a similar novel argument from the Commission in respect of the ERTA doctrine, where it argued that the "Open Skies" agreements included fifth freedom rights for US carriers so that they could

---

26.   See Opinion 1/94, point 86 (and not 89 as the Court said in point 57 of the Open Skies Case against Denmark, C-467/98).

transport passengers between two Member States, as long as the origin or destination was the USA, thus basically operating on intra-Community routes and thereby affecting the two main regulations on the Community aviation market, namely those on licensing of air carriers and on access to intra-Community routes. However, the Court rejected this as an "economic" and not an objective, "legal" affectation, since the scope of these regulations is limited to Community carriers and intra-Community air routes, thus excluding the fifth freedom rights of non-Community air carriers.[27] One wonders whether the Court has not driven "objectiveness", not to say legal formalism, too far here, given that as a consequence of fifth freedom rights both US and Community carriers operate on the market which is regulated by Community rules. The application of these rules, even if formally restricted to Community carriers, is certainly going to be affected by it in a real sense.

Whilst the Court thus rejected the application of the ERTA doctrine to the fifth freedom rights, following the guidance of its Advocate-General Tizzano, it accepted the application of the doctrine on the basis of an equally detailed and formalistic analysis of the Open Skies agreements in the light of a number of provisions of Community law relating to non-member countries and carriers, of which it had earlier said that they were not strong enough to demonstrate the inextricable link between internal and external competence under Opinion 1/76. Thus the Court concluded that the Open Skies agreements affected an implicit prohibition on third State carriers to introduce new products, which could be deduced from analyzing a number of specific provisions of Community law. Similarly, the Open Skies agreements affected a rule that subjected third country carriers to Community rules on computerized reservation systems (CRS's). On the other hand, some Member States escaped being sanctioned for affecting the slots regulation by their "Open Skies" accord.

Whatever the other merits of the Open Skies judgments[28], one may readily question whether establishing Community competence on such a detailed and meticulous analysis of specific provisions of Community law does not make the application of the doctrine of 1/76 and AETR so unpredictable as to exclude any operational application of it. Such an approach to the combined doctrines of Opinion 1/76 and ERTA was bound to result in any

27. Case C-471/98 (Belgium), p. 103.
28. It should be noted that the part of the Open Skies judgments dealing with the restriction of these agreements to aviation companies of the Member State that concluded them eventually had a very positive effect. The fact that these provisions were declared contrary to Article 49 of the EC Treaty finally resulted in a Community Open Skies agreement with the US, OJ L 134, 25.5.2007, p. 1.

attempt at applying the exclusive external Community powers in a Commission recommendation for negotiations turning into a huge internal battle with the Council. If the outcome of that battle was to opt for the negotiation of a mixed agreement – as would be likely given the prevailing mood of the Member States in the Council – the Commission would be confronted with the ugly choice of either going to Court or accepting that the definitive entry into force of the proposed agreement would have to wait until all of the now 27 Member States have completed their ratification processes – which could take three to four years at the very least.[29]

3.   Opinion 1/03 on the Lugano Convention

A.   Introduction

Under the old system of Community conventions relating to private international law under Article 293, fourth indent, of the EC Treaty, the Brussels Convention regulated the rules on the jurisdiction of Courts and the rules on the recognition and enforcement of judgments in civil and commercial matters. This Convention was placed under the jurisdiction of the European Court of Justice.[30] The regime of this Community Convention was extended to a number of countries closely associated with the Community, primarily Switzerland, by the so-called Lugano Convention.[31]

After the entry into force of the Treaty of Amsterdam, including the provisions on private international law and civil law cooperation in the Community, part of that Treaty, the Brussels Convention, was fairly quickly communitarized in a slightly modified version, and became Regulation 44/2001.[32] This "communautarization" of the Brussels I Convention had an immediate impact on EC external relations. In particular, it meant that, in accordance with the Court's case law,

---

29.   The Cotonou Agreement with 15 Member States on the Community side took 4 years to ratify, primarily because of the slowness of the 15 and not of the two-thirds of the 70-odd ACP States that had to ratify it before it could enter into force.

30.   See Protocol of 3 June 1971 on the interpretation of the Convention of 27 September 1968 (Brussels Convention), The consolidated text of the Brussels Convention and the consolidated text of the Protocol are to be found in OJ C27 of 26.1.1998, respectively at p. 1 and p. 28.

31.   The "old" Lugano Convention is to be found in OJ L 319, 25.11.1988, p. 9. A consolidated version of the "old" Lugano Convention as it is presently applied is at http://curia.europa.eu/common/recdoc/conventions/en/c-textes/lug-idc.htm. The "new" Lugano Convention which existed only in draft at the time of Court case, has now been signed (cf.OJ L 339, 21.12.2007, p. 1).

32.   OJ L 12, 16.1.2001, p. 1.

international agreements which contained provisions on the recognition and enforcement of judgments in civil and commercial matters would, to this extent, fall under the exclusive competence of the Community, and therefore could no longer be negotiated and concluded by the Member States acting alone.

After the entry into force of the Brussels I Regulation, it soon became clear that there were international agreements in a variety of policy areas, including transport policy or environmental policy, which now fell under exclusive Community competence insofar as they had links with the subject matter of the Brussels I Regulation. Generally, Community competence in such cases was not contested. Wherever possible, the Community was thus authorized to negotiate the relevant provisions. However, where a direct EC involvement of the EC in negotiations was no longer possible, or where the draft agreement in question did not provide for participation by the EC, other pragmatic solutions had to be found, sometimes even in the form of an authorization of the Member States to conclude the agreement on behalf of the EC.[33]

However, these were minor issues compared to the crucial question of whether the new Brussels I Regulation had to be extended in the same way as the Brussels Convention to the same circle of States insofar as they had not become Members of the Community or of the EEA in the meantime: this was to be the new Lugano Convention. The question immediately arose whether such a proposed Convention, which would be largely identical to the Community regime laid down in Reg. 44/2001 and extended to third countries, would be of such a nature as to be capable of affecting the relevant Community rules within the meaning of the ERTA doctrine and therefore fall wholly within exclusive Community competence. Since no clear view could be reached on this issue in the Council, as a minority consisting of the Commission and a few Member States supported this view and the large majority of Member States were opposed to it, the Council decided to request the Court for an Opinion under Article 300(6) of the EC Treaty.

In dealing with this request, the Court first gave a restatement of the doctrines developed in its case law since Opinion 1/76 and its ERTA judgment[34], and subsequently applied it to the two parts of the Lugano Convention, namely the part relating to the rules on the jurisdiction of

---

33. Cf. in greater detail the contribution by Hix in this book.
34. Points 114-113 of Opinion 1/03.

courts[35] and the part concerning the rules on the recognition and enforcement of judgments in civil and commercial matters.[36]

B.   The restatement of the law concerning the competence of the Community to conclude international agreements

The Court's restatement is very elaborate. First, it re-affirms the principle of implied external powers across the wide spectrum covered by the Treaty; then, it very briefly sets out the situation with respect to direct recourse to potential external powers; and finally, the Court makes a very elaborate restatement of its ERTA doctrine, nuancing and reorienting it in several ways compared to its earlier case law.

As to potential powers and its views developed since Opinion 1/76, the Court simply compresses into one single paragraph every turn of phrase that it has ever uttered on the subject, which results in the following:

> As regards exclusive competence, the Court has held that the situation envisaged in Opinion 1/76 is that in which internal competence may be effectively exercised only at the same time as external competence (see Opinion 1/76, paragraphs 4 and 7 and Opinion 1/94, paragraph 85), the conclusion of the international agreement being thus necessary in order to attain objectives of the Treaty that cannot be attained by establishing autonomous rules [...][37]

The concept of simultaneity has already been criticised above as needlessly restrictive where an indissoluble link would have been quite sufficient to indicate that internal competence cannot be properly or fully exercised without recourse to a potential external power. The most obvious recent example brought about by the Amsterdam Treaty is the indissoluble link between effective internal measures against illegal immigration, including repatriation of illegal immigrants (Article 63(3)(b) of the EC Treaty) and readmission agreements. The first can only be effective if there is a guarantee that the relevant third countries will accept the illegal immigrants that are to be repatriated to them, and to that end readmission agreements are absolutely indispensable. However, these agreements need to precede the internal measures, especially since a large number of them need to be concluded before the internal rules can be fully effective. The indissoluble link is there, but simultaneity in a strict sense cannot be maintained, especially now that the relevant internal measures have not yet

---

35.   Points 139-161 of Opinion 1/03.
36.   Points. 162-172 of Opinion 1/03.
37.   Opinion 1/03, para. 115.

been fully adopted.[38] Moreover, if simultaneity is supposed to be applied very strictly by the Court, what is then supposed to be the distinguishing feature between the 1/76 approach and the ERTA doctrine? Opinion 1/76 will simply be like the ERTA doctrine, but with the corresponding external power simply following (very) hard on the heels of internal legislation, with no longer an obligatory "first use" of potential external power, which as a result is no longer potential, but exclusive.

However, the Court's embellishment on Opinion 1/76 will be left for what it is, since the real core of the Opinion is the restatement of the ERTA doctrine. This restatement says much not only for the way in which it nuances or distinguishes earlier Court pronouncements, but also for the sequence in which this is done.

First of all, the Court goes back to the ERTA judgment itself (point 17 of it) in order to recall the core idea, namely that every time common rules have been adopted, Member States no longer have the right, individually or collectively, to undertake obligations with third States, which affect those rules. In other words: in such situations the Community has exclusive external competence. The Court also recalls in passing that this also applies in areas falling outside common policies and that all of this is underpinned by the principle of Article 10 of the EC Treaty.[39]

Secondly, the Court then goes directly to the passage from Opinion 2/91 concerning Part III of ILO Convention N° 170 in order to recall that

---

38. See Directive 2001/40/EC of 28 May 2001 on the mutual recognition of decisions on the expulsion of third country nationals, OJ L 149, 2.6.2001, p. 34 that would be repealed and expanded by the Commission Proposal for a Directive of the European Parliament and of the Council on common standards and procedures in Member States for returning illegally staying third-country nationals, doc. COM(2005) 391 that has not yet been adopted. It is intriguing to note that neither the minimalist directive of 2001 nor the broader one proposed in 2005 mention the issue of readmission anywhere, whilst it is perfectly clear that, if persons expelled or returned are not admitted in the third State concerned for whatever reason (usually arguable doubts about the person's nationality or country of residence) these directives are or will be wholly without practical effect. Note that the Member States in Council have never accepted fully that readmission agreements are an exclusive competence that must be exercised in order to reach an objective of the Treaty and the Commission has so far hesitated to bring a test case before the Court of Justice, though there are countless examples of Member States having concluded readmission agreements just before, or almost simultaneously with the granting of negotiating authority by the Council to the Commission under Article 300 of the EC Treaty. On readmission agreements in greater detail, see the contribution by Schieffer to this volume.
39. Opinion 1/03, paras. 115-118, quoting from para. 17 ERTA case and paras 10-11 of Opinion 2/91.

Community rules in an area largely covered by them, especially in the case of progressive harmonisation on the road to the internal market under simultaneous upholding of such values as the environment and human health, could be considered affected by international obligations in that area.[40]

Thirdly, the Court nuances the three situations which it recognized in Opinion 1/94 as additionally decisive for exclusive external competence (clauses concerning treatment of third State nationals, clauses granting negotiating powers with third States to the Community, normally the Commission, and situations of complete harmonisation of a sector), by arguing that those three situations were largely determined by the context of the cases in which they arose.[41] The Court now prefers to reason in more general terms and to refer back to ERTA itself where it said that the conclusion of an agreement by the Member States that is incompatible with the unity of the common market and the uniformity of Community law is not allowed.[42] On the other hand it compresses two of the three situations (namely clauses relating to third State nationals and clauses relating to the complete harmonisation of a particular issue) into one, namely situations where the nature of the existing Community provisions is such that any agreement in that area would necessarily affect the relevant Community rules within the meaning of the ERTA judgment.

The Court, however, continues to accept the minimum standards exception (but only in cases where both the Community law and the international convention contain minimum standards)[43] as well as the economic affectation exception. In this connection the Court places great emphasis on the need for a specific analysis of both the agreement envisaged and the relevant Community law in force possibly affected thereby.[44] What is important is to ensure a uniform and consistent application of Community rules and the proper functioning of the system they establish. This may not be affected by international obligations accepted by the Member States. The purpose of the exclusive external competence of the Community is primarily to maintain the integrity of Community law and the effectiveness of the Community system, according to the Court.[45]

---

40. Opinion 1/03, para. 120, referring to Opinion 2/91, paras 25-26.
41. Opinion 1/03, para. 121.
42. Opinion 1/03, para. 122, referring to para 31 of ERTA.
43. See my criticism of this point above in which it is implicit that only the presence minimum standards on the Community side is relevant, even in the approach of the Court.
44. Opinion 1/03, point 124.
45. Opinion 1/03, points 128 and 131.

This is clearly a minimalist approach by the Court and confirms what has been said above: the continued existence of the external sovereignty of the Member States is of prime importance, not the full parallelism between internal and external powers of the Community. The exception for minimum standards remains a clear sign in this connection.

There is, however, one very important restriction to this approach that is rejected by the Court, namely the notion that a so-called disconnection clause[46] or any exception in a Member State agreement in favour of Community law would automatically undo the fact that the agreement in question is otherwise capable of affecting Community law. The answer to that question must be established before the agreement is concluded and the Member States cannot exempt themselves from exclusive external Community competence by trying to undo the consequences of their (in principle) illegal action, however laudable the attempt may be.[47]

C.   The application of the restatement of the ERTA doctrine to the new Lugano Convention

The Court then proceeds to apply this restatement to Regulation 44/2001 in relation the projected Lugano Convention and thus follows its own prescription for a specific analysis of both the international and the

---

46. A disconnection clause is a clause in an international agreement which provides that the agreement in question will not prevent the Member States from applying among themselves Community law rather than the provisions of the agreement. This is a statement of great importance, when made by the Member States, in case the Community cannot become a party to the agreement in question, as was the case, when Member States were able to adhere to the first "Television without borders" convention of the Council of Europe. It enabled the Member States to continue to agree on and apply among themselves the "Television without borders directive" and give it priority over the CoE Convention. In that sense Member States and the Community were indeed "disconnected" from the Convention. In the present situation where most CoE Conventions are concluded in the form of mixed agreements, the clause merely serves to put the treaty partners of the Community Member States on notice that the Convention in question creates international obligations between the Member States and third States parties to the convention and also between the Community and third States, but not among the Member States themselves, who will be applying Community law among themselves, since it is the implementing law of the Convention text and presumably in conformity with it (since the Community is also a party to the convention). In short, there is no disconnection between the international convention and the Community and its Member States in any real sense.

47. See Case C-467/98 (Danish open skies case), point 101.

Community instrument involved. It proceeds with this analysis in two steps.

1. With respect to the rules of the Lugano Convention on the jurisdiction of Courts

The Court ventures to demonstrate by an analysis of Regulation 44/2001 alone that any agreement that sets up a similar unified system of rules on conflict of jurisdiction is capable of affecting that regulation. The Court argues that rules on the resolution of conflicts of jurisdictions between national systems governed by different linking factors for establishing jurisdiction are very complex so that the slightest difference or lacuna in the rules immediately leads to possible conflicts, but also to possible gaps in jurisdiction. In such a situation, an international agreement concluded by Member States with third States seeking to establish criteria for allocation of jurisdiction between the Courts of the parties would inevitably also lay down criteria for the exercise of jurisdiction not just for the courts of the non-Member country, but also for the courts of the Member State in question, and hence would cover matters covered by Regulation No. 44/2001.

This is the case, since after its much-commented Owusu ruling (on the Brussels Convention)[48] it is established that Regulation 44/2001 covers not only jurisdictional issues with an international aspect between Member States of the Community, but also cases where the possibly competing jurisdiction is that of a third country. Article 2 of the Brussels Convention and of Regulation No 44/2001 on the face of it is not restricted to Community nationals, when it says that persons domiciled in a Member State shall, whatever their nationality, be sued in the Court of that Member State. In the Court's view it is not only important for the functioning of the common market that the rules of jurisdictional conflict in choice of law situations are uniform as between the jurisdictions of the Community only, but also as between the jurisdictions of a Community Member State and a third state. It can also be very important that such judgments are exportable as between Member States.[49]

The Court in the course of this analysis also deals with a favourite argument of several Member States, namely that Article 4(1) of Reg. 44/2001 showed that there ought to be at least some Member State competence involved in the conclusion of the Lugano Convention. Article 4(1)

---

48.   Case C-281/02, Owusu, [2005] ECR I-1383.
49.   See Case C-281/02, Owusu, points 26 – 34.

provides that "if the defendant is not domiciled in a Member State, the jurisdiction of the courts of each Member State shall, subject to Articles 22 and 23, be determined *by the law of that Member State*."[50] The Court is not overly impressed by this reference to the law of a Member State as a basis for Member State competence and rejects it. The fact that the Regulation, like the Brussels Convention before it, refers to the law of the Member States, including the mentioned exceptions to that rule, does not automatically entail that it gives rise to Member State competence. The Court points out that a rule in a Member State agreement that respected the provision of Article 4(1) could still easily conflict with other provisions of Regulation No. 44/2001.[51]

It is important to note that the Court's analysis is less formalistic and more based on the effect in reality of the clause in question than was the case in the "Open Skies" case where, as we saw, the Court accepted that formal rules excluding non-Community carriers had to be taken at face value without looking at the real impact of the individual "Open Skies" agreement on the regulations in question.

The same realistic approach is also evident when the Court deals with the disconnection arguments of the Member States. The first argument is based on the general identical character of the provisions of the Lugano Convention with Regulation No. 44/2001. Thus consistency between the two is safeguarded and the Convention will not affect the Community rules. Here, the Court points out – and rightly so it would seem – that consistency with respect to rules, while extending to the participants in the system, may not lead to inconsistency, but does affect the operation of the rules in that jurisdiction, and may now, whilst applying the identical rules, rest with non-Community courts, whereas under the Regulation it would have rested with a Member State.[52]

The second argument relates to the disconnection clause as such, which had been carried over from the old Lugano Convention into the new one. This clause, now Article 64, states that the Lugano Convention shall not prejudice the application by the Member States of Regulation 44/2001.[53] Here, the Court returns to what it had already said in its restatement of the ERTA doctrine, namely that the inclusion of such a clause may provide an

---

50. Italics supplied.
51. Opinion 1/03, points 148 – 150.
52. Opinion 1/03, points 152 – 153.
53. Note that this drafting differs considerably from the kind of disconnection clause that had become customary in the Council of Europe Conventions and some UN-sponsored Conventions, see fn. 46 above.

indication that the agreement in question may affect the rules of Community law. Moreover, the Court points out that the non-prejudice clause suffers important exceptions, which clearly influence the application of Regulation No. 44/2001. To those who object that the outcome of the case should not hinge on the interpretation of exceptions, the Court opposes its earlier reasoning that the coexistence of the Lugano Convention with Regulation No. 44/2001 is *ipso facto* likely to affect the application of the latter. The Court's interpretation of the exceptions to the non-prejudice clause is merely confirmation of the bigger principle.[54]

2. With respect to the rules of the Lugano Convention on the recognition and enforcement of judgments

Here again, those who pleaded in favour of mixed competence took the view that in respect of this part of the Regulation 44/2001 there was a de facto disconnection since the recognition and enforcement of the regulation operated only among the Member States and that an agreement with a different scope, insofar as it concerns judgments external to the Community, would not be capable of affecting the Community rules.

Again, the Court meets these arguments with a very elaborate argumentation of its own that, once more, is based on analysis with less formal arguments than the Court tended to follow in the Open Skies case and more linked to how the Community Regulation and the projected agreement are going to interact in reality. Thus, the Court points out that the dichotomy between the jurisdiction and recognition parts of the Regulation should not be exaggerated, and that recognition based on mutual trust and without special procedure is possible precisely because of the stringent jurisdictional rules.

In short, the Court here returns in its detailed analysis of this aspect of the Community regulation and the projected Lugano Convention to its earlier announced idea that Community law should be able to function as a unified and coherent system (here: as between the jurisdiction and recognition aspects of that system). This would not be possible if Member States could conclude the Lugano Convention on their own or collectively. This is not prevented by the existence of a so-called disconnection clause – essentially for the reasons already given by the Court in its restatement of the ERTA doctrine.

Finally, the Court very simply, but effectively, refers to the core rule on recognition of the new Lugano Convention (now Article 33). This

54. Opinion 1/03, points 154 -160.

principle, whose effect is now extended beyond the circle of Community Member States to include the other parties to the new Lugano Convention, clearly affects Community rules within the meaning of the ERTA doctrine, since it increases the number of cases in which judgments delivered by courts of non-Community countries whose jurisdiction does not arise from the application of the provisions of Regulation No. 44/2001 will be recognized.

IV.   Some brief remarks on the consequences of the Lugano Opinion for other subjects of private international law

It requires only little imagination to see that that there are other situations in the field of private law co-operation that are very much like the Lugano situation. There are two other Conventions originally drafted under Article 293 of the EC Treaty that are in the process of being converted or just have been converted into Community regulations. These are the so-called Rome I Convention on the law applicable to contractual obligations[55] and the so-called Rome II Convention on the law applicable to non–contractual obligations.[56] These two Conventions, of which Rome II never entered into force, are generally regarded as an indissoluble whole with the Brussels Convention. Thus it was logical that the Commission, having presented the proposal for the Brussels I Regulation also presented proposals first for the Rome II Regulation, which was adopted on 11 July 2007[57] and later for a Rome I Regulation.[58]

It is not difficult to see that these regulations converted from Conventions are likely to have more or less the same "ERTA effect" on the external relations in the field of private international law as has had the conversion of the Brussels I Convention into the Brussels I Regulation. Bolstered by the Lugano Opinion, it is likely that all international conventions modelled on these regulations will in principle be a matter for the exclusive external competence of the Community – whether these are negotiated to draw neighbouring European States that have remained outside the EEA into an

55. A consolidated version of the Convention can be found in OJ C 27 of 26.1.1998, p. 34 – 46.
56. A text of this Convention can be found on the website of the European Group for Private International Law, http://www.gedip-egpil.eu/documents/gedip-documents-8pe.html
57. Reg. No. 864/2007 on the law applicable to non-contractual obligations, OJ L 199, 31.7.2007, p. 40.
58. Proposal for a Regulation of the European Parliament and the Council on the law applicable to contractual obligations, COM (2005) 650 final.

extended Community system of private international law, or whether the aim is to influence any broader international agreement within the framework of the Hague Conference on Private International Law, of which the European Community has recently become a Member next to its Member States[59].

Whether this will be easily accepted by the Member States remains to be seen. Especially in an area like the private international law of family law, where the Council adopted the Brussels II Regulation in 2003, but which entered fully into force on March 1, 2005[60], there is likely to be a fair amount of resistance because these matters are very much linked to national culture and belong to the core business of the Hague Conference (most of its Conventions relate to family law matters and the protection of the child). Some of this resistance is already evident from the carefully crafted provisions of the Regulation with various international instruments, as laid down in Articles 59- 63 (including a provision on concordats with the Holy See).

V.   Some conclusions on the ERTA doctrine after the Lugano Opinion

After the Lugano Opinion, it can be said that the restatement of the first exercise of potential external power under Opinion 1/76 has been reduced to such an extremely narrow hypothesis that it will seldom be reverted to in the future.

As to exclusive competence in external affairs after internal legislation under the ERTA doctrine, the restatement of the ERTA doctrine and the way it has been applied to the Lugano Convention brings some improvement in the application of the doctrine. In particular the analysis that the Court makes of the probable factual interaction between the possible Member State agreements and Community rules is based more on reality than was the rather formalistic reasoning the Court followed in the Open Skies cases and that is certainly an improvement. On the other hand, the same realistic approach has not yet broken through in respect to the problem of the so-called minimum rules. On that point it remains highly anomalous that the Court almost seems to encourage a total absence of the Community at the international level in areas where the Community

---

59.   The accession of the European Community became effective on 3 April 2007, according to the website of the Hague Conference, http://www.hcch.net.
60.   Reg. No. 2201/2003, OJ L 338, 23.12.2003, p. 1.

legislation may be very broad and intensive, simply because it is based on minimum rules. And this, merely because the Community <u>may</u> be "saved" by the Member States, if its minimum rules fall below the level agreed in the international agreement in question, thus encouraging the Member States instead of the Community to act in order to reach conformity with international standards.

However, given the fact that the ECJ continues to lay emphasis on the need for very precise analysis within their context of the proposed international agreement and of the possibly affected Community law, the application of the doctrine will never be easy and straightforward and clearly predictable as to its outcome. Hence the battle for external relations power will continue to be fought through the Court's case law.

It may, of course, be the case that the somewhat lapidary expression of the Union's powers to conclude international agreements with one or more third States in Article 216 of the Treaty on the Functioning of the European Union[61] will have profound consequences on the course of future case law in the field of external relations of the Union. That case law, already fairly summarily rendered above, has been further stultified by Article 216 as follows:

> The Union may conclude an agreement with one or more third countries or inter-national organisations where the Treaties so provide or where the conclusion of an agreement is necessary in order to achieve, within the framework of the Union's policies, one of the objectives referred to in the Treaties, or is provided for in a le-gally binding Union act or is likely to affect common rules or alter their scope.

This provision is supposed in quick succession to refer to explicit treaty-making power – of which there are now many more provisions than at the time when ERTA was first handed down – to Opinion 1/76 and to ERTA and their progeny.

Much will depend on whether the Court will actually feel constrained by these few words or whether it will see its case law as essentially having been codified by this provision and hence will lustily continue to develop it. All in all, the latter seems more likely.

---

61. Corresponding to Article 188 L in the numbering of the Treaty of Lisbon.

2. Mixed Agreements in the Field of Judicial Cooperation in Civil Matters: Treaty-Making and Legal Effects

Jan Peter Hix[1]

I.   Introduction

Legal issues relating to mixed agreements are among the recurrent issues in the practice of the Community institutions, the case-law of the Community courts, and the legal doctrine on Community law.[2] It is thus not surprising that these issues arise also in the context of agreements in the field of judicial cooperation in civil matters. Indeed, in this particular field the issues relating to mixed agreements may be even more accentuated than in some other fields of Community policies.

One of the reasons for the prevalence of mixed agreements in this field is the fact that judicial cooperation in civil matters is a relatively new and substantially limited Community policy, in which the development of the Community's external powers has been gradual and incomplete, with the Member States remaining partially competent. The Treaty establishing the European Economic Community did not confer powers on the Community for these matters. Judicial policy was considered to constitute an essential expression of national sovereignty. The rules on private

1.   The views expressed are those of the author and cannot be attributed to the Council of the European Union or its Legal Service. The final text of the contribution was submitted in May 2007.

2.   For general overviews see: David O'Keeffe/Henry G. Schermers (eds.), *Mixed Agreements* (1983); Iain MacLeod/Ian Hendry/Stephen Hyett, *The External Relations of the European Communities*, p. 142 (1996); Allan Rosas, Mixed Union – Mixed Agreements, in: Martti Koskenniemi (ed.), *International Law Aspects of the European Union*, p. 125 (1998); Allan Rosas, The European Union and mixed agreements, in: Alan Dashwood/Christophe Hillion (eds.), *The General Law of E.C. External Relations*, p. 200 (2000); Joni Heliskoski, *Mixed Agreements as a Technique for Organizing the International Relations of the European Community and its Member States* (2001); Piet Eeckhout, *External Relations of the European Union*, p. 190 (2004); Marianne Dony, Les accords mixtes, in: *Commentaire J. Mégret*, Vol. 12, p. 167 (2005); and the Reports in: Xenios L. Xenopoulos (ed.), *FIDE 2006, External Relations of the EU and the Member States: Competence, Mixed Agreements, International Responsibility and Effects of International Law* (2006).

international law and international civil procedures were laid down autonomously in the respective legal orders of the Member States or were established by international conventions concluded either among the Member States[3] or between Member States and third States, notably in the framework of the Hague Conference on Private International Law. These autonomous and conventional rules were subject to their compatibility with primary Community law, such as the non-discrimination principle laid down in Article 12 of the EC Treaty, and partially superseded or supplemented by specific provisions in the Community's secondary law.[4] It was only in 1999 that the Community acquired horizontal powers in the field of judicial cooperation in civil matters, on the basis of Articles 61 lit. c) and 65 of the EC Treaty, as amended by the Treaty of Amsterdam. However, the substantive scope of these provisions is limited to matters having cross-border implications and to measures being necessary for the proper functioning of the internal market, and has given rise to diverging interpretations.[5] Even when and where the Community adopted internal measures on this basis, the scope of the Community's external powers remained controversial within and among the institutions and the Member States. While the Commission pushed hard to ascertain the Community's external competence, there was a reluctance in some quarters to cede powers in this field to the Community institutions.[6] The Court of Justice had only recently the occasion to shed some light on the distribution of external powers in the field of judicial cooperation in civil matters. In its

3. Brussels Convention on jurisdiction and the enforcement of judgments in civil and commercial matters, which was concluded in the framework of Article 220 of the EEC Treaty (now: Article 293 ECT) (consolidated version: OJ C 27, 26.1.1998, p. 1); Rome Convention on the law applicable to contractual obligations (consolidated version: OJ C 334, 30.12.2005, p.1).
4. Cf. Michael Wilderspin/Xavier Lewis, Les relations entre le droit communautaire et les règles de conflits de lois des Etats membres, [2002] Rev. crit. dr. internat. privé, p. 1, p. 289. For a systematic analysis of the developments before the Treaty of Amsterdam, see Karl Friedrich Kreuzer, Die Europäisierung des internationalen Privatrechts – Vorgaben des Gemeinschaftsrechts -, in: Peter-Christian Müller-Graff (ed.), *Gemeinsames Privatrecht in der Europäischen Gemeinschaft*, p. 457 (2d ed. 1999).
5. Cf. Christian Kohler, Interrogations sur les sources du droit international privé européen après le traité d'Amsterdam, [1999] Rev. crit. dr. internat. privé, p. 1; Jürgen Basedow, The communitarization of the conflict of laws under the Treaty of Amsterdam, [2000] CMLRev, p. 687; Burkhard Heß, Die "Europäisierung" des internationalen Zivilprozessrechts durch den Amsterdamer Vertrag – Chancen und Gefahren, [2000] Neue Juristische Wochenschrift, p. 23.
6. For polemic views, see Eric Jayme, Zum Jahrtausendwechsel: Das Kollisionsrecht zwischen Postmoderne und Futurismus, [2000] Praxis des Internationalen Privat- und Verfahrensrechts, p. 165; Haimo Schack, Die EG-Kommission auf dem Holzweg von Amsterdam, [1999] Zeitschrift für Europäisches Privatrecht, p. 805.

Opinion 1/03 of 7 February 2006 the Court ruled that the conclusion of the new Lugano Convention on jurisdiction and the recognition and enforcement of judgments in civil and commercial matters, falls entirely within the sphere of exclusive competence of the Community.[7] This opinion may reduce – but cannot altogether eliminate – the uncertainties relating to the distribution of external powers between the Community and its Member States in this field.[8]

Another reason for the importance of mixed agreements in the field of judicial cooperation in civil matters resides in the fact that a considerable number of international agreements – in the areas of international transport, environment protection or other substantive subject matters – contain provisions on the applicable law, international jurisdiction and the recognition and enforcement of foreign judgments as a means of rendering the application of the substantive provisions of the agreements more effective. To the extent that the Community's exclusive competence is limited to such procedural provisions of the agreement and the Member States remain competent for the substantive provisions – either because there is no Community competence for the substantive provisions or because the Council chooses not to exercise a non-exclusive Community competence in this respect –, the agreement has a mixed character and must be concluded by both the Community and its Member States.[9]

7. [2006] ECR I-1145; cf. Alegría Borrás, Le droit international privé communautaire: réalités, problèmes et perspectives d'avenir, in: Académie de droit international, [2005] *Recueil des cours*, tome 317, p. 313, at pp. 481-490 (2006); Nicolaos Lavranos, Case law, [2006] CMLRev, p. 1087; Jan Asmus Bischoff, Besprechung des Gutachtens 1/03 des EuGH vom 7.2.2006, [2006] Europäische Zeitschrift für Wirtschaftsrecht, p. 295.

8. The present contribution does not address this issue. For a discussion of the respective competencies of the Community and the Member States in the field of judicial cooperation in civil matters, see the contribution by Pieter-Jan Kuijper, in this book; and Michael Wilderspin/Anne-Marie Rouchaud-Joët, La compétence externe de la Communauté européenne en droit international privé, [2004] Rev. crit. dr. internat. privé, p. 1.

9. An example is the (Cape Town) Convention on International Interests in Mobile Equipment (and its Protocols). This Convention provides for the constitution and effects of an international interest in mobile equipment for airframes, aircraft engines and helicopters as well as railway rolling stock and space property. Many of the substantive provisions of this Convention fall under the Member States' competence, while some provisions relating to the jurisdiction for claims brought under the Convention and to the effects of insolvency concern subject matters which fall under the exclusive Community competence, because they are capable of affecting the Community's internal rules laid down in Council Regulation (EC) No 44/2001 of 22.12.2000 on jurisdiction and the recognition and enforcement of judgments in civil and commercial matters (OJ L 12, 16.1.2001, p. 1) and Council Regulation (EC) No 1346/2000 of 29.5.2000 on insolvency proceedings (OJ L 160, 30.6.2000, p.1).

For the purposes of the present contribution, a mixed agreement is defined as an agreement between one or more third countries or international organisations of the one part, and the Community and/or one or more of its Member States of the other part, and the subject matter of which falls only partially within the exclusive competence of the Community, the other parts falling within a concurrent competence which the Council does not exercise, or within the Member States' competence.[10] The concept of "mixity" is thus attached primarily to the substantive question of competencies rather than to the formal question of the identity of the contracting parties on the Union side.[11] As will be demonstrated below, agreements in the field of judicial cooperation in civil matters provide for a particularly rich variety of imperfect mixed agreements that deviate from the typical scenario where the Community and all Member States are contracting parties on the Union side.

The structure of this contribution loosely follows the life cycle of mixed agreements, by examining first the treaty-making process, which starts with the negotiation of the agreement and ends with its conclusion (and entry into force), and second, the effects and the application of mixed agreements, with respect to third parties and to the Community internally.[12] The overarching principle, which informs the treaty-making process as well as the application of mixed agreements, is the principle of loyal cooperation between the Member States and the Community institutions, which results from Article 10 of the EC Treaty[13] and has also

---

10. The contribution will not address cases where an agreement is concluded by the Community and by some Member States, acting for their overseas territories (cf. in this context ECJ, Opinion 1/78, [1979] ECR 2871, para. 62; Opinion 1/94, [1994] ECR I-5267, para. 17). Such a case could arise, for instance, if the Community concludes an agreement with the Netherlands, acting on behalf of Aruba, and France, acting for Saint-Pierre-et-Miquelon and for Mayotte, in order to extend the rules of Council Regulation (EC) No 44/2001 to these overseas territories, for which the Brussels Convention is still applicable.
11. There is no agreed terminology for the different types of mixed agreements. For a detailed and nuanced analysis of different types of mixed agreements, see Allan Rosas, Mixed Union – Mixed Agreements, in: Martti Koskenniemi (ed.), *International Law Aspects of the European Union*, p. 125, at pp. 128-133 (1998).
12. The particular case of mixed participation of the Community and its Member States in international organisations is addressed with respect to the Hague Conference on Private International Law, in the contribution by Hans van Loon and Andrea Schulz in this book.
13. Cf. Astrid Epiney, Zur Tragweite des Art. 10 EGV im Bereich der Außenbeziehungen, in: Jürgen Bröhmer et al. (eds.), *Internationale Gemeinschaft und Menschenrechte*, p. 441 (2005).

been founded in relation to mixed agreements on the requirement of unity in the international representation of the Community.[14]

II.   Treaty-Making

A.   From the negotiating authorisation to the conclusion of mixed agreements

The negotiation and conclusion of mixed agreements may take place in the framework of an international organisation, in another multilateral context or bilaterally. The Community's practice in the field of judicial cooperation in civil matters relates mainly to agreements which were negotiated in international organisations, such as the Hague Conference on Private International Law, UNIDROIT, UNCITRAL, the Council of Europe or the International Maritime Organization. While the rules of these organisations, and the international law of treaties in general, determine the limits within which the Community and its Member States can act, the present contribution concentrates primarily on a Community law perspective.[15]

1.   *The negotiation of mixed agreements*

The EC Treaty addresses the negotiation of mixed agreements only to the extent that the agreement falls within the Community's competence, and remains incomplete with respect to the question of mixity.[16] It results, however, from the case-law of the Court of Justice, that the principle of close cooperation between the Community institutions and the Member States applies also to the negotiation phase of mixed agreements.[17]

---

14.   See, e.g., ECJ, Opinion 1/94, [1994] ECR I-5267, para. 108: "... where it is apparent that the subject-matter of an agreement or convention falls in part within the competence of the Community and in part within that of the Member States, it is essential to ensure close cooperation between the Member States and the Community institutions, both in the process of negotiation and conclusion and in the fulfilment of the commitments entered into. That obligation to cooperate flows from the requirement of unity in the international representation of the Community...".

15.   For an international law perspective of mixed agreements, cf. Delano R. Verwey, *The European Community, the European Union and the International Law of Treaties*, p. 155 (2004).

16.   An exception is Article 133(6) ECT concerning in particular agreements relating to trade in certain service sectors.

17.   Cf., e.g., ECJ, Opinion 1/94, [1994] ECR I-5267, para. 108.

With respect to subject matters of an envisaged mixed agreement which fall under the competence of the Community, it results from Article 300(1), first subparagraph, of the EC Treaty that the Commission takes the initiative by recommending to the Council that it be authorised to negotiate the agreement on behalf of the Community, and that the Council decides on such authorisation. The conduct of the negotiations by the Commission is subject to two legal constraints relating, in the first place, to the obligation to act within the framework of the negotiating directives which the Council may issue and, in the second place, to the obligation to consult the special committee which the Council appoints to assist the Commission in the negotiations. The Council acts by qualified majority, except in cases where the agreement covers a field for which unanimity is required for the adoption of internal rules and for association agreements. According to Article 67 of the EC Treaty, measures in the field of judicial cooperation in civil matters require unanimity only for aspects relating to family law.[18]

For subject matters of an envisaged mixed agreement which fall within the competence of the Member States, the Member States can decide on a common negotiator and common negotiating objectives and on the coordination of negotiating positions. They can act to this effect collectively by common accord of the Representatives of the Member States meeting within the Council.

In practice, the two sets of rules described in the two preceding paragraphs are often merged. The Council (and, as the case may be, the Representatives of the Member States meeting within the Council) may take decisions on the negotiating authorisation and directives, which comprise the entirety of the subject matters of the envisaged mixed agreement.[19] And the special committee acts during the negotiations as a consultative body and as the forum in which the negotiating positions of the Member States are coordinated among themselves and with the Commission.

The following observations relate to the Community's practice in the field of judicial cooperation in civil matters.[20] They must necessarily remain general, because the negotiating authorisations and directives are normally not publicly available and the coordination of the negotiating positions takes place behind closed doors.

---

18. Art. 67(5), second indent, in conjunction with Art. 67(1) and (2), first indent, ECT.
19. In such cases, the more restrictive voting rule, i.e. common accord, is required.
20. For a more horizontal account of mixed negotiations, see Jean Groux, Mixed Negotiations, in: David O'Keeffe/Henry G. Schermers (eds.), *Mixed Agreements*, p. 87 (1983).

a)   The negotiating authorisation

In the field of judicial cooperation in civil matters the Commission regularly submits recommendations for negotiating authorisations to the Council, including in matters which fall within the shared competence of the Community and the Member States.[21] In the early years after the entry into force of the Treaty of Amsterdam, such recommendations were sometimes submitted at a very late stage, after the substantial parts of the negotiations had already taken place. This may be explained by the fact that the negotiations had already started before the Community acquired its external competence in this field, or that the Commission learned too late of the fact that a particular instrument under negotiation contained also provisions relating to judicial cooperation in civil matters. There may also be cases where it is appropriate for the Commission to wait with the submission of a recommendation for a negotiating authorisation while entering into exploratory talks with third parties[22] or monitoring the direction into which negotiations in an international organisation are developing, in order to ascertain whether or not provisions on judicial cooperation in civil matters are to be included in the negotiations and whether any such provisions may affect internal Community rules.

Once the Commission has seized the Council with a recommendation for a negotiating authorisation, the recommendation is generally discussed in one of the Council's preparatory bodies, namely the Committee on Civil Law Matters, which will then transmit the draft, possibly in an amended form, to Coreper and to the Council for adoption. The Committee on Civil Law Matters frequently discusses the extent and nature of the Community's competence for the subject matters to be negotiated.[23] However, these issues do not necessarily need to be resolved at this stage. The Council can adopt the negotiating authorisation without prejudice to

---

21. For reasons which are not entirely clear, the Commission never submitted a recommendation for the negotiation of the Council of Europe Convention on Contact concerning Children, which was thus negotiated by the sole Member States, although the Commission later submitted a proposal for the signature of this Convention (COM(2002) 520 final of 2.10.2002); cf. Michael Wilderspin/Anne-Marie Rouchaud-Joët, La compétence externe de la Communauté européenne en droit international privé, [2004] Rev. crit. dr. internat. privé, p. 1, at p. 40.
22. Cf. Christian N. K. Franklin, Report on Norway, in: Xenios L. Xenopoulos (ed.), *FIDE 2006, External Relations of the EU and the Member States: Competence, Mixed Agreements, International Responsibility and Effects of International Law*, p. 165, at pp. 180-183 (2006).
23. In these cases, the Council Legal Service and the representative of the Commission, advised by its Legal Service, may express their opinions, which are not necessarily always identical.

the respective competencies of the Community and the Member States, which may be decided on at a later stage.[24]

This was so, for instance, in the case of the negotiating authorisation for the new Lugano Convention, where the Council authorised the Commission to negotiate the whole convention while referring the question of the correct division of competencies to the Court of Justice.[25]

The Council may also authorise both the Commission and the Presidency of the Council to conduct the negotiations. As it is often difficult in practice to determine precisely whether a particular negotiating area falls within the Community's or the Member States' competence, the negotiating authorisation does not necessarily need to specify the areas to be negotiated respectively by the Commission and the Presidency. In the case of the negotiation of the Hague Project for a Worldwide Judgments Convention, which later became the Hague Convention on Choice of Court Agreements, the Commission and the Presidency of the Council were jointly authorised to express the Community position, while the Member States were allowed to express their views to the extent that these views were compatible with the negotiating directives.[26]

In other cases, where the negotiations primarily concerned matters falling within the Member States' competence, the Council authorised the Commission to negotiate only those parts which fell within the Community's (exclusive) competence, such as those covered by Council Regulation (EC) No 44/2001 of 22 December 2000 on jurisdiction and the recognition and enforcement of judgments in civil and commercial matters (the "Brussels I Regulation").[27] In some of these cases, the authorisation did not address at all the negotiation of the other parts of the draft

---

24. Cf. Iain MacLeod/Ian Hendry/Stephen Hyett, *The External Relations of the European Communities*, pp. 151 et seq. (1996). This may, however, lead to the unsatisfactory situation that the other negotiating partners do not know who are to be the parties to the agreement on the EU side.
25. Cf. ECJ, Opinion 1/03, [2006] ECR I-1145.
26. Cf. the Joint Declaration of the Council and the Commission which was made at the occasion of the adoption of Council Regulation (EC) No 44/2001 and which laid down a working method to be used by the Community and the Member States for the negotiation of the Hague Project for a Worldwide Judgments Convention. The declaration is cited by Georges A. L. Droz/Hélène Gaudemet-Tallon, La transformation de la Convention de Bruxelles du 27 septembre 1968 en Règlement du Conseil concernant la compétence judiciaire, la reconnaissance et l'exécution des décisions en matière civile et commerciale, [2001] Rev. crit. dr. internat. privé, p. 602, at p. 624, note 30).
27. OJ L 12, 16.1.2001, p. 1.

agreement. The consequence was that the Member States were free to negotiate these parts on their own, having regard, however, for the principle of loyal cooperation.

The question as to who is to be authorised to negotiate a mixed agreement may also depend on the rules of the international organisation concerned, in particular on the question whether the Community is a member of the organisation or has at least observer status.[28]

b)   The negotiating directives

The Council generally adopts negotiating directives for mixed agreements together with the negotiating authorisation. The negotiating directives can be limited to matters falling within the Community's (exclusive) competence or comprise the entirety of the matters to be negotiated. The practice in the field of judicial cooperation in civil matters demonstrates that the degree of precision of such directives varies considerably. Negotiating directives can be very precise and may, under some circumstances, determine to a large extent the expected outcome of negotiations. This was the case with the negotiating directives for the new Lugano Convention, where a political agreement on the substantive provisions was already reached at the time of the adoption of the negotiating directives.[29] In other cases, negotiating directives have sometimes been limited to some specific instructions. For instance, the negotiating directives may state that the agreement to be negotiated should be consistent or compatible with internal Community acts, such as the Brussels I Regulation or Council Regulation (EC) No 1346/2000 of 29 May 2000 on insolvency proceedings,[30] that it should contain a disconnection clause safeguarding the application of such internal Community acts in the application between the Member States,[31] or that it should contain a clause which enables the Community to become a contracting party.

---

28. Cf. Part II.B.3.a), infra, on situations where the Member States are authorised to negotiate also in the interest of the Community.
29. Cf. ECJ, Opinion 1/03, [2006] ECR I-1145, paras. 20-25 on the history of the preparatory work for the Convention.
30. OJ L 160, 30.6.2000, p. 1.
31. See, generally, Alegría Borrás, Les clauses de déconnexion et le droit international privé communautaire, in: Heinz-Peter Mansel et al. (eds.), *Festschrift für Erik Jayme*, p. 57 (2004). On the significance of disconnection clauses for the determination of the respective powers of the Community and its Member States, see ECJ, Opinion 1/03, [2006] ECR I-1145, para. 130; cf. also Michael Wilderspin/Anne-Marie Rouchaud-Joët, La compétence externe de la Communauté européenne en droit international privé, [2004] Rev. crit. dr. internat. privé, p. 1, at pp. 21 et seq.

It has been observed that the Community and its Member States are sometimes perceived to be cumbersome negotiating partners, giving the impression that the real negotiations take place internally (by establishing negotiating directives or coordinated positions) and that the negotiating partners are left to accept or reject the outcome.[32] In particular in the context of multilateral negotiations, such as those in the framework of the Hague Conference on Private International Law, it may not be conductive to finding compromise solutions if the negotiating directives are too precise. If the negotiators of the Community and its Member States have to follow very detailed instructions which have been adopted by the Council before the negotiating sessions, they may be incapable of reacting appropriately during the negotiation sessions if negotiations take an unexpected turn and proceed in a direction not foreseen by the negotiating directives.[33] In such cases, it may be necessary to seize the Council again, which can at any time modify previous negotiating directives and adapt them to a specific negotiating situation. This was done, for instance, when it became clear that the scope of the Hague Project for a Worldwide Judgments Convention would be fundamentally reduced.

c)   *The coordination of negotiating positions and the conduct of negotiations*

For the negotiation of mixed agreements in the field of judicial cooperation in civil matters, the Committee on Civil Law Matters is generally appointed as the special committee in consultation with which the negotiations are conducted and where the negotiating positions are coordinated. Consultation and coordination can take place in Brussels or on the spot, in the margins of the negotiating sessions. In this case, it is often necessary for the Community delegation to meet in the morning of the negotiating sessions or during lunch break. The Hague Conference, in particular, has generally been very accommodating in enabling such internal meetings.

The Community's conduct of the multilateral (mixed) negotiations relating to judicial cooperation in civil matters has sometimes been criticised.[34] At a time when the Community and its Member States were still struggling among themselves with the division of powers in the field

---

32. See Piet Eeckhout, *External Relations of the European Union*, p. 216 (2004).

33. Cf. A.V.M. Struycken, Le droit international privé d'origine communautaire et les Etats tiers, [2001-2002] Rev. aff. europ., p. 469, at p. 477.

34. See, e.g., Herbert Kronke, Ziele – Methoden, Kosten – Nutzen: Perspektiven der Privatrechtsharmonisierung nach 75 Jahren UNIDROIT, [2001] Juristen Zeitung, p. 1149, at p. 1155, concerning the negotiations, in the framework of UNIDROIT, of the (Cape Town) Convention on International Interests in Mobile Equipment.

of private international law and when coordination between the Commission, the Council Presidency and the experts from the Member States was not yet fully efficient, there were times when third parties were puzzled by the idiosyncratic behaviour of the different actors on the Union side and found it hard to understand who spoke on behalf of whom. These initial difficulties now appear to have been reduced.

Furthermore, some observers regretted that notably in the context of the Hague Conference the representatives of the Member States – in many cases well known experts in the area of private international law – were prevented from developing creative ideas and submitting compromise texts, because they were instructed to follow the content of the interventions made by the Council Presidency and the Commission.[35] It is true that discussions could gain substantially from the experience, knowledge and intellectual capacity of the Member States' experts at the Hague Conference and elsewhere.[36] Although certain questions relating to important policy choices may need to be taken on a political level within the Community and expressed unequivocally in the negotiations, there should be ways of ensuring that Member States' experts can continue to express their observations on other points, at least in the initial stages of the negotiations, and to influence Community positions through the channel of the Community's internal coordination meetings.

2. The signing and conclusion of mixed agreements

The consent to be bound by an agreement may be expressed by signature, exchange of instruments, ratification, acceptance, approval or accession, or by any other means if so agreed.[37] In the context of mixed agreements such consent must be expressed by both the Community and the Member States. The conclusion by the Community of a mixed agreement presupposes that the agreement provides for the possibility for international organisations, Regional Economic Integration Organisations ("REIOs"), or – more specifically – the Community to become contracting parties. Recent treaty practice suggests that it has become increasingly common for international agreements to include REIO-clauses, the content of which may vary

---

35. Cf. A.V.M. Struycken, Le droit international privé d'origine communautaire et les Etats tiers, [2001-2002] Rev. aff. europ., p. 469, at p. 474.
36. Cf. also Jörg Pirrung, Europäische justitielle Zusammenarbeit, Haager Konferenz und Unidroit, in: Jürgen Basedow et al. (eds.), *Aufbruch nach Europa*, p. 785, at pp. 788 et seq. (2001), on the high qualifications of experts from Member States in the Hague Conference and Unidroit.
37. Cf. Article 11 of the Vienna Convention on the law of treaties.

however.[38] Examples of such REIO-clauses in agreements in the field of judicial cooperation in civil matters are the Hague Convention on the Law Applicable to Certain Rights in Respect of Securities held with an Intermediary[39] and the Hague Convention on Choice of Court Agreements.[40] The Council of Europe Convention on Contact concerning Children provides more specifically for the possibility for the Community to become a contracting party.[41] The insertion of REIO- or Community-clauses in draft agreements is possible even if the Community is not a member of the organisation within whose framework the agreement is negotiated.

Before the Community and its Member States can express their consent to be bound by a mixed agreement, they must comply with their respective internal procedures. With regard to the parts of the agreement which fall within the Member States' competence, the procedure for the conclusion is governed by the respective national law of the Member State concerned.[42]

With regard to the parts of the mixed agreement which fall within Community competence, the procedures are laid down in Article 300 of the EC Treaty. Article 300(2), first subparagraph, provides that the signing, which may be accompanied by a decision on provisional application before the entry into force, and the conclusion of an agreement is decided on by the Council on a proposal from the Commission. In the field of judicial cooperation in civil matters, such decisions require qualified majority or – for aspects relating to family law – unanimity.[43] The Council decision on the conclusion of the agreement requires the prior consultation of the

---

38. Cf. Delano R. Verwey, The *European Community, the European Union and the International Law of Treaties*, pp. 168-171 (2004).
39. Art. 18 of the Convention.
40. Art. 29 of the Convention. Other relevant examples of such clauses can be found in Art. 53 of the Convention for the Unification of Certain Rules for International Carriage by Air (the Montreal Convention); Art. 48 of the (Cape Town) Convention on International Interests in Mobile Equipment; Art. 19 of the Protocol of 2002 to the Athens Convention relating to the Carriage of Passengers and their Luggage by Sea, 1974; and Art. 27 and 28 of the Protocol on Civil Liability and Compensation for Damage caused by the Transboundary Effects of Industrial Accidents on Transboundary Waters.
41. Art. 22 of the Convention.
42. Cf. Joni Heliskoski, *Mixed Agreements as a Technique for Organizing the International Relations of the European Community and its Member States*, pp. 89-92 (2001); and Delano R. Verwey, *The European Community, the European Union and the International Law of Treaties*, pp. 172-175 (2004), for an analysis of the law and practice in some of the Member States.
43. Art. 300(2), first subparagraph, in conjunction with Art. 67 ECT.

European Parliament, pursuant to Article 300(3), first subparagraph.[44] However, the assent of the European Parliament is required in the cases described in Article 300(3), second subparagraph, notably if an agreement entails amendment of an act adopted under the co-decision procedure referred to in Article 251 of the EC Treaty.[45] Since the entry into force of the Treaty of Nice, which introduced the co-decision procedure for internal measures in the field of judicial cooperation in civil matters (other than those relating to family law), the assent requirement is considered to apply also to the conclusion of an agreement which entails amendment of the Brussels I Regulation and other acts in the field of judicial cooperation in civil matters (other than those relating to family law), even though the co-decision procedure did not yet apply when these acts were adopted.[46]

The case-law of the Court of Justice according to which the Member States and the Community institutions must ensure close cooperation also in the process of signing and concluding a mixed agreement does not specifically address the question whether the Community and its Member States must sign the agreement and deposit their respective instruments of acceptance simultaneously. In order to avoid situations of legal uncertainty, the Community and its Member States should collectively and in a coordinated manner at least deposit the instruments of acceptance,[47] because neither the Community nor its Member States are in a position to individually

---

44. The consultation procedure was applied, e.g., for the Council decisions relating to the conclusion of the International Convention for Bunker Oil Pollution Damage, 2001 (the Bunkers Convention), OJ L 256, 25.9.2002, p. 7; and the International Convention on Liability and Compensation for Damage in Connection with the Carriage of Hazardous and Noxious Substances by Sea, 1996 (the HNS Convention), OJ L 337, 13.12.2002, p. 55.

45. This would for instance be the case if it were decided to conclude the Hague Convention on the Law Applicable to Certain Rights in Respect of Securities held with an Intermediary, which may affect Directive 98/26/EC of the European Parliament and of the Council of 19.5.1998 on settlement finality in payment and securities settlement systems (OJ L 166, 11.6.1998, p. 45) and Directive 2002/47/EC of the European Parliament and of the Council of 6.6.2002 on financial collateral arrangements (OJ L 168, 27.6.2002, p. 43), both of which were adopted in the co-decision procedure.

46. The assent procedure was applied, e.g., to the Council decisions relating to the conclusion of the Protocol of 2003 to the International Convention on the Establishment of an International Fund for Compensation for Oil Pollution Damage, 1992 (the Fund Protocol of 2003), OJ L 78, 16.3.2004, p. 22; and the 2004 Protocol to the Paris Convention of 29 July 1960 on Third Party Liability in the Field of Nuclear Energy, OJ L 97, 1.4.2004, p. 53.

47. Cf. Marianne Dony, Les accords mixtes, in: *Commentaire J. Mégret*, Vol. 12, p. 185 (2005).

ensure the compliance with the entirety of the commitments contracted under a mixed agreement.[48]

Only under exceptional circumstances can it be envisaged that the Community and the Member States proceed individually and not simultaneously with the ratification or acceptance of a mixed agreement. Such circumstances may arise if the subject matters of the agreement fall within the parallel competence of the Community and its Member States or, where this is not the case, if the subject matters falling respectively within the Community's competence and the Member States' competence can clearly be distinguished and are not intrinsically linked, if the implementation of the agreement does not require a common and coordinated action by the Community and its Member States, and if the non-simultaneous ratification or acceptance by the Community for its part and by the Member States for their respective parts would not lead to a situation in relation to other contracting parties which would be contrary to the terms or the object and purpose of the agreement concerned.

The question of the necessity of a simultaneous signature and ratification was on occasion discussed in the Committee on Civil Law Matters or other preparatory bodies of the Council in respect of draft decisions on the signing and ratification of mixed agreements in the field of judicial cooperation in civil matters. In this field it is often difficult to clearly distinguish provisions falling within the Community competence from provisions falling within the Member States' competence. Even in cases where procedural provisions on the applicable law, international jurisdiction or the recognition and enforcement of foreign judgments (which may fall within the Community's competence) are laid down in formally separate parts of the agreement, they are often intrinsically linked to, and intended to ensure the effectiveness of, the substantive provisions of the agreement (which may fall within the Member States' competence).[49]

---

48. In any case, it appears to be the practice for some bilateral mixed agreements that the Community does not deposit its instrument of acceptance before all of its Member States have ratified the agreement; cf. Iain MacLeod/Ian Hendry/Stephen Hyett, *The External Relations of the European Communities*, p. 154 (1996); Piet Eeckhout, *External Relations of the European Union*, pp. 218 et seq. (2004); but see Joni Heliskoski, *Mixed Agreements as a Technique for Organizing the International Relations of the European Community and its Member States*, pp. 92-94 (2001), with contrary examples.

49. Cf. in this context, Ihor Tarko, in: Heinz Mayer (ed.), *Kommentar zu EU- und EG- Vertrag*, Art. 65, para. 80 (2003); Henrik Ringbom, EU Regulation 44/2001 and its Implications for the International Maritime Liability Conventions, [2004] Journal of Maritime Law & Commerce, p. 1, at p 6.

An example of the requirement for a simultaneous deposit of the instruments of acceptance is the Council's decision of 5 April 2001 on the conclusion by the European Community of the Convention for the Unification of Certain Rules for International Carriage by Air (the Montreal Convention)[50], which is founded on Article 80(2) of the EC Treaty, but also contains provisions on jurisdiction.[51] In the recitals to the decision, it is stated that "the Community and its Member States share competence in the matters covered by the Montreal Convention and it is therefore necessary for them simultaneously to ratify it in order to guarantee uniform and complete application of its provisions within the European Union."[52] Accordingly, Article 2 of the decision provides expressly that "the instrument [of acceptance on behalf of the Community] shall be deposited simultaneously with the instruments of ratification of all the Member States". There are examples of other Council decisions on the conclusion of mixed agreements in the field of judicial cooperation in civil matters, which impose the simultaneous deposit of the instruments of acceptance.[53] But this is not a general practice in this field.

A related question is whether it is legally possible to impose time-limits for the signature or ratification by the Member States of mixed agreements. On the one hand, Member States could argue that the Community cannot impose any obligation on them in the areas which fall within their competencies. On the other hand, it could be argued that an obligation to ratify a mixed agreement within certain time-limits would be justified in the light of the principle of loyal cooperation between the Community institutions and its Member States, at least in cases where a simultaneous ratification is required. Otherwise, one Member State could indefinitely postpone the signature and ratification by all the other Member States and the Community, and could thus prevent the entry into force of the

---

50. OJ L 194, 18.7.2001, p. 38.
51. See Articles 33 and 46 of the Convention.
52. Recital 4.
53. See Art. 3 of the draft Council Decision authorising the Member States to accede to, or ratify, in the interest of the European Community, the 1996 Hague Convention on Jurisdiction, Applicable Law, Recognition, Enforcement and Cooperation in respect of Parental Responsibility and Measures for the Protection of Children (Council doc. 14454/03 of 25.11.2003); Art. 2 of the Council Decision of 8.3.2004 authorising the Member States which are Contracting Parties to the Paris Convention of 29 July 1960 on Third Party Liability in the Field of Nuclear Energy to ratify, in the interest of the European Community, the Protocol amending that Convention, or to accede to it, OJ L 97, 1.4.2004, p. 53.

agreement, including its provisions which fall within the Community's exclusive competence.[54]

The Commission has in some instances proposed to impose time-limits on the ratification of mixed agreements by the Member States. An example is the Commission proposal for a Council decision concerning the conclusion by the European Community of the Protocol of 2002 to the Athens Convention Relating to the Carriage of Passengers and their Luggage by Sea, 1974,[55] which is founded on Articles 61 lit. c) of the EC Treaty. This Protocol contains provisions on jurisdiction and on the recognition and enforcement of judgments, which fall within the exclusive Community competence, and other provisions which fall within the competence of the Member States. Article 3 of the proposed Council decision provides that the "Member States shall take the necessary measures to become Contracting Parties to the Athens Protocol as soon as possible, and shall in any case have completed this procedure by 31 December 2005." The Council has not yet adopted the proposed decision.

The Council often appears to be reluctant to impose obligatory time limits for the ratification of mixed agreements by the Member States,[56] but some of the Council decisions authorising the conclusion of mixed agreements in the field of judicial cooperation in civil matters contain indicative time periods within which the Member States should, if possible, ratify the agreement.[57]

It has been observed that the delayed ratification by the Community and its Member States of mixed agreements containing provisions on judicial cooperation in civil matters has led to a loss of influence of the Community and its Member States in international organisations working for the unification of laws.[58] This coincides with the general observation that the

---

54. While the question as to whether the Council can impose such an obligation has not yet been resolved, it would in any case appear possible that in addition to the Council decision on the conclusion of a mixed agreement on behalf of the Community, time limits for the deposit of the instruments of ratification by the Member States are imposed by common accord of the Representatives of the Governments of the Member States meeting within the Council.

55. COM(2003) 375 final of 24.6.2003.

56. But see Art. 3 of the Council Decision of 19.12.2002 relating to the signing of the 1996 Hague Convention on the Protection of Children (OJ L 48, 21.2.2003, p. 1), which sets a binding date before which the Member States shall make the necessary arrangements for the Convention to be signed.

57. See the examples in part II.B.3.b, infra.

58. Alegría Borrás, La cooperation judiciaire en matière civile dans la Communauté européenne, Exposé to the Working Group X (Freedom, security and justice) of the European Convention, WG X -WD 8 of 4.11.2002, p. 10.

ratification of mixed agreements by 27 Member States can sometimes be time-consuming, in particular in Member States with a federal structure.[59] But in the field of judicial cooperation in civil matters there appears to be an additional problem, which results in the prolonged blocking of draft Council decisions on the signature or conclusion of some mixed agreements. In particular, although the Council authorised the Member States in December 2002 to sign the Hague Convention on the Protection of Children, and the signature took place in April 2003, the Council decision concerning the ratification of, or accession to, this Convention has yet to be adopted. The Secretary General of the Hague Conference has repeatedly urged the Council to overcome the remaining difficulties, which appear to be related to the issue of the application of the Convention to Gibraltar.[60] It is hoped that a satisfactory solution for these difficulties can be found in the near future.

B.   The negotiation and conclusion of imperfect mixed agreements

While a standard mixed agreement comprises on the Union side the Community and all of its Member States, and is applicable throughout the Community, there are areas or situations where this is not the case. I will refer to such agreements as imperfect mixed agreements.

A mixed agreement can be imperfect because only a limited number of Member States participate alongside the Community. If the agreement applies throughout the Community for the parts which fall within the Community's competence, but only to a limited number of Member States for the parts which fall within the Member States' competence, it could be called limping (asymmetric, incomplete or partial). By contrast, if the agreement, including the parts which fall within the Community's competence, applies only to the territory of the limited number of Member States which participate, it could be called a curtailed mixed agreement (with a limited territorial scope). Finally, if an agreement is concluded by the Member States only, but not by the Community, although its subject-matter falls partially within the Community's exclusive competence, it could be characterized as a concealed (or veiled) mixed agreement. There are examples of all these types of imperfect mixed agreements in the field of judicial cooperation in civil matters. Indeed, in this field, imperfect mixed agreements are the rule, rather than the exception.

---

59. See Piet Eeckhout, *External Relations of the European Union*, p. 218 (2004).
60. Cf. the letter of 25.10.2005 from Mr van Loon to the President of the Council of the EU (No 31848(05)VL/LJM), available on the website of the Hague Conference at http:/www.hcch.net.

1.   Limping mixed agreements

The requirement of unity in the international representation of the Community implies that mixed agreements must, in principle, be ratified by the Community and all of its Member States.

To the extent that the deposit of the respective instruments of acceptance of a mixed agreement by the Community and its Member States does not intervene in a coordinated and simultaneous manner, the mixed agreement remains incomplete until the last instrument of acceptance is deposited. The practice in the field of judicial cooperation in civil matters, as in other fields, shows that the coordination of ratification procedures does not always work satisfactorily and that Member States sometimes proceed to the ratification of, or accession to, mixed agreements in a disparate order, sometime even before the Council has adopted the decision on the conclusion of the agreement on behalf of the Community. After their accession to the EU, Hungary, Lithuania and Slovenia ratified, or acceded to, the 1996 Hague Convention on the Protection of Children,[61] though the Council had not yet adopted the decision authorising the Member States to ratify or accede to this Convention. Another example is the Bunkers Convention to which some, but not all Member States, have acceded.[62] This situation is unsatisfactory because it risks undermining the uniform application of Community law in the field of judicial cooperation in civil matters. It is unsatisfactory also from the point of view of international law, because the particular Member States for which a mixed agreement has already entered into force might not be in a position to fully apply and implement the agreement with regard to matters falling under the Community's competence.

Limping mixed agreements may moreover result from transitional situations, where some, but not all of the Member States had ratified an agreement before their accession to the EU or before the Community acquired or exercised competencies in the area covered by (parts of) the agreement. In this situation, Article 307(1) of the EC Treaty provides that the rights and obligations arising for third parties from such agreements shall not be affected. It follows, however, from Article 307(2) that the Member States concerned must eliminate, if necessary by renouncing the agreement, the incompatibilities of the agreement with the internal Community rules, unless the internal instruments expressly permit the continued application of such agreements by the Member States concerned,[63] or the Council adopts a

---

61.   Cf. the status table for this Convention at: http://www.hcch.net.
62.   Cf. the status table at: http://www.imo.org.
63.   See, for instance, Art. 71 of the Brussels I Regulation, OJ L 12, 16.1.2001, p. 1.

decision authorising the conclusion of such agreements.[64] In this latter case, the limping character of the agreement will continue until such time that the other Member States have also ratified the agreement. In the field of judicial cooperation in civil matters, the Community appears to have adopted a rather lenient approach with a view to finding practical solutions in this respect.[65]

Under the conditions described above with respect to the non-simultaneous ratification of mixed agreements,[66] there may be justification for the community to conclude a mixed agreement for the subject matters falling under its exclusive competence and for a limited number of Member States to ratify the agreement for the subject matters falling under their respective competence. As the obligations resulting from mixed agreements are partly to be performed by Member States and partly by the Community, third countries might insist in these cases that a declaration of competence be submitted by the Community, in order to allow them to understand the extent of the respective obligations of the Community and Member States concerned. Such a declaration of competence is not always easy to establish taking also into account the evolving character of the distribution of powers within the Community.

If the Council decision on the conclusion of a mixed agreement neither expressly provides for the simultaneous and coordinated deposit of the instruments of acceptance, nor for the exclusion of some Member States from the obligation to ratify the agreement, the question as to whether all Member States have to ratify alongside the Community may also depend on the nature of the agreement[67] or its specific rules. The (Cape Town) Convention on

---

64. See, for instance, the draft Council decision on the conclusion of the 1996 Hague Convention on the Protection of Children (Council doc. 14454/03 of 25.11.2003).

65. For a more elaborate discussion of these issues, see Michael Wilderspin/Anne-Marie Rouchaud-Joët, La compétence externe de la Communauté européenne en droit international privé, [2004] Rev. crit. dr. internat. privé, p. 1, at pp. 16-18; Alegría Borrás, Le droit international privé communautaire: réalités, problèmes et perspectives d'avenir, in: Académie de droit international, [2005] *Recueil des cours*, tome 317, p. 313, at pp. 508-510 (2006).

66. Part II.A.2, supra.

67. If the objective and the scope of application of a mixed agreement are limited by its very nature to a specific geographic area, the agreement can be concluded by the Community and only those Member States which are concerned by it (cf. Iain MacLeod/Ian Hendry/Stephen Hyett, *The External Relations of the European Communities*, pp. 144 et seq. (1996)). Such agreements, which do not appear relevant in the field of judicial cooperation in civil matters, relate for instance to the protection of rivers, seas or other geographic areas against pollution (e.g. Convention on the International Commission for the Protection of the Oder, OJ L 100, 15.4.1999, p. 21; Convention on the Protection of the Alps, OJ L 61, 12.3.1996, p. 32; Convention on the Protection of the Marine Environment of the Baltic Sea Area, OJ L 73, 16.3.1994, p. 20).

International Interests in Mobile Equipment provides in its Article 48(1) that a Regional Economic Integration Organisation that becomes a contracting party to the Convention shall have the rights and obligations of a Contracting State, "to the extent that that Organisation has competence over matters governed by this Convention". This has led some commentators to conclude that the Community could accede to the Convention alongside only some of its Member States.[68] As a matter of fact, Ireland acceded to the Convention and to its Protocol on Matters Specific to Aircraft Equipment, which entered into force for Ireland respectively on 1 November 2005 and 1 March 2006,[69] although the other Member States and the Community are not yet contracting parties. It is, however, difficult to see how Ireland can assume the entirety of the commitments under the Convention and the Protocol, including the commitments falling under the Community's exclusive competence, before the Community has become a contracting party.

2.   Curtailed mixed agreements (with a limited territorial scope)

a)   Objective justifications for a limitation of the territorial scope

Even in cases where the conditions for the conclusion of a mixed agreement by the Community and a limited number of Member States are fulfilled, the parts of the agreement which fall under the competence of the Community must in principle be applied throughout the Community in order to comply with the principle of uniform application of Community law in conjunction with the general principle of non-discrimination. A differentiated regime for these parts can be envisaged only if the differences are objectively justified.

The possibility to expressly provide for differentiated regimes was discussed in the Council's Committee on Civil Law Matters with respect to several mixed agreements in the field of judicial cooperation in civil matters. In one of these cases it was suggested to include an accession clause in the agreement according to which the Community would accede only in relation to the territory of those Member States that have themselves ratified the agreement. This suggestion was founded on the fact that the manufacturing and service sectors concerned by the agreement were located in some Member States only and that some other Member States had no interest in ratifying the agreement. The suggestion was rejected, however, because it was considered that economic circumstances

---

68.   See Christoph Henrichs, Das Übereinkommen über internationale Sicherungsrechte an beweglicher Ausrüstung, [2003] Praxis des Internationalen Privat- und Verfahrensrechts, p. 210, at pp. 216 et seq.

69.   See the status table for the convention and the protocol at: http://www.unidroit.org.

of this kind, which were subject to subsequent developments in the internal market, were not sufficient to justify a differentiated regime for those provisions of the agreement which related to judicial cooperation in civil matters and for which the Community was exclusively competent.

In other cases, where the Member States were authorised to conclude a mixed agreement in the interest of the Community (because the Community could not itself become a contracting party),[70] the exclusion of a Member State from such authorisation would have led to the non-application in this Member State of the particular rules of the agreement relating to jurisdiction, recognition and enforcement. This issue was discussed, inter alia, with respect to the International Convention on Civil Liability for Bunker Oil Pollution Damage, 2001 (the "Bunkers Convention"). It was apparently suggested that it would be inappropriate for Member States in a landlocked position and without any sea-going port, such as Austria, to ratify this convention.[71] However, this was not considered to justify an exception to the principle of uniform application of Community law, and the Council decision authorising the Member States to sign, ratify or accede to this convention was eventually adopted without any exceptions for such Member States.[72]

By contrast, a differentiated regime in the field of judicial cooperation in civil matters was considered to be justified with respect to the Protocol to amend the (Paris) Convention on Third Party Liability in the Field of Nuclear Energy of 29 July 1960, as amended by the Additional Protocol of 28 January 1964 and by the Protocol of 16 November 1982.[73] The Protocol contains provisions on jurisdiction in respect of a nuclear incident and on the recognition and enforcement of judgments. These provisions were capable of affecting the internal Community rules laid down in the Brussels I Regulation, and therefore fell within the Community's exclusive competence, while other provisions of the Protocol fell within the competence of the Member States. In its decision authorising the Member States which were contracting parties to the Paris Convention to ratify or

---

70. See Part II.B.3.b), infra.
71. See Gerhard Hafner, Report on Austria, in: Xenios L. Xenopoulos (ed.), *FIDE 2006, External Relations of the EU and the Member States: Competence, Mixed Agreements, International Responsibility and Effects of International Law*, p. 7, at p. 8 (2006).
72. Council Decision of 19.9.2002, OJ L 256, 25.9.2002, p. 7. Cf. Henrik Ringbom, EU Regulation 44/2001 and its Implications for the International Maritime Liability Conventions, [2004] Journal of Maritime Law & Commerce, p. 1, at p. 14.
73. Cf. Fabrizio Nocera, Recent European Union Legislation and the International Nuclear Third Party Liability Regime – Conflicts, Problems and Solutions, [2004] Rev. dr. unif., p. 83.

to accede to the Protocol in the interest of the Community,[74] the Council considered that:

- given the subject matter and the aim of the Protocol, the provisions of the Protocol which came under Community competence could not be dissociated from the provisions which came under the competence of the Member States,
- the Community could not itself become a contracting party, because the Convention and the amending Protocol were not open to participation of Regional Economic Integration Organisations, and
- only those Member States which were already contracting parties to the Convention should ratify the Protocol in the interest of the Community.

The Council justified this latter aspect, which implied the acceptance of a differentiated regime of jurisdiction within the Community, in the following recital: "... three Member States, namely Austria, Ireland and Luxembourg, are not Parties to the Paris Convention. Given that the Protocol amends the Paris Convention, that Regulation (EC) No 44/2001 authorises the Member States bound by that Convention to continue to apply the rules on jurisdiction provided for in it and that the Protocol does not substantially amend the rules on jurisdiction of the Convention, it is objectively justified that this Decision should be addressed only to those Member States that are Parties to the Paris Convention. Accordingly, Austria, Ireland and Luxembourg will continue to base themselves on the Community rules contained in Regulation (EC) No 44/2001 and to apply them in the area covered by the Paris Convention and by the Protocol amending that Convention."[75] As a consequence, "... the provisions of the Protocol, as regards the European Community, will be applied only by those Member States which are currently Contracting Parties to the Paris Convention and [this] is without prejudice to the position of Austria, Ireland and Luxembourg."[76]

This decision has been criticised by some commentators, because it would lead to an incoherent application of the Brussels I Regulation the provisions of which would be superseded by the Paris Protocol for a limited number of Member States only.[77] However, although this decision is not

---

74. Council Decision of 8.3.2004, OJ L 97, 1.4.2004, p. 53.
75. Recital 8 of the decision.
76. Recital 10 of the decision.
77. Cf. Michael Wilderspin/Anne-Marie Rouchaud-Joët, La compétence externe de la Communauté européenne en droit international privé, [2004] Rev. crit. dr. internat. privé, p. 1, at p. 30; Alegría Borrás, La cooperation judiciaire en matière civile dans la Communauté européenne, Exposé to the Working Group X (Freedom, security and justice) of the European Convention, WG X – WD 8 of 4.11.2002, p. 12.

entirely in line with legal orthodoxy, the creative legal construction, which allowed for an acceptable solution in a delicate political situation, appears legally defendable in view of the combined reasons set out in the above-cited recitals.

b)   The special position of the United Kingdom, Ireland and Denmark

A primary law limitation of the territorial scope of mixed agreements in the field of judicial cooperation in civil matters results from the Protocols respectively on the position of the United Kingdom and Ireland and on the position of Denmark.[78] Pursuant to these Protocols, these three Member States do not, in principle, take part in the adoption by the Council of proposed measures under Title IV of Part Three of the EC Treaty,[79] which includes the provisions on judicial cooperation in civil matters (Articles 61 lit. c) and 65). Furthermore, no measure adopted pursuant to this Title, no provisions of any international agreement concluded by the Community pursuant to this Title, and no decision of the Court of Justice interpreting any such provision or measure is, in principle, binding upon or applicable in these Member States.[80] However, the Protocol on the position of the United Kingdom and Ireland, contrary to the Protocol on the position of Denmark, provides procedures for an opt-in of the United Kingdom and Ireland before the adoption of a measure, or for the acceptance by these Member States of a measure after its adoption.[81]

The Protocols on the position of these three Member States have implications for the negotiation, signature and conclusion of mixed agreements by the Community and its Member States in the field of judicial cooperation in civil matters, to the extent that the Council decisions

---

78.   Protocol (No 4) and Protocol (No 5) annexed to the EU Treaty and the EC Treaty. Cf. The contribution by Bernd Martenczuk on Variable Geometry and the External Relations of the European Union in this book.
79.   Art. 1 of the respective Protocols.
80.   Art. 2 of the respective Protocols.
81.   Art. 3 and 4 of the Protocol on the Position of the UK and Ireland. Pursuant to Art. 7 of the Protocol on the position of Denmark, Denmark may inform the other Member States that it no longer wishes to avail itself of all or part of the Protocol.

relating to such agreements are founded on Articles 61 lit. c) of the EC Treaty.[82]

As concerns the United Kingdom and Ireland, these two Member States had originally announced their general intention of being fully associated with the Community's activities in relation to judicial cooperation in civil matters and have subsequently exercised their opt-in with respect to most – but not all – proposed measures in this field. In a situation where the United Kingdom and/or Ireland have availed themselves of the opt-in for a particular internal measure and are consequently bound by it, these Member States must arguably also participate in a measure relating to an international agreement capable of affecting the internal measure, in order to comply with the principle of uniform application of Community law to all Member States bound by the internal rules, and the principles underlying the ERTA case-law of the Court of Justice.[83] Taking into account that the United Kingdom and Ireland have exercised their opt-in in relation to the Brussels I Regulation, this opt-in therefore arguably applies automatically for any subsequent recommendation for a negotiating authorisation relating to, and any proposal for a Council decision on the signature and conclusion of, a (mixed) agreement which may affect the Brussels I Regulation.[84] Up till now, the United Kingdom

82. To the extent that the Council decisions relating to mixed agreements in the field of judicial cooperation in civil matters are founded on other legal bases, outside Title IV of Part Three of the EC Treaty, the position of the UK, Ireland and Denmark is no different from that of any other Member State. This is the case, e.g., for the Council Decision of 5.4.2001 on the conclusion by the European Community of the Montreal Convention for the Unification of Certain Rules for International Carriage by Air (OJ L 194, 18.7.2001, p. 38), which is founded on Article 80(2) of the EC Treaty; and the draft Council Decision concerning the signing of the Hague Convention on the Law Applicable to Certain Rights in Respect of Securities Held with an Intermediary (Council doc. 14836/04 of 29.11.2004), which is founded on Articles 47(2) and 95 of the EC Treaty. A more complex situation arises if the Council decision on the signing or conclusion of a mixed agreement is founded on Art. 61 lit. c), but also on another legal basis in a field for which the Protocols on the position of the UK and Ireland and the position of Denmark do not apply. For instance, the draft Council decision on the signature, on behalf of the European Community, of the Protocol on Civil Liability and Compensation for Damage caused by the Transboundary Effects of Industrial Accidents on Transboundary Waters (Council doc. 11811/03 of 12.9.2003) is founded on Art. 61 lit. c) and Art. 175(1) of the EC Treaty. In such cases, the Protocols apply only to those parts of the agreement, in respect of which Art. 61 lit. c) is the legal basis.
83. ECJ, Case 22/70, *Commission/Council*, [1971] ECR 263.
84. Cf. in this context, Pieter Jan Kuijper, The evolution of the third pillar from Maastricht to the European Constitution: institutional aspects, [2004] CMLRev, p. 609, at p. 623.

and Ireland have participated in the adoption and application of measures relating to mixed agreements in the field of judicial cooperation in civil matters. The question of the limitation of the territorial scope of such agreements has therefore not yet arisen in respect of these two Member States, but it is not excluded that it will arise in the future.

As concerns Denmark, the general exclusion of this Member State from the adoption and application of Community measures in the field of judicial cooperation in civil matters under Articles 61 lit. c) and 65 of the EC Treaty applies also with respect to mixed agreements in this field. Therefore, the territorial scope of such a mixed agreement, including its provisions on judicial cooperation in civil matters, is limited to the Community minus Denmark.

If a mixed agreement contains provisions for which the Member States are competent, as well as provisions on judicial cooperation in civil matters for which the Community is competent pursuant to Articles 61 lit. c) and 65 of the EC Treaty, Denmark remains free to negotiate, sign and conclude the entirety of the agreement on its own behalf.

However, it can be argued that the principle of loyal cooperation between the Member States and the Community institutions, enshrined in Article 10 of the EC Treaty, requires Denmark to at least inform or consult the other Member States within the Council on these matters.

More specific obligations of Denmark in this respect are laid down in the Agreement between the Community and Denmark on jurisdiction and the recognition and enforcement of judgments in civil and commercial matters, and the Agreement between the Community and Denmark on the service of judicial and extrajudicial documents in civil or commercial matters.[85] The aim of these agreements is to apply in the relations between the Community and Denmark and by virtue of international law, the provisions of the Brussels I Regulation and of Regulation (EC) No 1348/2000 of 29 May 2000 on insolvency proceedings,[86] which – as a consequence of the above mentioned Protocol – do not apply to Denmark by virtue of Community law. These agreements provide, in particular, that "Denmark will abstain form entering into international agreements which may affect or alter the scope of [the Brussels I Regulation and Regulation (EC) No 1348/2000] unless it is done in agreement with the Community

---

85. Council Decisions of 20.9.2005 on the signing of these agreements, OJ L 299, 16.11.2005, p. 61, and OJ L 300, 17.11.2005, p. 53. See also the Council Decisions of 27.4.2006 on the conclusion of these agreements, OJ L 120, 5.5.2006, respectively p. 22 and p. 23.
86. OJ L 160, 30.6.2000, p. 1.

and satisfactory arrangements have been made with regard to the relationship between this Agreement and the international agreement in question."[87] Furthermore, Denmark shall, when negotiating such international agreements "coordinate its position with the Community and will abstain form any actions that would jeopardise the objectives of a Community position within its sphere of competence in such negotiations."[88] These obligations of Denmark apply not only with respect to Community agreements in the field of judicial cooperation in civil matters, but also to mixed agreements in this field.

The situation of the United Kingdom, Ireland and Denmark for any particular mixed agreement in the field of judicial cooperation in civil matters is generally mentioned in the negotiating authorisation, in standard recitals of the Council decisions on the signature and conclusion of the agreement,[89] in the enabling terms of such decision,[90] and, as the case may be, in the declaration on the respective competencies of the Community and its Member States attached to the decision.[91]

3.   Concealed mixed agreements

A relatively large number of mixed agreements that contain provisions on judicial cooperation in civil matters have been negotiated, signed or concluded by the Member States alone, but not by the Community. To the extent that the subject matter of these agreements fell within the Community's exclusive competence, the Member States acted in the interest of the Community on the basis of a specific authorisation given by the Council.

This is in line with the case-law of the Court of Justice and the practice of the Community institutions in other fields. Although according to the ERTA case-law, Member States have in principle no right to negotiate or to undertake obligations with non-member countries, which may affect the internal Community rules and which therefore fall within the Community's exclusive competence,[92] the Court of Justice recognized that

87. Art. 5(2) of the Agreements.
88. Art. 5(3) of the Agreements.
89. See, e.g., the draft Council Decision on the signing by the Community of the Convention on International Interests in Mobile Equipment and its Protocol on Matters Specific to Aircraft Equipment (Council doc. 5720/04 of 17.2.2004), recitals 8 and 9.
90. Id., Art. 1(2) of the draft Decision: "in this Decision, 'Member State' shall mean all the Member States with the exception of Denmark."
91. Id., points I.3 and II.3 of the Annex to the draft Decision.
92. ECJ, Case 22/70, *Commission/Council*, [1971] ECR 263, para.17; Opinion 1/03, [2006] ECR I-1145, para. 116.

the Member States can exceptionally and under particular circumstances be authorised by the Council to conclude international agreements in the interest of the Community in areas falling within the Community's exclusive competence. Such circumstances may arise where a considerable part of the work carried out in the negotiations took place before the Community acquired exclusive competence as a result of the adoption of internal rules.[93] Such circumstances can also arise if the Community is not in a position to undertake international obligations itself, because the provisions of the agreement or the rules of the international organisation concerned do not enable the Community to act on its own.[94] Even in a case where the provisions of an international agreement falling within the Community's exclusive competence did enable the Community to conclude the agreement, the Member States were nevertheless authorised by the Council to conclude the agreement alongside the Community, in order to avoid temporary operational difficulties resulting from the procedural rules of the agreement.[95]

Loyal cooperation between the Community institutions and the Member States is all the more necessary in such situations where the Member States act in the interest of the Community by negotiating, signing or concluding mixed agreements.[96]

93. This was the case in the situation giving rise to the ERTA judgment where the Court stated that "in carrying on the negotiations and concluding the agreement simultaneously in the manner decided on by the Council, the Member States acted, and continue to act, in the interest and on behalf of the Community in accordance with their obligations under Article 5 [now: Article 10] of the Treaty." ECJ, Case 22/70, *Commission/Council*, [1971] ECR 263, para. 90.
94. This was for instance the case in the situation giving rise to the ECJ's Opinion 2/91 where the Court stated that "in any event, although, under the ILO Constitution, the Community cannot itself conclude Convention No 170, its external competence may, if necessary, be exercised through the medium of the Member States acting jointly in the Community's interest", ECJ, Opinion 2/91, [1993] ECR 1061, para. 5.
95. This was the case of the Council Decision of 24.9.2001 on the signing and conclusion on behalf of the European Community of the International Coffee Agreement 2001, OJ L 326, 11.12.2001, p. 22. The Decision is founded on Article 133, but states in its 5th recital that "notwithstanding the exclusive Community competence in this matter, and in order to avoid certain temporary operational difficulties, it is appropriate to authorise the Member States to conclude the Agreement at the same time as the Community and to participate on a temporary basis in the new arrangement." These considerations apply also with respect to the parts of a mixed agreement which fall under the Community's exclusive competence.
96. Cf. ECJ, Opinion 2/91, [1993] ECR I-1061, paras. 36-38.

a)   Negotiations by Member States in the interest of the Community

In the field of judicial cooperation in civil matters, an example of an authorisation for Member States to negotiate an agreement in the interest of the Community is the Council Decision of 11 May 2004 to authorise certain Member States, on behalf of the Community, to open negotiations for an Agreement on Liability arising from Environmental Emergencies to be annexed to the Protocol on Environmental Protection to the Antarctic Treaty.[97] The drafts of this instrument contained provisions on jurisdiction for which it was not excluded that they could potentially overlap with the internal Community rules laid down in the Brussels I Regulation. It can be supposed that the authorisation was given to certain Member States because the Community itself was not among the Consultative Parties to the Antarctic Treaty.

Another mixed agreement which was negotiated by the Member States, although it contained provisions falling under the exclusive competence of the Community, was the Bunkers Convention. While the negotiation on this Convention were ongoing in the framework of the IMO, the Council adopted the Brussels I Regulation. The problem of a potential overlap between the provisions of this Regulation and the draft provisions of the Bunkers Convention was highlighted only at the diplomatic conference which adopted the Bunkers Convention in March 2001. This was apparently too late for the Commission to present the Council with a recommendation for a negotiating authorisation. Although the Member States were thus not formally authorised to negotiate in the interest of the Community, the Council Presidency and the Commission attempted to arrive at a coordinated position during the conference, aiming at a provision which would allow the Member States to continue to apply the Brussels I Regulation in their mutual relations. It proved however impossible to modify the draft Convention at such a late stage. At the occasion of the adoption of the text of the Bunkers Convention, the Member States therefore made a declaration according to which the relationship between the Convention and recent Community legislation on jurisdiction and the recognition and enforcement of judgments would have to be addressed at the Community level.[98]

---

97.   Cf. point 2 of the draft Council minutes in Council doc. 9410/04 of 24.5.2004, in conjunction with point 1 of the list of A-items in Council doc. 9246/04 of 10.5.2004. Although the content of the authorisation decision is not publicly available, its title indicates that it is not the Commission, but certain Member States which were authorised to negotiate on behalf of the Community.
98.   Cf. the explanatory memorandum to the Commission proposal for a Council decision relating to the signing of the Bunkers Convention, COM (2001) 675 final of 19.11.2001.

b)   *Signing, ratification and accession by Member States in the interest of the Community*

In the field of judicial cooperation in civil matters the Council has fairly frequently authorised the Member States (or some Member States) to sign, ratify, or accede to mixed agreements in the interest of the Community.[99]

99. –   Council Decision of 19.9.2002 authorising the Member States, in the interest of the Community, to sign, ratify or accede to the International Convention on Civil Liability for Bunker Oil Pollution Damage, 2001 (the Bunkers Convention), OJ L 256, 25.9.2002, p. 7;
     –   Council Decision of 18.11.2002 authorising the Member States, in the interest of the Community, to ratify or accede to the International Convention on Liability and Compensation for Damage in Connection with the Carriage of Hazardous and Noxious Substances by Sea, 1996 (the HNS Convention); OJ L 337, 13.12.2002, p. 55;
     –   Council Decision of 19.12.2002 authorising the Member States, in the interest of the Community, to sign the 1996 Hague Convention on jurisdiction, applicable law, recognition, enforcement and cooperation in respect of parental responsibility and measures for the protection of children, OJ L 48, 21.2.2003, p. 1; and draft Council Decision authorising the Member States to accede to, or ratify, in the interest of the European Community, the 1996 Hague Convention on jurisdiction, applicable law, recognition, enforcement and cooperation in respect of parental responsibility and measures for the protection of children, Council doc. 14454/03 of 25.11.2003 (the 1996 Hague Convention on the Protection of Children);
     –   Council Decision of 2.3.2004 authorising the Member States to sign, ratify or accede to, in the interest of the European Community, the Protocol of 2003 to the International Convention on the Establishment of an International Fund for Compensation for Oil Pollution Damage, 1992, and authorising Austria and Luxembourg, in the interest of the European Community, to accede to the underlying instruments, OJ L 78, 16.3.2004, p. 22; and Council Decision adapting Decision 2004/246/EC by reason of the accession of the Czech Republic, Estonia, Cyprus, Latvia, Lithuania, Hungary, Malta, Poland, Slovenia and Slovakia, OJ L 303, 30.9.2004, p. 28 (the Fund Protocol 2003);
     –   Council Decision of 27.11.2003 authorising the Member States which are Contracting Parties to the Paris Convention of 29 July 1960 on Third Party Liability in the Field of Nuclear Energy to sign, in the interest of the European Community, the Protocol amending that Convention, OJ L 338, 23.12.2003, p. 30; Council Decision of 8.3.2004 authorising the Member States which are Contracting Parties to the Paris Convention of 29 July 1960 on Third Party Liability in the Field of Nuclear Energy to ratify, in the interest of the European Community, the Protocol amending that Convention, or to accede to it, OJ L 97, 1.4.2004, p. 53; Commission proposal for a Council Decision authorising the Republic of Slovenia to ratify, in the interest of the European Community, the Protocol of 12 February 2004 amending the Paris Convention of 29 July 1960 on Third-Party Liability in the Field of Nuclear Energy, COM(2006) 793 final of 13.12.2006 (the 2004 Protocol to the Paris Convention).

Such authorisations were necessary in cases where the agreements provided only for States, but not for regional organisations to become contracting parties.

The authorising decisions of the Council are similarly structured. The recitals state that certain provisions of the convention concerned – notably those on jurisdiction and the recognition and enforcement of judgments – fall within the Community's exclusive competence, whereas other – substantive – provisions fall within the competence of the Member States. Furthermore, it is noted in the recitals that the procedural and substantive rules of the convention cannot be dissociated. The enabling terms of the decisions contain a provision authorising the Member States (concerned) to sign, ratify or accede to the convention. This provision is in some instances followed by a provision on declarations to be made by the Member States at the time of the signing of the convention or the deposit of the instruments of acceptance. In addition, there are generally a cooperation clause, a transparency clause and a regularisation clause.

First, the authorisation provision in the first Article of the Council decision generally provides that the Member States are authorised to sign, ratify, or accede to the Convention "in the interest of the Community". These words express the fact that the Member States, whilst signing and ratifying the agreement in their own interest as concerns matters falling within their competence, also act in the interest of the Community for matters falling within the exclusive competence of the Community. The terms "in the interest of the Community", rather than "on behalf of the Community" were deliberately chosen, in order to avoid the wrong impression that the Member States act as a proxy for the Community and that the Community would become bound in relation to the other contracting parties. Some authorising provisions contain an additional qualification according to which the authorisation is given "without prejudice to the Community's powers" or "without prejudice to existing Community competence".[100] This is presumably meant to indicate that by authorising the Member States, the Council does not transfer the Community's competence to the Member States. In my view, this qualification is superfluous and may be misleading, because the Member States do not act without prejudice to the Community's competence, but in exercising the Community's competence.

---

100. Cf. Art. 1 of the Council decisions relating to the Bunkers Convention, the HNS Convention and the 2004 Protocol to the Paris Convention.

Second, a provision on the declarations to be made by the Member States may provide that, when signing, ratifying, or acceding to the convention the Member States shall make a declaration relating to the application of certain internal Community rules. Such a declaration may state, for instance, that "judgments on matters covered by the Convention shall, when given by a court of [a Member State], be recognised and enforced in [the Member State making the declaration] according to the relevant internal Community rules on the subject."[101] This provision is meant to safeguard the application of the internal Community rules, to the extent that the intra-Community recognition and enforcement of judgments is concerned. However, declarations of this kind, which could be construed to amount to reservations, can be problematic under international law if the convention concerned does not provide for a corresponding partial disconnection clause.[102]

Third, a provision in the authorising decision may provide for the manner in which the Member States shall coordinate the signing of the convention or the deposit of their respective instruments of ratification or accession. Article 3 of the Council decision on the signing of the 1996 Hague Convention on the Protection of Children sets a binding date before which the Member States shall make the necessary arrangements for the Convention to be signed, whereas other authorising decisions contain only best efforts obligations or indicative dates.[103] Whilst some authorising decisions expressly provide that the deposit of the instruments of acceptance is to be done simultaneously by the Member States,[104] others contain only coordination requirements such as the obligation of the

---

101. Art. 2 of the Council decisions relating to the Bunkers Convention and the HNS Convention. Cf. also the different declaration provided for in Art. 2 of the Council decision relating to the signing of the 1996 Hague Convention on the Protection of Children.
102. Cf. Henrik Ringbom, EU Regulation 44/2001 and its Implications for the International Maritime Liability Conventions, [2004] Journal of Maritime Law & Commerce, p. 1, at pp. 22 et seq.
103. Cf. Art. 3 of the Council decisions relating to the Bunkers Convention and the HNS Convention; Art. 3 of the draft Council decision on the ratification of the 1996 Hague Convention on the Protection of Children; Art. 2 of the Council decision relating to the Fund Protocol of 2003; Article 2 of the Council decisions relating to the 2004 Protocol to the Paris Convention.
104. Cf. Art. 3 of the draft Council decision on the ratification of the 1996 Hague Convention on the Protection of Children; Art. 2 of the Council decision on the ratification of the 2004 Protocol to the Paris Convention.

Member States to inform the Council and the Commission on the prospective date of finalisation of their ratification or accession procedures, or the exchange of information in this regard between the Member States.[105] Even where, in the latter case, the coordination requirements fall short of an express requirement of a simultaneous deposit of the instruments of acceptance, such requirement could be deduced from the fact that the Member States are authorised collectively to act in the interest of the Community for subject matters falling within its exclusive competence and that a single Member State cannot under these circumstances act individually.

Fourth, the authorising decision may contain an obligation for Member States to indicate to the other parties or the international organisation in the framework of which the convention was negotiated, the fact that the Community is exclusively competent for some of the matters falling under the convention, and that the Member States act, with regard to these matters, in the interest of the Community. These transparency clauses generally provide that Member States, when signing or ratifying the agreement, shall inform the depository in writing that such signing or ratification has taken place in accordance with the authorising decision. Such clauses are contained in the Council decisions relating to the Bunkers Convention,[106] the HNS Convention,[107] and the Fund Protocol of 2003,[108] where the written information is to be addressed to the Secretary-General of the International Maritime Organisation, in the Council decisions relating to the 2004 Protocol to the Paris Convention,[109] where the written information is to be addressed to the Secretary-General of the OECD, and in the Council decision on the signing of the 1996 Hague Convention on the Protection of Children,[110] where the written information is to be addressed to the Ministry of Foreign Affairs of the Netherlands.

Finally, the authorising decision may contain an obligation for Member States to use their best endeavours to ensure that the convention concerned is amended at a later stage in order to allow the Community to become a contracting party to it.[111] This provision, which would oblige the Member

---

105. Cf. Art. 3 of the Council decisions relating to the Bunkers Convention and the HNS Convention; Art. 2 of the Council decision relating to the Fund Protocol of 2003.
106. Art. 4.
107. Art. 4.
108. Art. 3.
109. Art. 3.
110. Art. 4.
111. Art. 5 of the Council decisions relating to the Bunkers and HNS Conventions; Art. 4 of the Council decision relating to the Fund Protocol of 2003.

States to attempt to regularize the situation, can be understood as a specific emanation of the principle of loyal cooperation, although it appears doubtful whether any such attempts will in a multilateral context be successful in the short or medium term. The Council decision relating to the signing of the 1996 Hague Convention on the Protection of Children and the draft Council decision relating to the ratification or accession to this convention, do not contain such a clause. The possibilities to overcome difficulties resulting from the absence of REIO-clauses in this and other Hague Conventions are addressed in more general terms in the declaration of the European Community, which is attached to its instrument of accession to the Hague Conference.[112]

III. Legal Effects

Mixed agreements raise a number of issues concerning their legal effects in relation to third parties and within the Community legal order. Some of these issues will be briefly examined below as regards, first, the international responsibility of the Community and its Member States for the performance of the agreement vis-à-vis third parties, second, the respective tasks and powers of the Community and its Member States in the implementation and application of the agreement, and third, the jurisdiction of the Court of Justice for the interpretation of the agreement. It can be noted at the outset that there is not yet much experience or case-law in this respect in the area of judicial cooperation in civil matters.

A. International Responsibility

The question of the international responsibility of international organisations in general and the Community in particular, as well as the specific question of the international responsibility for the performance of mixed agreements concluded by the Community and its Member States,

---

112. Cf. Annex III to the Council Decision of 5.10.2006 on the accession of the Community to the Hague Conference on Private International Law, OJ L 297, 26.10.2006, p. 1. Cf. also Alegría Borrás, Le droit international privé communautaire: réalités, problèmes et perspectives d'avenir, in: Académie de droit international, [2005] *Recueil des cours*, tome 317, p. 313, at pp. 511-513 (2006).

has given rise to a wide-ranging and on-going debate, notably within the framework of the International Law Commission.[113]

The prevailing view appears to be that the Community and its Member States are jointly (or even jointly and severally) liable for the performance of mixed agreements unless the agreement or a declaration of competence made at the occasion of the signature or conclusion of the agreement clearly indicates which commitments under the agreement were entered into respectively by the Community or the Member States.[114] This conclusion can be founded on the argument that both the Community and its Member States are bound vis-à-vis third contracting parties, by virtue of their acceptance or ratification of the agreement. Although third parties will in general be aware of the fact that the Community and its Member States share competence in the field covered by a mixed agreement, they cannot normally be expected to themselves investigate whether it is the Community or its Member States which would – under the internal Community rules – be competent to fulfil the obligations arising from the

113. The work of the International Law Commission on this subject is reported at http://untreaty.un.org/ilc/summaries/9_11.htm, with links to the Reports of the Special Rapporteur, the Drafting Committee, the comments of Governments and International Organisations, the Reports of the ILC and the General Assembly action on this matter. For an analysis of this work with respect to the international responsibility for the performance of mixed agreements, see Piet Eeckhout, General Report, in: Xenios L. Xenopoulos (ed.), *FIDE 2006, External Relations of the EU and the Member States: Competence, Mixed Agreements, International Responsibility and Effects of International Law*, p. 275, at pp. 297-303 (2006); cf. also Pieter Jan Kuijper/ E. Paasivirta, Further exploring international responsibility: the European Community and the ILC's project on responsibility of international organizations, [2004] International Organizations Law Review, p. 111.

114. Cf. Piet Eeckhout, *External Relations of the European Union*, pp. 222 et seq. (2004); Marianne Dony, Les accords mixtes, in: *Commentaire J. Mégret*, Vol. 12, p. 189 (2005); Iain MacLeod/Ian Hendry/Stephen Hyett, *The External Relations of the European Communities*, pp. 158 et seq (1996); all with further nuances.

agreement.[115] It has, however, been argued that this problem might be solved through procedural means, in particular by conferring on third parties the right to be informed by the Community and the Member States on their respective powers.[116]

The case-law of the Court of Justice has not yet given a definitive reply to these questions,[117] but it appears to confirm the principle of joint liability of the Community and its Member States for the performance of mixed agreements and the above-mentioned exceptions to this principle. In case C-316/91, the Court ruled that, under the particular circumstances of the Convention at issue "... in the absence of derogations expressly laid down in the Convention, the Community and its Member States as partners of

---

115. This conclusion appears to be confirmed by the rules of customary international law which are codified in the Vienna Convention on the law of treaties, although they apply to States only. If both the Community and the Member States are bound by a treaty, it would follow from Articles 26 and 27 of the Vienna Convention, that they must both perform the treaty in good faith, and that they may not invoke the provisions of the internal law – such as the ones relating to their respective powers under the EC Treaty – as a justification for the failure to perform the treaty. Furthermore, Art. 17 of the Vienna Convention provides that, without prejudice to the rules on reservations, the consent of a State to be bound by part of a treaty is effective only if the treaty so permits or the other contracting States so agree, and the consent of a State to be bound by a treaty which permits a choice between differing provisions is effective only if it is made clear to which of the provisions the consent relates. Finally, it follows from Art. 46 of the Vienna Convention that a party cannot invoke the violation of a provision of its internal law regarding competence to conclude treaties, as invalidating its consent unless that violation was manifest.

116. See, in particular, Joni Heliskoski, *Mixed Agreements as a Technique for Organizing the International Relations of the European Community and its Member States*, pp. 200-206 (2001). Cf. also Marise Cremona, Community Report, in: Xenios L. Xenopoulos (ed.), *FIDE 2006, External Relations of the EU and the Member States: Competence, Mixed Agreements, International Responsibility and Effects of International Law*, p. 319, at pp. 347 et seq. (2006); Eckhard Pasche/Joachim Bielitz, Das Verhältnis der EG zu den völkerrechtlichen Verträgen ihrer Mitgliedstaaten, [2006] EuR, p. 316, at pp. 320 et seq.

117. The positions of the Court's Advocates General also appear to be divergent. See, on the one hand, Opinion of Advocate General Jacobs in Case C-316/91, *Parliament/Council*, [1994] ECR I-625, para. 69: "Under a mixed agreement the Community and the Member States are jointly liable unless the provisions of the agreement point to the opposite conclusion." On the other hand, Opinion of Advocate-General Mischo in Case C-13/00, *Commission/Ireland*, [2002] ECR I-2943, para. 30: "..the very fact that the Community and its Member States had recourse to the formula of a mixed agreement announces to non-member countries that that agreement does not fall wholly within the competence of the Community and that, consequently, the Community is, a priori, only assuming responsibility for those parts falling within its competence."

the ACP States are jointly liable to those latter States for the fulfilment of every obligation arising form the commitments undertaken...".[118] On the other hand, in a case where there was a declaration of competence, the Court stated, in its Opinion 2/00, that "the extent of the respective powers of the Community and the Member States with regard to the matters governed by the Protocol determines the extent of their respective responsibilities in relation to performance of the obligations under the Protocol" and that the Protocol takes account of this by requesting Regional Economic Integration Organisations to make a declaration of competence.[119]

The application of these principles to mixed agreements which include provisions on judicial cooperation in civil matters must have regard to the provisions and the context of the particular agreement concerned.

As has been mentioned above, the Cape Town Convention on International Interests in Mobile Equipment provides in its Article 48(1) that a Regional Economic Integration Organisation, which accepts or approves the Convention, shall "have the rights and obligations of a Contracting State, to the extent that that Organisation has competence over matters governed by this Convention." Article 18(1) of the Hague Convention on the Law Applicable to certain Rights in Respect of Securities held with an Intermediary, and Article 19(1) of the Protocol of 2002 to the Athens Convention Relating to the Carriage of Passengers and their Luggage by Sea, also contain such clauses. These clauses, together with the declaration of competence which the Regional Economic Integration Organisation is obliged to deposit under these agreements, could lead to the conclusion that the Community and its Member States assume international responsibility only in respect of their respective competencies. However, this conclusion would be justified only if the declaration of competence is sufficiently precise in order to allow the other contracting parties to ascertain which of the commitments resulting from the agreement concerned fall within the competence of the Community and which other commitments fall within the competencies of the Member States. It is uncertain whether the declarations relating to the agreements mentioned above fulfil this condition. To the extent that the declarations merely state that the Community is competent to enter into commitments in matters which may affect, or which are covered by, certain internal instruments, third parties might find themselves unable to apply such statements to the specific commitments under the agreement. A more precise statement of

---

118. ECJ, Case C-316/91, *Parliament/Council*, [1994] ECR I-625, para. 29.
119. ECJ, Opinion 2/00, [2001] ECR I-9713 para. 16.

competence is the one envisaged for the conclusion of the Cape Town Convention and its Protocol on Matters Specific to Aircraft Equipment, which includes the indication that "the competence of the Member States concerning the rules of substantive law as regards insolvency are not affected".[120] This could arguably be sufficient to signal to third parties that the Community does not assume international responsibility in respect of the provisions of the Convention which establish substantive rules on insolvency.

As concerns conventions adopted in the framework of the Hague Conference on Private International Law, the provisions of the amended Statute of the Conference may also have an impact in this regard. The Statute provides that the Member States of a Regional Economic Integration Organisation shall be presumed to retain competence over all matters in respect of which transfers of competence have not been "specifically" declared or notified,[121] and it establishes the right of the Members of the Conference to request the Organisation and its Member States to provide information as to the distribution of competence in respect of any specific question which is before the Conference, and the obligation of the Organisation and its Member States to provide such information.[122]

In the absence of provisions which limit the rights and obligations of the International Regional Integration Organisation to matters falling within its competence, it appears more difficult to justify a limited international responsibility solely on the basis of a declaration of competence. In any case, a general declaration such as that provided for in the draft Council decision on the signing of the Council of Europe Convention on Contact Concerning Children, which would simply state that "certain provisions of the [Convention] fall under the competence of the Community", that "the Community signs the Convention to the extent that it falls within its competence" and that "Member States may sign the convention to the

---

120. Council doc. 13967/03 of 29.10.2003, Annex I to ANNEX I, Declarations I.5 and II.5. See also the draft Commission declaration in ANNEX IV which is intended for entry into the minutes of the Council meeting adopting the decision and for publication in the OJ, and which enumerates precisely the provisions of the Convention and the Protocol which are considered to fall within the Community's competence.
121. Art. 3(5) of the Statute, in its version resulting form the amendments which entered into force on 1.1.2007.
122. Art. 3(6) of the Statute, in its version resulting form the amendments which entered into force on 1.1.2007.

extent that if falls within their competence",[123] does not appear to be sufficient for this purpose.

In the particular case of concealed mixed agreements, which are concluded by the Member States in the interest (but not on behalf) of the Community, third parties must address any claim to the Member States concerned and cannot rely on any responsibility of the Community which, irrespective of the division of powers under the Community's internal legal order, is not a party to such agreements and is thus not bound by them under international law.

In other cases, where the above considerations lead to the conclusion that the Community assumes international responsibility for the performance of obligations arising from those provisions of a particular mixed agreement which fall within its competence, the issue is further complicated by the fact that the application of such provisions is not necessarily entrusted to the Community institutions. This complication is particularly visible in the field of judicial cooperation in civil matters, where the Community rules on conflict of laws or jurisdictions or on the recognition and enforcement of judgments are applied by the courts of the Member States.

This can be illustrated by a hypothetical example concerning the Cape Town Convention, under the assumption that the Community becomes a contracting party thereto. Chapter XII of the Convention lays down the rules on jurisdiction in respect of claims brought under the Convention. Some of these rules may affect the rules on jurisdiction laid down in the Brussels I Regulation. The Community would therefore, pursuant to the ERTA case-law of the Court of Justice,[124] be exclusively competent with respect to these provisions, and the Community would thus arguably assume the international responsibility for the performance of the commitments embodied in these provisions. Article 44 (in Chapter XII) of the Convention provides that the courts of the place in which the Registrar has its centre of administration shall have exclusive jurisdiction to award damages or make orders against the Registrar. If a court of a Member State of the Community takes jurisdiction for such a claim, in violation of this provision, the Community could be held responsible by the other contracting parties. The Community would then need to turn to the Member State concerned, which would be obliged under Community law to abide by the rules of the Convention. This would be in line with the Court's reasoning in the Demirel Case, according to which "in ensuring

---

123. Council Doc. 7625/1/03 of 22.4.2003, Art. 2.
124. ECJ, Case 22/70, *Commission/Council*, [1971] ECR 263, para.17; Opinion 1/03, [2006] ECR I-1145, para. 116.

respect for commitments arising form an agreement concluded by the Community institutions the Member States fulfil, within the Community system, an obligation in relation to the Community, which has assumed responsibility for the due performance of the agreement."[125]

B.　Implementation and Application

Mixed agreements are to be implemented and applied by the Community and its Member States within their respective fields of competence, on the basis of a close cooperation between them.[126] A close cooperation is particularly important in cases where the implementation and application of the agreement requires measures by both the Community and the Member States, and in cases of a mixed representation of the Community and the Member States in a body set up by the agreement.

For those provisions of a mixed agreement which fall within the Community's competence (such as certain provisions in the field of judicial cooperation in civil matters), the agreement is binding on the institutions of the Community and on the Member States, pursuant to Article 300(7) of the EC Treaty. Those parts are integrated into the Community legal order and take precedence over the provisions of secondary Community law,[127] such as the Brussels I Regulation. It is therefore not always legally necessary to adopt specific implementing acts. Whether or not implementing acts should nevertheless be adopted depends on the content and nature of the provisions of the agreement and of the pertinent internal Community rules, and is to be assessed on a case-by-case basis. In any case, the Community is obliged to apply such provisions of the agreement as a matter of compliance with its obligations under international law and Community law, and the Member States are obliged to apply these provisions as a matter of compliance with their obligations under Community law.[128]

---

125. ECJ, Case 12/86, Demirel, [1987] ECR 3719, para. 11. Cf. also ECJ, Case 104/81, *Hauptzollamt Mainz/Kupferberg*, [1982] ECR 3641, para. 13
126. Cf. ECJ, Ruling 1/78, [1978] ECR 2151, para. 36; Opinion 2/91, [1993] ECR I-1061, paras. 36-38, Opinion 1/94, [1994] ECR I-5267, paras. 107-109.
127. ECJ, Case 181/73, *Haegeman/Belgium*, [1974] ECR 449, para. 5; Case C-61/94, *Commission/Germany*, [1996] ECR I-3989, para. 52.
128. Cf. the example given supra in Part III. A, in fine. However, if the Member States concluded a (concealed) mixed agreement in the interest of the Community, the Community is obliged to comply with the provisions of the agreement, which fall within its competence, as a matter of Community law, and the Member States are obliged to comply with these provisions as a matter of international law and Community law.

For those parts of a mixed agreement which fall within the Member States' competence, it is for the Member States to assess, in the light of their respective internal legal orders, whether specific implementing action is necessary. In any case, the Member States must apply such provisions as a matter of compliance with their obligations under international law.

Some mixed agreements establish bodies which have different functions in the application of the agreement. The representation in such bodies is mostly "mixed", consisting of representatives of the Community (the Commission) and of the Member States.[129] The position to be taken by the Community and the Member States is generally established internally before the meetings of such bodies, sometimes on the basis of a general arrangement between the Council and the Commission, which represents the fulfilment of the duty of co-operation between the Community institutions and the Member States.[130] If a body established by a mixed agreement is called upon to adopt decisions having legal effects, the establishment of the Community's and the Member States' position is all the more important. As concerns matters falling under the Community's competence, Article 300(2), second subparagraph, of the EC Treaty provides that the position to be taken by the Community in the body is to be decided on by the Council on a proposal by the Commission.

In a body set up by a concealed mixed agreement, to which the Community is not a contracting party, only the Member States can be represented. However, to the extent that the body deals with matters falling within the Community's exclusive competence, the Member States act in this body in the interest of the Community. The HNS Convention, for example, establishes an Assembly consisting of the States party to the Convention.[131] Most of the functions of the Assembly appear to relate to subject matters falling within the Member States' competence. However, when the Assembly exercises its function to supervise the proper execution of the

---

129. Cf. Koen Lenaerts/Eddy De Smijter, The European Union as an Actor under International Law, [1999-2000] Yearbook of European Law, p. 95, at p. 128. See also ECJ, Opinion 1/76, [1977] ECR 741, para. 12, where the Court ruled that the structure given to the Supervisory Board to be established by a draft agreement and the arrangements for the decision-making procedure within that organ were not compatible with the requirements of unity and solidarity, because they would result in a surrender of the independence of action of the Community and a change in the internal constitution of the Community.

130. Cf., e.g., the arrangement which gave rise to the FAO case, ECJ, Case C-25/94, *Commission/Council*, [1996] ECR I-1469, para. 49.

131. Articles 25-28 of the International Convention on Liability and Compensation for Damage in Connection with the Carriage of Hazardous and Noxious Substances by Sea, 1996.

Convention,[132] the Member States should act in the Assembly in the interest of the Community to the extent that the supervision relates to the Convention's rules on jurisdiction which fall within the Community's exclusive competence.

C.   Jurisdiction of the Community courts

The jurisdiction of the Court of Justice and the Court of First Instance is limited to the interpretation and application of the EC Treaty.[133] Community courts have in principle no jurisdiction with respect to matters which fall outside the scope of the Treaty. If the Community courts are called upon to review or interpret mixed agreements, which may contain provisions falling outside the scope of Community law, it is therefore necessary to ascertain the extent of the courts' jurisdiction. In practice, this has become particularly relevant in the context of infringement proceedings pursuant to Article 226 of the EC Treaty and proceedings for a preliminary ruling pursuant to Article 234 of the EC Treaty.[134]

In cases where the Commission brings an action, pursuant to Article 226 of the EC Treaty, concerning the failure of a Member State to fulfil an obligation arising from the provisions of a mixed agreement, the Community courts must examine whether this obligation falls within the scope of Community law, because infringement proceedings can relate only to a failure to comply with obligations arising from Community law.[135] Mixed agreements have the same status in the Community legal order as purely Community agreements (and are thus subject to the jurisdiction of the Community courts) only "in so far as" the provisions fall within the scope of Community competence.[136] It would appear from the earlier case-law of the Court of Justice that it is sufficient in this respect that the provisions of the mixed agreement fall "in large measure within

---

132. Art. 26 lit. l) of the Convention.
133. Cf. Art. 220(1) ECT.
134. In the field of judicial cooperation in civil matters, Art. 234 applies, pursuant to Art. 68 of the EC Treaty, only to requests submitted by Member States' courts of last instance. For critical comments on this limitation, cf. Jürgen Basedow, Der Raum des Rechts – ohne Justiz, [2001] Zeitschrift für Europäisches Privatrecht, p. 437; Cédric Cheneviere, L'article 68 CE – Rapide survol d'un renvoi préjudiciel mal compris, [2004] CDE, p. 567. The Commission has suggested to adapt this provision on the basis of Art. 67(2), second indent, of the EC Treaty (COM(2006) 346 final of 28.6.2006).
135. Cf. ECJ, Case C-239/03, *Commission/France*, [2004] ECR I-9325, para. 23.
136. Ibid., para. 25.

Community competence".[137] By contrast, it could be inferred from the more recent judgment of the Court of Justice of 30 May 2006 that the Court's jurisdiction extends to such provisions only if they fall within the Community' exclusive competence or if the Community has exercised any non-exclusive (concurrent) competence by concluding the agreement.[138] In order to establish whether and to what extent the Community, by concluding a mixed agreement, exercised its external competence, the Court refers inter alia to the recitals of the Council decision on the conclusion of the agreement and to the declaration of competence annexed to this decision.[139]

In proceedings for a preliminary ruling pursuant to Article 234 of the EC Treaty, the case-law is more nuanced.[140] The Court has in some particular cases extended its jurisdiction to subject matters which did not fall within the Community's exclusive competence and has ruled that, where a provision of a mixed agreement applies both to situations falling within the scope of national law and to situations falling within that of Community law, the Court has jurisdiction to interpret it in order to forestall future differences of interpretation.[141] It would, however, be going too far to deduce from these particular judgments a principle according to which the Court's jurisdiction would extend in general to the entirety of the provisions of mixed agreements.[142]

The case-law mentioned above should also apply to cases where the Member States concluded a concealed mixed agreement in the interest of the Community. Independently of the fact that the Community is not a contracting party to such agreements, the parts of the agreements which fall under the Community's competence are part of the Community's legal order and as such subject to the jurisdiction of the Community courts.[143]

---

137. Cf. ECJ, Case C-239/03, *Commission/France*, [2004] ECR I-9325, paras. 27 to 31; Case C-13/00, *Commission/Ireland*, [2002] ECR I-2943, para. 16.
138. Cf. ECJ, Case C-459/03, *Commission/Ireland*, [2006] ECR 4635, para. 96.
139. Ibid., paras. 98 et seq.
140. Cf. Marianne Dony, Les accords mixtes, in: *Commentaire J. Mégret*, Vol. 12, pp. 192-198 (2005).
141. Cf. ECJ, Case C-53/96, *Hermès*, [1998] ECR I-3603; Joined cases C- 300/98 and C-392/98, *Christian Dior*, [2000] ECR I-11307.
142. For a contrary view, see Michael Wilderspin/Anne-Marie Rouchaud-Joët, La compétence externe de la Communauté européenne en droit international privé, [2004] Rev. crit. dr. internat. privé, p. 1, at p. 14.
143. In this sense also A.V.M. Struycken, Le droit international privé d'origine communautaire et les Etats tiers, [2001-2002] Rev. aff. europ., p. 469, at p. 477.

In order to ascertain whether any particular provision of a mixed agreement in the field of judicial cooperation in civil matters falls within the scope of the Community's (exclusive) competence, and whether the Community courts would thus assume jurisdiction in respect of such provision, account should be taken of the recitals of the respective Council decisions on the signature or conclusion of the agreement and the declarations of competence annexed to these decisions.

For instance, it is spelled out in the recitals of the Council decision relating to the conclusion of the Protocol of 2003 to the International Convention on the Establishment of an International Fund for Compensation for Oil Pollution Damage, that the Community has exclusive competence in relation to Articles 7 and 8 of the Protocol, insofar as these Articles affect the rules laid down in the Brussels I Regulation and that "the Member States retain their competence for matters covered by the Protocol which do not affect Community law".[144] Similar recitals can be found in other Council decisions relating to mixed agreements in the field of judicial cooperation in civil matters.[145] They appear to indicate that the Community did not intend to exercise any non-exclusive competence by concluding the agreements concerned.

Furthermore, the declaration of competence, which the Community is generally obliged to submit at the occasion of the signing or acceptance of a multilateral mixed agreements', may be helpful in examining whether the Community intended to exercise its non-exclusive external competence. If the declaration states that the Member States have conferred competence to the Community as regards matters which affect specific internal measures, such as the Brussels I Regulation or Regulation (EC) No 1346/2000 on insolvency proceedings,[146] it could be assumed that the Community did not intend to exercise any competence in respect of provisions of the agreement which do not affect these internal measures.

144. Recital 3 of the Decision of 2.3.2004, OJ L 78, 16.3.2004, p. 22.
145. Recitals 3 and 6 of the Council Decision of 19.9.2002 (Bunkers Convention), OJ L 256, 25.9.2002, p. 7; Recitals 3 and 6 of the Council Decision of 18.11.2002 (HNS Convention), OJ L 337, 13.12.2002, p. 55; Recital 4 of the Council Decision of 19.12.2002 relating to the signing of the 1996 Hague Convention on the Protection of Children, OJ L 48, 21.2.2003, p. 1; Recital 3 of the Council Decision of 2.3.2004 (Fund Protocol of 2003), OJ L 78, 16,3,2004, p. 22; Recital 4 of the Council Decision of 8.3.2004 (Protocol to the Paris Convention), OJ L 97, 1.4.2004, p. 53.
146. Cf. points I.5 and II.5 of the General Declarations concerning the competence of the Community, attached as Annex I to ANNEX I to the draft Council decision on the conclusion by the Community of the Convention on International Interests in Mobile Equipment and its Protocol on Matters Specific to Aircraft Equipment (Council doc. 13967/03 of 29.10.2003).

To the extent that the Community courts limit their jurisdiction, at least in infringement proceedings, to provisions of mixed agreements which fall within the Community's exclusive competence, such recitals or declarations may be taken into account by the courts in order to establish whether or not they have jurisdiction in a case relating to a mixed agreement in the field of judicial cooperation in civil matters.

IV. Conclusions

After the Community acquired powers in the field of judicial cooperation in civil matters, with the entry into force of the Treaty of Amsterdam, many of the actors in the Community institutions and the Member States underwent a learning process in order to understand, accept and apply to this field the Community's practice and the case-law of the Community courts relating to mixed agreements. Furthermore, it took some time for the negotiating partners in third countries and international organisations to understand the consequences of the specific internal structure of the Community for the negotiation, signing and conclusion of mixed agreements in this field.

The set-up, on the Union side, of some of the mixed agreements in the field of judicial cooperation in civil matters is exceedingly complicated, due to the combination of different types of imperfections, relating in particular to the exclusion of Denmark from measures in this field, the difficulties with the amendment of conventions to which only some Member States are contracting parties, and the absence of clauses which would allow the Community to become itself a contracting party. This is best exemplified in the Council decisions relating to the 2004 Protocol to the Convention on Third Party Liability in the Field of Nuclear Energy of 29 July 1960.[147]

Some of these imperfections may continue to require legally imaginative solutions in the future. However, it appears to be increasingly understood that the insertion of REIO- or Community-clauses in international conventions, which contain provisions in the field of judicial cooperation in civil matters, facilitates the signature and conclusion of mixed agreements by the Community and its Member States. Furthermore, the recent accession of the Community to the Hague Conference on Private International Law will further contribute to facilitating the exercise by the Community of its powers in the field of judicial cooperation in civil matters.

147. See part II.B.2.a, supra.

The Council and Commission Action Plan implementing the Hague Programme on strengthening freedom, security and justice in the European Union mentions the "continuation of negotiations and conclusion of international agreements relating to judicial cooperation in civil matters" among the items to be pursued by the Community.[148] More specifically, the Council agreed on 28 April 2006 on a general framework for a future strategy for the external dimension of judicial cooperation in civil matters, which envisages – in addition to the multilateral cooperation in the framework of the Hague Conference, the Council of Europe, UNIDROIT, UNCITRAL, and other organisations – the possible strengthening of bilateral cooperation, including the negotiation and conclusion of bilateral agreements with third States, such as the European Neighbourhood Policy countries.[149] It can be supposed that at least some of the future multilateral and bilateral agreements fall within the shared competence of the Community and its Member States and that mixed agreements in the field of judicial cooperation in civil matters will remain on the agenda of the Community for the foreseeable future.

148. OJ C 198, 12.8.2005, p. 1, at p. 22.
149. Council doc. 8140/06 of 11.4.2006.

3. The European Community and the Hague Conference on Private International Law

Hans van Loon and Andrea Schulz[1]

I. Introduction

On 3 April 2007, the European Community[2] became a Member of the Hague Conference on Private International Law[3]. In order to make this possible, the Statute of the Hague Conference, the intergovernmental organisation whose mandate it is to work for the progressive unification of the rules of private international law, had to be amended, because in its 1951 version it only allowed for States to become Members. The revised version of the Statute, which is now authentic in both English and French, opens the Conference to any "Regional Economic Integration Organisation" that is "constituted solely by sovereign States, and to which its Member States have transferred competence over a range of matters, including the authority to make decisions binding on its Member States in respect of those matters",[4] and the EC is the first organisation that made use of this new possibility.

Membership of the Hague Conference has to be distinguished from participation in treaty negotiations taking place within the Hague Conference. Such negotiations have always been open to Member States of the Conference as well as observers. Observers may include other intergovernmental organisations, international non-governmental organisations and non-Member States. The European Community has participated in Hague Conference meetings as an observer since the Ninth Session in 1960 (the first Session after creation of the European Economic Community).

Whether an observer can become Party to a Hague convention depends on the wording of the convention concerned. Traditionally, Hague conventions are open to Member States and non-Member States of the

---

1. The views expressed in this contribution are personal to the authors and do not necessarily reflect those of the Hague Conference on Private International Law.
2. Hereinafter also referred to as "the Community", or "the EC".
3. Hereinafter also referred to as "the Hague Conference" or simply "the Conference".
4. Article 3 (paragraphs 2 and 9) of the Statute (see *infra* note 9).

Conference. Moreover, the two most recent Hague Conventions (*Convention of 30 June 2005 on Choice of Court Agreements* and the *Convention of 5 July 2006 on the Law Applicable to Certain Rights in Respect of Securities held with an Intermediary*) provide for Regional Economic Integration Organisations (REIOs) to become a Party, although at the time of adoption of these two Conventions it was not yet possible for REIOs to become Members of the Hague Conference as such. The legal position of observers during negotiations, however, is formally weaker than that of Members – a fact that was felt to be more and more at odds with the growing external competence of the Community in the field of private international law.

In order to shed light on these three different aspects – membership of the Conference, participation in the negotiation of conventions and becoming a Party to a convention, this article is divided into two main parts. In Part II it will be described how the Community and its Member States participated in Hague Conference negotiations under the previous version of the Statute, using as an illustration the negotiations that resulted in the *Hague Convention of 30 June 2005 on Choice of Court Agreements*. Part III is dedicated to the content of the amendments to the Statute and the negotiations leading thereto. Moreover, it will highlight the important difference between being a Member of the Hague Conference, and being a Party to a Hague convention.

II. First Encounters: The role of the European Community in the negotiations on specific Hague instruments, in particular the *Convention on Choice of Court Agreements*

Since the entry into force of the Treaty of Amsterdam[5] and the resulting acquisition of competences in the field of private international law by the European Community, the Community has participated in the negotiation of a number of Hague conventions, namely the *Convention of 30 June 2005 on Choice of Court Agreements* and the *Convention of 5 July 2006 on the Law Applicable to Certain Rights in respect of Securities held with an Intermediary*. Particularly interesting as an example for the evolving relationship between the European Community and the Hague Conference is the *Convention on Choice of Court Agreements*. The negotiations that ultimately

---

5. See the EC Treaty as revised by the Treaty of Amsterdam, OJ C 340, 10.11. 1997, p. 1, which entered into force on 1 May 1999.

led to this Convention, which was unanimously adopted by the Twentieth Diplomatic Session of the Hague Conference on 30 June 2005, cover a time span of thirteen years – from 1992 to 2005 – during which the competence of the European Community with regard to private international law, and consequently also the Community's role in the negotiations in The Hague, changed considerably. These negotiations thus illustrate in an exemplary manner the creation and development of external competence of the European Community and its manifestation in multilateral negotiations with third States.

A.   The history of the negotiations and the evolving role of the European Community

In 1992, by letter from the Legal Adviser of the Department of State to the Secretary General of the Hague Conference, the United States of America proposed that the Hague Conference seek to prepare a new convention on the recognition and enforcement of judgments.[6] At that time, the Community's powers in the area of private international law were primarily governed by Article 220 of the Treaty establishing the European Community (EC Treaty) and therefore a subject of intergovernmental co-operation among the EC Member States as well as with third States. When the EC Treaty was amended by the Treaty of Maastricht[7] as of 1 November 1993, co-operation of the EU Member States in the field of Justice and Home Affairs became part of the newly-created so-called "Third Pillar", but remained a subject of intergovernmental co-operation.[8] There was no legal basis establishing competence for the Community to enact secondary Community law in this field and no external Community competence for private international law in relations with third States.

6.   See Peter H. Pfund, Contributing to Progressive Development of Private International Law, The International Process and the United States Approach, 249 [1994-V] *Recueil des cours* 9, p. 83; Andrea Schulz, International Organizations: The Global Playing Field for US-EU Cooperation in Private Law Instruments, in: Ronald A. Brand (ed.), *Private Law, Private International Law, & Judicial Cooperation in the EU-US Relationship*, p. 237 (2005), p. 257.

7.   See the consolidated version 1992 of the Treaty establishing the European Community, OJ C 224, 31.8.1992, p. 1.

8.   See Articles K.1 No 6 and K.3(2) c) of the Treaty on European Union as amended by the Treaty of Maastricht, OJ C 191, 29.7.1992, p. 1.

Until the late 1990s, the practice of the Hague Conference with regard to the elaboration of a new convention, based on its 1951 Statute[9] (which entered into force in 1955) and the Rules of Procedure, was to negotiate a preliminary draft convention in several meetings of a Special Commission, normally spread over a period of approximately three years. Discussions were often technical and not too politicised, and Member States often sent – exclusively or together with one or more civil servants – private international law scholars, high-ranking judges and experienced practising lawyers to The Hague to negotiate these conventions. At the last meeting of the Special Commission, a preliminary draft convention would be adopted by vote. After a period of internal consultation within the Member States of the Hague Conference, the next – and normally final – step towards the adoption of a new Hague convention would then be a Diplomatic Session, which normally took place about a year after the adoption of a preliminary draft convention by the Special Commission, and would also proceed on the basis of voting.[10]

1.   *Work on a global convention on jurisdiction, recognition and enforcement*

The Seventeenth Session of the Hague Conference on Private International Law, during the celebration of the Centenary of Hague Conference meetings in 1993, tentatively took a positive decision with regard to the United States proposal.[11] Preparatory work was carried out between 1992 and 1996, and the tentative decision was formally confirmed at the conclusion of the Eighteenth Session in 1996. It was decided "to include in the Agenda of the Nineteenth Session the question of jurisdiction, and recognition and enforcement of foreign judgments in civil and commercial matters".[12] Subsequently, the Secretary General of the Hague Conference convened a Special Commission, which held five meetings of one or more weeks between June 1997 and October 1999.[13] At a meeting in June 1999,

---

9.   For the full text of the 1951 Statute of the Hague Conference as well as of the amended version of 2007, see the website of the Hague Conference at < www.hcch.net > under "Conventions".

10.   See *infra* under III. C. 4.

11.   Final Act of the Seventeenth Session, Part B, No 2, Hague Conference on Private International Law, *Proceedings of the Seventeenth Session*, Tome I (1995), p. 43.

12.   Final Act of the Eighteenth Session, Part B, No 1, Hague Conference on Private International Law, *Proceedings of the Eighteenth Session*, Tome I (1999), p. 47.

13.   For further details, see Peter Nygh & Fausto Pocar, Report on the Preliminary Draft Convention on Jurisdiction and Foreign Judgments in Civil and Commercial Matters adopted by the Special Commission, Preliminary Document No 11, available at < www.hcch.net > under "Conventions", then "Convention 37", then "Preliminary Documents", p. 25 *et seq.*

the Special Commission was supposed to complete its work but some extra time was needed, and at an additional gathering in October 1999 the "preliminary draft Convention on Jurisdiction and Foreign Judgments in Civil and Commercial Matters"[14] was adopted by vote in accordance with the Hague Conference's Rules of Procedure. The draft contained rules on jurisdiction as well as on the recognition and enforcement of judgments given in a Contracting State by a court having Convention-based jurisdiction. A Diplomatic Session was expected to take place in 2000.

At the time of adoption of the preliminary draft Convention in October 1999, the Hague Conference on Private International Law counted 47 Member States, including all of the then fifteen Member States of the European Community. The Community was invited to participate as an observer. During the negotiations which led to the Choice of Court Convention, the Community delegation comprised representatives of the European Commission, the Council (including of the respective Presidency and the Council Secretariat) and the European Parliament.

On 1 May 1999, the Amsterdam Treaty revising the EC Treaty entered into force, and it had important consequences in the field of private international law: this field of law was moved from the Third to the First Pillar,[15] which meant that the Community was from now on entitled to enact regulations, directives and other acts of secondary Community legislation on private international law matters. Following the case law of the European Court of Justice,[16] this also had consequences for the external competence of EC Member States to negotiate with third States: if and to the extent that there is internal Community law for a certain subject matter, the Community consequently acquires exclusive external competence covering the same scope. Even if such Community law is not

14. The text of the preliminary draft Convention 1999 and its Explanatory Report by Nygh & Pocar have been published in Preliminary Document No 11 (*supra* note 13).
15. Article 61 *et seq.*, in particular Article 65, of the EC Treaty as revised by the Treaty of Amsterdam (*supra* note 5).
16. See in particular Case 22/70, *Commission/Council*, [1971] ECR 263; Opinion 1/76, *European laying-up fund*, [1977] ECR 741; Opinion 1/94, *WTO*, [1994] ECR I-5267; the Open Skies decisions: Case C-467/98, *Commission/Denmark*, [2002] ECR I-9519; Case C-468/98, *Commission/Sweden*, [2002] ECR I-9575; Case C-469/98, *Commission/Finland*, [2002] ECR I-9627; Case C-471/98, *Commission/Belgium*, [2002] ECR I-9681; Case C-472/98, *Commission/Luxembourg*, [2002] ECR I-9741; Case C-475/98, *Commission/Austria*, [2002] ECR I-9797, and Case C-476/98, *Commission/Germany*, [2002] ECR I-9855; and Opinion 01/03 on the competence of the Community to conclude the new Lugano Convention on jurisdiction and the recognition and enforcement of judgments in civil and commercial matters, [2006] ECR I-1145.

yet in place, but *could* be enacted because there is internal competence over a certain subject matter, the Council may decide under Article 300 of the EC Treaty that external Community competence should be exercised by way of negotiating a treaty between the Community and one or more third States on such matter.

Between 1997 and 1999, negotiations aiming at a revision of the very successful Brussels Convention[17] had taken place within the Community, and the result was adopted by the Council on Justice and Home Affairs on 27 May 1999, a few weeks after the entry into force of the Treaty of Amsterdam. The Council adopted the *substantive content* agreed upon by the working group charged with the revision. Concerning the *form* of the revised instrument, the Council, in light of the new legislative powers of the Community created by the Treaty of Amsterdam, invited the Commission to submit a proposal for a Community instrument which would incorporate the substantive results agreed. When the Special Commission reconvened in The Hague in June 1999 to finalise a preliminary draft Convention on jurisdiction and foreign judgments, a proposal for a Community Regulation covering the same ground was therefore imminent within the EC.[18]

At the time of the June 1999 meeting of the Special Commission, there were diverging views and some amount of uncertainty as to what this meant for the negotiations in The Hague. Until then, some delegates of EC Member States had been given almost "academic freedom" for the negotiations in The Hague by their respective States, and the multiplicity of contributions greatly enriched the discussion. Now the European

17. *Convention on Jurisdiction and the Enforcement of Judgments in Civil and Commercial Matters of 27 September 1968*, OJ C 27, 26.1.1998, p. 1.
18. It was presented two weeks after the Special Commission: see the Proposal of the Commission, Com (1999) 348 final, 14.7.1999, OJ C 376, 28.12.1999, p. 1, and the Revised Proposal, Com (2000) 684 final of 26.10.2000, OJ C 62, 27.2.2001, p. 243. On 1 March 2002, the Brussels Convention was replaced by Regulation (EC) No 44/2001 of 22 December 2000 on jurisdiction and the recognition and enforcement of judgments in civil and commercial matters, OJ L 12, 16.1.2001, p. 1 (the Brussels I Regulation), for 14 of the then 15 EC Member States. Since 1 May 2004, the Regulation also binds the ten new Member States that joined on that date, and since 1 January 2007 also Bulgaria and Romania which joined the Community on that date. The Brussels Convention remained in force between Denmark, which due to Protocol No 5 to the EC Treaty as revised by the Treaty of Amsterdam is not bound by Community law in this area, and the 14 EC Member States Parties to it. An agreement between the Community and Denmark along the lines of the Brussels I Regulation now replaced it on 1 July 2007 (see OJ L 299, 16.11.2005, p. 62 and OJ L 94, 4.4.2007, p. 70).

Commission gently started to allude to the duty of loyalty under Article 10 of the EC Treaty,[19] which might be of some importance while a Community instrument is under preparation. In June 1999, it was suggested that this might already apply to some extent where a proposal was not yet on the table but would be forthcoming in the very near future. At the October 1999 meeting of the Special Commission, this position was reiterated by the European Commission and was now based on its Proposal of July 1999 for a Brussels I Regulation.[20] However, the reference to Article 10 of the EC Treaty did not remain uncontested. Several delegates of EC Member States were of the view that external Community competence could only exist once there was a Community instrument in force which governed the same matter internally. And it was expected that the future Brussels I Regulation would only come into force after adoption of the new Hague Convention, which was envisaged for late spring/early summer 2000. In June 1999, practically no coordination took place among EC Member States. The one-week meeting held in October 1999 during the Finnish Presidency of the Council of the European Union, which adopted the preliminary draft Convention by vote, was the first Hague Conference meeting to see at least some formal coordination of EC Member States.[21]

Nevertheless, when the preliminary draft Convention was adopted by vote in October 1999, as provided by the Rules of Procedure, even this still rather limited coordination among EC Member States led to what was perceived by some other Member States of the Conference as "block voting". Moreover, the voting at the last meeting of the Special

---

19. EC Treaty as revised by the Treaty of Amsterdam (*supra* note 5).
20. See *supra* note 17.
21. It might be interesting to consult the Working Documents submitted during the negotiations, which are the basis for the discussions in The Hague. During the meetings of the Special Commission held in June 1997 (9½ working days) and March 1998 (8½ working days), the relationship between proposals made by one or more EC Member States and proposals made by non-EC States was 30% to 43% (1997) and 50% to 50% (March 1998). Nevertheless, the resulting text very much resembled the Conventions of Brussels (*supra* note 17) and Lugano (*Convention of 16 September 1988 on Jurisdiction and the Enforcement of Judgments in Civil and Commercial Matters*, OJ L 319, 25.11.1988, p. 9), which was not satisfactory to other delegations. Consequently, at the November 1998 meeting the relationship was 53% of proposals from non-EC States seeking to change this to only 15.6% proposals from EC States. Similarly, during the June 1999 (10 working days) and October 1999 (5½ working days) meetings, the EC Member States apparently felt little need to make proposals for amendments because the text already reflected their wishes. In June 1999, 36% of the working documents were submitted by non-EC States while about only 15% came from EC Member States; in October the percentage was even more telling: 45% to 16%.

Commission in October 1999 produced rather narrow majorities on many key articles, thus leaving a large number of delegations unhappy with the result. Consultations carried out in the Member States of the Hague Conference on the October 1999 preliminary draft Convention suggested that the draft was primarily acceptable for those States that were already Parties to the *Conventions of Brussels of 27 September 1968*[22] and *Lugano of 16 September 1988*[23] *on Jurisdiction and the Enforcement of Judgments in Civil and Commercial Matters*, but that it was unlikely to receive global support.[24] This, together with rising doubts whether traditional rules, relying very much on locating certain acts (place of performance of a contract, place of the injury etc.) would be able to deal appropriately with legal issues raised by the Internet and electronic commerce, and concerns of the United States of America that the Convention combined with the rather generous system on the recognition and enforcement of foreign judgments in the United States might create a serious imbalance in this respect, led Member States of the Hague Conference, in May 2000, to postpone the Diplomatic Session to June 2001, to suspend formal negotiations and to conduct informal discussions on how to reach consensus on specific issues, including intellectual property and e-commerce.[25] It was felt that more time than that available at a Diplomatic Session was needed to prepare the Convention, and it was therefore decided to split the Diplomatic Session in two. A first part of three weeks was to be held in June 2001 which should, moreover, no longer proceed by vote but by consensus.

22. *Supra* note 17.
23. *Supra* note 21.
24. For the concerns expressed by several States, see the letter from Jeffrey D. Kovar, then Assistant Legal Adviser for Private International Law at the United States Department of State, to the Secretary General of the Hague Conference of 22 February 2000, available at < http://www.cptech.org/ecom/hague/kovar2loon22022000.pdf >.
25. See Permanent Bureau of the Hague Conference, Informational note on the work of the informal meetings held since October 1999 to consider and develop drafts on outstanding items, Preliminary Document No 15, available at < www.hcch.net > under "Conventions", then "Convention 37", then "Preliminary Documents", para. 1.

2. Emerging Community competence and the search for consensus in The Hague

After a series of informal meetings hosted by individual States in 2000 and 2001,[26] delegations accordingly resumed their formal negotiations in June 2001. In the meantime, the Brussels I Regulation had been adopted,[27] thus creating an exclusive Community competence with respect to the matters governed by the Regulation. At the same time, membership of the Hague Conference had been constantly growing. While in 1993, at the beginning of the informal discussions on a global Convention on jurisdiction and enforcement, the Hague Conference counted 40 Member States, there were 47 of them in October 1999, and 53 in June 2001 when the so-called First Part of the Diplomatic Session took place. The number of proposals from non-EC Member States rose to an impressive 60% of all Working Documents submitted during this meeting, and the now almost daily coordination meetings of the EC Member States were to a large extent spent on the elaboration of common positions of the Community and its Member States on the proposals made by other delegations. Since there had not been any need to coordinate the positions of the EC Member States in the past, the views on some issues within the Community diverged widely. This division often ran parallel with the division between civil and common law, and the common law Member States of the Community tended to agree with other common law jurisdictions rather than with their civil law fellow Member States of the Community. There were also other dividing lines, however. The number of proposals stemming from the EC Member States remained at 18% of all working documents submitted, and therefore close to the rate at previous meetings. On the other hand,

26. Meetings in various compositions, sometimes open, sometimes limited to selected States and/or delegates, were held upon invitation by Canada, Scotland, Switzerland and the United States of America in Ottawa (Canada), Noordwijk (the Netherlands), Edinburgh (Scotland – United Kingdom), Basel and Geneva (Switzerland) and Washington, D.C. (United States of America). The Ottawa meetings focused on e-commerce and the Geneva meeting on intellectual property issues, while the others covered the whole range of issues under discussion in The Hague. See, for a summary description of the informal meetings, the report drawn up by the Permanent Bureau of the Hague Conference on Private International Law, Informational note, Preliminary Document No 15 (*supra* note 25).

27. See *supra* note 18.

external Community competence started to produce some effects: the number of joint proposals made by one or more EC States with one or more third States decreased significantly (to 5% as compared to 31% at the meeting before).[28] And it was the First Part of the Diplomatic Session in June 2001 which saw the first two working documents submitted by the European Commission.

The meeting produced a draft entitled "Interim Text".[29] The structure of the 1999 draft remained largely unchanged and therefore continued to resemble the structure of the Conventions of Brussels and Lugano. However, the consensus rule was applied strictly in June 2001. Wherever consensus on the previously achieved, European civil law-style rule was not possible, a second alternative paragraph, often following United States suggestions, was added. As a result, the text contains a large number of square brackets, options, variants and alternatives. It is rather difficult to understand, even for those having participated in the negotiations, and did not bring about much harmonisation. Rather than to converge, positions seemed to drift apart again. The wide range of issues covered by the draft made it seem doubtful, in particular in light of the ongoing globalisation of Hague Conference membership together with the ensuing growth of the number of Member States and of the variety of legal systems and traditions at the negotiating table, that consensus could be achieved on a text within any reasonable time.

3.   *Change of focus: consensus-based negotiations leading to the Choice of Court Convention*

In April 2002, therefore, the Commission on General Affairs (Commission I) of the Nineteenth Session of the Hague Conference (now comprising 59 Member States of the Conference) decided to change the working method: the Permanent Bureau was invited to establish an informal working group, reflecting the legal traditions of the Member States of the Hague Conference, including the new Member States such as, *e.g.*, Brazil, New Zealand, Russia and South Africa[30]. This informal working group was to try to draft a text that could serve as a basis for future work. The group was

28. At earlier meetings between 1997 and 1999 this rate had been 7%, 14%, 8% and 6%, respectively.
29. Available at < www.hcch.net > under "Conventions", then "Convention 37", then "Preliminary Documents" under "Interim Text".
30. This decision was prepared by several studies of the Permanent Bureau: see Preliminary Documents Nos 16, 17, and 18 preceding the Conclusions of Commission I of the Nineteenth Session, at < www.hcch.net > under "General Affairs and Policy".

supposed to work on a consensus basis and use a "bottom-up approach", starting from the one basis of jurisdiction in previous drafts that seemed the least controversial, namely choice of court clauses in business-to-business cases. The group was further invited to examine other bases of jurisdiction on which consensus seemed possible. As possible "candidates", the Special Commission on General Affairs and Policy listed: general defendant's forum, submission, counter-claims, branches, trusts and physical torts.[31]

Between April and September 2002, the informal working group was established, and the Permanent Bureau prepared a paper to facilitate the discussions of the group which dealt with choice of court clauses in business-to-business cases as well as with submission, counter-claims and the general defendant's forum.[32] The group held its first meeting in October 2002. It was chaired by Allan Philip from Denmark and comprised participants from Argentina, Brazil, China, Egypt, the European Commission, Germany, Italy, Japan, Mexico, New Zealand, Russia, South Africa, Spain, Switzerland, the United Kingdom and the United States of America. During the three meetings of the group between October 2002 and March 2003,[33] a text on exclusive choice of court clauses in business-to-business cases was drafted[34] while it was not possible to reach consensus on other bases of jurisdiction. Unlike its 1999 and 2001 predecessors which had resembled the Conventions of Brussels and Lugano, this new draft now more resembled the *New York Convention of 10 June 1958 on the Recognition and Enforcement of Foreign Arbitral Awards* – a development that seems logical since choice of court agreements and arbitration

---

31. This last expression was used in order to exclude mere financial damages and damages to intangible rights (intellectual property, reputation). See, for the Conclusions of the Commission, < www.hcch.net > under "General Affairs and Policy".

32. Andrea Schulz, Reflection paper to assist in the preparation of a convention on jurisdiction and recognition and enforcement of foreign judgments in civil and commercial matters, Preliminary Document No 19, available at < www.hcch.net > under "Conventions", then "Convention 37", then "Preliminary Documents".

33. See the reports of the three meetings (Preliminary Documents No 20, 21 and 22) at < www.hcch.net > under "Conventions", then "Convention 37", then "Preliminary Documents".

34. The draft text, accompanied by a report reflecting the discussions in the informal working group, has been published in: Andrea Schulz, Report on the work of the informal working group on the Judgments Project, in particular on the preliminary text achieved at its third meeting – 25-28 March 2003, Preliminary Document No 22. It is available at < www.hcch.net > under "Conventions", then "Convention 37", then "Preliminary Documents".

agreements both aim at enhancing party autonomy with regard to the choice for a certain dispute resolution system.

The text elaborated by the group was submitted to the Special Commission on General Affairs and Policy of the Conference[35] at its meeting in April 2003. This meeting, as well as further consultation subsequently carried out by the Secretary General of the Hague Conference among the now 62 Member States of the Conference in 2003, demonstrated that there was sufficient support for a Special Commission to be convened on the basis of the draft text. The Special Commission met in The Hague from 1-9 December 2003[36] and again from 21-27 April 2004 and produced a new preliminary draft Convention.[37] Like the informal working group, the Special Commission was chaired by Allan Philip from Denmark, and a considerable change of atmosphere was noticeable during the negotiations which had now returned to the formal stage. In the fourth year of Community external competence, the EC and its Member States had found an operable internal working method for coordination and were externally back on the scene as a proactive player. Moreover, the bi-polarisation of the negotiations between the EC and the United States of America, which had temporarily overshadowed the negotiations in The Hague, disappeared again, due *inter alia* to the fact that other voices now made themselves heard, *e.g.*, Australia, China, Japan, Korea, Russia and many more. Moreover, as a result of the growing diversity of legal systems represented, the consensus-based negotiations were now accepted as the appropriate

35. This is a plenary meeting of Member State representatives which has met to prepare the Diplomatic Sessions – since 2003 on an annual basis – and, increasingly, to decide on the work programme of the Conference. Under the revised Statute (Article 4, paragraph 1), as "Council on General Affairs and Policy", it now "has charge of the operation of the Conference".
36. The text produced at the December 2003 Special Commission (Working Document No 49 E Revised – Proposal by the Drafting Committee), together with an Explanatory Report drawn up by Trevor C. Hartley and Masato Dogauchi (Preliminary Document No 25), is available at < www.hcch.net > under "Conventions", then "Convention 37", then "Preliminary Documents".
37. The text produced at the April 2004 Special Commission (Working Document No 110 E Revised – Proposal by the Drafting Committee) together with an Explanatory Report drawn up by Trevor C. Hartley and Masato Dogauchi (Preliminary Document No 26), is available at < www.hcch.net > under "Bonventions", then "Convention 37", then "Preliminary Documents".

way to handle these matters within the Hague Conference.[38] The Chairman of the Special Commission, coming from Denmark as the only EC Member State[39] which is not bound by secondary Community legislation in the field of private international law, was able to build bridges between the negotiating parties. Being a renowned arbitrator himself, he moreover managed to allay any fears that may have existed in the world of international arbitration that a competing convention might be forthcoming, which would deprive them of cases and income.

Consultations among Member States of the Hague Conference (the EC of course presenting a common position following internal coordination among its Member States) led to an overall rather positive view on the prospective success of such an instrument. Moreover, in the meantime, the international business community and several national bar associations had pronounced themselves very strongly in favour of this prospective new Hague Convention. A draft Explanatory Report on the April 2004 draft was produced by Trevor C. Hartley (United Kingdom) and Masato Dogauchi (Japan) in December 2004,[40] and a Diplomatic Session was tentatively envisaged for January or February 2005. However, when Allan Philip, the Chairman, died unexpectedly in September 2004, the planning had to be reconsidered. With a view to preparing and facilitating the negotiations at the Diplomatic Session, the Drafting Committee met twice; once informally, once formally, in January and April 2005. The informal meeting in January 2005 was hosted by the European Commission in Brussels in connection with an EC public hearing on the preliminary draft Convention, which was also attended by several representatives of third States such as China, Russia and the United States of America. The formal meeting took place in The Hague in April 2005 and led to the production of language to "pick and choose from" for the various policy choices that

---

38. The *Convention on the Law Applicable to Certain Rights in Respect of Securities held with an Intermediary*, which was negotiated between 2000 and 2002 and thus fell "in between" the negotiations of the global jurisdiction and enforcement Convention, was the first Hague convention ever to be adopted on a consensus basis. The adoption of this Convention in December 2002 concluded the Nineteenth Session which had initially been dedicated to the elaboration of a global convention on jurisdiction, recognition and enforcement. For the text and status of the Convention as well as for further information, see < www.hcch.net > under "Conventions", then "Convention 36".

39. The United Kingdom and Ireland, although not automatically bound by Community law in this field, have reserved the possibility to opt in under Protocol No 4 to the EC Treaty as amended by the Treaty of Amsterdam.

40. See *supra* note 37.

still had to be made by the Diplomatic Session.[41] A Diplomatic Session –
the Twentieth – was convened for June 2005, and former Vice-Chair
Andreas Bucher from Switzerland (equally a European, albeit from a non-
EC Member State, not bound by EC coordination obligations and an
arbitrator himself), was elected Chairman.

During the Diplomatic Session, the EC delegation actively participated in
the negotiations. In its capacity of observer, the Community presented six
Working Documents, and six other Working Documents emanated from
the EC together with one or more other States. In one case, the total
number of States sponsoring a particular Working Document amounted to
ten third States plus the 25 EC States at the time – clearly a sign that the
meeting as a whole was now striving for co-operation and consensus.
Moreover, members of the delegations of EC Member States and of the
representation of the Community participated in all informal working
groups and presented the coordinated position of the Community there.
The Drafting Committee equally comprised delegates of EC Member States
as well as representatives of the European Commission.

B.   The Convention on Choice of Court Agreements

1.   *The content of the Convention in brief*

On 30 June 2005, the Twentieth Diplomatic Session unanimously adopted
the *Convention on Choice of Court Agreements*. The Convention applies in
international cases[42] and contains three basic rules addressed to three
different courts in Contracting States: provided that an exclusive[43] choice
of court agreement concluded between two or more parties is valid
according to the standards established by the Convention, (1) the chosen

---

41. See Andrea Schulz, Report on the meeting of the Drafting Committee of 18-20 of
April 2005 in preparation of the Twentieth Session of June 2005, Preliminary
Document No 28, available at < www.hcch.net > under "Conventions", then
"Convention 37", then "Preliminary Documents".
42. For the purpose of applying the Chapter on jurisdiction, a case is international unless
the parties are resident in the same Contracting State and the relationship of the
parties and all other elements relevant to the dispute, regardless of the location of the
chosen court, are connected only with that State (Article 1(2)). For the purpose of
applying the Chapter on recognition and enforcement, it is sufficient that the
judgment to be recognised or enforced is from another Contracting State
(Article 1(3), Article 8).
43. A choice of court agreement that designates the courts of a Contracting State, or one
or more specific courts of one Contracting State, is deemed to be exclusive unless the
parties have explicitly provided otherwise (Article 3 b)).

court has to take the case and may not decline jurisdiction in favour of another Contracting State that might be a more appropriate forum; (2) any court in a Contracting State other than that of the chosen court has to suspend or dismiss proceedings if it is seised in spite of the choice of court agreement; and (3) a judgment given by the chosen court has to be recognised and enforced in all other Contracting States. The Convention contains its own form requirements[44] for the choice of court agreements which exclude the application of any more rigid form requirements that might be contained in national law.[45] Although there is no autonomous Convention rule governing the substantive validity of the choice of court agreement, harmonisation of this aspect is achieved by way of a conflict-of-laws rule in the three key Articles addressed to the chosen court (Article 5), any court seised but not chosen in a Contracting State other than that of the chosen court (Article 6 a)), and any court before which the recognition or enforcement of a judgment given by the chosen court of another Contracting State is sought (Article 9 a)). All three courts have to apply the law of the State of the chosen court (including its choice-of-law rules) to the substantive validity of the choice of court agreement[46].

In spite of this rather straightforward content, the Convention contains 34 Articles. Its chapters on "General Clauses" (Chapter IV) and "Final Clauses" (Chapter V) include a number of provisions which are of great importance for the European Community. This concerns in particular the rules on the relationship with other instruments (Article 26) and the rules on the participation of REIOs in Articles 29 and 30. These latter two provisions will be discussed first because they are relevant for the status of the European Community and its Member States as Parties to the Convention.

---

44. See Article 3 *c).*
45. Should national law contain more generous form requirements, a choice of court agreement that does not comply with the Convention's form standards may still be valid under national law but would nevertheless not fall within the scope of the Convention.
46. See the Explanatory Report by Trevor C. Hartley and Masato Dogauchi which is available on the Hague Conference's website at < www.hcch.net > under "Conventions", then "Convention 37", then "HCCH Publications", at para. 94, and Andrea Schulz, The Hague Convention of 30 June 2005 on Choice of Court Agreements, 2 [2006] Journal of Private International Law 243, p. 251-253.

2.   *Participation of Regional Economic Integration Organisations in the Hague Choice of Court Convention*

Article 29 of the 2005 *Hague Convention on Choice of Court Agreements* allows an REIO to become a Party to this Convention. The provision is based on the precedent of the Hague Securities Convention,[47] which was adopted in 2002 and was the first Hague convention ever to contain an REIO clause. According to Article 29, an REIO which has competence over some or all of the matters governed by the Convention may equally sign, accept, approve or accede to it. The REIO shall in that case have the rights and obligations of a Contracting State to the extent that the organisation has competence over matters governed by the Convention. In the case of the European Community, this Article would be used in the case of shared or mixed competence, *i.e.,* where both the Community and its Member States are (partly) competent for the matters governed by the Convention and would therefore both join it. Article 30 of the 2005 *Hague Convention on Choice of Court Agreements* moreover contains a true novelty, going beyond Article 29 and its predecessors in earlier conventions, *e.g.,* in the Cape Town Convention[48] and the Hague Securities Convention adopted in 2002. Article 30 provides for the case where *only* the REIO and not its Member States also join the Convention. With regard to the European Community, this Article would be used in case of *exclusive* external competence of the European Community for *all* matters covered by the Hague Convention. In 2005, when the Convention was adopted, the European Court of Justice had not yet delivered its opinion on the competence to conclude the revised Lugano Convention[49] and consequently, there were concrete reasons for the Twentieth Diplomatic Session to draft for both cases – that of shared or mixed competence and that of exclusive Community competence. Moreover, the possibility to choose between these two Articles may prove useful for other REIOs in the future. Should the Community declare under Article 30 that it exercises competence over all the matters governed by the 2005 *Hague Convention on Choice of Court Agreements* and that its members will not be Parties to the Convention, the Member States would be bound by virtue of the signature, acceptance, approval or accession of the European Community (Article 30(1)).

---

47.   See *supra* note 38. Article 18 of the Hague Securities Convention was modelled on Article 48 of the *Convention on international interests in mobile equipment of 16 November 2001* (the Cape Town Convention), elaborated under the auspices of UNIDROIT.

48.   *Supra* note 47.

49.   *Supra* note 16.

3.   *The relationship between the Hague Choice of Court Convention and other international instruments*

a)   Overview

The 2005 *Hague Convention on Choice of Court Agreements* also contains a very comprehensive provision governing its relationship with other international instruments (including secondary Community legislation) in Article 26. In this paper, it is only possible to give an overview of the basic principles.[50]

The rules in Article 26(2)-(6) only apply in cases where both instruments, under their own terms, would cover the situation in question *and* such application would lead to incompatible results. Between the Hague Convention on the one hand, and the Conventions of Brussels and Lugano, or the Brussels I Regulation[51] on the other, such conflicts will be rare. They may arise, however, and it was necessary to provide a solution. The operation of the *lis pendens* rule in cases where a non-chosen court is seised first and the chosen court is seised second is the conflict case which is most likely to occur. The legal situation under the different instruments concerned and its solution in Article 26 of the Hague Convention will now be described in order to illustrate the operation of Article 26.

Article 17 of both the Brussels Convention and the Lugano Convention (and Article 23 of the Brussels I Regulation) contain a rule on choice of court agreements. Such an agreement is deemed to be exclusive and confers jurisdiction upon the chosen court. Although there is no explicit rule to this effect, any court other than the chosen court has to decline jurisdiction provided that the agreement is valid. In principle, therefore, the rules of the Conventions of Brussels and Lugano and the Brussels I Regulation do not seem to differ from Articles 5 and 6 of the Hague Choice of Court Convention. However, there are differences. Article 6 of the Hague Convention gives absolute priority to the *chosen court*. It obliges any court seised but not designated in the choice of court agreement to come to its own conclusions concerning the validity of the choice of court agreement,[52] and, in case of a positive result, to suspend or dismiss the case – regardless of whether it is the court first seised, or whether another court (in particular the chosen court) was seised first. The Conventions of Brussels

---

50. See also the Explanatory Report by Hartley/Dogauchi (*supra* note 46), paras 265-310. For a discussion of Article 26, see also Andrea Schulz, The Hague Convention of 30 June 2005 on Choice of Court Agreements, 2 [2006] Journal of Private International Law 243, p. 265-267.

51. See *supra* note 18.

52. In doing so, the court seised but not chosen has to apply the law of the State of the chosen court, including its choice-of-law rules (Article 6 *a*)).

and Lugano and the Brussels I Regulation, on the other hand, which have a wider scope and contain several bases of jurisdiction that are not necessarily mutually exclusive, contain a *lis pendens* rule. Here, according to the ECJ, the *court first seised* has absolute priority, and any court second seised – be it the chosen court or any other – has to suspend proceedings until the court first seised has declined jurisdiction, *e.g.*, because of a valid choice of court agreement in favour of the courts of another State.[53] For Article 17 of the Conventions of Brussels and Lugano and Article 23 of the Brussels I Regulation to apply, it is sufficient for *one* of the parties to be domiciled in the European Community or in a State Party to the Lugano Convention, respectively.[54] This means that a court designated in a choice of court agreement and situated in a State Party to both the new Hague Convention *and* the Brussels or Lugano Convention (or a State where the Brussels I Regulation applies) can be exposed to conflicting obligations under the two instruments in question if that same court is seised second.

Let us assume that the European Community and all its Member States, or the Community alone, join the Hague Choice of Court Convention along with Norway, Switzerland (both States Parties to the Lugano Convention) and the United States of America. Let us further assume that two private parties, one resident in the United States of America, the other in Norway, conclude a choice of court agreement in favour of the courts of Switzerland. If one party now sues the other before a Norwegian court instead, and subsequently the other party sues in Switzerland, the Swiss court would have to decide whether to apply the Hague Convention or the Lugano Convention. Under its own terms, the Lugano Convention does cover this case and would oblige the chosen court in Switzerland to stay or dismiss proceedings until the Norwegian court, which was seised first, has found that it lacks jurisdiction. Under the Hague Convention, which also covers the case, the chosen court in Switzerland would proceed with the case even if the Norwegian court has not (yet) dismissed the case pending before it. It may be expected that under both instruments, the Norwegian court will ultimately dismiss the case because of the choice of court agreement, and the Hague Convention has in principle opted for speed by allowing the chosen court to proceed with the case already before this decision of the Norwegian court.

---

53. See Case C-116/02 – *Gasser/MISAT*, [2003] ECR I-14693, at para. 54 on Article 17 of the Brussels Convention. The States Parties to the Lugano Convention have undertaken an obligation to observe the case law of the ECJ on the interpretation of the Brussels Convention also with regard to the application of the Lugano Convention.
54. Case C-412/98 – *Group Josi Reinsurance Company/Universal General Insurance Company*, [2000] ECR I-5925, at paras 57, 61.

However, there are situations where the Hague Convention gives way to the other instrument. In this respect, Article 26 of the Hague Convention distinguishes between other international treaties (paragraph 2) and Community instruments (paragraph 6) containing rules on jurisdiction which might lead to incompatible results. We will first explain the rule on international treaties in paragraph 2, which determines the relationship between the Hague Choice of Court Convention and the Conventions of Brussels and Lugano, as well as the Agreement between the Community and Denmark, which replaced the Brussels Convention as of 1 July 2007.[55]

b)   *The Hague Convention and other general treaties containing rules on jurisdiction, in particular the Conventions of Brussels and Lugano and the Agreement between the Community and Denmark*

Under Article 26(2), the Hague Convention gives way to other general (earlier or later) treaties where none of the parties are resident in a Contracting State that is not a Party to the other treaty. In other words, paragraph 2 allows other treaties to prevail over the Hague Convention in two groups of cases: cases which do contain an international element, but are not sufficiently connected to the Hague Convention to require it to prevail, and cases considered "internal" to another treaty. It is recalled that for the purposes of the Chapter of the 2005 Hague Convention on jurisdiction, a case is internal if the parties are resident in the same Contracting State and neither the relationship of the parties nor any other elements relevant to the dispute, regardless of the location of the chosen court, are connected with a State other than the State of residence of the parties.[56] It does not matter whether the parties to the choice of court agreement all reside in States that are Parties to both the Hague Convention and the other treaty, or in States Parties to the other treaty only. To give an illustration: Assuming that all States Parties to the Lugano Convention join the 2005 Hague Convention, the Lugano Convention would prevail in the courts of a State Party to both Conventions if all the parties are resident in a "Lugano State".[57] It would also prevail in the courts of a State Party to both Conventions if one of the parties is resident in a State Party to both

---

55. See *supra* note 18.
56. Article 1(2); see *supra* note 42.
57. This is in line with the general rule of *"Lex posterior derogat legi priori"*; see Article 30(3) of the *Vienna Convention of 23 May 1969 on the Law of Treaties*. For an in-depth discussion of these aspects of international treaty law, see Andrea Schulz, The relationship between the Judgments Project and other international instruments, Preliminary Document No 24, at < www.hcch.net > under "Conventions", then "Convention 37", then "Preliminary Documents".

the Lugano and the Hague Convention and the other in a State that is neither a Party to the Lugano Convention nor to the Hague Convention.

Only where the case (in terms of residence of the parties) has an element external to the other treaty *and* connected to the Hague Convention (because one of the parties resides in a State that is *only* a Party to the Hague Convention, but not to the other treaty), the Hague Convention prevails.[58] In the hypothetical example given above, which involves Norway, Switzerland and the United States, this would be the case because one of the parties to the choice of court agreement is resident in a State Party to the Lugano Convention that is also a Party to the Hague Convention (Norway) and the other party to the choice of court agreement is resident in a State Party to the Hague Convention only (the United States of America).

This is a logical and politically well-balanced solution because in the relations between two States Parties to the Hague Convention, this rule makes a treaty to which all States concerned by a particular case are Parties (the Hague Convention) prevail over another treaty to which not all of the States concerned are Parties, even though the latter treaty might cover the case in spite of this merely unilateral connection. However, this rule requires an "escape clause", which is illustrated by the following continuation of our above example: where one party to the choice of court agreement resides in a State Party to both the Lugano Convention and the Hague Convention (Norway in our example), and the *other* party resides in a State Party only to the Hague Convention (the United States in our example), the Hague Convention would prevail in the courts of the State Party to both instruments (Switzerland as the court chosen, but second seised in our example) under Article 26(2). However, as described above, it is possible that the two instruments impose conflicting obligations on the court concerned.[59] Article 26(3) of the Hague Convention therefore ensures that the State Party to both Conventions is not obliged to breach its *pre-existing* obligations under the other treaty (here: the Lugano Convention) vis-à-vis any State that is a Party to that other treaty but not to the Hague Convention. The chosen court in Switzerland will therefore be allowed to suspend or dismiss proceedings as required by Article 21 of the Lugano Convention until the Norwegian court first seised has found that it lacks jurisdiction.[60] This will also apply to the *revised* Lugano

---

58. Article 26(2).
59. See *supra* note 53 and the adjoining text.
60. The same would apply if the court first seised (but not chosen) was located in another State Party to the Lugano Convention which, unlike Norway in our hypothetical, has *not* also joined the Hague Convention.

Convention and the Agreement between the Community and Denmark, although those are *later* treaties as compared to the Hague Convention because of the specific rule in Article 26(3), second sentence.

c)   *The Hague Convention and Community instruments containing rules on jurisdiction, in particular the Brussels I Regulation*

The relationship between the Hague Convention and Community instruments (*e.g.* the Brussels I Regulation) is dealt with in Article 26(6). The rule is the same as the rule for international treaties in Article 26(2) just described for the Conventions of Brussels and Lugano and the Agreement between the Community and Denmark. There is no need, however, for an "escape clause" parallel to paragraph 3. Community law only allows the Community (in the case of exclusive external competence) or the Community and *all* its Member States (in the case of shared or mixed external competence) to join the Hague Convention. While it may happen that not all States Parties to the Lugano Convention join the Hague Convention, this is not conceivable for the Community Member States bound by the Brussels I Regulation. Consequently, even where Article 26(6) determines that the Hague Convention shall prevail over the Brussels I Regulation because one of the parties to the choice of court agreement is resident in a State Party to the Hague Convention which is not a Community Member State, a court of a Community Member State cannot be in a situation such as the Swiss court in the example described above, risking a breach of its obligations vis-à-vis another Community Member State under the Brussels I Regulation. Since necessarily both Community Member States concerned will be Parties to the Hague Convention, their mutual obligations under the Regulation will have been amended by the Hague Convention in those situations where the Hague Convention prevails because of the connection with another (third) State Party to the Hague Convention which is not an EC Member State. Consequently, no "escape clause" similar to Article 26(3) is needed here. Again, it has to be recalled that these rules will only need to be applied where both instruments in question would claim application according to their own terms, and would moreover lead to incompatible results. Such conflicts between the Brussels I Regulation and the 2005 Hague Convention are likely to be rare. Like for the Lugano Convention, the application of the *lis pendens* rule, which applies under the Brussels I Regulation but not under the Hague Convention, is an example.[61]

---

61. See *supra* note 53 and the Explanatory Report by Hartley/Dogauchi (*supra* note 46), paras 295-310.

By accepting that the Hague Convention prevails if one of the parties is resident in the European Community and the other in a non-EC State which is a Party to the Hague Convention, the European Community agreed to slightly reduce the territorial scope of Article 23 of the Brussels I Regulation which, according to its own terms, would already apply if one of the parties is domiciled in an EC Member State.[62] Moreover, the European Community Member States will no longer apply restrictions on choice of court agreements in business-to-business insurance cases where one of the parties is resident in a State Party to the Hague Convention that is not a Member State of the European Community.

This compromise was agreed upon for the benefit of achieving a global instrument. For non-EC States, such a global instrument would be of little interest if the Community Member States continued to apply the Brussels Regulation to cases where one of the parties to a choice of court agreement is resident or domiciled in a non-EC State, regardless of whether that State is linked to the EC and its Member States by this new Hague Convention. However, the impact on the Brussels I Regulation is limited to a minimum: the Regulation remains unaffected where both parties to the choice of court agreement are resident in a Community Member State and where one party is resident in a Community Member State and the other party in a third State that is not a Party to the Hague Convention. Only where the non-EC party is resident in a State Party to the Hague Convention does the latter prevail in case of conflict.

d)   *The Hague Convention and instruments containing rules on recognition and enforcement*

At the stage of recognition and enforcement, the Convention does not affect the application of other (earlier or later) treaties; however, the judgment shall not be recognised or enforced to a lesser extent than under the Hague Convention (Article 26(4)). Similarly, Article 26(6) *b)* states that the Convention does not affect the rules of an REIO on the recognition and enforcement of judgments as between its Member States. The restriction that the judgment may not be recognised and enforced to a lesser extent than under the Hague Convention does not apply to EC instruments; this is based on the assumption that these will normally be more generous as concerns recognition and enforcement.[63]

---

62.   See *supra* note 54.
63.   This is correct in most cases; insurance may be the only exception within the scope of the Hague Convention. See for further illustration Hartley/Dogauchi, Explanatory Report (*supra* note 46), paras 304-310.

e)   The Hague Convention and treaties on specific subject matters which contain rules on jurisdiction, recognition or enforcement

Treaties on *specific* subject matters which also contain rules on jurisdiction and/or recognition and enforcement are treated in paragraph 5 of Article 26. No matter whether they are earlier or later than the Hague Convention, these treaties remain unaffected; but only if the Contracting State concerned in the particular case has made a declaration in respect of the treaty under this paragraph. In that case, other Contracting States shall not be obliged to apply the Convention to that specific matter to the extent of any inconsistency, where an exclusive choice of court agreement designates the courts, or one or more specific courts, of the Contracting State that made the declaration.

4.   Concluding remarks

The history of the negotiations which led to the Choice of Court Convention, and the Convention itself, are an excellent illustration of the coming into being of external Community competence and its application in practice. New legal issues, such as the participation of the Community as a Party to a Hague convention and the relationship between a Hague convention and secondary Community legislation, arose during these negotiations, and after a somewhat painful transition period appropriate solutions were developed that also met the agreement of other States participating in the now consensus-based negotiations.

However, even if this particular Convention was eventually completed – and unanimously adopted – without the EC being a Member of the Hague Conference, it was felt that a more formalised solution was required, allowing for the Community to participate in the negotiations on an equal footing with other Members of the Conference and offering the same opportunity to future REIOs. The following part of this article will describe how this challenge was successfully mastered by amending the Statute of the Hague Conference.

III.   Formalising the Relationship: The Accession of the European Community to the Hague Conference on Private International Law

A.   Introduction

On 3 April 2007, during a ceremony at the new Academy Building on the grounds of the Peace Palace at The Hague, the President of the Council of the European Union (EU)[64], acting on behalf of the European Community[65], deposited the Community's instrument of acceptance of the Statute of the Hague Conference on Private International Law. Earlier that morning, the Council on General Affairs and Policy of the Conference[66] had unanimously decided to admit the European Community[67] as its first Member Organisation. As a result, the Community, which, as we have seen, until then formally had the status of an observing international organisation in the Hague Conference, became its 66th Member. This accession by the EC to the Statute left unaffected the status of the current 27 Member States of the Community in the Conference, all of which already were, and remain, Members of the Conference in their own right.

The accession of the EC to the Conference was prepared through negotiations among the Member States of the Conference, in which the EC took an active part. These negotiations started four years before in April 2003 and were concluded in June 2005, when the Twentieth Session of the Hague Conference on Private International Law[68] unanimously accepted a series of amendments to its original Statute. These amendments came into effect on 1 January 2007 and paved the way for the accession by the EC.[69]

64. As Germany held the Presidency of the European Union from 1 January–30 June 2007, it was the German Minister of Justice who deposited the instrument of acceptance in the hands of the representatives of the Statute's depositary, the Ministry of Foreign Affairs of the Kingdom of the Netherlands.
65. On the Community side, the accession of the EC to the Hague Conference was approved by Council Decision 2006/719/EC of 5 December 2006 (OJ L 297, 26.10.2006, p. 1). The European Parliament gave its assent to the accession, reflecting the fact that the Hague Conference constituted an organisational framework involving co-operation procedures within the meaning of Article 300(3) EC Treaty.
66. *Supra* note 35.
67. The Community, not the Union, since under the Treaty establishing the European Community, only the Community has legal personality (Article 281) and competence for matters of private international law (Articles 61 *et seq.*).
68. The First Session of the Hague Conference on Private International Law took place in 1893. Six more Sessions were held in 1894, 1900, 1904, 1925 and 1928, prepared by the Netherlands Standing Government Committee on Private International Law, but without the support of any permanent organisational structure. After a dormant period, the Hague Conference convened again in 1951, and it was then that it was established as an intergovernmental organisation with its own Statute. For a short description of the Conference, see Hans van Loon, The Hague Conference on Private International Law: an Introduction, in: Peter J. van Krieken & David McKay, *The Hague: Legal Capital of the World*, pp. 517-526 (2005).
69. See Final Act of the Twentieth Session of the Hague Conference on Private International Law, 30 June 2005, under C (pp. 24 *et seq.*), available at < http://www.hcch.net/upload/finalact20e.pdf >.

This negotiation process was prompted by a letter of 19 December 2002 co-signed by the President of the Council and by the Commissioner for Justice and Home Affairs at the time, and sent to the Secretary General of the Conference expressing the wish of the Community to join the Conference as a Member.

For a proper understanding of what follows, it is important to remember that, although the Conference's purpose is "to work for the progressive unification of the rules of private international law",[70] the Statute neither in its original nor in its amended version establishes a link between membership of the intergovernmental organisation, the Hague Conference on Private International Law, and the status of its Members – or any non-Members for that matter – in respect of each of the conventions[71] (and other instruments such as recommendations) negotiated under the auspices of the organisation. The question whether the EC, or any other REIO, or indeed any State – Member or not of the Conference – may sign or join any such convention is not determined by the Statute, but exclusively by each convention. As we have seen in Part II, *supra*, only two conventions adopted following the entry into force of the Treaty of Amsterdam on 1 May 1999 (but before the accession of the Community to the Conference), *i.e.*, the *Hague Convention of 5 July 2006 on the Law Applicable to Certain Rights in Respect of Securities held with an Intermediary*, and the *Hague Convention of 30 June 2005 on Choice of Courts Agreements*, make express provision for the Community to sign and join these Conventions.

Therefore, the main concern of the letter of 19 December 2002 – although it touched upon the question of "accession to instruments in areas where the Community is competent" – was not so much whether the Community could sign or become a Party to Hague conventions, but the legal position of the EC in the Conference in respect of ongoing and future negotiations on such conventions, and of decision-making on certain aspects of general affairs and policy of the Conference. Since the coming into force of the Treaty of Amsterdam, a practice had developed within the Conference according to which its Member States had implicitly accepted that the EC

---

70. Article 1 of the Statute (*supra* note 9).
71. Before 1951, the Conference adopted seven conventions on various topics of private international law in the field of legal co-operation and of family law. From 1951 till 2007, the Conference adopted thirty-six conventions in three broad areas: international legal co-operation and litigation; international protection of children, vulnerable adults, family relations and family property relations (including succession); and international commercial and finance law. See the website of the Conference at < www.hcch.net >.

took part in the negotiations very much as if it was *de facto* already a Member,[72] but the formal position remained that the Community participated in an observing capacity only. Yet, as the 2002 letter argued, this formal position risked increasingly being at odds with the expanding external competence of the EC, which under Community law led to increasing negotiating powers in relation to third States.[73] From the perspective of the Conference, it was important to encourage the EC, through an adequate organisational structure, to work within the framework of the Conference rather than without it.[74] This was all the more the case since private international law issues were increasingly taking on a global dimension that could no longer adequately be addressed through co-operation at the regional level only, which the Conference was being called upon to deal with.[75]

The request for Membership by the Community came at a critical moment in the life of the Conference. As was explained above,[76] the negotiations on a global Convention on jurisdiction and recognition and enforcement of judgments in civil and commercial matters (the "Judgments Convention") had reached a delicate stage. The challenge, therefore, was to conceive a working method that would enable the Conference to deal with the EC request for membership without upsetting the remainder of its heavy work programme, in particular the work on the Judgments Convention. Careful preparation and consultation were needed. Fortunately, there were a few precedents in other intergovernmental organisations, albeit not with a primary law-making mission, which had admitted the EC as a Member, and the EC letter itself made reference to the Community's accession to the United Nations Food and Agricultural Organization (FAO). The

---

72. This had been facilitated by the Conference's liberal practice for observers generally. Observers in the Conference have traditionally been allowed to speak and participate in the discussions, and make written proposals, but naturally without the right to vote; these participation rights are restrained only towards the end of the negotiations in order to restrict the final round of negotiations to the Members.
73. See *supra* under II. A.
74. This was certainly the view of the Permanent Bureau, the Hague Conference's secretariat; there was little explicit discussion of the basic objectives of EC Membership in the Conference during the negotiations, the focus being rather on its modalities.
75. See Hans van Loon, Unification of Private International Law in a Multi-Forum Context, in: Eva-Maria Kieninger (ed.), *Denationalisierung des Privatrechts, Symposium anlässlich des 70. Geburtstages von Karl Kreuzer*, pp. 33-52 (2005).
76. See *supra* under II. A. 2.

concurrence in time of the negotiations on the Judgments Convention and the admission of the EC, and the aim of bringing both to a conclusion at the Twentieth Session, were not without risk (for both projects), but indeed turned out to be a successful strategy.

Already during the meeting of the Special Commission on General Affairs and Policy held from 1-3 April 2003, it became clear that many Member States, in particular those that were not also Members of the EC, were concerned about the division of competences between the EC Member States and the EC, and the continuing evolution of this division. In practical terms, their concern was to be able to know, at any given moment during ongoing or future negotiations, whether it was the Community, or the EC Member States, that had authority to negotiate and to adopt a convention. In addition to this principal issue, other questions were raised: the modalities of participation and eligibility of the representatives of the EC as officers of drafting committees and other committees; the voting rights of the EC; and the financial implications of EC membership. A preliminary question concerned the need for formal amendments to the Statute, the Rules of Procedure and, possibly other bylaws of the Conference. And, in relation to the Conference's *"acquis de La Haye"*, the rich collection of Hague conventions drawn up since 1893, questions arose on the possible effect of continuing transfers of competence from the EC Member States to the EC, both on EC Member States that were Parties to such conventions, and on those that were not yet Parties but wished to join such instruments.

B.   The procedure established for dealing with the admission request

The 2003 Special Commission agreed that the Secretary General would convene an informal advisory group of experts which would examine the issues linked to the request, and assist him in the preparation of recommendations for the next meeting of the Special Commission in April 2004.[77] It was provided that this group should include "persons with experience in public international law as well as in the work of the Hague Conference, representing various regions in the world and different legal systems". The informal advisory group, chaired by the Ambassador of the People's Republic of China to the Netherlands, Mrs Xue Hanqin, first met

---

77. See the Conclusions of the Special Commission, available on the website of the Hague Conference at < www.hcch.net > under "Work in Progress", then "General Affairs", p. 10.

from 21-23 January 2004. On the second and third day, the group was joined by experts from the European Commission. The format and composition[78] of the informal group made it possible to address the issues both in a principled manner and with a focus on the specific characteristics and needs of the Conference. So, in relation to the question of competences on which the EC had provided further explanations, it soon appeared that the detailed and rigid model of the FAO, justified as this might be for the purposes of the FAO,[79] would be quite impracticable for extended negotiation processes on private international law matters such as take place within the Hague Conference.

There was an additional need for more flexibility, which was emphasized in particular by experts from non-EC Member States of the Conference: it was seen as a great potential loss if, as a result of transfers of competence to the Community combined with rigid adherence to the division of competences, the experts and delegates from individual EC Member States would no longer be in a position to give expression to the variety of European legal systems in the negotiations. This concern related especially to the early stages of discussions and negotiations, when it was important to obtain full pictures of, and perspectives from, the different legal systems represented in the Hague Conference. As will be seen, the outcome of the debate was indeed an agreement on a procedure that is flexible, but with the possibility of obtaining clarity at any given moment during the negotiations on the exact division of competences between the EC Member States and the EC.

The informal advisory group quickly agreed on the principle that membership of the EC should not lead to any additional voting power and that whenever the EC exercised its right to vote, its Member States should

78. The group included, in addition to its Chair, diplomatic representatives, government officials, judges and professors from Australia, Belgium, Brazil, Canada, Egypt, France, Germany, Italy, Japan, Netherlands, Russia, Spain, Sweden, United Kingdom, United States of America, as well as representatives of the European Community.
79. See, *e.g.*, Gerald Moore, The Alternative Exercise of Membership Rights – a Form of Membership for Regional Economic Integration Organizations in FAO [unpublished, on file with the authors], and Antonio Tavares de Pinho, L'admission de la Communauté économique européenne comme membre de l'organisation des Nations Unies pour l'alimentation et l'agriculture (FAO), No 370 [1993] Revue du Marché commun et de l'Union européenne 656, pp. 656-673; both authors were legal counsel of the FAO. For a critical assessment of the EC's FAO membership, as well as a more general analysis of EC membership of international organisations, from the perspective of a staff member of the European Commission, see Jörn Sack, The European Community's Membership of International Organizations, 32 [1995] Common Market Law Review 1227, pp. 1243-1247.

not exercise theirs, and conversely. However, agreement on the question as to how many votes the EC should have when it came to a vote, and under what conditions, turned out to be a much thornier issue. Some experts argued that the logic of the request for membership by the EC implied that the EC should have only one vote when it exercised its voting rights. The fact that since 2000 the Conference had been operating on the basis of consensus took off some of the pressure to reach an early agreement on the voting question. Nevertheless, it would take until the latest stages in the negotiations until agreement was finally reached on the voting rules.

On the basis of the Secretary General's report on the work of the informal advisory group, the 2004 Special Commission on General Affairs and Policy, which met from 6-8 April, unanimously expressed the view that, as a matter of principle, the EC should become a Member of the Conference. The Special Commission dealt with the preliminary issue of the need for a modification of the Statute, and decided that the admission of the EC would indeed require such a modification, as well as a modification of the Rules of Procedure of the Conference and, possibly, of the Regulations on Budgetary Matters – depending on whether the EC should contribute to the annual Budget as a Member or just cover administrative expenses arising from its membership. The modifications should not be limited to the admission of the EC but, following the example of the FAO, should allow for the admission of any Regional Economic Integration Organisation to which its Member States would have transferred competence on matters of private international law. It was furthermore decided that the occasion of amending the Statute should be used to undertake limited revisions of some other provisions, not related to the admission of REIOs, so that they might better conform to current practices as they had developed since the Statute came into force nearly fifty years before. The Secretary General was invited, with the assistance of the informal advisory group, to draw up a complete proposal for the next meeting of the Special Commission.[80]

The informal advisory group met for the second time on 16-17 December 2004, again with Mrs Xue Hanqin in the chair, and managed to narrow even further the areas where agreement was still lacking. On this basis, six draft Recommendations ultimately to be adopted by the Twentieth Session of the Conference in June 2005 were drawn up, which were submitted to the Special Commission on General Affairs and Policy held 31 March-

---

80. See Conclusions of the Special Commission held from 6-8 April 2004 on General Affairs and Policy of the Conference, available on the website of the Hague Conference at < www.hcch.net > under "Work in Progress", then "General Affairs", p. 10.

1 April 2005.[81] They related, among other matters, to amendments to the Statute, the establishment of an authentic English version of the amended Statute (the original Statute being authentic in French only), amendments to the Rules of Procedure, to certain assurances to be given by the Community, and to the decision to be taken to admit the EC as a Member. After a full debate, the Special Commission adopted the proposals, with few amendments.[82] The Twentieth Session, after extensive discussions, adopted the Recommendations which appear under C in the Final Act signed on 30 June 2005. Member States were invited to cast their votes on the amendments, and on 30 September 2006 the necessary two-thirds majority of votes by 44 Member States, including 23 of the current 27 EC Member States, was reached,[83] so that the amendments could come into force on 1 January 2007. This made it possible for the decision on the admission of the Community to take place on 3 April 2007 at the first meeting of the Conference's Member States on general affairs and policy following the entry into force of the amendments to the Statute.

C.   The issues posed by the admission request and their resolution

1.   REIO eligibility requirements

Article II, paragraphs 3 and 4, of the FAO Constitution[84] provided the starting point for the deliberations on the criteria for admission of an REIO

---

81.   See Preliminary Documents Nos 20, 21A and B of February 2005 for the attention of the Special Commission on General Affairs of March/April 2005, available on the website of the Hague Conference at < www.hcch.net > under "Work in Progress", then "General Affairs".

82.   See Preliminary Document No 32B of May 2005 for the attention of the Twentieth Session, available on the website of the Hague Conference at < www.hcch.net > under "Work in Progress", then "General Affairs".

83.   The 44 Member States that cast their vote before 30 September 2006 were Albania, Argentina, Australia, Austria, Belgium, Bosnia & Herzegovina, Bulgaria, Canada, China, Croatia, Cyprus, Czech Republic, Denmark, Egypt, Estonia, Finland, France, Germany, Greece, Hungary, Ireland, Italy, Latvia, Malaysia, Malta, Mexico, Monaco, the Netherlands, New Zealand, Norway, Panama, Peru, Romania, Russia, Slovakia, Serbia, Slovenia, Sweden, Switzerland, the former Yugoslav Republic of Macedonia, Turkey, Ukraine, the United Kingdom and the United States of America. The remaining four EC Member States, Luxembourg, Poland, Portugal and Spain, as well as Chile and South Africa, cast their votes before 3 April 2007.

84.   See Basic Texts of the Food and Agricultural Organization of the United Nations, Volumes I and II-2006 edition, Vol. I, A, Constitution, available at < http://www.fao.org/docrep/009/j8038e/j8038e00.htm >.

to the Hague Conference,[85] which ultimately resulted in the following provision of the amended Statute of the Conference (Article 3):

1. The Member States of the Conference may, at a meeting concerning general affairs and policy where the majority of Member States is present, by a majority of the votes cast, decide to admit also as a Member any Regional Economic Integration Organisation which has submitted an application for membership to the Secretary General. References to Members under this Statute shall include such Member Organisations, except as otherwise expressly provided. The admission shall become effective upon the acceptance of the Statute by the Regional Economic Integration Organisation concerned.

2. To be eligible to apply for membership of the Conference, a Regional Economic Integration Organisation must be one constituted solely by sovereign States, and to which its Member States have transferred competence over a range of matters within the purview of the Conference, including the authority to make decisions binding on its Member States in respect of those matters.

   [...]

A preliminary question had arisen during the negotiations prior to the Twentieth Session, namely whether it was appropriate to maintain the term "REIO" adopted by the FAO at a time when the EC's competences were still limited mainly to economic matters. Although those competences had evolved beyond the economic area, it was felt that "REIO" had become a term of art and, since the economic field still very much occupied the EC, should be maintained. Surprisingly, however, during the Twentieth Session, the Russian delegation, seconded by the observer from the Eurasian Economic Community,[86] insisted that the term should be

---

85. Many of these issues arose already in the context of the EC admission to the FAO, and, since they appeared there for the first time, were discussed in much greater depth than was necessary in the context of the Hague Conference. See the literature referred to *supra* note 79. These discussions remain relevant, as background for a full understanding of Articles 3 and 8 of the amended Statute of the Conference, in particular in those instances where the wording of the FAO texts did not give rise to discussion in the context of the Conference.

86. The Eurasian Economic Community is, as its name indicates, a trans-regional organisation; its purview, although mainly focused on economic matters, also extends, *e.g.*, into the development of common guidelines on border security.

broadened, so as to include other international organisations.[87] Although the EC was prepared to accept the Russian position, the United States and most other States preferred to retain the well-established term "REIO". In the end, a compromise was reached, and the following paragraph 9 was added at the end of Article 3:

> 'Regional Economic Integration Organisation' means an international organisation that is constituted solely by sovereign States, and to which its Member States have transferred competence over a range of matters, including the authority to make decisions binding on its Member States in respect of those matters.

Another issue of a political nature unexpectedly arose during the Diplomatic Session: the Chinese delegation, obviously concerned about the possibility of an Asian, or Asian-Pacific REIO to which Taiwan would have been admitted as a "sovereign State", insisted upon the inclusion of the word "solely" in paragraph 2 of Article 3, in an effort to exclude any such organisation from future membership of the Conference.[88] This proposal was accepted, and in the light of this history the adverb "solely" should be understood as qualifying the adjective "sovereign" only, and not the expression "sovereign States" as a whole (the EC, the REIO *par excellence*, consists not only of its Member States but, as a supranational body, also of an institutional framework of its own: Council, Commission, Parliament, Court etc., empowered to take decisions that are binding upon its Member States).

At the request of the EC, but contrary to Article II, paragraph 4, of the FAO Constitution, Article 3, paragraph 2, of the Statute as amended does not require that a majority of the REIO Member States be Members of the Conference. The EC view – supported by Member States from other continents such as Africa, where regional organisations were emerging with a possible interest in joining the Conference at a later stage – was that in a situation where an REIO had competence over a particular matter

87. The term "regional economic integration organisation" was coined in a series of treaties on environmental protection, including the *Geneva Convention on Long-range Transboundary Air Pollution* and the *Bonn Convention on the Conservation of Migratory Species of Wild Animals*, both from 1979. However, the 1982 *United Nations Convention on the Law of the Sea* uses the broader expression "international organization". Article 3, paragraph 9, of the amended Statute of the Conference, proposed by the Russian delegation, is an attempt to combine the two expressions.

88. It may be noted that, under Article XII of the Agreement Establishing the World Trade Organization, "Chinese Taipei" in 2002 acceded to the World Trade Organization, not as a State, but as "a separate customs territory possessing full autonomy in the conduct of its external commercial relations and of the other matters provided for in this Agreement and the multilateral trade agreements". See Agreement available at < http://www.wto.org/english/docs_e/legal_e/04-wto.pdf >.

within the purview of the Conference, it was irrelevant whether any of the Member States of the REIO were also Members of the Conference. Against this, it was argued that since the main "product" of the Conference, the conventions on private international law, depend for their implementation on courts, authorities and officials of States, it may be problematical for an REIO to ensure in its relations to Member States of the Conference that are not also REIO Members, that convention obligations are fully implemented by REIO Members that are not themselves also Members of the Conference.[89] The discussion on this point was, in its context, purely theoretical, since all EC Members were Members of the Conference. However, the Community obviously wished to create a precedent for future admissions of REIOs to organisations to which not all REIO Members did belong, and on this point the EC view prevailed.

It will be noted, finally, that, in line with the requirement for the admission of new Member States to the Conference, but in contrast with Article II(3) of the FAO Constitution, which requires a two-thirds majority, a simple majority of the Member States present at a "meeting concerning general affairs and policy" of the Conference,[90] is all that is required for the admission of an REIO to the Hague Conference.[91]

2.   *Declaration and exercise of competences*

As indicated in the Introduction to Part III, the question of how the Community competences should be declared and exercised was the principal issue to be resolved. The upshot of the negotiations is to be found in Article 3, paragraphs 3-7, of the Statute:

3. Each Regional Economic Integration Organisation applying for membership shall, at the time of such application, submit a declaration of competence specifying the matters in respect of which competence has been transferred to it by its Member States.

4. Each Member Organisation and its Member States shall ensure that any change regarding the competence of the Member Organisation or in its membership shall be notified to the Secretary General, who shall circulate such information to the other Members of the Conference.

---

89. Another argument advanced against deleting the words "a majority of which are Members of the Conference" was that this might have financial consequences, if REIOs were not to contribute to the budget.
90. *I.e.*, a meeting of the Council on General Affairs and Policy – see *supra* note 35 – or a meeting of the Diplomatic Sessions.
91. Provided the quorum (Article 3, paragraph 1) is reached.

5. Member States of the Member Organisation shall be presumed to retain competence over all matters in respect of which transfers of competence have not been specifically declared or notified.

6. Any Member of the Conference may request the Member Organisation and its Member States to provide information as to whether the Member Organisation has competence in respect of any specific question which is before the Conference. The Member Organisation and its Member States shall ensure that this information is provided on such request.

7. The Member Organisation shall exercise membership rights on an alternative basis with its Member States that are Members of the Conference, in the areas of their respective competences.

Article II, paragraphs 5-8, of the FAO Constitution[92] provided the basis for these rules. However, the FAO General Rules of the Organisation,[93] the Provisional Guidelines for the participation of the EC in FAO meetings,[94] and the Rules of Procedure of the Codex Alimentarius Commission (CAC),[95] a body jointly constituted by FAO and WHO, regulate in considerably more detail how within the FAO and the CAC the REIO/EC competences must be declared and exercised. Under these regulations there is an obligation for either the REIO or its Member States to indicate before any meeting which of them has competence in respect of any specific question to be considered in the meeting, and indeed, to declare so in respect of each agenda item,[96] preferably at least two working days beforehand; failure to do so will prevent the EC from effectively participating in the meeting.[97] It was readily agreed that requirements with such a level of detail would not work for comprehensive negotiations of a legislative nature, such as those undertaken by the Conference; issues were often interrelated and evolved in the course of the negotiations, especially in the early stages of discussions when the general orientation and the structure of a future convention are still to be determined, and it would be

---

92. *Cf. supra* note 84.
93. Article XLI, see Basic Texts of the FAO, *supra* note 84, Vol. I, B, General Rules of the Organization.
94. Available on the website of the Hague Conference at < www.hcch.net > under "Work in Progress", then "General Affairs" as Annex 2 to Preliminary Document No 21B of February 2005, < www.hcch.net/upload/wop/genaff_pd21be.pdf >.
95. Rule II, see Codex Alimentarius, Procedural Manual, Rules of Procedure of the Codex Alimentarius Commission, available at < ftp://ftp.fao.org/codex/Publications/ProcManuals/Manual_15e.pdf >, pp. 6, at pp. 6-7.
96. FAO Provisional Guidelines (*supra* note 94); CAC Rules of Procedure, Rule II, 5.
97. FAO Provisional Guidelines (*supra* note 94), p. 3 ("Implications of a failure to produce a statement of competence and voting rights").

difficult or even impossible to draw the line between Community and EC Member competences. On the other hand, it was clearly unacceptable to provide no mechanism at all for obtaining clarity on the distribution of competences. In this regard the FAO General Rules[98] and the Rules of Procedure of the CAC[99] were of assistance, because they provide that any Member may, at any time,[100] request a Member Organisation or its Member States to provide the necessary clarity, and the Member Organisation or the Member States concerned are obliged to provide such information. This rule, elevated to the level of a "constitutional" provision, now appears in Article 3, paragraph 6, of the Statute of the Hague Conference with a few minor amendments.[101]

The result is a system that is relatively simple and that should not cause any difficulties in the daily operation of negotiations in the Conference. At the outset, when the REIO applies for membership, there will be a declaration of competence (Article 3, paragraph 3). Such a declaration has indeed been deposited by the EC, first in general terms in its letter of 19 December 2002, subsequently in more detail when it joined the Hague Conference on 3 April 2007.[102] Any Member of the Conference may assume that the EC Members have retained competence over all matters in respect of which transfers of competence have not been specifically declared (paragraph 5). Any subsequent change of competence shall be notified to the Conference (paragraph 4), in the absence of which paragraph 5 will apply. If queries still remain, then paragraph 6 provides a remedy. Finally, paragraph 7 establishes the principle of non-additionality for the exercise of

---

98. Rule XLI, 1.
99. Rule II, 6.
100. *Cf.* FAO Provisional Guidelines (*supra* note 94), p. 4 (under "voting").
101. The request may be addressed to *both* the REIO *and* (not: or) its Member States (paragraph 6), because it was argued that one should not assume that in (future) REIOs other than the EC the transfer of competences would occur in a manner similar to that of the EC, and there might be REIOs, for example, where the REIO could only provide such information with the assistance of its Member States, or vice versa. For the same reason, paragraph 4 requires that the REIO *and* its Member States shall ensure that any change regarding the competence of the REIO (or its membership) shall be notified to the Conference.
102. The Declaration was approved by the EU Council of Ministers together with its approval of the EC's accession to the Hague Conference (OJ L 297, 26.10.2006, p. 4). The Declaration is equally available on the website of the Hague Conference at < www.hcch.net > under "Conventions", then "Statute of the Hague Conference", then "Status Table". In the list of Members, click on the "D" in the row concerning the European Community.

competence.[103] In the case of "mixed competence", where a subject matter dealt with by the Conference covers both issues within the competence of the EC and issues within the competence of its Member States,[104] both the EC and the Member States may take part in the negotiations, but they must each restrict themselves to the matters falling within their own spheres of competence.[105] Finally, it may be noted that at the end of the day, when the decision is to be made whether the Community and/or the EC Member States will join a Hague convention, the support of the Council will always be needed – this reduces to some extent the importance of the issue of competences in relation to the work of the Hague Conference.

3.   *Modalities of participation and eligibility for election*

At the 2005 meeting of the Special Commission on General Affairs and Policy of the Conference, the United States of America proposed that the Statute should clarify expressly that participation in meetings of REIO representatives and of those of its Member States should be on an alternative basis. While other delegations supported the wish to provide more clarity on "the exercise of membership rights" in what ultimately became paragraph 7, the view prevailed (for reasons similar to those that led to the rejection of detailed rules on the declaration and exercise of membership rights) that open discussion without rigid checks on competences, should be encouraged as a way to obtain full information and achieve consensus. It was felt that it could be left to the Chair of meetings to control the level of participation. In the end, the United States of America accepted to withdraw its proposal to insert in paragraph 7 the words "[membership rights] including participation in meetings".

We may conclude, therefore, that the principle of non-additionality as expressed in paragraph 7 applies generally in the Conference, including to participation and eligibility for election for offices such as membership of drafting committees or other subsidiary bodies, but is to be applied with some flexibility in order to achieve the best results in the negotiations. This

---

103. As Moore (*supra* note 79, at p. 11) points out in respect of EC membership of FAO, the essence of REIO membership is that there is "one single bundle of membership rights that should be exercised alternatively by the regional economic integration organization and its member states depending on which of the two ha[s] competence on any given matter. Of fundamental importance, both theoretically and politically, [is] the notion that on no occasion should the bundle of rights become larger or smaller, by whomsoever exercised".

104. *Cf.* FAO Provisional Guidelines (*supra* note 94), p. 2 (under "Declarations in respect of specific agenda items").

105. *Ibidem*, p. 4 (under "voting").

is in fact already current practice in the Conference: the EC has participated in drafting committees and in formal and informal working groups and this has generally given satisfactory results.[106] If more guidance were needed, it would always be possible, under Article 14 of the Statute, to draw up implementing regulations (inspiration for which could then be found in the aforementioned FAO Provisional Guidelines).

4. The right to vote

Traditionally, the Conference proceeded through voting, although there was always an understanding that in certain cases a vote could be reconsidered (the history of the Conference provides several examples of such reconsideration of a vote on a vital issue),[107] and wise Chairs always took consensus-building as their prime objective.[108] As was explained above,[109] since 2000 the Conference has adopted a different practice and has proceeded on the basis of consensus. The amended Statute provides that the Diplomatic Sessions and all other meetings (with the exception of those on the admission of Members and on financial matters) "shall, to the furthest extent possible, operate on the basis of consensus" (Article 8, paragraph 2); the Rules of Procedure have been amended accordingly. Nonetheless, *in extremis* voting may be unavoidable, and therefore the question of the voting rights of REIOs and their Member States had to be addressed. Article 3, paragraph 8, deals with this issue:

> The Member Organisation may exercise on matters within its competence, in any meetings of the Conference in which it is entitled to participate, a number of votes equal to the number of its Member States which have transferred competence to the Member Organisation in respect of the matter in question, and which are entitled to vote in and have registered for such meetings. Whenever the Member Organisation exercises its right to vote, its Member States shall not exercise theirs, and conversely.

As already indicated when we discussed the procedure for admission of the EC, the debate focussed on the number of votes the EC would have in the exceptional case where a vote had to be taken. The Community took the

---

106. See *supra* at II. A. 3.
107. A famous example is offered by the reconsideration of the vote on the issue of legal aid in the context of the *Hague Convention of 25 October 1980 on the Civil Aspects of International Child Abduction* (Article 26) – see the Explanatory Report by Elisa Pérez-Vera, in: *Proceedings of the Fourteenth Session*, Tome III, p. 426 (at p. 468) and for the reopening of the debate on the vote, *ibidem* (pp. 246-248).
108. See T. Bradbrooke Smith, Achieving results at international meetings: why the Hague Conference succeeds, in: Alegría Borrás *et al.* (eds.), *E Pluribus Unum, Liber Amicorum Georges A.L. Droz*, pp. 415-444 (1996).
109. See *supra* under II. A.

view that a vote cast by the EC in a Conference meeting would bind the EC Member States, whether present or not at the meeting, and not by proxy (as some delegations had argued) but directly, since the EC is a supranational entity. Therefore, they argued, the EC should always have as many votes as it has Members.[110] Other delegates drew the opposite conclusion: if *one* entity, then *one* vote only.[111] Many delegations, however, preferred the solution adopted in the Amendments to the Rules of Procedure of the CAC, according to which a Member Organisation may exercise a number of votes "equal to the number of its Member States which are entitled to vote in such meetings and present at the time the vote is taken". They felt that granting the EC as many votes as it had Members was unjustified since the voting tradition of the Conference supposed that each vote was based on an informed opinion about the issue in question. Moreover, if the Community view on voting was followed, individual EC Member States might feel discouraged to participate in meetings.

In the end, agreement was reached on a formula inspired by the FAO Provisional Guidelines according to which the number of votes of the REIO is "equal to the number of votes of its Member States [...] entitled to vote in and hav[ing] registered for the meeting in question".[112] This would mean that provided that any individual EC Member State has registered for the full duration of, for example, a Special Commission meeting, that State need not be actually present in the meeting room in order to be included in the number of votes the EC could cast at any special moment.

It may be noted that REIOs are not involved in the decisions on the admission of new Members to the Conference. Hence, they are excluded from voting on these matters. This applies equally to new Member States (Article 2, paragraph 2, of the Statute) and new Member Organisations (Article 3, paragraph 1): these decisions are to be taken by the Member

---

110. With possible qualifications in view of the special position of Denmark, and, possibly also of the United Kingdom and Ireland (see also *supra* notes 18 and 39).
111. This position was not pushed too hard, however. The FAO precedent also pointed in a different direction: the FAO Constitution provides that an REIO has a number of votes equal to the number of its Member States entitled to vote. There was also an indirect link between the number of votes an REIO would have in the Conference and the financial contribution of its Member States to the budget of the organisation; there was no wish to alter the basis of the latter which might have been the case if the "one vote only" policy had carried the day.
112. See FAO Provisional Guidelines (*supra* note 94) (under "Conduct of the meetings, Determining a quorum", p. 4), "[...] provided that any necessary formalities have been complied with, it is not required that each of the individual Member States actually be present in the meeting room for the EC to be able to vote".

States only. With regard to new Member States, there is a link with the financial aspects of membership, in which REIOs are also not involved.

5.   *Financial aspects*

Article 9 of the Statute deals with the budget of the Hague Conference. Following its amendment to take into account the consequences of the accession of REIOs, the provision now reads as follows:

1. The budgeted costs of the Conference shall be apportioned among the Member States of the Conference.

2. A Member Organisation shall not be required to contribute in addition to its Member States to the annual budget of the Conference, but shall pay a sum to be determined by the Conference, in consultation with the Member Organisation, to cover additional administrative expenses arising out of its membership.

3. In any case, travelling and living expenses of the delegates to the Council and the Special Commissions shall be payable by the Members represented.

The rule of paragraph 2 is in essence the same as that found in Article XVIII, paragraph 6, of the FAO Constitution.[113] It maintains the principle that the Member States are exclusively in control of the financial running of the organisation (and hence have an exclusive say over related matters, in particular the admission of new Member States). The word "additional" was added at the request of the Community in order to strictly limit the "sum" due by the REIO to the extra costs its membership implies for the Conference – which is fair enough. It does not, however, provide clear guidance as to how these extra costs should be calculated. In respect of the EC, these and other aspects will have to be clarified in further consultations. Ultimately the decision belongs to the Council of Diplomatic Representatives of the Conference (Article 10 of the Statute).

6.   *Effect of evolving EC competences on existing Hague conventions*

As mentioned in the Introduction to Part III, the evolving EC competences in the field of private international law may also have an effect on existing Hague conventions. New Community instruments may supersede such

---

113. "A Member Organization shall not be required to contribute to the budget [...] but shall pay to the Organization a sum to be determined by the [Organization] to cover administrative and other expenses arising out of its membership in the Organization. A Member Organization shall not vote on the budget."

conventions for those EC Member States that are Parties to them and in the relations between EC Member States only, to the extent that the EC instrument so prescribes and the Hague Convention so allows.[114] They may also affect the right of EC Member States that are not yet Parties to a certain Hague convention to join this convention, to the extent that as a result of the exercise of its competence by the Community, individual EC States are no longer free to join the Hague convention in question. Whether that is the case will depend on the nature and the subject matter of the Community instrument on the one hand, and of the convention in question on the other.

If the Community instrument and the convention both deal with applicable law rules – operating *erga omnes* –, one will in principle exclude the other: in so far as a Community instrument establishes applicable law rules on specific contracts such as sales or agency, they cannot coexist with Hague conventions on the same topics.[115] With regard to a Community instrument on jurisdiction and recognition and enforcement of judgments, a conflict may arise with a Hague convention in situations, usually involving EC Member States only, where both claim to be applicable.[116] To the extent that a Community instrument deals with judicial and administrative co-operation, it may supersede the convention (*i.e.* in the

---

114. *Cf.* Article 41 of the *Vienna Convention on the Law of Treaties*.

115. The *finesses* of the outcome of the negotiations on a Regulation on the law applicable to contractual obligations ("Rome I") will determine if, and to what extent this Regulation will be compatible with the *Hague Conventions of 1955* and *of 1986 on the law applicable to international sales* and *of 1978 on the law applicable to agency*, each of which are in force for a certain number of EC Member States. Similar remarks may be made in relation to the current negotiations for a Regulation on the law applicable to non-contractual obligations ("Rome II"), the *Hague Convention of 1971 on the Law Applicable to Traffic Accidents* and the *Hague Convention of 1973 on the Law Applicable to Products Liability*.

116. Examples include the Council Regulation (EC) No 2201/2003 of 27 November 2003 concerning jurisdiction and the recognition and enforcement of judgments in matrimonial matters and the matters of parental responsibility, repealing Regulation (EC) No 1347/2000 ("Brussels II *bis*"), in relation to the Hague Convention of 1996 on the International Protection of Children, and the Council Regulation (EC) No 44/2001 of 22 December 2000 on jurisdiction and the recognition and enforcement of judgments in civil and commercial matters ("Brussels I") in relation to the Hague Choice of Court Convention, see *supra* under II. B. 3. c).

relations with other EC Member States) if the convention so allows,[117] or it may coexist with it.[118] A more complete description and analysis of these various possibilities would exceed the limits of this contribution.

It is, however, of great significance that, as its legislative work in the field of private international law develops, the Community carry out an examination of the *"acquis de La Haye"*. Not only will this save the Community a duplication of efforts, it will also enable it to enrich its portfolio of Community instruments – the result of consultations among EC Members only, and binding upon EC Member States only – with Hague conventions which are the fruit of *global* negotiations and which, if ratified by both EC Member States and other States, provide important links with non-EC Members. Therefore – even though, as we have seen in the Introduction, the Statute of the Hague Conference does not make any direct connection between membership of the organisation and the Hague conventions –, it was important that in the context of the accession of the Community to the Hague Conference, the Community should accept to examine which Hague conventions it might be in the interest of the Community to join. Where necessary – because of the absence of a clause providing for the accession of an REIO – this may occur either through ratification by its Member States in the interest of the Community or through the adoption of a Protocol by all the States Parties to a Hague convention.

To this end, when it acceded to the Statute on 3 April 2007, the Community deposited the following Declaration:

> The European Community endeavours to examine whether it is in the interest of the Community to join existing Hague Conventions in respect of which there is Community competence. Where this interest exists, the European Community, in cooperation with the Hague Conference will make every effort to overcome the difficulties resulting from the absence of a clause providing for the accession of a Regional Economic Integration Organisation to these Conventions.

117. Examples include the Council Regulation (EC) No 1348/2000 of 29 May 2000 on the service in the Member States of judicial and extrajudicial documents in civil or commercial matters and the Council Regulation (EC) No 1206/2001 of 28 May 2001 on cooperation between the courts of the Member States in the taking of evidence in civil or commercial matters in relation to the Hague Service Convention of 1965 and the Hague Evidence Convention of 1970, respectively.
118. The idea of the provisions on children in the Brussels II *bis* Regulation (see *supra* note 116) is that they build on the 1980 *Hague Convention on the Civil Aspects of International Child Abduction*, while limiting, in accordance with Article 36 of this Convention, the restrictions to which the return of a child may be subject.

In order to facilitate consultations within the Community with a view to this examination, the Permanent Bureau prepared a document for the attention of the Community and its Members[119].

It is worth noting, that in a further effort to ensure good co-operation between the Community and the Hague Conference, the Community Declaration continues:

> The European Community endeavours to make participation possible of represent-atives of the Permanent Bureau of the Conference in meetings of experts organised by the European Commission where matters of interest to the Conference are being discussed.

Such combination of resources can only be beneficial to both the European Community and the Hague Conference.

IV. Concluding remarks

From the examination of the historic developments including the effect of emerging external Community competence for negotiations taking place within and conventions adopted by the Hague Conference on Private International Law, it has become apparent that the relationship between the EC and the Hague Conference is an evolving and multi-faceted one. The role of the Community in Hague Conference negotiations, membership of the EC in the Hague Conference as an intergovernmental organisation, and adherence of the EC to individual Hague conventions are separate, albeit related issues.

The creation and gradual expansion of external Community competence for issues of private international law, which initially had a factual impact upon the negotiation of conventions within the Hague Conference, eventually led to an amendment of the Conference's Statute and Rules of Procedure, and to the accession of the EC to the Conference.

A beginning has been made with the opening-up of meetings organised by the European Commission to representatives of the Permanent Bureau of the Hague Conference. As concerns Community participation in the two recent Hague Conventions open to REIOs, an impact assessment was prepared for the Securities Convention in 2006, and discussions within the Community are under way. Concerning the Choice of Court Convention, the Commission has launched an impact assessment in 2007, to be followed by a Commission proposal towards early 2008.

119. See < www.hcch.net > under "Work in Progress", then "General Affairs and Policy".

There remains the issue of the participation of the Community, or the collectivity of its Member States, in older Hague conventions which do not contain an REIO accession clause, but for which there is shared or mixed Community or even exclusive Community competence. It is hoped that in the near future, a solution can be found which takes into account the fact that many EC Member States are already Parties to the conventions concerned, and the benefit that adherence by the Community itself or all Community Member States to these conventions could bring by building bridges between the Community and the rest of the world. This, together with the fact that, on 3 April 2007, the European Community was unanimously welcomed as a Member of the Hague Conference on Private International Law, is reason enough to predict that the Hague Conference will continue to be a major forum for the elaboration and monitoring of private international law treaties linking the European Community and its Member States with the other States of the world.

Part III

Criminal Law

1. International Transfers of Data in the Field of JHA: The Lessons of Europol, PNR and Swift

Paul de Hert and Bart de Schutter¹

I. Introduction

A. What data protection is all about

As a result of the rapid development in computer technology, large amounts of information relating to individuals ('personal data') are routinely collected and used by public administrations and in every sector of business. Since the 1970s, several EU Member States have passed data protection legislation, that is, legislation protecting the fundamental rights of individuals and in particular their right to privacy, including *inter alia* protection from abuse resulting from the processing (i.e., the collection, use, storage, etc.) of personal data. In general, these laws specify a series of rights for individuals and demand good data management practices on the part of the entities that process data ('data controllers').

These basic practices or principles are also spelled out in the international legal data protection texts produced by institutions such as the United Nations,[2] the Organisation for Economic Cooperation and Development (OECD),[3] the Council of Europe,[4] and the European Union.[5] Each of these organisations produced what has become a classic basic data protection instrument, respectively the Guidelines on data protection, the

1. The authors wish to thank Gloria González Fuster (Institute of European Studies, Vrije Universiteit Brussels) for corrections and suggestions.
2. 1990 UN Guidelines Concerning Computerized Personal Data Files, UN Economic and Social Council, E/CN.4/1990/72, 20 February 1990.
3. Cf. OECD Guidelines Governing the Protection of Privacy and Transborder Data Flows of Personal Data, 23 September 1980 in OECD, *Guidelines Governing the Protection of Privacy and Transborder Data Flows of Personal Data*, 9-12 (1980); [1981] *International Legal Materials*, I., 317.
4. Convention for the protection of individuals with regard to automatic processing of personal data, Council of Europe, January 28, 1981, *European Treaty Series*, no. 108; [1981] *International Legal Materials*, 422
5. Directive 95/46/EC of the European Parliament and of the Council of 24 October 1995 on the protection of individuals with regard to the processing of personal data on the free movement of such data, OJ L 281, 23.11.1995, p. 31.

Convention and the Data Protection Directive. The latter has been supplemented by data protection provisions in the Telecommunication Privacy Directive 97/66/EC,[6] later replaced by Directive 2002/58/EC,[7] and in Directive 2000/31/EC on electronic commerce.[8] The EU has also included the right to data protection in the European Charter of Fundamental Rights.[9]

The ideas behind these legal instruments on data protection are similar. They all try to more or less reconcile fundamental but conflicting values such as privacy, free flow of information, governmental need for surveillance and taxation, etc. More concrete data protection takes the form of a set of principles governing the processing of personal data, whether in public or private sectors. Whenever there is processing of such data, the data protection principles apply. These principles are:[10] 1. the collection limitation principle;[11] 2. the data quality principle;[12] 3. the purpose specification principle;[13] 4. the use limitation principle;[14] 5. the

6. Directive 97/66 on the protection of privacy and personal data in the telecommunications sectors, which establishes specific legal and technical provisions for the telecommunications sector (OJ L 24, 30.1.1998. p. 1-8 (Telecommunication Privacy Directive).
7. Directive 2002/58/EC of the European Parliament and of the Council of 12 July 2002 concerning the processing of personal data and the protection of privacy in the electronic communications sector, OJ L 201, 12.7.2002, p. 37-47.
8. Directive 2000/31/EC of the European Parliament and of the Council of 8 June 2000 on certain legal aspects of information society services, in particular electronic commerce, in the Internal Market ("Directive on electronic commerce"), OJ L178, 17.7.2000, p. 1.
9. Charter of Fundamental Rights of the European Union, OJ C 364, 18.12.2000, p. 1.
10. W.J. Kirsch, 'The Protection of Privacy and Transborder Flows of Personal Data: The Work of the Council of Europe, the Organization for Economic Co-Operation and Development and the European Economic Community', 2 [1982] *Legal issues on European integration*, 31-32.
11. There should be limits to the collection of personal data and any such information should be obtained by lawful and fair means and, where appropriate, with the knowledge or consent of the data subject.
12. Personal data should be relevant to the purposes for which they are to be used, and, to the extent necessary for those purposes, should be accurate, complete, and up-to-date.
13. The purposes for which personal data are collected should be specified not later than at the time of data collection. Subsequent use should be limited to the fulfilment of those purposes or such others as are not incompatible with those purposes and as are specified on each occasion of change of purpose.
14. Personal data should not be disclosed, made available or otherwise used for purposes other than those first specified except: a) with the consent of the data subject; or b) by the authority of the law.

security safeguards principle;[15] 6. the openness principle;[16] 7. the individual participation principle;[17] 8. the accountability principle.[18]

Data protection is, however, still not internationally acknowledged as a global issue. There is no world treaty on data protection and many countries have no formal recognition of the need to protect personal data. The 1980 OECD Guidelines and the 1990 UN Guidelines are important at the global level, but they lack legally binding force. The OECD text is also less detailed compared to the European documents, being just a short document containing no more than a listing of the data protection principles. The mentioned European legal instruments widened the scope of 1980 OECD Guidelines in many respects and established the need for independent supervisory data protection authorities, which are unknown in the OECD Guidelines.

It is interesting to note that Europe has now developed two basic texts with regard to data protection. The approach of the Council of Europe Convention can be labelled 'guideline-oriented', whereas the EU rules are rather formalistic and bureaucratic in nature.[19] Different reasons have been suggested to explain this difference in approach between the two European documents.[20] The Directive came into place almost fifteen years after the Convention. In the meantime, data protection doctrine developed considerably. Almost all EU Member States (with the exception of Italy and Greece) had legislation in place based on the Convention. The Directive consequently benefited from all the practical experience accumulated in those years. The Convention and the Directive have a different nature and are part of different legal systems. While the Convention has a non-executive character and should be viewed in the framework of Public

---

15. Personal data should be protected by reasonable security safeguards against such risks as loss or unauthorized access, destruction, use, modification, or disclosure.
16. There should be a general policy of openness about developments, practices, and policies with respect to personal data. Means should be readily available for establishing the existence and nature of personal data, and the main purposes of their use, as well as the identity and usual residence of the data controller.
17. An individual should have the right of notification, access and rectification.
18. A data controller should be accountable for complying with measures that give effect to the data protection principles.
19. P. De Hert & E. Schreurders, 'The Relevance of Convention 108', available at http://www.coe.int/t/e/legal_affairs/legal_cooperation/data_protection/events/conferences/ (consulted July 2007), pp. 12-14.
20. D. Alonso Blas, 'Mechanisms for implementation and international co-operation in the context of data protection: existing mechanisms and mechanisms to be established', http://www.coe.int/t/e/legal_affairs/legal_cooperation/data_protection/events/conferences/ (consulted July 2007, p. 5.

International Law,[21] the Directive can impose much more specific obligations on the member states of the Union, which are then, under European Law, obliged to implement its provisions into national law.

Data protection is thus about controlling the actors processing personal data of citizens and this control is either done by the data subjects themselves or, in Europe at least, by data protection supervisory authorities. Controlling national actors is of course much easier than controlling actors outside the legal regime of the Member State of the data subjects.

B.   Objectives and outline of this contribution

In spite of increased attention to issues of data protection in the last 20 years, most citizens are still largely unaware of the extent to which their personal data are processed by police and judicial authorities. The reality, however, is that police and judicial databases are full of sensitive information, and one could consider all police data on persons to be sensitive. In fact, depending on the context, the sheer fact that someone appears in a police database may already be considered as sensitive information. Even fewer citizens are aware that their personal data are being transmitted by Member States to other Member States and to third countries outside the EU.

The naivety of citizens regarding their presence in police databases may well play into the hands of those who favour (new) security policies that infringe on fundamental rights.[22] Adequate data protection rules, on the level of the Member States and on the European level, contribute to the protection of fundamental rights and freedoms, notably the right to privacy, which is recognized both in Article 8 of the European Convention for the Protection of Human Rights and Fundamental Freedoms and in the general principles of Community law, as well as in the 2000 Charter of Fundamental Rights of the European Union.

In this contribution we look at the EU rules governing the processing of data in the field of Justice and Home Affairs (JHA), in particular with

---

21.   With regard to the "non-executive character" of the Convention: The ECHR has been considered as one of the most (if not *the* most) powerful human rights instruments also because the respect of its provisions is guaranteed by the authoritative rulings of the European Court (e.g., see Jack Donnelly, International Human Rights: A Regime Analysis, 40 [1986] *International Organization*, pp. 599-642

22.   EDPS, 'EU and the right to privacy', *EDPS Newsletter*, no. 6, 26 October 2006, 1-2 (www.edps.europa.eu.).

regard to data transfers to third countries. A fundamental distinction when it comes to protecting individual privacy within the EU ought to be made between the so-called First Pillar and Third Pillar (or JHA) processing. The latter category covers all crime-related and security-related processing of personal information. First Pillar processing normally covers all commercial processing of personal information. Whereas for First Pillar processing Directive 95/46/EC provides a common denominator for data protection, for Third Pillar processing such a common standard does not exist: instead, a patchwork of data protection regulations covers different sector-specific processing (the Schengen Agreement, SIS II, Europol, Eurojust and, recently, the Prüm Treaty). In the present paper we discuss briefly the EU regulatory framework on data protection and the choice between a comprehensive model of regulation and a sectoral or piece-meal approach, as is the case for the Third Pillar in its current state (section II).

Then we proceed with a basic question about the need for an EU approach with regard to transfers of personal data to third countries: *Is a European regulation of transfers of data to third countries necessary?* (Section III). After discussing this question in the context of the First Pillar (section III A), we will discuss the question in a subsequent paragraph with regard to Third Pillar processing (sections III B to E). We contend that the current data protection patchwork in the Third Pillar is not wholly satisfactory with regard to the issue of controlling transfers of data to third countries. We illustrate this with Europol, the PNR case and the Swift case. The latter PNR and Swift examples show that not all aspects of Third Pillar processing are covered by the current EU framework, as important aspects are delegated to the legal regimes of the different Member States. The Europol example shows us that the EU is in need of a general standard setting with regard to international transfers, complementing the current piece-meal approach.

Subsequently, this contribution will briefly outline the draft framework decision that was forwarded by the Commission to the Council in December 2005 (section IV). Finally, a summary and some concluding remarks will be in section V.

II.   The EU regulatory framework on data protection

A.   Directive 95/46/EC and Regulation (EC) No 45/2001

When pursuing its internal market objective at the beginning of the 1990s, the European Commission launched a package of measures for data protection. The core of these measures was a draft proposal for a Directive on the protection of personal data aiming at establishing the same level of protection within all Member States.[23] In 1995, after five years of discussions, the first and major instrument for data protection was established on European Community level by Directive 95/46/EC on the protection of individuals with regard to the processing of personal data and on the free movement of such data (Directive 95/46/EC).[24] This First Pillar instrument regulates the processing of personal data (defined as any information relating to an identified or identifiable natural person[25]) by laying down guidelines determining when the processing is lawful, and prohibiting the processing of special categories of data (e.g. personal data revealing racial or ethnic origin, political opinions, religious or philosophical beliefs, trade-union membership, and of data concerning health or sex life). The Directive specifies the information to be given to the data subjects and their rights, and establishes a series of other guidelines concerning the quality of the data, the legitimacy of the data processing, the data subject's right of access to data, the right to object to the processing of data, confidentiality and security of processing, the notification of processing to a supervisory authority and the right to a judicial remedy. Member States are asked to ensure that one or more public authorities (supervisory authorities) monitor the application within their territory of the provisions adopted pursuant to the Directive.

In the logic of Directive 95/46/EC, the transfer of personal data between EU states[26] is put on equal footing with transfer of data within one legal

23.   Draft Directive concerning the protection of individuals in relation to the processing of personal data (COM[90]314 final).
24.   Directive 95/46/EC of the European Parliament and of the Council on the protection of individuals with regard to the processing of personal data and on the free movement of such data, OJ L 281, 23.11. 1995, p. 31-50.
25.   "An identifiable person is one who can be identified, directly or indirectly, in particular by reference to an identification number or to one or more factors specific to his physical, physiological, mental, economic, cultural or social identity".
26.   We will come back *below* to the system of control set up with regard to transfers of data to Third Countries.

regime.[27] The Data Protection Directive applies throughout the EU, irrespective of whether the individuals concerned by the processing are EU citizens or not. The right to privacy of citizens has, as a result of the Directive, equivalent protection across the Union and at the same time, the Directive ensures that companies and other organizations will be able to transfer personal data throughout the EU. Jurisdiction also covers the EEA countries. Subjects wishing to control the use of their data in other Member States can call for assistance to their national data protection authority, which will call upon its colleagues to carry out the control. A similar logic was already built into Article 12 of the 1981 Council of Europe Convention. The second paragraph of this provision states that parties *"shall not, for the sole purpose of the protection of privacy, prohibit or subject to special authorisation transborder flows of personal data going to the territory of another Party"*.

Directive 95/46/EC was complemented by Regulation (EC) No 45/2001[28], which provides for criteria with regard to the lawfulness of processing personal data, the transfer of personal data within or between Community institutions or bodies, transfer of personal data to recipients other than Community institutions and bodies, but subject to Directive 95/46/EC, and transfer of personal data to recipients, other than Community institutions and bodies, which are not subject to Directive 95/46/EC. Like the 1995 Directive, the regulation defines 'personal data' and special categories of processing and provides all kinds of data regulations guidelines, e.g. on information to be given to the data subject. Nevertheless, the Community institutions and bodies can restrict the application of certain articles where the restriction constitutes, among other foreseen exemptions, a necessary measure to safeguard the prevention, investigation, detection and prosecution of criminal offences.

---

27. Cf. Directive 95/46/EC, Recital 3 "Whereas the establishment and functioning of an internal market in which, in accordance with Article 7a of the Treaty, the free movement of goods, persons, services and capital is ensured require not only that personal data should be able to flow freely from one Member State to another, but also that the fundamental rights of individuals should be safeguarded". Cf. also Recital 9 "Whereas, given the equivalent protection resulting from the approximation of national laws, the Member States will no longer be able to inhibit the free movement between them of personal data on grounds relating to protection of the rights and freedoms of individuals, and in particular the right to privacy (…)".
28. Regulation (EC) No 45/2001 of the European Parliament and of the Council of 18 December 2000 on the protection of individuals with regard to the processing of personal data by the Community institutions and bodies and on the free movement of such data, OJ L 8, 12.1.2001, p. 1-22.

Regulation (EC) No 45/2001 also established the European Data Protection Supervisor (EDPS), making him responsible for monitoring the application of its provisions to all processing operations carried out by a Community institution or body. Besides, each Community institution and Community body must appoint at least one person as data protection officer to cooperate with the European Data Protection Supervisor and in particular to inform him of certain sensitive data processing operations. The European Data Protection Supervisor is also requested to cooperate with the national supervisory authorities established under Directive 95/46/EC. According to his mission statement,[29] the EDPS has three sets of tasks: supervision (monitoring), consultation and cooperation.

B.   Directive 95/46/EC, Regulation (EC) No 45/2001 and JHA

According to its Article 3 (2), Directive 95/46/EC does not apply to the processing of personal data in the field of JHA. It explicitly does not apply to the processing of data in the course of an activity which falls outside the scope of Community law, such as those provided for by Title VI of the Treaty of the European Union. Like Directive 95/46/EC, Regulation (EC) No 45/2001 does not apply to activities falling completely within of the Third Pillar,[30] nor do its provisions apply to bodies fully established outside the Community framework. With regard to activities of the institutions under the Third Pillar, the European Data Protection Supervisor has no monitoring competence, since he is not competent to monitor the processing of personal data by bodies established outside the Community framework. The task of supervision by the EDPS relates exclusively to Community institutions and bodies and it is fulfilled by carrying out prior checks, informing data subjects, hearing and investigating complaints, conducting other inquiries and taking appropriate measures where needed.

However, both the Data Protection Directive and Regulation (EC) No 45/2001 do have an impact on the processing in the field of JHA. In this sense, it can be mentioned that, after 1995, the Directive caused a wave of reform of the then existing data protection laws in the Member States and, in most cases, that the reforms were of a general nature, affecting data protection principles that apply to all processing, including processing carried out by police and the judiciary. One can therefore assume that, as a result of the

---

29. As included in the Annual Reports of the EDPS over 2004 and 2005. Available at: www.edps.europa.eu.
30. Cf. Regulation (EC) No 45/2001, Recital 15.

Directive, differences between legal provisions of the Member States were reduced, including differences with regard to processing in the field of justice and home affairs.

Moreover, the Directive established a European Group of data protection Commissioners in its Article 29 of Directive 95/46/EC and this European Group is known as the "Article 29 Working Party". This unique data protection lobby is composed of a representative of the supervisory authority or authorities designated by each Member State and of a representative of the authority or authorities established for the Community institutions and bodies, as well as a representative of the Commission. The independent advisory body examines *any* question covering the application of the national measures adopted under the Directive in order to contribute to the uniform application of such measures, and advises the Commission on *any* proposed amendment of the Directive, as well as on any additional or specific measures to safeguard the rights and freedoms of natural persons with regard to the processing of personal data and on any other proposed Community measures affecting such rights and freedoms.[31] Therefore, the Working Party may, on its own initiative, make recommendations on *all* matters relating to the protection of persons with regard to the processing of personal data in the Community. The Article 29 Working Party has played an important role not only at Community level, but also regarding Third Pillar issues. Indeed, although originally established by a First Pillar instrument and as a First Pillar body, the Article 29 Working Party has tended to position itself as the watchdog of EU data protection in general[32] – especially until the establishment of the European Data Protection Supervisor in 2004. Moreover, it has established close cooperation with the EDPS, which is a full member of the Working Party, as well as with the Joint Supervisory Authority under the Schengen Convention.[33] It has intervened and drawn world attention to crucial data protection issues with Third Pillar relevance such as the PNR-case (*infra*) and the Swift case (*infra*) and has advised the European Parliament with regard to data retention regulation (*infra*).

31. Article 30 of Directive 95/46/EC.
32. In this sense, HIJMANS has noted that the Art. 29 WP has come to see itself as *"the independent EU Advisory Body on Data Protection and Privacy"* (H. Hijmans, "The European Data Protection Supervisor: the Institutions of the EC controlled by an independent authority", 43 [2006] *Common Market Law Review,* p. 1313.
33. There are some tensions between the national data protection authorities on the one hand and the EDPS on the other hand. These tensions will not be discussed here. Obviously the EDPS, being a new body (*infra*) has still to find his place, but this will probably be a question of time.

Even though we noted that the EDPS is in general terms not competent to supervise the processing of data performed in the context of the third pillar, the EDPS is competent for monitoring the data processing of the central part of the Schengen Information System of the second generation (SIS II), which will operate with Community financing. Also, the EDPS has the specific task of the supervision of the Central Unit of Eurodac (Article 20 of the Eurodac Regulation)[34] and, as Hijmans rightly observes, similar tasks are foreseen as regards other large scale information systems on persons in the area of freedom, security and justice.[35] In addition, Article 46(f)(ii) of Regulation (EC) No 45/2001 states that the EDPS has to cooperate with the national supervisory data protection bodies established under Title VI of the Treaty, allowing the EDPS to become an important actor in the organisation of Third Pillar data protection.

In his mission statement,[36] the EDPS describes his consultative task as follows: "*Advising the Community institutions and bodies on all matters relating to the processing of personal data, including consultation on proposals for legislation, and monitoring new developments that have an impact on the protection of personal data*". The EDPS understands the scope of the consultative task as being much wider than his supervisory task, which only covers the processing of personal data by Community institutions or bodies. This wide interpretation was confirmed by the European Court of Justice in the so called *PNR* case (see *below*). Indeed, the Court explicitly referred to Article 41(2) of Regulation 45/2001, according to which the EDPS is responsible for advising Community institutions and bodies on all matters concerning the processing of personal data. This includes, according to two orders of the Court of the First Instance, the connection between the legislation relating to data protection and that relating to the preservation of other interests.

---

34. Council Regulation (EC) No 2725/2000 of 11 December 2000 concerning the establishment of "Eurodac" for the comparison of fingerprints for the effective application of the Dublin Convention, OJ, L 316, 15 December 2000, p. 1-10.
35. H. Hijmans, above note 31, p. 1120 with ref. to Proposal for a Regulation of the European Parliament and of the Council concerning the Visa Information System (VIS) and the exchange of data between Member States on short stay-visas, COM(2004)835 final. And the three Proposals regarding the Second Generation Schengen Information System (SIS II),(COM(2005)230 final, COM(2005)236 final and COM(2005)237 final.
36. As included in the Annual Reports of the EDPS over 2004 and 2005. Available at: www.edps.europa.eu.

C. Data protection in the field of JHA: the current state

The foregoing may not blind us to the current general state of affairs. Whilst for First Pillar processing the EU legislative framework, together with some forty years of legislative history in some EU states (Germany, France, Sweden), has led to a well-regulated and clearly-defined processing environment for all commercial processing of personal information, unfortunately this is not the case with Third Pillar processing. The Data Protection Directive expressly excluded such processing from its scope (see *above*) and, although some EU Member States saw it fit to regulate such processing through their own national Data Protection Acts, this by no means constitutes the norm. Quite to the contrary, apart from a Council Convention of 1981 and a couple of Recommendations, the field is left basically unregulated. The EU Third Pillar patchwork is supplemented with the national rules on data protection in the field of JHA, but these rules are only consistent up to a certain degree (with very little attention to the problem of transfers to third countries). Criticism concerning this situation has lately become more pronounced.

In this sense, during the public seminar on transatlantic data transfers held at the European Parliament in March 2007[37], Yves Poullet expressed his concern regarding the absence of uniform data protection standards throughout all three pillars.[38] Peter Hustinx, the current EDPS, noted at the same seminar that the lack of the trans-pillar common framework creates problems during negotiations with third countries on, e.g. PNR agreements.[39] Indeed, the present situation raises the issue of a double standard with regard to, for instance, the US authorities, who are asked to respect the information privacy of Europeans in their anti-terrorist

37. Public Seminar: European Parliament: PNR/SWIFT/Safe Harbour: Are transatlantic data protected? (Transatlantic relations and data protection), Monday 26 March 2007 (see http://www.europarl.europa.eu/hearings/default_en.htm)
38. Y. Poullet, 'Transborder Data Flows and Extraterritoriality: The European Position', paper presented at Public Seminar: European Parliament: PNR/SWIFT/Safe Harbour: Are transatlantic data protected? (Transatlantic relations and data protection), Monday 26 March 2007, 17 p. (available at http://www.europarl.europa.eu/hearings/20070326/libe/poullet_en.pdf).
39. P. Hustinx, 'Concluding remarks', presented at Public Seminar: European Parliament: PNR/SWIFT/Safe Harbour: Are transatlantic data protected? (Transatlantic relations and data protection), Monday 26 March 2007, unpublished.

campaign, whereas the European institutions themselves do not necessarily follow those standards.[40]

It could be argued that the current Third Pillar situation is extremely problematic. Rather than proceeding rationally, by first establishing the general principles, the institutions and the definitions, and then entering into case-specific legislation (as has been the case within the First Pillar), the EU has already introduced case-specific regulations (Schengen, Europol, Eurojust) while still lacking any standard-setting piece of legislation. One could respond to this argument that a piece-meal approach has the advantage of depth and insight. Indeed, the Schengen Agreement, but also Europol and Eurojust Agreements, all include detailed data protection rules and processes in their own texts, very much along the lines of the Directive, but skillfully adapted to their specific purposes. A major drawback of this approach is that it requires that new legislation be introduced with each new technology or new processing operation, with the result that protection frequently lags behind.

We cannot discuss at great length this choice between a comprehensive model of regulation and a sectoral or piece-meal approach. Let us simply observe that both in the United States and the EU there seems to be a development towards a middle position, by using sectoral laws to complement comprehensive legislation with more detailed protections for certain categories of information, such as telecommunications, police files or consumer credit records. The Third Pillar situation contrasts with this. What we are effectively faced with today is a series of sectors that are well-regulated by means of their own texts of reference (Schengen, Europol, Eurojust), but without a uniform basis that would set the standards (e.g. definitions, administrative system, principles) when it comes to police and judicial processing of personal information, in the way that the Directive 95/46/EC performs this task for commercial communications. Some important standard setting took place in the 1981 Council of Europe Convention and Council of Europe Recommendation No R(87) of 17 September 1987 concerning the use of personal data in the police

---

40. Although it can be pointed out that the US authorities tend to use this argument of "double-standards" repeatedly, and also declared that EU applied "double-standards" in First Pillar matters while negotiating the Safe Harbor Agreement, because some breaches to the Data Protection Directive were believed to take place in the EU territory.

sector, but there may be reasons to question the accuracy of these documents for today's EU needs. One realizes that this discussion would take us far away from our subject matter. We certainly do not agree with those who say that there is currently a loophole in the EU data protection system, but it must be clear that there is reason to doubt the coherence and clarity of this system.

III. The need for a European regulatory framework on data transfers to third countries

Before drawing any conclusions, we return to our central topic and take one step back by asking one very basic question about the need for an EU approach with regard to transfers of personal data to third countries: *Is a European regulation of data transfers to third countries necessary?* Having discussed this question in the context of the First Pillar in the next paragraph (sub-section A), we shall discuss it in subsequent paragraphs with regard to Third Pillar processing (sub-sections B to D).

A. Centralised or de-centralised regulatory models for transfers of data to Third States and the choice of the Directive

The question whether a European regulation of data transfers to third countries is necessary was raised in the early nineties with regard to the First Pillar and is raised again today with regard to the Third Pillar. The choice is between letting Member States decide for themselves about protecting data transferred to Third States and creating European supervision of these transfers. Both options have their merit. The first option could be called the model of decentralized decision-making, i.e. the adoption of policies at the level of the EU Member States without any attempt at coordination. One can defend this model claiming that it will produce the most adequate results, as this decentralized approach may prevent bureaucracy and ensure a better fit between the kind of regulation involved and the specific local conditions, thus contributing to overall efficiency.

The second option is the one followed in Directive 95/46/EC. The Directive requires Member States to permit transfers of personal data only to countries outside the EU where there is adequate protection for such data.[41] The 'adequacy' criterion constitutes typical regulatory "gunboat

---

41. Article 25, Directive 95/46/EC.

diplomacy", which was by no means invented in the EU. The USA, for instance, has implemented the same approach in the case of the Semiconductor Chip Protection Act 1984. It is however the EU that applied this criterion in the data protection field in its relationships with third countries. According to the Data Protection Directive, "the Member States shall provide that the transfer to a third country of personal data which are undergoing processing or are intended for processing after transfer may take place only if, without prejudice to compliance with the national provisions adopted pursuant to the other provisions of this Directive, the third country in question ensures an adequate level of protection" (Art. 25.1). Article 25 also contains the procedure to determine whether there is an adequate regime.[42] It is striking that the Commission, and not the Member States, has the last say in the procedure, although the participation of a 'comitology' committee was incorporated in the decision-making process to reinforce control by national authorities.[43]

When there is no adequate protection, transfers may only take place in circumstances specified in Article 26. This will be the case, for example, if:

– an individual has given his unambiguous consent to the transfer;

– the transfer is necessary for the performance of a contract (e.g. employment contracts) or for the implementation of pre-contractual measures taken in response to his/her request (e.g. application for a job);

42. Cf. Article 25, paragraph 2, Directive 95/46/EC. Pursuant to this provision, the level of data protection should be assessed in the light of all the circumstances surrounding the data transfer operation or set of data transfer operations. The Working Party on Protection of Individuals with regard to the Processing of Personal Data has issued guidelines to facilitate the assessment: WP 4 (5020/97), *First Orientations on Transfers of Personal Data to Third Countries – Possible Ways Forward in Assessing Adequacy*, a discussion document adopted by the Working Party on June 26, 1997; WP 7 (5057/97) Working document: *Judging Industry Self-Regulation: When Does it Make a Meaningful Contribution to the Level of Data Protection in a Third Country?*, adopted by the Working Party on January 14, 1998; WP 9 (5005/98) Working Document: *Preliminary Views on the Use of Contractual Provisions in the Context of Transfers of Personal Data to Third Countries*, adopted by the Working Party on April 22, 1998; WP 12: *Transfers of Personal Data to Third Countries: Applying Articles 25 and 26 of the EU Data Protection Directive*, adopted by the Working Party on July 24, 1998, available at the website europa.eu.int/comm/internal_markt/en/media.dataprot/wpdocs/wp12/en.
43. Cf. Article 31, Directive 95/46/EC.

- the transfer is necessary or legally required for the establishment, exercise, or defence of legal claims;

- the transfer is necessary in order to protect the vital interests of the individual (e.g., transfer of medical data concerning an individual hospitalised in a non-EU country).[44]

Other exceptions are provided by the Directive and show that, even for data flows to those countries that do not ensure an adequate level of protection there are a great many bridges and doors. For some of these doors, the individual holds the key. However, the existence of exceptions is not enough to re-assure business. For the fact is that even in the best-case scenario a number of non-EU countries fall short of an adequate level of protection, and individuals may be reluctant to give their consent to the transfer to such countries of their personal data.

The Data Protection Directive pays due attention to this reality. Another door remains open even if the above conditions are not met, and this time the key to the door are held by the industry itself.[45] Companies operating worldwide may indeed wish to establish safeguards that make them less dependent on the good will of the legislators in a given country. Article 26 (second paragraph) recognises that adequate safeguards may be provided by the company itself and that these safeguards may in particular result from appropriate contractual clauses. When there is no adequate protection and the exemptions in Article 26 do not apply, the transfer must be forbidden ('blocked').

However, this radical step, possibly causing disruption to international data flows and commercial transactions, is not the general rule. Not only are there many exceptions and is there the possibility to adopt contractual clauses, but there is also a complex procedure concerning the possible decision to block: Member States must inform the Commission, which will start a Community procedure to ensure that any Member State decision to block a particular transfer is either extended to the EU as a whole or reversed.[46] Moreover, Article 25(4) of the Directive states that decisions to

---

44. As shown above, the Directive applies to transfers of data that take place in the course of direct contacts with individual consumers on the Internet. It might be argued that an individual transferring his own data has given his consent to such a transfer; one of the exemptions in Article 25 allowed by Article 26, provided that such an individual is properly informed about the risks involved. Cf. http://europa.eu.int/comm/internal_market/en/media/dataprot/backinfo/info.htm, November 3, 1998.
45. Cf. European Commission, *Data Protection: Background Information*, November 3, 1998, 10p. (www.europa.eu.int/comm/internal_market/en/media/dataprot/backinfo).
46. The Committee and the Working Party assist the Commission in this task.

block transfers are taken on specific individual cases. This implies that a decision to block a transfer would only apply to other transfers of the same type, not to all transfers to the country concerned. Everything in the Directive is designed to keep the scope of blocking decisions as narrow as possible.

B. The adequacy principle and the idea of a safe data protection harbour

The Directive requires all personal data transferred to countries outside the Union to benefit from 'adequate protection'. Transfers of personal data to countries outside the EU where there is *adequate protection* for such data cannot be blocked. The Data Protection Directive only prevents transfers of personal data to third countries where the level of data protection is considered 'inadequate'.

It must be pointed out that the European approach to the 'adequacy' requirement is not very strict and does not demand as high a level of protection as ensured under the First Pillar. As Poullet explains, according to the "Methology Paper" adopted by the Article 29 Working Group in 1998, the concept of "adequate protection" has to be distinguished from other concepts like "equivalent protection" or "sufficient protection". According to the paper: "With the adequate protection requirement, the question to be solved is ...: considering the specific privacy risks linked with a TBDF and taking into consideration the number and quality of the data transferred, the types of usages pursued by the transfer, the eventual onward transfers, etc., can we consider that the Data Protection of the data subjects is or not effectively ensured following the main requirements of the EU directive."[47] Therefore, Poullet characterises the European approach to the standard of adequate protection as pragmatic, relying on self-regulation, and functional and risk-oriented[48].

The overall policy of the Commission is to negotiate with countries that have a questionable reputation for data protection. The case of the US is well known. Because US data protection is non-statutory and there is no independent data protection authority, it is regarded as inadequate by definition. Yet, blocking the transfer of business data to the USA was widely considered to be unthinkable. Therefore, the European Commission adopted, on 26 July 2000, a decision on the adequacy of the level of data

---

47. Y. Poullet, above note 37, 8.
48. Y. Poullet, above note 37, 8-9.

protection in the US with the EU Data Protection Directive.[49] The decision, containing the Safe Harbour principles,[50] entered into force on 1 November 2000.[51] The Commission decision specifies the conditions for an adequate level of protection in the US concerning the transfer of data from the European Community to the United States. By agreeing to the Safe Harbour principles, US business will therefore be able to collect data and transfer personal data between the US and the EU Member States. In this way, US organisations can keep in line with the European data protection principles, create trust and confidence, and develop best business practice.

This construction is intended only for the US (and applies only to data transmitted from the EU to the US, and not *vice versa*). Major US business concerns, such as Microsoft, have accepted the principles, thereby allowing the transfer of personal data across the Atlantic. The software giant also goes a step further and uses the EU standards as a basis for its information transfers around the globe.[52] This voluntary extension may be interpreted as an indication of the potential of the Safe Harbour principles for international acceptance.

C.   The adequacy principle in the field of JHA?

The rule regarding transfers to third countries in the First Pillar is clear: transfers of personal data from a Member State to a third country are authorised only if the third country can guarantee an adequate level of protection. The question that needs to be addressed here is whether that rule should apply also in the Third Pillar. Against that position one could

---

49. Commission Decision of 26 July 2000 pursuant to Directive 95/46/EC of the European Parliament and of the Council on the adequate protection of personal data provided in Hungary, (2000/519/EC), OJ L215, 25.08.2000, p. 4-6

50. It is stipulated that US companies should comply with seven basic principles. Notably, they must inform customers and employees about why they collect and use information. Companies also must offer consumers the option to choose not to have their personal information disclosed (opt-out policy). Finally, companies must allow consumers or employees to access information collected about them so that they can correct, amend, or delete it. Important for what will follow is the provision in the Safe Harbour document stating that "Where, in complying with the Principles, an organization relies in whole or in part on self-regulation, its failure to comply with such self-regulation must also be actionable under Section 5 of the Federal Trade Commission Act prohibiting unfair and deceptive acts or another law or regulation prohibiting such acts".

51. For the principles, see: www.export.gov/safeHarbour/.

52. See 'Microsoft to adopt EU's data privacy rules', *Financial Times*, www.qlinks.net/items/qlitem10661.htm.

argue that law enforcement is of public interest, which in many cases deserves priority treatment over privacy considerations. One could add that law enforcement authorities are to be trusted to protect data as part of their duty to uphold professional secrecy; that these authorities only demand data on a case-by-case basis and that the judiciary especially is committed to a strong regulatory framework limiting the possible use of data received. Reference could be made to the fact that Interpol, the world's largest international police organization with 186 member countries, is working on the basis of self-imposed data protection principles.[53] Of course, one could object that Interpol, like Europol (see *below*) is not illustrative of a model of decentralized decision-making, but rather underpins the usefulness of a channelled approach with some supervision. Perhaps a better illustration of the decentralized model is given by the rules governing the exchange of data between judicial authorities. This kind of exchange was originally based on bilateral agreements, but later picked up on a supranational level through the European Convention on Mutual Assistance in Criminal Matters of 20 April 1959[54] and other Conventions. The EU complemented this framework with the EU 2000 Convention on Mutual Assistance in Criminal Matters between the Member States of the European Union,[55] which is particularly innovative with respect to personal data protection. Indeed, Article 23 of the 2000 Convention contains the first supranational rules establishing data protection requirements for the judiciary in their cross border activities – even though

---

53. Created in 1923, this organisation that has no formal legal basis in a convention, facilitates cross-border police co-operation, and supports and assists all organizations, authorities and services whose mission is to prevent or combat international crime. Interpol aims to facilitate international police co-operation even where diplomatic relations do not exist between particular countries. Action is taken within the limits of existing laws in different countries and in the spirit of the Universal Declaration of Human Rights. Interpol's constitution prohibits 'any intervention or activities of a political, military, religious or racial character.' For more than a decade this organisation, partly under pressure of host country France, has self-imposed data protection rules: On Rules adopted by the General Assembly at its 72nd session (Benidorm, Spain, 2003) in Resolution AG-2003-RES-04. Entered into force on 1 January 2004; Rules amended by Resolution AG-20054-RES-15 adopted by the General Assembly at its 74th session (Berlin, Germany, 2005), see http://www.interpol.com/public/icpo/default.asp. On Interpol, see P. De Hert & J. Vanderborght, *Informatieve politiesamenwerking over de grenzen heen* [Cross-border exchange of police data], Brussels, Uitgeverij Politeia nv., 1996, 635p.
54. Council of Europe, European Convention on Mutual Assistance in Criminal Matters signed at Strasbourg on 20 April 1959, *European Treaty Series.*, no. 30.
55. Convention established by the Council in accordance with Article 34 of the Treaty on European Union, on Mutual Assistance in Criminal Matters between the Member States of the European Union, OJ C 197, 12.07.200, p. 1-23.

they are very flexible and are clearly not intended to limit the work of the judiciary. According to Article 23, personal data communicated under the Convention may be used by the Member State to which they have been transferred:

(a) for the purpose of proceedings to which the Convention applies;

(b) for other judicial and administrative proceedings directly related to them;

(c) for preventing an immediate and serious threat to public security;

(d) for any other purpose, only with the prior consent of the communicating Member State, unless the Member State concerned has obtained the consent of the data subject.[56]

There is, as we can see, however, no requirement of adequacy. This requirement is certainly lacking in the many bilateral agreements on mutual assistance in criminal matters between the individual Member States and third countries. These agreements, which sometimes go back to the nineteenth century, traditionally ignore data protection principles and focus on more conventional principles of international criminal law, such as the principle of reciprocity and speciality. Moreover, the presence of an international agreement is not always mandatory, and some Member States engage in mutual assistance in criminal matters with third countries solely on basis of their national law and without any formal legal international or bilateral basis.

The foregoing shows that international cooperation in the field of JHA has functioned without requirement of adequacy and sometimes without data protection rules at all, and continues to do so. A requirement of adequacy in the field of JHA was, however, created with the 2001 Additional Protocol to the 1981 Council of Europe Convention.[57] The main purpose of this Protocol is to improve the application of the principles contained in the Convention by adding two substantial new provisions, one on supervisory authorities and one supplementing Article 12 of the Convention on transfer of data across national borders:[58] "*Each Party shall provide for the*

---

56. Article 23 paragraph 3 adds: "In the circumstances of the particular case, the communicating Member State may require the Member State to which the personal data have been transferred to give information on the use made of the data".

57. Additional Protocol to the Convention for the Protection of Individuals with Regard to Automatic Processing of Personal Data Regarding Supervisory Authorities and Transborder Data Flows, adopted by the Committee of Ministers on 23 May 2001, *European Treaty Series*, No. 179.

58. A. Blas, l.c., 7-8.

transfer of personal data to a recipient that is subject to the jurisdiction of a State or organisation that is not Party to the Convention only if that State or organisation ensures an adequate level of protection for the intended data transfer" (Additional Protocol, Article 2.1).

All the implications of this requirement in the Protocol are not immediately clear. What is its relationship with the bilateral agreements Member States have concluded with regard to mutual assistance in criminal matters with countries without data protection or adequate data protection? Can the EU, not being bound as such by the 1981 Council of Europe Convention, pursue a policy encouraging transfers to third countries in disrespect of the adequacy requirement? Is there a liability issue when the EU contributes to actions of Member States that disrespect this requirement? The examples of Europol, PNR and the Swift case may provide an answer to these questions.

D. Arguments in favour of the adequacy principle in JHA

1. Europol

The Europol Convention,[59] which formally established Europol, entered into force on 1 October 1998. Europol's tasks as they were defined were to facilitate the exchange of information between the Member States; to obtain, collate and analyse information and intelligence, to notify the competent authorities of the Member States without delay (via the National Units) of information that concerned them, and of any connections between criminal offences; to aid investigations in the Member States by forwarding all relevant information to the National Units; and to maintain a computerized system of collected information. Europol's data collection utilizes mainly three systems: an automatic information system, a work files system and an index system.[60] The information system contains all available data about persons suspected of or convicted for offences within Europol's mandate (Article 8 [1] Europol Convention). The work files refer to data about persons as mentioned in Article 8 (1) Europol

---

59. Convention Based on Article K.3 of the Treaty on European Union, on the Establishment of a European Police Office (Europol Convention). Available at: http://www.europol.eu.int/index.asp?page=legalconv, last consulted 24 August 2006. See T. Schalken, 'On Joint Investigation Teams, Europol and Supervision of Their Joint Actions' *European Journal of Crime,* 10 [2002] *Criminal Law and Criminal Justice,* p. 70.

60. P. De Hert, 'Les banques de données d'Europol', *Vigiles. Revue de droit de police*, 1996, no. 3, 36-44.

Convention as well as to possible witnesses, victims, or informants of such offences (Article 10 [1] Europol Convention).

With regard to data protection, each Member State acting within the framework of its national legislation, and Europol when collecting, processing and utilizing personal data, must take all necessary measures to ensure a standard that corresponds at least to the standard resulting from the implementation of the principles of the Council of Europe's 1981 Convention, and so doing, must take account of Recommendation No R(87) of 17 September 1987 concerning the use of personal data in the police sector. Each Member State must appoint a national supervisory body to independently monitor, and in accordance with its national law, the permissibility of the input, the retrieval and any communication to Europol of all personal data by the Member State concerned; it must also examine whether the rights of the data subject have not been violated. An independent joint supervisory body, the Europol Joint Supervisory Body, is set up to review the activities of Europol in order to ensure that the rights of the individual are not violated by the storage, processing and utilization of the data held by Europol.[61] This Joint Supervisory Body also monitors the permissibility of the transmission of data originating from Europol, and any individual has the right to request the Joint Supervisory Body to ensure that the manner in which his personal data have been collected, stored, processed and utilized by Europol is lawful and accurate.

In order to widen the exchange of information, Europol has over the years concluded numerous operational agreements[62] (including the exchange of personal data) and strategic agreements[63] (not including the exchange of personal data) with several third countries and organizations. The latter agreements, which are less interesting from a policing point of view, are reserved for countries with a questionable human rights or data protection track record.

By applying this double system, Europol appears to have taken the initiative to solve the data protection issue of international data transfers in the Third Pillar. On what basis does Europol distinguish between states with which operational agreements are concluded and states with which

---

61. Article 24.1 of Europol Convention. See on this body: http://europoljsb.ue.eu.int/.
62. Operational agreements signed: Bulgaria, Canada, Croatia (not yet ratified), Iceland, Norway, Romania, Switzerland, USA, FBI, United States Secret Service, Eurojust and Interpol. Operational agreement in progress: Albania, Australia, Bosnia Herzegovina, FYROM, Israel, Moldova, Monaco, Serbia & Montenegro and Ukraine.
63. Strategic agreements signed: Colombia, Russian Federation, Turkey, EU Commission, ECB, EMCDDA, OLAF, UNODC and WCO.

(only) strategic agreements are concluded? This is a relevant question, since the list of operational agreements is certainly too long from a data protection perspective. Given the lack of any provisions of general application, Europol has initiated exchanges with third countries that have not even been included in the list of countries that provide an 'adequate' level of protection according to the terminology and standards of the First Pillar (Directive 95/46). Moreover, the actual agreements that Europol has concluded are not satisfactory in terms of the protection of individual privacy (see, for instance, the agreement with the USA, and its inexplicably broad Articles 7 or 5).[64]

The foregoing shows that Europol has developed a system of self-regulation regarding international data transfers which though not wholly exempt from criticism constitutes an acceptable alternative in the light of the vacuum in which the organisation has to work and given the political pressure exercised on the organisation to cooperate with U.S. law enforcement agencies. Still, the situation is far from ideal since it puts the organisation in a delicate position.

Data protection provisions in the Europol Convention are impressively elaborate, and the overall image of how the Europol Joint Supervisory Body operates is rather positive. It might be that from a police perspective the existing rules are too strict, a situation that produces counter-productive results. There are signals for instance that Europol may be turning down requests by Member States to transfer data to third countries, while ignoring further action taken by these Member States. Rumour has it that if a Member State wants to transfer data via Europol to countries without data protection, say Nigeria, Europol will refuse to intervene and re-orient the case back to the Member State that took the initial initiative, with the message that it will have to consider the transfer based on its national legislation (which is quite often less strict in comparison with Europol). The Member State will then have to judge the legitimacy of the transfer in the light of its own regulations. This (possible) interplay between the European and the national level, which could eventually lead to forum shopping by police forces, is again far from ideal as far as data protection is concerned.

It should be said that the whole issue regarding Europol and data protection can be considered to be currently in a transitional phase, mainly for three reasons. Firstly, the so-called Third Protocol to the Europol

---

64. V. Mitsilegas, 'The New EU–USA cooperation on extradition, mutual legal assistance and the exchange of police data', 8 [2003] *European Foreign Affairs* Review, p. 515.

Convention, signed in 2003, has just entered into force.[65] It foresees a series of amendments to the Europol Convention, concerning inter alia the possibility of allowing data transfers to third bodies that do not ensure adequate levels of data protection.[66]

Secondly, with a view to changing the legal basis for the existence of Europol, the European Commission presented, on 20 December 2006, a proposal for a Council Decision establishing Europol, which should substitute the Convention.[67] Article 24 of the proposal allows communication of personal data to third bodies when deemed necessary for police purposes, and when 'the Union has concluded an international agreement with the third country, the international organisation or the third body concerned, which permits the communication of such data on the basis of an assessment of the existence of an adequate level of data protection ensured by that body'. The Union, and not Europol, will hence decide whether transfers can be allowed. It is uncertain whether this part of the proposal will be maintained. At a public hearing in the European Parliament,[68] it was said that Member States were opposed to this provision, without further explanation. At the same hearing, Europol officials observed that the new procedure would be more time consuming. Clearly, the law enforcement community has its reasons for opposing the proposals. However, from a data protection perspective, there is also reason for some criticism. Even if the proposal includes a provision allowing the Union to conclude international agreements with third bodies in which the assessment of an adequate level of data protection has been ensured, the foreseen assessment does not even require consultation of representatives of EU data protection authorities, and the adequacy criterion can suffer exemptions that do not even need to be communicated to those authorities.[69] Moreover, the proposal substantially modifies the general rules of decision-making for Europol – a change that has an impact

65. Council Act of 27 November 2003 drawing up, on the basis of Article 43(1) of the Convention on the Establishment of a European Police Office (Europol Convention), a Protocol amending that Convention, OJ C 2, 6.1.2004, p. 1.
66. Amending therefore Article 18 of the Europol Convention.
67. European Commission, Proposal for a Council Decision establishing the European Police Office (EUROPOL), COM (2006) 817, Brussels, 20 December 2006.
68. *Public Hearing on the The Future of Europol*, organised by the European Parliament, Committee on Civil Liberties, Justice and Home Affairs, Brussels, April 10, 2007.
69. See Opinion 07/07 of Europol Joint Supervisory Body with respect to the proposal for a Council Decision Establishing Europol, published 05/03/2007, available at: http://europoljsb.ue.eu.int/, p. 17.

also on the conclusion of data transfer agreements and that has not been unanimously welcomed.[70]

Thirdly, it has to be underlined that some of the provisions referring to data protection in the Europol legal instruments, notably those referring to international data transfers, might eventually contradict provisions in the currently discussed draft Proposal for a Framework Decision on data protection in police and judicial cooperation. Though the applicability of the draft proposal to Europol was originally not even envisaged, it now seems very probable, which raises the question of the relation between its provisions and Europol-specific provisions, particularly where international data transfers are concerned. It is indeed unclear which provisions would be applicable if contradictions occurred.

2.   The PNR Case

Since January 2003, European airlines flying into the United States are obliged to provide the U.S. customs authorities with electronic access to the data contained in their automated reservation and departure control systems, referred to as 'Passenger Name Records' (hereinafter 'PNR data'). In accordance with U.S. laws adopted following the terrorist attacks of 9/11, airline companies have to submit the data before or immediately after the airplane takes off and, if they fail to do so, they can be fined a maximum of $5,000 for each passenger whose data have not been appropriately transmitted. The PNR data comprise up to 34 fields of data, including not only names and addresses, but also contact details such as telephone numbers, email addresses, information about bank numbers and credits cards, and also about meals ordered for flights. The U.S. demand to access data held by European firms for billing purposes without passengers consenting to the transfer or without a proper legal basis for the transfer clearly violates European data protection regulations. The European Commission tried to solve the problem by negotiating with the U.S. officials a series of requirements, and later adopting a decision on adequacy based on Article 25 of the EC Directive on data protection,[71] the adoption of which meant that the Commission was convinced that that the US would

---

70. See Peers, Steve, "Europol: The final step in the creation of an "Investigative and Operational" European Police Force", available at www.statewatch.org/news/2006/oct/future-of-europol-analysis.pdf, p. 3-4.
71. Commission Decision 2004/535/EC of 14 May 2004 on the adequate protection of personal data contained in the Passenger Name Record of air passengers transferred to the United States' Bureau of Customs and Border Protection, OJ L 235, 6.7. 2004, p. 11.

ensure an adequate level of data protection for the transfers. This decision enabled the Council to adopt the Agreement of 17 May 2004 between the European Community and the United States of America[72] to officially allow the transfers.[73]

Obviously, the most difficult problem during the negotiations was the one related to the 'adequacy' criterion. Because the 'adequacy' of the suggested US processing of PNR data on European citizens had not yet been assessed, the Commission attempted to solve this problem as follows: it suggested to Council and Parliament that it would first issue a Decision incorporating an assessment of the US (CBP) processing in relation to the provisions of the Directive ("Adequacy Finding"), and that it would then enter an international agreement to deal with problems that would not be addressed by this Adequacy Finding – that is, the PNR Agreement. On February 23, 2004, the Council authorized the Commission to negotiate such an agreement with the USA and issued a series of negotiating guidelines. Accordingly, on March 17, 2004 the Commission made its final proposal to the Council so that the latter could issue a Decision *"on the conclusion of an Agreement between the European Community and the United States of America on the processing and transfer of PNR data by Air Carriers to the United States Department of Homeland Security, Bureau of Customs and Border Protection"*.

The first PNR Agreement was signed on May 28, 2004 in Washington. The Commission had previously issued its Decision *"on the adequate protection of personal data contained in the Passenger Name Record of air passengers transferred to the United States Bureau of Customs and Border Protection"*, and the Council had issued its own Decision, "on the conclusion of an Agreement between the European Community and the United States of America on the processing and transfer of PNR data by Air Carriers to the United States Department of Homeland Security, Bureau of Customs and Border Protection" [idem]. 'Adequacy' is guaranteed through a series of Undertakings by the US,[74] which constitute an integral part of the First PNR Agreement.

---

72. Council Decision 2004/496/EC on the conclusion of an agreement between the European Community and the US on the processing and transfer of PNR (*"Passenger Name Records"*) data, *Official Journal of the European Communities*, L 183, 20.5.2004, p. 83.
73. From a US perspective, the new instrument was intended to build upon the Aviation and Transportation Security Act of 2001.
74. See Secretary, Department of Homeland Security, 'Undertakings of the Department of Homeland Security Bureau of Customs and Border Protection (CBP)', *the Federal Register* (69 FR 41543-41547, 9 July 2004) Also; http://www.statewatch.org/news/2004/jul/PNR-Federal-REG-undertakings.pdf.

When negotiating these instruments, the Commission assumed that it was competent to do so on the basis of the provisions in Community law regarding transportation and data protection. However, the European Court of Justice, on 30 May 2006, annulled Council Decision 2004/496/EC and Commission Decision 2004/535/EC[75], arguing that they could not have their legal basis in EU transport policy (a First Pillar provision). A careful reading of the preamble to the EU-US agreement led the Court to conclude that its purpose was: to enhance security, to fight against terrorism, to prevent and combat terrorism; related crimes and other serious crimes, including organised crime; and to prevent flight from warrants or custody for those crimes. Thus, the Court held that the concerned data transfers fell within a framework established by the public authorities related to public security.[76] The Court judgement has been regarded as a failure for the European Parliament, which had launched the procedures, but mainly on a different ground, namely that Council Decision 2004/496/EC and Commission Decision 2004/535/EC accepted a disproportional transfer of data to the United States without proper data protection guarantees. This issue was simply not addressed by the Court,

---

75. European Court of Justice, Judgment of 30 May 2006, Joined Cases C-317/04 and C-318/04, European Parliament vs. Council and Commission, 2006 ECR I-4721.

76. L. Creyf & P. Van de Velde, 'PNR (Passenger Name Records): EU and US reach interim agreement', Bird & Bird Privacy & Data Protection Update, October 2006, no. 11, 2p. (http://www.twobirds.com/english/publications/newsletters/). On 3 July 2006, the Council and the Commission notified termination of the agreement with effect from 30 September 2006. On 7 September 2006, the European Parliament adopted a report in which it asked the Council to negotiate – under the Parliament's oversight – an interim agreement, whereby the Parliament wants to ensure that the US offers adequate protection of the passenger data collected and which should provide for a change to the "push"-system (under which US authorities must request specific data which will then be selected and transferred) instead of the present "pull"-system (whereby access is granted to the full database and airline passengers data are directly accessed online by the authorities concerned). In its report, the Parliament further requested joint decision-making rights over the negotiation of the final agreement with the U.S. On 6 October 2006, shortly after the Court-set deadline of 30 September, EU negotiators reached an interim agreement with their U.S. counterparts. The conflict of laws situation that existed since 1 October 2006 thereby appears to be, at least temporarily, solved. The interim agreement would ensure a similar level of protection of the PNR data as before and it would also comply with the US request that the PNR data can be more easily distributed between different US agencies. A move from the "pull"-system to the "push"-system should be undertaken at a later date. The nature of PNR data available to US agencies remains unchanged. The interim agreement will apply from its date of signature, which is due to be completed by 18 October, and will expire no later than 31 July 2007. By this date a new (superseding) agreement should be reached between the parties who meet again in November 2006 to begin discussions on that point.

which concentrated instead on the institutional arguments raised by the European Parliament. Even from this point of view, however, it is doubtful whether the outcome was really what the European Parliament was aiming for, since the result of the judgement was that any new agreement would have to be negotiated in the context of the Third Pillar, where the Parliament has less voice than in the First Pillar, and so it finds itself left out of the picture. Moreover, in the Third Pillar there is only limited control by the European Court of Justice, as its jurisdiction over these matters depends on whether each Member State has made a declaration allowing its national courts to refer questions to the European Court of Justice on Third Pillar issues.[77] Finally, there is the rejection of the 1995 Data Protection Directive as a proper legal basis. On the one hand, the European Court of Justice concluded that the collection of PNR data by the airlines falls within the scope of Community law, but on the other hand, it indicated that the data transfer for public security reasons of the same data does not benefit from the protection of the 1995 Data Protection Directive.[78] In his initial reaction to the PNR judgment, the European Data Protection Supervisor pointed out that this reasoning creates a loophole in the protection of citizens.[79] The judgement seemingly implies that the transmission of information to third countries or organisations from the future Visa Information System or SIS II would not be subject to the applicable rules of the 1995 Data Protection Directive, as long as the transmission is intended for police or public security use.

The practical results of the ECJ decision were, first, that the First PNR Agreement between the EU and the USA needed to be replaced, and, second, that the Second PNR Agreement would need to follow Third Pillar processes. Negotiations for the conclusion of the Second PNR Agreement began on July 2006, and were this time led by the Council. The Council authorised *"the Presidency, assisted by the Commission, to open negotiations for an Agreement with the United States of America on the processing and transfer of passenger name record (PNR) data by air carriers to the United States Department of Homeland Security"*. However, given the tight deadline and tense feelings raised within the EU by the Court's decision, its conclusion by September 2006 seemed unrealistic, so that an Interim PNR Agreement was suggested that would remain in effect until the end of 31 July 2007, when the second PNR Agreement should be concluded.

---

77. See Article 35 (3) EU Treaty.
78. In this light, the PNR judgment contrasts with the more liberal approach of the ECJ in its earlier judgment in the *Österreichischer Rundfunk* case.
79. EDPS first reaction to the Court of Justice Judgment, 31 mei 2006 <www.libertysecurity.org/article985.html>.

In accordance with Third Pillar procedures, negotiations between the USA and the (Finnish) Presidency, "assisted by the Commission", were completed on October 6, 2006. On October 16, 2006 the Council adopted a decision "authorising the Presidency to sign an Interim Agreement with the United States on the continued use of PNR data". The Interim PNR Agreement entered into force on October 18, 2006.

The Interim PNR Agreement accepts that "in view of the Undertakings issued on 11 May 2004 by DHS, Bureau of Customs and Border Protection, the United States can be considered as ensuring an adequate level of protection for PNR data transferred from the European Union concerning passenger flights to or from the United States". Consequently, the Undertakings upon which the First PNR Agreement was based are considered, for the Interim Agreement's purposes, as being still valid and ensuring an 'adequate' level of protection.

The distinction between pillars is a source of complexity, also with regard to data protection. From a legal point of view, the European Court of Justice has been clear in its judgement: the only factor to take into account in order to determine the scope of data processing is the nature of *the processing* itself, as opposed to the origin of the data. In this sense, the idea that the judgement creates *loopholes* in EU legislation could be discussed. Indeed, all processing either needs to be included in the exemptions to Directive 95/46/EC, or to fall under the terms of the Directive.

Despite the fact that such legal *loopholes* may not exist as such, it is undeniable that the *"use of commercial data for law enforcement purposes"* requires special protection provisions, different from those currently offered under the EU Third Pillar. As a result of the sectoral or piece-meal regulatory approach of data protection in this field, new legislation needs to be introduced with each new technology or new processing operation (*supra*). Again, this approach is not inherently wrong, although it may not always be desirable for the law to continually have to catch up with developing new practices. The real problem is that, in general, having to regulate data protection within Third Pillar institutions is far from easy and ideal. Member States have a greater say in the Third Pillar structure. So far, few commentators have defended the view that this structure has produced a good balance between security and privacy. This contrasts with the First Pillar, which offers institutional specificities such a reinforced participation of the European Parliament and a stronger role of the European Court of Justice, as well as more consistent data protection.

As we have seen, one of the major differences between EU data protection in the First and Third Pillars is that today there is no formal general requirement in the latter to declare that a third country ensures 'adequate' data protection to allow the transfer of data to said country. The second version of the PNR agreement signed between the EU and the US, approved in the framework of the Third Pillar, is nevertheless based on a Council Decision stating that 'adequate' protection will be provided by US authorities. The fact that such 'adequate' protection might indeed be provided is currently the subject of heated discussion, but it is probably impossible to prove. The general difficulties encountered by the EU in reviewing such 'adequacy' for US processing under the First Pillar, are compounded by the specific review limitations related to security matters. If it is not required by EU legislation to formally declare that the US authorities offer 'adequate' data, if it is possibly not even accurate and in any case subject to debate, then the point of making such a statement can be questioned.

3.   The Swift case

The credibility of the current EU data protection system has also been undermined by the so-called 'SWIFT case', which also showed that serious violations of data protection law manage to escape the supervision of the data protection authorities and finally need to be addressed at a different, political level. Swift ('Society for Worldwide Interbank Financial Telecommunication') is a worldwide financial messaging service that facilitates international money transfers. Swift stores all messages, including the personal data they contain (such as the names of payers and payees) for a period of 124 days at two operation centres, one within the EU and one in the USA – a form of data processing referred to as 'mirroring'. After the terrorist attacks of September 2001, the United States Department of the Treasury (UST) issued subpoenas requiring Swift to provide access to message information held in the USA. Swift complied with the subpoenas, although certain limitations to UST access were negotiated. Being a Belgian based cooperative, Swift is subject to Belgian data protection law implementing the 1995 Data Protection Directive. Moreover, the financial institutions in the EU using Swift's services are subject to national data protection laws implementing the Directive in the Member State in which they are established.

The case became public as a result of press reports in late June and early July 2006, leading to reactions by the Belgian government, the Belgian data protection authority, the EDPS and the Article 29 Working Party. Like most national supervisory authorities, the EDPS conducted an inquiry within its competence, focusing on the role of the European Central Bank.[80] The Article 29 Working Party called upon Swift and the EU financial institutions to take measures to remedy the illegal current state of affairs without delay. It declared, on 26 September 2006, that it considered it a *"priority to safeguard European data protection rights"*, that it criticised the lack of transparency surrounding the arrangements with the UST and that it called for clarification on the oversight on Swift.[81] On 22 November, the Article 29 Working Party unanimously adopted an opinion on the access by US authorities to EU banking data through Swift, in which the EU data protection authorities observed that both Swift and its client financial institutions shared joint responsibility, although in different degrees, for the processing of personal data as 'data controllers' within the meaning of Article 2(d) of the Directive. Although Swift bears the primary responsibility for the personal data transferred to the US, the financial institutions are also responsible for the way their clients' personal data are processed. This responsibility is now at stake, according to the Working Party, since continued transfer to the UST is a 'further purpose' not compatible with the original commercial purpose for which the personal data have been collected, within the meaning of Article 6(1)(b) of the Directive. The Article 29 Working Party stressed that in the Swift case there had been neither an adequate legal ground for the measures taken, nor independent control by data protection supervisory authorities. The hidden, systematic, massive and long-term transfers of personal data to third country authorities that had taken place, therefore constituted a violation of the fundamental principles of European data protection law.[82] Moreover, Swift could not rely on Article 25 of the Directive providing that the transfer of data to a third country might take place only if the third country in question ensures an adequate level of protection. None of the exemptions to this principle in Article 26 (1) of the Directive apply to the processing of data in the USA. Swift did not make use of the mechanisms

---

80. See EDPS, 'Swift case', EDPS Newsletter, no. 7, 14 December 2006, 1 (www.edps.europa.eu). All supervisory authorites decided to work on the Swift case in coordination in the framework of the Article 29 Working Party.
81. Article 29 Working Party, Opinion 10/2006 on the processing of personal data by the Society for Worldwide Interbank Financial Telecommunication (SWIFT) /06/EN WP128, 22 November 2006.
82. Neither Swift nor the financial institutions in the EU have provided information to data subjects about processing of their personal data, in particular as to the transfer to the USA, as required under Articles 10 and 11 of the Directive. The control measures put in place by Swift, in particular regarding UST access to the data, in no way replace the independent scrutiny that could have been provided by supervisory authorities established under Article 28 of the Directive.

under Article 26(2) of the Directive to obtain authorisation from the Belgian data protection supervisory authority for the processing operations.

It is not clear whether the Swift case will lead to court proceedings or not, as there seems to be little political will to go that far even if some contend that the Commission could take legal action against the Belgian government for failing to ensure Swift compliance with EC regulations.[83] It is clear however that all parties involved (Swift, financial institutions and Central banks) need to act to ensure that international money transfers occur in full compliance with data protection law, and to put an end to the regrettable lack of transparency which characterised the Swift case. The case is interesting because it highlights the legal uncertainty that governs EU data protection, especially after the PNR judgement. On the basis of the judgement, it could be argued that the 1995 Data Protection Directive does *not* apply, since the transfer serves enforcement purposes. This would imply that all depends on the national – especially Belgian – data protection laws. However, if the Directive does not apply, how could the Commission take legal action against national governments? There is a risk of 'loopholes' in the EU system of data protection, and there is most certainly a growing need to close them. Or is the EU again planning to create piece-meal regulation with specific data protection provisions? A question that has not been asked so far been raised is whether the Member States will always accept ad hoc interventions by the EU? What will happen if, in a case like the Swift case, one or more Member States oppose EU intervention and prefer to cooperate with third countries on their own terms (terms that will most likely not be supported by high data protection standards)?

IV. The draft Framework Decision on the protection of personal data in the field of JHA

Although some policy makers still question the need for a general data protection framework for the Third Pillar,[84] pressure by the European Parliament and growing insight into the matter has led to the elaboration

---

83. H. Spongenberg, 'SWIFT broke EU data laws', *EU Observer*, 23 November 2006. Available at: http://euobserver.com/9/22937/?rk= (last accessed 26 November 2006).
84. We repeat that there are good arguments for this position. The piece-meal regulation that has been produced so far is often of good data protection quality and in the case of Schengen, Europol and Prüm tailor-made in an exemplary manner.

of a new standard text on data protection in the Third Pillar, based on EU legal instruments (not on a Council of Europe Convention) to replace or complement the specific provisions governing initiatives such as Schengen, Europol and Eurojust.

On 4 October 2005, the Commission forwarded a proposal for a Council Framework Decision on the protection of personal data processed in the framework of police and judicial cooperation in criminal matters ("DPFD") to the Secretary-General of the Council.[85] On 13 December 2005, the Council consulted the Parliament on the proposal. The Parliament delivered its opinion on 27 September 2006. The European Data Protection Supervisor also delivered his opinion[86] on the proposal, which he presented to the Multidisciplinary Group on Organised Crime (MDG)-Mixed Committee on 12 January 2006. On 24 January 2006, the Conference of European Data Protection Authorities also delivered an opinion[87] on the proposal. The Commission presented its proposal to the meeting of the Council's *Multidisciplinary Group on Organised Crime* (MDG – Mixed Committee) on 9 November 2005. The MDG discussed the proposal at length and completed the third reading at its meeting on 15 and 16 November 2006. The work of the Commission and the interventions of the *Multidisciplinary Group on Organised Crime* was received with little enthusiasm. Lack of consensus within the group explained why in January 2007 the German Presidency, admitting that the Council had reached a stalemate, asked the European Commission to go back to the drawing board and prepare a 'revised' proposal.[88] At the meeting of the Article 36 Committee on 25 and 26 January 2007, the Presidency set out a series of basic guidelines[89] for revising the proposal, with the aim of removing outstanding reservations and making a real improvement in Third-Pillar data protection. The Presidency's revised draft of 13 March 2007 reflects

---

85. Commission, *Proposal for a Council Framework Decision on the protection of personal data processed in the framework of police and judicial cooperation in criminal matters*, (COM[2005] 475 final), 4 October 2005.

86. 16050/05 CRIMORG 160 DROIPEN 64 ENFOPOL 185 DATAPROTECT 8 COMIX 864.

87. 6329/06 CRIMORG 28 DROIPEN 12 ENFOPOL 26 DATAPROTECT 4 COMIX 156. 7315/07.

88. See page 4, point 7 in Presidency Note for discussion at the Article 36 Committee on 25-26 January: EU doc no: 5435/07.

89. 5435/07 CRIMORG 12 DROIPEN 4 ENFOPOL 5 DATAPROTECT 3 ENFOCUSTOM 9 COMIX 57.

those guidelines.[90] We first discuss briefly the general structure of the proposed text, and then address the provisions governing transfers of data to third countries.

The original 2005 proposal was drafted by the Commission along the lines of Directive 95/46. Taking into account that a solid instrument in the field of data protection already existed, that principles and national legislations were already in place and that the architecture of control was already established (supervising authorities, both at a national and at a European level) it would have appeared inconsistent if the proposed Framework Decision had not followed at least the pattern of the Directive.[91] Consequently, both the structure of the proposed Framework Decision and its approach to its subject matter is influenced by the Directive. The headings of the proposed Framework Decision are similar to those of the Directive and they cover scope and definitions in Chapter I, the general data protection principles in Chapter II, individual rights in Chapters IV, V and VI, the establishment of a Supervisory Authority (to be assisted by a Register) and a Working Party in Chapter VII. Only Chapter III of the proposed Framework Decisions, which defines the special types of processing and data transfers (principle of availability), is entirely unprecedented.

Like the Commission Proposal, the Presidency's revised draft of 13 March 2007 includes general rules on the lawfulness of the processing of personal data, provisions concerning specific forms of processing, rights of the data subject, confidentiality and security of processing, judicial remedies, liability, sanctions, national supervisory authorities, and the transfer to third countries. Modifications and amendments are suggested within all chapters of the draft; however, the most important and most far-reaching innovation made in this draft is the inclusion of article 26, which aims to combine the existing data protection supervisory bodies, which have hitherto been established separately for the Schengen Information System, Europol, Eurojust, and the Third-Pillar Customs Information System, into

90. COUNCIL OF THE EUROPEAN UNION, Proposal for a Council Framework Decision on the protection of personal data processed in the framework of police and judicial cooperation in criminal matters, Brussels, 13 March 2007 (15.03). The draft was submitted to the Article 36 Committee at its meeting on 22 and 23 March 2007. The first reading by the MDG was scheduled for 29 and 30 March 2007.
91. See Original Council Proposal, p.4. The Commission indicated that the Framework Decision "should not hamper consistency with the general policy of the Union in the area of privacy and data protection on the basis of the EU Charter for Fundamental Rights and of Directive 95/46/EC. The fundamental principles of data protection apply to data processing in the first and in the third pillar".

a single data protection supervisory authority, merging with it the advisory working party provided for in the earlier draft.

With regard to transfers of data to third countries, the October 2005 Commission proposal sets up a system similar to that of Directive 95/46, allowing some central control over the third countries to which national law enforcement agencies would send data. The *Multidisciplinary Group on Organised Crime* was very critical of this part of the proposal, preferring to leave the task of taking 'adequacy' decisions to Member States.[92] This position is echoed in the Presidency's revised draft of 13 March 2007. There is almost nothing in the draft on transfers to third countries. In the Preamble, it is said that where *"personal data are transferred from a Member State of the European Union to third countries or international bodies, these data should, in principle, benefit from an adequate level of protection"*,[93] but nowhere in the text is there an indication of the procedure or the criteria to be applied when assessing this norm. On the contrary, it is said that bilateral agreements undertaken by Member States are expressly not affected by the Framework Decision,[94] which could ultimately lead to problematic situations where, for instance, Belgium may deem that Nigeria provides 'adequate' protection, and thus exports its police records to it, while, at the same time, France thinks otherwise and prohibits such exports. In this example, a major problem could arise if Belgium acquired data from France under the principle of availability and wanted to send the data to Nigeria. For this type of situation, the Multidisciplinary Group on Organised Crime seems to have accepted as a last resort to require that "the competent authority of another Member State that has transmitted or made available the data concerned to the competent authority that intends to further transfer them has given its prior consent to their further transfer".[95] In the Presidency's revised draft of 13 March 2007, this consent requirement is incorporated in Article 14 ('Transfer to competent

---

92. See Art. 15 of Council's document 13246/13.11.2006 (available at: http://www.statewatch.org/eu-dp.htm).
93. Recital 12.
94. The final provisions (Chapter VII) now regulate the relationship to agreements with third countries saying that "This Framework Decision is without prejudice to any obligations and commitments incumbent upon Member States or upon the European Union by virtue of bilateral and/or multilateral agreements with third States" (Article 27).
95. See Art. 15(c) of Council's document 13246/13.11.2006 (available at: http://www.statewatch.org/eu-dp.htm).

authorities in third States or to international bodies').[96] Altogether, the model is weak and cannot be compared to the stronger central control of the First Pillar, and this even though the need for data protection is even more obvious in the Third Pillar than it is in the First Pillar.

V. Summary and Conclusion

The objective of this contribution was to assess the European Union's regulatory framework for data protection, in particular by comparing the approach under the First and Third Pillars. The starting point of the analysis was the fact that under the First Pillar, which covers all commercial processing of personal information, Directive 95/46/EC provides a common denominator for data protection, but that under the Third Pillar, which covers all crime-related and security-related processing of personal information, such a common standard does not exist at present, but that instead, a patchwork of data protection regulations covers different sector-specific processing (including the Schengen Agreement, SIS II, Europol, Eurojust and, recently, the Prüm Treaty).

In this contribution we have assessed the regulatory framework in the EU with regard to data protection, by contrasting the comprehensive model of regulation, as used for the First Pillar, with a sectoral or piece-meal approach, as is presently being used for the Third Pillar (section II). Section II A briefly highlighted the main features of the data protection system established by Directive 95/46/EC and Regulation 45/2001. It also briefly analysed the indirect impact of the First Pillar system on Third Pillar data transfers.

In sections III we discussed whether a European approach would be required to data transfers to third countries. Whereas such a European approach, based on the adequacy principle, is followed in the First Pillar, this is not the case for the Third Pillar. Though there may be arguments against such a European approach in the area of JHA (section III C), we analysed several cases, including the Europol, PNR and Swift cases, in which the absence of such a European approach was believed to have caused problems (section III D).

---

96. "Personal data received from or made available by the competent authority of another Member State may be transferred to third States or international bodies only if the competent authority of the Member States which transmitted the data has given its consent to transfer in compliance with its national law".

Without ignoring the benefits and arguments in favour of tailor-made regulations, we came to the conclusions that the example of Europol dealing with third countries, and of PNR and Swift, in part illustrated the lack of credibility of the current EU data protection system. Having to deal with externalities such as powerful third countries (in particular the U.S.) that do not always consult the EU officials when collecting 'European' data or data in (some) EU Member States, it would in our belief be beneficial to develop a general framework for data protection in the Third Pillar and for transfers of data to Third Parties with clear rules and responsibilities and a well-defined role for the EU institutions that live up to the European dimension behind cases such as PNR and Swift. We would even agree with Poullet that a uniform set of data protection standards applicable to all pillars would be desirable.

In this respect the 2005 Commission proposal for Council Framework Decision on data transfers to third countries was a welcome step forward. However, the scarcity of the provisions on transfers of data to third countries in the revised draft proposal for a Council Framework Decision on the protection of personal data processed in the framework of police and judicial cooperation in criminal matters of 13 March 2007 is not to be applauded and contrasts with the October 2005 Commission proposal setting up a Directive-like system, allowing some central control on the third countries to which national law enforcement agencies would send data. There might be good reasons for the *Multidisciplinary Group on Organised Crime* preferring to leave the task of taking 'adequacy' decisions to Member States. As a matter of fact there might be reasons to transfer data in the field of JHA even when there is no adequacy in a Third State, but these reasons do not justify the complete repudiation of a Directive-like system and its replacement by the current proposals. One can hope that the current choice for a system that relies on Member States will trigger a learning process between Member States leading, in the long-term, to the 'best' solutions becoming the rule.

In more general terms we have come to the conclusion that processing of personal data in the field of JHA is in need of a general framework with harmonized rules that avoid the risk of harmful regulatory competition between the regulatory regimes of the EU Member States, and that contribute to effective privacy protection by avoiding distortions resulting from the externalities which a purely decentralized model of implementation of data protection would risk ignoring. The European Commission presented its Proposal for a Council Framework Decision on the protection of personal data processed in the framework of police and judicial cooperation in criminal matters in October 2005.[97] The proposal did meet with strong resistance by the Member States, but it is our conviction that their alternatives are less satisfactory on the issue of regulating transfers of data to third countries. A net result of the latest proposal would be that the EU would be obliged to invent data protection standards on the issue, over and over again, with every new issue or demand to cooperate with third countries. This is clearly not an example of good regulation.

97. Commission, *Proposal for a Council Framework Decision on the protection of personal data processed in the framework of police and judicial cooperation in criminal matters,* (COM(2005) 475 final), 4 October 2005.

2. The EU-US Agreements on Extradition and on Mutual Legal Assistance

Guy Stessens[1]

I. Introduction and background to the negotiations

On 25 June 2003, Mr Petzalnikos, the Greek Minister of Justice, and Mr John Ashcroft, Attorney General of the United States of America, signed the EU-US Agreements on extradition and on mutual legal assistance in Washington D.C[2]. These agreements were the first to have been signed on behalf of the European Union on the basis of Articles 24 and 38 TEU. Over the past years, the European Union had already concluded a number of agreements on the basis of Article 24 TEU – a provision inserted in the Treaty on European Union by the Treaty on Amsterdam – but it was the first time that the European Union ventured to use this provision of the Treaty on European Union in the area of justice and home affairs (Title VI of the TEU), a possibility foreseen by Article 38 TEU.

In the immediate years following 25 June 2003, only on three other occasions similar agreements were signed by the EU, namely the Agreement of 19 December 2003 between the European Union and the Republic of Iceland and the Kingdom of Norway on Mutual Assistance in Criminal Matters between Member States of the European Union and the 2001 Protocol thereto, the Agreement of 28 June 2006 between the European Union and the Republic of Iceland and the Kingdom of Norway on the surrender procedure between the Member States of the European Union and Iceland and Norway[3], and the Agreement of 26 October 2004 between the European Union, the European Community and the Swiss Confederation concerning the latter's association to the implementation, application and development of the Schengen Acquis[4].

---

1. The opinions expressed in this contribution are personal to the author and do not necessarily coincide with those of the institution he works for.
2. OJ L 181, 19.07.2003, p. 1.
3. Both agreements have been published, together with the Council Decisions, in OJ L 26, 29.01.2004, p. 1 and L 292, 21.10.2006, p. 1.
4. OJ L 368, 15.12.2004, p. 26 (on the signing on behalf of the EU) and OJ L 370, 17.12.2004, L 370 (on the signing on behalf of the EC).

The EU-US Agreements came about as an immediate consequence of the terrorist attacks on the United States of America of 11 September 2002. The European Council, in its extraordinary meeting of 21 September 2001, made an offer to the US President to negotiate an agreement on judicial co-operation in criminal matters. Whereas the United States were initially foremost interested in facilitating extradition procedures (notably by removing or at least reducing the scope of the political offence exception and the nationals exception), the European Union was more keen to modernise mutual legal assistance methods. The offer to open negotiations was made in a spirit of great transatlantic solidarity following the tragic events of 11 September 2001, but the negotiations and especially the end of these (in the first half of 2003) were fraught with the transatlantic tensions caused by the Iraq war.

Hereafter the specific legal nature of the agreements will be discussed first, with particular attention to the role of the European Union as a Contracting Party and the relation to bilateral agreements. Thereafter, the main substantive provisions of both agreements will be briefly analysed.

II. The nature of Article 24-38 Agreements

A. Legal basis

1. *The European Union as a Contracting Party and the negotiation procedure*

a) *The European Union as a Contracting Party*

Article 24 was introduced into the Treaty on European Union by the Treaty of Amsterdam. It provides for a procedure for the negotiation and the conclusion of Agreements, but interestingly and contrary to what is the case for Community Agreements under Article 300 TEC, does not specify on behalf of whom these agreements are negotiated and concluded. The background to this is the discussion within the Intergovernmental Conference (ICG) which led to the Amsterdam Treaty. The reluctance of some Member States to recognise a legal personality for the European Union eventually led to a compromise, under which a procedure for the negotiation and the conclusion of agreements for matters falling under Title VI TEU was laid down, but the European Union was not mentioned as such[5]. This has inevitably raised the question on whose behalf these agreements are negotiated and concluded. The thesis that Article 24 TEU merely provides for a collective negotiation procedure for the Member States and that hence these agreements are contracted by the Member States does not seem tenable. Whilst paragraph 5 of Article 24 TEU indeed provides for a possibility for a Member State to make a statement in the Council to the effect that the agreement shall not be binding upon it until it has complied with the requirement of its own constitutional procedure, this does not amount to requirement of ratification by the Member States of the agreements thus concluded. Indeed, the overwhelming majority of agreements based on Article 24 TEU (over 70 at the time of writing) have been concluded without a Member State making use of the possibility of Article 24(5) TEU. (However, as will be discussed under (2), the vast majority of the Member States have made use of this possibility with regard to the EU-US Agreements on Extradition and Mutual Legal Assistance.) Title V of the Treaty on European Union taken as a whole demonstrates that the Union can act in a distinct manner from the Member States. Under the terms of Article 11 TEU it is the Union which 'shall define and implement a common foreign and security policy'. Agreements based on Article 24 TEU, which are concluded 'in implementation of this title' (Article 24(1) TEU) must therefore also be considered as binding on the European Union. It is the Union, and not the Member States, which is the Contracting party to such an agreement.

Article 24(4) TEU indicates that the provision of that Article shall also apply to matters falling under Title VI, which is confirmed by a provision of that Title, namely Article 38 TEU.

The fact that it is the Union, and not the Member States, which is the Contracting Party to an agreement concluded on the basis of Article 24 TEU gave rise to particular difficulties in the context of the negotiations of the EU-US Agreements. Whilst it was the Union which was contracting obligations under international law, it was clear to everyone that the execution of these obligations would be incumbent upon the Member States as it were their authorities which would be handling the extradition and mutual legal assistance cases. From a strictly EU law point of view this was not a problem as the Member States would be bound, by virtue of EU law, by the obligations contracted by the Union. For the US side, it did, however, pose a problem with regard to the relationship of the EU-US Agreement to the bilateral

---

5. See on this background: de Kerchove, Gilles and Marquardt, Stephan, Les accords internationaux conclus par l'Union européenne, in : *Annuaire Français de Droit International* (2004), pp. 806-807.

agreements. Apart from this problem, which will be discussed under (B), this particular situation in which the practical execution of the treaty obligations would, for the EU side, not be incumbent upon the Contracting Party, but upon the Member States, also created a terminological problem. As for many provisions it was not possible to refer to the 'Contracting Parties', the neutral term 'States' was chosen instead to refer to, one the hand, the United States of America and on the other, to the Member States, which would have to execute the obligation under the agreements.

b)   The negotiation procedure

The negotiation and conclusion of agreements based on Article 24 TEU are decided by an EU institution: the Council. The Council can act either as an EC institution or an EU institution, but in principle never acts on behalf of the Member States. It is clear that under Title V the Council acts as an EU institution.

Article 24 TEU states that the Council may authorise to open negotiations for an agreement 'when it is necessary (*i.e. when the Council deems it expedient*) to conclude an agreement with one ore more States or international organisations'. Paragraph 2 indicates that unanimity is required when the agreement covers an issue for which unanimity is required for the adoption of internal decisions.

The first decision to be taken by the Council is an authorisation for the Presidency to open negotiations with a third State. As a matter of practice, this authorisation is given by the Council with a number of negotiation instructions to the Presidency and is therefore also commonly referred to as the 'negotiation mandate'. Regarding the EU-US Agreements this decision was taken by the Council on 26 April 2002. The negotiation mandate is obviously a confidential document, which is not even communicated to the Parliament. The Parliament has no role in the negotiation and conclusion of Article 24 agreements, but in the case of the EU-US Agreements the Parliament was informally kept abreast of the development of the negotiations by the Presidency. The first negotiation session took place at the end of the Spanish Presidency in June 2002, but the bulk of the negotiations was conducted by the Danish and Greek Presidencies of the Council. In accordance with Article 24(1) TEU, the Presidency was assisted by the Commission. As has been pointed out elsewhere, the assistance of the Council Secretariat is of at least equal importance in the negotiation of this type of agreements[6].

---

6.   See de Kerchove, Gilles and Marquardt, Stephan, *l.c.*, 806.

During the negotiations, the Presidency at regular intervals reported to the relevant Council Working Parties on the state of play of the negotiations. Towards the end of the Greek Presidency, the EU and US sides eventually agreed on the texts of the agreements. At its meeting on 6 June 2003, the Council agreed to the texts as presented by the Presidency and adopted a Decision authorising the signing of the agreements. Article 24 TEU itself does not refer to this type of decision, but merely states that 'such agreements shall be concluded by the Council on a recommendation from the Presidency'. However, as it was clear that a large number of Member States would avail themselves of the possibility of making constitutional declarations under Article 24(5)TEU, the agreements could not yet be concluded, that is ratified by the European Union. At the same time, the United States needed to negotiate bilateral instruments with the Member States and needed to submit the agreements and the bilateral instrument to the US Senate for ratification.

The agreements can enter into force only once all Member States have gone through their constitutional procedures and the Council has adopted a second Council Decision, namely to authorise the Presidency to conclude the agreements. According to the provisions of the agreement concerning entry into force, the agreements shall enter into force on the first day following the third month after the date on which the Contracting Parties have exchanged instruments indicating that they have completed their internal procedures for this purpose. The agreements (Article 22 Extradition, Article 18 MLA) specify that these instruments must also indicate that the United States and all Member States have entered into bilateral instruments.

2.   The nature of constitutional declarations under Article 24(5) TEU

The fact that Article 24(5) TEU provides for a possibility for a Member State to make a statement in the Council to the effect that the agreement shall not be binding upon it until it has complied with the requirements of its own constitutional procedure, has given rise to some controversy. As argued above, the fact that it is a possibility, which in the vast majority of Title V agreements concluded on the basis of Article 24 TEU has not been used, demonstrates that this does not amount to a requirement of ratification by the Member States of the agreements. In reality it refers to a transitory situation in which Member States are not ready to apply the agreement precisely because they still need to comply with certain requirements of their constitutional proceedings. The fact that the Union is the Contracting Party and not the Member States of course begs the question why Member States would need to comply with certain constitutional proceedings, but this is ultimately a matter of domestic constitutional law and not of EU law. It seems that this question has equally puzzled Member State authorities. Given the fact that these agreements were the first agreements based on Articles 24 and 38 TEU, many Member States seemed unsure as to whether their constitution required them to follow certain constitutional procedures. However, only four Member States did not avail themselves of the possibility of Article 24(5) TEU: Austria, France[7], Greece and Romania. However, some of the other Member States, which did make a statement, eventually decided that their constitution did not require them to go through certain constitutional procedures with regard to the agreements. As to those Member States that have gone through constitutional procedures, it seems that they have opted to follow the same or similar procedures as those that are required in case of a treaty to which they as a State are a Contracting Party.

B.   Relationship to existing and future bilateral agreements

In the field of mutual legal assistance and extradition, the existing law enforcement relationships were moreover based on bilateral treaties between the Member States and the United States of America. At the time of negotiation, all Member States had bilateral extradition treaties in place with the United States of America and so had the ten plus two Member States that later joined the European Union. In the field of mutual legal assistance, eleven[8] out of fifteen Member States had a mutual legal assistance treaty (hereinafter referred to as 'MLAT') with the United States of America, as well as six of the ten plus two later Member States. For those Member States for which there was no MLAT with the United States of America, mutual legal assistance took place on the basis of reciprocity (comity).

Faced with this patchwork of bilateral treaties, some of which dated back to the beginning of the 20th century, the negotiators were faced with various options. The most drastic option would have been the replace all the bilateral treaty relationships with one (or two) EU-US Agreement(s) that would have covered all aspects of extradition and mutual legal assistance hitherto dealt with in the bilateral treaties. This option was not

---

7.   The French government decided this upon advice of the *Conseil d'Etat*: Avis n° 368.976.
8.   A twelfth Member State, Germany, finalised its bilateral negotiations on an MLAT with the United States, during the EU-US negotiations.

chosen, nor has it been seriously considered, probably because it would have implied that all the specificities of bilateral co-operation arrangements as expressed in the bilateral extradition treaties and MLATs would have been superseded by a 'one-size-fits-all' EU-US Agreement. Not only would such an approach have created important legal difficulties for (some) Member States, but to relinquish their complete treaty-making powers on extradition and mutual legal assistance to the European Union with a partner as important as the United States of America would also have been politically unacceptable to many Member States. Nor is it certain that the United States would have wanted to go down this avenue.

A second option would have been to establish a Mutual Legal Assistance Agreement between the European Union and the United States that would have applied only for those Member States that had not yet a bilateral mutual legal assistance treaty with the United States. Apart from the fact that such an approach would have applied only to mutual legal assistance an not to extradition (where all Member State already had bilateral treaties with the United States), it is questionable whether this approach would have been compatible with Article 24 TEU, which sets out the procedure for the Union *as a whole* to negotiate and conclude agreements. Whilst the voting procedure laid down in Article 23(1) TEU allows for 'constructive' abstention by one (or more) Member States, it does not seem possible to use the provision of Article 24 TEU to conclude an Agreement that would apply only to a number (in this case a minority) of Member States.

The option which was eventually chosen to determine the relationship between the EU-US Agreements and the bilateral treaties is laid down in Article 3 of both Agreements and is one by which the provisions of existing bilateral treaties are either substituted or supplemented by the provisions of the EU-US Agreements. This option will be discussed more in detail hereafter (1). The option to build upon the maze of existing bilateral treaties raised a number of questions, which will also be discussed hereafter: the question whether the grounds of refusal available under those bilateral treaties can still be invoked (2), at which level (EU or Member State level) operational difficulties will be resolved (3) and the question whether bilateral treaties can be further developed at bilateral level after the EU-US Agreements (4).

1.   *Substituting and supplementing bilateral extradition and mutual legal assistance agreements*

Articles 3(1) of both agreements stipulate the way in which each of the substantive provisions of both agreements shall be applied in relation to bilateral treaties in force at the time of entry into force of the agreements. Basically three different modes have been provided for in Article 3(1) in order to determine that relationship: (1) to apply the provisions of the agreements only in the absence of existing bilateral treaty provisions on the subject-matter, (2) to substitute the provisions of the agreements for the existing bilateral treaty provisions, or (3) to apply the provisions of the agreements both in lieu and in the absence of existing bilateral treaty provisions on the subject-matter.

The three different 'legislative' approaches all seek to arrive at more uniform rules on extradition and mutual legal assistance between the Member States and the United States of America. The differences between the three approaches reflect different attitudes towards the existing body of extradition and mutual legal assistance law in the bilateral treaties. For a number of subject matters the provisions in the bilateral treaties were deemed sufficient, but some bilateral treaties did not contain provisions on the subject matter and therefore only those bilateral treaties needed to be supplemented. Basically the first two 'modes' outlined above reflect this approach, as the substitution of the provisions of the EU-US agreements for existing bilateral provisions is normally restricted to 'old-fashioned' provisions. For some provisions (notably on capital punishment), the option was left to the Member States to apply them both in lieu and in the absence of existing bilateral treaty provisions on the subject matter. (For one provision, Article 7 on the transmission of extradition requests, it is specified that it shall apply in addition to bilateral treaty provisions, but with an exception for one Member State (Germany)[9]. Regarding the data protection provision of the Mutual Assistance agreement, it is specified in Article 9 itself that a requested State may apply the use limitation provision of the applicable bilateral mutual legal assistance treaty in lieu of this Article, where doing so will result in less restriction on the use of information and evidence than provided for in Article 9. In order to safeguard the data protection provision of the US-Luxembourg MLAT, Article 9(5) of the EU-US MLA agreement stipulates that 'where a bilateral mutual legal assistance treaty in force between a Member State and the

---

9.   The fact that this provision was meant to apply solely to one Member State was not spelt out in the text of the Agreement itself, but was made clear in the negotiation documents (including all relevant Council document) leading up to the Agreement.

United States of America on the date of signature of this agreement, permits limitation of the obligation to provide assistance with respect to certain tax offences, the Member State concerned may indicate, in its exchange of written instruments with the United States of America described in Article 3(2), that, with respect to such offences, it will continue to apply the use limitation provision of that treaty'.

The *chapeau* of Articles 3(1) tasks both the European Union and the United States of America with ensuring that provisions of the EU-US agreements are applied in relation to the bilateral treaties in accordance with the terms specified for each of the articles in that paragraph and paragraph 2 of the same provisions requires them to ensure that this is done by way of 'written instruments' between each Member State and the United States. It was thus up to each Member State and the United States of America to stipulate in a 'written instrument' the way in which the EU-US provisions relate to the existing 'bilateral' provisions.

The requirement of additional bilateral 'written' instruments was one that was inserted in the EU-US agreements at the request of the US side. The American negotiators had several concerns that led them to insist on this requirement. The paramount concern was one of clarity; the US negotiators thought it should be made absolutely clear to US prosecutors and US courts how the provisions of the EU-US agreement would relate to those of the bilateral instruments and thought this should be done by way of a bilateral instrument with the Member State concerned. It cannot be excluded, however, that at the background there were some fears that US courts would be reluctant to accept the binding force for a Member State of provisions of an umbrella agreement that was not concluded by the Member State concerned, but by the European Union. The clear preference of the US negotiators was also that these written instruments take the form of Protocols to the existing bilateral treaties (or, in the absence of an MLAT, of a Treaty). The European negotiators were loath to accept this demand, as an obligation to enter into separate bilateral treaties would undermine (or at least could be perceived as undermining) the legal binding force of the EU-US agreements. The European Union, which did not see the need for such additional, bilateral instruments, would have preferred to refer to the possibility of a bilateral exchange of letters between each Member State and the United States of America.

The compromise solution that was eventually found was the requirement in Articles 3(2) that there be a 'written' instrument between the United States and each Member State, including future Member States of the European Union. This compromise solution left it to each Member State to determine, together with the United States, the nature of such 'written instrument'. Attempts under the Italian Presidency of the Council in 2003 to arrive at a common EU position which would have bound all Member States to interpret the Article 3(2) requirement of concluding 'written instruments' in the same manner, failed. The result is that all Member States were free to construe this requirement in a manner which best suited their needs and policies. Whereas an important number of Member States have termed these bilateral instruments simply 'instruments', a minority has chosen to give these the forms of Protocols or even Treaties[10]. From the point of view of international law, the result is probably the same as all Member States were already bound by the EU-US agreements and all bilateral instruments, whatever their denomination, are binding on the (Member) States that have entered into these instruments. A possible difference lies at the domestic, constitutional level, as the constitutional requirements (e.g. ratification) may differ according to whether these instruments are termed instruments or Protocols. However, it appears that most Member States, regardless of the denomination of the bilateral instruments they have entered into with the United States of America, have chosen to follow a constitutional procedure of some kind with regard to those instruments[11].

2.   Non-derogation clauses and the death penalty

Given the fact that the choice was made not to replace the bilateral treaties with full-fledged EU-US agreements, the question whether the grounds for refusal available under bilateral treaties could continue to be invoked, had to be answered. Both agreements contain a non-derogation clause, which allows the further invocation of those grounds for refusal. Article 17 of the EU-US Extradition Agreement qualifies the non-derogation clause by stating that the grounds of refusal are available only 'relating to a matter not governed by this Agreement'. It is unclear what is meant by this qualification, which does not feature in Article 13 of the EU-US Mutual Legal Assistance Agreement. It does not seem to make sense that the matters governed by the EU-US Agreement, which are intrinsically linked to those governed by the bilateral treaties, would not be subject to the same

---

10.   This is the case for Austria, the Czech Republic, Estonia, Finland, Germany, Greece, Hungary, Latvia, Lithuania and Malta. Estonia and Latvia have incorporated the provisions of the EU-US Agreement on extradition into new Extradition Treaty with the United States of America.

11.   Apparently only three Member State did not have to go through a parliamentary approval or ratification procedure for the bilateral instruments: Denmark, Malta and France (the latter went through a simplified procedure).

rules. At any rate, such a limitation does not seem to be present in the bilateral written instruments.

The non-derogation clause had a particular importance with regard to the discussion on the risk of imposition and/or execution of the death penalty, which was probably the most sensitive topic in the negotiations. In the context of *extradition*, some Member States, and in particular one Member State with a very old extradition treaty (1909 – Portugal), deemed it necessary that the EU-US Agreement on extradition would also allow for the invocation of grounds of refusal not provided for in their bilateral treaty, but flowing from their constitution. In particular the risk of life imprisonment for the extradited person, which is not provided for in the bilateral Portuguese-American extradition Treaty, but for which the – subsequent – Portuguese Constitution demands specific guarantees in order for an extradition to be admissible. The US side obviously resisted any attempt to use the EU-US Agreement as a means to add grounds for refusal not provided for in the bilateral treaties. The obligation under Article 17(2) of the EU-US Agreement in cases where the 'constitutional principles of, or final judicial decisions binding upon, the requested State may pose an impediment to the fulfilment of its obligation to extradite' is therefore limited to a consultation between the States concerned.

The conceptualisation of the non-derogation clause was more difficult with regard to mutual legal assistance than with regard to extradition, as not all Member States had an MLAT to which could be referred. Therefore, in those cases where there is no MLAT between the United States and the Member State concerned, Article 13 of the Mutual Legal Assistance Agreement also allows a State to refuse mutual legal assistance on foot of 'its applicable legal principles, including where execution of the request would prejudice its sovereignty, security, ordre public or other essential interests'. Whilst this is in reality no more than the acknowledgment of the *status quo ante* as, in the absence of a treaty obligation, all mutual legal assistance based on comity can always be refused by the requested state, it is a very important treaty provision. The reason for this is that the EU negotiation mandate required the Presidency to discuss with the United States the possibility of a treaty provision that would allow refusing mutual assistance that could lead to the imposition of death penalty, whereas the prohibition of the death penalty was traditionally entrenched only in extradition law, and not in the international law of other forms of co-operation in criminal matters. The initial reaction of the United States to this EU demand was very negative. It seemed that, where problems had arisen in the past, American and Member State authorities had been able to resolve this type of problem on an ad hoc basis in a manner that was satisfactory to the Member State concerned. Piecemeal information presented by some Member States to the Presidency indicated that, in some instances, before granting mutual assistance to the United States, Member States had requested and obtained assurances from the United States that the evidence they provided would not be used in a procedure leading to the imposition of the death penalty[12]. Whilst acknowledging and even accommodating the concerns of some EU Member States in this respect, the US authorities were not willing to accept a treaty provision that, in line with what was an established treaty practice in the extradition relationships between the United States, would effectively allow Member States to demand assurances that the evidence that they provided would not lead to the imposition of the death penalty. The United States clearly preferred to handle matters on an *ad hoc* basis, rather than through a treaty provision.

The EU preference for dealing with the matter through a general clause rather than on an *ad hoc* basis therefore had a undeniably political undertone: the European Union wanted to "export" its human rights *acquis* to the United States by way of a provision that would prohibit US authorities to use evidence from EU Member States in a procedure that could lead to the imposition of the death penalty[13].

Such a provision would, however, have flown into the face of the American criminal justice system, as it would have curbed the powers of US prosecutorial authorities to seek the death penalty or even to prosecute for offences punishable by death in every case where evidence that originated from an EU Member State was used. From a legal point of view, it would have been very difficult to draft a clause that would attain the goal that the European Union had set itself. At the moment mutual legal assistance is requested and/or granted, it is rarely clear whether the evidence will be used in a procedure that will lead to the imposition of the death penalty, as the imposition of the sentence by a judge takes place only at the end of criminal proceedings. At the moment mutual legal assistance is granted it may not even be clear against whom the evidence will be used and it cannot be excluded that evidence may be used to exculpate a defendant.

---

12. This is confirmed by press reports: Chambon, "La France accepte de coopérer avec la justice américaine sur le cas de Zacaraias Moussaoui", *Le Monde*, 29 November 2002.
13. On the role of the EU acquis in negotiations with third countries, see more in detail: Stessens, Guy, The EU-US Agreements on Extradition and on Mutual Legal Assistance: how to Bridge Different Approaches, in: Gilles de Kerchove and Anne Weyembergh, *Sécurité et justice: enjeu de la politique extérieure de l'Union européenne* (2003), pp. 269-273.

The law of evidence is moreover a state competence in the United States, which at any rate made it impossible for the US federal government to guarantee that American courts would exclude "European" evidence in case it could lead to the imposition of the death penalty. It seems that the only way in which the US Department of Justice could guarantee that evidence could not be used in a procedure that leads to the imposition of the death penalty, is through an agreement with the prosecutorial authorities of the state concerned. Although the US authorities had used this method on a number of occasions in the past, they were not willing to institutionalise it by laying it down in a treaty provision.

Various reasons can be adduced to explain this. A first, obvious reason is that such a clause would have been politically unacceptable to the United States, as it would have constituted a major interference in the way American (often state) courts handle criminal procedures in general and in particular a drastic curb on the sentencing powers of US courts. To gauge the impact of such a hypothetical clause, one has to bear in mind that, within the purely domestic context of the United States, the US federal government as a rule does not have the power to impose limits on the sentencing powers of state courts. It was therefore unrealistic to expect that the US government would accept such a clause. Indeed, had the US government accepted to insert such a clause into the EU-US Mutual Legal Assistance Agreement, it might very well have meant that the US Senate would have refused to ratify the agreement. An additional reason that made it highly unlikely that the US authorities would ever accept such a clause, is the precedential value that such a clause in an agreement that binds the United States with 27 Member States would have for the United States for their mutual legal assistance relationships with other countries.

The only 'solution' that ensured that Member States could refuse to provide assistance in case this might lead to the imposition of the death penalty and that at the same time accommodated the US concern not to elevate this into a general rule, was therefore the non-derogation clause of Article 13 of the EU-US on Mutual Legal Assistance, which refers to the "ordre public" clause. Thus, a Member State whose assistance is requested in circumstances where the requested Member State considers that granting assistance would violate its fundamental human rights obligations has the possibility to refuse mutual legal assistance. Where information or evidence is being furnished to the US authorities, but a Member State has reasons to believe that the evidence could be used in circumstances that are unacceptable to that Member State, it may, by way of exception, demand that the information be used only for the purpose for which the information or evidence was transmitted (Article 9(2) of the EU-US Agreement[14]).

3.   *Consultation clauses*

There is a general duty upon the Contracting Parties to both agreements (Article 15 Extradition, Article 11 MLA) to consult each other in order to 'enable the most effective use to be made of th[e] Agreements[s], including to facilitate the resolution of any dispute regarding the interpretation or application'. The consultation duty is on the Contracting Parties, that is, as far as the European side is concerned, the European Union and not the Member States. This flows logically from the structure of the agreements and at the same time it affords the US authorities an additional lever in case operational difficulties under the agreement(s) cannot be solved at bilateral level. This general consultation duty upon the European Union, obviously does not, and was indeed not meant to, prevent the Member States to consult at bilateral level with the United States of America regarding any operational difficulty they might encounter in the course of mutual legal assistance or extradition relationships with the United States. Article 17(2) of the Extradition Agreement acknowledges this by obliging the requested and requesting States to consult each other in case "the constitutional principles of, or final judicial decisions binding upon, the requested State may pose an impediment to fulfilment of its obligation to extradite, and resolution of the matter is not provided for in this Agreement or the applicable bilateral treaty". Here, the specific consultation duty rests upon the Member State concerned and not the European Union as the subject matter for resolution stems from the Member State's law and not from the EU-US Agreement.

The EU-US Mutual Legal Assistance Agreement provides for a specific consultation duty in two cases where the operation of a provision of the agreement may result in extraordinary burdens on requested State. Both with regard to the identification of bank accounts (Article 4) and of mutual legal assistance to administrative authorities (Article 8), the Contracting Parties are asked to take measures to avoid the imposition of extraordinary burdens on requested States. Where extraordinary burdens on a requested State nonetheless result from the operation of these provisions, the Contracting Parties shall immediately consult with a view to facilitating the application of these provisions, including the taking of such measures as may be required to reduce pending and future burdens.

14.   See infra III.B.5.

4. Future bilateral agreements

These agreements being the first agreements the United States entered into with the European Union in the area of extradition and mutual legal assistance, the United States wanted to avoid that these agreements would preclude the further development of extradition and mutual legal assistance relationships at the bilateral level with Member States. The United States made it clear it could not accept a situation in which the EU-US Agreements would prevent them from elaborating a tailor-made solution for a specific Member State, in case operational difficulties would demonstrate the need for such a bilateral solution.

The European Union on the other hand could not accept that Member States would be able to deviate, at the bilateral level, from the provisions of the EU-US Agreements, which would form part of the EU *acquis*, binding on all Member States.

The identical provisions of both agreements (Article 18 Extradition, Article 14 MLA) on the possibility to enter into future bilateral agreements constitutes the outcome of the endeavour to reconcile the concerns of both sides. Both agreements explicitly stipulate that they do 'not preclude the conclusion, after its entry into force, of bilateral Agreements between a Member State and the United States of America consistent with th[e] Agreement'. An explanatory note to both agreements refers to the above-mentioned US concerns, but, in an attempt to accommodate the EU concerns, clearly accords priority to consultation as a mechanism to resolve any operational difficulties that may rise between the United States and a Member State over the conclusion of a new bilateral treaty or protocol. The explanatory note states the following:

> Should any measures set forth in the Agreement create an operational difficulty for either one or more Member States or the United States of America, such difficulty should in the first place be resolved, if possible, through consultations between the Member State or Member States concerned and the United States of America, or, if appropriate, through the consultation procedures set out in this Agreement. Where it is not possible to address such operational difficulty through consultations alone, it would be consistent with the Agreement for future bilateral agreements between the Member State or Member States and the United States of America to provide an operationally feasible alternative mechanism that would satisfy the objectives of the specific provision with respect to which the difficulty has arisen.

The provision on future bilateral agreements is also legally logical as the subject matter covered in both agreements falls under the (legislative) competence of both the European Union and the Member States. Article 38 TEU provides the Union with the competence to enter into agreements with third countries, whenever the Council deems this necessary, for any matters covered by Title VI. However, the competences dealt with in Title VI TEU are shared between the Member States and the Union. Hence Member States can continue to legislate and, as far as international relations are concerned, to enter into agreements with third countries. Of course, in exercising their legislative and treaty-making competence, Member States need to respect the *acquis* of the European Union and therefore both agreements provide that any future bilateral treaty must be consistent with the EU-US Agreement[15].

III.   The substance of the agreements

Hereafter the most important substantive aspects of both agreements will be briefly discussed.

A.   The extradition agreement

1.   *Creating an EU-wide level playing field for extraditable offences*

Some of the older bilateral extradition treaties with the United States still operate on the basis of the list approach, that is by listing all extraditable offences in the treaty. The more recent extradition treaties follow the threshold approach, by which the threshold for extradition was set at all offences punishable under the laws of the requesting and requested States by deprivation of liberty for a maximum period of more than one year or by a more severe penalty. The effect of Article 4 of the EU-US Extradition Agreement is to replace all list-approach provisions of the bilateral treaties with this threshold approach. Thereby Article 4 in effect creates an EU-wide level playing field for extraditable offences as the threshold for extradition will be the same between all 27 Member States and the United States of America as from the entry into force of the EU-US Extradition Agreement.

2.   *Simplifying the extradition procedure*

The EU-US Extradition Agreement endeavours to simplify the extradition procedure in several ways, mainly by simplifying the rules on transmission of documents. A first simplification is that Article 5(2) provides that documents "that bear the certificate or seal of the Ministry of Justice, or

---

15.   See on this also de Kerchove, Gilles and Marquardt, Stephan, *l.c.*, pp. 821-822.

Ministry or Department responsible for foreign affairs, of the requesting State shall be admissible in extradition proceedings in the requested State without further certification, authentication, or other legalisation". This is a major practical improvement with regard to the situation that still existed under many bilateral extradition treaties, where US (and European) judges, in the absence of such a treaty provision, were entitled to require some kind of separate certification for each document transmitted in the context of an extradition procedure.

Two other improvements relate to the provisional arrest, that is the arrest of a person pending the arrival of the proper extradition request. First, Article 6 allows for requests for provisional arrest to be sent directly from Ministry of Justice to Ministry of Justice as opposed to the diplomatic channel, which is the normal channel of transmission for extradition requests. In addition, Article 7 creates a new, speedier way of transmission of the proper extradition request and supporting documents once the person is under provisional arrest in the requested state. This period of provisional arrest is limited in time (under most bilateral extradition treaties, to 40 days) and sometimes it is difficult to gather all the necessary supporting extradition papers within the mandatory time period. As the non observance of the time limit laid down in the bilateral extradition normally leads to the release of the person concerned, it is imperative to meet this time limit. Therefore Article 7 of the EU-US Extradition Agreement allows the requesting State to 'satisfy its obligation to transmit its request for extradition and supporting documents through the diplomatic channel "[…] by submitting the request and documents to the Embassy of the requested State located in the requesting State". Article 7 goes on to clarify that in such case, the date of receipt of such request by the Embassy shall be considered to be the date of receipt by the requested State for purposes of applying the time limit that must be met under the applicable extradition treaty to enable the person's continued detention.

3. Temporary surrender

Article 9 supplements those bilateral treaties that did not yet allow for the temporary surrender of a person who is being proceeded against or is serving a sentence in the requested State. Article 9 stipulates that the person so surrendered shall be kept in custody in the requesting State and shall be returned to the requested State at the conclusion of the proceedings against that person, in accordance with the conditions to be determined by mutual agreement of the requesting and requested States. The provision allows for, but, interestingly, does not impose, the deduction of the time spent in custody in the territory of the requesting State from the time remaining to be served in the requested State.

4.   *Capital punishment*

The provision on capital punishment was without any doubt the most difficult to negotiate and also the most controversial. Whereas most of the extradition rules are of a highly technical nature, this issue is one which, because of the strong legal and political differences on both sides of the Atlantic, was bound to give rise to controversy. At the outset of the negotiations, all Member States (and some of the Acceding States) had clauses in their bilateral extradition treaty that allowed[16] them to refuse extradition for an offence punishable by death in the requesting state (i.e. the USA) if the offence is not punishable by death in the requested state (i.e. the Member State) unless assurances were provided by the requesting state to the effect that death penalty would not be imposed or, if imposed, not carried out. The negotiation mandate for the EU Presidency, however, demanded to negotiate a provision that would allow refusing extradition in the event of a risk of imposition of death penalty. This part of the negotiation mandate had a clear political undertone, as the system of assurances on a case-by-case basis had never given rise to any practical difficulties and the US authorities had always respected the assurances they had provided to Member State authorities.

Apart from the fact that the United States of America did not see any reason to change a clause which, certainly from a US point of view, had been working well, the US authorities invoked procedural difficulties that made it difficult for them to accept to the EU demand for a general condition of non-imposition of the death penalty. Whereas the US federal authorities are able to make the handing over of an extradited person to state authorities contingent on the condition that the death penalty will not be *executed*, the US federal authorities do not have control on the sentencing powers of state courts. As, under some state legislation, it is impossible for prosecutors to prosecute for some grave offences (e.g. murder) without seeking the death penalty, the federal structure of the US criminal justice system gives no leverage to federal authorities to guarantee in an absolute manner that the death penalty will never be imposed. Therefore Article 13 of the EU-US Agreement on Extradition states that "the requested State

---

16.   Only the bilateral extradition treaty between Spain and the United States of America obliges the requested state to refuse extradition in case these guarantees are not provided: Article VII of the Treaty on extradition between Spain and the United States of America, signed at Madrid on 29 May 1970.

may grant extradition on the condition that the death penalty shall not be imposed on the person sought, or if for procedural reasons such condition cannot be complied with by the requesting State, on condition that the death penalty if imposed shall not be carried out". The exception for "procedural reasons" covers in fact two situations: (i) that of those states where certain offences cannot be prosecuted without seeking the death penalty and (ii) that where the extradited person was already sentenced to the death penalty prior to his extradition. Article 13 increases the level of human rights protection in a second respect as the non-execution (and non-imposition) of the death penalty does not depend on guarantees to be provided on an *ad hoc* basis by the US government, but that if the requesting State accepts extradition subject to conditions pursuant to this Article, it has to comply with the conditions.

The fact the European Union was able to obtain such a clause is no mean feat, which is demonstrated by the fact that only two Member States[17] had managed to insert this type of condition in its bilateral extradition treaty with the United States. The criticism, which sometimes has been voiced with regard to this provision, to the effect that it is not sufficiently protective as it only allows, but does not impose to refuse extradition without these conditions being met, shows a failure to understand both the political and legal realities of extradition between EU Member States and the United States of America. At the political level, a mandatory provision by which both Contracting Parties would have bound themselves to refuse extradition in case of risk of the death penalty, would amount to a moral condemnation by the United States of its own legal system. At the legal level, the optional nature of Article 13 does not prevent Member States from providing under its domestic law that this condition shall always be sought.

B.   The Mutual Legal Assistance Agreement

The content of the EU-US Mutual Legal Assistance Agreement was to a certain extent inspired by a number of the 'modern' MLA provisions from the EU Convention of 29 May 2000 on Mutual Assistance in Criminal Matters between the Member States of the European Union[18]. In some cases, the US negotiators were, however, not willing to accept all elements of the EU rules and simply wanted to have a so-called enabling provision,

---

17.   Austria and Lithuania.
18.   OJ C 197, 12.7.2000, p.1.

which allowed EU Member States and the United States to enter into the type of co-operation envisaged.

The fact that the EU-US Mutual Legal Assistance Agreement is not a full-fledged MLAT, but only provides for more modern MLA provisions was a matter of some disappointment for some, especially new, Member States that did not have an MLAT with the United States. This results in the somewhat odd situation that for some Member States only these modern types of mutual legal assistance are regulated, whereas there is no general mutual legal assistance framework between these Member States and the United States of America.

1.   *Identifying bank accounts*

Article 4 of the EU-US MLA Agreement is inspired by Article 2 of the Protocol of 16 October 2001[19] to the EU Convention of 29 May 2000 on Mutual Assistance in Criminal Matters between the Member States of the European Union. It allows requesting another State to ascertain if the banks located in its territory possess information on whether an identified natural or legal person suspected of or charged with a criminal offence is the holder of a bank account or accounts. The requested State is under an obligation to do so promptly and communicate promptly the results of its enquiries to the requesting State. However, this provision only serves to find out whether a person holds a bank account and is not a conduit for obtaining bank records concerning the accounts or transactions thus identified: Article 4(6) explicitly refers to the provisions of the applicable MLAT in force between the States concerned, or in the absence thereof, the provisions of the domestic law of the requested State.

Ascertaining whether a person holds bank account may be requested for one of the three following purposes: (i) identifying information regarding natural or legal persons convicted of or otherwise involved in a criminal offence; (ii) identifying information in the possession of non-bank financial institutions; or (iii) identifying financial transactions unrelated to accounts.

The Member States must designate the authorities which shall be competent to deal with such requests (either central authorities responsible for mutual legal assistance, or national authorities responsible for investigation or prosecution of criminal offences). The United States of America have, under most bilateral instruments, designated three authorities: the U.S. Department of Justice, the U.S. Drug Enforcement

---

19.   OJ C 326, 21.11.2001, p.1.

Administration, the U.S. Department of Homeland Security, Bureau of Immigration and Customs Enforcement, and the U.S. Department of Justice, Federal Bureau of Investigation, the latter having the residual competence for all matters not falling under the jurisdiction of the two former.

Article (4) allows a State to limit its obligation to provide assistance to a category of offences ((i) offences for which there is double criminality; (ii) offences punishable by a penalty involving deprivation of liberty or a detention order of a maximum period of at least four years in the requesting State and at least two years in the requested State; or (iii) designated serious offences punishable under the laws of both the requested and requesting States). This limitation, which is specified for each Member State in its bilateral instrument with the United States, cannot however exclude the obligation to identify accounts associated with terrorist activity and the laundering of proceeds generated from a comprehensive range of serious criminal activities, punishable under the laws of both the requesting and requested States.

2. *Joint investigation teams*

Article 5 of the EU-US Agreement on Mutual Legal Assistance is an enabling clause, which obliges the Contracting Parties to take ' such measures as may be necessary to enable joint investigative teams to be established and operated in the respective territories of each Member State and the United States of America for the purpose of facilitating criminal investigations or prosecutions involving one or more Member States and the United States of America where deemed appropriate by the Member State concerned and the United States of America'.

Contrary to what is the case for Article 13 of the EU Mutual Assistance Convention of 29 May 2000 (or the Framework decision of 13 June 2002 on joint investigation teams), the provision does not regulate the procedures under which such joint investigation teams are to operate, but simply states that 'the composition, duration, location, organisation, functions, purpose, and terms of participation of team members of a State in investigative activities taking place in another State's territory shall be as agreed between the competent authorities responsible for the investigation or prosecution of criminal offences, as determined by the respective States concerned.' Under Article 5 (3), the communication regarding the establishment and operation of such team shall in principle take place directly between the competent authorities, except 'where the exceptional complexity, broad scope, or other circumstances involved are deemed to require more central coordination as to some or all aspects'.

Like Article 13 of the EU Mutual Assistance Convention of 29 May 2000, this provision stipulates that where the joint investigation team needs investigative measures to be taken in one of the States setting up the team, a member of the team of that State may request its own competent authorities to take those measures without the other States having to submit a request for mutual legal assistance.

3. *Video conferencing*

Article 6 of the EU-US Agreement on Mutual Legal Assistance is also an enabling clause, which obliges the Contracting Parties to take 'such measures as may be necessary to enable the use of video transmission technology between each Member State and the United States of America for taking testimony in a proceeding for which mutual legal assistance is available of a witness or expert located in a requested State'. The provision itself contains very little in terms of modalities governing such procedure, but refers to the applicable MLAT in force between the States concerned, or, in the absence of an MLAT, to the law of the requested State. Paragraph 3 also states that the requesting and requested States may consult 'in order to facilitate resolution of legal, technical or logistical issues that may arise in the execution of the request'. It is also clarified that this provision is without prejudice to the use of other means for obtaining of testimony in the requested State available under applicable treaty or law.

Regarding costs, paragraph 2 stipulates that unless otherwise agreed by the requesting and requested States, the requesting State shall bear the costs associated with establishing and servicing the video transmission. Other costs arising in the course of providing assistance shall be borne in accordance with the applicable provisions of the MLAT, or in the absence of an MLAT, as agreed upon by the requesting and requested States.

4. *Mutual legal assistance to administrative authorities*

Under Article 8, mutual legal assistance shall also be afforded to a national administrative authority, 'investigating conduct with a view to a criminal prosecution of the conduct, or referral of the conduct to criminal investigation or prosecution authorities, pursuant to its specific administrative or regulatory authority to undertake such investigation'. Furthermore, this provision allows for (but does not oblige) mutual legal assistance to other administrative authorities under such circumstances. An explanatory note to Article 8 clarifies that the obligation to afford mutual legal assistance extends solely to US federal administrative authorities and to requesting national administrative authorities of Member States, but that the mutual legal assistance *may* also be made available to other, that is non-federal or local, administrative authorities.

It is also clearly stated in the article that assistance shall not be available for matters in which the administrative authority anticipates that no prosecution or referral, as applicable, will take place. However, the explanatory note indicates that the criterion must be assessed at the time of making the request. It is explicitly stated that 'the fact that, at the time of making the request referral for criminal prosecution is being contemplated does not exclude that, other sanctions than criminal ones may be pursued by that authority. Thus, mutual legal assistance obtained under Article 8(1) may lead the requesting administrative authority to the conclusion that pursuance of criminal proceedings or criminal referral would not be appropriate. These possible consequences do not affect the obligation upon the Contracting Parties to provide assistance under this Article'.

As is made clear by the explanatory note, this limitation was not just a matter of choice for the negotiators, but was also imposed by the legal confines of the European Union under Title VI TEU, under which the Union has competence only with regard to assistance in criminal, and not in administrative, matters.

As to the channels for transmission of such requests for assistance, paragraph 2 specifies that they shall be transmitted between the central authorities designated pursuant to the bilateral mutual legal assistance treaty in force between the States concerned, or between such other authorities as may be agreed by the central authorities. In the absence of a treaty, requests shall be transmitted between the US Department of Justice and the Ministry of Justice or comparable Ministry of the Member State concerned responsible for transmission of mutual legal assistance requests, or between such other authorities as may be agreed by the Department of Justice and such Ministry.

5. Data protection

The clause on data protection phrases the limitations on the use of information obtained under the EU-US Agreement on mutual legal assistance in terms which are very similar to those of Article 24 of the EU Mutual Assistance Convention of 29 May 2000. It is said that the requesting State may use any evidence or information obtained from the requested State:

(a) for the purpose of its criminal investigations and proceedings;

(b) for preventing an immediate and serious threat to its public security;

(c) in its non-criminal judicial or administrative proceedings directly related to investigations or proceedings:

    (i) set forth in subparagraph (a); or

    (ii) for which mutual legal assistance was rendered under Article 8;

(d) for any other purpose, if the information or evidence has been made public within the framework of proceedings for which they were transmitted, or in any of the situations described in subparagraphs (a), (b) and (c); and

(e) for any other purpose, only with the prior consent of the requested State.

Paragraph 2, however, allows the requested State to impose additional conditions in a case where the particular request for assistance could not be complied with in the absence of such conditions. Where additional conditions have been imposed, the requested State may require the requesting State to give information on the use made of the evidence or information. Generic restrictions with respect to the legal standards of the requesting State for processing personal data may, however, not be imposed by the requested State as a condition under that article to providing evidence or information.

As is clarified by the explanatory note on Article 9(2)(b), this is meant to ensure that refusal of assistance on data protection grounds may be invoked only in exceptional cases. Such a situation could arise if, upon balancing the important interests involved in the particular case (on the one hand, public interests, including the sound administration of justice and, on the other hand, privacy interests), furnishing the specific data sought by the requesting State would raise difficulties so fundamental as to be considered by the requested State to fall within the essential interests. This in effect means that the requested state cannot impose limitations on the use of information or evidence by the requesting state because it deems the requested state's data protection system inadequate. Thus, the fact the requesting and requested States have different systems of protecting the privacy of data (such as that the requesting State does not have the equivalent of a specialised data protection authority) or have different means of protecting personal data (such as that the requesting State uses means other than the process of deletion to protect the privacy or the accuracy of the personal data received by law enforcement authorities), may as such not be imposed as additional conditions under Article 9(2a).

This statement in the explanatory note on Article 9 was inspired by a similar statement in paragraph 268 of the Explanatory Report to the Convention on Cybercrime of 23 November 2001 of the Council of Europe[20].

Paragraph 3 allows the requested State which, following disclosure to the requesting State, becomes aware of circumstances that may cause it to seek an additional condition in a particular case, to consult with the requesting State to determine the extent to which the evidence and information can be protected.

IV. Conclusion

The EU-US Agreements of 26 June 2003 constitute a first, ambitious step by the European Union in the area of extradition and mutual legal assistance with third countries. It is a step which was made possible only by the tragic events of 11 September 2001, but which has paved the way for other so-called Article 24-38 agreements in the future.

From a legal point of view, the elaboration of the agreements was complicated by the fact that an existing maze of bilateral treaties had to be taken into account. That the Union is the Contracting Party does not alter the fact that the practical execution of the treaty obligation is incumbent on the Member State authorities. The fact that the negotiation of such an agreement can take place by the Union affords however additional leverage, which would be lacking for many Member States in case they were to negotiate as individual Member States. Notably on the issue of the death penalty, the outcome of the negotiations demonstrate the added value of negotiations by the Council.

20. *E.T.S.*, No. 185.

3. The External Relations of Europol – Political, Legal, and Operational Considerations

Dick Heimans

I.   Introduction

On 1 December 1999, the Dutch newspaper "Trouw" ran a front-page publication under the headline: "Europol to do business with countries that practise torture".[1] The article inter alia notes: "The European Police Agency Europol is allowed to exchange data world-wide on suspects and criminals. To this end, Europol will negotiate agreements with countries like Turkey and Morocco which regularly violate human rights. The European Union Ministers will authorise Europol tomorrow to start negotiations with 22 countries and three international organisations". The main thrust of the article was critical, claiming that Europol would be able to receive and store data from all over the world, and also disseminate data on Europeans world-wide. The question was raised how to control what happens with this information. Also, human rights organisations were quoted as saying that this would give Europol the right to store information on suspects without being able to verify whether that information is trustworthy. Consequently, the Dutch Parliament called an emergency session of its Committee on Justice and Home Affairs dealing with the issue, and instructed the Minister of Justice to lay down a parliamentary reservation against the Council Act on which the newspaper reported.

If nothing else, this historic incident highlights the political sensitivity of the subject of this contribution at a time when the first steps in Europol's external relations were being taken. Since its inception, Europol's press has not been as positive as might be expected of an organisation which was set up, in the terminology of the Amsterdam treaty, to make a significant contribution to an area of freedom, security and justice in Europe.

This contribution focuses firstly on the legal framework for Europol's co-operation possibilities with third States and organisations. In order to do that, a brief tour through the history of the setting up of Europol will be taken, and some detail on the main legal instruments which lay down the

---

1.   "Trouw", 1 December 1999.

framework within which Europol operates will be provided. Special attention will be paid to the provisions on the processing of personal data, and the applicable control procedures. Against that background, the specific topic of this contribution – Europol's co-operation with third States and international organisations, or Europol's external relations – will be considered more in detail. This will include a description of the development of these relations over recent years and a glance at what the future may bring under the Commission's proposal for a new legal basis for Europol. Some final remarks will conclude this chapter.

II. Europol's History

Europol is quite a young organisation, as the original idea of establishing a specialised European Intelligence Agency to enhance international police co-operation was conceived only at the beginning of the nineties. The first "official" mention of Europol was in the Maastricht Treaty, concluded in 1992. In its Article K.1 (9), this Treaty stated that the Member States of the European Union "shall regard the following areas as matters of common interest: police co-operation for the purposes of preventing and combating terrorism, unlawful drugs trafficking and other serious forms of international crime, including if necessary aspects of customs co-operation, in connection with the organisation of a Union-wide system for exchanging information within a European Police Office (Europol)". Article K.3 of the Maastricht Treaty provided the possibility for the Member States to draw up conventions on these subjects, to be adopted in accordance with their respective constitutional requirements. The current legal basis for Europol's activities, the Europol Convention, was drawn up on the basis of this Article.

The negotiations on the Europol Convention could eventually be successfully concluded in the summer of 1995.[2] During the ratification process of the Convention, a number of important implementing regulations under the Convention were prepared for formal adoption by later Council decisions. These implementing regulations also covered Europol's possibilities of international co-operation. The Convention itself stipulated that these regulations, and a number of others, should be adopted and enforced before Europol could take up its activities. The Convention came into force on 1 October 1998, and Europol was able to take up its activities on 1 July of 1999. In the meantime, the Amsterdam

2.   OJ C 316, 27.11.1995, p. 1.

Treaty was negotiated, resulting in a further development of the description of Europol's tasks at the highest level in Articles 29 and 30 TEU.

III. Europol's Tasks and Organisation

One of the peculiarities which flows from the fact that Europol was set up on the basis of a separate Convention, is that it is a fully fledged international organisation, not an agency of the European Union. As a consequence it has full legal personality, including the capacity to enter into binding agreements under international law. This is the basis on which Europol's external relations have been built, and the starting point for considering its special position within the framework of EU-wide law enforcement co-operation. At the same time, this does not mean that Europol functions completely independently from normal EU co-operation mechanisms, as will be clarified later – political, legal and financial control over Europol are all firmly embedded within the existing Council structures.

Although over the past few years there have been on-going discussions on Europol's role and its tasks, firstly in the context of the debate on the Constitutional Treaty, and more recently as part of the political discussion on Europol's future started by the Austrian Presidency of the Council (first semester 2006), its basic function and tasks have not changed significantly since 1999. And the recent entry into force of three Protocols amending the Europol Convention has also not brought dramatic changes in this respect. In fact, Europol is still a centralised, multidisciplinary criminal intelligence organisation tasked to support the law enforcement authorities of the Member States in combating international organised crime.

One of the unique features of Europol is that, within its organisation, representatives of almost all national law enforcement organisations work closely together. This is achieved through the so-called Europol liaison officers. Each Member State has appointed one or more of these liaison officers to represent their respective organisations at Europol. These liaison officers are not formal Europol officials, but continue to work under the responsibility of their seconding authorities. This also means that the data processing by liaison officers is subject to national legislation, not to the Europol legal framework.

Europol is a centralised organisation not only in the sense that there is a centralisation of law enforcement information at European level – the

Europol Convention also calls for national centralisation. This works through the "Europol National Units" set up in all Member States to act as Europol's sole contact with the national law enforcement organisations.

Another important point to remember is that Europol is a support organisation. Although there has been much debate about Europol as a "European FBI", and careful steps have been taken in the Amsterdam Treaty – and in the Constitutional Treaty – to give Europol more operational powers, under the current legal framework, Europol has no investigative authority of its own. This is unlikely to change in the near future. The support which Europol provides to national authorities is mainly of a co-ordinating and analytic nature, and functions through the so-called Analysis Work Files where information from the national law enforcement authorities can be brought together. The information can then be analysed for links between information already available, and eventually returned to the Member States for appropriate action at the national level. Further co-ordination of activities is achieved through the use of the Europol Information System, which is directly accessible by all Europol national units in the Member States, and which contains personal data on persons convicted of criminal activities or suspected of being involved in such activities. This information is put into the system by the Member States directly.

It is important to realise that at the early stage of investigations not all information that can be supplied for the analysis projects mentioned before has already been verified. Some of the information may be so-called "soft" data. Usually, the data will also be very sensitive. This may be because of the subject matter, but also because of the way the information was obtained. It could, for instance, be the result of telephone tapping, or it could have been supplied by informants. Data may also be sensitive within the meaning of Article 6 of the Council of Europe Convention on Data Protection, revealing for instance racial origin, or political beliefs. An important point to keep in mind here is that Europol is only allowed to process data if such data can also be legally processed by the Member State supplying the information.[3] Also, the Member States are responsible for ensuring that data they supply have been legally collected.[4]

Europol is unique in that it offers the possibility of processing such data within a well-established legal framework, which caters both to the needs of data protection in the civil liberties sense, and in the sense of the operational need for protecting information from sensitive sources. In this

3.   Article 10 (3) Europol Convention.
4.   Article 15 (1) Europol Convention.

respect, a strict data protection regime is beneficial from both an operational and organisational point of view, both for Europol and for the law enforcement organisations with which it co-operates. One simple example to illustrate this point: the data protection requirement of having regular checks on the accuracy and relevance of information is not only beneficial from the point of view of ensuring that information is not kept longer than necessary, but should also help ensure that information used is relevant and up-to-date, which is clearly also a requirement for successful investigations.

IV. Europol's Control Mechanisms

The main general control mechanism of Europol is its Management Board. This Management Board consists of high level representatives of the Member States, most of them from the Ministries of Interior or Justice, but also some from operational law enforcement organisations. The tasks of the Management Board are laid down in quite some detail in Article 28 of the Europol Convention. For now, the main point is that the Management Board has a significant role to play in controlling all of Europol's activities. As such, it is also the main conduit between Europol and Council structures. All issues relating to Europol which have to be decided upon at the level of the EU Council of Ministers go through the Management Board before going, via the Article 36 Committee and Coreper, to the Council. In addition to its task of preparing Council decisions, the Management Board also has some direct authority in deciding on Europol issues. Of particular importance for the subject of this contribution is the Management Board's task of identifying priorities for negotiations with third States and bodies, as well as its advisory role relating to the international relations of Europol.

The Joint Supervisory Body – Europol's data protection control authority – is also of direct practical relevance for Europol's work, including its international relations. This independent body consists of representatives of national Supervisory Bodies. Its main task is to "review the activities of Europol in order to ensure that the rights of the individual are not violated by the storage, processing and utilisation of data held by Europol".[5] Like the Management Board, the Joint Supervisory Body has an important role to play in preparing co-operation agreements with third States and bodies. It has a particular responsibility in ensuring that these agreements provide for appropriate safeguards in the area of data protection. As we shall see

5. Article 24 Europol Convention.

when looking at the particular provisions put in place by the Council for reaching such agreements, the Joint Supervisory Body must advise the Management Board on the data protection aspects of any co-operation agreement to be reached.

V.   Europol's Data Processing and Data Protection Regime

Europol's data protection regime should be seen as complementing the systems already in place in the Member States. As stated above, Member States may only transmit data to Europol which have been collected, and are processed, in accordance with national legislation. To ensure that this level of legislation is adequate, the Europol Convention requires that the Member States take appropriate measures to ensure an adequate standard of data protection. This standard should at least correspond to the standard resulting from the implementation of the principles of the 1981 Council of Europe Convention, and take account of Council of Europe Recommendation R (87) 15[6] concerning the use of personal data in the police sector.

Within this context, reference should also be made to Article 23 of the Europol Convention, which requires Member States to appoint a national supervisory body, responsible for independently monitoring the acceptability of the input, retrieval and communication to Europol of personal data. Representatives of these national supervisory bodies have an important task as well as members of the so-called Joint Supervisory Body.

The national obligations in this respect are complemented by Article 15 of the Europol Convention, which contains a division of responsibility in data protection matters between Europol and the Member States. The Member States are responsible for the legality of the collection of data and their transmission to Europol. Also the input of data, their accuracy, their up-to-date nature and the verification of storage time-limits lies with the Member States, for data which they supplied to Europol, or have put into the Europol Information System.

Europol, on the other hand, is responsible for these same issues for the data received from third parties – which include third States and international organisations – and the data produced by analyses conducted by Europol. In addition, Europol has general data protection responsibility for all the

---

6.   Published at the Council of Europe website www.coe.int – data protection – recommendations

data it receives, whether such data are in the Information System, the Analysis Work Files, or the Index System. The latter provides for an indirect access to the Analysis Files, and allows for the verification of whether data on a particular person or object is included in one of the Analysis Work Files.

The main elements of Europol's data protection regime are also familiar features of other international instruments. As expected, there is the duty to maintain an audit system for retrievals of personal data from the Europol Systems (Article 16 Europol Convention). There is also a specific provision on the use of data, and on any restrictions which may be imposed in this respect. There is a detailed regulation on regular verification of data included, and maximum time limits for storage are laid down. No data protection system would be complete without a provision on the technical measures needed for data protection, and this can be found in Article 25.[7] And then, of course, there are the important provisions on the right of access, correction and deletion, and the respective roles within these procedures for Europol itself, the National Supervisory Bodies and the Joint Supervisory Body.

VI. International Co-operation Possibilities

Against this general background, Europol's possibilities of international co-operation can now be discussed. Again, with relation to this subject, we must first look at the relevant provisions included in the Convention. A number of Articles are of particular importance here. First of all, Article 42 is of relevance for the procedure to be followed. This Article explicitly establishes Europol's right to engage in co-operative relations with third States and bodies. Again, there is the "division of labour" between the Management Board and the EU Council of Ministers: the Management Board is responsible for establishing rules for contacts with European Union related bodies, and the Council is responsible for establishing rules on co-operation with other third bodies and third States. On these rules, the Management Board must advise the Council.

The rules referred to in Article 42 are the general co-operation rules. For the transmission and receipt of personal data, other Articles in the Convention come into play. For the receipt of personal data, Article 10 (4) requires that the Council should establish rules- again after consultation

---

7.   Article 25 includes details on the measures to be taken to prevent e.g. unauthorised access to, unauthorised usage or modification of personal data.

with the Management Board. For the transmission of personal data from Europol to third countries, Article 18 (2) is the important provision. The Convention clearly considers that this issue requires additional data protection, and while specifying that the same procedure should be followed, it also provides for the Joint Supervisory Body to be consulted by the Management Board.

A.   The Implementing Rules

On the basis of the procedures described above, four regulations have been adopted: three by the Council, and one by the Management Board. These regulations include:
– Rules concerning the receipt of information by Europol from third parties (adopted by the Council on 3 November 1998);[8]
– Rules governing Europol's external relations with third States and non-European Union related bodies (adopted by the Council on 3 November 1998);[9]
– Rules governing the transmission of personal data by Europol to third States and third bodies (adopted by the Council on 12 March 1999);[10]
– Rules governing Europol's external relations with European Union-related bodies (adopted by the Management Board on 15 October 1998)[11].

Not all of the details pertaining to these regulations can be discussed here. Apart from the issue of data protection, a few points are worth mentioning nonetheless. First, all regulations foresee the possibility for Europol to enter into formal agreements with third States and bodies, and a formal agreement is always required for the stationing of liaison officers of third States or bodies at Europol, and for Europol liaison officers to be stationed in a third State or with a third body. Second, although formal agreements are signed by the Europol Director – since he is Europol's legal representative – for all agreements to be negotiated with third States and bodies, the prior authorisation of the Council is required. Finally, a formal agreement authorised by the Council is also required for any exchange of information which is "protectively marked", which in Europol terminology means classified.

8.   OJ C 26, 30.1.1999, p. 3.
9.   OJ C 26, 30.1.1999, p. 4.
10.   OJ C 88, 30.3.1999, p. 1.
11.   OJ C 26, 30.1.1999, p. 10.

B.   Receipt of Personal Data

From both the point of view of operational law enforcement needs and the point of view of data protection, the most important issue, however, is what Europol's possibilities are for exchanging personal data with third States and bodies. The receipt of personal data by Europol is the less-complicated side of this coin, and the applicable regulations are far less detailed than those that apply to the transmission of personal data. First of all, Article 10 (4) gives a limitative listing of the bodies and States from which Europol may receive information. Although the list is limitative, in practice it offers possibilities for the receipt of information from almost all public international bodies and all third States. An exception is made for non-governmental bodies and private persons. It would appear that on the basis of this Article, personal data from such bodies or persons may not be received directly by Europol.

The specific regulation on the receipt of personal data, mentioned above, does not contain many restrictions either, with a few exceptions. The regulation, for instance, prescribes the "standard" procedure for reaching agreements on the receipt of personal data, which requires the unanimous authorisation of the Council for the start of the negotiations and the approval of the Management Board. An important point to note here, however, is that the regulation does not specify that an agreement is an absolute necessity for the receipt of information, including personal data. In practice, this offers some possibilities for co-operation even where formal agreements have not yet been reached.

On the content of the information which may be received, Article 3 of the regulation specifies that Europol shall ask the third State or third body submitting information to assess that information and its source, as far as possible. In this sense, the provision helps Europol to comply with Principle 3 of Recommendation R (87) 15, which states that data should be distinguished in accordance with their degree of accuracy, and data based on facts should be distinguished from data based on opinions or personal assessments.

Furthermore, Article 4 provides for some important mechanisms to ensure that the information received continues to be up-to-date after its transmission to Europol. Whenever an agreement is concluded, it must contain mutual obligations for the partners to inform each other in cases where information is corrected or deleted. An interesting point to note here is that there is no strict obligation for Europol to delete information if it has information itself which is more extensive than the information received from third States and bodies.

Article 4 also contains the important provision that Europol is not allowed to store, either in its Information System or in its analysis files, data which have clearly been obtained by a third State in obvious violation of human rights. Although one can imagine that there will be both practical and political difficulties in the application of this provision, it is a clear political statement on Europol's obligations in this respect.

C.   Transmission of Personal Data

The restrictions imposed on the transmission of personal data by Europol to third States or bodies are far stricter than those imposed on the receipt of information, which is understandable because the regulations in place reflect the overriding concern of Member States to ensure that no personal data are transmitted by Europol without their consent. One might even suspect that Europol's possibilities in this respect are far more limited than those of the Member States' authorities themselves. Looking at the provisions in more detail, it is obvious that this restrictive approach stems from the two main elements identified earlier, i.e. the protection of sensitive information from an operational point of view, and general data protection principles.

The most logical starting point for the examination of the provisions dealing with this issue is Article 18 of the Europol Convention. The first paragraph of this Article already points to a number of fairly obvious restrictions. First of all, the same limitations that were discussed with regard to the receipt of information also apply to the States and bodies to which personal data may be transmitted,. On top of that, communication must be necessary "in individual cases for the purposes of preventing or combating criminal offences for which Europol is competent".[12] Also, an adequate level of data protection must be ensured in the State or body to which the personal data are to be transmitted (this provision caused much debate at a later stage). And thirdly, transmission should be permissible under the general rules adopted by the Council.

On the adequacy of the level of data protection, the third paragraph of Article 18 provides some interesting pointers. In general, all circumstances

12.   Article 18 (1) Europol Convention.

which play a part in the communication of personal data should be taken into account, and in particular:
- the nature of the data;
- the purpose for which the data are intended;
- the duration of the intended processing; and any general or specific provisions applying to the third State or body.

A very clear indication of the Member States' concern with respect to direct transmission of personal data by Europol can be found in paragraph 4 of Article 18. Under that paragraph, Europol can only communicate personal data supplied by a Member State once it has obtained that Member State's consent. Fortunately, the Article also foresees the possibility that such consent may be given in general terms, so that it would not be necessary to contact the Member State for each individual transmission. Even where the data are not supplied by a Member State, Europol must satisfy itself that the communication of data is not liable to obstruct the proper performance of tasks falling within a Member State's sphere of competence. Nor should the data transmission jeopardise the security and public order of a Member State or otherwise prejudice its general welfare.

Within this context, account should also be taken of Article 10 (8) of the Convention. Although this provision is not specifically concerned with external contacts, it does provide for further limitations, since it deals with the dissemination of the results of Europol's analyses. The important sentence here is that any dissemination or operational use of analysis data shall be decided on in consultation with the participants in the analysis. Since this provision applies to any dissemination, it is relevant for the dissemination of data to Member States as well as to third States and bodies. In practice therefore, even if all legal preconditions have been met, the transmission of analysis data will only be possible with the agreement of all Member States involved in the analysis.

As expected, Europol is explicitly made responsible for the legality of authorising the transmission of data. It must also keep a record of such communications and why they took place. A further restriction is that the recipient must give an undertaking that the data will only be used for the purpose for which they were transmitted. It is also specified that this shall not apply to the communication of personal data required for a Europol inquiry. This provision appears to be aimed at the situation in which Europol, in order to obtain an answer to an enquiry, must supply some personal data, e.g. when enquiring whether the recipient has information regarding a specific person.

In addition to these provisions of the Europol Convention, the general Rules on the transmission of personal data by Europol, as referred to earlier, come into play. One of the most important points to make in this respect is the great importance attached to negotiating formal co-operation agreements. The general principle is that there can be no transmission of personal data without there being such an Agreement. The only exception concerns cases in which the transmission of data is absolutely necessary to safeguard the essential interests of the Member States, or to prevent imminent danger associated with crime. The inspiration for this provision was clearly drawn from Principle 5.4 of Recommendation R (87) 15, although the text is not followed literally. In essence, this exception clause can only be used in very limited cases. The example often given is the case where Europol might have information concerning a terrorist act being prepared in a third State. In such cases, the interest of the possible victims clearly outweigh the right to data protection of the possible perpetrators. As an additional safeguard, the Director of Europol is obliged to inform both the Management Board and the Joint Supervisory Body in cases where he has decided to use his authority to transmit data without an agreement.[13] Through this procedure, we know that the Director of Europol used this possibility at least once, shortly after the 9-11 attacks in the United States, when no formal agreements between Europol and the US had been put in place.[14]

D.   Co-operation Agreements

Given these restrictions, any structural operational co-operation between Europol and a third State or body, including the exchange of personal data, must clearly be based on a formal co-operation agreement. Article 2 (1) of the Rules specifies that the minimum elements to be regulated in such agreements must concern the recipients of data, the type of data to be transmitted, and the purposes for which the data are to be transmitted or used.

As was briefly mentioned earlier, the procedure to reach such agreements involves the Council as the main authority, and the Management Board and the Joint Supervisory Body as advisor to the Council and the Management Board respectively. The procedure starts with the Council determining

---

13. Article 4 Rules on the transmission of personal data by Europol to third States and third bodies.
14. See JSB document 02/08, 6 March 2002, available at the JSB website at http://europoljsb.ue.eu.int/

with which States and bodies agreements are to be negotiated. This must be done by unanimous decision. The Council is also entitled to specify particular conditions when reaching its decision. Also, the Council is obliged to take account of the "law and administrative practice of the third State or body in the field of data protection, including as to the authority responsible for data protection matters".

To complete the procedure, again the Council must unanimously authorise the Director to sign the Agreement. At this stage, the Joint Supervisory Body must have been consulted by the Management Board, hereby ensuring that sufficient attention has been devoted to data protection issues. Only after this stage of the procedure has been completed can an agreement be signed and enter into force. In some cases, entry into force may be further delayed by national ratification requirements by the State with which the Agreement was negotiated, but this depends on the applicable national legislation in the third State in question.

E.   Provisions on Content

Apart from these procedural rules, there are some more substantive issues to be found in the Rules under discussion. These relate in particular to the competent authorities to whom data may be transmitted, the purposes for which data may be transmitted, the issue of correction and deletion, and liability. A few words should be said about each of these subjects.

As for the competent authorities, the first point is that personal data can only be transmitted to competent authorities within the third State. These should be bodies which, under national law, are responsible for preventing and combating criminal offences. Any onward transmission of data received by a competent authority is also restricted to authorities endowed with this specific task. Within this context, there is a clear interest, both from a practical and from a data protection point of view, to have one central authority within the third State, which acts as the national contact point between Europol and the competent authorities. Under the Rules, this is an objective which Europol should try to achieve. When these Rules were discussed, however, the drafters realised that this may not always be possible, especially when co-operation is with States with a federal organisation. Therefore, there is not here a strict obligation of result.

An interesting additional provision, which should be of help in ensuring that the data protection principles are adhered to by the third State, is the provision of Article 5 (3) of the Rules, which deals with the issue of onward transmission. This obliges Europol to ensure that the recipient of the data gives an undertaking that onward transmission of data by the initial recipient shall be limited to competent authorities, and that it will take place under the same conditions as those that apply to the original transmission. To further ensure that data are not being transmitted beyond the intended recipients, the third State must also give an assurance that it will not communicate data received from Europol to other third States or bodies. Clearly these last two provisions are practical examples of a further implementation of the principle that data should only be used by the appropriate authorities, in line with Principle 5.4 of the Recommendation R (87) 15.

As far as the purposes are concerned for which data may be transmitted, there is the prohibition to transmit data if there is no indication of the purpose of and reason for the request. There is also a particular provision on the transmission of the categories of sensitive data specified in Article 6 of the Council of Europe Convention: this is limited to absolutely necessary cases. Here again, the Director must inform the Management Board and the Joint Supervisory Body of such cases. The provisions on the purpose for which data may be transmitted end with the basic purpose limitation principle: Europol must ensure that the recipient gives an undertaking that the data will be used only for the purposes for which they were transmitted.

Along the same lines of basic data protection principles, Article 7 of the Rules contains the procedures specified for ensuring that data are kept accurate and up to date. As is the case in the Rules on the receipt of data, there are mutual obligations to keep one another informed when data that have been transmitted prove to be incorrect, or should not have been transmitted in the first place. Again, it is the responsibility of the Director to inform the Management Board and the Joint Supervisory Body of Europol's activities in this field. Any agreement which is concluded must contain provisions on these subjects. Europol should also ensure that the third State gives an undertaking that any data transmitted will be deleted when they are no longer necessary for the purpose for which they were transmitted.

Finally, agreements should contain provisions on liability. This is of particular importance in respect of any cases brought to the judicial authorities for damage suffered as a consequence of incorrect or illegal data processing.

VII. The Starting Phase: The 2000 Council Decision[15]

The first real test of all the provisions and procedures described above came in 1999, when the first Council Decision was prepared marking the start of Europol's external relations strategy. It was at this time that the newspaper article with which this contribution started was published and, as stated before, this illustrated the difficulties which had to be solved before Europol's external relations could really take off. In addition to the general legal issues, a political compromise needed to be found concerning the question of which third States and organisations Europol should develop relations with. Already at that stage, there were considerations with respect to the human rights situation in the third States with which co-operation was contemplated, and in particular with respect to data protection provisions. For many Member States, and for Europol, however, an equally important consideration was the operational benefit that could be expected from a possible co-operation.[16]

Within that context, a number of criteria were devised, which needed to be considered when deciding on candidates for co-operation. These included first of all the more operational question whether or not the third State concerned was a direct neighbour of the European Union, and whether or not crime from the third State had a direct effect on the Member States. Another practical point, which was logically taken into consideration, was whether or not the third State had expressed an interest in establishing co-operative relationships. Also, for practical reasons, it was considered important to start co-operation with Interpol as soon as possible, given the obvious synergies that could come from rapidly starting with close co-operation.

In addition, the general external relations policy of the European Union had to be considered. In general, there was no Member State at that time that supported a direct link between Europol's external relations policy and the EU's external policy, which meant that Member States recognised that Europol needed to have some room for manoeuvre. Nevertheless, account needed to be taken of the Council's declaration, which had been made at the time when the Europol Convention was agreed. This declaration stated that Europol should – as a matter of priority – establish relations with the competent bodies of those States with which the European Communities and their Member States had established a structural dialogue, which thus included all candidate countries at the time.

15. OJ C 106, 13.4.2000, p. 1.
16. See recital 2 of the preamble to the 2000 Decision.

In the end, the 2000 Council Decision not only established the first list of countries and organisations with which Europol could enter into negotiations; it also provided for further procedural safeguards to ensure that careful consideration be given to the data protection situation in the third States in. In particular, the Decision provides that whenever an agreement, including provisions for the exchange of personal data, is contemplated, the Director of Europol may only start negotiations after the Council has unanimously decided, on the basis of a report submitted to it by the Europol Management Board, that there are no obstacles that might prevent such negotiations from taking place.[17] The Management Board, for its part, is required to consult the Joint Supervisory Body on these reports, which should enable this data protection authority to express its opinion even before the start of the negotiations. The 2000 Council Decision also marks the start of the distinction between agreements which include the possibility of exchanging personal data –generally referred to as "operational" agreements – and those which do not provide for this possibility –referred to as "strategic" agreements. This distinction has proven to be useful in those cases where there is a political need to establish formal relationships, but a full "operational" agreement is not (yet) possible because of the data protection situation in the third country concerned.

As a final procedural safeguard, Article 3 of the Council Decision also clarifies that the Management Board should first be satisfied that the negotiations are adequately prepared before they can start. The Management Board is also given the authority to provide the Director with further instructions as necessary in such cases. Perhaps more importantly, the Decision also clearly establishes the power of the Management Board to decide on the prioritisation of the negotiations – taking account of the previously mentioned Council's declaration on Article 42 of the Convention. The Management Board first used these powers when it established, on 5 April 2000, that it was satisfied that negotiations with all of the third States and bodies mentioned in the 2000 Decision had been adequately prepared – with the logical exception of negotiations on the transmission of personal data – and that Europol should give priority to entering into negotiations with the accession candidates, the Schengen co-operation partners Norway and Iceland, Switzerland and Interpol. In addition to these third States and bodies, the 2000 Decision included Bolivia, Canada, Colombia, Morocco, Peru, the Russian Federation, Turkey and the US as third States with which Europol could enter into

17.   Article 1 (5) of the Council Decision 27 March 2000, OJ C 106, 13.4.2004, p. 2.

negotiations – other international organisations included the UNDCP (later renamed to ODCCP – The United Nations Office for Drug Control and Crime Prevention) and the World Customs Organisation.

After its adoption in 2000, the Council Decision was amended seven times to add new Sates and organisations to the list, most recently in February 2007[18]. Through these amendments, Monaco, Albania, Bosnia and Herzegovina, Croatia, The Federal Republic of Yugoslavia, FYROM, Moldova, Ukraine, Australia, Israel, China, Liechtenstein and Montenegro have been added to the list.

VIII. Practical Implementation – The First Agreements

In accordance with the Decision of the Council and the Management Board, a small but dedicated team at Europol started the preparation of the first elements of Europol's external relations strategy. Given that the first priority was to enter into agreements with the candidate States of the European Union, an approach was devised to deal with as many of those as possible in the shortest possible period of time. This approach also needed to take account of the fact that these States were at different stages in their preparations to become fully fledged members of the European Union, which also had its implications on their preparedness to enter into negotiations with Europol.

The first step was the organisation of a seminar, on 26 and 27 April 2000, to which representatives of all those States were invited. At that seminar, information was provided on many aspects concerning Europol, including its functioning as an organisation, the complex procedures for coming to a co-operation agreement, and a number of operational issues, including the possibilities of stationing liaison officers at Europol. In some cases, it was also the first opportunity to meet with the representatives of those organisations which would be involved in the procedures to come to a co-operation agreement. At that stage, the candidate States were also asked to provide further information on their state of preparedness to enter into a co-operation agreement. On that basis, it was possible to first concentrate efforts on those States which were most advanced, particularly in the area of data protection, since that was going to be one of the main requirements for a speedy conclusion of the procedure. After this stage, the States in question were visited one by one by a small team of Europol officials, usually consisting of one legal and one law enforcement expert. On the

18.   OJ L 51, 20.2.2007, p. 18.

basis of the information already provided previously and the results of the evaluation visit, a report was prepared by Europol on the data protection situation in the State in question, following a standard lay-out determined at the start of the procedure. These reports then went via the Management Board, CATS and Coreper to the Council, having previously been seen and commented upon by the Joint Supervisory Body. They served to identify not only the state of play in the State in question, but also provided an opportunity for all organisations involved to provide comments which could be taken into consideration during the negotiating process. For example, if a particular provision was not yet provided for under the national law of that State in question, this could be addressed through an appropriate provision in the co-operation agreement. In some cases, the States concerned took the opportunity to change their legislation or organisational arrangements in order to address the specific comments that were made during this procedure.

For most of the candidate States, this procedure did not cause many problems. Most of them were at the time well advanced in the process of becoming member States of the European Union, which meant that they were well acquainted with the EU principles on data protection, which they also knew through their membership of the Council of Europe. In practice, they were already in the process of ensuring that their national legislation on data protection would be in line with both the 1981 Council of Europe Convention and EU Directive 95/46[19] on the processing of personal data. Throughout the whole procedure of evaluation of the data protection legislation, only a few detailed changes would normally have been required to ensure consistency and compliance with the established norms. The situation was basically the same for Iceland, Norway and Switzerland, which are all signatories to Council of Europe Convention 108 and which all have well-elaborated systems of personal data protection in place. For all of these States, then, authorisation from the Council to start negotiations on co-operation agreements, including provisions on the exchange of personal data, was granted as a matter of course.

Once the negotiating stage was reached, negotiations were simplified by the fact that Europol had elaborated, in co-operation with the Member States, a Model Agreement which was used as a starting point in its negotiations with third States. For the negotiations with third bodies, an adapted version of that document was used. This Model Agreement is in fact nothing more than a compilation of all the issues which Europol is bound to take into consideration under the elaborate system described

19.   OJ L 281, 23.11.1995, p. 31– 50.

above, including the considerable number of very specific pre-conditions which must be met before an actual exchange of personal data can take place. The Model Agreement aims at clarifying these preconditions for Europol's negotiation partners. Although the document itself is neither binding, nor formally accepted by the Council, the idea behind its preparation was to ensure that, before the start of any negotiations, there would at least be some clear indication of what sort of agreement would be acceptable to the EU side. Since the Model Agreement was elaborated with this in mind, it should come as no surprise that it is very much centred on Europol's needs and obligations. Although there is very little room for manoeuvre on issues on which the Council has already laid down binding provisions, there is room for incorporating into specific agreements any issues that are requested by negotiating partners, or any amendments to those provisions of the Model Agreement which are not linked to binding obligations. In practice, the Model Agreement has proven to be a very useful tool indeed, and many agreements which have to a large extent been concluded have been based on the Model Agreement.

With hindsight, one can perhaps question the value of the agreements reached with the candidate States, for the simple reason that these agreements have lost their meaning after the accession of these States to the European Union and (through a separate procedure) to the Europol Convention. However, both the negotiating procedure and the implementation of the agreements have brought tangible benefits both to Europol and the States involved. The benefit for the States involved was to become closely associated with EU efforts in combating organised crime, well before those States became fully fledged Members. For Europol, the benefit was that it could rely on law enforcement information made available by those States at an earlier stage. Also, early agreements facilitated the transition to full membership of the States concerned.

IX. A Special Case – Co-operation with the United States

No contribution on the external relations of Europol would be complete without at least a few words on the relations between Europol and the United States of America. In sharp contrast to the relatively simple and non-political nature of the relations of Europol with the candidate States, Norway, Iceland and Switzerland, the conclusion of formal co-operation agreements with the United States proved to be a more challenging task. After 9-11, it was clear that the European Union needed to respond to the increased threat from terrorism, and it was equally clear that the development of relations between the US and Europol would need to be incorporated into the overall EU response. The Conclusions of the special JHA Council of 20 September 2001 invited the Director of Europol to take all the measures necessary to establish informal cooperation with the United States, pending the conclusion of a formal agreement. The Council also invited the Director of Europol to finalise a formal agreement with the United States as quickly as possible. The Council specified that this agreement should provide, inter alia, for an exchange of liaison officers between Europol and US agencies that are active in the policing sector. At the same time, the Director of Europol was invited to take the necessary steps to open negotiations with the United States on the conclusion of an agreement which included the transmission of personal data.

Under the immense political pressure of the time to come up with concrete measures to demonstrate the EU's solidarity with the US, the first "strategic" agreement between the United States and Europol was negotiated in the shortest time limits, and it was possible to conclude the agreement already on 6 December 2001. Although the agreement does not include provisions allowing for the exchange of personal data, it does provide for the exchange of technical and strategic information, and it regulates the difficult issue of exchanging classified information. It also provides the legal basis for the stationing of liaison officers through a separate agreement – a possibility that was used at a later stage, e.g. to station the first Europol Liaison Officers outside the European Union at the EU representation in Washington in August 2002.

At the same time, discussions on a farther reaching agreement, which would provide for the possibility to exchange personal data, continued at a frantic pace. The difficulties in this area are now well-known and resulted from the clear differences in the approach taken by the EU and the US in the area of personal data protection. Especially since the adoption of Directive 95/46, these different approaches have led to difficulties whenever the exchange of personal data is discussed.[20] Given the strong emphasis placed on personal data protection by Europol's legal framework, and the detailed nature of the provisions that need to be observed before personal data can be exchanged, many believed at the time that it would be impossible to reconcile these different approaches and come to an acceptable result. In spite of these difficulties, it did prove possible to arrive at an agreement which satisfied Europol, the Council, the Joint Supervisory Body and of course the US authorities. The second (or supplemental)

---

20. As recently demonstrated by the difficulties surrounding the exchange and usage of so-called PNR data (cf. contribution by de Schutter/de Hert in this book)

agreement between Europol and the US was signed on 22 December 2002, after intense last minute exchanges of views, which necessitated the signature of a side letter as well.[21]

A complete analysis of the second agreement would go well beyond the scope of this contribution, but a few points are worth highlighting all the same. Firstly, although the agreement has been criticised for not being in line with the EU data protection *acquis*, it does contain a number of significant data protection safeguards, which had not previously been agreed to by US authorities. These include the purpose limitation principle, contained in Article 5 (1) (a) of the Agreement, according to which information obtained for a specific purpose may only be used for that purpose. These also include a specific provision on so-called "sensitive" data (data revealing race, political opinions, religious or other beliefs, or concerning health and sex life, Article 6) which provides that such data may only be transmitted upon the transmitting party's determination that such information is particularly relevant for the purpose for which this information is transmitted. Another ground breaking provision is included in Article 7 (1), which not only stipulates that all federal authorities to which information may be provided under the Agreement are bound by it, but also that the information may only be transmitted to State or local law enforcement authorities, provided that they agree to observe the provisions of the Agreement. This was the only solution conceivable to deal with the fact that the US has thousands of competent law enforcement authorities, which cannot all be bound through an Agreement at the federal level. Other limitations included in Article 7 concern a prohibition of onward transmission without prior consent of the transmitting party, which constitutes another important safeguard. Important data protection provisions concerning the accuracy of information are also included in Article 9 of the Agreement, which provides for mutual obligations to inform the other party in case it is discovered that incorrect data have been transmitted, as well as to inform other recipients that the data received are in fact incorrect. The Europol-US Agreement was arguably the first such international Agreement in which US authorities agreed to apply such specific data protection provisions.

---

21. Text available via the Europol website at www.europol.europa.eu.

X. Concluding Remarks

The external relations of Europol are highly specific to the organisation for a number of reasons. One of these is the relative independence of the organisation from the normal Council structures. This is due to the fact that Europol was set up as a classic international organisation on the basis of a Convention which provides full legal personality to Europol as an organisation, including the right to conclude valid agreements under international law.

At the same time, the independence of the organisation in its external relations is highly relative. As was demonstrated before, the procedures, which need to be followed before Europol can enter into formal relations with third countries, ensure that political, legal and data protection control is actually exercised at all stages of the procedure. In fact, no agreement can be signed by the Director of Europol without at least three Management Board and Council Decisions, and two consultations of the Joint Supervisory Body when the agreement includes the exchange of personal data. In addition, the terms of the agreements and the conditions imposed ensure that Europol cannot transmit any personal data supplied by a Member State, without that Member State's consent. Although it can be argued that this procedure reflects a lack of trust in the organisation, the restrictions and limitations are more understandable when considering the context within which Europol works – clearly all safeguards have been put in place to ensure not only the protection of personal data, but also the operational effectiveness and protection of sources required when combating serious criminal threats such as terrorism and organised crime.

The system is also set up to ensure that possible infringements of the right to privacy, which cannot be excluded in any law enforcement work, are balanced by an elaborate system of norms to prevent data abuse. Effective control mechanisms are put in place to ensure that in cases where abuses do occur, corrections can be made. This system of norms also helps law enforcement authorities manage their information. Any system which improves the level of accuracy of data, the proper administration of data processing, and an increased awareness of the dangers inherent in processing sensitive data can only help to increase the effectiveness of law enforcement activities. It is also quite clear that this system of norms is indispensable for the political and public acceptance of Europol. Without such acceptance, it would be impossible for Europol to exist, let alone function effectively.

In addition, Europol's external relations are clearly influenced by the existence of Interpol – the world-wide police organisation which already EU law enforcement authorities with opportunities to exchange crime related information, including personal data, with other States across the world. When considering Europol's external relations, the point has often been made that Europol should not become a duplication of Interpol, or in other words, there might be no need for Europol to establish relations with the whole world. The selective and careful approach adopted so far reflects the point that, only where international relations can actually provide added value for Europol and the Member States should they be established. In other cases co-operation through Interpol can provide a viable alternative.

A final point worth mentioning is that the system described here may well change in the near future. After the start of the political discussion on the future of Europol during the Austrian Presidency (first semester 2006), the Commission adopted a proposal in December 2006[22] for a new legal basis for Europol, which includes a significant departure from the currently applicable system. Particularly striking is the idea that Europol would no longer be allowed to negotiate and sign international agreements, and that instead, its external relations should be managed through agreements negotiated by the European Union. This approach is clearly intended to ensure that Europol's external relations are brought closer in line with the general external relations in the JHA field. Discussions on the Commission proposal are on-going at the time of writing, and the Council Working Group dealing with the proposal has not yet discussed this aspect in depth. This is just the final step in the on-going debate on Europol's external relations. If the Commission's proposal for a new legal basis for Europol is adopted, it should also bring simplification to the current system which is indeed in need of an overhaul. As was demonstrated in this contribution, the main difficulty is that the different norms which are currently applicable are distributed over a large number of different legal instruments, making the system in its entirety difficult to comprehend and apply. Although this is understandable within the context of the historic development of the system, it is certainly urgent to simplify the system and maybe rethink its crucial points once again. Hopefully, on-going discussions on the new legal basis for Europol will make a simplified and better system a reality in the near future.

22.   COM(2006)0817, 20 December 2006.

Part IV

Horizontal Issues

1. EU-US Relations in Justice and Home Affairs

Jonathan Faull and Luigi Soreca[1]

I.   Introduction

The European Union and the United States are global, political and economic partners. Together they represent just 10 % of the world's population yet account for approximately 40% of global trade and 60% of Gross Domestic Product. Their close economic, cultural and political ties can be explained by the successive waves of European emigrants received by the United States over the last 200 years in particular. More recently in the aftermath of the Second World War, the United States has been a key supporter of integration between the nations of Europe, embodied today in the European Union.

Diplomatic relations between the United States and European Union (or its forerunners) have been maintained since 1953. For example, the United States mission to the European Communities (now the European Union) was established in Brussels in 1961. Since 1953, a Delegation in Washington has represented the European Commission in its relationships with the United States Government. The present partnership between the United States and the European Union therefore draws on common values and a long history of transatlantic cooperation.

The USA and the EU also have close ties in the area of Justice, Freedom and Security. Relations have grown rapidly in this field over the last few years. Cooperation had already started in the mid-90s, when, under the umbrella of the New Transatlantic Agenda, a specific vehicle for Justice, Freedom and Security cooperation was created in the form of bi-annual "informal" Justice and Home Affairs "Troika" meetings.

The EU and the US have long had a regular dialogue in the area of JHA, not only in general terms, but also on topical issues, such as terrorist financing, radicalisation, travel document security, visa issues and the sharing and protection of information. This dialogue is based on mutual trust and shared values, and even though the EU and the US have differences of

---

1.   The authors express their personal views, which do not necessarily reflect official positions of the European Commission.

opinion and operation, there is a clear understanding that in today's globalised world they have a shared interest in working together to protect their citizens.

Two recent events dramatically increased EU-US cooperation in the area of Justice, Freedom and Security in terms of both political significance and concrete effectiveness. The first was the signature (and entry into force) of the Treaty of Amsterdam (1999), which transferred regulatory competencies on a number of JHA issues from the Member States to the EU. This inevitably triggered an exploration of the external implications of these newly "Europeanised" policy areas, which again resulted in more intensive cooperation also with the USA in areas such as document security and visa policy. The second was no doubt the dramatic terrorist attack on selected economic, political and defence targets in the USA on 11 September 2001 (9/11), which resulted in an intensification of co-operation and a proliferation of legal instruments formalising the modalities of that co-operation. These two driving forces behind more intensive EU-US cooperation in the area of JHA will be further discussed in section II.

As a result of these two driving forces, eight ground-breaking agreements, which show the EU and US working together on an equal footing, have been signed since 11 September 2001: two police cooperation agreements between Europol and US law enforcement authorities (signed respectively in 2001 and in 2002), two agreements on judicial criminal cooperation regarding extradition and mutual legal assistance (signed in 2003), one agreement on the Container Security Initiative (CSI, signed in 2004), three agreements on the transfer of passenger data (PNR, signed respectively in 2004, 2006 and 2007), and, in November 2006, an agreement on judicial cooperation between Eurojust and US Department of Justice. These agreements will be further discussed in section III.

Section IV gives an overview over the main actors and institutions of EU-US Cooperation in the area of justice and home affairs. A brief summary of the paper and its main conclusions will be offered in section V.

II.   The Treaty of Amsterdam and 9/11: driving forces of the EU-US relationship

A.   The "Europeanisation" of immigration, asylum, border control and visa policies and their growing external dimension

The free movement of people in an area without borders, where freedom of circulation is the norm and where any restrictions to cross-border movements are the exception, is one of the European Union's greatest achievements. It was clear from the outset that this completion of an internal market without frontiers and the creation of an area of justice, security and liberty, would have to go hand in hand with satisfying the need of securing the EU's external borders and of tackling at a Community level internal security risks, which had previously been tackled at national level.

In the 1997 Treaty of Amsterdam, the EU Member States entrusted the European Union with regulatory powers in areas traditionally part of national sovereignty such as visa policy, protection of external borders, asylum and migration. By giving the European Community powers to legislate and act in these areas, the Member States of the Union decided the time had come to establish common policies and implement common standards at Union level and to exploit the added value of pooling resources and expertise among their national authorities.

By 1999, the European Commission had started exercising its right of initiative and had presented several legislative proposals and measures to put in place operational networks among national authorities for exchange of information and best practices. Henceforth, JHA came to be regarded as a legitimate field for cooperation at Union level. Incorporation into the EU of the so-called "Schengen acquis" has put additional tools at the disposal of the Union.

It was also clear from the outset that the newly created Community powers and responsibilities would have policy implications not only at EU level but also in relations with third countries. In fact the common internal approach meant that the European response to migration from outside the EU had to be sophisticated enough to work across borders. Cooperation with third countries began in all those areas and significant developments have been made in the areas of document security and visa policies.

The entry into force of the Treaty of Amsterdam has changed the role of the EU in its relations with the US in the areas of immigration, asylum, border control, and visa policies.

The successful development of EU-US cooperation must be seen in the wider context of the externalisation of the internal security of the EU. This has been triggered by the opportunities provided by improvements in transport and communication technologies, the emergence of trans-national criminal organisations engaged in world-wide illegal trafficking and, more recently, by the growth of global terrorism. All this has had an impact on structures, methods and content of the policy-making process in the field of Justice and Home Affairs in Europe, providing a fundamental legitimising argument for action at EU level.

European policy makers and legislators have understood the need to pursue the external dimension of internal security measures and how an effective external security strategy may substantially contribute to the successful building of the internal area of freedom, security and justice. In today's world, challenges are global and security indivisible. The EU's external relations promote democracy, development, the rule of law and respect for fundamental rights and international obligations. In pursuing these objectives, the EU seeks to project its core values and create conditions in which its internal policies have the greatest chance of success.

B.   After 9/11: Strengthening cooperation in counter-terrorism

The threat of global terrorism has recently reconfirmed the depth of European–American shared values and interests more than any other issue since the Cold War. Terrorist attacks taught democracies on both sides of the Atlantic brutal lessons about their vulnerabilities.

Transatlantic cooperation has been robust since 2001 in particular and continues to grow. Alliance and partnership do not conceal differences of view and emphasis. In some cases, differences run deeper than just tactics, such as the European hostility to the death penalty or the inclusion of certain groups in terrorist lists or the characterisation of the fight against terrorism[2].

2.   Kristin Archick, US-EU Cooperation Against Terrorism, CRS Report for Congress, 24.1.2006, US Department of State Website: http://fpc.state.gov/documents/organization/61436.pdf, accessed 30.7.2007 p. 5.

To address the rising threat of terrorist attacks within Europe, the EU has developed its counterterrorism capabilities dramatically over the past ten years. Two of the most evident changes have been the emergence of an increasingly unified European approach to terrorism and the virtual elimination of internal border controls on the Continent. After September 11th, European governments directed resources of the EU into the fight against terrorism. They used the EU's still limited powers on internal security matters to implement a Europe-wide arrest warrant,[3] draw up a common definition of the crime of terrorism,[4] and establish rules for more joint operations between national police forces.[5] Governments gave Europol (the European Police Office) extra resources and staffed a new Europol Counter-Terrorism Task Force with officers from their own national police and intelligence services.[6]

The European Union understood that this new, virulent strain of terrorism demanded a broader and more comprehensive strategy. In an action plan developed just 10 days after September 11, 2001, the EU expressed its solidarity with the United States and instituted greater cooperation among its Member States.[7] On 20 September 2001, the Council of Justice and Home Affairs Ministers adopted a series of conclusions including measures to improve transatlantic relations in the fight against terrorism.[8] An extraordinary European Council meeting adopted an EU Action Plan on the Fight against Terrorism, on 21 September 2001. The Action Plan contains specific references to the need to improve EU-US relations.[9]

Since 2001, the EU has built steadily on that foundation by developing a multifaceted campaign to thwart terrorism. The annual EU-US Summit and

---

3. Council Framework Decision of 13 June 2002 on the European Arrest Warrant and the Surrender Procedures between Member States, OJ L 190, 18.07.2002, p. 1.
4. Council Framework Decision of 13 June 2002 on Combating Terrorism, OJ L 164, 22.06.2002, p. 3.
5. Council Act of 28 November 2002 drawing up a Protocol amending the Convention on the establishment of a European Police Office (Europol Convention) and the Protocol on the privileges and immunities of Europol, the members of its organs, the deputy directors and the employees of Europol, OJ C 312, 16.12.2002, p. 1.
6. Council Decision 2003/48/JHA of 19 December 2003 on the implementation of specific measures for police and judicial cooperation to combat terrorism in accordance with Article 4 of Common Position 2001/931/CFSP, OJ L 16, 22.1.2003, p. 68.
7. 'Extraordinary European Council Meeting Conclusions and Plan of Action' SIC (2001) 990 - Brussels, 21/09/2001.
8. Bulletin 2001/9; formally adopted in the Council Framework Decision supra n. 4.
9. 'Extraordinary European Council Meeting Conclusions and Plan of Action' supra n. 7.

Ministerial meetings regularly discuss terrorism, justice, freedom and security issues. The EU-US Summit of 26 June 2004 adopted a comprehensive joint declaration on combating terrorism including financing, preventive measures and transport security.[10] More recently, the EU adopted a revised counter-terrorism strategy in December 2005 which included actions divided into four main categories: prevention, protection, pursuit and response.[11]

The Union has also acknowledged that the development of a true Area of Freedom, Security and Justice in the EU will be successful only if it is underpinned by a partnership with key foreign countries. Therefore, in December 2005, the Union also adopted a strategy for the external dimension of justice, freedom and security, which seeks to confront the inter-linked threat and challenges posed by terrorism, organised crime, corruption, drugs and illegal migration flows.[12] It promotes the respect of human rights, the rule of law and international obligations, strengthens judicial and law enforcement capacities and cooperation and supports bilateral and multilateral approaches to give effect to policies in the area of freedom, security and justice.

Partnership with the US is an integral part of this strategy. As Europe moves from a reactive to a proactive approach in dealing with the global challenges it faces, including terrorism, strategic cooperation with the US must continue to improve. This collaboration is of paramount importance. 12 million Europeans travel to the United States every year. EU-US trade is worth 420 billion € per year,[13] foreign direct investment by EU countries in the US is 702.9 billion € (2004 figures), while US companies invested 802 billion €[14] (total investment in each other's economies was 1.5 trillion € in 2006).[15] By way of comparison, there is more US investment in Ireland than in China, more in the Netherlands than in China and India combined.

---

10. EU-US Declaration on Combating Terrorism, signed at EU-US Summit, Ireland 26 June 2004.
11. EU Counter-Terrorism Strategy (doc. 14469/4/05 REV 4) adopted in Presidency Conclusions to Brussels European Council 15/16 December 2005 (doc. 15914/1/05 REV 1).
12. Strategy for the external dimension of JHA: Global Freedom, Security and Justice (Council doc. 15446/05 JAI 488 RELEX 741) 06.12.2005.
13. "United States Barriers to Trade and Investment: Report 2006" European Commission February 2007, p. 5.
14. European Commission External Relations Website: http://ec.europa.eu/comm/external_relations/us/economic_relations/index.htm, accessed 14.6.2007.
15. "United States Barriers to Trade and Investment: Report 2006", supra n. 13.

Experience shows that the most effective way to promote security cooperation is information exchange between law enforcement and other authorities. This has led to mutual benefits for both the US and the EU, as shown by recent successes concerning threats to flights from London to the USA in August 2006, which led to restrictions on liquids. Counterterrorism efforts have benefited from law enforcement and prosecution improvements, even if problems still exist when it comes to bringing terrorists to justice.

The use of intelligence information in trials of terrorist suspects is still problematic because it is often either inadmissible as evidence or likely to compromise sensitive sources and methods. Authorities must weigh the costs and benefits of exposing confidential information in return for obtaining a conviction. Prosecuting terrorists has become an increasingly international endeavour. Frequently, suspects have ties to individuals and organizations abroad, and international cooperation with foreign governments is often necessary to obtain a conviction. Unfortunately, not all countries have laws that allow them to prosecute terrorism suspects effectively.

The agreements signed between the EU and its agencies and the US authorities have helped to fill in some of these gaps. It will be important to ensure full and rapid implementation of these agreements, as well as effective monitoring of their application, because as the terrorist threat evolves, counterterrorism laws and agreements will need to be reviewed regularly.

It is important to counter the perception that American and European counterterrorism efforts are at odds with each other. By focusing on commonalities, the US-EU partnership can be enhanced to improve both tactical and strategic cooperation. The EU's role in coordinating counterterrorism policy among Member States goes hand in hand with this notion, and will help develop overarching solutions to a shared challenge.

III. Main Areas of EU-US Cooperation

A. Document security

New technology provides opportunities for improvement in document security. The European Union has taken several measures to make travel and residence documents more secure. It has put forward a harmonised system of security features for EU visa and residence documents, to help protect against forgery and counterfeiting.[16] In addition, a European image-archiving system called FADO (false and authentic documents) is being developed to exchange information on genuine and false documents.[17] Finally, the skills, equipment and training for detecting false documents are being boosted at document issuing centres[18] and points of entry into the European Union.[19]

The EU and the US are consulting closely on secure passports which incorporate biometric data such as facial imagery. On 28 February 2005, the Commission adopted the first part of the technical specifications for storing the passport holder's facial image in a chip in the passport.[20] This image is protected by "Basic Access Control", which means that the part of the passport to be read by a machine must first be scanned in order to unlock the chip for reading.

The US requirement that travellers with passports issued after 26 October 2005 must have biometric passports, as part of the Visa Waiver Programme (see below under II.A.2), was initially a contentious EU-US issue. However, the US postponed the deadline to 26 October 2006, and this minimised the potential impact on EU citizens travelling to the US because EU Member States have in the meantime started issuing biometric passports. EU citizens holding a passport issued by a visa waiver country after 28 August 2006 can therefore continue to travel to the US without a visa.

On 28 June 2006, the Commission adopted the second part of the technical specifications for passports and other travel documents issued by Member

16. Council Decision of 27 March 2000 on the improved exchange of information to combat counterfeit travel documents, OJ L 81, 1.04.2000, p. 1.
17. Joint Action 98/700/JHA of 3 December 1998, concerning the setting up of a European Image Archiving System (FADO), OJ L 333, 9.12.1998, p. 4.
18. Council Recommendation 99/C 140/01 of 29 April 1999 on the provision for the detection of false or falsified documents in the visa departments of representations abroad and in the offices of domestic authorities dealing with the issue or extension of visas, OJ C 140, 20.5.1999, p. 1.
19. Council Recommendation 98/C 189/02 of 28 May 1998 on the provision of forgery detection equipment at ports of entry to the European Union, OJ C 189, 17.06.1998, p. 19.
20. Commission Decision establishing the technical specifications on the standards for security features and biometrics in passports and travel documents issued by Member States. 28/02/2005 C (2005) 409.

States[21] pursuant to Council Regulation (EC) 2252/2004.[22] This relates to the additional storage of two fingerprints on the passport chip. The Commission considered these data more sensitive and decided to protect them by "Extended Access Control", a system which works with a Public Key Infrastructure (PKI).

Therefore, by June 2009, two fingerprints will be added to the microchip that will already contain a facial image. The EU countries are among the first in the world issuing passports with a high level of protection against unauthorized access by providing 'Extended Access Control,' whilst at the same time complying with the recommendations of the International Civil Aviation Organization (ICAO) in order to ensure interoperability. The harmonised introduction of biometric identifiers in passports of EU citizens will ensure that the identity of the holder can be easily established and will protect against identity fraud.

Another area of practical cooperation between the EU and US is the exchange of information on stolen and lost passports. Launched in 2003, with the aim of contributing to a central database of stolen and lost passports at Interpol headquarters in Lyon (France), this joint EU-US initiative has proved successful. On the basis of the Common Position on exchanging certain data with Interpol adopted by the Council of the European Union in January 2005, Member States routinely send data to Interpol on issued and blank passports that are stolen, lost or misappropriated.[23]

According to Interpol statistics, before the Common Position was implemented, the 15 EU Member States had entered 4,567,267 entries in the Interpol database. By June 2006, there were 8,129,327 entries from 23 EU Member States. EU searches of the database rose from 3955 to 102,632 over the same period, and the number of "hits" had risen from 173 to 610[24].

21. Commission Decision establishing the technical specifications on the standards for security features and biometrics in passports and travel documents issued by Member States, 28/06/2006, C(2006) 2909.
22. Council Regulation (EC) No 2252/2004 of 13 December 2004 on standards for security features and biometrics in passports and travel documents issued by Member States, OJ L 385, 29.12.2004, p. 1.
23. Council Common Position on exchanging certain data with Interpol, 2005/69/JHA of 24 January 2005, OJ L 27, 29.1.2005, p. 61.
24. Statistical data provided by the International Criminal Police Organisation –ICPO (Interpol) (see website www.interpol.int).

B.   US Visa Waiver programme and EU's reciprocity regulations

In line with the principle of free movement of persons,[25] visa policy for the EU is regulated at European level. In particular, Regulation (EC) no 539/2001[26] establishes the joint lists of third countries whose citizens are exempted from the visa requirement by the Schengen Member States.

The United States of America is listed in Regulation (EC) no 539/2001, so American citizens can travel to all EU countries without a visa.

The United States continues to impose a visa obligation on nationals of 12 EU Member States: Czech Republic, Estonia, Latvia, Lithuania, Hungary, Poland, Slovakia, Greece, Malta, Cyprus, Romania and Bulgaria. The US considers that those countries do not satisfy all the criteria necessary for acceptance into the US Visa Waiver Programme (VWP).

This programme[27] allows nationals from 27 participating countries to enter the US as temporary visitors for business or leisure without first obtaining a visa from a US consulate.[28] The eligible countries are designated by the Secretary of Homeland Security in consultation with the Secretary of State. The US has emphasised that the requirements for a country's acceptance into the United States Visa Waiver Programme (VWP) have been established by Congress as a matter of law[29] and that countries desiring to participate in the Visa Waiver Programme must individually satisfy all of these criteria, any changes to the current criteria requiring an Act of Congress.

US visa policy therefore creates a distinction between the oldest EU Member States, and those which have joined since 2004 (plus Greece,

---

25. Art. 39 EC Treaty.
26. Council Regulation (EC) No 539/2001 of 15 March 2001 listing the third countries whose nationals must be in possession of visas when crossing the external borders and those whose nationals are exempt from that requirement, OJ L 81, 21.3.2001, p. 1–7.
27. The Visa Waiver Program (VWP) was established as a temporary program by the Immigration Reform and Control Act of 1986 (P.L. 99- 603). Congress periodically enacted legislation to extend the program's authorization. Finally, the program gained permanent status on 30 October 2000, by the adoption of the Visa Waiver Permanent Program Act (P.L. 106-396).
28. Immigration and Nationality Act (8 U.S.C 1101,1187), specifically sections 101(a)(15)(B) and 217.
29. The conditions are set by the Immigration and Nationality Act (U.S.C. 1187), the Border Security Act, and the Enhanced Border Security and Visa Entry Reform Act.

minus Slovenia). Regulation (EC) no 851/2005[30] requires reciprocity in precisely this situation. The regulation applies to all non-EU countries, not merely the United States. Where its citizens suffer from a situation of non-reciprocity, the Member State concerned must notify the European Commission, which then begins negotiations with the non-EU state's authorities in order to ensure visa-free travel.

As part of its negotiations under this Regulation, the EU has put the issue of visa reciprocity on the agenda of EU-US meetings at all levels up to, and including, the Summit. The Commission has published regular reports on visa reciprocity and has alluded to possible retaliation measures. These reports highlight the need for clear, detailed and verifiable criteria for participation in the Visa Waiver Programme, in particular through a transparent process and detailed implementation plans aimed at ensuring visa exemption for all EU citizens as soon as possible. The US authorities acknowledge the importance of the issue and it is hoped that implementation of new legislation adopted in the US in 2007 will solve this matter.

Prior to this legislation, President Bush had proposed a Visa Waiver Programme "roadmap" in February 2005 to focus and guide joint efforts towards future participation in the Visa Waiver Programme for the 12 excluded Member States.[31] Joint consular working groups were established and met regularly in all of the EU Member States concerned.

The roadmaps were said to be shaped to the circumstances of each country but contained a number of common elements, including:
– A US agreement to review the visa application process;
– Removing all pre-1989 cases from overstay calculations;
– The need to meet the technical requirements of US legislation (e.g.: overstay and non-immigrant visa refusal rates, biometrics, lost and stolen passport reporting, etc);
– The need for public campaigns to increase awareness of the requirements and obligations associated with travel to the US.

The roadmaps were, however, not comprehensive. They did not cover all the criteria for a judgement on a country's VWP eligibility and, in some cases, the criteria were essentially subjective. The US acknowledges this. In

---

30. Council Regulation (EC) No 851/2005 of 2 June 2005 amending Regulation (EC) No 539/2001 listing the third countries whose nationals must be in possession of visas when crossing the external borders and those whose nationals are exempt from that requirement as regards the reciprocity mechanism, OJ L 141, 4.6.2005, p. 3–5.
31. "Process for Admitting Additional Countries into the Visa Waiver Program" US Govt. Accountability Office, Report GAO-06-835R, 5 September 2006, p. 1.

addition, some of the statistical data on which the criteria are measured (e.g. overstays) were acknowledged to be imperfect.

During his visit to Tallinn in November 2006, President Bush announced that he intended to seek modifications to the VWP that would strengthen and enhance the security of VWP travel and allow the US to accelerate the entry of new countries into the programme. In January 2007, two draft bills tabled in Congress were merged into a single bill, entitled "Improving America's Security by Implementing Unfinished Recommendations of the 9/11 Commission Act of 2007".[32]

On 26 July 2007 the US Senate and on 27 July 2007 the US House of Representatives passed the bill[33]. Section 711 of the Act covers the "Modernisation of the Visa Waiver Program". Its key elements are: (1) the introduction of an Electronic Travel Authorisation (ETA) system for which a fee may be charged, (2) flexibility on the non-immigrant visa refusal rate up to 10%, only once an air exit system, using biometrics, is in place that can verify the departure of not less that 97 % of foreign nationals that exit through US airports, (3) the eligibility of travelling to the USA under the VWP is not a determination that the person is admissible to the USA, (4) reporting on lost and stolen passports either through Interpol or other means, (5) third countries should accept repatriation of any citizen, former citizen or national against whom is issued a final executable order of removal, and finally (6) bilateral agreements with third countries on passenger information exchange. The Act was signed by President Bush on 3 August 2007.

The Commission had issued its first report on the reciprocity situation on 10 January 2006.[34] After deliberations at various levels the Council adopted conclusions on the report on 21 February 2006, which endorse

---

32. `Improving America's Security Act of 2007'. (110th Congress, 1st Session, S. 4) passed Senate 13.3.2007.
33. See the H.R.1 Congressional Record at http://hsgac.senate.gov/_files / ConferenceReportinRecord.pdf.
34. Report from the Commission to the Council on visa waiver reciprocity with certain third countries in accordance with Article 2 of Council Regulation (EC) No 851/2005 of 2 June 2005, OJ C 49, 28.2.2006, p. 23.

the Commission's appreciation.[35] A second report was issued by the Commission on 3 October 2006.[36] Both Commission reports underlined the need to ensure that the transatlantic economy remains competitive and a driver of global growth. Visa reciprocity plays an important role and can be considered a key feature of EU-US relations. As many as 14 million jobs, on both sides of the Atlantic, depend on transatlantic commercial ties. Likewise, increased travel can bring substantial social and economic benefits to both tourists and their destination states. It is therefore important that the issue of visa reciprocity be resolved speedily and without undue impediment to the security and movement of travel across the Atlantic.

C.   The Agreements between Europol and the US

In the aftermath of the events of 9/11, two agreements were signed between Europol and the US..[37] The first agreement, signed on 6 December 2001, was designed to enhance the cooperation of EU Member States, acting through Europol, and the US in preventing, detecting and investigating serious forms of international terrorism and organised crime. These forms are unlawful drug trafficking, trafficking in nuclear and radioactive substances, illegal immigrant smuggling, trafficking in human beings, motor vehicle crime, crimes committed or likely to be committed in the course of terrorist activities against life, limb, personal freedom or property, forgery of money and means of payment, as well as illegal money laundering activities in connection with these forms of crime or specific manifestations thereof and related criminal offences. The agreement provided for the exchange of strategic and technical information. It did not

35.   Council conclusions on visa waiver reciprocity mechanism, CS/2006/6390,21.2.2006, adopting Report from the Commission to the Council on visa waiver reciprocity with certain third countries in accordance with Article 2 of Council Regulation (EC) No 851/2005 of 2 June 2005 amending Council Regulation (EC) No 539/2001 listing the third countries whose nationals must be in possession of visas when crossing the external borders and those whose nationals are exempt from that requirement as regards the reciprocity mechanism, OJ C 49, 28.2.2006, p. 23.
36.   Report from the Commission to the European Parliament and the Council on on cases where visa waiver non-reciprocity is maintained by certain third countries in accordance with Article 1(5) of Council Regulation (EC) No 539/2001 listing the third countries whose nationals must be in possession of visas when crossing the external borders and those whose nationals are exempt from that requirement, as amended by Regulation (EC) No 851/2005 as regards the reciprocity mechanism, Bulletin /2006/10/ 1.19.2, COM/2006/568/FINAL, 3.10.2006.
37.   For more detail on the external relations of Europol, cf. the contribution by Heimans in this book.

authorise the transmission of data related to identified or identifiable individuals.

A second agreement allowing for the sharing of personal data was signed in December 2002. Europol and the United States are now able to fully implement their existing co-operation at a more operational level. This agreement supplements the existing bilateral co-operation arrangements between the US and EU Member States.

Since then, fruitful operational cooperation has developed between Europol and the US Department of Justice, FBI and Secret Service. Since 2005, the FBI and the Secret Service have posted liaison officers at Europol's headquarters in The Hague, while Europol has posted two liaison officers in the European Union Delegation in Washington.[38]

Europol and the US intend to implement common standards on clearances and develop measures for the exchange of classified information. Best practices are already shared and exchange programmes for analysts take place on a regular basis in strategic and joint operational activities.[39]

D.   The EU-US Agreements on Extradition and Mutual Legal Assistance

On 20 September 2001, JHA Council agreed to start negotiations for an EU-USA judicial cooperation agreement in criminal matters based on Articles 24 and 38 of the Treaty on European Union.[40] The signature of two agreements, one on extradition[41] and one on mutual legal assistance in criminal matters,[42] took place on 25 June 2003.

These agreements underline the importance of the EU-US relationship, as they are the first agreements between the EU and a third country in the field of judicial co-operation in criminal matters. Cooperation includes

---

38.   Report from Europol to the Council of the European Union, Cooperation between the United States of America and Europol: Prevention and suppression of transnational organised crime- Evaluation of the cooperation agreements, CS/2005/11502, 27 July 2005, p. 7.

39.   Europol Press Release, Enhanced Cooperation with the USA, The Hague 24.4.2006, Europol   Website: http://www.europol.europa.eu/index.asp?page=news&news=pr060424.htm, accessed 30.7.2007.

40.   On these agreements, cf. also the contribution by Stessens in this book.

41.   Agreement on extradition between the European Union and the United States of America OJ L 181, 19.7.2003, p. 27.

42.   Agreement on mutual legal assistance between the European Union and the United States of America OJ L 181, 19.7.2003, p. 34.

identification of bank information, joint investigation teams and video conferencing. Criteria are listed for dealing with competing requests, e.g. a US request for Mutual Legal Assistance and a request of another Member State under the European Arrest Warrant. The agreements build upon, supplement and, in a few cases, replace provisions in many EU Member States' bilateral treaties with the US.

The Mutual Legal Assistance (MLA) Agreement, which contains extensive provisions on data protection and the provision of evidence and information, is mainly aimed at:
- giving EU law enforcement authorities access to bank accounts throughout the US (and vice versa) in the context of investigations into serious crimes, including terrorism, organised crime and financial crime;
- improving practical co-operation by reducing delays in mutual legal assistance and allowing for the creation of Joint Investigative Teams and videoconferencing;
- allowing EU Member States to continue to apply their grounds for refusal under their bilateral mutual legal assistance treaties or other provisions of domestic law; and
- allowing EU Member States that at present do not have a mutual legal assistance treaty with the US to refer to their *ordre public* (public policy, security, sovereignty, or other essential interests of the requested State) in order to refuse to communicate information in certain cases.

The Extradition agreement is intended to:
- reduce delays in the handling of requests, through an alleviation of legalisation and certification requirements, and simplification of documentation to be provided;
- improve channels of transmission for extradition requests, in particular in urgent cases concerning provisional arrest, and facilitate direct contacts between central authorities;
- broaden the range of extraditable offences by allowing extradition for every offence punishable by more than one year's imprisonment;
- allow EU Member States to continue to apply grounds of refusal from their bilateral extradition treaties;
- enshrine the right to a fair trial of an extradited person by an impartial tribunal established by law;
- allow Member States to make extradition contingent upon the condition that the death penalty will not be imposed;

- provide for consultations to determine the extent to which sensitive information contained in an extradition request can be protected by the requested State; and to
- set out a detailed list of criteria that a requested State needs to take into account when dealing with competing extradition requests from several States, or in case of competition between a US extradition request and a European arrest warrant (this provision does not have bearing on the International Criminal Court: a Member State that deems that it should surrender a person to the ICC rather than extradite him or her to the US will be able to do so).

Unfortunately, neither of the two agreements has yet entered into force. Under Article 3 of both Agreements, all Member States need to exchange "written instruments" with the U.S. in order to acknowledge the way in which the provisions of the EU-US Agreements are implemented at the bilateral level (one on mutual legal assistance and one on extradition).

25 Member States have signed such bilateral instruments with the United States, but several Member States still need to go through the domestic procedures with regard to these bilateral instruments. The US needs to go through a ratification procedure as well. On 29 September 2006, the US President transmitted the two Agreements, plus the bilateral instruments per Member State, for ratification to the US Senate.

It appears that all bilateral instruments which have been negotiated between the Member States and the United States contain a provision which stipulates that they will, after completion of the necessary internal procedures, only enter into force at the same time as the EU-US Agreements. This implies that all ratification procedures with regard to the bilateral instruments will need to have taken place before the exchange of ratification instruments for the EU-US Agreements can take place. These delays are highly regrettable.

E.   Border and Transport Security

The aftermath of 11 September 2001 saw new security measures imposed by governments around the world also in the area of border and transport security. The challenge was to strike a balance between heightened security requirements and the continuation of open and secure trade and passenger transport. Smoother trade and more effective security are not contradictory.

US policy after 9/11 was basically to create virtual borders for goods and people at their points of departure. The actual US border became the 'last line of defence'. This policy included issues such as use of sky marshals, deploying immigration officers overseas, advance passenger screening, capturing biometric information at entry points, etc. The US wished to work more closely with the EU on many of these issues. Contacts at formal and informal levels were substantially enhanced and, in spring 2004, a new forum was established under the name of the "EU-US Policy Dialogue on Border and Transport Security" (PDBTS).

This forum, which first met in April 2004, now meets bi-annually, bringing together officials from both sides of the Atlantic. On the EU side, the Presidency of the Union, the Council General Secretariat and the Commission take part, while for the US side the Departments of State, Justice and Homeland Security are involved. The goal of the PDBTS is to enhance mutual understanding and complementarity of EU-US security policies and to improve security in land, air and maritime environments. It is also used as an early warning mechanism whereby each side can notify the other about relevant new initiatives.

In 2002, the United States began bilateral negotiations with several EU Member States on container security. These talks culminated in the admission of Belgium, France, Germany and the Netherlands to the United States' Container Security Initiative in June, and by January 2003 the United Kingdom, Italy, Spain and Sweden had followed. The individual bilateral agreements entitled US Customs agents to search all containers leaving EU ports bound for the United States.[43]

However, this move infringed the European Community's exclusive legislative competence in the area of customs and trade, so in December 2002, the European Commission began infringement proceedings against the relevant Member States Consequently, on 22 April 2004, the European Community and the United States expanded the scope of a 1997 co-operation agreement[44] by concluding an agreement to include transport security co-operation, and in particular co-operation as regards the US

---

43. "EU member states by-pass Commission to give US access to containers at ports," Statewatch News Online 27.5.2003, Statewatch Website: http://www.statewatch.org/news/2003/feb/05contain.htm, accessed 31.7.2007.
44. The European Community and the United States concluded in 1997 an agreement on customs co-operation and mutual assistance in customs matters. The agreement provided the framework for customs co-operation and establishes the EC-US Joint Customs Co-operation Committee (JCCC). The Joint Committee can adopt decisions and recommendations to strengthen co-operation or to strive for the solution of problems encountered in the application of customs rules to transatlantic trade.

Container Security Initiative (CSI)[45], within the scope of the EU/US customs co-operation and relations[46]. As a consequence, the infringement proceedings were discontinued, and did not reach the European Court of Justice.

The agreement is aimed at improving security on a reciprocal basis for both parties. It strikes a balance between trade facilitation and security by (1) ensuring that general customs control of legitimate trade takes due account of security concerns, and (2) creating equal levels and standards of controls for US and EU operators. The agreement establishes a working group to elaborate the necessary operational elements of expanded co-operation, such as minimum standards for CSI ports, common risk criteria and trade partnership programmes.

Following the 2004 agreement, two expert working groups were established with specific tasks: one group focused on furthering joint efforts in security standards, and the other on the comparison of trade partnership programmes. A series of meetings were held to identify and define programmes and activities that would achieve these objectives. The outcome of these meetings is a joint list of recommendations for the initiation of a series of measures concerning, inter alia, the establishment of minimum standards for risk-management techniques, agreed operating procedures for customs controls and CSI requirements for EU ports.[47]

---

45. The Container Security Initiative (CSI) pre-selects, according to risk assessment criteria, containers destined for the USA prior to loading on the ship in a foreign port. The U.S. has also published a regulation on advanced cargo manifest information, the so-called "24 hour rule". This regulation obliges carriers to provide electronic manifest data to CBP, 24 hours before loading sea containers bound to the USA. For air cargo, information should be made available straight after take off. This enables CBP to select high-risk shipments via their automated target system.
    CSI is currently operational in the following European ports: Antwerp and Zeebrugge, (Belgium); Le Havre and Marseille (France); Bremerhaven and Hamburg (Germany); Piraeus (Greece); La Spezia, Genoa, Naples, Gioia Tauro and Livorno (Italy), Rotterdam (The Netherlands); Lisbon (Portugal); Algeciras (Spain); Gothenburg (Sweden); Felixstowe, Liverpool, Thamesport, Tilbury, and Southampton (United Kingdom).
46. Council Decision (EC) No 634/2004 of 30 March 2004 concerning the conclusion of the Agreement between the European Community and the United States of America on intensifying and broadening the Agreement on customs cooperation and mutual assistance in customs matters to include cooperation on container security and related matters, OJ L 304, 30.9.2004, p. 32.
47. EC Press Release: Customs: EU and US adopt measures to strengthen maritime container security, IP/04/1360, 15/11/2004, Rapid Website: http://europa.eu/rapid/searchAction.do, accessed on 30.7.2007.

F.   Passenger Name Records

Again in the aftermath of 11 September 2001, the US Congress passed a law requiring air carriers operating passenger flights to or from the United States to make Passenger Name Record (PNR)[48] information available to the Customs Service (now the Bureau of Customs and Border Protection [CBP], which is part of the Department of Homeland Security). After several postponements requested by the European Commission, CBP indicated its intention to start sanctioning airlines that did not comply with this obligation from 5 March 2003.

Since then the Commission has been working with the US to implement a sound and durable legal framework for transfers of PNR data to the US. The Commission announced, in its Communication to the Council and the Parliament of 16 December 2003,[49] that it would launch the formal procedures to set up a framework. This framework consists of a bilateral EU-US International Agreement and a Decision by the Commission, adopted on 14 May 2004 under the Data Protection Directive, establishing the adequacy of the protection granted to PNR data transferred to CBP[50]. Then, on 28 May 2004, the European Community and the United States signed an international agreement providing for the transfer of air passenger data to the US, under certain conditions. It entered into force immediately.[51]

48.   The Passenger Name Record (PNR) is the generic name given to the files created by the airlines for each journey any passenger books. They are stored in the airlines' reservation and departure control databases. PNR allows all the different agents within the air industry (from the travel agent and the computer reservation systems (CRS) to the carrier and the handling agents at the airports) to recognise each passenger and have access to all relevant information related to his/her journey: departure and return flights, connecting flights (if any), special services required on board the flight, etc. The number and nature of fields of information in a PNR system will vary from airline to airline and from passenger to passenger and could expand to approximately 60 fields and sub-fields.

49.   Communication from the Commission to the Council and the Parliament – Transfer of Air Passenger Name Record (PNR) Data: A Global EU Approach, OJ C 122, 30.4.2004, p. 40.

50.   Commission Decision (EC) 535/2004 of 14 May 2004 on the adequate protection of personal data contained in the Passenger Name Record of air passengers transferred to the United States' Bureau of Customs and Border Protection, OJ L 235, 6.7.2004, p. 11–22.

51.   Agreement between the European Community and the United States of America on the processing and transfer of PNR data by air carriers to the United States Department of Homeland Security, Bureau of Customs and Border Protection, OJ L 183, 20.5.2004, p. 84–85.

On 21 April 2004, the European Parliament brought two actions before the European Court of Justice. The first asked for the annulment of the Council Decision 2004/496/EC of 17 May 2004 on the conclusion of an Agreement between the European Community and the United States.[52] Likewise the second sought to invalidate the Commission Decision 2004/535/EC of 14 May 2004 on the adequate protection of personal data contained in the PNR of air passengers transferred to the United States Bureau of Customs and Border Protection.[53] The European Parliament was supported in its action by the European Data Protection Supervisor.

The Court of Justice gave judgment on 30 May 2006[54] annulling the Commission's adequacy finding decision and the Council's decision concluding the agreement. The Court held that the legal basis (Article 95 of the EC Treaty, read in conjunction with Article 25 of the Directive 95/46/EC)[55], was inappropriate for security or law enforcement matters. In essence, the subject-matter fell outside the EU's "first pillar." The Council Presidency, the Commission and the US administration started then a new round of negotiations to implement the ECJ's decision and to replace the annulled agreement with a new framework that could meet US statutory and security needs as well the EU's privacy concerns.

On 6 October 2006, an interim agreement on the processing and transfer of PNR data by air carriers to the US Administration was concluded and approved by the Council ten days later.[56] The interim agreement was valid until 31 July 2007. The interim agreement pursued the fight against terrorism and serious transnational crime. It complied with European fundamental rights, notably privacy. Although passenger information

---

52. Council Decision of 17 May 2004 on the conclusion of an Agreement between the European Community and the United States of America on the processing and transfer of PNR data by Air Carriers to the United States Department of Homeland Security, Bureau of Customs and Border Protection, OJ L 183, 20.4.2004, p. 83.
53. Commission Decision of 14 May 2004 on the adequate protection of personal data contained in the Passenger Name Record of air passengers transferred to the United States' Bureau of Customs and Border Protection (notified under document number C(2004) 1914) (1), OJ L 235, 6.7.2004, p. 11.
54. Joined Cases C-442/03 P and C-471/03 P: Judgement of the Court (Third Chamber) of 1 June 2006 — P&O European Ferries (Vizcaya) SA v Diputación Foral de Vizcaya, Commission of the European Communities OJ C 178, 29.07.2006, p. 1.
55. Directive 95/46/EC of the European Parliament and of the Council of 24 October 1995 on the protection of individuals with regard to the processing of personal data and on the free movement of such data, OJ L 281, 23.11.1995, p. 31.
56. Agreement between the European Union and the United States of America on the processing and transfer of passenger name record (PNR) data by air carriers to the United States Department of Homeland Security, OJ L 298, 27.10.2006, p. 29–31.

could be passed on by the Department of Homeland Security (DHS) to other US agencies with counter-terrorism functions, as under the 2004 agreement, none of these agencies had direct electronic access to PNR data and they had to respect data protection standards comparable to those followed by the DHS.

The interim agreement enabled PNR data in the reservation systems of air carriers to continue to be transferred to the US in the same way as under the previous agreement. The US administration could electronically access PNR data from air carriers' reservation/departure control systems located within the territory of the EU Member States, in accordance with specific undertakings. This system was to be replaced in due course by one under which airlines in the EU will send the required data to the US[57].

The interim agreement responded in a balanced way to the challenges of terrorism and serious trans-national crime, whilst ensuring a high level of protection of passengers' personal data in line with European standards on fundamental rights and privacy.

Negotiations on a long-term agreement started on 26 February 2006 and ended on 26 July 2007 with the signature of the Agreement by both sides[58]. The agreement is divided into three parts: (i) an agreement signed by both parties, (ii) a letter from the USA to the EU in which it sets out assurances on the way in which it will handle EU PNR data and (iii) a letter from the EU to the USA acknowledging receipt of the assurances and confirming that, on that basis, it considers the level of protection of PNR data in the U.S. as adequate. This agreement is valid for seven years, thus providing for a considerable period of legal certainty.

The number of PNR data has been reduced from 34 to 19 as a result of rationalisation. Air carriers will make available the PNR data of all persons who fly to and from the U.S. The U.S. authorities will use only the 19 PNR elements as defined in the Agreement, and only if the passenger has made available information corresponding to these PNR elements. In practice, the number of PNR elements about a passenger given to an airline and made available to the US authorities is more limited than the 19 provided for in the agreement.

---

57. The US Administration will continue to process PNR data received and treat data subjects concerned by such processing in accordance with undertakings given in 2004.
58. See the Agreement at htpp://www.dhs.gov/xlibrary/assets/pnr-2007agreement-usversion.pdf.

As to sensitive data, the U.S. Department of Homeland Security (DHS), the agency which receives the data, will filter out and not use sensitive information contained in PNR data, save in exceptional cases where life is at risk. Sensitive information means data revealing racial or ethnic origin, political opinions, religious or philosophical beliefs, trade union membership or concerning the health or sex life of the individual.

Much of the information contained in PNR is already included in airline tickets and other travel documents. The missing information can generally be requested by airline staff on departure or US border officials on arrival. The DHS will keep the data for seven years from the date of collection in an active database, following which the data will be moved to an inactive status for eight years, to be accessed only in exceptional circumstances and under strict conditions. Protections provided for in the US Privacy Act will be extended through administrative procedures to non-US citizens, in particular with regard to redress and correction.

Finally, the Commissioner for Justice, Freedom and Security and the US Secretary of Homeland Security will be responsible for the review system.

The agreement between the European Union and the USA is intended to meet security and data protection requirements through assurances provided by the USA. This provides a Europe-wide solution, legally binding in all Member States, and the necessary legal certainty for all concerned.

G.   The EU-US Eurojust Agreement

Following a series of discussions and negotiations, Eurojust and the US Department of Justice signed an agreement on 6 November 2006, aiming to facilitate co-operation, co-ordination and the exchange of information between EU and US prosecutors on terrorism and cross-border criminal cases.[59]

This agreement, which again demonstrates close co-operation based on mutual trust, will allow Eurojust, the European Union's Judicial Co-operation Unit, to exchange information with its US counterparts on cases under investigation and will facilitate co-operation between EU Member States and the US.

---

59.   See the Agreement at http://eurojust.europa.eu/official_documents/Agreements/061106_EU-US_co-operation_agreement_pdf.

The agreement provides for the protection of personal information and individual privacy for citizens of the US and the EU. A US Liaison Prosecutor will shortly be posted to Eurojust headquarters in The Hague to facilitate law enforcement co-operation between the US and the EU on a day-to-day basis.

H.   *Information and data exchange: liberty and security, sharing and protecting data*

EU-US cooperation has developed rapidly in recent years. It has now reached a point where it is necessary to tackle new challenges, especially regarding personal information exchange and data protection.

Sharing personal data for law enforcement purposes is one of the most difficult issues in the EU-US relationship. The common goal is to guarantee high levels of protection of personal data and at the same time foster meaningful data exchange to support the secure flow of persons and goods, and fight against terrorism and crime. Arrangements in this respect have already been agreed in the context of the Europol, Eurojust, MLA and PNR but they are case-specific and do not provide for a comprehensive framework. There is a clear need for an overall framework for information sharing.

Today's reality is that more data are available and transferred across jurisdictions. New technologies have made it possible to exchange in a few seconds a lot of information, including personal data. These data require protection. Some of this information is at the same time of vital interest for law enforcement officers to help them tackle terrorism and serious trans-national crime.

Law enforcement systems need the best possible tools to make use of relevant data while ensuring that the protection of personal data is guaranteed. Failure is not an option. The EU and the US have to work together to find legally sound and practical arrangements to govern transfers of personal data for the purposes of law enforcement and the prevention of terrorism. They share the belief that the fight against terrorism must be anchored in a legal framework that respects fundamental human rights and international humanitarian law and is built on the principles of democracy, good governance and the rule of law. Despite the common values which underpin EU–US cooperation in the fight against terrorism and other international criminal activity, their cultures of data protection are different, especially in operational terms.

The effective protection of personal data should not be a barrier to efficient law enforcement cooperation. On the contrary, it compels police to manage data intelligently.

It is time to start thinking about "commonalities" rather than the differences between the EU and the US. Interference with private life can be justified only if it is in accordance with the law, is necessary in a democratic society for the pursuit of legitimate aims, and is not disproportionate to the desired objective. The EU and the US need to agree on general requisites of appropriateness and proportionality, and in so doing identify a limited number of essential, basic principles for transatlantic transfer of personal data for the fight against terrorism and serious trans-national crime.

The initiative taken at the EU-US ministerial Troika on 6 November 2006 in Washington D.C. to establish a high level Contact Group to discuss data sharing and data protection for law enforcement purposes is therefore welcome. The Contact Group is charged with (1) identifying the issues at stake and perceived problems, and (2) exploring how the data protection policies and systems accomplish the protection of personal data in the wake of security challenges. Its overall aim is to work towards the elaboration of a joint text that lays down the personal data protection basic principles that are common to both EU and US in a language that is shared by both, and provide solutions to bridge differences of approach.

At this stage of the works of the Contact Group it appears premature to forecast the results of the negotiations and, in particular, to elaborate on the possible legal form that the final outcome will take.

IV. Institutions and actors of EU-US Cooperation

In the mid-1990s a specific vehicle for Justice, Freedom and Security cooperation was created in the form of bi-annual "informal" Justice and Home Affairs "Troika" meetings. These meetings addressed a wide range of JHA issues, notably trafficking in human beings, drugs, cyber-crime and fight against organised crime, but also immigration and asylum issues. Following the entry into force of the Treaty of Amsterdam and the events of 9/11, the bi-annual informal JHA meeting has become an important platform for EU-US counter-terrorism cooperation and has been supplemented by a growing number of formal consultation mechanisms.[60]

The movement into the "first pillar" of many areas of Justice and Home Affairs cooperation has given the Commission a more prominent role in relationships with third countries. In those areas, the Commission is now entitled to negotiate international agreements on behalf of the European Community and to establish direct relationships with third countries' administrations. In the areas of cooperation still governed by the provisions of Title VI of the Treaty of the European Union (police and judicial cooperation in criminal matters), the Commission assists the Presidency of the Council of the European Union when it enters into international relationships.

In September 2004, it was agreed to hold an annual JHA Ministerial meeting bringing together on the EU side the Presidency of the Union (accompanied by the Council General Secretariat) and the Commissioner responsible for Justice, Freedom and Security, and on the US side the Attorney General and the Secretary of Homeland Security. Consultations at Ministerial level have addressed topical issues of common concern such as biometrics in passports, the US VISIT programme, visa issues, the sharing of information and judicial cooperation in criminal matters. These consultations have proven highly valuable for early warning, up-front consultation and avoiding potential conflicts.[61]

The bi-annual informal JHA meeting at working level gives a good opportunity to go into details on a wide range of JHA issues, notably trafficking in human beings, drugs, cyber-crime and the fight against organised crime, together with immigration and asylum issues.

Regular meetings between EU and US officials, from ministerial level to working level, have now become the norm and provide a useful opportunity to compare notes on ideas and processes, to reach agreement when necessary, and to understand that, while Europe and America share the same objectives, methods sometimes differ. European officials rub shoulders with their American colleagues, exchange information rapidly and plan joint operations more easily. US officials are now much more at

---

60. Counter-Terrorism: Statement of EU-US shared objectives and close cooperation, 18.5.1998, Delegation of the European Commission to the United States Website: http://www.eurunion.org/partner/summit/ Summit9805/counter.htm, accessed 30.7.2007.
61. Justice, Freedom and Security high on US-EU Transatlantic Agenda, DG for Justice, Freedom and Security Website http://ec.europa.eu/justice_home/ fsj/external/usa/ fsj_external_usa_en.htm, accessed 30.7.2007.

ease working with the EU institutions on counter-terrorism and law enforcement issues. The Commission has appointed an official dedicated to Justice and Home Affairs at its Washington delegation and Europol has posted two officers to Washington to liaise with the US services. The US mission to the EU in Brussels follows JHA issues closely.

Since its creation in 2003, the Department of Homeland Security (DHS) has played a major role in the EU-US relations. Being responsible for border control, travel security, critical infrastructure protection, preparedness and response in case of terrorist attacks as well as immigration, it has become a fundamental partner both in day-to-day business with the services of the Member States and the European Institutions, and in engaging in negotiation with the EU for important international agreements such as the two PNR and the Container Security agreements.

The Department of Justice (DOJ) is a long-standing actor in EU-US relations in the JHA area, being responsible for law enforcement and judicial cooperation, both in criminal and civil matters. Its officials successfully negotiated the EU-US MLA and extradition agreements, as well as the Europol and Eurojust agreements, and daily contact takes place between EU and DOJ colleagues on common challenges such as terrorist financing, counterfeiting and piracy, fight against cyber-crime, trafficking in human beings and organised crime.

V.   Conclusions: towards a common EU-US space for Justice Freedom and Security

The EU and the US have an impressive track record in transatlantic security cooperation in the area of Justice and Home Affairs, drawing on shared values, a history of transatlantic migration and the realities of modern business and tourism travel.

Two recent events have had a considerable impact on the way the relationship has developed. The tragic terrorist attacks of 9/11 made security and cooperation in the fight against terrorism a foremost priority, while successive Treaty reforms in Europe made the EU responsible for many aspects of Justice and Home Affairs.

As a result, the EU-US relationship has progressed significantly. Eight agreements have been signed, providing for cooperation between the EU and the US on issues of extradition, mutual legal assistance, container security, transfer of passenger data, and police and judicial cooperation.

By strengthening their strategic cooperation in this way, the EU and the US have also shown that they share the same long-term objectives. Their mutual goals are to guarantee high levels of protection of personal data and at the same time foster meaningful data exchanges to support the flow of people and trade and the borderless fight against terrorism and crime.

While Europeans and Americans share many values, differences on some issues still exist, presenting challenges to development of closer transatlantic cooperation. For example, conflicting views on the death penalty have affected areas of judicial cooperation such as the extradition of suspects, whilst differences of approach on data protection and privacy issues have made PNR agreements controversial.

In addition, an added layer of complexity is brought by the fact that the EU and the US are very different political entities. Lawyers and political scientists examining the EU often lack categories to define it, instead considering that it inhabits a class of its own. Europeans sometimes find their own institutional arrangements opaque and bewildering. How then can one expect foreign countries, such as the USA in the grip of a major struggle with international terrorism in the aftermath of 11 September 2001, to react easily and confidently to this unique and rapidly expanding[62] three-pillared entity?

Despite these difficulties, continued confidence and cooperation between the European Union and the United States are clearly necessary. The benefits of the relationship include improved security in the face of the common terrorist threat, as the risks of future attacks can be diminished by pooling intelligence, and undertaking preventative measures together. Increased EU-US collaboration has also eased transatlantic trade and travel, bringing numerous financial and social benefits to both sides. Finally mutual legal assistance and enhanced police cooperation can ensure safer and fairer societies on both sides of the Atlantic.

The EU and the US cannot allow their differences to have an impact on the way they respond to the global, strategic challenges they both face. They are partners bound by common values, common interests and common responsibilities in the world. In particular, they need each other to counter terrorism effectively. They can diminish the risks of future attacks by pooling intelligence. The US's annual $30 billion dollar intelligence budget cannot piece the whole intelligence picture together by itself.

---

62. The European Union enlarged from 15 Member States in 2001, to 25 in 2004 and 27 in 2007.

On matters of principle, the two sides should look for practical ways to work around their differences, building upon existing commonalities and agreeing on the importance of strengthening Euro-Atlantic cooperation on security, justice and protecting fundamental rights. On this basis, whilst never compromising the values with respect to fundamental rights that they also share, they may take on any challenge.

The EU and the US should keep working together to ensure European and American citizens' freedom of movement across the Atlantic, with a high-level security in place. They should step up their common efforts to make the Atlantic an area where security and freedom are fully implemented and respected.

This achievement requires the establishment of a set of mutually recognised, high-level standards of cooperation. Much has already been done, such as in the area of document security, while the recent establishment of the High Level Contact Group on data protection gives hope to those who believe that that the two sides must focus their efforts on identifying common principles that can be translated into common action.

Nevertheless, despite the EU's complexities, the record shows that, while the US has many links with individual Member States in the JHA field, it sees considerable added value in the EU's ability to deliver cooperation with all 27 countries and is therefore happy to work with Brussels. Many examples are given in this chapter. To stress just one category among many, when problems occur at the interface of data sharing for law enforcement purposes and data protection (privacy), it is to the EU institutions that the US and EU Member States turn for solutions. PNR and Swift are recent examples, which have in turn led to calls for an overall settlement of these issues based on "commonalities" between European and US rules and principles. Work is under way on the identification of such commonalities. If successful, it will remove many problems from the negotiation table when specific issues are discussed.

Border management, visa policy, civil law, criminal law, drugs, crime and terrorism: these are all major challenges for the EU internally and externally and regular features of EU-US discussions at all levels. It could hardly be otherwise. Global challenges require global responses. Transatlantic cooperation is a cornerstone of endeavours to fashion and implement those responses, based on mutual respect and a common commitment to the rule of law.

2. The EU and the Council of Europe in the Justice and Home Affairs Area: Competition or Cooperation?

Philippe Boillat and Stéphane Leyenberger

I. Introduction

In 1949, on the ashes and ruins of the Second World War, ten European countries decided to definitely put aside the risk of a new tragedy, by building a common European home based on human rights, the pre-eminence of law and pluralistic democracy. The Council of Europe has developed its action ever since, remaining faithful to these fundamental values that have been extended to forty-seven European States (that is to say, nearly the whole of our continent[1]) within an intergovernmental framework. A few years later, six States set up the European Economic Communities to build a common economic area as the first stage of a reinforced political union. Fifty years later, the European Union has evolved considerably: its twenty-seven members (all members of the Council of Europe) have agreed to transfer part of their sovereignty and powers to an entity that has no equivalent in the world.

Two different European institutions, two different vocations, two different development methods, but stemming from "*the same idea, the same spirit, the same ambition*[2]". Thus the Preamble to the Treaty of Rome, in which the States declared to be "*determined to lay the foundations of an ever closer union among the peoples of Europe*" and "*resolved to ensure the economic and social progress of their countries by common action to eliminate the barriers which divide Europe*", echoes Article 1 of the Statute of the Council of Europe: "*The aim of the Council of Europe is to achieve a greater unity between its members for the purpose of safeguarding and realising the ideals and principles*

---

1. The Holy See benefits from the status of permanent observer with the Organisation. The accession process of Belarus has been frozen. All other European States are members of the Council of Europe.
2. Report by Jean-Claude Juncker, Prime Minister of Luxembourg, to the attention of the Heads of State or Governments of the member States of the Council of Europe: "Council of Europe – European Union: a sole ambition for the European continent" (11 April 2006).

which are their common heritage and facilitating their economic and social progress".

Today, however, one could be tempted to have cause for opposing the European Union and the Council of Europe, in particular in matters concerning justice, freedom and security, which are the original missions of the Strasbourg institution and which have gradually imposed themselves in Brussels. While "good governance" has become a watchword, can European States afford to have two different structures with similar competences? Is there not a risk of damaging the coherence and necessary rationalisation of the European standard-setting device? And what about the command of public expenditure? Does the financial situation of the European States reasonably allow for the parallel development of two structures?

These are certainly legitimate questions. It would nonetheless be simplistic, not to say dangerous for the future of our democratic societies to answer too rashly and inconsiderately. Such an approach would be irresponsible if we consider what is at stake and the reality of both institutions – with the specificity that makes up their complementarity.

Firstly, there can be no competition when it comes to defending fundamental rights that directly affect European citizens in their everyday life. Today, one may get the impression that some Europeans are wary of European standards; that Europe is no longer everyone's dream; that Europeans are suspicious of measures taken far away from their own capital cities. The temptation to withdraw into oneself may be becoming increasingly attractive in some sections of the population. These are just as many reasons not to adopt such attitudes however. To improve the human rights situation and the rule of law in the new democratic States of Central and Eastern Europe, as well as in countries with older democratic traditions will only be possible if people combine their efforts and vigilance and put together their means of action and of persuasion. We must repeat it over and over again: in matters of human rights and democracy, nothing can ever be taken for granted.

Another reason is that justice, freedom and security are issues that transcend European Union borders. If these concepts do not come into force on the whole of our continent, it is likely that they will not take root in the twenty-seven European Union States either, since we now live in a global world where borders – including virtual borders and cyberspaces – are wide open.

Finally, one has to admit that the possibility, for States as well as for European institutions, of relying on the expertise and experience of other institutions in order to keep the best of them and reinforce their own principles and structures actually amounts to "good governance". As we hope to develop a more humane Europe more closely in touch with its citizens, we should also rely on communication between people and on the exchange of know-how and good practices.

Cooperation between the European Union and the Council of Europe is therefore the most secure and most efficient way of achieving the European construction. While progress made in consolidating an area of justice, freedom and security common to the twenty-seven EU member States must be welcomed, it should also be stressed that the Council of Europe and the European Union naturally share the same values and the same aim to promote human rights, the rule of law and the setting up of true democracies. Those are the foundations of a lasting peace on the whole continent which in turn is the *sine qua non* of any economic, social and cultural development.

This is the sense of the message conveyed by the Heads of States and Governments of the member States of the Council of Europe, who met at the 3rd Summit in Warsaw in 2005 and asserted their will *"to create a new framework for enhanced co-operation and interaction between the Council of Europe and the European Union in areas of common concern, in particular human rights, democracy and the rule of law*[3]". It is also the subject of the report prepared at their request by the Prime Minister of Luxembourg, Jean-Claude Juncker[4], who recommends a series of concrete measures *"necessary, because of their significant lever effect"* in order to strengthen the *"partnership between our two different but complementary organisations."*

---

3.   Warsaw Declaration, 17 May 2005.
4.   See above.

In this spirit, the Council of Europe and European Union recently signed a "Memorandum of Understanding[5]" that defines a *"new framework for enhanced co-operation and political dialogue"*, calling for the development of reinforced partnership and complementarities, taking into account the respective comparative advantages, competences and expertise of both institutions, while defining the practical aspects of such cooperation.

II.   The contribution of the Council of Europe to the *acquis* of the European Union

A.   The normative acquis of the Council of Europe...

Two hundred conventions[6] and hundreds of recommendations by the Committee of Ministers to the member States make up the Council of Europe's normative *acquis* today; they concern virtually all areas of the Europeans' everyday lives. In accordance with the fundamental principle of treaty law, *pacta sunt servanda,* the Council of Europe's treaties legally ratified by the member states are binding upon the parties and must be performed by them in good faith. The recommendations do not have the same binding force, but in spite of their soft law character, they actually make it possible to set out strong standards, adopted by the Committee of Ministers and passed on to the national policy-makers as common denominators between the States belonging to the same family of European democracies.

This *acquis* is the result of nearly sixty years of steadily enriched work and expertise. It is also the result of the special attention given to the evolution of societies in Europe and in the world. The Council of Europe is a remarkable laboratory of ideas. This is true, for instance, in the area of

---

5.   The Memorandum of Understanding between the Council of Europe and the European Union was prepared according to the Action Plan adopted by the Third Summit of the Heads of State and Government of the Council of Europe (Warsaw, 16 – 17 May 2005). It was signed for the Council of Europe on 11 May 2007 by Fiorenzo Stolfi (President of the Committee of Ministers of the Council of Europe) and Terry Davis (Secretary General of the Council of Europe) and for the European Union on 23 May 2007 by Günter Gloser (for the Presidency of the Council of the European Union) and Benita Ferrero-Waldner (Member of the European Commission in charge of External Relations and European Neighbourhood Policy). The Memorandum defines the purposes and principles of cooperation between the two European institutions, their shared priorities and focal areas as well as the arrangements for cooperation.

6.   See website: http://conventions.coe.int.

medical and biotechnological progress, which requires legal answers to complex ethical issues. Another example is the development of cyberspace, which is an important factor of communication and openness, but which needs to be regulated to avoid exploitation for criminal purposes. Similarly, the protection of privacy must be guaranteed, in particular as we cannot allow "Big Brother" to bring it to heel simply because new technologies make it possible.

An essential part of that *corpus* of norms concerns human rights and legal questions, and we can say that the European standards in this area are those of the Strasbourg Organisation. The "Memorandum of Understanding" between the Council of Europe and the European Union[7] states that *"the Council of Europe will remain the benchmark for human rights, the rule of law and democracy in Europe"*. These standards are prepared and made applicable within a Europe without dividing lines, where States are treated as equals. The Council of Europe thus plays a fundamental role in the creation of an area of justice, freedom and security on the continent, or even beyond – while the Council of Europe is not destined to conduct lasting activities outside our continent, it develops and promotes universal values that may be used and applied in other countries[8].

B.   ... contributes to European Union's acquis

As from 1993, the Copenhagen criteria – in which the Council of the European Union had laid down the conditions for the entry of new member States – explicitly referred to Council of Europe standards in order to build stable institutions that would guarantee the respect of democracy, the rule of law and human rights.

---

7. See above.
8. For instance, the principles and the expertise of the Venice Commission in constitutional matters enabled South Africa (who benefits from the special cooperation status with the Commission) to carry out fundamental reforms during its democratic transition; it can also be noted that Chile, the Republic of Korea and Kirghizstan are full members of that body. As well as the Group of States against Corruption (GRECO) among whose members can be found the United States of America, or countries of Maghreb, Middle-East and South-Eastern Asia who are interested in the methodology for the evaluation of the functioning of justice established by the European Commission for the Efficiency of Justice (CEPEJ).

Thus, a few dozen Council of Europe conventions are closely related to the *acquis* of the European Union in the area of justice and home affairs[9]. It is the case in particular of conventions for the protection of fundamental rights and individual freedoms, around the European Convention on Human Rights[10], the European Convention for the Prevention of Torture[11], the European Social Charter[12], treaties on the protection of national minorities[13] and the protection of personal data[14] – the ratification of the latter, for instance, is mandatory before a State can belong to the Schengen area[15]. Conventions on nationality[16] and biomedicine[17] are also concerned.

9. For the purpose of this article, the authors have deliberately considered the EU acquis as a whole, irrespective of the division between the areas belonging to the second and third pillar of the European Union – and thus under the jurisdiction of the Council of the European Union – and the areas belonging under the first pillar, which fall under the jurisdiction of the European Community.

10. Convention for the Protection of Human Rights and Fundamental Freedoms (STE N°5), Additional Protocol (STE N°9), Protocol N°4 (STE N°46), Protocol n°6 on the Abolition of the Death Penalty (STE N°114), Protocol N°7 (STE N°117), as amended by Protocol n°11 restructuring the control machinery established by the Convention (STE N°155); Protocol n°12 (STE N°117); Protocol n°13 on the Abolition of the Death Penalty in all Circumstances (STE N°187); Protocol n°14 to the Convention amending the control system of the Convention (STE N°194).

11. European Convention for the Prevention of Torture and Inhuman or Degrading Treatment or Punishment (STE N°126) as amended by Protocols n°1 and n°2 (STE N°151 and 152).

12. European Social Charter (STE N°35), Additional Protocol (STE N°128), Protocol amending the European Social Charter (STE N°142), Additional Protocol Providing for a System of Collective Complaints (STE N°158); European Social Charter (revised) (STE N°163).

13. European Charter for Regional or Minority Languages (STE N°148); Framework Convention for the Protection of National Minorities (STE N°157).

14. Convention for the Protection of Individuals with Regard to Automatic Processing of Personal Data (STE N°108); Protocol regarding Supervisory Authorities and Transborder Data Flows (STE N°181).

15. Article 126 of the Schengen Agreements of 14 June 1985.

16. Convention on the Reduction of Cases of Multiple Nationality and Military Obligations in Cases of Multiple Nationality (STE N°43); European Convention on Nationality (STE N°166).

17. Convention for the Protection of Human Rights and Dignity of the Human Being with regard to the Application of Biology and Medicine: Convention on Human Rights and Biomedicine (STE N°164), Additional Protocol with regard to the Application of Biology and Medicine, on the Prohibition of Cloning Human Beings (STE N°168), concerning the Transplantation of Organs and Tissues of Human Origin (STE N°186), concerning Biomedical Research (STE N°195).

A second set of instruments concerns criminal justice cooperation[18], the protection of victims[19], the fight against terrorism[20], large-scale crime[21], cybercrime[22] and corruption[23]. Other instruments, finally, relate to civil

18. European Convention on Extradition (STE N°24) and its Additional Protocol (STE N°86 and N°98 – Strasbourg); European Convention on Mutual Assistance in Criminal Matters (STE N°30) and its Additional Protocols (STE N°99 and N°182); European Convention on the Transfer of Proceedings in Criminal Matters (STE N°73); European Convention on the Supervision of Conditionally Sentenced or Conditionally Released Offenders (STE N°51); European Convention on International Validity of Criminal Judgments (STE N°70); Convention on the Transfer of Sentenced Persons (STE N°112) and its Additional Protocols (STE N°167-Strasbourg).
19. European Convention on the Compensation of Victims of Violent Crimes (STE N°116).
20. European Convention on the Suppression of Terrorism (STE N°90) and its amending Protocol (STE N°190); Council of Europe Convention on the Prevention of Terrorism (STE N°196); Council of Europe Convention on Laundering, Search, Seizure and Confiscation of the Proceeds from Crime and on the Financing of Terrorism (STE N°198).
21. Convention on Laundering, Search, Seizure and Confiscation of the Proceeds from Crime (STE N°141); Agreement on Illicit Traffic by Sea, implementing Article 17 of the United Nations Convention against Illicit Traffic in Narcotic Drugs and Psychotropic Substances (STE N°156); Council of Europe Convention on Action against Trafficking of Human Beings (STE N°197).
22. Convention on Cybercrime (STE N°185) and its Additional Protocol concerning the Acts of a Racist and Xenophobic Nature Committed through Computer Systems (STE N°189).
23. Criminal Law Convention on Corruption (STE N°173) and its Additional Protocol (STE N°191); Civil Law Convention on Corruption (STE N°174).

and commercial law[24], family law[25], administrative and fiscal law[26], to the movement of people, asylum-seekers and refugees[27].

It goes without saying that, while the member States of the European Union are bound by these Council of Europe provisions once they have ratified them, it is still possible, not to say desirable, that a more extended protection be offered within the context of the European Union. Conversely, the Council of Europe may be a particularly suitable place to extend European Union standards beyond its twenty-seven member States. This new trend, which ought to be encouraged and developed, is reflected for example in the Convention on Information and Legal Co-operation concerning "Information Society Services" (STE N° 180).

In any case, it is essential that both institutions act as partners, working on standards in a coordinated manner. Double standards cannot become a feature of the implementation of their common principles. Legal and political difficulties may be overcome only through sustained and regular dialogue.

One particular question that arises here in is that of the relevance of the Council of Europe's conventions in a European Union that goes beyond the principle of national sovereignty alongside other traditional concepts of international public law, at least when it comes to the relations between EU member States. Hence, the "disconnection clauses", which mean that EU

24. European Convention on Information on Foreign Law (STE N°62); Convention on the Establishment on a Scheme of Registration of Wills (STE N°77); European Agreement on the Transmission of Applications for Legal Aid (STE N°92) and its Additional Protocol (STE N°179); Convention on Insider Trading (STE N°130); Convention on Information and Legal Co-operation concerning "Information Society Services" (STE N°180).

25. European Convention on the Adoption of Children (STE N°58); European Convention on the Legal Status of Children Born out of Wedlock (STE N°85); European Convention on Recognition and Enforcement of Decisions concerning Custody of Children and on Restoration of Custody of Children (STE N°105); European Convention on the Exercise of Children's Rights (STE N°160); Convention on Contact concerning Children (STE N°192).

26. European Convention on the Service Abroad of Documents relating to Administrative Matters (STE N°94); European Convention on the Obtaining Abroad of Information and Evidence in Administrative Matters (STE N°100); Convention on Mutual Administrative Assistance in Tax Matters (STE N°127).

27. European Agreement on Regulations governing the Movement of Persons between Member States of the Council of Europe (STE N°25); European Convention on the Abolition of Visas for Refugees (STE N°31); European Agreement on Travel by Young Persons on Collective Passports between the Member Countries of the Council of Europe (STE N°37); European Agreement on Transfer of Responsibility for Refugees (STE N°107).

member States – among themselves or between member states and the European Community – cannot directly rely on and apply the rights and obligations stemming from an international convention that fall into the Community's sphere of competence, where community legislation exists. This *sui generis* right of the European Union is constantly changing and has to be articulated with classic international law. Only discussions carried out prior to any legislative initiative can guarantee a harmonious evolution between the two logics.

The example of the draft framework decision on certain procedural rights granted to defendants in criminal proceedings[28] shows the importance of sound coordination. This project within the scope of the EU sets out some principles and rules that have already been laid down by the European Convention on Human Rights and the case-law of the Strasbourg Court. The articulation between the two legal instruments thus raises questions: what is the respective scope of each text? How can one guarantee a level of protection at least identical to that of the European Convention on Human Rights as interpreted by the European Court of Human Rights? How can one settle the potential contradictions between the interpretation given by the Court of Justice of the European Communities and that of the European Court of Human Rights? Having heard the experts of the Council of Europe, the working group of the European Union in charge of preparing the draft framework decision acknowledged the need to work on an instrument that would be compatible and coherent with the European Convention on Human Rights. Preliminary consultation is essential here in order to ensure the prior compatibility of standards.

So we can only hope for the generalised cross-participation of experts of the European Union and the Council of Europe in the respective work (and committees) of the two institutions. While this practice is already widely in use, it ought to be made systematic, reciprocally, to avoid any lack of coherence in European standards. Hopefully, the above-mentioned "Memorandum of Understanding" and the Agreement on the Cooperation between the Agency for Fundamental Rights of the European Union and the Council of Europe that is being discussed, will help reinforce this cooperation.

The enhanced coherence of the European legislative system is no doubt also inherent to the accession of the European Community to a greater number of Council of Europe conventions. Eleven of the fifty Council of Europe instruments to which the European Community has access have

---

28. 2004/0113 (CNS)

been actually been used by the European Community, although only one of those instruments is concerned with "justice and home affairs"[29]. Conventions on the rights of children, bioethics, the prevention of terrorism, the fight against trafficking in human beings and corruption could all be accessed by the European Community. Legal solutions exist in order to facilitate access to other conventions, including the European Convention on Human Rights. Much depends on political will. Hopefully, for the sake of the 800 million European citizens, there will be a new European initiative that will tip the scales in favour of increased cooperation.

III. Optimising the use of the Council of Europe's know-how and structures

A. Reinforcing the mechanisms for the protection of human rights

Once the principle of supremacy of Council of Europe standards on the protection of human rights has been laid down, mechanisms should be organised and reinforced accordingly, in order to guarantee the unicity, validity and efficiency of European principles.

An observer would possibly be surprised to see here the creation of separate mechanisms for the European Union, alongside those for the European Court of Human Rights, while the lack of means of the latter to deal with the exponential growth of litigation is regularly and accurately put forward. How can one ensure the uniformity of the enforcement of human rights in forty-seven European States if the EU's own authorities rule on the same rights as those of the Convention? How can one avoid case-law conflicts between the decisions of the Luxembourg and Strasbourg Courts, in particular when human rights are to be legally consecrated in the Union's treaties? How can the Agency for Fundamental Rights based in Vienna articulate its work to keep it consistent with the case-law of the Strasbourg Court and the solutions of other control and monitoring mechanisms of the Council of Europe?

The Vienna Agency is a reality and will surely play a significant role in the reinforcement of politics in favour of human rights in Europe. The aim is to promote the implementation of fundamental principles and the

---

29. Convention on Information and Legal Co-operation concerning "Information Society Services" (STE N°180).

protection of individual freedom within the context of the European Union. However, in its activity, the Agency will duly take into account the Council of Europe's instruments, of which the first is the European Convention on Human Rights, as well as the work of the relevant authorities of the Council of Europe (i.e. intergovernmental and monitoring committees, the Commissioner for Human Rights) which the Agency will expressly refer to. As for the Council of Europe, it should take part in the work of the Agency on the basis of a cooperation agreement between both institutions that should be reached soon.

Moreover, it would be important for EU authorities to have the possibility to submit all questions on human rights not covered by the existing mechanisms to the Commissioner for Human Rights of the Council of Europe, as put forward by the Prime Minister Jean-Claude Juncker in his report[30].

However, the accession of the European Union to the European Convention on Human Rights remains the best guarantee of coherence in the implementation of human rights and legal safety, and thus the best assurance for all European citizens to see their rights effectively protected. That fact was asserted by the Heads of States and Governments of the member States of the Council of Europe– and thus of the European Union – in Warsaw, and reiterated in the above-mentioned "Memorandum of Understanding". This accession would not amount to subordinating one institution to another, but would establish instead an external control to the Union of the implementation of fundamental rights within the Union itself, while allowing the Union to come forward as a party in disputes before the Strasbourg Court for EU law-related questions. The draft Treaty establishing a Constitution for Europe was paving the way for such a solution, and this possibility has been preserved by the Reform Treaty.[31] On the Council of Europe's side, Article 59 of the European Convention on Human Rights, as amended by its 14th Protocol, extends a clear invitation to the European Union which "may accede to this Convention"[32].

---

30. See footnote N°2, above.
31. According to Article 6 of the EU Treaty in the form of the Reform Treaty, the European Union shall accede to the European Convention on Human Rights. However, unlike the Constitution, the Reform Treaty provides that this accession shall not come into force until it has been approved by the EU's Member States in accordance with their respective constitutional requirements (Article 218 para. 8 of the Treaty on the Functioning of the European Union).
32. Protocol N°14 to the European Convention for the Protection of Human Rights and Fundamental Freedoms amending the control system of the Convention is not as yet in force.

We must then hope that the political, institutional and legal logic will be materialised by the budgetary logic, in order to allow for an effective and coherent development of the device for the protection of human rights in Europe, whatever the competent institution.

B.   Relying on accepted and effective control mechanisms

Besides the European Convention on Human Rights and its control mechanisms (including the enforcement mechanisms of the Court's decisions, falling into the Committee of Ministers' sphere of competence), the European Union may rely on other Council of Europe's authorities whose expertise, know-how and efficiency are acknowledged by national and international policy-makers, relevant professional organisations and the NGOs involved. Reinforcing synergies between these Council of Europe's mechanisms and the competent authorities of the European Union is also necessary both to guarantee the effectiveness and coherence of the political message conveyed to the States by the European institutions and to avoid duplications which would be useless and expensive.

This way, the European Committee for the Prevention of Torture and of Inhuman or Degrading Treatment or Punishment (CPT) carries out essential work checking whether the Convention and the principles of its protocols are observed. The recommendations contained in its reports, of which the publicity is usually ensured, have to be implemented by the contracting States. These reports also represent a valuable source of information- and provide the basis for political decisions, which the authorities of the Council of Europe and of the European Union rely on. The same applies to other monitoring mechanisms of the implementation of fundamental rights and individual freedoms, such as the European Commission against Racism and Intolerance (ECRI), the Consultative Council for the Framework Convention for the Protection of Minorities or the European Committee of Social Rights.

In the field of constitutional reforms, the Venice Commission plays a crucial role in looking at the compliance of the States' fundamental legal norms with European values and standards. Its first-rate role in the prevention and management of conflicts on our continent is also widely accepted. The European Commission is regularly represented there. It would be advisable to take further steps towards an institutionalised cooperation.

Also in the fight against crime, the peer pressure mechanisms constituted by GRECO – in charge of monitoring the implementation of European instruments against corruption – and MONEYVAL – in matters of measures against money laundering – are obvious references: their monitoring reports are directly usable within the European Union and can be the object of an enhanced cooperation with EUROJUST. Therefore, beyond the participation or the financial support of the European Commission, which are certainly greatly appreciated, rapid access of the European Community to these mechanisms appears necessary. This would strengthen the institutional logic. Other mechanisms are to be developed soon, like the mechanisms that can be used in the prevention and fight against terrorism, or the GRETA for the fight against trafficking in human beings. Close cooperation with the relevant EU authorities would also be highly desirable here, as Europe can only speak as one on such important subjects by allocating its resources and expertise to common goals.

Finally, when it comes to the functioning of justice, the European Union can rely for its own needs on the work of the European Commission for the Efficiency of Justice (CEPEJ), which is entrusted with the evaluation of the functioning of justice in the forty-seven member States. The position expressed by Mr Franco Frattini, Vice-President of the European Commission in charge of Justice, Freedom and Security, who considered the work of the CEPEJ an essential element for the reinforcement of mutual trust between the judicial systems of the Union States in as much as it guarantees the smooth implementation of the community mechanisms for judicial cooperation,[33] is to be welcomed in this context.

The member States of the European Union and the Council of Europe, as well as the respective executive and parliamentary authorities of both institutions, will have shared responsibility for following up the reports, opinions and recommendations of these authorities. To keep the institutions working closely together whenever it is possible is an additional and necessary step to assert a firm and coherent political position in the construction of an area of justice, freedom and security on the whole continent.

C.   Acting together and cooperating in the field

The smooth articulation between the normative devices and the implementation and monitoring mechanisms must eventually find a tangible outcome in the everyday action and in the field. This is important in order for the twenty-seven States concerned (and for candidate States)

33.   7th plenary meeting of the CEPEJ, Rome, 6 – 7 July 2006.

and for the peoples placed under their jurisdiction to live in harmony with the fact that they belong both to the Council of Europe and to the European Union. But this is also necessary for the development of an immediate neighbourhood policy for the European Union: the Council of Europe offers an irreplaceable forum to build a common legal area from Brest to Vladivostok and from Reykjavik to Nicosia.

Sustained dialogue and regular cooperation in several fields are well established at the institutional level. This cooperation amounts to regular meetings at high political level (quadripartite meetings bringing together the Council of the European Union, the European Commission, the Presidency of the Committee of Ministers of the Council of Europe and the Secretary General) or at technical level (meetings between the representatives of the Directorate General of Human Rights and Legal Affairs with the Committee for Article 36 of the Council of the European Union; inter-service meetings etc.) and the reciprocal participation of representatives and experts of the different committees. For instance, EUROJUST and the European Network for Judicial Cooperation in Criminal Matters are regular partners for the committees of the Council of Europe in charge of criminal matters. The same applies to the partnership between the European Network for Judicial Cooperation in Civil Matters and the European Commission for the Efficiency of Justice (CEPEJ) or between the European Judicial Training Network and the Lisbon Network[34] of the Council of Europe. As was mentioned above, this device can and should be completed and extended to all areas in which a planned action is necessary in order to reinforce the normative and political coherence. The new "Memorandum of Understanding" sets out the means to accomplish this ambition. It must now be fully implemented.

Moreover, what should be stressed – with satisfaction – are the substantial cooperation efforts that have been or are now being made between the European Commission and the Council of Europe to promote human rights and legal reforms in several member States of our Organisation, in particular in the Russian Federation, Ukraine, and in the countries of Southern Caucasus and South-East Europe. The common European values and standards shared by the Council of Europe and the European Union must take root in the day to day reality of these States, which must be supported in the fulfilment of their commitments to the Organisation at the time of their accession. For more than ten years, Joint Programmes have been negotiated by the Council of Europe and the European Commission

---

34. Network bringing together the judicial training structures of the forty-seven Council of Europe member States.

together with the beneficiary States. They are substantially financed by Brussels which, in turn, entrusts the Council of Europe with their management and implementation. These programmes are based on the Council of Europe's standards and promote human rights in the training of parties involved in activities at local level (judges, prosecutors and other legal professions, police forces, ombudsman, NGOs, etc.). The focus is on institutional (for example, Ministries of Justice, high councils for the judiciary, financial intelligence agencies, institutions for the fight against corruption) and legal reforms (codes in penal, civil or administrative matters, or more specific legislation – e.g., on the status of judges, data protection legislation or measures against money laundering), as well as on the legal training of the players concerned and the setting up and development of training institutions (judicial training schools, police academies, prison staff training schools, etc.). A specific programme has also been set up with Turkey to improve the judicial and prison systems. These Joint Programmes concretely and effectively reveal the necessary inter-institutional cooperation that is to be pursued in this same spirit of complementarity for the sake of common goals.

IV. Conclusion

The Council of Europe, being the largest and oldest European political institution, and the guardian of the founding values of the European pact, cannot and may not be considered as a rival of the European Union. Nor should the powerful economic and political Union be seen as casting doubt on the legitimacy of the Council of Europe, which would then soon be confined to playing the part conferred upon it by General De Gaulle of "la belle endormie au bord du Rhin où on l'a laissée". Neither should the Council of Europe be seen simply as the "anteroom" of the European Union in which candidate members acquire their democratic passport. The Council of Europe remains the reference as far as human rights, and the pre-eminence of law and democracy are concerned. In the complex context of the European construction, the Council of Europe and the European Union must evolve in a way which is complementary in matters of human rights, pre-eminence of law and legal cooperation[35] – a guarantee for the development of an area of European law that will be stronger, fairer and more efficient for 800 million Europeans.

"There are broad areas where worthwhile co-operation between the two organisations is natural, and the added value of a renewed partnership seems to me undeniable", claimed Jean-Claude Juncker in his report. It is thus the responsibility of policy-makers and civil servants of both our institutions to progress hand in hand for a more humane Europe, and one that is forever closer to its citizens.

35. The Memorandum of Understanding refers in particular to the protection of people belonging to national minorities, the fight against torture and bad treatment, the fight against discrimination, racism, xenophobia and intolerance, the fight against trafficking of human beings, the protection of children, the promotion of education to human rights and freedom of speech and of information, as well as the security of individuals, in particular in the context of the fight against terrorism, organised criminality, corruption, money laundering and other modern challenges, including those resulting from the development of new technologies.

3. UN Anti-Terrorism Sanctions and EU Human Rights: The lessons of European integration

Servaas van Thiel[1]

I.   Introduction

The European Union can perhaps best be described as an ongoing integration process between the European states. From the outset there were strong political reasons not to leave the further shaping and implementation of this process entirely in the hands of the participating governments (as in a classical international law approach). Therefore the responsibility for the integration process was entrusted to a newly created European governance structure with its own institutional framework and legislative, executive and judicial powers (Community approach). Throughout the years the integration process has widened to 27 Member States and deepened with the acceptance of broad policy objectives including an internal market without frontiers, an Economic and Monetary Union, an area of Justice, Liberty and Security and a Common Foreign and Security Policy.

Early on in this European integration process the problem arose that the newly created EU institutions were competent to adopt binding legal acts that potentially violated human rights of individuals. The EU was itself, however, not bound by international human rights instruments, nor did its own basic treaties contain such human rights protection elements.

This created a dilemma for the national supreme courts of the Member States, which were obliged to apply Community law and to give it priority over national law, including national constitutional human rights standards, even though this could possibly cause a human rights protection deficit. Particularly interesting in this regard is the way in which the German Constitutional Court grappled with the question to what extent national courts should feel obliged to accept the primacy of those Community law rules which it considered to fall short of the human rights protection standards guaranteed by the domestic constitution.

The same political considerations that lay at the origin of the European integration process have played a role in the setting up of post war global

1.   The article expresses the personal view of the author only.

437

governance structures. The Bretton Woods institutions, for instance, were clearly meant as an international institutional guarantee against a repetition of the pre-war experience, that an economic crisis in one major economy, could deepen and spread around the globe, and result in domestic economic policy reactions that would ultimately contribute to the eruption of a world war.

More importantly, to prevent any further war, the UN Charter provided clear rules and endowed the Security Council with sweeping powers to maintain international peace and security. The UN Charter, for instance, obliges states to settle their disputes by peaceful means and to abstain from the threat or use of force (Chapter I, article 2), and it allows the Security Council to take a pro-active role in settling disputes between members (Chapter VI, articles 33 to 38). But more than that, to prevent disputes from deteriorating into armed conflict, the UN Charter mandates the Security Council to determine when a threat to the peace occurs, and, in that case, to decide any measures to maintain international peace and security (Chapter VII, articles 39 to 51). UN Members may be called upon to apply economic or diplomatic sanctions[2], and if these do not have the desired effect, they may be requested to (collectively) use force[3]. UN Members have all agreed to accept and carry out the decisions of the Security Council in accordance with the UN Charter,[4] which means, inter

2. Article 41 UN Charter provides that the Security Council may decide what measures not involving the use of armed force are to be employed to give effect to its decisions, and that it may call upon the Members of the United Nations to apply such measures. It further specifies that these measures may include complete or partial interruption of economic relations and of rail, sea, air, postal, telegraphic, radio, and other means of communication, and the severance of diplomatic relations.

3. Article 42 provides: "Should the Security Council consider that measures provided for in Article 41 would be inadequate or have proved to be inadequate, it may take such action by air, sea, or land forces as may be necessary to maintain or restore international peace and security. Such action may include demonstrations, blockades, and other operations by air, sea, or land forces of Members of the United Nations."

4. Under Article 24(1) of the 1945 UN Charter the members of the United Nations 'confer on the Security Council primary responsibility for the maintenance of international peace and security, and agree that in carrying out its duties under this responsibility the Security Council acts on their behalf'. Under Article 25 of the UN Charter "[t]he Members of the United Nations agree to accept and carry out the decisions of the Security Council in accordance with the present Charter". Article 48(2) of the UN Charter provides that the decisions of the Security Council for the maintenance of international peace and security "shall be carried out by the Members of the United Nations directly and through their action in the appropriate international agencies of which they are members".

alia, that they have fully accepted the primacy of the Charter over other international agreements, which again implies that binding Security Council Resolutions supersede over other obligations of the members.[5]

Since the early 1990ies, the UN Security Council has assumed a broader understanding of its role to maintain peace and security, and it has directed its actions also against threats to the peace that emanate from private persons or organisations engaged in terrorist activities. There is, as a consequence, a long list of Security Council Resolutions that provide for sanctions, such as visa bans or asset freezes, to be applied to listed individuals or private sector organisations. The problem is that the listing of individuals at UN level, which has serious implications for their ability to travel and to dispose over their assets, typically takes place on the basis of procedures that fall short of the normal human rights protection standards that would apply in a similar domestic context. Nevertheless, under the UN Charter UN Members are obliged to carry out these Resolutions, and interestingly, the Community, though not itself a UN Member, has assumed full responsibility for implementing Security Council sanction resolutions, presumably at the request and on behalf of the Member States.[6]

As a consequence, it is now the Community that is facing claims from individuals that they have been wrongly listed by UN Security Council Resolutions and thus unlawfully deprived of their rights by the parallel EU restrictive measures. In a way, the European Courts now find themselves in a situation similar to the one in which the German Supreme Court found itself in the early days of the European integration process: how to solve the dilemma between, on the one hand, the desire to uphold the protection of human rights in accordance with internal constitutional rules, and on the other hand the need to avoid undermining the effectiveness of an international or supra-national governance structure, to which one committed itself and the decisions of which one is, under the applicable supra-national normative framework, obliged to implement.

---

5. See Article 103 of the UN Charter ("In the event of a conflict between the obligations of the Members of the United Nations under the present Charter and their obligations under any other international agreement, their obligations under the present Charter shall prevail") as interpreted by the International Court of Justice in the Lockerbie case, ICJ Reports 1992, page 16 paragraph 39.
6. The Commission website (http:/europa.eu.int/comm/external_relations/cfsp/sanctions/) provides an overview of sanctions that are currently in force, and a consolidated list of persons and entities concerned.

This paper investigates possible ways in which that European dilemma could be solved, also in the light of the past experience at the intra-Community level. For that purpose, section II will briefly outline the ways in which European and national institutions have dealt with this potential human rights protection deficit (A), by recalling the different phases in the development of an effective human rights protection framework at European level (B), and the parallel developments in the case law of the German Constitutional Court (C). This will be a good illustration of how the European Union, as a complex multi-layered governance structure with multiple actors, "constitutionalizes" gradually by means of a series of decisions of the Courts and the constitutional legislator that, over time, fill the constitutional gaps that were left open by the "founding fathers" when they drafted the initial treaties.

Section III of this paper will outline the human rights protection deficit that has arisen at UN level and that has caused a dilemma for the EU, when implementing UN Security Council Sanctions Resolutions that order smart sanctions against terrorists. After having outlined the basic principles applying to the EU sanctions policy (A) and the flaws in the UN procedures that nevertheless have the outcome of obliging UN Members to implement targeted sanctions against listed individuals and groups (B), it will be briefly discussed how the European Courts are struggling with this dilemma in the Kadi case (C).

In a final section IV possible solutions will be discussed that could perhaps help achieving an appropriate balance between the simultaneous obligations on the EU to respect and protect human rights and to reinforce the global governance structures and in particular the functioning of the UN Security Council.

II.   The human rights protection deficit in the European integration process and how it was gradually remedied

A.   Complex European governance structures with a potential human rights protection deficit

After the second World War, the Council of Europe was set up including a supranational governance structure to ensure that European states would fully respect the human rights of their citizens. Apart from formulating these human rights in a European Convention on Human Rights (ECHR), a supervisory mechanism was created consisting of political and judicial elements, and allowing individual complaints against states for violations of the rights spelled out in the ECHR.

In a separate but parallel track some European states engaged in a deep economic integration process with the clear objective of tying themselves so tightly together that they could no longer afford armed conflict. To ensure the success of this strategy the responsibility for this integration process was placed in the hands of a newly created European governance structure that disposed of its own legislative, executive and judicial powers, and its own institutions and budget to exercise these powers.

Interestingly, the European Communities themselves did not adhere to the ECHR, nor did the Treaties establishing the European Communities provide for the protection of human rights. Consequently, there was a potential deficit in the European system of human rights protection, because citizens had no effective recourse against acts of European institutions that would violate their human rights as guaranteed by the ECHR and the constitutions of the Member States. It would take many years of combined action by the Court and the Constitutional legislator to gradually fill that constitutional gap (section II B).

In the absence of a European human rights protection system that could satisfy the standards of the domestic constitutions of the Member States and the ECHR, the human rights dimension of a Community act was bound to end up in the national courts. The position of the German Constitutional Court is a good illustration of the dilemma which arises when national courts are obliged to accept the primacy of rules of Community law which are considered to fall short of the human rights protection standards guaranteed by the domestic constitution (section II C).

B. The European institutions gradually moving towards a closed system of human rights protection in the Union

History has shown that the potential gap in the European system of human rights protection could only be closed in a gradual process in which all European actors have, at different stages of the integration process, made their contribution to a solution that ultimately can be qualified as a guaranteed constitutional system of protection of human rights in the European Union.

Starting point of this historic process has been the European Court of Justice, which has tackled this constitutional issue in several steps. First, in a more general line of case law, it has always assumed that the Community is based on the rule of law and that all governance levels and institutions are accountable to an independent judiciary[7]. European citizens are, like the Member States, subjects of this new European legal order, and they may derive not only obligations but also rights from the Treaty on which they can rely in all national courts (direct effect)[8] which must ignore incompatible national law (primacy of Community law[9]). In addition, the Community law principle of judicial protection of individual rights, requires that citizens must have access to national courts and that Member States may be held liable for the damages caused by their breaches of the law[10]. Therefore, the Court recognised from the outset that the Community, as a new legal order, grants European citizens rights which they enjoy in an overall constitutional context.

Secondly, in a more specific line of case law, the Court gradually acknowledged the principle of protection of human rights in the sense that there should be a nucleus of the citizen's private sphere on which the European institutions cannot trespass. Though the initial treaties did not contain specific references to human rights, the ECJ, after initial reluctance[11], gradually developed a protection doctrine[12] based on the premise that fundamental human rights form part of the general principles

---

7. Opinion 1/91 EEA [1991] ECR I-6079; Case 294/83 Les Verts [1986] ECR 1339.
8. Case 26/62 van Gend & Loos [1963] ECR 1; Case 6/64 Costa v. ENEL [1964] ECR 585.
9. The primacy of Community law was confirmed in early case law including Case 6/60 Humblet [1960] ECR 559, Case 26/62 van Gend & Loos [1963] ECR 1, Case 6/64 Costa v. ENEL [1964] ECR 585, Case 48/71 Commission v. Italy [1972] ECR 527, Case 106/77 Simmenthal [1978] ECR 629.
10. Joined Cases C-6 and C-9/90 Francovich and Bonifaci [1991] ECR I-5357; Case C-224/01 Köbler [2003] ECR I-10239.
11. In Case 1/58 Stork v High Authority [1959] ECR 17, the Court refused to consider the argument that a decision of the High Authority violated basic rights protected by German constitutional law. Likewise in Joined Cases 36, 37, 38, and 40/59 Geitling v High Authority [1960] ECR 423, the Court not only rejected the relevance of fundamental rights protected by German constitutional law, but also dismissed the suggestion that Community law might itself protect such rights.
12. De Witte B (1993): "The Past and Future Role of the European Court of Justice in the Protection of Human Rights" in Alston P. (1993): "The EU and Human Rights", Oxford University Press at 866. The Court's change of hart was probably motivated as much by its desire to protect human rights as by its desire to overcome opposition against its primacy doctrine by the German and Italian constitutional courts (see German Constitutional Court decisions of 29 May 1974, Solange I; 22 October 1986, Solange II; 12 October 1993, Maastricht; and 7 June 2000, Bananas).

of Community law which are protected by the Court[13]. In determining the substance of those rights the Court was inspired by the constitutional traditions common to the Member States[14] and by international human rights treaties[15], such as the European Convention on Human Rights[16]. The Court ultimately reached the point that fundamental rights were, in the Community legal order, protected against intrusive acts of the Community institutions, and of the Member States when they implement Community rules[17], and that both are obliged by Community law to respect those rights[18].

Therefore, human rights were protected in the Community legal order well before they were first explicitly referred to in the 1986 Single European Act (SEA)[19]. It was nevertheless this first legislative reference that reinvigorated the European Parliament's call for the adoption of a Community catalogue of human rights, which it subsequently included in its 1989 draft Constitution in the form of a Declaration of Fundamental

---

13. Case 29/69 Stauder v City of Ulm [1969] ECR 419 at 425.
14. Case 11/70 Internationale Handelsgesellschaft [1970] ECR 1125. Meehan M.: "(Un) Chartered Waters: The Legal Background to Fundamental Rights Protection in the EU", in Feus K. (2000): "An EU Charter of Fundamental Rights: Text and Commentaries", London 2000 at 85 pointed out correctly that these constitutional traditions were very different which made it problematic to clearly define individual rights at the Community level.
15. Case 4/73 Nold [1974] ECR 491.
16. Case 36/75, Rutili [1975] ECR 1219. In Case C-13/94 P v S and Cornwall County Council [1996] ECR I-2143 the ECJ referred for the first time to ECHR case law. More recently, Case C-274/99 P *Connolly* v *Commission* [2001] ECR I-1611 point 37, and Case C-94/00 Roquette Frères [2002] ECR I-9011 point 25.
17. Joined Cases 60 and 61/84 Cinétheque [1985] ECR 2605; Case 12/86 Demirel [1987] ECR 3719; Case 5/88 Wachauf [1989] ECR 2609; Case 260/89 ERT [1991] ECR I-2925; Case C-168/91 Konstantinidis [1993] ECR I-1191; Case C- 299/95 Kremzow v Austria [1997] ECR I-2629; Case C-309/96 Annibaldi [1997] ECR I-7493.
18. Case C- 260/89 ERT & POSP v Dimotiki Etairia Pliroforissis et al. [1991] ECR I-2925.
19. The SEA refers in its preamble to the fundamental rights recognized in the constitutions and laws of the Member States, the European Convention on Human Rights and the Social Charter.

Rights.[20] In spite of this parliamentary activism, the 1992 Maastricht Treaty merely codified the Court's decision that the Union must respect fundamental rights common to the constitutional traditions of the Member States as general principles of Community law (ex Article F (2)), while also explicitly conditioning EU Membership on respect for human rights.[21]

The longstanding debate continued whether the EU should codify human rights in a Community specific bill of rights or simply accede to the Council of Europe and its European Convention on Human Rights (ECHR). Part of the literature favoured an EU-specific catalogue[22] on the grounds that it would allow for an update of the 1950 ECHR, strengthen the position of individuals, and increase the transparency and visibility of the European commitment to human rights. Others, however, including

20. In 1973, the European Parliament invited the Commission to report on how it intended to protect fundamental rights common to the Constitutions of Member States (OJC 26 of 30 April 1973). In its 1976 report to the Parliament, the Commission favoured a written catalogue of fundamental rights, and it particularly underlined the need for developing economic and social rights (EC Commission Report, "The Protection of Fundamental Rights as Community Law is Created and Developed", EC Bull. Suppl. 5 of 1976). In 1979, the Commission submitted a Memorandum on Accession of the Communities to the European Convention for the Protection of Human Rights and Fundamental Rights (EC Bull. Supplement 2 of 1979), which the Court, however rejected in the constitutional context of the time. See Rack R. and Lausegger S.; "The Role of the European Parliament: Past and Future", and Bradley K.: "Reflections on the Human Rights Role of the European Parliament", both in Alston P. (1993); "The EU and Human Rights", Oxford University Press at 801-37 and at 845.
21. See Nowak M.: "Human Rights 'Conditionality' in Relation to Entry to and Full Participation in the EU", in Alston P. (1993): "The EU and Human Rights" at. 687 and 698.
22. Weiler J.J.H. (1999): "The constitution of Europe, "Do the new clothes have an emperor?" and other essays on European integration", Cambridge University Press at 15; Oddvar E. and Fossum J.E. (2000): "Democracy in the European Union: integration through deliberation?", Routledge, London, 2000 (ISBN 0-415-22592-2). Lindfelt M.: "A Bill of Rights for the European Union", Institute for Human Rights, Abo Akademi University, http://www.abo.fi/instut/imr/norfa/mats_billofrights.pdf.

the Commission, favoured accession to the ECHR[23] as this would avoid confusion over applicable standards (which were anyway constantly updated by the European Court of Human Rights), and would make the ECJ accountable to the Human Rights Court (like domestic supreme courts). Lenaerts at the time proposed a hybrid solution under which acts of a Member State that were outside the scope of Community law would be controlled by the European Court of Human Rights, whereas Community acts or Member State acts within the scope of Community law, would be controlled by the ECJ (which would have to follow the interpretation of the ECHR).[24]

In its 1996 Opinion, the Court clarified that the constitutional context at the time did not allow Community accession to the European Convention for lack of Community competence and because no specific arrangements had been made concerning the way in which the Community would become subject to judicial control by the ECHR.[25] Whereas the Court's insistence that accession could take place only by way of Treaty

23. O'Leary S. (1996): "Accession by the European Community to the European Convention on Human Rights-The Opinion of the ECJ", European Human Rights Law Review 4 of 1996 at 375; Toth A.G. (1997): "The European Union and Human Rights: the Way Forward", 34 Common Market Law Review of 1997 at 501; Commission Communication SEC (90) 2087 of 19 November 1990; Betten, Lammy and Grief (1998): "EU Law and Human Rights", London 1998 at 114; Sislova N.: "The outline of some Current Issues of the Human Rights Protection at EU Level", http://www.ecsanet.org/ecsaworld6/contributions/others/Siskova.doc.; Cooper J. and Pillay R. (): "Through the Looking Glass: Making Visible Rights Real" in Feus K. (2000): "An EU Charter of Fundamental Rights: Text and Commentaries", London at 117; House of Lords Select Committee on the European Union (2003):"The Future Status of the EU Charter of Fundamental Rights" Session 2002-03, 6th Report, HL Paper 48 at 29; Goldsmith: "Consolidation of Fundamental Rights at EU Level-the British Perspective", in Feus K. (2000): "An EU Charter of Fundamental Rights: Text and Commentaries", London at 35.
24. Lenaerts K. (1991): "Fundamental Rights to be included in a Community Catalogue", 16 European Law Review of 1991 at 377 to 381.
25. Opinion 2/94 [1996] ECR I- 1759. Kokott J. and Hoffmeister F. (1996): "Opinion 2/94, Accession of the Community to the European Convention for the Protection of Human Rights and Fundamental Freedoms", 90 American Journal of International Law of 1996 at 667. Arnull A. M. (1996): "Opinion 2/94 and its Implications for the Future Constitutions of the Union", in: The Human Rights Opinion of the ECJ and Its Constitutional Implications, University of Cambridge, CELS Occasional Paper No 1, June 1996.

amendment was severely criticised in the literature[26], members of the Court insisted that it had to be understood as an appeal to amend the constitutional character of the Community's legal order", rather than as opposition by the Court to the principle of accession.[27] In other words, the European Court put the responsibility for change on the constitutional legislator.

The Amsterdam Treaty, which entered into force in 1999, merely reiterated that: "The Union is founded on the principles of liberty, democracy, respect for human rights and fundamental freedoms, and the rule of law, principles which are common to the Member States" (Article 6 paragraph 1) and it authorised the Council to take measures against Member States which infringed those rights (Article 7 TEU and Article 309(2) ECT), and to act against discrimination based on sex, racial or ethnic origin, religion or belief, disability, age or sexual orientation (Article 13[28]). But the Amsterdam Treaty did not solve the controversy over whether the Community should have its own bill of rights or accede to the ECHR.

At the June 1999 Cologne European Council, European Heads of State and Government took a further step forward when they invited a "Convention", presided by former German President Roman Herzog, to draft a European Charter for Human Rights. On 7 December 2000, in Nice, the Presidents of the European Parliament, the Council and the Commission were able to sign and proclaim the Charter, which set out in

26. Craig P. and de Burca G.(1998): "EU Law: Text, Cases, and Materials", Oxford 1998 at. 337 and 338; Weiler, J.H.H. and Fries S.C: "A Human Rights Policy for the European Community and Union: The Question of Competences", in: Alston P. (1993): "The EU and Human Rights", London at 150. Burrows N. (1997): "Question of Community Accession to the European Convention Determined", 22 European Law Review of 1997 at 61. Tridimas T. (1999): "The General Principles of the EC Law", Oxford 1999 at 242. Bulterman M. (2001): "Human Rights in the Treaty Relations of the European Community", Antwerpen 2001 at. 88.
27. Lenaerts K. (2000): "Fundamental Rights in the European Union", 25 European Law Review of 2000 at 575; Jacobs F.G. (2002): "The EU Charter of Fundamental Rights" in Arnull A. and Wincott D. (eds.) (2002), "Accountability and Legitimacy in the European Union", at 289.
28. Bell M. (1999): "The New Article 13 EC Treaty: A Sound Basis for European Anti-Discrimination Law?", Maastricht Journal of European and Comparative Law of 1999 at 5; Flynn L.: "The Implications of Article 13 EC – After Amsterdam, Will Some Forms of Discrimination be More Equal than Others?", 36 Common Market Law Review of 1999 at 1127; Gearty, Conor A., "The Internal and External 'Other' in the Union Legal Order: Racism, Religious Intolerance and Xenophobia in Europe" in Alston, Philip (1993): "The EU and Human Rights, at 327-58; Ellis E.:"The Principle of Non-Discrimination in the Post-Nice Era" in Arnull A. and Wincott D. (2002): "Accountability and Legitimacy in the European Union", Oxford, 2002 at 291-305.

a single text the full range of civil, political, economic and social rights of European citizens. The Charter was, however, neither incorporated in the Nice Treaty nor legally binding[29]. Nevertheless frequent authoritative references to the Charter (inter alia by the Court of First Instance[30], the Council of Ministers[31], and the European Court of Human Rights[32]), complicated the already lively discussion on the protection of human rights in the EU[33].

The drafters of the now defunct Constitution resolved the long debate by simultaneously taking several steps towards an appropriate level of human

29. The EP Draft Report on the Treaty of Nice and the future of the European Union noted that Denmark, Finland, Ireland, the Netherlands, Sweden, and the United Kingdom rejected the idea of incorporating the Charter into the Treaties, Committee on Constitutional Affairs, 22 March 2001, doc. PE 294. 755.
30. Judgments of 30 January 2002 in Case T-54/99 Max-mobil Telecommunications Service GmbH v Commission [2002] ECR II-313 and Case T-177/01 Jego-Quere v Commission [2002] ECR II-2365.
31. Council Decision 2002/187/JHA of 28/2/2002, OJ L 63, 6.3. 2002, p. 1.
32. See Goodwin v United Kingdom, judgment of 7 July 2002, Reports 1996-II, point 100.
33. Jacobs, Overy, Claire and White (2002): "European Convention on Human Rights", Oxford 2002 at 446; Kyriakou T. (2001): "The Impact of the Fundamental Rights on the EU system of Protection of Rights: much ado about nothing?", Web Journal of Current Legal Issues Ltd, of 2001 at http://webjcli.ncl.ac.uk.; Douglas-Scott (2004), "The Charter of Fundamental Rights as a Constitutional Document", European Human Rights Law Review 1 of 2004 at 40; Eeckhout P. (2002): "The Charter of Fundamental Rights and the Federal Questions", 39 Common Market Law Review of 2002 at 947; Wiener A. (2001): "The Constitutional Significance of the Charter of Fundamental Rights", German Law Journal of 2001 at http://germanlawjournal.com.; Lenaerts K. and De Smijter E (2001): "A 'Bill of Rights' for the European Union", 38 Common Market Law Review of 2001 at 298-99; Groussot X. (2003): "A Third Step in the Process of EU Constitutionalization: A Binding Charter of Fundamental Rights?", Europarattslig Tidskrift of 2003 at 538; Liisberg, Jonas Bering, "Does the EU Charter of Fundamental Rights Threaten the Supremacy of Community Law? Article 53 of the Charter: A Fountain of Law or just an Inkblot?" Jean Monnet Working Paper 4/01 at p. 7; Tesauro G.: "Some thoughts on the Charter of Fundamental Rights", available at http://www.ecln.net/rome2002/tesauro.pdf.; McBride J.: "Protecting Fundamental Rights in Europe: A Legal Analysis" in Arnull A. and Wincott D. (2002): "Accountability and Legitimacy in the European Union", Oxford at 265; Eeckhout P.: "The Proposed EU Charter of Fundamental Rights: Some Reflections on Its Effects in the Legal Systems of the EU and of its Member States", in Feus K. (2000): "An EU Charter of Fundamental Rights: Text and Commentaries", at 104; Menendez A.J. (2002): "Chartering Europe: Legal Status and Policy Implications of the Charter of Fundamental Rights of the European Union", 40 Journal of Common Market Studies of 2002 at 476; de Gucht K.: "The Charter of Fundamental Rights", in van Thiel, Lewis and De Gucht (2006): "Understanding the New European Constitutional Treaty" published by the Brussels Institute for European Studies, Globalisation Series (www.ies.be).

rights protection in the Union. They first ensured that the Constitution would mention fundamental rights amongst its objectives and values (Preamble and CA I-1 to I-3) and that it would take the logical consequences of accepting human rights as a general foreign policy steer (CA I-40), of conditioning accession to the Union on respect for human rights (CA I-58) and of sanctioning non-respect by Member States (CA I-59).

Secondly, as regards European citizens, the drafters chose the maximum approach in CA I-9 which simply combined all the alternatives that had been debated in the literature. Following the recommendation from the relevant Convention working group that "a building block as central as fundamental rights should find its place in the EU constitutional framework"[34], the Constitution on the one hand obliged the Union to recognise the rights, freedoms and principles of the Charter, which it integrated as an EU specific bill of rights, into part II of the Constitution. On the other hand, the Constitution also obliged the Union to accede to the ECHR and it provided that fundamental rights constitute general principles of Union law, which the Court should protect when assuring that the law is observed (CA I-29). To reconcile this multilevel European system of human rights protection (constitutions of the Member States, EU general principles, ECHR, other international treaties), the Constitution (CA II-111 to 114) contained a number of rules of thumb. In line with the suggestion of Lenaerts, the European bill of rights would apply to Union acts and to Member State acts that implement Union law. Moreover, the Constitution provided that the protection available under the ECHR would be the minimum standard (the Union not being prevented from providing a more extensive protection). Finally, the Constitution explicitly referred to the explanations drawn up by the Convention Praesidium as an interpretative guide which should be taken into account by the Community and national courts.[35]

34. Working Group Final report p.2 (CONV 354/02).
35. The old CA II-112 para 7 provides that the explanations drawn up as a way of providing guidance in the interpretation of the Charter of Fundamental Rights shall be given due regard by the courts of the Union and of the Member states. The Praesidium explanations are published in: Council of the European Union (2004): "Draft Treaty establishing a Constitution for Europe as approved by the Intergovernmental Conference on 18 June 2004, Volume II: Protocols and Declarations", at 379 to 438. See also Official Journal C 303, 14.12. 2007, p. 17.

However, subsequent to the French and Dutch no-votes to the Constitution in June 2005, the project was abandoned and Europe disappeared in one of its recurrent stages in which reflection rather than action is the key word. It took exactly 2 years for the Union to come back on its Constitutional project and to replace it with a simpler Reform Treaty. The text of this Reform Treaty was adopted at the intergovernmental Conference on 19 October 2007 and signed in Lisbon on 13 December 2007 (with entry into force expected in early 2009 before the next European Parliament elections). The essential provisions in the area of human rights are that the provisions of the Charter will not be integrated in the text of the Treaties, but will continue to form a separate text, which will, however, be binding on the European Union and the Member States,[36] albeit with a limited opt out for the UK.[37]

This means that the human rights protection deficit in the EU is finally closed and that, in addition to adhering to the ECHR, the EU will itself have a binding Human Rights Charter that essentially provides for the protection of 50 civil, political, economic and social rights and principles,

36. Article 6 of the Reform Treaty provides that the Union recognises the rights, freedoms and principles set out in the Charter of Fundamental Rights of 7 December 2000, and that the Charter shall have the same legal value as the Treaties. It also provides that the Union shall accede to the ECHR, and that the fundamental rights, as guaranteed by the ECHR and as they result from the constitutional traditions common to the Member States, shall constitute general principles of the Union's law.
37. The UK, with a largely uncodified Constitution, was strongly against making the Charter legally binding, but in the end could not convince its partners and obtained a limited opt out. Poland made a unilateral declaration about the Charter stating that: "The Charter will not affect in any way the right of Member States to legislate in the sphere of public morality, family law as well as the protection of human dignity and respect for human physical and moral integrity". (see Council Conclusions, p.25, footnote 18 and Presidency Conclusions, footnote 18).

under six headings: dignity[38], liberty[39], equality[40], solidarity[41], citizen's rights[42] and justice[43]. As to the interpretation of these rights, the Praesidium explanation that is added to the Charter[44] clarifies that the classical rights (in the chapters dignity, freedoms, equality and justice) are

38. Five articles on Dignity declare human dignity inviolable and confirm the right to life, the right to the integrity of the person, the prohibition of torture and inhuman or degrading treatment or punishment, the prohibition of slavery and forced labour including trafficking in human beings (Articles 1 to 5 of the Charter).

39. Fourteen articles on liberty in physical, spiritual, social and economic terms, provide the right to liberty and security of person, the right to asylum and protection in the event of removal, expulsion or extradition, the protection of personal data, the freedom of thought, conscience and religion, the freedom of expression and information, the freedom of the arts and sciences, the right to education, the right to respect for private and family life and the right to marry and found a family, the freedom of peaceful assembly and of association the right to own property, the freedom to choose an occupation and the right to engage in work, and the freedom to conduct a business including the freedom to contract (Articles 6 to 19 of the Charter).

40. Seven articles on equality which provide for equality before the law, prohibit any discrimination based on physical characteristics (such as sex, race, colour, ethnic origin, genetic features, birth, disability, age, sexual orientation), socio-political characteristics (such as social origin, language, religion, political or other opinion, membership of a minority) or nationality, prescribe respect for cultural, religious and linguistic diversity (including the status of churches and non-confessional organisations), ensure gender-equality and protect or respect the rights of vulnerable groups of the population such as children (based on the 1989 New York Convention on the rights of the child), the elderly, and persons with disabilities (Articles 20 to 26 of the Charter).

41. Twelve articles on solidarity confirm the right of collective bargaining, the prohibition of child labour, protection in the event of unjustified dismissal, right to fair and just working conditions, the right of workers to information and consultation within the undertaking, the right to a good balance between family and professional life, the right to social security and social assistance, and to access to placement services, the right of access to health care, the right of access to services of general economic interest, and the right to high levels of environmental protection and consumer protection (Articles 27 to 38 of the Charter).

42. Citizen's Rights include the right to vote and to stand as a candidate at EP and municipal elections, the right to good administration, the right of access to documents, the right to refer cases of mal-administration to the Ombudsman, the right to petition the European Parliament, the freedom of movement and of residence, and the right to diplomatic and consular protection (Articles 39 to 46 of the Charter).

43. Four articles on justice include the right to an effective remedy and a fair trial, including the right to a fair and public hearing within a reasonable time by an independent tribunal, the presumption of innocence, the rights of defence, the principles of legality and proportionality of criminal offences and penalties, ne bis in idem (Articles 47 to 50 of the Charter).

44. "Explanations relating to the Charter on fundamental rights", OJ C 303, 14.12. 2007, p. 17 to 35.

the same[45] or slightly broader[46] as those provided by the ECHR and are thus to be interpreted in the same way. For many of the social rights (in the "solidarity" chapter) reference is made to the European Social Charter[47] and for the other Articles reference is often made to the Community acquis (including secondary Community law and rulings of the ECJ) and to common constitutional traditions of the Member States, or other international conventions. Moreover, as regards the effect of these rights it is clarified that the classical human rights and freedoms are fully justiciable, and can be restricted only by law and in accordance with the principles of necessity and proportionality[48], while most of the individual

45. Constitutional rights that correspond to the rights provided by the ECHR include the right to life (Article 2 ECHR), the prohibition of torture (Article 3 ECHR), the prohibition of slavery and forced labour (Article 4 ECHR), the right to liberty and security of person (Article 5 ECHR), respect for private and family life (Article 8 ECHR), the freedom of thought, conscience and religion (Article 9 ECHR), the freedom of expression (Article 10 ECHR), the right to property (Article 1 of ECHR Protocol), the right to protection in the event of removal, expulsion or extradition (Article 3 ECHR and 4 of Protocol 4 ECHR), the presumption of innocence and right of defence (Article 6 ECHR), and the principle of legality and proportionality of criminal offences and penalties (Article 7 ECHR).

46. Constitutional rights that go beyond those provided by the ECHR include the right to marry and found a family (the Charter has a wider scope than Article 12 ECHR because it protects other forms of marriage if provided by national legislation), the freedom of assembly and association (the Charter has a wider scope than Article 11 ECHR as it is extended to EU level), the right to education (the Charter goes beyond 11 ECHR because it also covers vocational and continuing training), the right to an effective remedy and a fair trial (the Charter goes beyond 6 ECHR because the limitation to the determination of civil rights and obligations or criminal charges do not apply as regards Union law and its implementation), and the ne bis in idem rule (the Charter goes beyond 4 of Protocol 7 ECHR because it is extended to EU level).

47. See, for instance, the Praesidium explanation on the Articles concerning the rights of the elderly, the integration of persons with disabilities, workers right to information and consultation, right of collective bargaining and action, right of access to placement services, protection in the event of unjust dismissal, fair and just working conditions, prohibition of child labour, family and professional life balance, social security and assistance, and health care.

48. In particular, the Charter provisions on human dignity, life, integrity of the person, torture, liberty and security, private and family life, protection of personal data, marriage and family life, thought, conscience and religion, expression and information, assembly and association, freedom of arts and sciences, occupation and business, property, asylum, protection in case of removal, expulsion or extradition, equality and non discrimination, collective bargaining and action, prohibition of child labour, the citizen's rights (to vote, to good administration, to access to institutions and documents, to free movement and residence, to diplomatic and consular protection), to an effective remedy and a fair trial, presumption of innocence, non-retroactivity of criminal law, ne bis in idem.

or collective social rights and principles clearly require further articulation in secondary law.

Of specific relevance to this paper on sanctions is that the Charter explicitly confirms certain substantive human rights that had already been accepted by the European Court in its case law, such as the right to own property[49], the freedom to choose an occupation and the right to engage in work[50], and the freedom to conduct a business including the freedom to contract[51]. The Charter also seeks to ensure that justice is done in the Union, by means of due process rights. Key provisions are the right of any European citizen to an effective remedy in case of violation of his or her constitutional rights, including fundamental due process concepts such as the right to a fair and public hearing within a reasonable time by an independent tribunal.[52] In the case of criminal charges, there are the presumption of innocence, the right to a fair trial and the rights of defence as well as the principles of legality and proportionality of criminal offences and penalties and the right not to be tried or punished twice in criminal proceedings for the same criminal offence (ne bis in idem).[53]

C. The German constitutional court between direct effect of secondary Community law and human rights protection standards of the German Constitution.

The drawn-out European process of addressing the human rights protection deficit caused a serious dilemma for the constitutional courts of the Member States. On the one hand, they were obliged, under the primacy doctrine of the European Court of Justice, to apply Community law and set aside incompatible national law, even if of a constitutional nature. On the other hand, they were obliged to assure the full protection of the human

---

49. See for instance Case 44/79 Hauer [1979] ECR 3727.
50. See for instance Case 4/73 Nold [1974] ECR 491 points 12 to 14; Case 44/79 Hauer [1979] ECR 3727; Case 234/85 Keller [1986] ECR 2897 point 8.
51. See for instance Case 4/73 Nold [1974] ECR 491 point 14; Case 230/78 Eridiana [1979] ECR 2749 points 20 and 31; Case 151/78 Sukkerfabriken Nykobing [1979] ECR 1 point 19; Case C-240/97 Spain v. Commission [1999] ECR I-6571 point 99.
52. See for the right to an effective remedy for instance Case 222/84 Johnston [1986] ECR 1651; Case 222/86 Heylens [1987] ECR 4097; Case C-97/91 Borelli [1992] ECR I-6313.
53. See for instance Joined Cases 18 and 35/65 Gutmann v. Comission [1966] ECR 149 and Case T- 305/94 Limburgse Vinyl Maatschappij v. Commission [1999] ECR II-931; Case C-187/01 Gözütok [2003] ECR I-1335.

rights listed in their domestic constitutions and in the European Convention on Human Rights.

In particular, the German Federal Constitutional Court grappled with this dilemma because it was regularly called upon to rule on the relation between Community law and the German constitution or "GrundGesetz" (Basic Law) as it is called.[54] In 1967, the German Court recognised, along the lines of the case law of the European Court, that the Community was not itself a State, but a Community of a special nature engaged in a process of continuing integration and with inter-governmental institutions, to which the Member States had transferred particular sovereign rights. The German Court thus recognised that a new public power had been created, independent and autonomous in relation to the State power of the individual Member States. It dismissed as inadmissible a complaint addressed directly against a regulation of the Community, but it did not yet address the underlying question to what extent European institutions are bound by the fundamental-rights order of the Federal Republic of Germany"[55].

In 1974, however, the German Court did reach that point when it considered that the European standards of human rights protection fell short of those guaranteed by the Basic Law. In its "Solange" I judgement, the German Court reserved the right to review the constitutionality of secondary Community law, so long as the protection of fundamental rights in the EEC had not been secured.[56] It recognized the existence of German and European law as two legal spheres, but contrary to the case law of the European Court, it denied the binding effect of the case-law of the ECJ on a national Constitutional Court. Its argument was that while the ECJ reviews the conformity of a Community Act with primary and secondary Community law, the German Constitutional Court needs to deal with the question of compatibility of any acts with the German Basic Law. In case of a conflict between secondary Community law and the German Basic Law, German courts would be obliged to first refer to the European Court to rule on the validity of the Act under Community law, and subsequently to the German Constitutional Court. And the German Court gave priority to national human rights law by ruling that "as long as" the European integration process had not resulted in a catalogue of fundamental rights,

---

54. For a good overview see Winfried Hassemer, Vice-President of the Federal Constitutional Court: "Case-law of the Federal Constitutional Court regarding: The Position of Constitutional Courts following Integration into the European Union", at http://www.us-rs.si/en/index.php.
55. BVerfGE 22, Judgment of 1967, at 298 et seq.
56. *Solange I*, BVerfGE 37, at 271 et seq., Judgment of 29 May 1974.

which is adequate in comparison with the catalogue of fundamental rights contained in the Basic Law, secondary Community law will still be reviewed according to standards of the Basic Law.

In 1986, in its "Solange II" decision, the German Federal Constitutional Court took a step back. It considered that the European case law had developed and matched, as regards the concepts, contents and implementation, the human rights protection standards provided for by the Basic Law. It noted that all the Community institutions recognised that they were under a legal duty to respect basic rights when exercising their competences and pursuing the goals of the Community. Even in the absence of a catalogue of fundamental rights at Community level, this justified a suspension of the national judicial review of the compatibility of Community acts with the Basic law "for the time being".[57]

This opened the way for the European Court of Justice, to rule explicitly in October 1987, in the unrelated Foto Frost case (concerning the ex post recovery of customs duties), that national courts have no jurisdiction to declare acts of Community institutions invalid, as this would jeopardise the uniform application of Community law and legal certainty, and because the Treaty established a complete system of judicial protection which entrusts the European Court with the task to review the legality of Community acts.[58]

In the early 1990ies, when faced with a challenge to the Maastricht Treaty, the German Court took another step in the direction of leaving human rights protection in relation to European Acts, to the European institutions. As such it repeated in the "Maastricht – decision"[59] that in the EU the effective protection of fundamental rights is generally guaranteed to German citizens, also against the sovereign powers of the Community, and that this protection at European level is substantially similar to the

---

57. *Solange II*, BVerfGE 73 at 339 et seq., Judgment of 22 October 1974. The German Court held: "As long as the European Communities, in particular European Court case law, generally ensure effective protection of fundamental rights as against the sovereign powers of the Communities which is to be regarded as substantially similar to the protection of fundamental rights required unconditionally by the Constitution, and in so far as they generally safeguard the essential content of fundamental rights, the Federal Constitutional Court will no longer exercise its jurisdiction to decide on the applicability of secondary Community legislation cited as the legal basis for any acts of German courts or authorities within the sovereign jurisdiction of the Federal Republic of Germany, and it will no longer review such legislation by the standard of the fundamental rights contained in the Basic Law."
58. Case 314/85 Foto Frost [1987] ECR 4199.
59. BVerfGE 89, 155 ff ("Maastricht") Judgment of 12 October 1993.

minimum protection required by the Basic Law. It further placed its reserved competence to review the applicability of secondary Community law, in the framework of the "cooperative-relationship" between the European Court and national courts, whereby the European Court should guarantee the protection of fundamental rights in each individual case for the whole territory of the Community, so that the Federal Constitutional Court could therefore limit itself to decide whether the minimum protection standards of the basic law are protected. The German Court concluded that the European Court was competent for the protection of fundamental rights of German citizens against the regulations of national (German) public power which were adopted on the basis of secondary Community law, and that it would itself take action only in cases in which the ECJ would not observe the standards of the fundamental rights established in the "Solange II – decision".

In that same decision, the German Court rejected the claim that the Maastricht Treaty violated the basic competencies of the German Parliament and thus the right of citizens to participate in the legitimation of the state power through elections. It held that the German Parliament retained sufficient substantial powers and that in the European legal order constitutional democratic principles were sufficiently considered. The Union was no state but a confederation of states, in which the task of democratic authority and supervision, at least regarding the crucial points, goes to the parliaments of the Member States, and in which the Council of Ministers should primarily carry out Community powers, as only its members have a democratic authority through the Parliaments of the respective Member States. At the same time, however, the German Court retained the power to review, also in the future, whether "legal acts of the European institutions and bodies stay within the limits of their allowed sovereign rights, or they exceed such".

The outcome of this case law is that a claim before the German Federal Constitutional Court as regards the violation of a fundamental right through secondary Community law must demonstrate that the European human rights protection standards have declined below the minimum standard of the Basic Law so that the inalienably minimum protection of fundamental rights is in general not guaranteed.[60]

---

60. BVerfGE 102, 147 ff. ("Regulation on the Market of Bananas), Judgment of 7 June 2000.

D.   Summary and conclusions

From these two aspects of the historic development of Community law, it is clear first that the creation of supra-national governance structures with legislative powers is likely to cause concerns over the continued application of highly developed domestic standards on democracy, the rule of law and respect for human rights, when faced with regulatory acts emanating from the supra-national level. This again is likely to cause friction between the various constitutional actors at these different levels, and this friction will have to be dealt with depending on the circumstances.

Secondly, what is interesting in the European experience is that the developments were, to a certain extent, influenced by the fact that the problem was that the normative framework (i.e. a list of human rights) was in place at national and Council of Europe level, but not at Community level. On the other hand, the institutional framework was fully developed at both national and Community levels. The friction caused by the absence of a normative framework at supra-national level could thus initially be dealt with by the two supreme courts, both taking a moderate stance and awaiting action by the constitutional legislator. In fact, though the German Court reserved itself the right to test secondary Community law against the German human rights standards, it did not actually do so, but rather allowed the European Court to fill in the gap by gradually introducing the human right standards common to the Member States, into its review of legality of Community action. The very moment this case law had sufficiently developed, and the European institutions had indeed accepted that they were also bound to respect fundamental rights, the German Court could take a step back and leave the testing of the human rights compatibility of European acts largely to the European level.

In the space created by this judge-made truce between the two systems, the European constitutional legislator could take the time required to come to an agreement on how to complete the normative framework at European level, and he ultimately chose for a combination of solutions. The first solution is the inclusion in the Reform Treaty of a reference to the binding human rights Charter (Article 6 Reform Treaty cited in footnote 32). This ensures that Citizens' human rights are protected also against intrusive acts of the European Union institutions, which gives a political confirmation and democratic legitimacy to what had hitherto been the result of a mere judicial desire to protect basic rights at Union level. The second solution, accession to the ECHR, which is recognised as the minimum standard of protection of civil and political rights below which neither European nor national governments can go, guarantees an external specialised human rights scrutiny of the acts of all Union institutions including the European Court of Justice and presumably the European Council[61]. This is not unimportant taking into account that both institutions are powerful but not infallible.

At the same time, we see sufficient guarantees against an excessively intrusive effect of the Charter in the legal orders of the Member States. For one, the Charter primarily addresses European institutions and Member States when implementing European law and explicitly provides that its inclusion cannot extend the competencies of the Union. Also, there is the distinction between rights and principles (of which the latter require implementing legislation), and there are the guidelines on interpretation drafted by the Praesidium of the Convention. Finally, most human rights listed in the Charter are not absolute, but can be limited by legislative acts.[62]

In conclusion, even though the constituent European Treaties did not refer to the protection of human rights, the very nature of the Community as a supranational governance structure obliged the ECJ to review Community acts and measures for any possible violation of fundamental human rights, and it did so from 1969 onwards[63]. Under this review, the Court requires both the EC institutions and the Member States, when they act within the framework of EC law, to respect human rights, thereby taking as a reference framework the constitutional traditions of the Member States, the European Convention on Human Rights, and other international human rights instruments to which the Member States are a party. The totality of these "European Union" human rights was first codified in the 2000 Nice Charter, which was subsequently integrated almost verbatim into Part II of the Constitution (CA I-2 and II – 61 to II – 114 inclusive), and which will, in accordance with the agreement reached at the European Council of June

61. See for case law on the applicability of the ECHR to Community institutions and acts: EctHR, 18 February 1999 Matthews v. UK, App. No. 24833/94 (exclusion Gibraltar citizens from the right to vote) and ECtHR Senator Lines v. 15 Member States of the EU, App.No. 56672/00.
62. Von Danwitz T. (2003): "The Charter of fundamental rights of the European Union between political symbolism and legal realism", 29 Denv. J. Int'l L; & Pol'y 4 of 2003 at 289 – 304 (at 298, 299) correctly noted that the possibility to limit human rights is traditionally conditioned on an act of legislation so as to ensure that limitations involve Parliament thus giving them democratic legitimacy.
63. See for an explicit reference to human rights as part of the Community legal order Case 29/69 Stauder v. Stadt Ulm [1969] ECR 419, in which the Court held that a provision of Community law contained "nothing capable of prejudicing the fundamental human rights enshrined in the general principles of Community law and protected by the Court" (para. 8).

2007, become a self standing Charter with legal force (except for the UK), once the two new European treaties, the Treaty on European Union and the Treaty on the functioning of the European Union, will have entered into force.[64]

III. EU Sanctions Policy and its human rights deficit

A. EU Sanctions policy

The EU applies sanctions (also referred to as restrictive measures)[65] to achieve the objectives of its Common Foreign and Security Policy (CFSP). Apart from inward looking objectives such as "safeguarding the common values, fundamental interests, independence and integrity of the Union" and "strengthening the security of the Union in all ways", the CFSP is also geared towards achieving outward looking or transcendent objectives such as "to preserve peace and strengthen international security, in accordance with the principles of the United Nations Charter ..." and "to promote international cooperation and to develop and consolidate democracy and the rule of law and respect for human rights and fundamental freedoms".[66]

Sanctions regularly have a cross pillar character. Generally a Common Position is first adopted by the Council by unanimity under Article 15 EUT. If the Common Position introduces economic and financial

---

64. The Lisbon Reform Treaty is published in OJ C 306, 17.12. 2007, p. 1.
65. Types of sanctions include: diplomatic sanctions (expulsion of diplomats, severing of diplomatic ties, suspension of official visits); suspension of cooperation with a third country; boycotts of sport or cultural events; trade sanctions (general or specific trade sanctions, arms embargoes); financial sanctions (freezing of funds or economic resources, prohibition on financial transactions, restrictions on export credits or investment); flight bans; and visa and travel bans. On the latter, see also the contribution by Martenczuk on visa policy in this book.
66. Article 11 EU Treaty provides in para (1): 'The Union shall define and implement a common foreign and security policy covering all areas of foreign and security policy, the objectives of which shall be: to safeguard the common values, fundamental interests, independence and integrity of the Union in conformity with the principles of the United Nations Charter; to strengthen the security of the Union in all ways; to preserve peace and strengthen international security, in accordance with the principles of the United Nations Charter, as well as the principles of the Helsinki Final Act and the objectives of the Paris Charter, including those on external borders; to promote international cooperation; to develop and consolidate democracy and the rule of law, and respect for human rights and fundamental freedoms'. Interestingly, in point 5 of its Kadi decision, the Court of First Instance only cites the first part of Article 11 up to and including the words: "the United Nations Charter".

sanctions, implementation at Community level is governed respectively by Article 301 (economic sanctions), and Article 60 EUT (financial restrictions).[67] Council Regulations imposing sanctions and implementing Commission Regulations are directly applicable in the Member States and take precedence over conflicting legislation of the Member States.

EU sanctions have traditionally been imposed on governments of third countries and taken the form of arms embargoes[68] or other trade restrictions.[69] However, since the 1990s, EU sanctions have increasingly targeted non-state entities and individuals, such as terrorist groups and their respective organisational structures, and taken the form of financial restrictions and restrictions on admission such as visa or travel bans. Targeted (or smart) financial sanctions address specific persons, groups and entities and typically comprise an obligation to freeze funds and economic resources and a prohibition on making funds or economic resources available to them. Restrictions on admission (visa or travel ban) prevent third country nationals to enter into, or transit through, Member States territories (except if needed on humanitarian grounds or to comply with obligations under international law). EU sanctions are imposed either

67. In these cases, the Commission has to make a proposal for a Council Regulation, which the Council can adopt by a qualified majority. Where restrictive measures target persons, groups and entities which are not directly linked to the regime of a third country, Articles 60, 301 and 308 of the Treaty establishing the European Community have sometimes been relied on as legal basis, but this is disputed. In this case, adoption of the Regulation by the Council requires unanimity and prior consultation of the European Parliament.

68. Arms embargoes typically seek to stop the flow of arms to conflict areas or to questionable regimes and generally comprise a sales and export ban of arms and related materiel (included in the EU Common Military List) and a ban on financial and technical assistance or services related to military activities (except for approved humanitarian assistance, institution-building programmes, crisis management operations, de-mining operations and protective equipment for international personnel). Although trade in manufactured goods falls under exclusive Community competence, Article 296 ECT allows for an embargo relating to military goods to be implemented by Member States using national measures. It is, therefore, common practice that arms embargoes are imposed by a Common Position and enforced on the basis of export control legislation of Member States (although the prohibitions on providing related financial or technical assistance are implemented through a Regulation).

69. Other trade restrictions may consist of the withdrawal of tariff preferences, or export and/or import bans, flight bans, and restrictions on investment, payments and capital movements, and they have to be applied by all natural and legal persons doing business in the EU, and all EU nationals and enterprises doing business outside the EU.

on an autonomous basis or to implement binding UN Security Council resolutions adopted under Chapter VII of the UN Charter.[70]

In 2004, the EU Council of Ministers agreed the "**Basic Principles** on the use of Restrictive Measures (Sanctions)"[71] so as to ensure a more effective use of sanctions. These principles on the one hand reflect the fundamental and constitutionally guaranteed EU foreign policy objective to support and strengthen, whenever possible, the United Nations as a global governance system, by means of coordinated action on the adoption and implementation of sanctions.[72] Member States agreed to do this in accordance with the EU common foreign and security policy, as set out in Article 11 TEU, and in full conformity with their obligations under international law (principle 3). Also, the Council committed to using sanctions as part of an integrated, comprehensive policy approach which should include political dialogue, incentives, conditionality and could even involve, as a last resort, the use of coercive measures in accordance with the UN Charter (principle 5).

70. In the case of autonomous sanctions, the European Court does test the human rights compatibility of sanctions regulations of the Council. See for instance Case T-47/03 Sison, judgment of the CFI of 11 July 2007, in which the Court of First Instance annuls Council Decision 2006/379/EC implementing Council Regulation 2580/2001 and listing Mr Sison as a person suspected of terrorism whose funds should be frozen, on the ground that "no statement of reasons has been given for the contested decision and that the latter was adopted in the course of a procedure during which the applicant's rights of defence were not observed. What is more the Court is not, even at this stage of the procedure in a position to undertake the judicial review of the lawfulness of that decision in the lights of the other pleas in law…" (paragraph 226). See also Case T-327/03 Stichting Al-Aqsa, Judgment of the CFI of 11 July 2007; T-228/02 OMPI Judgment of the CFI of 12 December 2006 [2006] ECR not yet reported.

71. Council document 10198/1/04.

72. As such, the EU Member States commit themselves to the effective use of sanctions as an important way to maintain and restore international peace and security in accordance with the principles of the UN Charter and the Council committed to work continuously to support the UN and fulfil "our" obligations under the UN Charter (principle 1). More specifically the Member States agreed that they would seek to further intensify their efforts within the UN, in line with Article 19 TEU, to coordinate their actions on sanctions. They agreed to ensure full, effective and timely implementation by the European Union of measures agreed by the UN Security Council and to establish a dialogue with the UN to this effect (principle 2). They moreover agreed, if necessary, that the Council would impose autonomous EU sanctions in support of efforts to fight terrorism and the proliferation of weapons of mass destruction and as a restrictive measure to uphold respect for human rights, democracy, the rule of law and good governance.

On the other hand, the 2004 Basic principles reflect the equally fundamental EU foreign policy objective to ensure the full compliance with international human rights protection standards. As such, the Basic Principles refer to the need for sanctions to be proportional and respectful of human rights. Principle 6, for instance, provides that sanctions should be targeted so as to reduce to the maximum extent possible any adverse humanitarian effects or unintended consequences for third parties or countries. More explicitly Principle 7 provides as regards sanctions against non-state actors: "We will carry this forward in full respect of human rights and the rule of law (principle 7)". Also, the Council agreed to clearly define the objectives in the enabling legislation, to regularly review sanctions as to their continued contribution towards their stated objectives, and to terminate them once the objectives were met, in accordance with the EU Guidelines (principle 9).

Restrictive measures are applied and enforced by the competent authorities of the Member States and the Commission. In 2005, the EU Council agreed "**Guidelines on implementation**" as well as a set of "**Best practices** on effective implementation of financial restrictive measures.[73]

The **Guidelines** address a number of general issues and present standard wording and common definitions that may be used in the legal instruments implementing restrictive measures. They clarify that the EU imposes sanctions to bring about a change in policy or activity by the targeted country or persons, in line with the objectives set out in a Common Position, which is implemented either by national measures (in particular in case of arms embargoes) or by a Community Regulation (including in the case of targeted sanctions). The Guidelines also indicate a preference for targeted sanctions and clarify respective Community competencies.[74] Most important for this paper is that the Guidelines explicitly provide that the introduction and implementation of restrictive measures must always

---

73. Respectively Council Doc. 15114/05 of 2 December 2005 (as revised) and Council Doc. 15114/05 of 2 December 2005 (as replaced by Council Doc. 11679/07).

74. Points 44 to 47 clarify that where restrictive measures are being considered, a case by case assessment needs to be made of Community competence, taking the EC Treaty's attribution of powers to the Community into account. It is noted that the European Community can adopt legislative implementation measures through a Regulation based on Articles 60 and 301 of the EC Treaty (or Articles 60, 301 and 308), and that where the Community has no competence it is up to each of the Member States to adopt the necessary legislation or implementing measures. The current practice is recalled that the Council indicates in the CFSP instrument that "action by the Community is needed to implement certain measures" to invite the Commission to propose a Regulation implementing the measures falling within the remit of the Community.

respect international law, the principle of proportionality and human rights.

First, restrictive measures must be in accordance with international law and respect the international obligations of the European Community and its Member States (point 9). Even though the Guidelines refer in particular to the obligations resulting from the WTO Agreements (point 11)[75], this reference must be assumed to also include other norms of international law to the extent applicable. The Guidelines further specify rather timidly that if EU measures are in conflict with the international obligations of the EC or its Member States, "a common approach for dealing with such conflicts may have to be developed" (point 12).

Second, the restrictive measures must be proportionate to their objective (point 9). In this respect the Guidelines specify that when deciding on restrictive measures it is important to consider which measure or package of measures is most appropriate (point 13). They also provide that the measures should be targeted (based on clear criteria and identifyers for listed persons) rather than indiscriminate, so as to minimise adverse consequences for those not responsible for the objectionable actions (points 14, 18 to 22). Furthermore, they refer to the need to include sunset provisions either in the form of an expiration date or a review (points 27 to 32). Finally, since targeted financial sanctions must be implemented by all private actors concerned, the guidelines refer to the Commission website (point 23) which provides, *inter alia*, a consolidated list of persons and entities subject to financial sanctions[76] and an overview of the restrictive measures in force.[77]

Third, the Guidelines explicitly provide that restrictive measures must respect human rights and fundamental freedoms, "in particular due process and the right to an effective remedy" (point 9). They should be drafted "in light of the obligation under Article 6(2) TEU for the EU to respect fundamental rights, as guaranteed by the European Convention on Human Rights and as they result from the constitutional traditions common to the Member States, as general principles of Community law"

---

75. The GATT and GATS apply when restrictive measures affect trade in goods or services with third countries. Article XXI of GATT allows for import and export restrictions which are either applicable to arms and military equipment, or imposed in pursuance of obligations under the UN Charter for the maintenance of international peace and security. Article XIV bis of GATS provides for a similar exception. Measures restricting trade which do not fall under these categories, have to meet the conditions laid down in Article XX of GATT and Article XIV of GATS.
76. http://europa.eu.int/comm/external_relations/cfsp/sanctions/list/consol-list.htm
77. http://europa.eu.int/comm/external_relations/cfsp/sanctions/measures.htm

(point 10). This implies, in particular, that proper attention is given to the protection and observance of the due process rights of the persons to be listed (point 17) and that restrictive measures make provision for humanitarian exemptions (point 24 and 25).[78]

The EU "**Best Practices** for the Effective Implementation of Restrictive Measures" (Council Doc 10533/06 of 14 June 2006) are non-binding recommendations for effective implementation of restrictive measures "in accordance with applicable Community/Union law and national legislation." (point 5). They first concern the correct identification of targeted persons (points 7 to 19) on the basis of as many identifyers as possible and the ongoing review of their correctness. They recognise that wrong persons may be listed and provide that claims of mistaken identity should be examined by the competent authorities, who should share the outcome with the person or entity concerned and the other Member States and the Commission (points 10 to 15). If restrictive measures implement UNSC Resolutions, and a claim of mistaken identity is not manifestly unfounded but its correctness cannot be established by the competent authorities, Member States and the Commission should be informed and the UN Sanctions Committee (and where possible, through that Committee, the State that made the listing proposal) should be consulted, and "where appropriate, the matter could be referred to that Committee for an authoritative finding" (point 17). If, however, a Member State court decides on a mistaken identity claim, the Best Practices provide merely that: "it could be communicated by the competent authorities of that State to all other Member States and the Commission". Finally, they note that a transparent and effective de-listing procedure is essential and that measures should be kept under constant review (point 19).

Secondly, the Best Practices Paper concerns the freezing measures (points 20 to 61), and provides that these should concern all funds and economic resources over which the listed person or entity can lawfully dispose (or which he can transfer without owning them), and, that these, though not involving a change of ownership, do override all incompatible contractual arrangements. The restrictive measures should be carried out by all

---

78. Point 25 provides: " The competent authorities should grant exemptions on a case by case basis, which will allow them to assess all interests concerned and to impose conditions to ensure that the exemptions do not frustrate or circumvent the objective of the restrictive measure. The exemptions should be granted on the basis of the relevant legislative instruments. If there are grounds to grant an exemption from one restrictive measure (e.g. financial restrictions) this does not by default justify granting an exemption from another measure (e.g. restrictions on admission) which affects the person or entity concerned..."

economic operators, and national legislative frameworks should allow the freezing without delay and even pending EU decisions to implement UNSC resolutions (point 21). When granting "humanitarian exemptions", meant to ensure the continued satisfaction of basic needs, competent authorities must take into account fundamental rights and listed persons do retain their right to work, but wages must be monitored and paid into a frozen account.

B.   Sanctions imposed as a result of UN Security Council Resolutions and due process

The UN Charter confers on the Security Council powers to decide, in a manner binding for all UN members, restrictive measures required in order to maintain or restore international peace and security. UN Members are obliged to carry out these measures and in case of conflict with other international obligations, the obligations under the UN Charter prevail.[79]

Since the early 1990s, the UN Security Council has assumed a broader understanding of its role to maintain peace and security, and in this respect it has directed its actions also against private persons or organisations, in particular international terrorists. There is, as a consequence, a long list of Security Council Resolutions providing for restrictive measures, such as visa bans or financial freezes, in respect of listed individuals or private sector organisations. For the purposes of this paper, the key UNSC Resolutions include Resolution 1267 (1999) which ordered restrictive measures (flight ban and freezing of funds) against Usama bin Laden, the Al-Qaida network and the Taliban and established the UNSC Sanctions Committee, Resolution

---

79.   Under Article 24(1) of the 1945 UN Charter UN members "confer on the Security Council primary responsibility for the maintenance of international peace and security, and agree that in carrying out its duties under this responsibility the Security Council acts on their behalf". Under Article 25 of the UN Charter "[t]he Members of the United Nations agree to accept and carry out the decisions of the Security Council in accordance with the present Charter". Article 41 of the UN Charter provides in a non exhaustive way that measures taken by the UNSC may include complete or partial interruption of economic relations and of rail, sea, air, postal, telegraphic, radio, and other means of communication, and the severance of diplomatic relations. Under Article 48(2) of the UN Charter the decisions of the Security Council for the maintenance of international peace and security "shall be carried out by the Members of the United Nations directly and through their action in the appropriate international agencies of which they are members". According to Article 103 of the UN Charter "[i]n the event of a conflict between the obligations of the Members of the United Nations under the present Charter and their obligations under any other international agreement, their obligations under the present Charter shall prevail".

1333 (2000) which strengthened these restrictive measures and instructed the Sanctions Committee to maintain an updated list of designated persons and entities (of which it published a first version on 8 March 2001 and to which it added Mr Kadi on 19 October 2001), and Resolution 1390 (2002) which renewed the list, extended the sanctions and applied them to persons and groups without connection to a particular state territory.

UN Members are under the Charter obliged to carry out these Resolutions and thus to freeze without delay the funds and other financial assets of individuals and entities associated with Usama bin Laden, the Al-Qaida network and the Taliban, as listed by the Sanctions Committee. At the same time, however, the listing of individuals, which has serious implications for their ability to travel and to dispose over their assets and thus potentially clashes with substantive human rights, typically takes place on the basis of procedures that fall short of the normal human rights protection standards that would apply in a similar domestic context.[80]

First, as regards the substance, it may be clear that the smart sanctions potentially violate certain human rights that are traditionally recognised in international human rights instruments and national constitutions.[81] Most directly affected is the right to own and dispose of *property*. The freezing of all funds and economic resources of a listed individual, even though in strict legal terms not involving a loss of property, may well be qualified as a denial of the peaceful enjoyment of possessions or a deprivation of the right to enjoy property. This is the more so because there in effect is no time limit to these sanctions, and even though there is a review mechanism, removal from the list may be difficult because until the end of 2006 it had to be requested by a state (since December 2006 affected individuals may also address the Sanctions Committee) and it requires the agreement of all 15 SC Members. On the other hand, most human rights protection systems allow for fairly far going restrictions on property rights in the public interest. The question thus arises to what extent the freezing of all assets and resources, with the exception of a humanitarian "basic needs" minimum, would fall short of the principle of proportionality, i.e. the

---

80. See for an in depth analysis: Cameron I. (2006): "The European Convention on Human Rights, due process and UN Security Council counter terrorism sanctions", Report prepared for the Council of Europe, available at www.coe.int.

81. The right to own, use and inherit property, the right to private and family life, the right to reputation, the right to a fair trial, including the right to "nulla poena sine praevia lege", the right to be presumed innocent, the right of access to all evidence against you, the limits on admissibility of evidence, the right to a fair hearing, the right to legal remedies in the form of administrative or judicial appeal, the right to effective remedies in case of human rights breaches.

principle that the measure should be necessary (for maintaining peace and security) and that there should be a fair balance between the interference in the individual rights and the public interest objective (the positive effect on peace and security). Another right that could be indirectly affected by the sanctions is the right to a *private and family life*, but in view of the inclusion in the later SC Resolutions of the humanitarian exemptions that should allow for provision of basic needs, the question arises whether the possible adverse effects could be considered to be proportional to the objectives. In the same sense the control on the paying of a wage to a listed person (into a frozen account), may have the effect of barring him from any new private sector employment, which again is likely to adversely affect his private and family life.

Second, as regards the procedure, one can say in general terms that it is a political process without any of the legal safeguards that usually apply when individuals are deprived of property or liberties.[82] A first procedural flaw is that both the adoption of the Resolutions ordering the sanctions, and the concrete shaping of those Resolutions by means of listing individuals, is done by the same actors, i.e. the 15 members of the Security Council, albeit partly in the Security Council and partly in the Sanctions Committee. There is thus *no separation of legislative and executive powers* which is common in any system based on the rule of law.

A second procedural flaw is that the listing of the persons routinely takes place on the basis of intelligence information submitted by the Members. That information, and thus the motivation for listing a person, is however generally available neither to the public, nor to the persons concerned, and sometimes it has not even been available to the members of the Sanctions Committee. There is generally no active and independent verification of the information on which the listing is based, let alone an independent review of the legitimacy, necessity and proportionality of the sanctions. Resolution 1617 has responded somewhat to these "secrecy concerns" by allowing the release of information on a case-by-case basis and with the prior consent of the source State. In the meantime the Sanctions Committee also accepted listing and delisting guidelines which structure decisions and clarify criteria,

---

82. There is a discussion ongoing on whether suspicions of engagement in terrorist activities, on which the restrictive measures are based, should be considered as criminal charges to which the normal criminal law guarantees should be applied mutatis mutandis, or whether the restrictive measures are merely administrative in nature. We consider this a rather semantic discussion, the real question being whether one believes that the law should provide guarantees in the case individuals are deprived of their right to enjoy their property, or whether such a sanction can be decided in a purely political process, beyond legal safeguards and control.

but these procedures remain discretionary and without legal safeguards for the individuals concerned.[83] There are no clear rules of law describing in a sufficiently detailed way the conduct that can result in a person being listed (substance), nor does there seem to be a presumption of innocence. Nor are there rules on the way in which a conclusion of wrongdoing by a certain person can be reached. There is no "police" type decision to launch an investigation, no "public prosecutor" type procedure to collect evidence and formulate the complaint, and no adversorial procedure in which an independent person hears two sides that are legally assisted and, on the basis of clear rules on evidence, comes to a conclusion that balances the rights and interests of the individual against the public interest of dealing efficiently with crime and terrorism. In short, there is *no fair trial*.

A third procedural flaw is that, once persons have been listed by the Sanctions Committee, they have no effective legal remedies. There is at the UN level no access to administrative or judicial review of those decisions and thus *no independent judicial control*. Until the end of 2006, listed persons could not even directly address the Sanctions Committee with a request to be removed from the list, but they had to rely on some sort of diplomatic protection whereby their own state had to intervene with one of the 15 Members of the Security Council and convince that state to request delisting, which could be approved only if none of the other Members opposed.[84]

In the light of this analysis it is rather astonishing that the listing procedure and the Sanctions Committee as institutional framework, when they were set up by the Security Council actually passed the scrutiny of the UN Legal Service. After all, fundamental due process requirements are fully embedded in the UN human rights instruments, which the Security Council presumably wants to respect. Article 14 of the ICCPR for instance obliges states to ensure that any person tried for a crime be given a "fair and public hearing by a competent, independent and impartial tribunal established by law." Article 14 also specifies some of the guarantees that must be incorporated into any criminal proceeding, such as the right to counsel. While international law permits the derogation of certain rights in a state of emergency, any such derogation is permitted only to "the extent strictly required by the exigencies of the situation."

---

83. See www.un.org/Docs/sc/committees.
84. Discussions to improve the standing of individuals before the Committee revealed a lack of consensus between the SC Members. SC/8602 of 23 December 2005 and para 18 of Resolution 1617. However a change to the procedure was agreed at the end of 2006.

Unsurprisingly, the UN Sanctions procedure, and in particular the absence of administrative and judicial appeal, caused constitutional concerns at Community level since it was the Community that implemented the UN Security Council sanction resolutions by means of regulations of the Council and the Commission.

C.   The Kadi case and the position taken by the European Courts

The three abovementioned UNSC Resolutions concerning Usama bin Laden, the Al-Qaida network and the Taliban were duly implemented at Community level by a series of Common Positions and Regulations.[85] The most important of these, for this specific case, are Regulation 467/2001, which listed Mr Kadi as a person suspected of supporting terrorism whose funds and resources should be frozen, and the successor Regulation 881/2002 which continued to list Mr Kadi as a person suspected of supporting terrorism whose funds should be frozen.[86] As a result Mr Kadi, a resident

---

85. See for a complete listing the Judgment of the Court of first instance of 21 September 2005 in Case T-315/01 Kadi v. Council and Commission (paragraphs 10 to 36), [2005] ECR II-3649.

86. Council Regulation (EC) No 467/2001, OJ L 67, 9.3.2006, p. 1 (adopted on the basis of Articles 60 and 301 ECT and repealing Regulation 337/2000, OJ L 43, 16.2.2000, p. 1) prohibiting the export of certain goods and services to Afghanistan, strengthening the flight ban and extending the freeze of funds and other financial resources in respect of the Taliban of Afghanistan, replaced by Regulation 881/2002, OJ L 139, 29.5.2002, p. 9 (adopted on the basis of Articles 60 EC, 301 EC and 308 EC). See also Council Common Position 2002/402/CFSP (OJ L 139, 29.5.2002, p. 4) concerning restrictive measures against Usama bin Laden, members of the Al-Qaida organisation and the Taliban and other individuals, groups, undertakings and entities associated with them (repealing Common Positions 96/746/CFSP, 1999/727/CFSP, 2001/154/CFSP and 2001/771/CFSP), which again gave effect to S/RES/1267(1999) of 15 October 1999, S/RES/1333(2000) of 19 December 2000, and S/RES/1390(2002) of 16 January 2002 which were adopted by the UNSC under Chapter VII of the UN Charter to maintain peace and security. The Resolutions provide, inter alia, that all States are to take measures to freeze the funds and other financial assets of individuals and entities listed by the Sanctions Committee, including as from 19 October 2001, Mr Kadi. UNSC Resolution 1452(2002), provided for the possibility for States to allow humanitarian exceptions to the freezing of funds on condition that the Sanctions Committee was notified and did not object (or gave its consent). These humanitarian exceptions were implemented by Council Common Position 2003/140/CFSP Concerning exceptions to the restrictive measures imposed by Common Position 2002/402/CFSP (OJ 53, 28.2.2003, p. 62) and Council Regulation (EC) No 561/2003 amending, as regards exceptions to the freezing of funds and economic resources, Regulation (EC) No 881/2002 (OJ, L 82, 29.3.2003, p. 1).

of Saudi Arabia, was as from October 2001 listed by the UNSC Sanctions Committee and by the implementing Council Regulations as a person suspected of supporting terrorism[87], whose funds and other financial resources should be frozen.[88]

In December 2001 Kadi appealed to the Court of First Instance against his inclusion in the list, arguing inter alia[89] that the regulation breached a number of his fundamental rights. He submitted, first, that he had been deprived of his right to a fair hearing because he was never given the opportunity to make his views known to the Council and the Commission.[90] He, secondly, claimed a breach of the fundamental right to respect for property and the principle of proportionality, essentially because the Community legislator had acted without being able to weigh

---

87. Kadi's name was added by Commission Regulation (EC) No 2062/2001 of 19 October 2001, amending, for the third time, Regulation (EC) No 467/2001, OJ L 277, 20.10.2001, p. 25.

88. The regulation provides that all funds and other financial resources belonging to, or owned or held by, a listed natural or legal person, group or entity shall be frozen except for funds needed for food, medical expenses and reasonable legal fees, on condition that the Sanctions Committee has been notified and has not objected.

89. The pleas concerning the legal basis of the contested regulation will not be discussed in this paper.

90. As regards his right to a fair hearing, Kadi acknowledged that, on account of the very nature of the original measure freezing his assets, no prior notice could have been given of its implementation. He claimed, nevertheless, that he was denied the right to make his views known to the Council and the Commission with a view to obtaining the removal of his name from the list, contrary to the general principle of Community law that persons affected by decisions of public authorities must be given the right to make their points of view known (Case 17/74 *Transocean Marine Paint Association* v *Commission* [1974] ECR 1063, paragraph 15). The right to a fair hearing, which is a principle of a fundamental nature, must be ensured in all proceedings likely to affect the person concerned and to entail adverse consequences for him (Case 85/87 *Dow Benelux* v *Commission* [1989] ECR 3137, and Case C-49/88 *Al-Jubail Fertilizer and Another* v *Council* [1991] ECR I-3187). See Judgment of the CFI, paragraphs 141 to 143. Kadi argues that, in the circumstances of this case, the contested regulation is clearly in breach of those fundamental principles, in that it makes it possible for the Council to freeze the applicant's funds indefinitely without giving him any opportunity to make known his views on the correctness and relevance of the facts and circumstances alleged and on the evidence adduced against him.

the evidence.[91] Thirdly, he argued a breach of his right to effective judicial review because the contested Regulations did not provide for such review.[92] Kadi also rejected the Council's argument that he had been subjected to mere administrative measures and not to any criminal penalty or confiscation under the protection of Article 6 ECHR. He noted that he had been accused of the most serious form of criminal wrongdoing, namely, involvement in a terrorist organisation responsible for the attacks of 11 September 2001, that his reputation had been destroyed and his property frozen without quantitative or time limit, and this all without the Council considering the evidence against him, providing him with any opportunity to dispute the measure and asserting that the Court could not investigate the correctness of the freezing decision. Kadi added that he had exhausted all other remedies (Sanctions Committee, the Saudi Arabian Ministry of Foreign Affairs, US Office of Foreign Assets Control) and that the possibility of an appeal to the CFI was not sufficient because the Court could not investigate the validity of the evidence (paragraphs 149 to 152).

The Council and the Commission, first, argued that the Community was bound by international law to give effect to UNSC Resolutions without any reservation and that national law could not stand in the way of implementing measures. The Community could not exclude listed individuals from the implementing measures (as that would contravene international law and the principle of comity of nations, disrupt international relations, and affect the uniformity of application of UNSC Resolutions), and even if the regulation violated human rights, this did not make the act unlawful (reference to Article 48 para 2 UN Charter) because fundamental rights may, as provided for in the appropriate international legal instruments, be temporarily suspended in time of emergency (paragraphs 153 to 164). Under Article 103 of the UN Charter the obligation imposed on the Community and its Member States by the UN

---

91. With reference to Article 1 of the First Additional Protocol to the ECHR and the general principles of Community law, including the principle of proportionality, Kadi complains that his funds are frozen because he was listed by the UN Sanctions Committee, but without the Community institutions having the possibility of assessing the available evidence or actually having weighed the interests involved, so that the Court has no means to assess whether the contested regulations justify the draconian measures taken against the applicant's property (paragraphs 144 and 145).

92. With reference to Case 222/84 *Johnston* [1986] ECR 1651, paragraph 18, in which the Court confirmed the right to effective judicial review as a general principle of Community law, Kadi notes that he is deprived of any opportunity for such a review, and that, if there were such a review, he would be in a position to demonstrate that the allegations against him have no basis (paragraphs 146 to 148).

Charter prevailed over every other obligation of international, Community or domestic law (paragraph 177).

The Council and the Commission, secondly, denied a violation of human rights. As mere implementing actors without room for political evaluation, they had to implement UNSC Resolutions and could not add any mechanism to review those measures. Moreover, the right to respect for property was not absolute but subject to public policy restrictions, and, in the light of the need to comply with UNSC measures to ensure that individuals' assets cannot be used to promote terrorism, the freezing measures, though severe, were not disproportionate. Kadi had and made use of his right to judicial review by means of the appeal to the CFI and a full judicial review would run the risk of undermining the UN system, seriously damaging international relations and resulting in a failure of the Community to respect international law. Also Kadi had the possibility to approach the Sanctions Committee via Saudi Arabia (paragraphs 165 to 175).

On 21 September 2005 the Court of First Instance rejected Kadi´s claims.[93] It held first that Security Council resolutions adopted under Chapter VII of the UN Charter prevail over rules of Community law,[94] that Member States must leave unapplied any provision of Community law that raises any

---

93. Case T-315/01 *Kadi v Council and Commission* [2005] ECR II-3649.
94. The Court of First Instance essentially found that Community law, and in particular Article 307 ECT (that the EC Treaty does not affect prior obligations of the Member States under international law) and Article 224 ECT (common action to prevent distortions to the common market as a result of carrying out obligations to maintain peace and security), recognises and accepts the primacy of UN Charter obligations as laid down in international law and more specifically in customary law and Article 27 of the 1969 Vienna Convention and Article 103 of the UN Charter (which provides: "In the event of a conflict between the obligations of the Members of the United Nations under the present Charter and their obligations under any other international agreement, their obligations under the present Charter shall prevail."). It is generally recognised that this obligation extends to binding Security Council decisions (Article 25 of the UN Charter, cited above). See the Order of 14 April 1992 of the International Court of Justice in *Questions of Interpretation and Application of the 1971 Montreal Convention arising from the Aerial Incident at Lockerbie (Libyan Arab Jamahiriya v. United Kingdom), Provisional Measures*, Order of 14 April 1992, I.C.J. Reports 1992, p. 3, at paragraph 39.

impediment to the proper performance of UN Charter obligations,[95] and that this obligation, by virtue of Community law, extended to the Community.[96]

Secondly, while recognising that the Community is based on the rule of law and that judicial control reflects a general principle of law[97], the CFI held

95. In paragraphs 189 to 191, the CFI recalls the primacy and the binding nature of UN SC Resolutions under Chapter VII of the UN Charter, so that Member States must therefore take all measures necessary to ensure that those resolutions are put into effect (Opinions of Advocate General Jacobs in Case C-84/95 *Bosphorus* [1996] ECR I-3953, at I-3956, paragraph 2, and Case C-177/95 *Ebony Maritime and Loten Navigation* [1997] ECR I-1111, at I-1115, paragraph 27), and must leave unapplied any incompatible provisions of Community law (reference to Case C-124/95 *Centro-Com* [1997] ECR I-81 in which the Court of Justice allowed national measures contrary to the common commercial policy under the security exception of Article 307 EC, if they were necessary to ensure compliance with the UN Charter and UNSC Resolutions).

96. In paras 192 to 208, the CFI concludes that even though the Community is not directly bound by the UN Charter, it must be considered to be bound in the same way as its Member States for several reasons: by concluding the EC Treaty Member States could not transfer to the Community more powers than they possessed or withdraw from their obligations to third countries under that Charter, (by analogy, Joined Cases 21/72 to 24/72 *International Fruit Company and Others* ('*International Fruit*') [1972] ECR 1219, paragraph 11), but they made clear their desire to fulfil their obligations under that Charter (Article 224 and Article 234 para 1, *International Fruit*, paragraphs 12 and 13, and the Opinion of Advocate General Mayras in those cases, ECR 1231, at page 1237), implying a duty on the Community institutions not to impede the performance of the obligations of Member States which stem from that Charter (Case 812/79 *Burgoa* [1980] ECR 2787, paragraph 9). In so far as the Community assumed powers previously exercised by the Member States (in the case of sanctions on the basis of Article 301), the Charter binds the Community and the Community is thus, by virtue of Community law itself, required to give effect to UNSC Resolutions (para 207).

97. In paragraphs 209 to 211, the CFI recalls that the EC is based on the rule of law, inasmuch as neither its Member States nor its institutions can avoid constitutional review of their acts (Case 294/83 *Les Verts* v *Parliament* [1986] ECR 1339, paragraph 23; Case 314/85 *Foto-Frost* [1987] ECR 4199, paragraph 16; Case C-314/91 *Weber* v *Parliament* [1993] ECR I-1093, paragraph 8; Joined Cases T-222/99, T-327/99 and T-329/99 *Martinez and Others* v *Parliament* [2001] ECR II-2823, paragraph 48; see also Opinion 1/91 of the Court of Justice of 14 December 1991, ECR I-6079, paragraph 21) and that judicial control is a general principle (*Johnston*, paragraph 18; Case C-97/91 *Oleificio Borelli* v *Commission* [1992] ECR I-6313, paragraph 14, Case C-1/99 *Kofisa Italia* [2001] ECR I-207, paragraph 46; Case C-424/99 *Commission* v *Austria* [2001] ECR I-9285, paragraph 45, and Case C-50/00 P *Unión de Pequeños Agricultores* v *Council* [2002] ECR I-6677, paragraph 39), which finds expression in Mr Kadi's right under Article 230 EC para 4 to appeal regulations of direct and individual concern to him.

that it had no authority to review the implementing regulation and thus to indirectly review the lawfulness of Security Council resolutions[98], including their compatibility with fundamental rights as protected by the Community legal order.[99]

In a third step, however, the CFI considered, with reference to the Vienna Convention's provision that treaties are void if in conflict with "a peremptory norm of general international law" (Articles 5, 53 and 64 VC), that it was nevertheless allowed to asses the conformity of the Security Council resolutions with the principle of *jus cogens,* which covers "the mandatory provisions concerning the universal protection of human rights, from which neither the Member States nor the bodies of the United Nations may derogate because they constitute "intransgressible principles of international customary law".[100]

In paras 233 to 292 it then nevertheless rejects all claims. The CFI first rejects the claim of breach of the right to property, essentially because the possibility of humanitarian exemptions shows that the freezing of the funds does not amount to inhuman or degrading treatment (thus not constituting a breach of ius cogens), but rather amounts to a temporary

---

98. In paragraphs 212 and following, the CFI holds that such an indirect review of UN SC Resolutions would be incompatible with Articles 25, 48 and 103 of the UN Charter and 27 of the Vienna Convention, as well as with Articles 5, 10, 297, 307 para 1 ECT and the principle that Community powers must be exercised in accordance with international law (reference to Case C-286/90 *Poulsen and Diva Navigation* [1992] ECR I-6019, paragraph 9, and Case C-162/96 *Racke* [1998] ECR I-3655, paragraph 45. See also Case T-184/95 *Dorsch Consult* v *Council and Commission* [1998] ECR II-667).

99. In paras 224 and 225, the CFI adds that, with particular regard to Article 307 EC and to Article 103 of the Charter of the United Nations, reference to infringements either of fundamental rights as protected by the Community legal order or of the principles of that legal order cannot affect the validity of a Security Council measure or its effect in the territory of the Community (see, by analogy, Case 11/70 *Internationale Handelsgesellschaft* [1970] ECR 1125, paragraph 3; Case 234/85 *Keller* [1986] ECR 2897, paragraph 7, and Joined Cases 97/87 to 99/87 *Dow Chemical Ibérica and Others* v *Commission* [1989] ECR 3165, paragraph 38), so that UN SC resolutions fall, in principle, outside the ambit of the Court's judicial review and that the Court has no authority to call in question, even indirectly, their lawfulness in the light of Community law. On the contrary, the Court is bound, so far as possible, to interpret and apply that law in a manner compatible with the obligations of the Member States under the Charter of the United Nations.

100. Reference in para 231 to the Advisory Opinion of the International Court of Justice of 8 July 1996, The Legality of the Threat or Use of Nuclear Weapons, ICJ Reports 1996, p. 226, paragraph 79; and Advocate General Jacobs's Opinion in *Bosphorus,* paragraph 65.

measure that serves the important campaign against international terrorism, and that is subject to review including at the initiative of the person concerned through the State of his nationality. The CFI secondly denies the alleged breach of the right to be heard by the Council, because that right is correlated to the exercise of discretion which the Council does not have when implementing UN SC Resolutions[101], and by the Sanctions Committee, because the SC Resolutions set up a review mechanism allowing affected persons to address a request through their national authorities (reference to the Guidelines of the UN Sanctions Committee and UN SC Resolutions), which satisfies their right to be heard, even though they do not have the right themselves to be heard[102] and even though they have no opportunity effectively to make known their views on

101. In paras 255 to 260, the CFI recalls that the right to a fair hearing, in all proceedings initiated against a person which are liable to culminate in a measure adversely affecting that person, is a fundamental principle of Community law which must be guaranteed even in the absence of any rules governing the proceedings at issue and which requires that any person on whom a penalty may be imposed must be placed in a position in which he can effectively make known his views on the evidence on the basis of which the sanction is imposed (see, to that effect, Case C-135/92 *Fiskano* v *Commission* [1994] ECR I-2885, paragraphs 39 and 40; Case C-32/95 P *Commission* v *Lisrestal and Others* [1996] ECR I-5373, paragraph 21, and Case C-462/98 P *Mediocurso* v *Commission* [2000] ECR I-7183, paragraph 36). But that right applies in areas such as competition law, anti-dumping action and State aid, but also disciplinary law and the reduction of financial assistance, in which the Community institutions enjoy extensive powers of investigation and inquiry and wide discretion, and is thus correlated to the exercise of discretion by the authority which is the author of the act at issue (Case C-269/90 *Technische Universität München* [1991] ECR I-5469, paragraph 14). It does not apply to the sanctions area where the Council has no discretion, and the Council was thus not obliged to hear the applicant on the subject of his inclusion in the list of persons and entities affected by the sanctions, in the context of the adoption and implementation of the contested regulation.

102. In paras 267 to 274, the CFI recognises that the persons concerned depend on the diplomatic protection afforded by the State of their nationality, but deems that, in the light of the mandatory prescriptions of the public international order, "it is normal that the right of the persons involved to be heard should be adapted to an administrative procedure on several levels, in which national authorities play an indispensable part", and that "Community law itself recognises the lawfulness of such procedural adaptations in the context of economic sanctions against individuals (see, by analogy, the order of the President of the Second Chamber of the Court of First Instance of 2 August 2000 in Case T-189/00 R *Invest Import und Export and Invest Commerce* v *Commission* [2000] ECR II-2993)."

the correctness and relevance of the facts and on the evidence.[103] Finally, the CFI rejects the alleged breach of the right to effective judicial review, essentially because Kadi was able to bring an annulment action before the CFI, and because the decision of the Security Council not to provide for judicial review at international level and the resulting lacuna is not in itself contrary to jus cogens, and because the right to access to courts is not absolute and the limitation in this case inherent in the immunity from jurisdiction enjoyed by UN SC Resolutions.[104] The CFI also considers that, in the absence of an international court having jurisdiction to ascertain whether acts of the Security Council are lawful, the setting-up of a body such as the Sanctions Committee and the opportunity of applying at any time to that committee in order to have any individual case re-examined, by means of a procedure involving both the 'petitioned government' and the 'designating government', constitute another reasonable method of affording adequate protection of the applicant's fundamental rights as recognised by *jus cogens* (para 290).

On appeal to the ECJ, in November 2005, Kadi reiterated the claim that his human rights were breached, and the Council and the Commission reiterated that the regulation was necessary for the implementation of

103. In paras 273 and 274, the CFI reasons that: "Those facts and that evidence, once classified as confidential or secret by the State which made the Sanctions Committee aware of them, are not, obviously, communicated to him, any more than they are to the Member States of the United Nations to which the Security Council's resolutions are addressed" and "None the less, in circumstances such as those of this case, in which what is at issue is a temporary precautionary measure restricting the availability of the applicant's property, the Court of First Instance considers that observance of the fundamental rights of the person concerned does not require the facts and evidence adduced against him to be communicated to him, once the Security Council or its Sanctions Committee is of the view that that there are grounds concerning the international community's security that militate against it."

104. In para 287 and 288, the CFI recalls that the right of access to the courts (recognised by both Article 8 of the Universal Declaration of Human Rights and Article 14 of the International Covenant on Civil and Political Rights), can be limited at a time of public emergency which threatens the life of the nation (Article 4(1) of that Covenant), and that certain restrictions must be held to be inherent in that right, such as the limitations generally recognised by the community of nations to fall within the doctrine of State immunity (see, to that effect, the judgments of the European Court of Human Rights in *Prince Hans-Adam II of Liechtenstein* v *Germany* of 12 July 2001, *Reports of Judgments and Decisions* 2001-VIII, paragraphs 52, 55, 59 and 68, and in *McElhinney* v *Ireland* of 21 November 2001, *Reports of Judgments and Decisions* 2001-XI, in particular paragraphs 34 to 37) and of the immunity of international organisations (see, to that effect, the judgment of the European Court of Human Rights in *Waite and Kennedy* v *Germany* of 18 February 1999, *Reports of Judgments and Decisions,* 1999-I, paragraphs 63 and 68 to 73).

binding Security Council resolutions, and that the Community Courts should not assess the conformity of the regulation and the UNSC Resolutions with fundamental rights. In response to that argument, Kadi contended that neither Article 103 of the UN Charter[105] nor SC resolutions could preclude European courts from reviewing implementing measures on their conformity with fundamental rights. He submitted that "so long" as the United Nations do not provide a mechanism of independent judicial review that guarantees compliance with fundamental rights of decisions taken by the Security Council and the Sanctions Committee, the Community Courts should review Community measures on their conformity with fundamental rights as recognised in the Community legal order[106].

In his Opinion of 16 January 2008, Advocate-General Poiares Maduro first (points 17 to 24) rejects the argument that Community courts should not test the human rights conformity of secondary Community law implementing SC Resolutions. Even if the application and interpretation of Community law is guided by the presumption that the Community wants to honour its international commitments[107] and Community Courts therefore carefully examine the international obligations of the Community,[108] the Community legal order is autonomous[109] with the

---

105. According to Article 103 of the Charter of the United Nations, '[i]n the event of a conflict between the obligations of the Members of the United Nations under the present Charter and their obligations under any other international agreement, their obligations under the present Charter shall prevail'.
106. Case C-84/95 Bosphorus [1996] ECR I-3953.
107. Case 41/74 *Van Duyn* [1974] ECR 1337, paragraph 22, and Case C-286/90 *Poulsen and Diva Navigation* [1992] ECR I-6019, paragraphs 9 to 11.
108. AG Maduro refers to Case C-431/05 *Merck Genéricos-Produtos Farmacêuticos* [2007] ECR I-0000; Case C-300/98 *Dior and Others* [2000] ECR I-11307, paragraph 33; Case C-162/96 *Racke* [1998] I-3655; Joined Cases 21/72 to 24/72 *International Fruit Company and Others* [1972] ECR 1219; and *Poulsen and Diva Navigation*. AG Maduro also mentions cases in which the Court held that an international agreement did not have effect within the Community legal order because based on the wrong legal basis (*Parliament* v *Council and Commission*. Joined Cases C-317/04 and C-318/04 [2006] ECR I-4721; Case C-327/91 *France* v *Commission* [1994] ECR-3641), cases in which the Court has held that Member States and Community institutions are under a duty of loyal cooperation when entering into international commitments, (Ruling 1/78 of 14 November 1978 [1978] ECR 2151, paragraph 33; Opinion 2/91 [1993] ECR I-1061, paragraphs 36 to 38; and Case C-25/94 *Commission* v *Council* [1996] ECR I-1469, paragraphs 40 to 51), and cases in which the Court verified whether Community acts implementing international commitments were in compliance with general principles of Community law (Case C-122/95 *Germany* v *Council* Bananas [1998] ECR I-973).
109. Case 26/62 *Van Gend en Loos* [1963] ECR 1, at p. 12.

Treaty as the 'basic constitutional charter'.[110] In the final analysis, therefore, it is for the Community Courts to determine the effect of international obligations within the Community legal order, and, although the Court takes great care to respect the international law obligations of the Community, it seeks, first and foremost, to preserve the constitutional framework created by the Treaty.[111] The AG thus disagrees with the Council and the Commission that, once the Community is bound by a rule of international law, the Community Courts must apply it unconditionally in the Community legal order. International law can permeate the Community legal order only under the conditions set by the constitutional principles of the Community.

Secondly (points 25 to 40), AG Maduro investigates whether Community Acts implementing UNSC Sanction Resolutions would be exempt from the normal constitutional constraints imposed by Community law. He sees no legal base for that reasoning and also denies that the Bosphorus decision can be taken as a precedent,[112] because in that case the Court did not deny jurisdiction but rather implicitly accepted the Advocate General's view that 'respect for fundamental rights is ... a condition of the lawfulness of Community acts' (Bosphorus Opinion point 53). He also rejects the UK suggestion that such immunity from review can be derived from a combination of Article 307 EC, which grandfathers rights and obligations arising from agreements concluded by Member States before 1 January 1958, and the loyalty obligation of Article 10 EC, which would impose on the Community an obligation not to impair Member State compliance with Security Council resolutions. Even if the Court would annul the Regulation Member States would be free to implement the UN Resolution

---

110. Case 294/83 *Les Verts* [1986] ECR 1339, paragraph 23.
111. Reference to Opinion 2/94, cited in footnote 22, paragraphs 30, 34 and 35.
112. In *Bosphorus* the impounding of an aircraft of Bosphorus Airways took place in accordance with Security Council Resolution 820(1993). The UN Sanctions Committee had decided that a failure on the part of the authorities to impound the aircraft would amount to a breach of the resolution. The Court assessed whether a regulation that was adopted to implement a Security Council resolution which imposed a trade embargo on the Federal Republic of Yugoslavia infringed fundamental rights and the principle of proportionality. The Court did not explicitly rule on the question of its jurisdiction and held that the interest of 'putting an end to the state of war in the region and to the massive violations of human rights and humanitarian law in the Republic of Bosnia-Herzegovina' outweighed the interest of a wholly innocent party to be able to pursue its economic activities using assets it had leased from a company based in the Federal Republic of Yugoslavia. The Court did not say that it might not have powers of review because the regulation was necessary in order to implement a sanctions regime that was drawn up by the Security Council.

themselves,[113] albeit within the limits of Community law and in full respect for human rights.[114] Moreover, Article 307 EC cannot derogate from Article 6(1) EU, according to which 'the Union is founded on the principles of liberty, democracy, respect for human rights and fundamental freedoms, and the rule of law', nor can Member States, even when implementing SC Resolutions, escape their obligations to respect human rights, whether under national law[115] or under Community law.[116] AG Maduro in fact reverses the implications of the duty of loyal cooperation, by deriving therefrom an obligation on Member States to exercise their powers and responsibilities in an international organisation in a manner compatible with Community law[117]. Therefore, Member States, and particularly Security Council members, must, as far as possible, prevent the adoption of UN decisions that are liable to conflict with the core principles of the Community legal order. The Advocate General also rejects the argument of the Commission, the Council and the United Kingdom that the specific subject-matter at issue in the present case is "political" and does not lend itself to judicial review or only to the most marginal kind of review. Even

113. Member States are allowed, under the Treaty, to adopt measures which, though affecting the functioning of the common market, may be necessary for the maintenance of international peace and security, Articles 297 EC and 60(2) EC. See also: Case C-70/94 *Werner* [1995] ECR I-3189; Case C-83/94 *Leifer and Others* [1995] ECR I-3231; and the Opinion of Advocate General Jacobs in Case C-120/94 *Commission* v *Greece* [1996] ECR I-1513.

114. The powers retained by the Member States in the field of security policy must be exercised in a manner consistent with Community law (Case C-124/95 *Centro-Com* [1997] ECR I-81, paragraph 25) and in full respect of human rights (Case C-260/89 ERT [1991] ECR I-2925. See also Case C-368/95 *Familiapress* [1997] ECR I-3689 and Case C-60/00 *Carpenter* [2002] ECR I-6279).

115. AG Maduro notes that in certain legal systems, it seems very unlikely that national measures for the implementation of Security Council resolutions would enjoy immunity from judicial review and he refers to the case law of a number of courts of the Member States.

116. It is settled case law that the Community guarantees a complete system of judicial protection in which fundamental rights are safeguarded in consonance with the constitutional traditions of the Member States. As the Court stated in *Les Verts*, 'the European Community is a community based on the rule of law inasmuch as neither its Member States nor its institutions can avoid a review of the question whether the measures adopted by them are in conformity with the basic constitutional charter, the Treaty'. More straightforwardly, in *Schmidberger* (Case C-112/00 *Schmidberger* [2003] ECR I-5659, paragraph 73), the Court reaffirmed that 'measures which are incompatible with the observance of human rights ... are not acceptable in the Community'. See also Case C-203/03 *Commission* v *Austria* [2005] ECR I-935, paragraph 59.

117. The AG refers to Opinion 1/94 [1994] ECR I-5267, paragraphs 106 to 109, and *Commission* v *Council* paragraphs 40 to 51)

the claim that a measure is necessary for the maintenance of international peace and security cannot operate so as to silence the general principles of Community law and deprive individuals of their fundamental rights. He recognises that extraordinary circumstances may justify unusual restrictions on individual freedom, but when the risks to public security are believed to be extraordinarily high, the pressure is particularly strong to take measures that disregard individual rights, especially in respect of individuals who have little or no access to the political process. Therefore, in those instances, the courts should fulfil their duty to uphold the rule of law with increased vigilance.

AG Maduro thirdly (points 41 to 55) investigates the alleged breaches of fundamental rights and whether they could be justified for reasons relating to the suppression of international terrorism. In a first step, he rejects the argument that the Court should not apply normal standards of review, but instead should – in the light of the international security interests at stake – apply less stringent criteria for the protection of fundamental rights (similar to the jus cogens approach by the Court of First Instance). He sees this argument as yet another expression of the belief that the Court is not in a position to deal adequately with "political" questions of international significance and that any intervention of the Court might upset globally-coordinated efforts to combat terrorism. He agrees that the Court ought not to be institutionally blind, but be mindful of the international context in which it operates and conscious of its limitations. The Court must, where possible, recognise the authority of institutions, such as the Security Council, that are established under a different legal order than its own and that are sometimes better placed to weigh certain fundamental interests. He underlines, however, that the Court cannot turn its back on the fundamental values that lie at the basis of the Community legal order and that respect for other institutions is meaningful only if it can be built on a shared understanding of these values and on a mutual commitment to protect them. Consequently, in situations where the Community's fundamental values are in the balance, the Court may be required to reassess, and possibly annul, measures adopted by the Community institutions, even when those measures reflect the decisions of the Security Council. The fact that the measures at issue are intended to suppress international terrorism should not inhibit the Court from fulfilling its duty to preserve the rule of law. In doing so, rather than trespassing into the domain of politics, the Court is reaffirming the limits that the law imposes on certain political decisions. Its responsibility is to guarantee that what may be politically expedient at a particular moment also complies with the rule of law without which, in the long run, no democratic society can truly prosper. The AG sees no reason, therefore, for the Court to depart, in the present case, from its usual interpretation of the fundamental rights invoked by the appellant. The only novel question is whether the concrete needs raised by the prevention of international terrorism justify restrictions on the fundamental rights of the appellant that would otherwise not be acceptable.

In a second step, AG Maduro turns to Mr Kadi`s problem that all his financial interests within the Community have been frozen, without time limit and without adequate means to challenge the assertion that he is guilty of wrongdoing. The AG notes that the indefinite freezing of someone's assets constitutes a far-reaching interference with the peaceful enjoyment of property, even where arrangements are made for basic needs. Though that effect may explain why 'smart sanctions' are used to prevent terrorist acts, it also underscores the need for procedural safeguards that require the authorities to justify such measures and demonstrate their proportionality. In the absence of those safeguards, the freezing of someone's assets for an indefinite period of time infringes the right to property.

The AG then recalls that the right to be heard by the administrative authorities taking the decision[118] and the right to effective judicial review by an independent tribunal[119] constitute fundamental rights that form part of the general principles of Community law. He recognises that certain restrictions on those rights may be envisaged for public security reasons, but a complete denial is never allowed. In the case at hand, Mr Kadi had no

---

118. According to settled case-law, 'observance of the right to be heard is, in all proceedings initiated against a person which are liable to culminate in a measure adversely affecting that person, a fundamental principle of Community law which must be guaranteed even in the absence of any rules governing the proceedings in question ... That principle requires that the addressees of decisions which significantly affect their interests should be placed in a position in which they may effectively make known their views'. Case C-32/95 P *Lisrestal and Others* [1996] ECR I-5373, paragraph 21. See also Article 41(2) of the Charter on Fundamental Rights of the European Union.

119. As the Court has held: 'The European Community is ... a community based on the rule of law in which its institutions are subject to judicial review of the compatibility of their acts with the Treaty and with the general principles of law which include fundamental rights. ... Individuals are therefore entitled to effective judicial protection of the rights they derive from the Community legal order, and the right to such protection is one of the general principles of law stemming from the constitutional traditions common to the Member States'. (Case C-50/00 P *Unión de Pequeños Agricultores* v *Council* [2002] ECR I-6677, paragraphs 38 and 39). See also Article 47 of the Charter on Fundamental Rights and Articles 6 and 13 ECHR.

right to present his views, neither to the Community institutions nor to the UN Sanctions Committee, nor did he have even minimal access to the information on which the listing decision was based. According to the AG, this absence of the right to be heard also hinders Mr Kadi to defend his rights effectively and thus has significant adverse effects on his right to effective judicial protection. Again, while certain limitations on that right might be permitted if there are other compelling interests, it is unacceptable in a democratic society to impair the very essence of that right.[120] Fact is that Mr Kadi has been listed, and subject to severe sanctions, for several years on the basis of extremely serious allegations against him, but that he has neither been heard nor had access to an independent tribunal assessing the fairness of these allegations and the reasonableness of these sanctions. The mere existence of a real possibility that the Community sanctions may be disproportionate or even misdirected, and might nevertheless remain in place indefinitely, is anathema in a society that respects the rule of law.

The AG recognises that, had there been a genuine and effective mechanism of judicial control by an independent tribunal at the level of the United Nations, this might have released the Community from the obligation to provide for judicial control of implementing measures that apply within the Community legal order. However, he notes that no such mechanism currently exists, and that the decision whether or not to remove a person from the United Nations sanctions list remains within the full discretion of the Sanctions Committee – a diplomatic organ.[121] In those circumstances, the right to judicial review by an independent tribunal has not been secured at the level of the United Nations. As a consequence, the Community institutions cannot dispense with proper judicial review proceedings when implementing the Security Council resolutions in question within the Community legal order. AG Maduro concludes that the appellant's claim that the contested regulation infringes the right to be heard, the right to judicial review, and the right to property is well founded and that the Court should annul the contested regulation in so far as it concerns the appellant.

120. The AG refers to the European Court of Human Rights, which held in *Klass and Others*, 'the rule of law implies, inter alia, that an interference by the executive authorities with an individual's rights should be subject to an effective control which should normally be assured by the judiciary, at least in the last resort, judicial control offering the best guarantees of independence, impartiality and a proper procedure'. ECtHR, *Klass and Others*, cited in footnote 42, § 55.
121. See Security Council Resolution 1730(2006) of 19 December 2006 and the Sanction Committee's Guidelines for the Conduct of its Work, available at http://www.un.org/sc/committees/1267/index.shtml.

IV. Conclusions

First, in general terms, it is clear from European and international experience that the process of setting up supra-national governance structures is far from perfect and often follows the logic of "doing first and thinking later" (Weiler)[122] especially in times of political turmoil. There is often no extensive preparation at public sector level by means of a sophisticated interplay between institutions that have clearly allocated powers in the legislative and executive processes. Nor is there a democratic or societal debate in which stakeholders can provide their own input. Instead, supra-national governance is often created by governments that feel the political need to react to current events. The preparatory negotiations often take place in closed circuits between the very governments that seek to set up the structures concerned. Unsurprisingly, therefore, these newly created supranational governance structures often reflect the monolithic character of their creators while lacking the basic mechanisms and guarantees to ensure that decision making is open, legitimate and democratic, and that the output of the decision making process satisfies fundamental standards that are common to developed systems governed by the rule of law and respect for human rights.

Second, in the historic process of constructing the European Union, one of the problems at supra-national level has been that a human rights protection deficit arose because there was no European bill of rights that applied to the acts of the European institutions. In view of the fact, however, that the institutional and procedural framework at European level was "complete", because there was a constitutional legislator, a legislator, an executive and an independent judiciary, the deficit could be handled by the various actors concerned over time and in a gradual way. In fact, once the problems became apparent, some of the domestic supreme courts of the Member States could signal that they would reserve the right to test the human rights conformity of European acts as long as such a judicial verification did not take place at European level. This allowed the European Court, in response, to develop a line of case law in which it clarified that it would test whether European acts respected human rights, as common to the constitutional traditions of the Member States and the European Convention on Human Rights. When this was accepted by the domestic supreme courts, the European Court could develop its Foto Frost

---

122. Weiler J.J.H. (1999): "The constitution of Europe, Do the new clothes have an emperor?, and other essays on European integration", Cambridge University press at 3 (ISBN 0521585678).

rule that national courts cannot invalidate Community acts, inter alia because the Treaty establishes a complete system of judicial protection in which the European Court reviews the legality of Community acts. This judicial solution balanced the need for Member States to give priority to Community law, with their obligation to respect human rights, and allowed the constitutional legislator to develop a European bill of rights and thus to fill the constitutional gaps by allocating human rights protection tasks to both domestic courts and the European Courts, which rule on the basis of catalogues of human rights that are authoritative in both legal orders (domestic Constitutions, Charter, ECHR) and under the final supervision of a pan-European Human Rights Court.

The international experience with the establishment and functioning of the UN as the global governance structure to maintain international peace and security, has been similar to the European experience in that structures such as the Security Council and the Security Council Sanctions Committee were created and endowed with sweeping powers, without necessarily providing simultaneously for a full set of guarantees as regards respect for democratic values, the rule of law and human rights. Unlike at European level, however, the human rights protection deficit of the functioning of the UN Security Council and its Sanctions Committee, results not so much from the fact that the normative framework at that level is lacking (one could after all assume that the UN itself is bound to respect the provisions of the UN Charter, the Universal Declaration and the Human Rights Covenants and Treaties), but rather that the institutional framework is very incomplete and falls short of the normal safeguards that apply under domestic constitutions. It is after all the Security Council that calls for the sanctions which all States are obliged to implement (legislative function), that also, through its Sanctions Committee, lists the individuals to which the sanctions must be applied (executive function), and that, finally receives, through diplomatic protection channels, any claims from listed individuals, which it than itself decides on (judicial review function). In short, a procedure that is at odds with all the usual safeguards that apply at domestic level, and in particular with the requirement of independent administrative review and/or judicial control over acts of the executive. Therefore, unfortunately, at international level the constitutional discussion that is needed to solve the resulting human rights protection deficit – a discussion that in the case of human rights should be reserved to an independent judiciary- cannot have its proper course, because neither the International Court of Justice nor any other independent institution or person have been given a sufficient role.[123] It is in the end the same Members of the Security Council and the Sanctions Committee that are simultaneously responsible for prescribing sanctions, for listing the persons to be sanctioned, and for hearing mistaken identity and other claims. Unsurprisingly, if the constitutional discussion cannot properly take place at international level, it is automatically shifted to the domestic level of those states and organisations that are obliged to implement the Resolutions.

Third, in the constitutional discussion at the level of the European Union, the first question really is whether Community Courts, in principle, should or should not reserve themselves the right to test the human rights conformity of secondary Community law that implements Security Council Resolutions. The dilemma here is whether the appropriate balance between safeguarding the effectiveness and uniform application of UNSC Resolutions for the maintenance of international peace and security, and the domestic constitutional human rights protection safeguards of the Community and the Member States, should be solved at the "jurisdictional" level, or whether, assuming jurisdiction, it should be addressed at the level of the substantive questions.

In this dilemma, the Council and the Commission, taking account of the fact that sanctions resolutions form part of the unique and necessarily powerful role of the UN Security Council in maintaining peace and security, place themselves squarely behind the UN Security Council essentially by arguing, as AG Poiares Maduro noted, that, when the Security Council has spoken under Chapter VII of the UN Charter, domestic Courts must remain silent.[124] This unreserved acceptance of the "primacy" of SC Resolutions over Community law is understandable for institutions which constitute, directly and indirectly, the very actors who adopted the sanction measures at Community and at international level. More importantly, this view has the advantage of fully supporting the UN Security Council and the international Community in its fight against terrorism. Furthermore, it clearly reflects the intention of the drafters of the UN Charter, who, in their drive to ban war, created a supranational Security Council and endowed it with extensive powers. In a way therefore, the position taken by the Commission and the Council, is the position that

---

123. See for the relationship between the Security Council and the International Criminal Court, Neha Jain (2005): "A separate law for peacekeepers: the clash between the Security Council and the International Criminal Court", 16 EJIL 2 at 239-254.
124. Case C-402/05 P Yassin Abdullah Kadi v.Council of the European Union and Commission of the European Communities, Opinion of AG Poiares Maduro of 16 January 2008.

everybody would probably like to support, and that also, in EU – UN relations, fully reflects the Foto Frost rule which the ECJ itself applies in the relation between Member States and the Community.

Interestingly, the CFI follows the Commission and Council view to a large extent. It in fact assumes primacy of UNSC Resolutions over Community law (on the basis of both international and Community law), and reasons logically that as a consequence, first Community Courts cannot test the conformity of those Resolutions with Community law, and, second, Member States must leave unapplied Community law if it would prevent them from complying with UN Charter obligations (para 190). Nevertheless the CFI adds a nuance, by assuming that domestic courts may test the conformity of UN action, including any action by the UN Security Council, not with domestic law, but with certain peremptory norms of international law (jus cogens). This approach seems rather elegant, because there is full support for, and acceptance of, the full discretion of the UN Security Council in its important role to maintain peace and security, and it safeguards the required unity of application of SC Resolutions. At the same time, it leaves a small escape to address situations in which the UN Security Council possibly would derail, for instance, by adopting a Resolution that would oblige all Members to torture terrorist suspects in order to prevent imminent terrorist attacks. Also, the CFI, in a way, itself seems to fill the institutional gap at international level, by, so to say, substituting for the non-existent international judiciary that would presumably, if it existed, test the actions of UN organs on their conformity with the most important rules of international law. One of the downsides of this approach, however, is that the exact meaning of jus cogens is disputed, and that in any case, jus cogens has much less content than the basic safeguards on democracy, the rule of law and respect for human rights, which are constitutionally guaranteed in the Community context.[125] The CFI thus accepts a human rights protection deficit when it concerns the implementation by the Community of UNSC Resolutions, and it seems to do so without caveats. This is surprising, also in the light of Community law, because Article 11 EUT lists, as CFSP objectives, not only security and support for the UN but also the consolidation of the rule of law and human rights, and both the Sanctions Guidelines and the Best Practices explicitly

---

125. See Orakhelashvili A. (2005): "The impact of premptory norms on the interpretation and application of UN Security Council Resolutions", 16 EJIL 1 of 2005 at 59-88. He refers to the Tadic Decision of the ICTY Appeals Chamber that the right to fair trial is an unconditional limitation on the Security Council's powers and that its observance is conditio sine qua non for the validity of SC measures (at 65 and 66).

provide that sanctions must respect human rights, in line with Article 6 EUT.

Advocate General Maduro takes the opposite view and reasons that, while the Community must certainly honour its international commitments, it is ultimately for the Community Court to determine the effect of international obligations within the Community legal order. Community courts cannot give up their responsibility to review the legality of Community acts, including their conformity with constitutionally protected human rights. International law can permeate the Community legal order only under the conditions set by the constitutional principles of the Community. This approach has the advantage of allowing the Community courts, as gate keepers, to uphold constitutional principles including the rule of law and respect for human rights. It also seems a logical consequence of Foto Frost, because if the European Courts would stop testing the human rights compatibility of secondary Community law, the domestic supreme courts of the Member States may have to come back to their "solange" decisions. The problem of this approach, however, is that if every state follows this example, and starts testing the conformity of UNSC Resolutions with its own basic constitutional rules, not much will be left of the Security Council as supreme organ to maintain peace and security. This "effet utile" was the reason why the European Court at the intra-Community level, in Foto Frost, clearly barred domestic courts from the possibility to declare Community acts unlawful.

On this first question of jurisdiction, we agree with the Council and the Commission that the most desirable solution would be to defer to the UN whenever action is needed for the maintenance of peace and security. But we also believe that, though no effort should be spared to arrive at a situation in which that would be possible without reservations, time is not yet ripe for a "Foto Frost rule" at UN level. Unlike at Community level, where supreme Courts of the Member States could solve the issue together with the European Court, there is no judicial counterpart at the UN level with whom a temporary truce can be reached, allowing (and encouraging) the international "constitutional actors" to fill the gaps. In the words of Foto Frost, there is, at UN level, no "complete system of legal protection" as there is at Community level. In fact there is, at UN level, no independent gate keeper who tests the human rights conformity of the actions of UN organs such as the Security Council, and thus no rule of law. In that situation the choice, whether to unreservedly accept international decisions with human rights deficits and to make them have effect within the Community legal order, or whether to use all Community powers to defend the rule of law and respect for human rights at home, and to seek to bring those constitutional guarantees to the international level, is perhaps not so difficult to make. It seems self-evident to prefer enlarging the scope of application of sound constitutional principles, rather than to allow external decision-making centres to intrude into a rule of law system, with actions that carry the risk of falling short of the most basic procedural standards. This is also how we would understand that the balancing act between the various CFSP objectives listed in Article 11 EUT (and between Articles 6 and 11 EUT) could best be made. We thus fully understand AG Maduro´s position that in principle no supra-constitutional status can be given to Community law that implements UNSC Resolutions (points 25 and following), that the Court cannot turn its back on the fundamental values underlying the Community legal order, and that respect for other institutions, such as the Security Council, is meaningful only if built on a shared understanding of those values and a mutual commitment to protect them (point 44).

Fact is that there a serious institutional and procedural gap at UN level, and that this should in itself be sufficient reason not to blindly accept what comes out of that procedurally flawed international decision-making process. This is the more so, if we realise, leaving the legal sphere for a moment, that the Security Council is of course not an abstract body that takes all the decisions objectively needed to maintain peace and security, but that it is essentially a political body composed of 15 States, including 5 permanent members, who act through it collectively. Unfortunately, at least two of the five permanent members are criticised for not always respecting basic democratic values, the rule of law and human rights themselves, and one further permanent Member, though often a staunch defender of human rights, has recently been under fire for sacrificing civil liberties in the "war on terrorism". Moreover, the information on which the listing takes place is supplied by secret services of the States requesting the listing. With all due respect for the hard work these services put in, it is unsettling to realise that even wars have started on the basis of intelligence information which subsequently appeared to be incorrect. In those circumstances, the option advocated by the Council and the Commission, and to a large extent by the CFI, looks decisively less attractive, and seems more in tune with what would be desirable tomorrow than with what could be realistically acceptable today.

Nevertheless, there is no reason to believe that tomorrow could not be here relatively soon. In fact, it could well be that, if there would be some kind of an independent review of UNSC acts that have implications for individuals, the European Courts might relinquish their gate keeper role and leave the human rights conformity testing up to those higher instances, in much the same way as the German Federal Constitutional clarified that it would come back on stage only if fundamental values were no longer respected at the higher Community level. In other words the institutional gap at UN level can be repaired, and the two EU Member States that are Permanent UNSC Members, can act (and have in fact acted), with the other Member States, to ensure that global governance structures with decision making powers, are set up along the European constitutional principles. In this respect we also agree with AG Maduro that the Member States are under an Article 10 ECT loyalty obligation (in relation with Articles 6 and 11 EUT) to ensure that global governance structures are set up in respect of those constitutional principles.

In conclusion on the first question of jurisdiction, it would be premature at this point in time and in the light of the ongoing UN institution-building process, to agree that once the Security Council has spoken through its Resolutions under Chapter VII of the UN Charter, or more specifically through its Sanctions Committee listing decisions, domestic courts of the Members, including the ECJ, must remain silent. So long as the procedural guarantees for the full respect of human rights are not in place at UN level, the Community courts will continue to bear full responsibility for verifying the lawfulness of actions by Community institutions, even if those are the result of actions by the UN Security Council. It is up to the EU Member States to ensure that the procedural and institutional gaps in the UN decision-making process are repaired as soon as possible so that any incompatibilities with Community law are avoided.

Fourth, assuming that it is too early for the Community Courts to relinquish their gate keeper role as regards the effects in the Community legal order of UNSC Resolutions adopted under Chapter VII, the second main question that arises is how the balance should be struck between the simultaneous needs to support the UN as a global governance structure, to combat terrorism and to protect human rights. In other words, the question of substance is to what extent limits on human rights can be justified by reference to the UN Charter and the need to combat terrorism.

As a preliminary remark it should perhaps be recalled here that this balancing act, though essentially of an intra Community constitutional nature, necessarily needs to take place within its proper international context. After all the European Court has always shown great respect for international law and there is no reason to believe it would change its approach in this particular case. It would probably fully recognise the significance of the fact that the UN Security Council Resolutions in question are Chapter VII Resolutions. That means inter alia, that these

Resolutions reflect the political assessment of the competent UN organ that the measures concerned are necessary for the maintenance of international peace and security. This also means that the Court would probably take account of the fact that these Resolutions are binding on all UN members, and that, being binding SC Resolutions under Chapter VII, they supersede any other obligations of the EU Member States (Articles 25, 41, 103 UN Charter). The Court would probably also factor in the possible grave consequences for the international legal order if the judiciary of any UN member, and in particular the judiciary of the EU, would decide not to respect those Resolutions.

In general terms, therefore, the Court can probably be expected to recognise the preservation of international peace and security, by means of UN Security Council Resolutions and implementing measures, as an overriding public interest reason that could justify restrictions on the intra Community movement of goods, persons and capital, that would in normal circumstances be qualified as restrictions contrary to the fundamental rights to free movement and non discrimination guaranteed by the Treaty. Likewise the Court can probably be expected to recognise that, whereas some human rights are absolute in the sense that no derogations are admissable, other human rights can be limited in the case of overriding public interest concerns (legitimacy test) and in proportional ways (proportionality test).[126] In this classical approach, certain human rights, such as the right to life and the prohibition of torture, clearly have a different status, than other rights, such as the right to enjoy property. The proportionality of any derogations from the second category of rights would probably have to be considered in light of the overall objective of the measures in question and the need to act urgently in a critical situation.

More specifically, as regards the right to respect for property, the CFI, using the marginal jus cogens test, denies a breach of that right, essentially because there was no arbitrary deprivation but a freezing of funds in the framework of the fight against terrorism, and the humanitarian exceptions ensured that the freezing did not amount to inhuman or degrading treatment. On the other hand AG Maduro, relying on European constitutional principles, concludes that the indefinite freezing of assets, even with humanitarian exceptions, infringes the right to property if there

---

126. On the proportionality of the measures, the UN has been concerned from the beginning about the need to respect human rights while fighting terrorism (see report of UNSGA/57/1, 2002 p.1; UN organs (see A757/18, 2002 p106-7), OEA/ser.L./V/IL. 116, Doc. 5 rev. 1 corr. See also Article 51 UN Charter (counter-measures; see US-France Air Services Agreement Arbitration, 54 ILR p.303 and 337) self-defence (Nicaragua case, ICJ Reports 1986 p. 14, 94 and 103).

are no procedural safeguards to assure the correctness of the measure. As regards the substantive right to respect for property, it is perhaps, in the light of the far-reaching limitations that can be imposed in the public interest and that have been routinely accepted by human rights courts, not so difficult to accept that a temporary freezing of funds, with a humanitarian basic needs exception, is not disproportionate in the case of a person who is suspected of supporting terrorism (assuming that the correctness of this claim can be tested before an independent person and that the sanctions are regularly reviewed and lifted if there is not enough evidence).

As regards the right to be heard and to an effective review by an independent tribunal, to assess the correctness of the claims, the CFI sees no breach: the Council does not exercise any discretion when implementing UNSC Resolutions, and the UN Sanctions Committee does hear a listed person indirectly through the diplomatic protection interventions by the state of his nationality. Moreover, Kadi had the possibility to appeal to the CFI against the Regulation which was recognised as of direct and individual concern to him. AG Maduro disagrees and, while accepting that these rights may be restricted in the national interest, he considers a complete denial, as in the present case, unacceptable. Mr Kadi had no opportunity to present his views and he is sanctioned on the basis of severe allegations without the right to judicial review being secured at UN level. In those circumstances, Community institutions cannot dispense with proper judicial review proceedings when implementing UNSC Resolutions in the Community legal order. As regards these procedural rights, it should be clear that without them, a severe sanction can be put in place against individuals on the basis of unverifiable information supplied by secret services, and can stay in place for a long time, without the person concerned having any chance to challenge that sanction, and without an in-built procedure in that sanctioning mechanism to at least independently and objectively assess the correctness of the evidence. In our view the right to be heard and to effective judicial review are precisely meant to prevent any possibility that Community sanctions may be falsely imposed or disproportional, and there is no immediate reason why this should be different for Community sanctions implementing UNSC Resolutions. Only from the moment that, at the level of the UN, a genuine and effective mechanism would be created to exercise such independent and objective control over the correctness of the evidence and the lawfulness of the sanction, could the Community Courts relinquish their gatekeeper role. It is to be hoped that EU Member States will sooner rather than later be successful in New York in adding such a control procedure to the UN Security Council institutional framework dealing with sanctions.

In the mean time it seems wise, while those minimum procedural guarantees are gradually being set up at international level, to provide for them at least at Community level. That would imply first of all that Community acts implementing UNSC sanctions should be properly motivated and communicated to those concerned or publicised, so that targeted individuals have full knowledge of the reasons why action was taken against them or their assets. Secondly, the persons concerned should have a right to present evidence that could possibly discharge them from the suspicions of being engaged in the support of terrorist activities. Third, there should be an independent verification of the evidence presented by both sides, preferably a control point that would have a different composition from the structure taking the listing decisions in the first place. Fourth, if sanctions are nevertheless imposed, there should be access to administrative and subsequently judicial review, under the normal right of individuals to appeal to the CFI against Community acts that are of direct and individual concern to them. Fifthly, sanctions should be regularly reviewed and, subsequent to review, a new motivated decision should be taken to either continue or to discontinue the sanction measures concerning a particular person. Finally, this all assumes that there would be a minimum of access of the Community instances responsible for implementing UNSC sanction Resolutions, to the evidence produced in support of a claim to the UN Sanctions Committee. Also, if during any of these procedural steps doubts arise as to the (ongoing) correctness of a listing decision of the UN Sanctions Committee, it would be up to the EU, through its UNSC members to ensure that corrective action is taken at UN level, or new evidence is produced from that side.

A fifth and final remark is that it is clear from European and international experience that "constitutionalism" has a meaning beyond the nation-state context. In our transitional era of globalisation, constitutional theory, though nurtured within the context of national states, can and must flourish in other contexts in particular those integration movements that establish new structures of governance that are complementary to and build upon more traditional forms of self-organisation of the people or society.[127] True, as the European experience has shown, this is a gradual process to which all actors will have to autonomously contribute in a considered way that interlocks with and takes account of the full spectre of concerns of other actors, but with the clear longer-term objective to build a system that respects the basic values to which they all subscribe and by which they, in the end, all want to be bound. Only when that objective is reached, can the Member States, the Community and the UN act as network actors in mutual cooperation without the EU having recourse to the claim that it has to measure external actions on the basis of domestic constitutional standards.[128]

127. Petersmann E.U. (1997): "Constitutionalism and International Organizations", 17 Northwestern Journal of International Law of 1997 at 398-469; Pernice I. (2002): "Multilevel Constitutionalism in the European Union", 27 EURLR 5 of 2002 at 511-529; Di Fabio U. (2001): "A European Charter: towards a Constitution for the Union", Columbia Journal of European Law Spring 2001; Verhoeven A. (2004): "The European Union Search of Democratic and Constitutional Theory", lecture at the Free University Brussels in the framework of the 2004 IES lecture series on the Convention and the Constitution.
128. Nettesheim M. (2006): "UN sanctions against individuals, a challenge to the architecture of European Union governance", contribution to the Conference: "Rechtschutz gegen den UN-Sicherheitsrat zwischen Europa- und Völkerrecht", Humboldt University, Berlin (8 December 2006). Also published in 44 CMLR 3 of 2007 at 567-600.

4. Variable Geometry and the External Relations of the EU: The Experience of Justice and Home Affairs

Bernd Martenczuk[1]

I.   Introduction

The Treaty of Amsterdam introduced the goal of the creation of an area of freedom, security, justice (Article 2 EU, Article 61 EC). At the same time, the Amsterdam Treaty transferred most of the relevant powers, with the exception of police and judicial cooperation in criminal matters, from the Third Pillar of the EU to the European Community. The relevant provisions are found in Title IV of Part III of the EC Treaty (hereinafter: Title IV), under which the EC may take measures in a number of fields relevant to justice and home affairs, including the abolition of internal borders and the control of external borders, asylum and immigration policy, and judicial cooperation in civil matters.

However, this "communitarisation" of a sizeable proportion of justice and home affairs would not have been possible without a high degree of variable geometry. This was partly because of the sensitive character of justice and home affairs, which were perceived by some Member States as part of their traditional sovereign prerogatives. For this reason, Denmark, the United Kingdom, and – partially also because of its traditional links with the United Kingdom – Ireland obtained far-reaching derogations ("opt-outs") from the new Community policies under Title IV. At the same time, the Schengen acquis was integrated into the framework of the Community. Since the United Kingdom and Ireland were not participating in Schengen, whereas the non-EU countries Norway and Iceland were, this added an additional layer of variable geometry to the field. Finally, a further element of complexity was added by the most recent enlargements of the European Union, since the 12 new Member States could not initially fully apply the Schengen acquis.

Accordingly, the "area of freedom, security and justice" is not identical with the territory of the European Community. Rather, it can take on

---

1.   The article expresses the personal views of the author only.

different configurations depending on the specific policies and measures concerned. At the same time, justice and home affairs has become one of the most active areas for the Community's external relations. The present contribution will examine how the variable geometry under Title IV has affected the EC's external relations in the field. The purpose of this examination is twofold: on the one hand, the contribution will try to shed some light on the numerous legal questions created by the various opt-outs and opt-ins, in particular in relation to the negotiation and conclusion of international agreements by the EC, and will examine how these questions have been solved in the EC practice; on the other hand, the contribution will also try to draw some conclusions regarding the impact of variable geometry on the capacity of the EU to act efficiently in international relations.

The first section of this contribution will introduce a number of general concepts, and place the variable geometry of Title IV in the overall context of differentiation and "flexibility" in European integration (II). The second part will present the various opt-outs applicable under Title IV (III). On this basis, the paper will examine a number of legal problems created by the opt-outs for the EC's international relations, in particular as regards the negotiation and conclusion of international agreements (IV). Finally, the paper will take a look at the Reform of the EU Treaties and its likely impact on the variable geometry in justice and home affairs (V), before drawing some general conclusions (VI).

II.   Concepts and Applications

In a Union of by now 27 Member States, it has become more and more difficult to find solutions which are both adequate and politically acceptable for all Member States. A possible solution discussed in recent years to this conflict between the deepening and widening of integration is the idea of "flexibility" or "differentiation" in European integration. The idea is that Member States no longer all need to participate in steps of integration. The present section will recall some general concepts and applications of differentiated integration as background for the discussion of the variable geometry of Title IV.

A.   Concepts of Differentiated Integration

In the discussion about differentiated integration, there is wide terminological variety, in which expressions such as "flexibility", "reinforced cooperation", "variable geometry", "multi-speed Europe", or "Europe à la carte" are used interchangeably and not always consistently.[2] However, the different expressions may sometimes conceal important differences as regards the underlying objectives of integration. According to a categorization by *Stubb,* it is possible to distinguish three basic conceptions of differentiated integration, namely multi-speed Europe, variable geometry, and Europe à la carte.[3]

Multi-speed Europe may be regarded as the potentially mildest form of differentiated integration. According to this model, the differentiation results from the need to accommodate transitional difficulties in certain Member States, which make their full and immediate participation impossible. According to the concept of multi-speed Europe, derogations should only be temporary and not politically motivated; the final goal remains the participation of all Member States. The concept of variable geometry takes the idea of differentiated integration a step further. According to this concept, it is accepted that there is, for the foreseeable future, no realistic prospect for participation of all Member States in particular policy areas. Accordingly, derogations are typically not time-bound, and there may not be a final objective of participation of all Member States. On the other hand, variable geometry remains limited to particular policy areas, and therefore should not affect core Community policies and the *acquis communautaire.* The most far-reaching conceptions are discussed under the notion of „Europe à la carte". According to "Europe à la carte", all policy areas would in principle be open for participation or non-participation of Member States; participation in European Integration

---

2.   Cf. Florence Chaltiel, Pour une clarification du débat sur l'Europe à plusieurs vitesses, 1995 Revue du Marché Comun 5 et seq.; Eberhard Grabitz/Constantin Iliopoulos, Typologie der Differenzierungen und Ausnahmen im Gemeinschaftsrecht, in Eberhard Grabitz (ed.), *Abgestufte Integration,* 31 et seq, (1984); Bernd Martenczuk, Die differenzierte Integration nach dem Vertrag von Amsterdam, 1998 Zeitschrift für europarechtliche Studien 451 et seq.; Alexander Stubb, A Categorization of Differentiated Integration, 1996 JCMS 285 et seq.; Nina Ost, Flexibilität des Gemeinschaftsrechts – Vom Notantrieb zum Vertragsprinzip?, 1997, 495 Die öffentliche Verwaltung 496 et seq.
3.   Cf. Stubb (above footn. 2); cf. equally Claus-Dieter Ehlermann, Increased Differentiation or Stronger Uniformity, in Jan A. Winter/Deirdre M. Curtin, *Reforming the Treaty on European Union – The Legal Debate,* p. 27 et seq. (1996).

would follow the "pick and choose" principle. This last concept is generally rejected as harmful to European integration.[4]

As will be seen, the opt-outs under Title IV in favour of Denmark, the United Kingdom, and Ireland resemble most closely the concept of "variable geometry", although the various opt-in possibilities also introduce an element of Europe "à la carte".[5] In contrast, the temporary non-participation of the new Member States in certain parts of the Schengen acquis could be argued to constitute an example of a "multi-speed Europe". However, the purpose of the present paper is not to categorise the various opt-outs and opt-ins, or to create new categories. Rather, the present article will examine the real implications of differentiated integration for the external relations of the European Community. In this respect, the analysis in the present paper can be regarded as relevant for all conceptions of differentiated integration, regardless of their theoretical underpinnings.

B.   External and Internal Differentiations

Applications of differentiated integration can also occur in different forms, with different implications for the external relations of the European Union.

A first distinction concerns the question whether the differentiation takes place inside or outside the institutional framework of the European Union.[6] The derogations applicable with respect to Title IV are differentiations implemented inside the framework of the Union. In contrast, the European Patent Convention or the original Schengen Convention would be examples of cooperation between Member States taking place outside the institutional framework of the Union.[7] A more recent example is the Prüm Convention on the stepping up of cross-border cooperation, particularly in combating terrorism, cross-border crime and

---

4.   Vgl. Chaltiel (above footn. 2), 6 f.; Justus Lipsius, The 1996 Intergovernmental Conference, 1995 ILR 235, 244. On the impact of differentiated integratoin on the federal structure of the EU, cf. Bernd Martenczuk, Die differenzierte Integration und die föderale Struktur der Europäischen Union, 2000 Europarecht 351.

5.   Critical A.G. Toth, The Legal Effects of the Protocols Relating to the United Kingdom, Ireland and Denmark, in: Tom Heukels/Niels Blokker/Marcel Brus (ed.), *The European Union after Amsterdam*, 227, 244 (1998), who speaks of "Europe à la carte on a full scale".

6.   Cf. Martenczuk, above footn. 2, pp. 453 et seq.

7.   Of course, cooperation which originates outside the EU may eventually be integrated into the framework of the Union, as occurred for the Schengen Convention.

illegal immigration, which was concluded by Belgium, Germany, Spain, France, Luxemburg, the Netherlands and Austria in 2005.[8] Such cooperation outside the framework of the Union is not attributable to the Union, and does not therefore normally affect the external relations of the Union. It is therefore not further considered in the present contribution.[9]

Another important distinction is between the non-participation of EU Member States in certain policy areas and the selective participation of third countries in certain EU policies. The partial inclusion of third countries into specific policy areas of the Union, such as the association of Norway and Iceland with the Schengen acquis, is also sometimes regarded as a form of variable geometry.[10] However, the association of third countries with EU policies raises a different set of problems than the non-participation of EU Member States in certain EU policies. For instance, an important question in this regard is the possibility for third countries to participate in the debates of the EU institutions leading to the adoption of legal acts to be applied by them. These institutional questions resulting from the association of third countries with EU policies in the field of justice and home affairs are not discussed in the present contribution.[11] However, this does not mean that the existence of associated countries may not also have complicating effects on EU external relations, in particular as regards the need to ensure a degree of coherence in the external dimension of the European area of freedom, security and justice. To this extent, the impact of the association of third countries with Title IV on EU external relations will also be considered in the present contribution.

C.   Policy fields

Title IV is one of the most important examples of variable geometry in the law of the European Union. The other prominent example is monetary

---

8. On this Convention, cf. Daniela Kietz/Andreas Maurer, Vertiefungs- und Fragmentierungstendenzen in der Justiz- und Innenpolitik der EU, 2006 Integration 201. The integration of the Prüm Convention into the EU framework is explicitly envisaged in Article 1 (4) of the Convention.
9. This does of course not mean that such extra-EU cooperation may not raise legal or political questions. On possible legal limitations on Member States for engaging in such extra-EU cooperation, cf. Martenczuk, above footn. 2, pp. 454, 464.
10. Ulrich Becker, Differenzierung der Rechtseinheit durch „abgestufte Integration", 1998 Europarecht, Supplement 1, 29; Hans R. Krämer, Abgestufte Integration und differenzierte Integration, in: Gedächtnisschrift Eberhard Grabitz, p. 307 et seq. (1995).
11. On this, cf. contribution by Filliez in this book.

union, in which currently only 15 out of 27 Member States are fully participating.[12] However, unlike under Title IV, the EU has not developed major external relations activities in the field of monetary policy. In particular, it has not concluded any significant international agreements in this area.[13] For this reason, Title IV remains the best possibility to study the implications of variable geometry on EU external relations.

Since the Amsterdam Treaty, Articles 43 EU and 11 EC also contain the procedures and conditions under which Member States may establish, within the framework of the European Union, enhanced cooperation for specific subject matters.[14] These provisions were reviewed by the Nice Treaty with the objective of facilitating their utilisation. In addition, the Nice Treaty also introduced specific provisions on enhanced cooperation in the field of the common foreign and security policy (Article 27a to 27e EU).[15] These mechanisms have so far not been used, and therefore not given

12. Taking into account the adoption of the Euro by Cyprus and Malta on 1.1.2008. Another example of variable geometry was constituted by the non-participation of the United Kingdom in the European Social Charter concluded in 1989. However, this differentiation came to an end when the United Kingdom fully signed up to the social provisions of the Treaty of Maastricht (cf. Martenczuk, above footn. 2, p. 457 et seq.).

13. Generally on the external relations of EMU cf. Christoph W. Herrmann, Monetary Sovereignty over the Euro and External Relations of the Euro Area: Competences, Procedures and Practice, 7 [2002] European Foreign Affairs Review 1; Bernd Martenczuk, Die Außenvertretung der Europäischen Gemeinschaft auf dem Gebiet der Währungspolitik, 59 [1999] Zeitschrift für ausländisches öffentliches Recht und Völkerrecht 93.

14. On the provisions introduced by the Amsterdam Treaty, cf. Becker, above footn. 10, 29; Florence Chaltiel, Le traité d'Amsterdam et la coopération renforcée, 1998 Revue du marché comun 289; Vlad Constantinesco, Les clauses de „coopération renforcée": Le protocole sur l'application des principes de subsidiarité et de proportionalité, 1997 Revue trimestrielle du droit européen 751; Claus Dieter Ehlermann, Engere Zusammenarbeit nach dem Amsterdamer Vertrag: Ein neues Verfassungsprinzip?, 1997 Europarecht 362; Giorgio Gaja, How Flexible is Flexibility under the Amsterdam Treaty?, 1998 CMLR 855; Helmut Kortenberg, Closer Cooperation in the Treaty of Amsterdam, 1998 CMLR 835; Martenczuk, above footn. 2.

15. Cf. Thomas Jaeger, Enhanced Cooperation in the Treaty of Nice and Flexibility in the Common and Foreign Security Policy, 7 [2002] European Foreign Affairs Review 297; Tobias Bender, Die verstärkte Zusammenarbeit nach Nizza, [2001] Zeitschrift für ausländisches öffentliches Recht und Völkerrecht 729.

rise to any difficulties for EU external relations.[16] However, a first activation of enhanced cooperation is currently being discussed for the integration of the Prüm Convention into the framework of the European Union.

Finally, it is important to note that the variable geometry is currently limited to the first pillar of EU Justice and Home Affairs, but does not extend generally to the third pillar.[17] Due to the intergovernmental framework of the third pillar, Member States have apparently seen no reason for having greater recourse to variable geometry. However, this may change with the possible integration of the Prüm Treaty – which covers third and first-pillar matters – into the EU framework. Moreover, the situation will change further with the "communitarisation" of the Third Pillar upon entry into force of the Treaty of Lisbon.[18]

Accordingly, Title IV is still rather unique as a policy area which combines a strong degree of variable geometry with an important external dimension. However, it is unlikely to remain unique in this sense, and may therefore provide general insights into the potential impact of variable geometry on EU external relations.

III. Variable Geometry under Title IV

The present section will give an overview of the opt-outs applicable under Title IV.[19] The relevant rules are contained in three protocols: the Protocol

16. However, on the basis of Article 6 of the Protocol on the position of Denmark, Denmark has not participated in a number of CFSP measures with defence implications; cf. for instance Council Joint Action 2004/551/CFSP on the establishment of the European Defence Agency, OJ L 245, 17.7.2004, p. 17; Council Decision 2004/197/CFSP establishing a mechanism to administer the financing of the common costs of European Union operations having military or defence implications, OJ L 63, 28.2.2004, p. 68.

17. The only exception are theoretically the parts of the Schengen acquis which fall under the third pillar, in which the UK and Ireland in principle are not obliged to participate. In practice, however, the UK and Ireland have systematically opted into the third-pillar measures of the Schengen acquis.

18. OJ C 306, 17.12.2007, p. 1. On this, cf. below Section VI.

19. Cf. also Steven Peers, *EU Justice and Home Affairs Law*, 2nd ed., pp. 55 et seq. (2006); Toth, above footn. 5; Martin Hedemann-Robinson, The Area of Freedom, Security and Justice with Regard to the UK, Ireland, and Denmark: The 'Opt-in Opt-outs' under the Treaty of Amsterdam, in: David o'Keeffe/Patrick Twomey (ed.), *Legal Issues of the Amsterdam Treaty*, pp. 289 et seq. (1999); Jaap de Zwaan, Opting in and Opting Out of the Rules concerning the free movements of persons: Problems and Practical Arrangements, 1 [1998] Cambridge Yearbook of European Legal Studies 107.

integrating the Schengen acquis into the framework of the European Union (hereinafter: Schengen Protocol);[20] the Protocol on the Position of the United Kingdom and Ireland (hereinafter: Anglo-Irish Protocol); and the Protocol on the Position of Denmark (hereinafter: Danish Protocol). The present section will first explain the rules governing the participation of Member States and third countries in the Schengen acquis, as integrated into the framework of the Union; subsequently, it will address the rules concerning the application of the remainder of Title IV to Denmark, the United Kingdom and Ireland.

A.   The Schengen acquis

The Schengen acquis was integrated into the framework of the European Union by the Schengen Protocol.[21] In essence, the Schengen acquis contains the rules regarding the abolition of border controls between the participating states, and rules concerning the control of external borders, including the issuing of short-term visas.[22] The original Schengen Convention was concluded in 1985 by only 5 Member States, namely Belgium, Germany, France, Luxemburg, and the Netherlands. By the time of the Amsterdam Treaty, most EU Member States were either a party to Schengen or in the process of acceding to it, with the notable exception, however, of the United Kingdom and Ireland. An additional complication was created by Denmark, which, although a Member of Schengen, did not wish to submit to the Community disciplines of Title IV. Finally, Schengen also included all Members of the Nordic Passport Union, which, besides the EU Members Denmark, Finland and Sweden also included two third countries, namely Norway and Iceland. Since it was not intended that the participation of the three Nordic EU members should disrupt the Nordic Passport Union, an arrangement including Norway and Iceland also had to

20. As regards the United Kingdom and Ireland, the Schengen Protocol is flanked by the Protocol on the application of certain aspects of Article 14 of the EC Treaty to the United Kingdom and Ireland. This Protocol allows the United Kingdom inter alia to maintain controls at its external borders, and Ireland and the United Kingdom to maintain a Common Travel Area, and is to this extent the corollary of the non-participation of the United Kingdom and Ireland in the abolition of internal border controls under Schengen.

21. On this integration in more detail cf. Peers, above footn. 19, p. 44 et seq.; Pieter Jan Kuijper, Some Legal Problems Associated with the Communitarization of Policy on Visas, Asylum and Immigration under the Amsterdam Treaty and Incorporation of the Schengen Acquis, 37 [2000] CMLR 345.

22. I.e. visas covering stays of up to three months. In more detail on the Schengen acquis, cf. Contribution above on Visa Policy and EU External Relations.

be found. The complex rules of the Schengen Protocol were designed to accommodate these various interests and circumstances.

1.   Denmark

Together with the other Members of the Nordic Passport Union, Denmark had signed an accession treaty to Schengen in 1996. However, due in part to the negative experience with the first referendum on the Maastricht Treaty, Denmark was unwilling to accept any new EU competences in the field of justice and home affairs. The resulting arrangements reflect this somewhat contradictory motivation. In accordance with Article 1 of the Schengen Protocol, Denmark is authorised, together with the other Member States, to participate in the Schengen cooperation. However, unlike for all other Member States, the Schengen acquis shall not apply to Denmark as part of Community law. Rather, Article 3 of the Protocol provides that even after the identification of Community and third pillar legal bases for the Schengen acquis in accordance with Article 2 of the Protocol,[23] the Schengen acquis shall continue to apply to Denmark via international law only. In other words, Denmark, although a Member of the EU and fully participating in the Schengen cooperation, is involved in the Schengen cooperation as if it were a third country associated with this cooperation under public international law.

As regards measures building upon the Schengen acquis adopted under Title IV, Article 5 of the Danish Protocol provides that Denmark must decide within a period of 6 months whether it will apply the measure.[24] If it does so, this decision will create an obligation under international law between Denmark and the other Member States participating in Schengen. If Denmark decides not to apply the measure, the Member States shall consider appropriate measures to be taken. Up until now, however, Denmark has decided to apply all measures building on the Schengen acquis.

23.   On the identification of the first and third-pillar legal bases of the Schengen acquis, cf. Kuijper, above footn. 21, pp. 346 et seq.

24.   Interestingly, Article 5 of the Danish Protocol does not contain any specific mention of measures building on the Schengen acquis which fall under the third pillar. A possible explanation of this approach is that it may have been assumed that Union law does not constitute a separate legal order from public international law. Whether this assumption is correct as a matter of Union law is questionable. In practice, however, Denmark has participated in the adoption of third-pillar Schengen measures and applied them like any other EU Member.

2. The UK and Ireland

As for the UK and Ireland, the driving force behind the opt-outs is the United Kingdom, which, partially also on account of its insular status, did not wish to abolish border controls with other Member States, and correspondingly also not to engage in common policies regarding the control of external borders. The United Kingdom and Ireland also maintain a common travel area, which explains why Ireland adopted a similar approach to the United Kingdom.[25]

The United Kingdom and Ireland are in principle not bound by the Schengen acquis. However, according to Article 4 of the Schengen Protocol, the United Kingdom and Ireland may at any time request to take part in some or all of the Schengen acquis. The participation is not automatic, but requires a decision of the Council, which must be unanimous. Upon their request, the United Kingdom[26] and Ireland[27] have been allowed by the Council to participate in a number of provisions of the Schengen acquis. However, these provisions mainly concern the criminal law and police provisions of Schengen, as well as provisions on irregular migration. In contrast, the United Kingdom and Ireland do not participate in measures relating to border controls or visa policy.

As regards proposals to build upon the Schengen acquis, Article 5 (1) of the Schengen Protocol merely states that such proposals "shall be subject to the relevant provisions of the Treaties", and further provides that if the United Kingdom and Ireland have notified in writing within a reasonable period that they wish to take part, the authorization of closer cooperation under Articles 11 EC or 40 EU shall also be deemed to extend to them. This somewhat enigmatic formula has led to disagreement as to which rules should apply for the opt-in by the UK or Ireland into rules which build on parts of the Schengen acquis. Is has been argued that in such a case, it is not the Schengen Protocol which applies, but rather Article 3 of the Anglo-Irish Protocol, which provides for an opt-in possibility without prior approval by the Council.[28] However, it appears that the Schengen Protocol

---

25. Cf. de Zwaan, above footn. 19, p. 108.
26. Council Decision 2000/356/EC, OJ L 131, 1.6.2000, p. 43; Council Decision 2004/926/EC, OJ L 395, 31.12.2004, p. 70.
27. Council Decision 2002/192/EC, OJ L 64, 7.3.2000, p. 20.
28. Cf. Peers, above footn. note 19, p. 58.

is *lex specialis* as regards the participation of the UK and Ireland in the Schengen acquis.[29]

Alternatively, it has been argued that a participation in acts building upon the Schengen acquis could take place on the basis of Article 5 of the Schengen Protocol.[30] However, it does not appear that Article 5 can be applied to acts building upon the Schengen acquis independently from Article 4 of the Schengen Protocol.[31] First, there is nothing in the wording of Article 4 of the Schengen Protocol, which refers to participation in some or all of the provisions of the Schengen acquis, which would indicate that this includes only the Schengen acquis as it stood at the time of the Treaty of Amsterdam, but not subsequent measures amending or building on that acquis. Second, the application of Article 5 independently of the participation by the United Kingdom and Ireland in the underlying Schengen measures pursuant to Article 4 would lead to a further fragmentation of the Schengen acquis.

Accordingly, for all measures building on the Schengen acquis, Article 4 of the Schengen Protocol applies.[32] This means that when examining the participation of Ireland and the United Kingdom in a measure under Title IV, it is necessary first to determine whether the measure constitutes a part of the Schengen acquis, or a development thereof. If this is the case, the applicable rules are those of the Schengen Protocol; if not, the rules of the Anglo-Irish Protocol will apply. If a measure contains both aspects falling under the Schengen acquis and aspects which fall under other areas of Title IV, it may be necessary to apply both protocols simultaneously.

29. Cf. Article 7 of the Anglo-Irish Protocol, according to which Articles 3 and 4 of this Protocol are without prejudice to the Schengen Protocol. This has been confirmed by the ECJ in its judgments of 18.12.2007 in cases C-77/05 and C-137/05, in which it dismissed reference by the UK to the Anglo-Irish Protocol and assessed the possibility of the UK to opt into two measures which constituted a development of the Schengen acquis exclusively on the basis of the Schengen Protocol (cf. Case C-77/05, para. 76 et seq.; Case C-137/05, para. 55 et seq.).
30. This view has been advanced by the United Kingdom in two disputes before the ECJ (Cases C-77/05 and C-137/05, UK/Council).
31. In the same sense, the Court held in its judgments of 18.12.2007 that "the second subparagraph of Article 5 (1) of the Schengen Protocol must be interpreted as applicable only to proposal and initiatives to build upon an area of the Schengen acquis in which the United Kingdom and/or Ireland have been authorised to take part in pursuant to Article 4 of that protocol" (Case C-77/05, para. 68; Case C-137/05, para. 50).
32. Cf. Toth, above footn. 15, p. 237 et seq.

3.   The Schengen Associates

In 1996, Norway and Iceland had, together with the three Nordic EU Member States Denmark, Sweden and Finland, signed an agreement on their accession to the Schengen area. In order not to disrupt the existing Passport Union between the five Nordic countries, it was therefore necessary to find an arrangement allowing the continued participation of Norway and Iceland in the Schengen cooperation despite its integration into the EU framework.

The legal basis for this association was laid by Article 6 (1) of the Schengen Protocol. In accordance with this provision, and in derogation from the normal treaty-making procedures of Article 300 EC, the Council negotiated and concluded an agreement on the association of Norway and Iceland with the Schengen acquis.[33] Under this agreement, Norway and Iceland shall fully apply the Schengen acquis. This also applies to measures adopted by the EU institutions amending or building on this acquis.[34] On the basis of Article 6 (2) of the Schengen Protocol, an Agreement has also been concluded by the Council on the establishment of rights and obligations between Norway and Iceland and the United Kingdom and Ireland in respect of those parts of the Schengen acquis which apply to these Member States.[35]

In the meantime, Switzerland has also expressed the wish to become associated with Schengen. Given the cross-pillar nature of the Schengen acquis, this required an agreement involving both the European Community and the European Union. The corresponding agreement has recently been concluded.[36] This agreement also allows for the accession of Liechtenstein, which will then equally become associated with the Schengen acquis.[37]

4.   The New Member States

A final complication as regards the territorial application of the Schengen acquis has been added by the most recent enlargements of the European

---

33.   OJ L 176, 10.7.1999, p. 35.
34.   Cf. Article 2 (3) in conjunction with Article 8 of the Agreement. If Norway or Iceland do not accept to apply such a measure, the Agreement shall normally be considered terminated, cf. Article 8 (5) of the Agreement. So far, Norway and Iceland have accepted and applied all provisions building on the Schengen acquis.
35.   OJ L 15, 20.1.2000, p. 1.
36.   Cf. OJ L 53, 27.2.2008, pp. 1, 50. On the association of Switzerland cf. Contribution by Filliez.
37.   Cf. Article 16 of the Agreement concerning the Association of Switzerland.

Union. According to Article 8 of the Schengen Protocol, the Schengen acquis must be accepted by all new Member States in full. However, given the complex nature of the Schengen acquis, there was a need to allow for transitional periods in the full application of the Schengen acquis by the new Member States. As a consequence, the 2004 Act of Accession provides that certain parts of the Schengen acquis, including those regarding the abolition of internal borders and the issuance of Schengen visas, shall, while binding on the new Member States from the date of accession, be applied in a new Member State only pursuant to a Council decision to be taken after a verification process.[38] A corresponding provision is also contained in the Protocol of Accession for Bulgaria and Romania.[39]

On 6 December 2007, the Council adopted a decision which renders the Schengen acquis fully applicable to all of the 10 new Member States having acceded in 2004, with the exception of Cyprus.[40] Accordingly, as of 2008, only Bulgaria, Cyprus and Romania will be concerned by the transitional arrangements foreseen in the accession treaties.

B.   The Remainder of Title IV

Special arrangements also apply to Denmark, Ireland and the United Kingdom as regards the remainder of Title IV.[41]

1.   *Denmark*

According to Article 1 of the Danish Protocol, Denmark shall not take part in the adoption of any measures under Title IV. Article 2 further specifies that no measure adopted under Title IV, including any international agreement, shall be binding upon or applicable in Denmark. Denmark accordingly benefits from an almost complete opt-out from Title IV. The only exception to this is Article 4 of the Danish Protocol, which provides

---

38.   Cf. Article 3 (2) of the 2004 Act of Accession (OJ L 236, 23.9.2003, p. 1). Cf. in more detail Peers, above 19, pp. 60 et seq.
39.   Cf. Article 4 (2) of the Accession Protocol (OJ L 157, 21.6.2005, p. 29).
40.   OJ L 323, 8.12.2007, p. 34.
41.   There is no systematic association of third countries with measures adopted under Title IV outside the Schengen acquis. However, Norway and Iceland have been associated with the "Dublin Regulation" concerning the criteria and mechanisms for establishing the State responsible for examining a request for asylum (cf. the Agreement concluded between the Community, Norway and Iceland on the basis of Article 63 [1] EC, OJ L 93, 3.4.2001, p. 38). Moreover, the envisaged Lugano Convention will provide for the extension of the Brussels Regulation to Norway, Iceland, and Switzerland (cf. contribution by Kuijper in this book).

that the opt-out does not apply to measures determining the third countries whose nationals must be in possession of a visa when crossing the EU external borders, and measures relating to a uniform format for visas.[42]

However, it subsequently appeared that this complete opt-out from Title IV exceeded even the wishes of Denmark.[43] This applies in particular to the area of civil cooperation. For instance, Denmark was a party to the "Brussels I" Convention on jurisdiction and the recognition and enforcement of judgments in civil and commercial matters. Following the entry into force of the Amsterdam Treaty, this Convention was "communitarised" through the adoption of Council Regulation 44/2001.[44] Even though the Brussels I Convention continued to apply between Denmark and the other Member States, this would nonetheless have put Denmark into an awkward situation, since the Brussels I Convention is not entirely identical to the Brussels I Regulation, and subsequent case law of the Court of Justice on the Regulation would equally not have applied to Denmark. To close this gap, a "parallel agreement" was negotiated, pursuant to the procedures of Article 300 EC, between Denmark and the EC.[45] This Agreement renders the Brussels I Regulation as well as any subsequent amendments and implementing measures applicable to Denmark.[46] The agreement also confers jurisdiction on the Court to render preliminary rulings on request from Danish courts concerning the interpretation of the Brussels I Regulation, and empowers the Commission to bring cases against Denmark for non-compliance with any obligation under the agreement.[47] As regards international agreements concluded by the Community in the area covered by the Brussels I regulation, the agreement provides that such agreements shall not be binding on Denmark; however, the agreement also provides that Denmark shall abstain from negotiating agreements which could affect the Brussels I regulation without the consent of the Community and shall coordinate its position with the Community when negotiating such international

---

42. This are the measure for which a Community competence already existed since the Treaty of Maastricht.
43. On this and the following cf. Pieter-Jan Kuijper, The Evolution of the Third Pillar from Maastricht to the European Constitution: Institutional Aspects, 41 (2004) CMLR 609, 621.
44. OJ L 12, 16.1.2001, p. 1.
45. For the decision concluding the agreement, cf. OJ L 120, 5.5.2006; the text of the agreement is attached to the decision on the signature of the agreement, OJ L 299, 16.11.2005, p. 61.
46. Articles 2 to 4 of the Agreement.
47. Articles 5 and 6 of the Agreement.

agreements.[48] Similar "parallel agreements" have also been concluded with Denmark for a number of other measures under Title IV.[49]

Even though they create obligations for Denmark only under international law, rather than under Community law, these parallel agreements put Denmark in almost the same situation as if it were fully participating in the EC policies in question. Although this outcome might be welcomed, given also Denmark's integration into the Schengen area, the parallel agreements are nonetheless subject to certain doubts. First, the recourse to Article 300 EC for the conclusion of an international agreement with a Member State is rather unusual.[50] However, it might be argued that Denmark is, for the purposes of Title IV, essentially in the same legal position as a third country. Second, it could be questioned whether the parallel agreements do not constitute a circumvention of the Danish protocol, which – with the exception of the Schengen acquis – does not foresee any possibility for Denmark to opt into measures under Title IV. Finally, and most importantly, the question could be raised whether the conclusion of parallel agreements may not remove any incentive for Denmark to integrate more fully under the policies under Title IV, for instance by renouncing parts of its Protocol.[51]

2.   The UK and Ireland

Articles 1 and 2 of the Anglo-Irish Protocol are identical in substance with Articles 1 and 2 of the Danish Protocol. However, unlike the Danish Protocol, the Anglo-Irish Protocol provides these two Member States with the possibility to "opt into" measures adopted under Title IV.[52] According to Article 3 of the Anglo-Irish Protocol, if the UK or Ireland notify the President of the Council within three months of the presentation of a proposal that it wishes to take part in the adoption and application of the

48. Article 5 of the Agreement.
49. Cf. the Agreement on the application of Regulation 1348/2000 on the service of documents in civil or commercial matters, OJ L 300, 17.11.2005, p. 53 (signature) and OJ L 120, 5.5.2006, p. 23 (conclusion); Agreement concerning the extension to Denmark of Regulations 343/2003 (Dublin II) and 2725/2000 (Eurodac), OJ L 66, 8.3.2006, p. 37.
50. It is noted that whereas Article 300 (1) EC refers to "States", Article 300 (7) provides that international agreements are binding on the Community and its "Member States". Article 300 EC does therefore not normally cover the conclusion of international agreements between the Community and its Member States.
51. Article 7 of the Danish Protocol allows Denmark to renounce all or part of its Protocol.
52. As discussed above, this does not apply to measures which constitute a development of the Schengen acquis.

measure, it is entitled to do so. Unlike under the Schengen protocol, no form of approval is required. However, if, after a reasonable period of time, the proposal cannot be adopted with the UK or Ireland taking part, the Council may adopt the measure without the participation of these Member States.

Moreover, under Article 4 of the Anglo-Irish Protocol, the UK or Ireland may also, at any time after the adoption of a measure pursuant to Title IV, notify its intention to the Council and the Parliament to accept the measure. In this case, however, the procedure of Article 11 (3) EC shall apply, which means *inter alia* that the Commission has to decide on the request presented by the Member State concerned.

In practice, the United Kingdom and Ireland have, pursuant to Article 3 of the Protocol, opted into all measures in the field of civil cooperation, and into numerous measures on asylum and illegal immigration, but generally not into measures concerning visas, border controls, or immigration policy.[53]

IV. EC-Treaty Making and Variable Geometry under Title IV

In this section, a number of legal problems created by the various derogations, opt-outs and opt-ins for EU external relations will be examined. The analysis will primarily focus on problems regarding the negotiation and conclusion of international agreements by the EC.

A. External Competence and Territorial Application

In a first step, it shall be examined what are the legal effects of the non-participation of certain Member States on international agreements concluded under Title IV. In this regard, it is important to distinguish between the situation under Community law and the situation under public international law.

1. Community law

Any international agreement concluded by the EC will become an integral part of the EC legal order, and will, in accordance with Article 300 (7) EC, become binding on the institutions of the Community and its Member

---

53. Cf. with further detail Peers, above note 19, p. 56.

States. Accordingly, an international agreement will normally apply to the entire territory of the Community, as defined in Article 299 (1) EC.

However, this principle is modified by the opt-outs of Denmark, Ireland and the United Kingdom. According to Articles 2 of the Anglo-Irish and the Danish Protocol, no provision of any international agreement concluded by the Community under Title IV shall be binding upon or applicable in Denmark, the United Kingdom or Ireland.[54] These provisions modify Article 300 (7) EC Treaty, as well as Article 299 (1) thereof, and thus limit the territorial application of any international agreement concluded by the Community under Title IV.

Of course, this does mean that the EC does not have external competence in matters relating to Title IV. Where the Community has a competence to adopt internal measures, it is also competent to conclude international agreements where this is necessary to attain the objectives of the Treaty.[55] Moreover, if the Community has adopted internal legislation, this competence may also become exclusive, in accordance with the ERTA case law of the Court of Justice.[56] However, the EC is competent only to represent the EC with the territorial limitations which result from the opt-outs. In other words, variable geometry in EC law has the consequence that the EC becomes an international actor whose territory varies depending on the subject matter of the agreement.

A different analysis, however, must apply to the derogations contained in the Acts of Accession for the 10 New Member States[57] and the Protocol of Accession of Bulgaria and Romania in respect of the Schengen acquis. Contrary to the Danish and Anglo-Irish Protocols, the accession arrangements provide explicitly that even those parts which are temporarily not applied by the new Member States remain nonetheless binding on them.[58] This will equally apply to any international agreement amending or developing the Schengen acquis concluded by the Community. Of course, in concluding such agreements, the Community is obliged to ensure that it does not accept commitments which the new

---

54. This also includes any international agreement which constitutes a development of the Schengen acquis.
55. Cf. Opinion 1/76, Laying-up Fund for Inland Waterway Vessels, [1977] ECR 741, para. 3; Opinion 2/91, ILO Convention No. 170, [1993] ECR I-1061, para. 7.
56. Case 22/70, ERTA, [1971] ECR 263, para. 22.
57. As of 2008, the Schengen acquis is fully applied by all of the 10 Member States having acceded in 2004, with the exception of Cyprus.
58. Cf. above footn. 38 and 39.

Member States, given the partial suspension of the Schengen acquis on their territory, cannot implement.

The distinction between the situation of the three opt-out Member States and the New Member States is illustrated by the Memorandum of Understanding concluded between the Community and China on visa and related issues concerning tourist groups from China (ADS Agreement).[59] This Agreement deals inter alia with the issuance of short-term Schengen visas to Chinese tourists, which is a matter falling under the Schengen acquis. For this reason, Denmark, Ireland and the United Kingdom could not participate in the adoption and application of the agreement, and are therefore explicitly excluded from the scope of the agreement.[60] There are merely two non-binding declarations which call for the conclusion of bilateral agreements between these Member States and China. In contrast, the Agreement does apply to the territory of the ten new Member States which acceded in 2004. However, since the new Member States did not yet issue Schengen visas, specific arrangements had to be made with respect to them. This is achieved through a Protocol annexed to the Agreement, which provides that as long as the ten new Member States[61] do not issue Schengen visas, they shall issue national visas to the Chinese tourist groups. For the rest, the Agreement is fully applicable to the new Member States. This means that in the issuance of the national visas under the ADS Agreement, they must also observe the procedural provisions contained in Article 4 of the Agreement.

2. *Public International Law*

However, account must be taken not only of the situation under Community law, but also of the situation under international law. Article 29 of the Vienna Convention on the Law of Treaties, which can be regarded as a codification of customary international law, provides that unless a different intention appears from the Treaty or is otherwise apparent, a treaty is binding upon each party in respect of its entire territory.

Accordingly, public international law does not exclude that upon conclusion of an international agreement, a party may exclude the

---

59. OJ L 83, 20.3.2004, p. 12. The term "ADS" stands for "Authorised Destination Status". A very similar model has also been followed for the visa facilitation agreement with Russia OJ L 129, 17.5.2007, p. 25 and Ukraine OJ L 332, 18.12.2007, p. 66.
60. Article 1 (a) and (c) of the Agreement. On the issues relating to the Anglo-Irish opt-in, cf. the following section.
61. The same applies by analogy also for Bulgaria and Romania.

application of a treaty in part of its territory. However, this must be made clear at the time of conclusion, and must be accepted by the other party. In case of doubt, the treaty will be presumed to apply to the entire territory of the contracting party.[62]

For the EC acting under Title IV, this means that utmost care must be taken to correctly describe the territory to which an international agreement shall apply. Frequently, EC international agreements contain a territorial clause which defines the territory of the EC in terms identical to Article 299 (1) EC. In the case of agreements under Title IV, these clauses have to be adapted in order to take account of the various opt-outs, which has been done in a number of agreements negotiated under Title IV.[63]

In contrast, if the Community does not include explicit territorial exclusions into its international agreements even though an internal opt-out applies, it runs the risk that the other contracting party might argue that the non-application of the agreement to this extent constitutes a breach of the agreement. Given the extreme complexity of the variable geometry under Title IV, it would probably be difficult to argue that a resulting territorial exclusion should have been obvious to the third country concerned.[64]

B.   The UK and Irish Opt-in

The resulting situation is still relatively clear for Denmark, which must be excluded from the scope of any agreement concluded under Title IV.[65]

---

62. Cf. Anthony Aust, Modern Treaty Law and Practice, 163 (2000).
63. Cf. Article 20 of the Readmission Agreement with Sri Lanka, OJ L 124, 17.5.2005, p. 41; Article 21 of the Readmission Agreement with Albania, OJ L 124, 17.5.2005, p. 21.
64. By way of analogy, reference can be made to Article 46 of the Vienna Convention on the Law of Treaties, according to which a violation of an internal rule concerning competence to conclude treaties does not give rise to the invalidity of a treaty unless the violation was manifest and concerned a rule of fundamental importance; a violation will be manifest if it would be objectively evident to any State conducting itself in accordance with normal practice and good faith. Given the highly intricate character of the variable geometry under Title IV, it is not certain that a violation of an opt-out under Title IV would be manifest in this sense.
65. Theoretically, Denmark should decide to apply an agreement constituting a development of the Schengen acquis under Art. 5 of its Protocol. However, such an application could merely concern the obligations of the Community, but not have the effect of creating corresponding obligations of the third country in respect of Denmark. It is therefore not clear that Article 5 of the Danish Protocol can be applied to international agreements.

However, considerable difficulties for the negotiation and conclusion of Community agreements are created by the opt-in possibilities for the United Kingdom and Ireland, which shall be discussed hereunder.

1.   *Schengen Protocol or Anglo-Irish Protocol?*

The first question is already which Protocol is applicable for a potential opt-in of the UK or Ireland into an agreement under Title IV. This issue arose in connection with the ADS Agreement with China,[66] which – besides the issue of tourist visas, which falls under the Schengen acquis – also deals with the readmission of Chinese tourists, which is not a development of the Schengen acquis. The United Kingdom and Ireland had expressed a wish to opt into this agreement even though they do not participate in the Schengen acquis for the issuance of visas. However, this was rejected by the Council. The Council decision concluding the agreement refers in this regard to both the Schengen and the Anglo-Irish Protocol.[67] This reflects the fact that to the extent that the agreement constitutes a development of the Schengen acquis, the opt-in provisions of the Schengen Protocol are *lex specialis*. According to Article 4 of the Protocol, the Council was therefore entitled not to accept the request by the United Kingdom and Ireland. Moreover, the conditions of the opt-in were not fulfilled, since the Member States concerned were not participating in the Schengen acquis concerning the issuance of tourist visas, and could therefore not have implemented part of the agreement, which called for the issuance of Schengen visas.[68] A partial opting into the non-Schengen parts of the Agreement would not have been possible either, since the readmission of tourists was the counterpart of the facilitation of the issuance of tourist visas. Accordingly, the United Kingdom and Ireland remained excluded from the application of the ADS Agreement.

66. On this case, cf. also Kuijper, above footn. 43, p. 623; Annalisa Meloni, The Development of a Common Visa Policy under the Treaty of Amsterdam, 42 [2005] CMLR 1357, 1364.

67. Council Decision 2004/265/EC (recital 4), OJ L 83, 20.3.2004, p. 12. The same formula also appears in the Council decision regarding the conclusion of the visa facilitation agreement with Russia (Council Decision 2007/340/EC, OJ L 129, 17.5.2007, p. 25).

68. This is different from the situation of the New Member States, which, although not yet issuing Schengen visas, are bound by the Schengen acquis in this regard.

2.   Internal Measures and International Agreements

The example of the ADS Agreement raises a more general point, which is also relevant to the Anglo-Irish Protocol, namely the link between the participation in internal measures and the possibility to opt into agreements which affect these internal measures. This question can arise in two directions: on the one hand, it may be asked whether the UK and Ireland can opt into an international agreement if they have not opted into the corresponding internal measure; on the other hand, the question arises whether they still have the freedom not to participate in an international agreement which affects an internal act into which they have opted.

The answer to the second question is arguably more straightforward than the answer to the first. According to the ERTA case law of the Court of Justice, where an international agreement affects an internal act of the Community, the EC has exclusive competence to conclude this agreement.[69] This means that where the United Kingdom has opted into a measure adopted under Title IV, it can no longer accept international commitments affecting such measure. Logically, this must mean that the competence to conclude such commitments with effect for the United Kingdom passes to the Community.

This consequence has in practice been accepted by the United Kingdom and Ireland, which have indicated their willingness to opt into all international agreements negotiated by the EC affecting the measures adopted by the EC under Title IV. A question remains, however, as to whether the opt-out provisions are still applicable in such a case. A number of decisions concerning international agreements in the area of private international law, where the UK and Ireland are participating in the internal measures, still indicate that the United Kingdom and Ireland are taking part pursuant to Article 3 of the Anglo-Irish Protocol.[70] This formula would seem to suggest that whereas the UK and Ireland may be obliged to opt into the international agreement in question, they will not be bound

---

69.   Above footn. 56.
70.   Cf. Council Decision 2006/719/EC on the Accession to the Hague Conference, OJ L 297, 26.10.2006, p. 1 (recital 12); Council Decision 2006/325/EC on the conclusion of the parallel agreement with Denmark on the Brussels I Regulation, OJ L 120, 5.5.2006, p. 22 (recital 4); Council decision of 2006/326 on the conclusion of the parallel agreement with Denmark on the service of documents in civil or commercial matters, OJ L 120, 5.5.2006, p. 23 (recital 4).

unless they actually notify their intention to participate. In contrast, in a number of other cases, it has simply been stated that the UK and Ireland are bound by the internal instrument and are therefore participating in the decision concerning the international agreement.[71] This latter formula seems to be the correct one. Once the United Kingdom or Ireland have transferred competence to the EC by opting into a measure under Title IV, they must accept the consequences of this transfer for all international agreements affecting the internal measure. To this extent, the opt-in provisions of the Anglo-Irish Protocol are no longer applicable.

As concerns the reverse constellation, the situation is less clear. If the Community concludes an international agreement affecting an internal act into which the UK or Ireland have not opted in, it clearly has exclusive competence to do so; equally clearly, the UK or Ireland will not be bound by this agreement. However, the question is whether they UK and Ireland, despite their non-participation in the internal measure, could still opt into the corresponding international agreement.

It could be argued that the internal measure and the decision concluding the international agreement are both "measures" within the meaning of Article 3 of the Anglo-Irish Protocol, and that a separate opt-in possibility should therefore exist in respect of each.[72] However, such a strict reading could lead to odd results, since it would, for instance, permit opting into a measure which amends another measure, without participation in the original measure.[73] Similar problems could also arise in relation to international agreements, where such agreements build upon, or amend, the rules applicable within the Community. However, in the absence of

---

71. Council Decision 2004/294/EC authorising the Member States to ratify the Paris Convention, OJ L 97, 1.4.2004, p. 53 (recital 11); Council Decision 2004/246/EC authorising Member States to accede to the FIPOL Convention, OJ L 78, 16.3.2004, p. 22 (recital 6). Council Decision 2002/762/EC authorising Member States to ratify the Bunkers Convention, OJ L 256, 25.9.2002, p. 7 (recital 9) simply states that the United Kingdom and Ireland are participating without providing any further explanation.

72. This is supported by the fact that the United Kingdom and Ireland have opted into a number of readmission agreements concluded by the EC without any prior internal legislation (cf. Meloni, above note 66, p. 1364 et seq.).

73. It should be noted that in this respect, the terminology of Article 4 of the Schengen Protocol is somewhat different, since it refers to the participation in "provisions of the acquis".

clear rules in the Anglo-Irish Protocol, it is not entirely clear where the legal limitations lie. In the final analysis, much may also depend on the content of the legal acts involved, and on whether an application of the agreement without participation in the underlying Community act would create legal difficulties.

3.   Timing of Opt-in

Considerable difficulties also exist as regards the timing of the opt-ins in relation to the various steps of the Community treaty-making procedure under Article 300 EC. Article 3 of the Anglo-Irish Protocol foresees that a single notification to be made within three months after the proposal is presented to the Council. However, Article 300 EC envisages several major steps in the treaty-making procedure, namely the authorisation to open negotiations, which is issued by the Council upon recommendation from the Commission, and the approval of the signature and/or conclusion of the agreement, which is decided by the Council on the basis of a proposal from the Commission.

It is not clear from the Anglo-Irish Protocol at which stage of the treaty-making procedure the notification is required. This lack of clarity is regrettable. As has been explained, any territorial exclusions resulting from opt-outs normally have to be included in the text of the agreement under negotiation. Therefore, before concluding the negotiations and submitting the agreement to the Council for approval, the Commission acting as the negotiator needs to know which Member States will participate and which will not. Therefore, it would appear appropriate that the notification be provided before the negotiating directives are issued, and remain binding on the Member States with respect to the subsequent signature and conclusion of the agreement.

However, the practice has not followed this line. For all readmission agreements which have been negotiated by the Community, the United Kingdom and Ireland participated in the adoption of the authorisation to negotiate, and the negotiating directives foresaw the application of the agreements to these Member States. Accordingly, all readmission agreements concluded by the EC provide only for the exclusion of Denmark. At the time of signature and conclusion of the agreements, however, only the United Kingdom consistently notified its intention to participate.[74] Only in the case of the readmission agreement with Hong Kong did both the UK and Ireland opt into the decision.[75]

C.   Splitting of Decisions

Difficulties can also be created by the variable geometry under Title IV in the case of international agreements which, besides matters falling under Title IV, also cover other matters falling under EC competence. An example are the two protocols to the UN Convention against Transnational Organised Crime (UNTOC) on the Smuggling of Migrants by Land, Sea and Air (the Smuggling Protocol) and the Prevention, Suppression, and Punishment of Trafficking in Persons (the Trafficking Protocol). These protocols largely fall under Title IV, in particular under Community competence regarding external border controls and immigration policy. However, at the same time, the Protocols also contain provisions which fall under the EC's development and cooperation policies pursuant to Articles 177 and 181a EC, to which no opt-outs apply.

The Council considered that it was not possible to base the decisions concluding the Protocols both on Title IV and on provisions outside of Title IV. The reason for this position was that according to Article 1 of the Anglo-Irish Protocol and the Danish Protocol, the non-participating Member States must not take part in the voting in the Council. However, it is unclear which voting rules should apply if a measure falls both under Title IV and under other provisions of the Treaty. In order to avoid this problem, the Council eventually adopted two decisions for each Protocol. The first decision is based on Title IV, and does not apply to Denmark, the United Kingdom and Ireland, whereas the second decision is based on

---

74. Cf. Council Decision 2004/424/EC, OJ L 143, 30.4.2004, p. 97 (Macao); Council Decision 2005/372/EC, OJ L 124, 17.5.2005, p. 41 (Sri Lanka); Council Decision 2005/371/EC, OJ L 124, 17.5.2005, p. 21 (Albania); Council Decision 2007/341/EC, OJ L 129, 17.5.2007, p. 38 (Russia); Council Decision 2007/839/EC, OJ L 332, 18.12.2007, p. 46 (Ukraine); Council Decision 2007/817/EC, OJ L 33, 19.12.2007, p. 1 (Macedonia); Council Decision 2007/818/EC, OJ L 33, 19.12.2007, p. 25 (Montenegro); Council Decision 2007/819/EC, OJ L 33, 19.12.2007, p. 45 (Serbia); Council Decision 2007/820/EC, OJ L 33, 19.12.2007, p. 65 (Bosnia and Herzegovina); Council Decision 2007/826/EC, OJ L 33, 19.12.2007, p. 148 (Moldova).
75. Cf. Council Decision 2004/80/EC, OJ L 17, 24.1.2004, p. 23.

Articles 179 and 181a EC and applies to all Member States.[76] With each decision, the Council approved also the declaration of competence which the EC was required to submit upon accession, which is identical with respect to each Protocol. However, despite the separate decisions, only one instrument of acceptance and one declaration of competence were submitted for each protocol. This was important in order to avoid any misconception on the part of third states that the EC was acting as two separate entities.

This need to split the conclusion of multilateral agreements into two or more separate acts constitutes another unwelcome consequence of variable geometry. In EC internal legislation, it may be feasible to draft legal acts in such a way that they stay within the boundaries of Title IV. However, it cannot be expected that international agreements, and in particular multilateral agreements, will necessarily respect the lines of the EC's internal policies and their variable geometry. It is therefore likely that the example of the UNTOC Protocols may not remain an isolated case.

D.   International Organisations

Similar problems arise in the context of multilateral organisations of which the EC is a Member. Where the EC is a Member of an international organisation alongside its Member States, it typically exercises a number of votes equivalent to the number of its Member States which are members of the organisation.[77] However, with variable geometry, this simple equation no longer necessarily holds. For this reason, when the Community negotiated its accession to the Hague Conference on Private International Law,[78] the traditional clause had to be adapted further compared to the traditional model. As a consequence, Article 2A (8) of the revised Statute of the Hague Conference now provides that a Member Organisation may exercise on matters of its competence a number of votes "equal to the number of Member States which have transferred competence to the

---

76.   For the Smuggling Protocol, cf. Council Decisions 2006/616/EC and 2006/617/EC, OJ L 262, 22.9.2006, pp. 24 and 34; for the Trafficking Protocol, cf. Council Decisions 2006/618/EC and 2006/619/EC, OJ L 262, 22.9.2006, pp. 44 and 51. For the UK and Ireland, the situation was in fact even more complicated, since the Protocols also affected certain parts of the Schengen acquis in which the UK and Ireland were participating (cf. recital 5 of each of the Title IV-Decisions).
77.   Cf. Article IX (1) WTO Agreement; more generally, cf. Jörn Sack, the European Community's Membership of International Organizations, 32 [1995] CMLR 1227.
78.   On this, cf. the contribution in this book by van Loon/Schulz.

Member Organisation in respect of the matter in question".[79] This reference to a "transfer of competence in respect of the matter in question" was specifically intended to address the problems of the opt-outs. Accordingly, the Community will exercise in the Hague Conference a varying number of votes, depending on which of its Member States participate in the underlying measures.[80]

E.   Association Agreements and Mixed Agreements

In recent years, the EC has also begun including provisions on justice and home affairs in association agreements which it concludes with third countries on the basis of Article 310 EC. Frequently, such clauses concern the readmission and repatriation of illegal immigrants.[81]

To the extent that such clauses concern matters falling under Title IV, the question is how such association agreements relate to the opt-outs under this Title. In particular, the question arises whether an agreement concluded on the basis of Article 310 EC could bind Denmark, Ireland, or the UK even in respect of matters which would normally fall under Title IV. From a formal point of view, it could be argued that Article 310 EC is a self-standing legal basis, which is not referred to in any of the opt-out Protocols. On the other hand, it must be considered that the very nature of an "association" also implies that the EC has powers over the area covered by the association. This is confirmed by the case law of the Court of Justice, which has held that Article 310 empowers the Community "to guarantee commitments towards non-member countries *in all the fields covered by the Treaty*".[82] Accordingly, since the Community does not have the power to bind Denmark, the UK and Ireland under Title IV, it must not do so either through the conclusion of association agreements.

The practical significance of this question could be relatively minor, since most association agreements are concluded as mixed agreements, to which

79.   OJ L 297, 26.10.2006, p. 7. A similar formula was also used in Article 19 (2) the Protocol of 2002 to the Athens Convention Relating to the Carriage of Passengers and their Luggage by Sea (for the Commission proposal for conclusion of this Protocol, cf. COM [2003]375 final).

80.   In certain cases, namely when the Hague Conference deals with matters falling under other Community policies than Title IV, the EC might also exercise 27 votes. This was for instance the case for the Hague Collaterals Convention, which fell under Articles 47 (2) and 95 EC, to which no opt-out applies (for the Commission proposal for signature of this Convention, cf. COM[2002]783 final).

81.   Cf. also contribution by Schieffer in this book.

82.   Case 12/86, Demirel, [1987] ECR 3719, para. 9 (emphasis added).

both the EC and its Member States are party. However, in recent years, the opt-out Member States under Title IV have begun insisting on the inclusion of recitals in the decisions concluding association agreements according to which the provisions of the agreements falling under Title IV do not bind them as part of the Community, but as separate contracting parties.[83] These recitals are superfluous, since the EC and its Member States have traditionally never indicated which of them is responsible for the execution of the obligations under an association agreement, and have treated this question as an internal matter. However, the insistence on the explicit identification of opt-outs in the context of association agreements provides an additional example for the disintegrating effect of variable geometry on the EC's external relations.

F.   Coherence and Coordination

To the extent that Member States do not participate in policies under Title IV, in principle they retain the power to conclude international agreements in this area. The same also applies to the non-EU Member States Iceland and Norway even in areas where they are associated and participating in the Schengen acquis.

However, a side-by-side of independent external policies could lead to difficulties where Member States or third countries are nevertheless participating in the relevant Community policies without being bound by the EC's international agreements. An obvious example is provided by the Schengen area. In an area without internal borders, in which individuals can therefore travel freely, it is not desirable for readmission agreements to apply only to part of the area, since this would provide illegal immigrants with an incentive to move to those Member States where the readmission agreements do not apply. Similarly, the conditions for granting Schengen visas should be applied uniformly by all Schengen Member States in order to avoid visa-shopping; accordingly, visa facilitation agreements should equally apply uniformly to the entire area.

---

83. Cf. Council Decision 2005/40/EC/Euratom concerning the conclusion of the association agreement with Croatia, OJ L 26, 28.1.2005, p. 1 (recital 3); Council Decision 2004/635/EC concerning the conclusion of the association agreement with Egypt, OJ L 304, 30.9.2004, p. 38 (recital 2). No corresponding recital, in contrast, is found in the conclusion decision for the agreement with Algeria (OJ L 265, 10.10.2005, p. 1), although this agreement also contains provisions falling under Title IV.

However, given the variable geometry of Title IV, there is no single actor who could act on behalf of the entire Schengen area. This can give rise to an increased need for cooperation and coordination between the EC and the other Member States or third countries concerned. The relevant rules shall be examined hereafter separately for the Schengen acquis, and for the remainder of Title IV.

1.   The Schengen acquis

Denmark, though a Member State, applies the Schengen acquis only under international law, and is therefore not bound by international agreements concluded by the EC. The same is also true for Iceland and Norway.[84] However, this does not mean that these countries may freely conclude international agreements affecting the Schengen acquis. Article 136 (2) of the Schengen Implementing Convention provides that no contracting party shall conclude international agreements with third countries simplifying or abolishing border checks. This provision illustrates the need for a common external policy in all matters relating to the application of the Schengen. This does not merely apply to border controls, but to all matters governed by the Schengen acquis, including the issuing of Schengen visas. For instance, it does not appear that Denmark, Iceland or Norway could still negotiate visa agreements derogating from provisions of the Schengen acquis, since such derogations would violate their obligation to fully apply the provisions of the Schengen acquis.

Inversely, where the Community has concluded an international agreement with a third country on matters relating to the Schengen acquis, it will be necessary that a similar agreement also be concluded by Denmark and the Schengen associates. For instance, on the occasion of the conclusion of the ADS Agreement with China, the parties issued joint declarations which call for the conclusion of parallel agreements between China and Denmark, Iceland and Norway. Similar declarations were also made in relation to the visa facilitation agreement with Russia. Arguably, these declarations at the same time constitute the expression of the agreement of the EC to the conclusion of such agreement by the three countries concerned.

As regards the United Kingdom and Ireland, except in areas where they have opted into the Schengen acquis, they remain in principle free to conduct their own external relations. The United Kingdom and Ireland are

---

84.   As well as Switzerland and Liechtenstein upon their accession to the Schengen acquis.

not part of the Schengen area, and maintain their own external borders; therefore, there is no compelling need to conduct a common external policy with the Community on matters of visa policy or border controls. This notwithstanding, both with respect to the ADS Agreement and the visa facilitation agreement with Russia, declarations were issued according to which the conclusion of similar agreements with the United Kingdom and Ireland is "desirable".[85]

2.   *The Remainder of Title IV*

For the remainder of Title IV, there is also a certain need for uniformity and coherence in external action. One example is the conclusion of readmission agreements, which, although not a development of the Schengen acquis, has nonetheless implications on that acquis given the possibility of illegal immigrants to move freely through the Schengen area. Accordingly, on the occasion of the conclusion of all readmission agreements concluded by the EC, declarations were issued which called for the conclusion of parallel readmission agreements between Denmark, Iceland, Norway, and the third countries concerned.

Outside such Schengen-related matters, the opt-out Member States and third countries remain relatively free in the conduct of their external relations. Of course, to the extent that the United Kingdom and Ireland opt into a Community measure, they lose the corresponding power to negotiate international agreements. Similarly, for those measures for which Denmark has concluded "parallel agreements", the parallel agreements contain explicit provisions which oblige Denmark to closely coordinate any international negotiations on the covered subject matters with the Community.

An interesting question is whether Denmark, Ireland and the United Kingdom are also bound to coordinate their positions with those of the Community for matters on which they have not exercised an opt-in, or concluded a parallel agreement. A legal basis for such a duty could result from Article 10 EC. A certain measure of coordination is certainly appropriate, and should also occur naturally given the presence of these

---

85.   In the case of the visa faciliation agreement with Russia, a justification for this declaration could be seen in the fact that the visa faciliation agreement is linked to the readmission agreement (cf. Article 15 (1) of the Visa faciliation agreement, according to which the agreement shall enter into force only if the Readmission agreement has also entered into force). Since it is envisaged that the United Kingdom and Ireland will also opt into the readmission agreement, it is therefore appropriate that these countries should equally grant corresponding visa facilitations to Russia.

Member States in the Council. However, Article 10 EC may also not override the opt-outs contained in the Protocols to the Treaty. Accordingly, if no common position can be found, the opt-out Member States are not precluded from taking diverging positions from those of the EU.[86]

VI. The Treaty of Lisbon

The Treaty of Lisbon,[87] signed on 13 December 2007, marks the end of a long and difficult process of reforming the EU treaties. It will bring about significant changes for EU justice and home affairs; in particular, it will abolish the current third pillar, which will become a regular policy area of the European Union. Before concluding, it is therefore useful to briefly consider the impact of Treaty of Lisbon on the variable geometry in the field of Justice and Home Affairs.

As regards the scope of the opt-outs, a first question arises from the envisaged "communitarisation" of the current third pillar, which is supposed to become a policy area of the Union subject to the same decision-making procedures as all other areas of justice and home affairs. For Denmark, Protocol 20 to the Constitution already foresaw an extension of the current opt-out also to the areas covered by the former third pillar, and this is also contained in the Treaty of Lisbon. In contrast, Protocol No. 19 to the Constitution originally transposed the provisions of the current Anglo-Irish Protocol without any major changes. This would have meant that despite the "communitarisation" of the current third pillar, the scope of the Anglo-Irish opt-outs would have remained limited to the scope of the current Title IV, and would not have been enlarged. However, this positive aspect of the Constitutional Treaty was not maintained in the Treaty of Lisbon. Accordingly, under the modified treaty, Denmark, Ireland and the UK will have an opt-out from all areas of EU justice and home affairs, including the area of the former third pillar.[88]

As regards the mechanics of the opt-outs, the opt-in provisions of the Anglo-Irish Protocol, which have been the source of some difficulties both internally and internationally, are maintained without changes, and will now also apply to the former third pillar. In contrast, the opt-in provisions of the Schengen Protocol will be replaced by a highly complex multi-step

---

86. By analogy, cf. Declaration No. 25 to the Treaty of Maastricht on the coordination between the Community and the Member States which ensure the international representation of the overseas countries and territories.

87. OJ C 306, 17.12.2007, p. 1.

procedure involving the Council of Ministers, the European Council and the European Commission.[89] It is at this stage not easy to see how this complex procedure could be applied to the negotiation and conclusion of international agreements constituting a development of the Schengen acquis.

Moreover, once it has accepted the new Protocol in accordance with its constitutional requirements, Denmark will equally be able to avail itself of a new Protocol, which is drafted very much along the lines of the Anglo-Irish Protocol.[90] The main difference between the current Danish protocol and the new protocol is that the latter contains, in its Articles 3 and 4, opt-in provisions identical to those of Articles 3 and 4 of the Anglo-Irish Protocol. This means that the opt-in provisions of the Anglo-Irish Protocol may also become applicable to Denmark.

Overall, the Treaty of Lisbon is therefore likely to increase, rather than decrease, the variable geometry of EU justice and home affairs, and its potential impact on EU external relations in the field.

88. However, acts which had originally been adopted under the third pillar and thus are binding for Denmark, the UK and Ireland remain in principle binding for these Member States. Therefore, specific procedures were foreseen concerning the applicability to the UK and Ireland of such an amendment to such acts (cf. Article 4a of the Anglo-Irish Protocol in the form of the Treaty of Lisbon). As for DK, Art. 1 of the Danish Protocol in the form of the Treaty of Lisbon foresees that amendments to former third-pillar acts will be binding on Denmark; however, this will apply only until the entry into force of a new Danish Protocol modelled on the Anglo-Irish Protocol, which will then contain an analogous provision to Article 4a of the Anglo-Irish Protocol.
89. Cf. Art. 5 of the Schengen Protocol as amended by the Treaty of Lisbon.
90. The new protocol was originally foreseen as an Annex to Protocol 20 to the Constitution, and will now become a protocol annexed to the current Danish Protocol.

V. Conclusion

It seems fair to conclude that the variable geometry of Title IV has turned out to be a considerable complicating factor for the EU's external relations in justice and home affairs. This has not prevented the EU from imparting a very active dimension to the area of justice and home affairs. In fact, creative solutions have been found to deal with many of the difficulties generated by the opt-outs, even though sometimes the price to pay has been very complex arrangements, as illustrated for instance by the ADS Agreement with China. Of course, some problems also continue to elude solutions, most notably the difficulties created by the Anglo-Irish opt-in possibilities.

However, even where solutions have been found, the toll imposed on EU external relations should not be underestimated. The EU still remains an unusual international actor, and frequently needs to spend its negotiating capital on questions of status and competence, which other States do not need to address in their international relations. With variable geometry, the EU now has to tax the patience of the international community with another complication. It is already hard to convince third countries that the EC, in the context of mixed agreements, should exercise 27 votes rather than one vote. Clearly, this task is not facilitated if EC negotiators also need to explain why the EC may in fact have to exercise 24, 25, or 26 votes, as the case may be.

Clearly, these complications do not mean that variable geometry will soon disappear. In the area of justice and home affairs, with the entry into force of the Treaty of Lisbon, the scope and complexity of variable geometry is likely to increase further. Moreover, with an increasingly heterogeneous EU of more than 27 Members, variable geometry is likely to also find its way into other EU policy areas. Accordingly, the difficulties discussed in the present contribution may well spread to other policy areas of the EU.

In the immediate future, it should be attempted to at least minimise the impact of internal derogations on EU external relations. For this purpose, derogations should be clear and simple. Opt-in provisions of the type of the Anglo-Irish Protocol are difficult to manage in the context of international relations, and should therefore as far as possible be avoided. Moreover, it may also be preferable for opt-outs to be determined simply in relation to specific policy areas, rather than to specific legal acts or instruments.

More generally, in any future discussion on differentiated integration, the impact on EU external relations should also be kept in mind. The EU cannot become an efficient international actor and at the same time remain internally fragmented and divided. "Europe à la carte" is not compatible with effective external action.